GREAT

MASS-MEETING

TO-NIGHT, at 7.30 o'clock,

AT THE

HAYMARKET, Randolph St., Bet. Desplaines and Halsted.

Good Speakers will be present to denounce the latest atrocious act of the police, the shooting of our fellow-workmen yesterday afternoon.

Attention Workingmen!

HAYMARKET SCRAPBOOK

A Profusely Illustrated Anthology in Honor of the 125th Anniversary of the Haymarket Affair

When the People took to the streets to demand the right to Fair Labor Conditions and an end to Oppression.

Edited by FRANKLIN ROSEMONT and DAVID ROEDIGER

AK PRESS
EDINBURGH · OAKLAND · BALTIMORE

"The Anarchists of Chicago": Memorial drawing by Walter Crane, 1894

HAYMARKET SCRAPBOOK

EDITED BY
DAVE ROEDIGER
&
FRANKLIN ROSEMONT

CHICAGO
Charles H. Kerr Publishing Company
1986

Original title page from the 1986 edition, courtesy of Charles H. Kerr Company

Haymarket Scrapbook, Anniversary Edition
Edited by Franklin Rosemont and David Roediger

This edition © 2012 AK Press / Charles H. Kerr Company
ISBN: 978-1-84935-080-8 (print)
Library of Congress Control Number: 2011936330

AK Press
674-A 23rd Street
Oakland, CA 94612
U.S.A.
www.akpress.org
akpress@akpress.org

AK Press UK
PO Box 12766
Edinburgh EH8 9YE
Scotland
www.akuk.com
ak@akdin.demon.co.uk

Charles H. Kerr Company
1726 West Jarvis Avenue
Chicago, IL
U.S.A.
www.charleshkerr.com
arcane@ripco.com

The above addresses would be delighted to provide you with the latest AK Press distribution catalog, which features
several thousand books, pamphlets, zines, audio and video recordings, and gear, all published or distributed by AK Press.
Alternately, visit our websites to browse the catalog and find out the latest news from the world of anarchist publishing:
www.akpress.org | www.akuk.com
revolutionbythebook.akpress.org

Printed in the United States with union labor.

Cover design by John Yates | www.stealworks.com
Original interior design courtesy of Charles H. Kerr Company.

ACKNOWLEDGMENTS

We are especially grateful to William J. Adelman, Carl Aniel, Federico Arcos, Carolyn Ashbaugh, Paul Avrich, Martin Blatt, Flavio Costantini, Sam and Esther Dolgoff, George Esenwein, Philip Foner, Joseph Giganti, Robert Green, Joseph Jablonski, Gina Litherland, John Logue, Blaine McKinley, David Montgomery, O. W. Neebe, Les Orear, Hal Rammel, Sally Rosemont, Beryl Ruehl, Allen Ruff, Sal Salerno, E. P. Thompson, Michael Vandelaar, Theodore Watts and Fred Woodworth for their advice, encouragement and assistance throughout this project.

Conrad Amenhauser of the Wisconsin Labor-Farm Party; Heiner Becker of the International Institute of Social History; Sharon Darling of the Chicago Historical Society; Marianne Enckell of the Centre Internationale de Recherches sur l'Anarchisme; Paul and Elizabeth Garon of Beasley Books; Kenan Heise of Chicago Historical Bookworks; Dione Miles of the Archives of Labor and Urban Affairs, Walter P. Reuther Library at Wayne State University; Ed Weber of the Labadie Collection of the University of Michigan; and the staffs of the Beni Memorial Library; the Illinois Labor History Society; the Industrial Workers of the World; the Kansas State Historical Society; *The Match!*; the Newberry Library; Northwestern University Library; Rare Books and Manuscripts Division, the New York Public Library; the Tamiment Library of New York University; the Union Printers' Historical Society; and the State Historical Society of Wisconsin kindly helped us locate many of the illustrations reproduced in these pages.

Thanks, too, to the Estate of Irving Abrams, the American Institute of Marxist Studies, Lee Baxandall, the Estate of Ray Ginger, *Guangara Libertaria*, the *Industrial Worker*, *Jewish Currents*, *Massachusetts Review*, *Solidaridad* and Frederick Schmidt for permission to reprint material in their possession, as indicated in the text.

—The Editors

TABLE OF CONTENTS

III. THE HERITAGE

Introductory material by Blaine McKinley, Howard S. Miller and the editors

WITH ADDITIONAL DOCUMENTS BY

JANE ADDAMS, JOHN P. ALTGELD, PAUL CAMS, JAKE FALSTAFF, JOHN GLOY, FRANK HARRIS, ROBERT HERRICK, WILLIAM HOLMES, H. TAMBS LYCHE, JOHN REED, RUDOLF ROCKER, CHARLES EDWARD RUSSELL, MICHAEL J. SCHAACK, UPTON SINCLAIR, "BOXCAR BERTHA" THOMPSON & JOSEPHINE TILTON

POEMS

ILLUSTRATIONS

ROBERTO AMBROSOLI, J. A. ANDREWS, JACOB BURCK, RALPH CHAPLIN, D. CHUN, FLAVIO COSTANTINI, WALTER CRANE, ROBERT GREEN, GEORGE GROSZ. GEORGE HERRIMAN, J. F. HORRABIN, ROLLIN KIRBY, MIKE KONOPACKI, MAN RAY, ROBERT MINOR, ALFREDO MONROS, THOMAS NAST, F. B. OPPER, PASHTANIKA, ERNEST RIEBE, LOUIS SCUTENAIRE, MITCHELL SIPORIN, I. SWENSON, T. DE THULSTRUP, "DUST" WALLIN, TRUE WILLIARNS, ART YOUNG

TRANSLATIONS

ROBERT D'ATTILIO (FROM THE ITALIAN OF PIETRO GORI), MAX ROSENFELD (FROM THE YIDDISH OF DAVID EDELSHTAT), DIANE SCHERER (FROM THE CHINESE OF BA JIN)

SPRING FORWARD

Preface to the Anniversary Edition of *Haymarket Scrapbook* by Dave Roediger

Twenty-five years ago, Franklin Rosemont and I completed editing *Haymarket Scrapbook*, overwhelmingly thorough Franklin's inspiration and effort, just in time for the centennial of the events the book dramatizes. Back then the timing, and placing in Chicago, of the origins of May Day made special sense to me. I had spent most of a decade in Chicago, after growing up at the other, warmer end of Illinois.

The uniquely brutal winter of 1978–79 was part of that decade. It seemed perfectly logical that the celebration of surviving what seemed to be impossibly long and harsh winters would help generate all manner of hopes for renewal when spring finally came. Franklin and I were much-influenced by the great old Industrial Workers of the World (IWW) historian Fred Thompson's musings to us on the tragedy of (green) Earth Day being considered separate from (red) May Day. Franklin would soon take a leading role in IWW/Earth First! efforts to make the two traditions one. The many references by participants in the May 1, 1886 protests to wanting eight hours of leisure to enjoy nature and warmth—the appeals of what 1886er and later socialist humorist Oscar Ameringer called "buds and blue hills beckoning"—could not have failed to register with us.

Indeed in many ways the centuries-old traditions of peasants' May Day celebrations, replete with garlands and play was a pagan spring alternative to Easter and the post-Haymarket May Days of revolutionaries were secular (and pagan) alternatives. Warmth meant the start of the building season—making May Day an occasion for new labor agreements, and often for labor conflicts, long before the 1886 strikes and the events at Haymarket. Spring meant reasonable weather in which to relocate, making it logical that May Day would be moving day for many working class renters. Spring, flowers, and love cohabited, so that May Day also was a day on which charms predicting romance were traditionally most sold. Change was in the warming air. When I soon moved to Minneapolis, where May Day is still wonderfully marked on largely pagan grounds, the even bigger and longer chill of winter there convinced me that May Day, and Haymarket itself, were the products of their season. A wonderful recent May 1 in Winnipeg did nothing to change this view.

The relation of sunshine, spring, and revolt looks a little different now. 2011's marvelous Arab Spring can hardly be said to have been animated by coming in from the cold. Indeed its clearest comparison to the Haymarket events lies in the open-endedness of revolt. The threat of the strike wave described in this book was not only that it was huge but also that it was spreading wildly and unpredictably, much as Arab Spring has done and continues to do. The possible reanimation of May Day in the U.S. was born out of the 2006 immigrant rights protests, spearheaded by peoples without traditions of harsh winters. In the world today, May Day is as much and as militantly celebrated in the global South, where it marks the start of winter, as it is north of the equator. Because the call of Thompson and others to make the world a good place to live has not only gone largely unheeded but also uncomprehended, the start of summer in the overdeveloped world is now as likely to call to mind tornadoes, hurricanes, and deadly heat as it is to signal gentle warmth and renewal, even in Chicago.

The refusal by humans to be estranged from nature—the questioning of capital's alternating currents of regarding the rest of the world as a "resource" and as the enemy—is fundamental to any meaningful assertion of what Paul Lafargue has called the "right to be lazy." It is a vital part of the playful heritage of Haymarket. That right has been fundamental to workers' abilities, locally and globally, to live through the assaults on bodies and spirits that alienated labor necessitates. It increasingly is the condition for the planet's survival as well.

November 2011

MAY DAY RECONSIDERED

Foreword to the Anniversary Edition of Haymarket Scrapbook by Peter Linebaugh

In considering the history of May Day… How are we to bring together the three forces for social change—students, immigrants, and power? To begin with we need a methodology.

METHODOLOGY

Our first methodological principle starts with Aneurin Bevan, the Welsh coal miner who went on to install the national health system in Britain. He would remind himself and everyone else, not to forget that everything starts "at the point of the pick." This was in the days before the continuous miner when coal was hewed, even "crafted" he said, from the underground coal-face. The energy of industrialization began there. The methodological principle puts the worker at the center of history, and the coal miner at the center of the industrial working class.

We need a symbol of reproduction, and Vandana Shiva, the feminist advocate of India, can suggest one, for she issued the international warning against the taking of the seeds from the women and thus their power. "The seed, for the farmer, is not merely the source of future plants and food; it is the storage place of culture and history." The bowl of seeds had to be hidden against the "scientific" agronomists who were in the pay of Monsanto or other international genetic engineers ("the knights of the gene snatchers," quips Alan). The invisible work of reproduction surrounds history. The commons, often invisible and generally in the care of women is the second methodological principle.

So (the hammer and the sickle having had their day), let us proceed in our methodology on the basis of "the point of the pick" and "the seeds in the bowl." Because the pick takes things apart, it may act as a metaphor for analysis, and because the bowl holds stuff together it may stand for synthesis. If the Pick be analysis and the economics of production, it thrives in the realm of the inanimate. If the Bowl be synthesis and social reproduction, its realm is the animate.

These are both crucial operations of historical thinking. Consider the history of May Day.

MERRY MOUNT

In north America it began with immigrants, the English immigrants to Massachusetts, and they were of two minds. The gloomy Puritans wanted to isolate themselves ("the city on the hill") and having accepted hospitality of the native people either made them sick or went to war against them. Thomas Morton, on the other hand, arriving in 1624, wanted to work, trade, and enjoy life together with the natives. He envisioned life based on abundance rather than scarcity. Three years later he celebrated May Day with a giant Maypole, "a goodly pine tree of eighty feet long was reared up, with a pair of buckhorns nailed on somewhat near unto the top of it."

· A · GARLAND · FOR · MAY · DAY · 1895 ·
· DEDICATED · TO · THE · WORKERS · BY · WALTER · CRANE ·

William Bradford, coming over on the Mayflower, landed at Plymouth Rock. He thought Indians were instruments of anti-Christ. Of Thomas Morton and his crew, he wrote, "They also set up a maypole, drinking and dancing about it many days together, inviting the Indian women for their consorts, dancing and frisking together like so many fairies, or furies, rather; and worse practices. [It was] as if they had anew revived the celebrated the feats of the Roman goddess Flora, or the beastly practices of the mad Bacchanalians…"

Because Morton taught the Indians how to use firearms, the Puritan, Myles Standish, attacked and destroyed this early rainbow gathering. Morton was twice deported by the Puritans, and twice exonerated in England. He died in Maine.

Bradford gets one thing right. May Day is very old, and nearly universal (in one form or another). It is a festival of planting, of fertility, of germination. It is a community rite of social reproduction. Years later Nathaniel Hawthorn bemoaned this road not taken. Not taken yet, we might add. The circular bowl of seeds symbolizes the day in several senses. Picking away at time we easily find the commons.

HAYMARKET

From Merry Mount (1627) to Haymarket (1886) two and half centuries passed. An empire diminished (England 1776), a nation was founded, bankers established themselves, slavery advanced, an army and a navy manifested "destiny." With the pick of analysis we take up with the coal miners, the railroad builders, the ditch diggers. With the bowl of synthesis we apprehend how all together make a force in history. As a force it includes the commons, the space of autonomy, independent of capital and privatization.

In 1886, the iron workers of the Molder's Union struck at the Mc-Cormick Works in Chicago setting in motion the events that led to the infamous Haymarket bombing, the hanging of four workers, and our modern May Day. Let's pick it apart. First, these workers struck for an 8-hour day. This had been at the center of the post Civil War movement of industrial workers:

> We want to feel the sunshine;
> We want to smell the flowers
> We're sure God has willed it.
> And we mean to have eight hours.
> We're summoning our forces from
> Shipyard, shop and mill;
> Eight hours for work, eight hours for rest.
> Eight hours for what we will.

Second, many of them were Irish immigrants and as such brought knowledge of the Famine and knowledge of the struggle by the Molly Maguires in the anthracite fields of Pennsylvania the decade earlier. They remembered the Day of the Rope (June 1877), the first of a series of more than twenty hangings against the Irish coal miners of Pennsylvania.

Third, in Chicago the workers were making a machine to reap the grasses, the grains of the north American prairies. The machine presupposed the robbery of lands from the indigenous people—the Lakota, the Comanche, the Apache, the Metis in Canada—this is the fourth point of analysis. Its so-called productivity would result in a) the globalization of food as both grain and meat passed through Chicago and the Great Lakes into the hungry bel-

Eight Hours Work, Eight Hours Rest, Eight Hours Play was the slogan of the labor unions.

lies of Europe, and b) the short-sighted agriculture which would result in the disastrous Dust Bowl two generations hence. Chicago was a hub of world food organization as well as a forward base in the conquest of the common lands of the prairies.

The strike was suppressed by soldiers and a worker was killed. The class conscious workers of Chicago protested. Irish and Poles, socialists and anarchists, Catholics and communards, former Blues (Yankees) and former Grays (Confederates) joined in a howl of outrage. Albert Parsons, the former Confederate soldier whose consciousness was awakened by the Civil War to join forces with the former slave-slaves and present wage-slaves (marrying Lucy Parsons, part African American, part Native American), summarized the Haymarket gathering: "We assembled as representatives of the disinherited."

Truly, in one way or another the immigrants had been dispossessed, not only from their present means of production (capital), but from their past subsistence (commons) in the lands of their origins. Furthermore, the soldiers attacking the Chicago workers had learned how to kill in the Indian wars and to expropriate the indigenous peoples from their communal systems. This was the era when the critique of capitalism was elaborated by many hands. Few at the time swung the pick with greater point than Karl Marx who, unlike pure theorists, asked the workers what they thought in an inquiry of more than a hundred questions. This was to become the essence of subsequent student movements.

At Haymarket in Chicago, a stick of dynamite was thrown into the crowd (did the police do it? was it the deed of an anarchist or socialist activist?) and all hell broke loose. A spectacular and terrible trial was held, unfair in every respect, and Sam Fielden, Augustus Spies, Albert Parsons, Oscar Neebe, Michael Schwab, Adolph Fischer, George Engel, and Louis Lingg were found guilty. On 11 November 1887, despite an international campaign, four of them were hanged, preparing the way for the Gilded Age of American capitalism.

Chicago has never been the same, nor has the world labor movement: on the one hand, Chicago became the center of brutish capitalism, led by gangsters such as Al Capone, on the other hand a multi-ethnic working class arose from Mississippi, Mexico, Poland, or Ireland and writers such as Carl Sandburg, Nelson Algren, or Richard Wright told us about it. The "Chicago Idea" is not quite dead, the notion that revolutionary unionism can combine militant union with mass action. In remembrance of "los martires" May Day became the world-wide day of the workers and the 8-hour day.

The pick (the workers) and the bowl (the commons) must take us to the jubilee of SDS and SNCC. But the path is not direct. The coal miners had to overcome the ethnic and language civilizations deliberately instilled by the bosses. The United Mine Workers of America was formed in 1890. Mother Jones was born on May Day 1838 in county Cork, Ireland. In 1901, she was in Pennsylvania urging the wives of the miners to form a militia wielding brooms and banging pots and pans. The prosecutor called her "the most dangerous woman in America." In 1905, in Chicago, she helped found the Wobblies, the I.W.W., or Industrial Workers of the World, whose preamble stated: "The working class and the employ-ing class have nothing in common. There can be no peace so long as hunger and want are found among millions of working people and the few, who make up the employing class, have all the good things of life." Mother Jones herself urged us "to pray for the dead and fight like hell for the living."

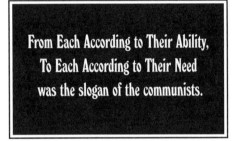

From Each According to Their Ability, To Each According to Their Need was the slogan of the communists.

Common lands was not within their program. Yet, the commons (of land and labor) became an anti-capitalist dream. The rulers will try to establish control over repro-duction with walls, fences, ICE, terror, detention. The rul-ers will do so by population policy, controlling birth rates and death rates, eugenics, family allowance, maternity leave, abortion, and what John Ruskin called "illth" or the opposite of health and wealth alike. The rulers attempt to organize the structures of labor markets, the skill-sets and levels by education and immigration policies. In Ameri-can history, slaughter and disease are weapons against the indigenous; slavery and immigration are weapons against workers. In fact terror has always been the instrument against the commons.

I believe in its early agreements with the bosses that, in addition to his own birthday, the coal miner's mother's and mother-in-law's birthdays were paid days off. It indicates

that a community of women backed up the miners. Oscar Ameringer, an immigrant, often called "the Mark Twain of American socialism" wrote for the miner's union in Illinois under the pseudonym of "Adam Coaldigger." He acknowl-edged that the miner had access to the commons, hunting and fishing, yet he couldn't do both at once, mine all day and half the night and then go hunt and fish! It was the coal miners who backed the union organizing during the Great Depression.

The epic, the decisive, event of the 20th century (at least one of them) was the Bolshevik Revolution in Russia of 1917. The Cold War of the U.S.A. against the USSR seemed to occupy the ideas, the institutions, and the poli-tics of the world. (The U.S.A. went so far as to shift the workers' holiday to the first of September and pretended that May Day was a Russian holiday!)

After the Russian Revolution, Communism was in-terpreted as a matter of State or the government far, far removed from actual commoning experiences which were dismissed as belonging to either a "primitive social forma-tion" or "backward," "undeveloped," economies. This began to change in 1955 as the second great theme of the 20th century—the national liberation struggles of colonies from European empires—congealed on the world stage. These two themes—the Com-munist Revolution and the national liberation struggles—provide essen-tial background for the birth of SNCC and SDS.

Again, let us take up the pick and the bowl.

INDONESIA

In 1955, a group of Asian and African nations met in In-donesia. They were seeking a third way, neither Commu-nist nor Capitalist, aligned with neither the USSR nor the U.S.A. Chou en Lai, Nehru, Nasser, Sukarno were some of the leaders present. This movement of ex-colonies devel-oped the block of non-aligned nations in 1960 that met in Belgrade.

Led by Sukarno, Nehru, and Tito, the attempt on the one hand was to find a third way between socialism and capitalism during the Cold War impasse, and on the other hand it was to assert the independence of the third world liberation forces. In either case these independent entities were results of that liberation, Yugoslavia after World War One, India and Indonesia after World War Two.

Richard Wright was the writer who understood racism, the working-class, and Chicago. He was born in 1908 in Mississippi, the grandchild of slaves. He moved to Chicago and joined the Communist Party. His 1940 photo essay of the workers in the American South was an eloquent visual preliminary to the Civil Rights movement of the Rosa Parks generation and the Montgomery bus boycott. In 1940, too, he composed *Native Son*, the unparalleled study of male proletarian rage in a racist society. In the Sixties, however, Third Worldism was the American optic of internationalism. It was deliberately and self-consciously revolutionary in its rejection of the U.S.A.

Richard Wright was present at Bandung, Indonesia, in 1955 and wrote a book about it, *The Color Curtain*. It was the first meeting of the third world countries, neither capitalist nor communist. He saw it as a meeting of "The despised, the insulted, the hurt, the dispossessed—in short, the underdogs of the human race were meeting." Of the American newsmen he met, "they had no philosophy of history with which to understand Bandung." He prepared himself for the trip by devising a questionnaire and using it as a basis of conversation with fellow travelers on trains and planes (78 of these questions are included in *The Color Curtain*): Were you educated by missionaries? What do you think of capital punishment? Is it ever justifiable to use the atomic bomb? Do national inferiority feelings find expression in your country? Do you want to see your country industrialized? Do you think that a classless society, in an economic sense, is possible? Here again is the empirical pick at work: the student asks questions, the student interrogates her subject, and then listens.

"With us land has always been communal," replied one Indonesian. Not one of the Asians he spoke to defended "that most sacred of all Western values: property." An Indonesian man summed up the recent history of his country, "Now the common people are not getting benefits from that revolution. That's why today we are threatened with another revolution."

Ninety percent of the land in the outer islands was under shifting cultivation or swidden agriculture; they had no notion of private property in land nor was production for commerce. High bio-diversity is maintained, with very high nutrient content stored in soil and in the biotica. The swidden plot is not a "field" but a miniature forest. By contrast Java and inner Indonesia under rice cultivation or *sawah* depends on terraces and elaborate irrigation systems carrying water, algae, and nitrogen. Seeds from nurseries instead

of broadcast. Pepper, rubber, coffee part of plantation. The 1870 Agrarian Land Law proclaimed that "waste" land was government property. It inaugurated the Corporate Plantation. Then the external pre-emption of village lands. The involution of life, ranking system, changing content of village rights. In the 1950s, local peasants took over roughly half the plantations but made dense, vague, and dispirited communities.

Pramoedya Ananta Toer (1924–2006), the Indonesian novelist of Dutch imperialism, was imprisoned on Buru island between 1965 and 1979. He describes life there in *The Mute's Soliloquy*, "But the Buru interior was not empty; there were native people living off that piece of earth long before the arrival of the political prisoners forced them to leave their land and huts behind. Then, as the prisoners converted the savanna into fields, the native people watched their hunting grounds shrink in size. Even the area's original place names were stolen from them and they, too, were calling the area 'Unit 10.'" He was lucky I suppose, because perhaps one million, certainly several hundred thousand, Indonesians were massacred between 1965 and 1966. Henry Kissinger and the CIA were complicit in this mass slaughter.

KENYA

In 1952, the indigenous movement for independence from the British empire began in Kenya. Guerrilla forces in the forests attacked the imperialists on the plantations. They formed the Land and Freedom Army, but the British called them Mau Mau, and the name stuck. The colonials ruling Kenya adopted the Swynnerton Plan in 1954, a massive land grab.

Cash cropping and land titling destroyed traditional communal economies in favor of a system based on commodity production. It effectively led to the confiscation of lands and "the consolidation and enclosure." Moreover the terracing of lands forced labor to make coffee plantations. Public grazing lands were closed. "One no longer feared to push aside traditional customs." Women and children suffered most. Women's entitlement to communal lands disappeared. A million men and women were forced into detention centers and concentration camps. It is against a background of mass hangings and concentration camps, part of the notorious British campaign against the Land Freedom Army, or Mau Mau. Male leaders failed to articulate a position in favor of women's access to land. Kenya attained independence in 1963.

The experience of Mau Mau is partly described in Ngugi wa Thiong's *Weep Not Child* (1964) and *A Grain of Wheat* (1967). In Detroit, 14 February 1965, Malcolm X explained that the Mau Mau frightened the white man throughout the colonial world. The U.S. FBI Counterintelligence Program and J. Edgar Hoover warned that "an effective coalition of black nationalist groups might be the first step toward a real 'Mau Mau' in America, the beginning of a true black revolution." Malcolm, our shining black prince, was assassinated a week later.

Si Se Puede! was the slogan of the immigrants in 2006.

SNCC

The number of students doubled in the decade; there were more students than farmers. The University had become the focal point of national growth. These youngsters were militants, the militants were students. University at the time didn't cost much. There were, however, fewer of them. Still, students were relatively privileged.

In the spring of 1960, there was the execution in San Quentin of Caryl Chessman by gassing. There was the Sharpeville massacre in South Africa. These shocked the young idealists of the time. Then there was the approval of the birth control pill which seemed to open the way to massive love-making. Ed Sanders wrote, "two roads seemed to split the American vista: fun & revolution."

Revolution or fun were the alternatives in America. The fun corrupted into porn, the revolution into violence. The American vista became an ugly horizon of terror. The Jubilee we observe is one for students, not for the New Left which in any case began in 1956. SNCC and SDS sang their songs, expressed their hopes, plotted their campaigns, danced their dances, took the hand of history saying goodbye to the old steps. These new dances started out as a cup of coffee at a lunch counter. It was fifty years ago. Now fifty years is the jubilee of something. Jubilee used to mean (the pick digs deep) emancipation, debt cancellation, return of lands, the reclamation of commons, and rest. In bringing it back and taking it forward, we could do worse than these ancient near eastern practices.

February 1, 1960: the sit-in at the Woolworth lunch counter in Greensboro, North Carolina, and a few weeks later in April, Ella Baker brought together the students who founded SNCC. Howard Zinn, a young professor, helped out the SNCC students. He wrote of them, "They have no closed vision of the ideal community. They are fed up with what has been; they are open to anything new and are willing to start from scratch." "They are young radicals; the word 'revolution' occurs again and again in their speech. Yet they have no party, no ideology, no creed." They believed in action, and their actions spoke louder than words.

A 19-year-old white student wrote, "the University is not much different than a giant marketplace of mediocrity, an extension of a corrupt, warped, illusion-ridden, over-commercialized, superficial society whose basic purpose seems to be turning out students to be good citizens dead, unconscious automatons in our hysterically consuming society... I want to work in the South as this seems to be the most radical (to the core), crucial, and important place to begin to try and enlarge the freedom of humanity."

SNCC stood for non-violent direct action, the "beloved community," and for anti-racism. As students they stayed up all night talking about existentialism, philosophy, theology, French literature. They did it in jail, not the classroom. From its credo composed at Raleigh, N.C., 1960: "We affirm the philosophical or religious ideal of nonviolence as the foundation of our purpose, the presupposition of our faith, and the manner of our action. Love is the central motif of nonviolence." They appealed to conscience and the moral nature of human existence. It was philosophy; or spirituality, or a love that enabled them to take a beating and by doing so beat down segregation.

Howard Zinn wrote that the best approach is "boldness in moving into a situation where interracial contact will take place, and then patience in letting them develop." Things began to get desperate in the winter of 1960–61 in McComb County, Mississippi, as local forces prevented even Federal food from being provisioned to the hungry and starving. Instead caravans of clothing and food from Michigan, some from Ann Arbor, began to arrive. This was a kind of commoning, though no one called it that at the time.

Staughton Lynd remembers a SNCC staff meeting on 12 June 1964. He wrote, "Several staff members said this week: I'm ready to die, but I need a program worth dying for. I think that both for the movement's effectiveness and for its morale there really must be more thinking as to program." A few days later Goodman, Schwerner, and Chaney were assassinated. So, voter registration and membership in the Democratic Party became the "program" as a default for want of having done that thinking as to program, and even they were betrayed at the Atlantic City convention that summer, by the Dems, the liberals, and the UAW. The question remains, What is the Program to Die for?

SDS

In 1901, Upton Sinclair spoke at the founding of the Intercollegiate Socialist Society which was to become the League for Industrial Democracy. "Since the professors would not educate the students, it was up to the students to educate the professors." Early on Jack London said, "Raise your voices one way or the other; be alive."

In August 1959, SLID (Student League for Industrial Democracy) changed its name to SDS and in the following spring the first SDS convention was held here in Ann Arbor. "Human Rights in the North" was the conference's name.

SNCC vitalized the meeting. The students were black and white, from the north and south. The UAW provided a grant, "to look for radical alternatives to the inadequate society."

Dwight MacDonald spoke on "The Relevance of Anarchism." The students asked, "What is happening to us, where are we going, what can we do?"

The preamble to its constitution affirmed that SDS "maintains a vision of a democratic society, where at all levels the people have control of the decisions which affect them and the resources on which they are dependent." At the beginning they were drawing upon and revising classic socialist and anarchist ideas but without taking a stand in the stultifying Cold War ideologies. Al Haber wrote in 1961, "The synthesis continually in our mind is that which unites vision and relevance."

Ed Sanders, the poet, summarized the "Port Huron Statement" (1962), which, he writes, "cut free of Cold War commie-noia & free of the do-nothing component of the labor movement." It was produced in an interesting way. In the summer of 1961, questionnaires were sent out to the entire membership asking for its views. The answers were then sent to all asking for changes. These became the basis of another submission to the membership and further review. Tom Hayden prepared a draft for the Port Huron conference. There, workshops discussed each issue, and both big issues (bones) and little ones (widgets) were sub-

mitted for discussion and vote at a plenary meeting. This then became the basis of a final draft.

"We are the inheritors and the victims of a barren period in the development of human values." "The role of the intellectuals and of the universities (and therefore, I think, SDS) is to enable people to actively enjoy the common life and feel some sense of genuine influence over their personal and collective affairs."

"Student" comes from Latin, meaning to be eager or zealous, or diligent. SDS members were questioners whose investigations thoughtfully and empirically gathered knowledge in a way similar to that followed by Karl Marx or Richard Wright. And then they attempted to put this knowledge to work.

SDS formed economic research and action projects (ERAP). SDS stood for participatory democracy and anti-anti-communism. SNCC stood for anti-racism and the "beloved community." Thus each came close to naming the commons. However, both skirted the idea in important ways, one with a nimbus of spirituality and the other with the convolution of a double-negative (anti-anti-communism) which made it difficult to grasp and develop the idea.

After the summer of 1964, the Movement began to change under the impact of the looming war in Vietnam and then the nefarious activity of the COINTEL program of the FBI. SNCC began to respond to the call for "Black Power" which issued from the black proletariat of the northern cities and, at the same time, it became increasingly conscious of the international dimension of national liberation movements. Martin Luther King moved to Chicago. SDS began to disintegrate after the Democratic Convention of 1968 when the blue meanies of Chicago ran amok.

BLACK PANTHERS

Although the symbol itself arose from the voter registration campaigns of the south (Lowndes county), the Black Panther Party, founded in 1966, quickly became an organization of the urban north and west, Chicago, Los Angeles, Detroit, San Diego, Denver, Newark, New York, Boston, Philadelphia, Pittsburgh, Cleveland, Seattle, Washington D.C. The Party's Ten Point program included employment, housing, health care, justice, peace, and education. It began as a self-defense organization against police brutality and quickly developed other forms of autonomous living, most notably, the free breakfast programs for children, the free medical clinics for the sick and infirm, the door-to-door health services, and the free schooling.

In Chicago, Fred Hampton was effective in bringing about a nonaggression pact among the street gangs persuading them to desist from crime and by teaching the elements of solidarity in the class struggle. He formed alliances with other organizations. It was he who coined the expression "the rainbow coalition." The Chicago police and the FBI assassinated him in December 1969. He had said, "You can kill the revolutionary but not the revolution."

Now, having sketched the history of May Day and linked it to the jubilee of SNCC and SDS, we arrive at the third task of this sketch, the invitation to Pres. Barack Obama to join the immigrants rights march in Detroit the afternoon of May Day in 2010 having finished addressing the students at Michigan's Big House. By all means let him come, but let him come as one man, a person among many, but not as President. As such he is too entangled in the toils of the ruling class. No so long ago, for instance he directed the largest immigration raid in American history, 800 officers of ICE (Immigration and Customs Enforcement) in South Tucson.

Hooray! Hooray! The First of May! Outdoor Loving Begins Today! was the slogan of the hippies.

OBAMA AND YOU

Obama's book, *Dreams from My Father: A Story of Race and Inheritance* (1995), is a compelling autobiography, and it remains a commercial success. Notice it is about "dreams." It is a "story." It is about an "inheritance." The biographical approach underestimates historical forces. In searching for his father in Indonesia, Kenya, and a father-like patrimony in Chicago, he underestimates the historical experience of the fathers. Both in Kenya and in Java, they avoided the deaths attendant on the terrorizing enclosure of common lands, but the defeat nevertheless affected them, even while they seemed to prosper in new petroleum-related jobs.

People who grow up with their parent's defeat take that as the norm. Their personality is shaped accordingly and so it has been with Obama. Personalities are not fixed forever. We are a collective subjectivity. The surge of historical change makes it possible in long lifetimes to pass through several. Can we grasp the living spirit of human experience, hold it in our hand? America is full of second-acts, and make-overs. We want to see through Obama as if he were a window and not a mirror of our projections. To do this we need to understand the dreams of his father's generation, which had been killed even before he was born. They survived terror, massacre, imprisonment, loss.

Our identity stems not just from our fathers, it is not just our family; our humanity must scale upwards beyond genetic lineages. Who are we to become? The big forces—war, globalization, climate change, automobilism, expropriation from land—arise through time and the conflict of classes: between the rulers and the ruled (power), the many and the few (numbers), the haves and the have-nots (possessions), the working-class and the capitalist class (20th century), the privatizer and the commoner (21st century). Prophetic generalization requires us to adhere to historical specificity.

When the boy, Obama, arrived in Indonesia, his stepfather fetched him. "We stopped at the common, where one of Lolo's men was grazing a few goats…" Obama learned how to box, to take a punch, and to deal with beggars, but the commons was being expropriated. Otherwise silence awaited him. What were the dreams, not from his father, but of his father? Obama's step-father in Indonesia had survived the massacres of 1965–66 by silence. Moreover, he prospered to the extent that he obtained employment in the petroleum industry. By the time he enters the young Obama's life, he has put the past behind him. Yet, the present is nothing more than the accumulated past.

Obama's biological father in Kenya also survived and prospered during the struggle for freedom from the imperial government of Great Britain. Franz Fanon taught us to understand these movements as both freedom movements or movements of bourgeois nationalism. What were the aspirations of Mau Mau? For if bourgeois nationalism expressed the right-wing aspect of the liberation struggle, what was the left-wing aspect? It depended on a relationship to the forest and commoning. They were smashed by British terrorism, i.e. concentration camps and hangings.

When Obama came to the continental U.S.A. to begin to search for authorities here, how was he going to fit in? Eventually, after several colleges, many chameleon changes, he settled in Chicago, and here too he fell into a time of silence, repression, defeat.

In Indonesia, Africa, and Chicago, Toer, Fanon, Wright provide us the materials, the clue, to understanding the structural silences. For in all of those writers it is not difficult to discern elements of commoning as a relation to land, to community, and to class. The anchors of doctrine or union or schooling provide no purchase in the storm. It is one where hope is chimerical, unrelated to either political programs or the movements to the commons.

Class consciousness is the knowledge that emancipation is ours. Class struggle is the fight for it, the fight to be a class and then the fight to abolish the class system. It is not economistic; it is historical. It was concrete not abstract. It was expressed in real voices, voices of the past and voices of the present. The skill is in the listening.

The pick pierces the soil or shale. The pick also acts as a lever. Thus, the usefulness of the pick arises from two functions. It penetrates its subject, and it dislodges it. As historians we do the same. It takes an energy from the past to heat and light the present. The lever-and-fulcrum uses distance to increase force. The class of working people can move the world. We need to recognize one another. The bowl of seeds is an artefact of preservation. It permits a future life. So, look at these seeds from our past—the 8-hour day, commoning, non-violent direct-action, one big union, song, satyagraha, participatory democracy—and watch them grow. They require sufficient aereation which we provide by talking and debate; they require plenty of watering which our considered and righteous action supplies. Then, they germinate in many forms: horizontal unionism, solidarity economics, commoning, autonomous living, Social Forums…

Fellow-worker Obama is welcome, but not his executive power. Our power arises from our class and it is that which we must make. Hence, you and I are urgently needed…

FURTHER READING

Leigh Brownhill, *Land, Food, Freedom: Struggles for the Gendered Commons in Kenya* (Africa World Press: Trenton, N.J., 2009)

Clifford Geeru, *Agricultural Involution: The Process of Ecological Change in Indonesia* (Berkeley, 1963)

James Green, *Death in the Haymarket: A Story of Chicago, the first Labor Movement and the Bombing that Divided Gilded Age America* (Pantheon Books: New York, 2006)

Andrei Grubacic (ed.), *From Here to There: The Staughton Lynd Reader* (Oakland: PM Press, 2010)

Thomas Morton, *The New English Canaan* (1637)

Barack Obama, *Dreams from My Father: A Story of Race and Inheritance* (New York, 1995)

Kirkpatrick Sale, *SDS* (New York, 1973)

Ed Sanders, *America: A History in Verse: The 20th Century*, 4 volumes (Woodstock, N.Y., 2000, 2004, 2008)

Vandana Shiva, *Stolen Harvest: The Hijacking of the Global Food Supply* (Boston: South End Press, 2000)

Pramoedya Ananta Toer, *The Mute's Soliloquy*, translated by Willem Samuels (Penguin, 1999)

Richard Wright, *The Color Curtain: A Report on the Bandung Conference* (Cleveland, 1956)

Howard Zinn, *SNCC: The New Abolitionists* (South End Press, 2002)

PREFACE

In January, 1887 Friedrich Engels considered American realities as he wrote the preface for a U.S. edition of his *The Condition of the Working Class in England*. Using a strikingly modern, if rather bourgeois, image, Engels highlighted the extent to which the May 1, 1886 strikes, Haymarket and the labor successes at the polls in November, 1886 had transformed the American calendar:

May and November have hitherto reminded the American bourgeoisie of the payment of the coupons of U.S. bonds; henceforth May and November will remind them, too, of the dates on which the American working class presented *their* coupons for payment.

Writing ten months before the judicial murder of the Haymarket martyrs, Engels nonetheless perceived that "brutal class-justice" had already characterized capitalist response to the May 1 strikes. The Haymarket executions, which would reveal the full extent of such brutality, would soon put another November mark on the American calendar and the world's.

This is very much a May and November book. Its orientation differs little from that of Engels' remarks except in emphasizing that working people were changed even more profoundly than coupon-clippers by the May and November events surrounding Haymarket, and that these changes were international in scope. What Jack London, in *The Iron Heel*, called "the classic instance of. . .ferocious and wanton judicial murder" was a decisive factor in making the first of May World Labor Day, and in making November a month of workingclass militant memorials.

It is customary in introducing new works to disparage older ones on the subject. We want to do just the opposite. The writings of William Adelman, Carolyn Ashbaugh, Paul Avrich, Henry David, Philip Foner, Sid Lens, Bruce Nelson and others make Haymarket the best-studied event in U.S. labor history. However, what these studies do not do—individually, as a group, or in combination with the present collection—is to exhaust the drama and significance of the Haymarket events.

Our aim has been to focus on less-well-known aspects of these events, and we have therefore minimized such incidents as the trial and Altgeld's pardon, which have been treated in detail elsewhere.

Important factual gaps remain. We had hoped to be able to include, for example, something on Chicago's Polish and Scandinavian revolutionaries of the 1880s, on the later history of the Central Labor Union and its affiliates, and on many other individuals—from John Swinton to A. J. Muste—who were involved in or influenced by Haymarket. Moreover, no study has quite situated Haymarket within the broader history of labor in the Gilded Age. The spectacular scenario in which the American Federation of Labor's predecessor, the Federation of Organized Trades and Labor Unions, led its supposedly conservative and craft-conscious affiliates in an attempt to cooperate in an eight-hour campaign with the revolutionary and class-conscious International Working People's Association deserves close consideration.

Internationally, we would like to have had articles on the impact of Haymarket in France and in South America—where a once-flourishing anarcho-syndicalism drew so appreciably on "Chicago Idea" traditions—and in Japan, where the executions of Shusui Kotoku and eleven others in 1911 was so reminiscent of Haymarket; and something, too, on the development of England's Freedom Press, which, like the publisher of this *Scrapbook*, is celebrating its centennial this year. The fact that this volume has reached ample proportions even without such material emphasizes that the subject is indeed inexhaustible. We anticipate that some of these omissions will be covered by the special Haymarket issue of *International Labor and Working Class History* scheduled for publication this year.

One index of the continuing fascination of Haymarket is the enthusiastic response of contributors to this collection. When we began to put it together eighteen months ago, we foresaw a book of considerably more modest dimensions. Given the numbers and political heterogeneity of the contributors, we also feared that missed deadlines and quarrels over editing would be the rule. Instead we were treated to timely responses, superb suggestions and forebearance by those who wrote this volume.

Readers will note that footnote citations vary in number and style throughout the book. Our original impulse was to discourage frequent footnotes, in keeping with the "scrapbook" format. When most contributions did come in with extensive and instructive notes, deadlines precluded full standardization.

If the *Haymarket Scrapbook* revives something of the rich international tradition signified by the Wobblies' motto, "In November We Remember," and helps workers recall the heroism of the many labor organizers martyred in that month, we shall be immensely pleased. If it recaptures something of the fighting spirit of May 1, we shall be all the happier.

Dave ROEDIGER
Franklin ROSEMONT

April, 1986

ABOUT THE EDITORS

DAVE ROEDIGER gives episodic attention to the hard problem posed by the Welsh historian Gwyn A. Williams: "the relevance of our historical experience to our blind-bat present." Co-author with Philip Foner of *American Labor and the Working Day* (forthcoming), he has also edited and introduced *Dreams and Dynamite: Selected Poems of Covington Hall*, published by Charles H. Kerr. His recent work appears in *Science and Society, Journal of Social History, Labor History, Negro History Bulletin, Labour/Le Travail, Pan-Africanist, History Workshop Journal, Massachusetts Review, Guardian, The Progressive, Southern Exposure, Mid-America, Chicago Sun-Times, Tennis* and elsewhere. Roediger teaches Southern and workingclass history at the University of Missouri. Once the Books Editor at *In These Times*, he is a former member of the Students for a Democratic Society and of collectives too frivolous to mention. With his wife, Jean Allman, he is currently active in movements to support the emergence of a new society in Southern Africa, and hopefully elsewhere.

After hitch-hiking some 20,000 miles all over the U.S. in the early 1960s, **FRANKLIN ROSEMONT** went to Paris and joined the Surrealist Group. Author of two books of poems and numerous essays on labor history and popular culture, he has edited and introduced a 600-page collection of writings by André Breton, the founder of surrealism, and organized the World Surrealist Exhibition in Chicago in 1976. He has also edited and introduced volumes of selected works by socialist anti-war agitator Mary E. Marcy, dancer Isadora Duncan and IWW cartoonist Ernest Riebe; his compilations of writings by anarchist poet Voltairine de Cleyre and Wobbly humorist T-Bone Slim are forthcoming. A contributor to such publications as the *Industrial Worker, Typographical Journal, Radical America, City Lights Anthology, Free Spirits, Living Blues* and *The Match!*, and one-time editor of the Chicago Typographical Union's organizing paper, he is on the Board of Directors of the Illinois Labor History Society and is a member in good standing of the National Puzzlers League.

PART I.
THE MARTYRS &
THEIR MOVEMENT

One of a series of Haymarket drawings by Mitchell Siporin

Chicago, May 3rd, 1886: Painting by Flavio Costantini

THE BOMB AT HAYMARKET

The Long Strike of 1875 and the Railroad War of 1877 were defensive actions to avert wage cuts at a time when the advance of organized labor generally was sliding backward. The national strike for the eight-hour day that began on May 1, 1886, marked a change in proletarian direction. The movement had expanded since the setbacks of the 1870s and was poised for a major leap forward, the accomplishment of a dream held for generations.

The *National Laborer* had expressed the belief back in 1836, when the workday was still twelve hours long and often more, that "eight hours daily labor is more than enough for any man to perform." The demand was heard more frequently in the 1850s through the efforts of a few special groups launched specifically to win that objective and proclaimed at many labor meetings. Then in 1863 the Machinists and Blacksmiths Union and the Boston Trades Assembly jointly appropriated $800 to lobby for eight hours, entrusting the task to a relatively young machinist in his early thirties, Ira Steward. For Steward, who devoted his life to this one goal, the shorter workday was more than a means of gaining leisure; it would give the workingman an opportunity to study politics and formulate plans to check the "corruptions of capital." It was the only means, said Steward, to preserve democracy and emancipate workers "from slavery and ignorance and the vices and poverty." Steward's wife, Mary, composed a couplet, soon to be heard on thousands of lips:

> Whether you work by the piece or work by the day,
> Decreasing the hours, increases the pay.

On Steward's initiative hundreds of Eight-Hour Leagues were formed fom 1865 to 1868, fifty in California alone, and together with the National Labor Union—founded by one of the noblest of labor leaders, William H. Sylvis—the agitation was accelerated. Responding to the *vox populi* six states and a number of cities legislated eight-hour labor laws in 1868, and Congress passed a bill covering its own employees. Most of the laws, however, were full of glaring loopholes—some requiring, for instance, that both the worker and the employer concur before the shorter workday could become operative. In other instances wages were cut proportionate to the cut in hours, thus making the law meaningless. In the end the entire effort turned out to be a pyrrhic victory.

But the idea of the eight-hour day, which was latent during the bleak 1870s, became overt in the 1880s—as a combination of prosperity and interunion rivalry gave it momentum. The 1880s, despite the 1883-85 slump, witnessed fabulous economic expansion. Capital invested in manufacture zoomed from $2.8 billion to $6.5 billion, the number of factory hands doubled and five and a quarter million immigrants came to these shores seeking surcease from Europe's sorrow. Though labor shared minutely, if at all, in the materialist glories of the decade—President Grover Cleveland in 1888 spoke of the poor being "trampled to death beneath an iron heel"—no nation on earth was doing nearly so well over-all as the United States. There was a feeling in proletarian circles that capital

could afford the shorter day (at the old pay) without too much strain, and that now was the time to get it.

The union rivalry referred to above was more subtle. It was between two organizations with unwieldy names—the Federation of Organized Trades and Labor Unions of the United States and Canada, formed in 1881 under the guiding hand of a Dutch-Jewish cigarmaker born in London, Samuel Gompers; and the Noble Order of the Knights of Labor, secretly established in 1869 by nine garment workers in Philadelphia. Neither was particularly massive in membership at the beginning of the decade, but by 1886 the Knights had spurted to 700,000 members, probably more than all the previous labor federations combined. A strike in 1885 against the three rail lines controlled by Jay Gould—the Wabash, the Missouri Pacific, and the Missouri, Kansas and Texas—had gained for the Knights a quick victory, restoration of a 15 percent wage-cut, and such acclaim that its national membership increased thirteenfold from what it had been in 1883.

Albert Parsons by True Williams (*The Chicago Riot*, 1886)

August Spies addressing strikers at McCormick's
(from Schaack)

Ironically, the Knights were opposed to strikes in principle. Terence V. Powderly, the vain but able former mayor of Scranton who headed the organization in its most productive years, considered the strike "a relic of barbarism." It might be, he conceded, necessary on occasion, but was to be avoided as much as possible since it offered only "temporary relief." This thesis flowed inexorably from Powderly's doctrine that while there was friction between workers and capitalists, especially the greedier ones among the latter, there was no *fundamental* conflict between the two. And the strength of this attitude was reinforced by a long list of disasters: defeat of the telegraphers in 1883; of 4,000 coal miners in Hocking Valley after two years on the picket line; of 5,000 textile operatives in Fall River whose ranks were sundered by the import of Swedish strikebreakers; of building tradesmen in Buffalo; of molders and cigarmakers in Cincinnati, and so on.

Instead of strikes, then, the Knights of Labor concentrated on "uplift." It created two hundred producer and consumer co-operatives, agitated on the legislative front for such reforms as free land, the eight-hour day, abolition of child labor, the income tax, public ownership of railroads. And when it took action against rapacious capitalists, it was in the form of boycotts far more than strikes. In its day the Knights conducted the most successful labor boycotts in history—against newspapers, manufacturers and retailers of beer, flour, cigars, stoves, shoes, clothing, carpets, pianos, etc.

Naive as this program of co-operation, reform, and boycott seems today, it excited working people passionately in the 1880s. The slogan of the Knights, "an injury to one is the concern of all," welded men and women into an almost religious solidarity that neither the AFL nor the CIO have ever been able to match. Many a socialist who believed in revolution rather than "uplift" joined the Knights because of its "beautiful watchword"—as one socialist put it.

In 1884 Powderly's organization was on the ascendancy, the Federation of Organized Trades and Labor Unions, though only three years old, in decline. Eschewing both "uplift" and revolution, the federation, formed by representatives of about one hundred local and national organizations, promoted what became known as "simple" unionism. Its basic philosophy—and that of the AFL later on—was contained in a statement made to the Senate Committee on Education and Welfare in 1883: "We have no ultimate ends. . . . We are fighting only for immediate objects that can be realized in a few years. We are opposed to theorists. . . . We are practical men." Not that these men were hostile to radicalism. To the contrary, Sam Gompers, as a young cigarmaker in New York, used to read socialist tracts to his fellow workers as they rolled the noxious weed, and boasted he was a socialist sympathizer. Peter J. McGuire, secretary of the carpenters' union, was a card-carrying member in the socialist movement. But they believed that there was a time and a place for revolutionary propaganda, a time and a place for trade-union activity, and the two were mutually exclusive. Being practical, they also rejected "uplift" as pie in the sky. They argued that the goals of labor ought to be mundane—higher wages, shorter hours—and the primary instrument for achieving them, when negotiations failed, the strike.

Much to the chagrin of the simple unionists, the American worker was not yet buying their notion of practicality. Succeeding federation conventions attracted a maximum of twenty-six and as few as nineteen delegates. In an effort, therefore, to save itself from extinction the federation inaugurated an eight-hour campaign in 1884. Next year the federation renewed its proposal and set May 1, 1886 as the date for a general strike nationwide, to attain the shorter workday. The federation, of course, was in no position to undertake such a venture on its own—its membership at most was 25,000—and the leadership of the Knights of Labor, while advocating an eight-hour day, intended to win on the legislative front, not through "relics of barbarism" such as the strike. Nonetheless the call had electrifying impact, and if Powderly shunned it, the "general assemblies" of the Knights, at the grass roots, embraced it jubilantly. So did another force, the anarcho-syndicalists of Chicago, whose role in the impending walkout was to prove more important than that of any other.

The slogan "Eight Hours to Constitute a Day's Work" was so popular that thousands of laborers brought and wore

"Eight-Hour Shoes," smoked "Eight-Hour Tobacco," and sang an "Eight-Hour Song":

We mean to make things over;
    we're tired of toil for naught,
But bare enough to live on:
    never an hour for thought.
We want to feel the sunshine;
    we want to smell the flowers;
We're sure that God has willed it,
    and we mean to have eight hours.
We're summoning our forces
    from shipyard, shop and mill:
Eight hours for work, eight hours for
    rest, eight hours for what we will!

As the appointed day for the strike approached excitement ran high everywhere and particularly in the metropolis of Chicago, where the anarcho-syndicalists were in the vanguard of events.

II

May 1, 1886, was a beautiful Saturday in Chicago—clear, with a bright sun beaming on the quiet panorama below. On Michigan Avenue near the lake, thousands of men, women, and children exchanged pleasantries and joshed with each other as they waited for the parade to begin. Elation was in the air: employers had already granted the shorter workday to 45,000 workers in the city, including 35,000 in the packinghouses. All told in the next couple of days, 340,000 men and women would down tools in 12,000 establishments nationally, almost a quarter of them in Chicago.

Waiting with the multitude was Albert Parsons, the young man who during the great strikes of 1877 had been warned by Chicago's police chief to leave town or be hung "to a lamp post." Parsons was now thirty-eight years old, a national figure in the labor and radical movement, idol of both the native and foreign-born workers in his city. On the Sunday before, April 25, he and his close friend August Spies had addressed a massive rally of 25,000 in preparation for this parade and the accompanying strike. On the morning of May 1, the Chicago *Mail* gave the city an editorial warning that

There are two dangerous ruffians at large in this city; two skulking cowards who are trying to create trouble. One of them is named Parsons; the other is named Spies. . . . Mark them for today. . . . Make an example of them if trouble does occur.

With Parsons on Michigan Avenue were his lovely wife, the former Lucy Ella Gathings, and their two children, Lulu Eda, seven, Albert, eight. Parsons, a trim, high-spirited man, logical in thought, poetic in expression—he often ended a speech with a recitation of poetry—was as much fitted, by his early background, to be a reactionary as a blazing radical. Youngest of three children in a solid middle-class Yankee family that traced its American heritage back to 1632, he was born in 1848 in Montgomery, Alabama, to which his parents emigrated immediately after their wedding in New England. Orphaned at five, he was sent to live on the ranch of his oldest brother in Texas, and was brought up by a black slave, Aunt Esther, who, he later recalled, was "my constant companion and had always given me a mother's love." At eleven Albert was apprenticed as a printer in Galveston and at thirteen, though short in stature, went to fight with the Confederate

cavalry in the Civil War. A good horseman and an excellent shot, he remained with the southern forces until the end of hostilities.

Returning after four years of war, Parsons had second thoughts about having fought to uphold slavery; he could not face his Aunt Esther, now freed from bondage. Ultimately he had a talk with the black woman who had virtually been his mother; it was, he said later, the turning point in his life. He started publishing a small weekly in Waco, Texas, the *Spectator*, espousing the rights of liberated blacks. For a long time none of his white friends would talk to him; he received repeated threats of lynching. Nonetheless he continued publishing the paper until his money was gone, and often stumped for the Republican Reconstructionists—"scalawags"—who had similar views. By the simple process of extending his humanism from the race issue to social problems generally, Parsons became an ardent socialist.

In 1872 he married a comely girl of Black and Mexican-Indian extraction, who had been living with a former slave. Lucy Gathings was not only to be Albert Parsons' wife but political comrade, and an important leftist figure on her own right many years after Albert had been hanged from the gallows. The two newlyweds departed from Texas for Philadelphia in 1873, then Chicago. Here, as they were getting settled and Parsons took a job as typesetter for the Chicago *Times*, they observed the effects of the depression on the

Police firing on McCormick strikers
(from McLean)

underclasses: the misery, the hunger, the demonstrations and police clubbings, the denial of free speech. They pored over the works of Karl Marx and Lewis Henry Morgan to find an explanation for such tragedies, and in 1876 joined the Workingmen's Party. A year later, as already noted, Parsons was embroiled in the 1877 riots. He emerged with a national reputation and was called upon to address workingclass meetings as far west as Nebraska and as far east as New York.

Meanwhile the socialist movement was in another of its interesting upheavals, enmeshed in a dispute between those who held that the party (now rechristened the Socialistic Labor Party) could seize state power through elections, and those who claimed that elections or no, the bourgeoisie would never yield its position, unless compelled to do so by "armed resistance." Though Parsons had run for alderman in Chicago in 1877 and had put a local ticket on the ballot in 1880, he was one of the key figures that seceded from the SLP in 1881 to launch the Revolutionary Socialist Party. It was not a large group—5,000 or 6,000 members at its peak, one third of them in Chicago—and it was seriously divided

REVENGE!

Workingmen, to Arms!!!

Your masters sent out their bloodhounds—the police—; they killed six of your brothers at McCormicks this afternoon. They killed the poor wretches, because they, like you, had the courage to disobey the supreme will of your bosses. They killed them, because they dared ask for the shortening of the hours of toil. They killed them to show you, ' Free American Citizens'', that you must be satisfied and contended with whatever your bosses condescend to allow you, or you will get killed!

You have for years endured the most abject humiliations; you have for years suffered unmeasurable iniquities; you have worked yourself to death; you have endured the pangs of want and hunger; your children you have sacrificed to the factory-lords — in short: You have been miserable and obedient slave all these years: Why? To satisfy the insatiable greed, to fill the coffers of your lazy thieving master? When you ask them now to lessen your burden, he sends his bloodhounds out to shoot you, kill you!

If you ar men, if you are the sons of your grand sires, who have shed their blood to free you, then you will rise i your might. Hercules, and destroy the hideous monster that seeks to destroy you. To arms we call you, to arms!

Your Brothers.

Rache! Rache!

Arbeiter, zu den Waffen!

Arbeitendes Volk, heute Nachmittag morbeten die Bluthunde Eurer Ausbeuter 6 Eurer Brüder draußen bei McCormid's. Warum morbeten sie diejelben? Weil sie den Muth hatten, mit dem Loos unzufrieden zu sein, welches Eure Ausbeuter ihnen bejchieden haben. Sie forderten Brob, man antwortete ihnen mit Blei, eingedenk der Thatjache, daß man damit des Volk am wirkjamsten zum Schweigen bringen kann! Viele, viele Jahre habt Jhr alle Demüthigungen ohne Wlberjpruch ertragen, habt Euch vom frühen Morgen bis zum späten Abend gejchunden, habt Entbehrungen jeder Art ertragen, habt Eure Kieder jelbst geopfert — Alles, um die Schapkammern Eurer Herren zu füllen, Alles für sie! Und jetzt, wo Jhr vor sie hintretet, und sie erjucht, Eure Bürde etwas zu erleichtern, da hepen sie zum Dank für Eure Opfer ihre Bluthunde, die Polizei, auf Euch, um Euch mit Bleitugeln von der Unzufriedenheit zu kurtren Sklaven, wir fragen und bejchwören Euch bei Allem, was Euch heilig und werth ist, nicht tiefen schrecklichen Mord, den man heute an Euren Brüdern beging, und vielleicht morgen schon-an Euch begehen wird. Arbeitendes Volk, Herkules, Du bist am Scheidewege angelangt. Wofür entjcheidest Du Dich? Für Sklaverei und Hunger, oder für Freiheit und Brob? Entjcheidest Du Dich für das Lehtere, dann säume keinen Augenblick; dann, Volk, zu den Waffen! Vernichtung den menjchlichen Bestien, die sich Deine herrscher nennen! Rücksichtslose Vernichtung ihnen — das muß Deine Losung sein! Dent' der Helden, deren Blut den Weg zum Fortjchritt, zur Freiheit und zur Menschlichkeit gebängt — und strebe, ihre würdig zu werden!

Eure Brüder.

The "Revenge" Circular: May 3, 1886.
The text was written by August Spies, but the heading "Revenge" was added by the typesetter.

from the outset. An eastern wing, led by Johann Most, advocated "propaganda of the deed" and shunned existing unions; a western wing, led by Parsons and Spies, considered unions the embryo of the future society and work within them indispensable for creation of the "workers' commonwealth." Both subscribed to the theory that the state *per se* was the enemy of social progress and that tomorrow's society would be run by some kind of loose federation of producers' groups. But Parsons believed that the Revolutionary Socialists had to work to alleviate the lot of the worker immediately as well as for tomorrow; and it was this concept which propelled his Chicago anarcho-syndicalists into national prominence.

Taking to their task with vigor the revolutionists founded five journals in 1884 and thereafter: the semi-monthly *Alarm* in English (2,000 circulation, Parsons as editor), the daily *Arbeiter-Zeitung* (3,600 circulation, edited by Spies, assisted by Michael Schwab), two other German sheets (*Vorbote* and the *Fackel*) and one in Bohemian, the *Budoucnost*. Within a year the anarcho-syndicalists doubled their influence, and what was more, weaned away enough unions from the conservative Amalgamated Trades and Labor Assembly, and unionized enough in their own organizations to become the dominant force in the labor movement. Their Central Labor Union boasted twenty-two affiliates, including the eleven largest locals in Chicago. They provided, in addition to ideology and militancy, men of unquestioned talents for leadership—Parsons, August Spies, Michael Schwab, Spies' assistant on the *Arbeiter-Zeitung*, Samuel Fielden, who many years earlier had been a lay preacher, Adolph Fischer, a printer. It was such men as these who gave the eight-hour movement its primary impetus in 1886. Had it not been for the Haymarket affair on May 4, this effort might have become the rallying point for the national labor movement. The American Federation of Labor, organized that year, had but 138,000 adherents, and the Knights of Labor was already beginning its decline into oblivion. What happened at Haymarket, however, halted anarcho-syndicalist aspirations for the time being.

III

Parsons could not have suspected this on that warm Saturday, May 1, as he, Lucy and the two children marched in the front lines of the procession to the lake front. There was an ominous atmosphere surrounding the parade: on the rooftops along the route, police, Pinkertons and militiamen were deployed with rifles poised, and in the city's armories 1,350 National Guardsmen were waiting nervously for a call to action. But no one paid much attention to the sinister gunmen, and the parade took place without incident. At the meeting-site speakers vented their feelings on the eight-hour day in a potpourri of languages: German, English, Bohemian, Polish. Spies, thirty-one years old, with blue eyes and exceptionally white skin, made a loud, dramatic speech that won the greatest applause. Parsons spoke eloquently, discoursing with his usual logic about the need for proletarian unity if labor were to become invincible. The crowd went home encouraged and enlivened.

With the parade over, Chicago tightened to meet the bigger crisis—the strike for the eight-hour day. Once again the city was in a state of semi-paralysis. The building industry

Two views of the arrival of the police at the Haymarket meeting. The sketch above is from Lucy Parsons' *Life of Albert R. Parsons* (Chicago, 1889); the one below from George N. McLean's *Rise and Fall of Anarchy in America* (Chicago, 1888).

The most widely-reproduced—and most far-fetched—picture of the Haymarket "Riot," this drawing by T. de Thulstrup ("from sketches and photographs provided by H. Jenneret") appeared as a two-page center-spread of *Harper's Weekly* (May 15, 1886).

This dramatic portrayal of the aftermath of the Haymarket meeting is reproduced from the *Nordstjerens Aarsrevue* (Denmark, 1886).

and metal foundries were silent. Lumber-laden ships had tied up at the docks and three hundred more were expected to follow suit. Some of the rail yards had already been shut down by a strike over another issue. Within a day or two 65,000 to 80,000 workers were walking picketlines. Employers, in small and large groups, were meeting frantically at the Hotel Sherman and elsewhere, to plan retaliatory strategy. Except for police clubbings to break up meetings, however, there was as yet no serious violence.

Trouble came on the afternoon of May 3—from another quarter. At the McCormick Harvester Works on the south side, 1,400 workers had been locked out since mid-February and were partly replaced by three hundred strikebreakers. Unrelated to that event, 6,000 lumber-shovers, on strike for eight hours, were meeting near Black Road, a few hundred yards away, to select a committee for talks with the employers. While August Spies addressed them, the workshift changed at McCormick's, and some of the lumber-shovers drifted toward the harvester plant to help the locked-out workers heckle and attack the scabs. In a few minutes two hundred police arrived, and what had been a minor skirmish now became serious. Hearing gunfire and watching patrol wagons rush by, Spies and many others in his audience hastened to the scene—to be greeted with clubs and a hail of bullets. As the crowd scattered, at least four workmen lay dead, and more were wounded.

Blazing with anger, Spies headed for the *Arbeiter-Zeitung*'s printshop, where he issued a fiery circular in English and German. Headed, "Revenge! Workingmen, to Arms!!!," the text read:

The masters sent out their bloodhounds—the police; they killed six of your brothers at McCormick's this afternoon. They killed the poor wretches because they, like you, had the courage to disobey the supreme will of your bosses. . . . They killed them to show you, "Free American Citizens," that you must be satisfied with whatever your bosses condescend to allow you, or you will get killed . . . . If you are men, if you are the sons of your grand sires, who have shed their blood to free you, then you will rise in your might, Hercules, and destroy the hideous monster that seeks to destroy you. To arms, we call you, to arms.

It was signed "Your Brothers." A second leaflet issued next morning, May 4, called for a mass protest that evening at Haymarket Square on Randolph Street.

On the fourth, police continued their attacks on strikers—at Eighteenth Street and Morgan, at Thirty-Fifth Street and elsewhere. In the evening 3,000 people showed up at Haymarket. Parsons, just back from a trip to Cincinnati, took Lucy and the two children to the event, expecting no trouble. When he arrived, Spies was speaking, and the crowd, on seeing Parsons, burst into applause. He mounted the wagon which served as a platform and told the audience: "I am not here for the purpose of inciting anybody, but to speak out and tell the facts as they exist." He finished at 10 p.m. and soon left for a nearby saloon with his wife and children and some friends.

Mayor Harrison, who attended part of the meeting to see how things were going, left at about the same time, and advised police at the Desplaines Street Station, a half-block away, that everything was in order. The meeting's attendance was by now about a third of its original size, partly because it was late in the day and partly because a raw wind was blowing and rain beginning to fall. Just as Sam Fielden was concluding a rambling speech the crowd suddenly noticed Captain John Bonfield coming at them with 180 policemen. The Captain, not known for his subtlety and dubbed "clubber" by working people, gruffly commanded the assemblage to disperse "immediately and peaceably." "But Captain," said Fielden, "we are peaceable." In that moment, without warning, there was an earsplitting explosion. Someone had thrown a bomb, probably from an alley, into police ranks. One policeman was killed on the spot, seven died later, sixty were wounded.* In the maddening confusion that followed, police fired wildly and clubbed everyone in sight. A number of citizens were killed by the police—how many is unknown— and two hundred were injured.

To this day it has never been determined who threw the bomb. Police of course attributed it to an anarchist; Parsons claimed it was the work of an *agent provocateur*. "The possibility of an *agent provocateur*," comments Samuel Yellen in his chronicle, *American Labor Struggles* (1936), "must not be dismissed offhand. The police officials in

---

* Most of the police casualties, however, were not inflicted by the bomb, but by bullets. Moreover, "all or nearly all of the policemen who had suffered bullet wounds had been shot by their fellow officers and not by civilians in the crowd." Paul Avrich, *The Haymarket Tragedy* (Princeton, 1984), 208-9. See also Carolyn Ashbaugh, *Lucy Parsons: American Revolutionary* (Chicago, 1976), 7, 79-80.

"The Charge of the Police" (from *The Chicago Riot*, 1886)

A scene from the Haymarket Trial (from Schaack). Note Judge Gary's several female companions, with whom he exchanged jokes and pleasantries throughout the proceedings.

Chicago were at this time quite equal to such a scheme." Another hypothesis, favored by the prosecution, was that the bomb had been produced by Louis Lingg, a carpenter and an anarchist leader, and thrown by Rudolph Schnaubelt, Michael Schwab's brother-in-law. But Schnaubelt was twice arrested and twice released. Governor John P. Altgeld, when he pardoned the three surviving convicted men in 1893—destroying his career in the process—postulated that "the bomb was, in all probability, thrown by someone seeking personal revenge," rather than as a political manifestation. Altgeld gave as justification

that for a number of years prior to the Haymarket affair there had been labor troubles, and in several cases a number of laboring people, guilty of no offense, had been shot down in cold blood by Pinkerton men, and none of the murderers were brought to justice.

It did not much matter who actually threw the bomb, however, since the ten men indicted for the crime (one left the country, another was released) were not charged with the actual murder, but with conspiracy to commit murder. What was on trial, it developed, was inflammatory speeches, writings, a political philosophy that called for liberation through violence. Only Fielden and Spies had been on the scene at the time of the explosion, but under the wide-ranging doctrine of "conspiracy" the other seven anarcho-syndicalist leaders could be tried for inciting the act. "Convict these men," cried State's Attorney Julius S. Grinnell, "make examples of them, hang them, and you save our institutions."

In the days that followed Haymarket, the newspapers, both in Chicago and throughout the nation, opened the floodgates of hysteria about unionism. "These serpents," shouted the Chicago *Tribune*, ". . .have been emboldened to strike at society, law, order, and government." From the epithets hurled at the anarchists—"Dynamarchists," "Red Flagsters," "Bomb Slingers"—the general impression was that Parsons and his friends had themselves tossed the explosive, and so it was believed by a considerable segment of the population. The Chicago police immediately initiated a reign of terror. They arrested twenty-five printers at the *Arbeiter-Zeitung*, wrecked presses, took subscription lists—used for further arrests—invaded radical offices, meeting halls, private homes, and beat and tortured conspiracy suspects while in jail. "Make the raids first and look up the law afterwards," Grinnell instructed the minions of the law. Everywhere the police announced they had found pistols, swords, rifles, ammunition, anarchist literature, dynamite, red flags. Nor was repression confined to Chicago: In Milwaukee the whole executive board of the local Knights of Labor was incarcerated, as were four officials of the Knights in Pittsburgh. Leaders of District Assembly 75 in New York were held on charges of "conspiracy" for conducting a strike against the Third Avenue Elevated.

Parsons, expecting the worst, went into hiding at once and only surfaced six weeks later when he calmly walked into court to stand trial with his comrades. Meanwhile Spies, Schwab, Fielden, Lingg, Fischer, George Engel, a toymaker, and Oscar Neebe, a yeastmaker who had earlier organized the beer-wagon drivers' and other unions, had been picked up and in quick order indicted for conspiracy to kill patrolman Mathias J. Degan.

18

The trial in Judge Joseph E. Gary's courtroom was a travesty. Candidates for the jury had been chosen by a special bailiff, instead of being selected at random. One of those picked, after the defense had exhausted its peremptory challenges, was a relative of a police victim. Others frankly conceded their prejudice against the accused but were permitted to serve anyway. Altgeld, in his later pardon message, asserted that "much of the evidence given at the trial was a pure fabrication. . ." Witnesses contradicted each other, some obviously lied. The jury was inundated with anarchist writings and documents, indicating that what was really on trial was a philosophy, not men charged with specific crimes. And, as expected, the jury found all eight guilty. Seven were sentenced to be hanged. Neebe was given a fifteen-year prison sentence.

On November 11, 1887, after all appeals had been exhausted, Spies, Engel, Fischer and Parsons mounted the gallows. Lingg had already cheated the hangman by exploding a dynamite cap in his mouth. Schwab and Fielden had asked for executive clemency and had had their sentences commuted to life imprisonment by Governor Richard Oglesby. The other four were executed. With nooses around their necks, waiting for the traps to be sprung, Fischer cried out: "Hurrah for Anarchy! This is the happiest moment of my life." Parsons said: "Will I be allowed to speak, O men of America? Let me speak, Sheriff Matson! Let the voice of the people be heard! O—" From inside his hood, Spies made a short statement which would be heard for decades in workingclass circles: "The time will come when our silence will be more powerful than the voices you strangle today."

Sidney LENS

Haymarket Square in 1889, shortly after the police statue was erected
(photo courtesy of Chicago Historical Society)

Haymarket Martyrs' Memorial lithograph issued by the Chicago *Arbeiter-Zeitung*, 1893

AUGUST SPIES

August Spies (1855-1887) came first when Prosecutor Julius S. Grinnell listed the Haymarket defendants in order of their guilt during the closing arguments in their trial. If we add that guilt implied, for Grinnell, able leadership in the anarchist movement and not conspiracy to murder, Spies' name was well-placed.

A German, born in Landeck, Spies emigrated at age seventeen. He settled a year later in Chicago where he worked as an upholsterer, setting up his own shop in 1876.

He began to study socialism in Chicago in 1875 and, radicalized in part by the Great Strike of 1877, became an active member of the Socialistic Labor Party and the armed Lehr-und-Wehr-Verein. A frequent SLP political candidate, Spies became manager of the socialist Arbeiter-Zeitung in 1880 and later edited that newspaper, which became the most widely circulated German-language daily in the city. He broke gradually from political socialism in the early 1880s. He was a delegate to the 1881 Chicago Congress which formed the Revolutionary Socialistic Party and presided at the opening of the Con-

from the Chicago Knights of Labor

gress. In 1883 he served as delegate to the Pittsburgh Congress which founded the International Working People's Association.

An excellent speaker and writer in German and English, dedicated, brilliant and funny, Spies was a leading figure in the Chicago IWPA. He addressed the huge crowd of strikers on Black Road on May 3, 1886 and witnessed the bloodshed that day when police fired into a group of his listeners who had left Spies' speech to confront strikebreakers at the nearby McCormick plant. Spies composed the text, though not the incendiary headline, of the celebrated "Revenge Circular" which reacted to the deaths on Black Road. He opened the ill-fated May 4 protest meeting at Haymarket commemorating the Black Road victims.

Throughout the trial, Spies was an exemplary figure. His long address to the court while under sentence of death in October, 1887, was perhaps the most eloquent speech ever made in America under such circumstances.

Spies' last line, as he was about to be hanged on November 11, 1887, was prophetic: "There will come a time when our silence will be more powerful than the voices you strangle today!"

DR

A LECTURE ON SOCIALISM

Socialism is simply a resume of the phenomena of the social life of the past and present traced to their fundamental causes, and brought into logical connection with one another. It rests upon the established fact that the economic conditions and institutions of a people form the groundwork of all their social conditions, of their ideas—aye, even of their religion—and further, that all changes of economic conditions, every step in advance, arises from the struggles between the dominating and the dominated class in different ages. . . .

The necessity of common ownership in the means of toil will be realized, and the era of socialism, of universal cooperation begins. The dispossessing of the usurping classes—the socialization of these possessions—and the universal cooperation of toil, not for speculative purposes, but for the satisfaction of the demands which we make upon life; in short, cooperative labor for the purpose of continuing life and of enjoying it—this, in general outlines, is socialism.

This is not, however, as you might suppose, a mere "beautifully conceived plan," the realization of which would be well worth striving for if it could only be brought about. No; this socialization of the means of production, of the machinery of commerce, of the land and earth, etc., is not only something desirable, but has become an im-

perative necessity, and wherever we find in history that something has once become a necessity, there we always find that the next step was the doing away with that necessity by the supplying of the logical want.

Spies' autograph as reproduced on the cover of
Reminiscenzen von Aug. Spies

Our large factories and mines, and the machinery of exchange and transportation, have become too vast for private control. Individuals can no longer monopolize them.

Everywhere, wherever we cast our eyes, we find forced upon our attention the unnatural and injurious effects of unregulated private production. We see how one man, or a number of men, have not only brought into the embrace of their private ownership a few inventions in technical lines, but have also confiscated for their exclusive advantage all natural powers, such as water, steam and electricity. Every fresh invention, every discovery belongs to them. The world exists for them only. That they destroy their fellow-beings right and left they little care. That, by their machinery, they even work the bodies of little children into gold pieces they hold to be an especially good work and a genuine christian act. They murder, as we have said, little children and women by hard labor, while they let strong men go hungry for lack of work.

People ask themselves how such things are possible, and the answer is that the competitive system is the cause of it. The thought of a cooperative, social, rational and well-regulated system of management irresistibly impresses the observer. The advantages of such a system are of such a convincing kind,

21

so patent to observation—and where could there be any other way out of it?

According to physical laws a body always moves itself, consciously or unconsciously, along the line of least resistance. So does society as a whole. The path to cooperative labor and distribution is leveled by the concentration of the means of labor under the private capitalistic system. We are already moving right in that track. We cannot retreat, even if we would. The force of circumstances drives us on to socialism.

August SPIES

from a lecture
to Congregational clergymen,
at the Grand Pacific Hotel;
published in *The Alarm*,
January 9, 1886

Sketch by Art Young

A REMINISCENCE OF AUGUST SPIES

[August Spies] was undoubtedly the most gifted of all the indicted anarchists, and he had a most intelligent appearance; his forehead was well developed. Temperance in eating and drinking was one of his qualities, but as regards his intellectual activity, I regret to say that this was not the case. Many of his articles betrayed nervous over-excitement. In the beginning of the year 1886, all intellectual work was forbidden him by his physician, and for a few weeks he followed his advice.

He was full of compassion for the poor and wretched, and he helped them wherever he could. Concerning his charities he observed strict silence. Any reference to them was disagreeable to him, and made him angry. A man who had once rudely offended him without cause, being in distress, Spies obtained work for him. I came to the knowledge of this by accident. One of the employees of the *Arbeiter-Zeitung* who received but a small salary told me that Spies out of his own pocket gave him for some months $2.00 a week to pay a doctor and procure medicine. The salary of Spies was only $19.00 a week, and from this he supported his mother.

Spies was of a very tender nature, and what his comrades thought of his blood-thirstiness may be gathered from the following anecdote. A certain man by the name of Matzinger had translated an article from the French, "The Day After the Revolution," and Spies asked an acquaintance of mine, "What would you do the day after the revolution?" The answer was, "I should imprison you till all was over, for your sentimentality would prevent us from any energetic methods." The bystanders laughed; Spies flushed and said nothing.

Michael SCHWAB

from "A Convicted Anarchist's
Reply to Professor Lombroso,"
The Monist, July 1891

August Spies in his cell at Cook County Jail

COMRADE SPIES

Although a ready and efficient speaker, especially in his native tongue, Comrade Spies was not an orator in the sense that Parsons was. As a writer, however, he had few equals.

His style was vigorous, terse and logical. He could put a great deal in a short paragraph. His thorough knowledge of history—ancient and modern, of philosophy and of economics gave him a great fund of information, which his excellent memory enabled him to draw from at will.

He was apparently a tireless worker; after attending to his duties as editor and business manager [of the Arbeiter-Zeitung] *during the day, he would often be found at night addressing group or mass-meetings upon the social question.*

Spies was a thorough radical, advocating a complete change in all the relations of mankind—political, sexual, social and economical.

William HOLMES

*from "Reminiscences,"
Free Society
(Chicago, November 6, 1898)*

22

"THE ARBITRARY WILL OF THIS LAWLESS COURT"

Anarchism does not mean bloodshed; does not mean robbery, arson, etc. These monstrosities are, on the contrary, the characteristic features of capitalism. Anarchism means peace and tranquility to all. Anarchism, or socialism, means the reorganization of society upon scientific principles and the abolition of causes which produce vice and crime. Capitalism first produces these social diseases and then seeks to cure them by punishment. . . .

Now, if we cannot be directly implicated with this affair, connected with the throwing of the bomb, where is the law that says "that these men shall be picked out to suffer"? Show me that law if you have it. If the position of this court is correct, then half of this city—half of the population of this city—ought to be hanged, because they are responsible the same as we are for that act on May 4th. And if not half the population of Chicago is hanged, then show me the law that says "eight men shall be picked out and hanged as scapegoats"! You have no such law. Your decision, your verdict, our conviction is nothing but an arbitrary will of this lawless court.

It is true there is no precedent in jurisprudence in this case. It is true we have called upon the people to arm themselves. It is true that we have told them time and again that the great day of change was coming. It was not our desire to have bloodshed. We are not beasts. We would not be socialists if we were beasts. It is because of our sensitiveness that we have gone into this movement for the emancipation of the oppressed and suffering. . . .

This seems to be the ground upon which the verdict is to be sustained:

But when a long train of abuses and usurpations pursuing invariably the same object evinces a design to reduce the people under absolute despotism, it is their right, their duty, to throw off such government and provide new guards for their future safety.

This is a quotation from the Declaration of Independence. Have we broken any laws by showing to the people how these abuses, that have occurred for the last twenty years, are invariably pursuing one object, *viz:* to establish an *oligarchy* in this country as strong and powerful and monstrous as never before has existed in any country?

I can well understand why that man Grinnell did not urge upon the grand jury to charge us with treason. I can well understand it. You cannot try and convict a man for treason who has upheld the constitution against those who try to trample it under their feet. It would not have been as easy a job to do that, Mr. Grinnell, as to charge "these men" with murder.

Now, these are my ideas. They constitute a part of myself. I cannot divest myself of them, nor would I, if I could. And if you think that you can crush out these ideas that are gaining ground more and more every day, if you think you can crush them out by sending us to the gallows—if you would once more have people to suffer the penalty of death because they have dared to tell the truth—and I defy you to show us where we have told a lie—I say, if death is the penalty for proclaiming the truth, then I will proudly and defiantly pay the costly price! Call your hangman. Truth crucified in Socrates, in Christ, in Giordano Bruno, in Huss, in Galileo, still lives—they and others whose number is legion have preceded us on this path. We are ready to follow!

August SPIES

from *Anarchism: Its Philosophy and Scientific Basis* (Chicago, 1887)

Office of the anarchist daily *Arbeiter-Zeitung* on Wells Street

LETTER TO THE GOVERNOR OF ILLINOIS

Chicago, Nov. 6, 1887

The fact that some of us have appealed to you for justice (under the pardoning prerogative) while others have not, should not enter into consideration in the decision of our cases. Some of my friends have asked you for an absolute pardon. They feel the injustice done them so intensely that they cannot conciliate the idea of a commutation of sentence with the consciousness of innocence. The others (among them myself), while possessed of the same feeling of indignation, can perhaps more calmly and dispassionately look upon the matter as it stands. They do not disregard the fact that through a systematic course of lying, perverting, distorting and slandering, the press has suceeded in creating a sentiment of bitterness and hatred among a great portion of the populace that one man, no matter how powerful, how courageous and just he be, cannot possibly overcome. They hold that to overcome that sentiment or the influence thereof would almost be a psychological impossibility. Not wishing, therefore, to place your excellency in a still more embarrassing position between the blind fanaticism of a misinformed public on the one hand and justice on the other, they concluded to submit their case to you unconditionally.

I implore you not to let this difference of action have any weight with you in determining our fate. During our trial the desire of the prosecution to slaughter me and to let my co-defendants off with slighter punishment was quite apparent and manifest. It seemed to me then, and to a great many others, that the prosecution would be satisfied with one life—namely, mine. Grinnell in his argument intimated this very plainly.

AUGUST SPIES

I care not to protest my innocence of any crime, and of the one I am accused of in particular. I have done that, and I leave the rest to the judgment of history. But to you I wish to address myself now, as the alleged archconspirator (leaving the fact that I have never belonged to any kind of a conspiracy out of the question altogether); if a sacrifice of life must be, will not my life suffice? The state's attorney of Cook County asked for no more. Take this, then; take my life. I offer it to you that you may satisfy the fury of a semibarbaric mob, and save the lives of my comrades. I know that every one of my comrades is as willing to die and perhaps more so than I am. It is not for their sakes that I make this offer, but in the name of humanity and progress, in the interest of a peaceable, if possible, development of the social forces that are destined to lift our race upon a higher and better plane of civilization.

In the name of the traditions of our country I beg you to prevent a sevenfold murder upon men whose only crime is that they are idealists; that they long for a better future for all. If legal murder there must be, let one, let mine suffice.

A. SPIES

from George N. McLean,
The Rise and Fall of Anarchy
(Chicago, 1888)

LIBERTY

The greatest crime known to American courts, capitalists and editors, is that of being a revolutionist, i.e., a man who will not be convinced that the world has come to a standstill, since the bourgeoisie have arranged everything so nicely. . . .

* * *

If I teach certain doctrines with which my neighbor is displeased, does that give him the right to suppress me, because it is "license," and because he has the power to suppress me? Where there is liberty there can be no license! But the suppression of liberty in any and every form is license! License and privilege are twins. Equality and liberty are twins. Our constitution speaks not of liberty and license. Liberty can have no other but natural restrictions. How monstrous to think that a policeman may decide where "liberty" ends and where "license" begins! How monstrous—when we consider that the average policeman is very little, if at all, above the common brute!

* * *

It may surprise some of our American citizens to learn that in this country of "free speech" there is no easier thing in the world than to sentence persons to death for expressing their views. . . .

August SPIES

Autobiography,
"Notes & Letters"
(Chicago, 1887)

Linocut from *Solidaridad* (Uruguay)

from a police photograph

24

ABRAHAM BISNO

Abraham Bisno (1866-1929), a Russian emigrant, came to the United States in 1881 and to Chicago the following year. He became active in Jewish radical causes and in the labor movement during the middle and late 1880s, and was particularly influenced by August Spies. Bisno, a tailor, helped to found the Workingmen's Educational Society in 1888 and and became the first president of the Chicago Cloak Makers Union in 1890. He served under Florence Kelley as a state factory inspector during John Peter Altgeld's governorship in Illinois and helped make the inspection agency such a model of efficient enforcement of labor legislation that the laws under which it operated were quickly repealed. Bisno later was a leading official in the Cloakmakers' division of the International Ladies' Garment Workers' Union. The texts below are reprinted from his posthumously published memoirs.

DR

WHAT I LEARNED FROM AUGUST SPIES

A mass meeting was called to explain the nature of the strike and encourage our membership. By that time there were already a great many of us that were in actual want for food, house wants, etc., and when that meeting was called a man was invited to speak to us in the German language and he made a wonderful speech. August Spies was his name.

He was the editor of a German socialist or anarchist newspaper. He was then engaged in the agitation for the eight-hour movement, but he didn't only advocate an eight-hour movement. He advocated something much more significant. He told us that we were experiencing now in the modern industrial life a class struggle; that we, all of us, were on the side of the poor; that the capitalists, the employers of all kinds, traders and storekeepers of all kinds, the government, legislators, judges and policemen and clergymen were all classed as either capitalists or their henchmen and were arrayed against us; that humanity was suffering because humanity was disinherited; that the property of the country belonged all to that one class and their henchmen; that the great body of the people, the working man and the poor, had no property, and depended for their living only on wages that they received from the employing classes; that under the present economic order of things there was such a thing as an iron law of wages which meant that no working man got more than bare subsistence for his work so that he might be able to live and work for his boss and reproduce, in his children, working men for ever after to keep his employer in wealth—nay, he said, even in riotous luxury; that the employers were maintaining their horses and their dogs in better houses than their men; that the employers worked their horses less than they did their men and that was because when a horse died because of being exhausted the employers lost something, while if the working man died, he was easily replaced with no damage to the boss.

August Spies went on to say that we are now living in an industrial age that keeps on developing itself, that working men are acquiring more and more significance as the real producers of all wealth; that the employers, tradesmen and their henchmen, clergymen and government officials, are all a useless lot, bound to be overthrown by labor in the course of time, and that historically labor was assigned the mission to overthrow the capitalist class, and that while he wished us good luck in our strike to establish a regular working day, raise the price for our work, and enforce decent treatment on the part of the employers, he thought that this was only a minor effort and that the real effort to be made by us [was] to destroy root and branch the present capitalist order of things and establish a co-operative commonwealth.

He advised us to read anarchist and socialist newspapers and books on the labor movement. There were then and there in the hall a number of German socialists and English socialists and anarchists who distributed amongst us appeals, leaflets, newspapers, in both German and English, and we were advised to read them so that we might educate ourselves in the cause of labor, the theories of socialism and anarchism, and on the general labor movement. He spoke in a very plain German, and since Yiddish is only a dialect of German, I understood almost every word he said and it made a great impression on me.

On that night when I went home I was aflame; the whole argument struck me like lightning and went all through me. I had heard ideas that I had never heard before in my life and they seemed to express the very thoughts that were in my inner consciousness. He's right, I thought; we are disinherited, the property of the country does belong to the rich; all we get out of it is a bare living for very hard work; there must be a chance to improve conditions; there are so many of us, there ought to be no division of opinion amongst us; we ought to all unite, all the working people from all trades, and support what he calls the Labor Movement for the purpose of getting redress.

Abraham BISNO

From *Abraham Bisno, Union Pioneer*
(Madison, 1967)

AUGUST SPIES'

AUTO-BIOGRAPHY;

His Speech in Court,

AND GENERAL NOTES.

Bound in Paper, 25 Cents.

Bound in Cloth, 65 Cents.

PUBLISHED BY

NIÑA VAN ZANDT,
CHICAGO, ILL.

Title-page of *August Spies' Autobiography*, 1887

THE DAY AFTER

On May the fifth, 1886, an event happened that had a great influence on the fortunes of our strike. It was known to us that the manufacturers had taken into their own downtown shops a number of our own people to do the work inside instead of in the outside shops. In doing so, they were able to satisfy their trade and prolong the strike for an indefinite time. When we got together in the hall in conversation between ourselves, it was made clear that unless we could go downtown and stop these shops, we would be obliged to lose the strike; but that was a big job. The manufacturers had their factories on the upper floors of great big buildings. To break into these buildings it would be necessary to have a great many men. It was necessary to overawe the nonunion people in the shops, and make them come down in the hope that we might win the strike.

A consensus of opinion was formed that in this special case the committee to stop those shops must be composed of our entire membership. About six hundred of us left the De Koven Street Hall, which was about a mile or more distant from the factory, and walked in a body downtown. When we crossed the Van Buren Street bridge, something happened that we had not expected to happen at all, namely, patrol wagons came in on us from all sides of the city in large numbers; hundreds, probably thousands of policemen were unloaded in very short order in the cloak district; every policeman had a billy and they began to chase us and beat us unmercifully. Within ten or fifteen minutes the whole neighborhood there was cleared; none of us were arrested, none of us had time to do anything that would warrant an arrest. We simply were there, but a great many of us were beaten up very badly, and we ran for our lives.

When we finally got back into the hall, and got over our astonishment at the treatment we received at the hands of the police, we bound up the wounds of those of us that were badly hurt and tried to find some explanation for what had happened. We found the following. One of our men was able to read German. He said that he read in the newspaper that there was a great big factory about a mile away called the McCormick Harvester Works; that the people over there were out on a strike for an eight-hour day; that two or three days past they had had a meeting near the factory; that the policemen had tried to disperse them and they killed a number of men; that yesterday these men held a meeting at Haymarket Square and the policemen there, too, tried to disperse them; that someone threw a bomb under the policemen's patrol wagon, which killed a number of policemen and wounded a great many more; that the police were out to stop those gatherings and were looking for the men who threw the bomb; that it was said in the newspapers that the men who threw the bomb were anarchists; that one of them was this same August Spies who had lectured before us, and because of that, any assembly on the street by working men was prohibited, and the fact that so many of us had gone downtown at the same time made the police think we were anarchists prepared to throw bombs and make riots and therefore they treated us the way they did. . . .

After May 5th, 1886, picketing became absolutely impossible. The police arrested all pickets, even two or three. The attitude on the part of the police was practically the same as though the city was under martial law. Labor unions were raided, broken up, their property confiscated, the police used their clubs freely. Arrests were made without any cause, and the life of a working man was not quite safe when out on strike.

Abraham BISNO

from *Abraham Bisno: Union Pioneer*
(Madison, 1967)

Die Fackel was the Sunday edition of the *Arbeiter-Zeitung*.

MY FRIEND AUGUST SPIES

I have been charged with personal friendship for August Spies. Of this crime I plead guilty—guilty to the fullest extent. But not alone that—I am even proud of that friendship. I say it with pride, and say it to everyone who wants to hear it, that among the large number of my fellow-turners and other personal friends I have to look long before I find one worthy to be compared to August Spies, notwithstanding the fact that in political matters I do not agree with my friend Spies on many important points. . . .

I ask you, can you name me a man (I allow you to search ancient and modern history) who, in the face of an infamous death, showed more courage, more character, and more fidelity to his convictions, than Spies and his associates have shown?

Those men have compelled the admiration of the whole world, and even forced their bitterest enemies to give them the respect they deserve. . . . Indeed, a community which knows no better how to treat those men than to hang them—well, but may everyone finish the thought himself. . . .

On the 4th of May there was a public open-air meeting held in Chicago. While the police are making the unlawful attempt to disperse this meeting an unknown person throws a bomb, which kills and wounds several men. In the trial following this event seven men are sentenced to death and one to fifteen years imprisonment in the penitentiary, notwithstanding the fact that the thrower of the bomb has not been discovered to this day.

Several months afterward, after the ending of a strike in the stockyards, shots were fired from a railroad train into a crowd of people. One man is killed; several others are wounded. It was known who hired those men, who paid them, who armed them—yes, even the very men who did the shooting were known—and yet there was not even an indictment found.

Now, turners, whoever can call this justice without blushing and without sinking into the earth for very shame, let him come forward.

John GLOY

Amerikanische Turner-Bund
Chicago District

ALBERT R. PARSONS

Albert Richard Parsons (1848-1887) went from Confederate soldier to America's foremost native-born revolutionary labor leader in just two decades. Born in Montgomery, Alabama, Parsons lost his parents as a youth. Apprenticed as a printer in Texas before the Civil War, he followed the brother who had raised him into service in the Rebel army.

But after the war Parsons came to embody many of the conservative South's worst nightmares. He served the radical Republican cause in Texas (which he later described as a "labor party" for Blacks there) both as an officeholder and as editor of the Waco Spectator. *From 1869 to 1871, he worked for the Internal Revenue Bureau in Texas. Around 1872 Parsons capped his apostasy by marrying the lovely Lucy Gathings, a woman of Black, Indian and Mexican ancestry.*

After the defeat of Republican power in Texas, Parsons settled in Chicago, probably in late 1873. His work as a printer and editor, and especially his activities in labor and radical causes, are treated at some length in the articles on Parsons by Henry Rosemont, Alexander Yard and Dave Roediger in the present volume.

from the Chicago *Knights of Labor*

Parsons twice moved from the wings to the center stage in the Haymarket tragedy. On May 2, 1886 he addressed a huge eight-hour

rally in Cincinnati. Just back in Chicago, he devoted May 4 to napping and to discussing strategies for organizing women sewing workers with a few associates at an evening meeting of the American section of the IWPA. Only after the Haymarket meeting had started was Parsons located at the gathering of the American section and recruited to speak at Haymarket. He addressed the crowd there for almost an hour, stressing self-defense and the eight-hour day while arguing that individual terror was futile. He then introduced Samuel Fielden and retired to Zepf's Hall to escape the rain. Thus he was not in the square when the bomb exploded.

Parsons eluded police after the bombing, making his way to Waukesha, Wisconsin where he lived under an assumed name until he chose again to enter the Haymarket drama. On June 21, 1886 he voluntarily returned to Chicago to stand trial with his seven co-defendants. Never again out of police custody, Parsons was hanged by the state of Illinois on November 11, 1887. "Let the voice of the people be heard!" he demanded, seconds before his own was stilled.

DR

WHAT IS ANARCHISM?

Anarchy is anti-government, anti-rulers, anti-dictators, anti-bosses. . . . Anarchy is the negation of force; the elimination of all authority in social affairs; it is the denial of the right of domination of one man over another. It is the diffusion of rights, of power, of duties, equally and freely among all the people.

But Anarchy, like many other words, is defined in Webster's dictionary as having two meanings. In one place it is defined to mean "without rulers or governors." In another place it is defined to mean, "disorder and confusion." This latter meaning is what we call "capitalistic anarchy," such as is now witnessed in all portions of the world and especially in this courtroom; the former, which means without rulers, is what we denominate communistic anarchy, which will be ushered in with the social revolution.

Socialism is a term which covers the whole range of human progress and advancement . . . I think I have a right to speak of this matter, because I am tried here as a socialist. I am condemned as a socialist. . . . If you are going to put me to death, then let the people know what it is for.

Socialism is defined by Webster as "a theory of society which advocates a more precise, more orderly, and more harmonious

arrangement of the social relations of mankind than has hitherto prevailed." Therefore everything in the line of progress, in civilization in fact, is socialistic.

There are two distinct phases of socialism in the labor movement throughout the world today. One is known as anarchism, without political government or authority; the other is known as state socialism or paternalism, or governmental control of everything. The state socialist seeks to ameliorate and emancipate the wage-laborers by means of law, by legislative enactments. The state socialists demand the right to choose their own rulers. Anarchists would have neither rulers nor lawmakers of any kind. The anarchists seek the same ends [the abolition of wage-slavery] by the abrogation of law, by the abolition of all government, leaving the people free to unite or disunite as fancy or interest may dictate, coercing no one. . . .

We are charged with being the enemies of "law and order," as breeders of strife and confusion. Every conceivable bad name and evil design was imputed to us by the lovers of power and haters of freedom and equality. Even the workingmen in some instances caught the infection, and many of them joined in the capitalistic hue and cry against the anarchists. Being satisfied of ourselves

that our purpose was a just one, we worked on undismayed, willing to labor and to wait for time and events to justify our cause. We began to allude to ourselves as anarchists and that name, which was at first imputed to us as a dishonor, we came to cherish and defend with pride. What's in a name? But names sometimes express ideas, and ideas are everything.

What, then, is our offense, being anarchists? The word anarchy is derived from the two Greek words *an*, signifying no, or without, and *arche*, government; hence anarchy means no government. Consequently anarchy means a condition of society which has no king, emperor, president or ruler of any kind. In other words, anarchy is the social administration of all affairs by the people themselves; that is to say, self-government, individual liberty. Such a condition of society denies the right of majorities to rule over or dictate to minorities. Though every person in the world agree upon a certain plan and only one objects thereto, the objector would, under anarchy, be respected in his natural right to go his own way. . . .

The great natural law of power derived alone from association and cooperation will of necessity and from selfishness be applied by the people in the production and distribu-

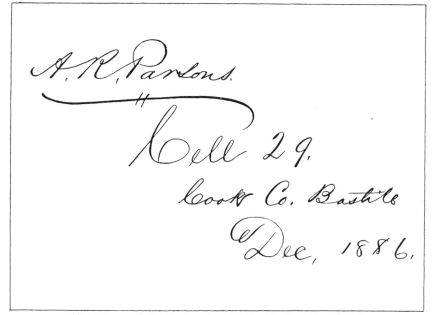

Albert Parsons' signature and his address in Cook County Jail

tion of wealth, and what the trades unions and labor organizations seek now to do, but are prevented from doing because of obstructions and coercions, will under perfect liberty—anarchy—come easiest to hand. Anarchy is the extension of the boundaries of liberty until it covers the whole range of the wants and aspirations of man. . . .

The anarchists are the advance-guard in the impending social revolution. They have discovered the cause of the worldwide discontent which is felt but not yet understood by the toiling millions as a whole. The effort now being made by organized and unorganized labor in all countries to participate in the making of laws which they are forced to obey will lay bare to them the the secret source of their enslavement to capital. Capital is a thing—it is property. Capital is the stored up, accumulated savings of past labor . . .the resources of life, the means of subsistence. These things are, in a natural state, the common heritage of all for the free use of all, and they were so held until their forcible seizure and appropriation by a few. Thus the common heritage of all, seized by violence and fraud, was afterwards made the property—capital—of the usurpers, who erected a government and enacted laws to perpetuate and maintain their special privileges. The function, the *only* function of capital is to confiscate the labor-product of the propertyless, non-possessing class, the wage-workers. The origin of government was in violence and murder. Government disinherits and enslaves the governed. Government is for slaves; free men govern themselves. . . .

The right to live, to equality of opportunity, to liberty and the pursuit of happiness,

is yet to be acquired by the producers of all wealth. . . . Legalized capital and the state stand or fall together. They are twins. The liberty of labor makes the state not only unnecessary, but impossible. When the people —the whole people—become the state, that is, participate equally in governing themselves, the state of necessity ceases to exist. . . .

Anarchy, therefore, is liberty; is the negation of force, or compulsion, or violence.

OUR CRIMES

There is no evidence that I or any of us killed, or had anything to do with the killing of, policemen at the Haymarket. None at all. But it was proven clearly that we were, all of us, anarchists, socialists, communists, Knights of Labor, unionists. It was proven that three of us were editors of labor papers; that five of us were labor organizers and speakers at workingmen's mass meetings. They, this class court, jury, law and verdict, have decided that we must be put to death because, as they say, we are "leaders" of men who denounce and battle against the oppression, slaveries, robbery and influences of the monopolists. Of these crimes against the capitalist class they found us guilty beyond any reasonable doubt, and, so finding, they have sentenced us.

Albert R. PARSONS

from a letter,
The Alarm,
August 11, 1888

It is the precise reverse of that which those who hold and love power would have their oppressed victims believe it is. . . .

The great class-conflict now gathering throughout the world is created by our social system of industrial slavery. Capitalists could not if they would, and would not if they could, change it. This alone is to be the work of the proletariat, the disinherited, the wage-slave, the sufferer. Nor can the wage-class avoid this conflict. Neither religion nor politics can solve it or prevent it. It comes as a human, an imperative necessity. Anarchists do not make the social revolution; they prophesy its coming. Shall we then stone the prophets?. . .

In the line of evolution and historical development, anarchy—liberty—is next in order. With the destruction of the feudal system, and the birth of commercialism and manufactories in the sixteenth century, a contest long and bitter and bloody, lasting over a hundred years, was waged for mental and religious liberty. The seventeenth and eighteenth centuries, with their sanguinary conflicts, gave to man political equality and civil liberty, based on the monopolization of the resources of life. . . .

All over the world the fact stands undisputed that the political is based upon, and is but the reflex of the economic system, and hence we find that whatever the political form of the government, whether monarchical or republican, the average social status of the wage-workers is in every country identical.

The class struggle of the past century is history repeating itself; it is the evolutionary growth preceding the revolutionary denouement. Though liberty is a growth, it is also a birth, and while it is yet to be, it is also about to be born. Its birth will come through travail and pain, through bloodshed and violence. It cannot be prevented. . . .

An anarchist is a believer in liberty, and as I would control no man against his will, neither shall anyone rule over me with my consent. Government is compulsion; no one freely consents to be governed by another—therefore, there can be no just power of government.

Anarchy is perfect liberty, is absolute freedom of the individual. Anarchy has no schemes, no programmes, no systems to offer or to substitute for the existing order of things. Anarchy would strike from humanity every chain that binds it, and say to mankind: "Go forth! you are free! Have all, enjoy all!"

Albert R. PARSONS

from Albert R. Parsons,
*Anarchism: Its Philosophy and
Scientific Basis, as Defined by
Some of its Apostles*
(Chicago, 1887)

"No Book of 1889 Will Live So Long as This Vivid Biography"

THE LIFE OF ALBERT R. PARSONS

There is a weird fascination about this *Life of Albert R. Parsons* [by Lucy E. Parsons, Chicago, 1889]. Few stories in our literature are told with such dramatic power as this. No book of 1889 will live so long as this vivid biography.

It is a tale of chivalry so exalted, with an ending so tragical and pathetic, that it reads like a romance by Stevenson or Haggard. In all the ideal knighthood of Sir Walter Scott, there is not a high-born Templar or Crusader whose heroism can be compared to the self-devotion and chivalry of this indomitable puritan, who was merely a Knight of Labor without crest, coat of arms, or any other heraldry of barbarian aristocracy.

Americans cannot study the character of Parsons without admiring his integrity and courage, however much they may condemn the doctrines for which he forefited his life. Out of this admiration for his personal qualities will spring the question which sooner or later must be answered by every American conscience. Was it necessary to put this man to death? Was it just? Was it legal? To every one of these questions the answer must be, No. The sacrifice of Parsons was a political tragedy casting over the labor question a storm-cloud, which grows darker and more ominous as time adds to the glamor of the catstrophe.

That the death of Parsons should become an epoch in the labor movement and pass into history as a part of it, is due to the mad vengeance of the men who hanged him. By this blunder they exalted him to the rank of a representative, not of anarchy, but of labor. On the morning of the execution a laborer was riding on the front platform of a North State Street car. Passing the jail, he said to the driver, "What is anarchy?" "I don't know," was the answer. "I understand it means more wages and less hours of labor for the working man". . . .

A grotesque horror is added to the drama by the concession that Parsons was entirely innocent of any knowledge of the crime for which he was condemned, and of all participation in it, excepting that he had preached the gospel of anarchy. . . .

Parsons was an enthusiast, cherishing the ideal of a perfect social system. . . . He was a man of genius, refined in manner, and possessed of rare poetical and oratorical powers. His eloquence was magnetic, and his argument clear. He could use sarcasm with fine effect, and in denunciation he was forcible and keen. There was no cruelty in his nature, and his private life was pure. . . .

Few braver things are found either in fact or fiction than the manly act of Parsons, who, out of a place of safety in Wisconsin, came to Chicago and, walking into the courtroom, quietly said to the judge, "I present myself for trial with my comrades, your honor." This magnanimity was answered by a sentence of death, executed with ceremonial cruelty in the state of Abraham Lincoln, whose immortal glory is written in the inspired words, "With charity for all, with malice towards none"—a sentiment harshly reversed in the Anarchist Case, where judgment was executed with malice towards all, with charity for none.

Gen. M. M. TRUMBULL

The Open Court
(April 10, 1890)

Cover of the First Edition, 1889

FROM A LETTER

Cell No. 29
Cook County Bastille
Chicago, July 29, 1886

Whether we live or whether we die, the social revolution is inevitable. The boundaries of human freedom must be enlarged and widened. The seventeenth century was a struggle for religious liberty, the eighteenth for political equality, and now in the nineteenth century mankind is demanding economic or industrial freedom. The fruition of this struggle means the social revolution. We see it coming. We predict it, we hail it with joy! Are we criminals for that?

Albert R. PARSONS

from Lucy E. Parsons,
The Life of Albert R. Parsons
(Chicago, 1889)

FREEDOM

Toil and pray! Thy world cries cold;
Speed thy prayer, for time is gold;
At thy door Need's subtle tread;
Pray in haste! for time is bread.
And thou plow'st and thou hew'st,
And thou rivet'st and sewest,
And thou harvestest in vain;
Speak! O, man; what is thy gain?
Fly'st the shuttle day and night,
Heav'st the ones of earth to light,
Fill'st with treasures plenty's horn—
Brim'st it oe'r with wine and corn.
But who hath thy meal prepared,
Festive garments with thee shared;
And where is thy cheerful hearth,
Thy good shield in battle dearth?
Thy creations round thee see—
All thy work, but nought for thee!
Yea, of all the chains alone
Thy hand forged, these are thine own.
Chains that round the body cling,
Chains that lame the spirit's wing,
Chains that infants' feet, indeed,
Clog! O, workmen! Lo! Thy meed.
What ye rear and bring to light,
Profits by the idle wight,
What ye weave of diverse hue,
'Tis a curse—your only due.
What ye build, no room insures,
Not a sheltering roof to yours,
And by haughty ones are trod—
Ye, who toil their feet hath shod.
Human bees! Has nature's thrift
Given thee naught but honey's gift?
See! the drones are on the wing,
Have you lost the will to sting?
Man of labor, up, arise!
Know the might that in thee lies,
Wheel and shaft are set at rest
At thy powerful arm's behest.
Thine oppressor's hand recoils,
When thou, weary of thy toils,
Shun'st thy plough; thy task begun
When thou speak'st: Enough is done!
Break this two-fold yoke in twain;
Break thy want's enslaving chain;
Break thy slavery's want and dread;
Bread is freedom, freedom bread.

Albert R. PARSONS

SOCIALISM!

JUSTICE, EQUALITY, FRATERNITY.

MASS MEETING!

EVERY PERSONS' DUTY!

The Workingmen and Citizens of Columbus, O., will hold a Grand Mass-meeting

FRIDAY & SATURDAY EVENINGS, FEBRUARY 12 & 13,

At 7:30 o'clock, in the City Hall.

A. R. PARSONS, the Chicago Socialist,

Will address the meeting. Subject: "The Emancipation of the Wage-Slave; How to Achieve It." Every workingman and woman should be present. Free discussion. Everybody invited.

THE COMMITTEE.

Group No. 1, International Working People's Association.

SOCIALISMUS!

Alle Arbeiter u. Arbeiterinen von Columbus sind freundlichst eingeladen am Freitag u. Samstag-Abend, 7:30 Uhr, in der City Halle, zu erscheinen. Discussion u. Eintritt frei.

Das Comite der Gruppe No. 1, J. A. A.

Anarchist Meeting on the Chicago Lakefront: Fielden and Parsons Speaking
from Lucy Parsons' *Life of Albert R. Parsons*

ALBERT R. PARSONS:
The Anarchist as Trade Unionist

Albert Parsons was for a short time a Confederate soldier, a Radical Republican office-holder, a socialist political candidate, and an anarcho-syndicalist activist. More durable than any of these commitments was his membership in trade unions, which stretched over at least a decade and perhaps a quarter century. There would be no more important figure in the Chicago labor movement until the emergence of John Fitzpatrick early in the twentieth century.

Parsons' first trade union contacts go back at least to 1861 when, not yet a teenager, he worked as an indentured apprentice at the Galveston *Daily News*. He subscribed during that year to the *The Printer*, the official organ of the National Typographical Union. His printing career interrupted by the war, Parsons returned to the trade as a typesetter and, in 1868, as editor of the (Waco) *Spectator*. It is unclear whether he held a union card while working in Texas. His autobiography relates that on coming to Chicago in 1872, he "at once became a member of Typographical Union No. 16," suggesting he may have obtained a traveling card in Texas. Rodney Estvan's useful study of Parsons holds that the autobiography may err on this point since Parsons' membership in No. 16 became the object of a vote in April, 1877 after his application had been held in abeyance more than three years. The most likely explanation for the lapse of time is that Parsons was working in a nonunion, indeed fiercely anti-union, shop at the Chicago *Times* during this period, under a secret "permit" from No. 16.[1]

In any case, Parsons was a No. 16 member when he addressed demonstrators on behalf of the socialist Workingmen's Party-USA during the Great Railroad Strike of 1877. The chairman of the union's Executive Committee, S.A.

Manion, stood by Parsons during the repression which followed the latter's militant speeches during the strike but Parsons nonetheless lost his *Times* job and fell victim to an effective blacklisting in Chicago printing shops. Ironically, the *Times* accused Parsons of being a "rat" (that is, scab) who joined the union only to gain support for campaigns in electoral politics, before firing him for his union activities.[2]

While seldom able to find work as a printer, Parsons remained an active and respected No. 16 member. In January, 1878 he became one of the local's three delegates to the city central labor union. He was reappointed to that position as late as April, 1883, long after he had become active in the anarchist Social Revolutionary Clubs. Parsons often spoke at union meetings, especially on the eight-hour movement, and appropriately, given his personal situation, he led union efforts to find work for unemployed printers. Especially in 1879, he successfully encouraged No. 16's participation in Socialistic Labor Party demonstrations.[3]

Throughout the last decade of his life, Parsons was also a member of the Knights of Labor. He came into the Knights in 1876 while that organization was still a secret society. Initiated in Indianapolis before there was a Chicago branch, Parsons was probably, as Bruce Nelson has recently emphasized, Chicago's first Knight. He joined Local 400 in Chicago and switched membership in 1885 to Local 1307. By his own account, he served two terms as delegate to Knights' District Assembly 24. He may also have once been Master Workman. Parsons' writings appeared in the Knights' *Journal of United Labor*. He remained a Knight until his execution.[4]

Albert R. Parsons

Parsons' most vital trade union activity came at the city-wide level. He led the Council of Trade and Labor Unions of Chicago, a group founded late in 1877 to bring together more than a dozen organized trades. As tensions over socialism, ethnicity and admission of secret societies developed, Parsons helped heal a series of factional fights and at least one split in the city central in 1878 and 1879. He later recalled that he thrice served as president of the city central. Interestingly, Parsons was considered a "compromise" leader, acceptable to both socialists and "pure and simple" unionists, to Knights and craft unionists, to Germans and the American-born.[5]

Indeed, it was in large part Parsons' commitment to aggressive trade unionism which ultimately led him away from the electoralism and reform politics of the Socialistic Labor Party and toward anarchism. He first clashed with Chicago SLP leader Tommy Morgan in 1878 over the latter's refusal to countenance secret societies in central labor bodies. Their more bitter quarrel, a year later, focused on reaction to the speech of the great eight-hour working-day advocate, Ira Steward, at the SLP's 1879 July 4 celebrations. Steward spoke, as he almost always did, on the shorter working-day as a key to labor unity and social transformation. Morgan countered with the position that reforms in wages and work would be unimportant until workers began "to organize politically and set their own men to making laws." Parsons, who publicly debated Morgan on the issue, held that the trade unions "sought to organize all workers for the purpose of securing better homes, better food, clothing and surroundings for all, and this would be affected through reduction of the hours of labor."[6]

Stewardism gave Parsons, as it gave many other trade union socialists, a way to link an immediate working-class concern, the eight-hour day, with the ultimate transformation of society.[7] It also led him, and many others, away from the single-minded electoral emphasis which characterized the Socialistic Labor Party. "In 1880," Parsons recalled in his autobiography,

I withdrew from all active participation in the political Labor party, having been convinced that the number of hours per day that the wage-workers are compelled to work. . .amounted to their practical disenfranchisement as voters.

In one of his last bursts of political activity, Parsons acted as a labor lobbyist in Washington, D.C., joining other trade unionists appointed by the National Eight-Hour Association to press unsuccessfully for enforcement of the eight-hour law applying to federal government workers.[8]

Parsons' further disagreements with the Socialistic Labor Party leadership hinged on his belief in the necessity for armed defense of strikes and labor organizations. Parts of Parsons' commitment to self-defense likely stemmed from his having witnessed the use of terror against black Radical Republicans in Texas. He further witnessed the use of terror against the labor movement during the bloody police attacks which left eighteen dead during the Great Railroad Strike of 1877 in Chicago. Given these experiences, it is hardly surprising that Parsons wished to raise the "arming question" among trade unionists, and that he apparently had joined the *Lehr-und-Wehr-Verein*, a workers' militia, by 1879.[9]

In short, many of the tenets of "Chicago-idea" anarchism had coalesced for Parsons well before he met Johann Most and joined the International Working People's Association in 1883. His commitments to the labor union as an agency of social transformation, to the armed defense of strikes and to economic rather than political action were established more through experience than through theory. Indeed, in the questions he raised, and in some of the answers he gave, Parsons was not unlike several other radical craft unionists who had undergone similar experiences with strikes and with political action by the early 1880s. Figures such as Samuel Gompers and Peter J. McGuire shared Parsons' emphasis on trade union organization and his growing distrust of legislative solutions to labor problems, though they opposed revolution, anarchism and the IWPA.[10]

In Chicago, a breach was to open between Parsons and the craft unionists. The anarchists and some socialist unionists there responded to the October, 1883 refusal of the Chicago Trades and Labor Assembly to recognize delegates from the Cigarmakers' Progressive Union No. 15 by forming their own citywide labor body, the Central Labor Union. Parsons quickly became a leader of the CLU, which rivaled the Knights of Labor and the Trades and Labor Assembly in influence, and possibly in membership, by April, 1886. But the breach was for a long while far from a total one. Parsons apparently quit the Trades and Labor Assembly only in April, 1884 and left the Chicago Typographical Union—almost certainly by means of a withdrawal card—only weeks before Haymarket. He not only practiced dual unionism in the sense that he supported a labor federation separate from the existing labor movement, but he was also a dual (and, counting the Knights, triple) unionist in terms of simultaneous organizational affiliations.[11]

Though a convinced anarchist, Parsons had good reasons to cut old ties slowly. The 1879 split in the Trades and Labor Assembly had been short, partly due to Parsons' peace-making intervention, and there was reason to think that the division which began in 1883 might be similarly brief. Parsons would also have seen continued affiliation with the Knights and even with craft unions as providing a forum for spreading anarchist ideas. He spoke often under Knights of Labor auspices. As an American-born and English-speaking radical, Parsons would have been increasingly cut off from English-speaking workers had he only had CLU connections. While *The Alarm*, the English-language paper Parsons edited, claimed a circulation of 2500, English, Irish and American-born membership in the CLU was small, especially in comparison to such membership in the Trades and Labor Assembly and the Knights of Labor.[12]

But Parsons likely saw the non-CLU unions, especially the Knights, as more than just audiences of potential recruits. Like later Chicago syndicalists, especially William Z. Foster, Parsons both railed at the practices of existing nonrevolutionary unions and predicted that events and social forces would make such unions revolutionary. Amidst diatribes, especially directed against the Trades and Labor Assembly, Parsons' *Alarm* still held that "every labor union is . . .a

school of true civilization and a wedge driven into the body of the present infamous system of society." The IWPA, Parsons added in *The Alarm*,

recognizes in the Trades Union the embryonic group of the future "free society." Every trade union is, *nolens volens* an autonomous commune in process of incubation. . . . No, friends, it is not the unions but the methods which some of them employ with which the International finds fault.[13]

The passages on unions in the IWPA's 1883 Pittsburgh Manifesto allowed that it might be at some point necessary to "attack and seek to destroy all those [unions] who stand on reactionary principles." *The Alarm* sometimes verged on applying this stricture to the Chicago Trades and Labor Assembly, which was bitterly accused, with some justice, of excluding radicals from labor celebrations, of class collaboration, especially in the support of capitalist politicians, and of failing to build the local movement for the May 1, 1886 eight-hour strike.[14] *The Alarm* also began an interesting critique of craft unionism generally. It emphasized that organizing according to craft had achieved only limited success. By one uncharitable *Alarm* estimate, only one Chicago trade in twenty-five had actually been thoroughly organized through the craft union strategy. Moreover, craft union prospects would worsen, according to *The Alarm*, as employers found ways to dispense with skilled workers. Ironically enough, *The Alarm* considered craft unionism to be unstable, arguing that the "principles and practices of the socialistic

Handbill, 1885

THE ALARM.

"WORKINGMEN OF ALL COUNTRIES, UNITE!"

No. 25   CHICAGO, SATURDAY, JUNE 27, 1885   Price, 5 Cents.

labor movement furnish the only safe and reliable foundation for keeping working people within trades' unions.'' Such a formulation is of interest not only for its sectarianism but also for its suggestion that socialism served trade unionism rather than vice versa. But especially in relations with the Knights of Labor, the Chicago IWPA never did require open espousal of socialism as a criteria for its supporting a labor organization.[15]

The Knights, whose egalitarianism and tendencies towards industrial unionism exempt them from many criticisms which *The Alarm* made of conservative craft unions, did draw fire for their failure to give support as a national organization to the May 1, 1886 strikes and for their later refusal to defend the Haymarket prisoners. Nonetheless, Parsons held an open, nonsectarian and even forgiving attitude toward the Knights, one much like later Chicago syndicalists, including

Albert R. Parsons in disguise in Waukesha, Wisconsin

Lucy Parsons, would hold toward the AFL. Lucy Parsons herself was still organizing sewing women into the Knights, not into anarchist unions, as late as May 3, 1886. *The Alarm* even maintained that the Knights' constitution made certain that the organization would become a socialist one. Parsons reiterated the latter position from jail, in a public letter written in August, 1886:

The foundation principle of socialism or anarchy is the same as the Knights of Labor, viz., ''the abolition of the wages system'' and the substitution in its stead of an industrial system of universal cooperation.

Two months later, in an autobiography written for the local *Knights of Labor* newspaper, Parsons suggested that the Knights, rather than the IWPA, would be at the center of revolutionary change in the U.S.:

The Knights of Labor unconsciously stand upon a state socialist programme. They will never be able to seize the state by the ballot, but when they do seize it (and seize it they must), they will abolish it.[16]

Parsons not only retained a commitment to trade unionism, of both anarchist and non-anarchist kinds, but he remained one of the best disciples of Ira Steward. Three years after Steward's death and two months before Haymarket, Parsons wrote that if the eight-hour day were won

then the employing class will have to pay us as much for eight hours' work as they do now for ten. Employers will put labor-saving machinery to work instead of the high-priced laborers. The laborers will then for the same reason that they reduced the hours to eight, have to reduce them to six hours per day. A voluntary reduction of the work hours is a peaceful solution to the labor problem. . . . Wages in this way will increase until they represent the earnings, instead of, as now, the necessities, of the wage-laborer. This would result in. . .a system of universal cooperation and distribution.[17]

Here is Stewardism undiluted, a defense of the same concepts Parsons had embraced in 1879. Here also is the main reason that Parsons was slow to support the May 1, 1886 campaign. He certainly did not oppose a shorter working day, the quest for which he characterized as ''a class movement against domination, therefore historical, and evolutionary and necessary.''[18] Nor is it likely that Parsons enthusiastically embraced the IWPA's briefly held position—one he sometimes articulated in editorials—that eight hours was a ''compromise. . .a virtual concession that the wage system is just.'' For Parsons the crux of the matter was that the eight-hour call was, without tremendous—and, he argued, armed—agitation, ''doomed by the very nature of things to defeat.''[19] This was so because, according to Parsons, eight hours was essentially a *revolutionary* demand capable of uniting all workers and leading to further sweeping transformations.

As George Schilling later recalled, Parsons had ''been a student of the philosophy of Ira Stewart [Steward] for years, and was one of a few men who understood the full impact of reduced hours.'' Parsons, seeing the eight-hour demand as anything but the ''soothing syrup'' that, according to

34

Schilling, some other IWPA leaders initially considered it, could not believe that capital would fail to use its full arsenal against the May 1 movement.[20] He thus feared that "defenseless men, women and children [would] finally succumb to the power of the discharge, black-list and lockout. . .the militiaman's bayonet and the policeman's club."[21] At first this fear led to a hesitation to plunge into support for the May 1 strikes. Later it led to an emphasis on armed defense of the strikes.

As Bruce Nelson's recent and excellent study of the IWPA shows, many anarchists besides Parsons had substantial records of labor leadership in pre-CLU craft unions, in the CLU and even in the Knights. The charge that conservative unionists and prosecutors made against Parsons and his associates—that they used trade unions for socialist purposes—could have made little sense to the IWPA unionists who had come to see their unionism and their socialism as one.[22] What is certain is that Parsons and others used trade union principles and trade union experiences to forge their view of the world and of the possibility of changing it.

Dave ROEDIGER

1. *The Printer,* 3 (Feb. 1861), as cited in Henry Rosemont's notes on Parsons, Union Printers' Historical Society, Chicago.; Philip S. Foner, ed. *The Autobiographies of the Haymarket Martyrs* (New York 1969), 28-30; Rodney D. Estvan, "The Political Thought of Albert Parsons" (unpublished paper at the Chicago Historical Society), 34ff. 2. Estvan, "Parsons," 58ff; *Chicago Times* (July 24, 1877). 3. See the minutes of Chicago Typographical Union Number 16 (hereafter, CTU Minutes), held at the Chicago Historical Society, esp. for April 30, May 28, June 25, and October 29, 1879. 4. Foner, ed., *Autobiographies,* 35; Bruce Nelson, "Socialists, Anarchists and the Labor Movement," the second chapter of Nelson's doctoral dissertation on Chicago anarchism (Northern Illinois University, 1985); George Schilling, "History of the Labor Movement in Chicago" in Lucy Parsons, ed. *Life of Albert R. Parsons* (Chicago 1903), xxxiv; Albert Parsons, "Labor vs. Capital," *Journal of United Labor* (July 1883), 331-32; Albert Parsons, in Lucy Parsons, ed. *Life,* 125. On the Knights in Chicago, see Richard Schneirov, "The Knights of Labor in the Chicago Labor Movement and Municipal Politics" (unpublished doctoral dissertation, Northern Illinois University, 1984). 5. CTU Minutes (January 30, May 28, and June 26, 1878 and April 29, 1883); Estvan "Parsons," 83; Foner, ed. *Autobiographies,* 35. 6. *Chicago Socialist* (May 24 and July 5, 1879); Carolyn Ashbaugh, *Lucy Parsons: American Revolutionary* (Chicago 1976, 35-36. I have argued elsewhere that much of Steward's great influence over labor thought stemmed from his ability to apply antislavery critiques to the conditions of free labor during the postbellum years. Paul Avrich's superb recent work attributes Parsons' radicalization to a similar merging of critiques of chattel and wage slavery. See Avrich, *The Haymarket Tragedy* (Princeton 1984), 19, 42-43; Roediger, "Ira Steward and the Antislavery Origins of the Eight-Hour Theory," forthcoming in *Labor History.* 7. Kenneth Fones-Wolf, "Boston Eight-Hour Men, New York Marxists and the Emergence of the International Labor Union," *Historical Journal of Massachusetts,* 9 (June 1981), 47-59. 8. Foner, ed. *Autobiographies,* 37; Henry David, *The History of the Haymarket Affair* (New York 1963), 142; see also William Holmes' reminiscences in *Free Society* (November 6, 1898). 9. Estvan, "Parsons," 86; Ashbaugh, *Parsons,* 14; Philip S. Foner, *The Great Labor Uprising of 1877* (New York, 1977), 139-56. 10. Stuart B. Kaufman, *Samuel Gompers and the American Federation of Labor, 1848-1896* (Westport, 1973), esp. 51ff; Mark Erlich, "Peter J. McGuire's Trade Unionism: Socialism of a Trades Union Kind?" *Labor History,* 24 (Spring 1983), 165-97; David, *Haymarket Affair,* 91-92 and Estvan, "Parsons," 111. 11. CTU Minutes (April 27, 1884 and March 26, 1886), as cited in Eric Hirsch, "Revolution or Reform?: The Chicago Eight-Hour Movement in the Mid-1880s" (unpublished paper presented at Chicago Labor History Group, 1980), 29. 12. On ethnicity in the Chicago labor movement at the time, see Nelson, "Socialists, Anarchists and the Chicago Labor Movement," esp. Table 2:2 and Schneirov, "Knights of Labor in Chicago," esp. 472-74. Throughout Parsons' editorship, *The Alarm* ran articles supportive of strikes of the Knights and other non-anarchist unions. Notices of CLU meetings and of Knights' meetings ran side-by-side, as for example in *The Alarm* (October 31, 1885). On Lucy Parsons' later syndicalism, see Ashbaugh, *Parsons,* 230-31. 13. Foster, *The Road to Trade Unionism* (Chicago n.d.), passim; *The Alarm* (February 1, 1884 and April 4, 1883). 14. The Pittsburgh Manifesto is most accessible as an appendix to Richard Ely, *The Labor Movement in America* (New York 1886); see also *The Alarm* (September 19 and October 17, 1885). 15. *The Alarm* (Feb. 7 and Sept. 19, 1885). 16. Parsons in (Detroit) *Labor Leaf* (Sept. 1, 1886); Foner, ed. *Autobiographies,* 45; Lucy Parsons, ed. *Life,* 125; *Chicago Tribune* (May 4, 1886); *The Alarm* March 7 and April 4, 1885 and March 20 and April 3, 1886); "Albert Parsons to William Holmes" (May 22, 1886) as reprinted in *Free Society* (November 29, 1899), a misdated issue which, in sequence, should bear the date November 5, 1899. In the last cited source Parsons held the hope that all unions, not just Knights' organizations, would be made revolutionary by events. 17. *Chicago Daily News* (March 13, 1886). 18. Foner, ed. *Autobiographies,* 47. 19. Estvan, "Parsons," 162-67. Cf. *The Alarm* (Nov. 28, 1885). See also Ashbaugh, *Parsons,* 67-68 and David, *Haymarket Affair,* 147-50. 20. Foner, ed. *Autobiographies,* 47; Schilling, "Labor Movement," xxxii. 21. Foner, ed. *Autobiographies,* 47; *The Alarm* (October 31, 1885); Lucy Parsons, ed. *Life,* 145. 22. Nelson, "Socialists, Anarchists and the Labor Movement." See also Oscar Neebe's explicit, and a little puzzled, response to the charge that the anarchists did not support trade unionism in Foner, ed. *Autobiographies,* 167.

A FABLE FOR WORKERS

A farmer had gathered his herd of sheep into a pen preparatory to shearing them of their wool. Finally, one sheep, becoming more bold than his timid comrades, seeing the farmer standing at the gate with his long shears in his hand, addressed him thus:

"Pray, sir, why do you huddle us together in this style? Will you not let us out to play and gambol on the hillside? It is hot, dusty and dry, and very uncomfortable to be cooped up in this pen."

Farmer: "Certainly, certainly. But before I turn you out I must shear you of your wool."

Sheep: "Pray, sir, what harm have we ever done you that you should now take the covering from our backs, and leave us unprotected from the storms of winter and the heats of summer?"

Farmer: "You ungrateful wretches! Have you no sense of gratitude for the many favors I have always shown you? If it were not for me how could you exist at all? Don't I furnish you the green pasture upon which you browse and play? Besides that, when I shear

Drawing by Mitchell Siporin

off your present coating of wool are you not permitted by my generosity to graze upon my fields and soon supply yourselves with another coating?"

The rest of the timid and thoughtless herd, overhearing the conversation, immediately set up a great "hurrah" for their supposed benefactor, and one and all calmly and patiently and with apparent satisfaction submitted themselves to the process of being "fleeced of their wool."

Moral: When capitalists and their lying preachers, teachers and politicians set themselves up as the benefactors of their wage-slaves, and begin their long-winded discourses upon the "harmony" of capital and labor, you may be sure that they are merely preparing their wage-slaves for a quiet submission while they "fleece" them of their labor product.

Albert R. PARSONS
from Lucy E. Parsons,
The Life of Albert R. Parsons
(Chicago, 1889)

HENRY P. ROSEMONT

The youngest son of Bay Area pioneers, Henry P. Rosemont (1904-1979) learned the "art preservative of all arts" at his father's printing office on Rosemont Street in San Francisco, and joined the city's Typographical Union in 1926. When he deposited a traveling card with Chicago Typographical Union No. 16 later that year, the young journeyman, interested in history since childhood, enjoyed meeting many old-timers—the Gritzmacher brothers, John C. Harding, Alexander Spencer and others—who had been members of Illinois' oldest union for almost a half century and had known Albert R. Parsons personally. Rosemont found that all of them spoke of their martyred fellow unionist with the greatest respect, and some with evident admiration.

Over a decade later he met Lucy Parsons when she appealed to No. 16's Executive Committee for funds; everyone present contributed appreciably to the aged widow's relief.

Organizer of printers' support for the Newspaper Guild strike against the Hearst papers in 1938-40, and strategist of No. 16's historic October 1945 strike for the 7¼-hour day in the job-shops, Rosemont was one of

his union's best known, best loved and most influential figures. In organized labor's first major battle against Taft-Hartley—No. 16's 22-month-long newspaper strike of

1947-49—he was given charge of publicity for the duration, and authored a large share of the ITU's anti-Taft-Hartley literature (no AFL or CIO union was hit harder by the infamous "slave labor law" than the ITU). During that struggle, he edited the strike paper, The Picket; *wrote innumerable press*

releases and handbills; and scripted the nightly WCFL radio show, "Meet the Union Printers."

Rosemont's short history of No. 16 in the union's 1952 centennial souvenir book included a sketch of Parsons. He projected a comprehensive history of printing trade unionism, for which he assembled a vast amount of material in years of research at libraries throughout the country. But he lived to complete only an important preliminary study: Benjamin Franklin and the Philadelphia Typographical Strikers of 1786—*the first detailed look at a strike historians have recognized as the earliest in the U.S. Published in the journal* Labor History *in 1981, this was later made available as a pamphlet by the Union Printers' Historical Society.*

The text on Parsons reprinted here was written as a speech for the then-president of No. 16 at a trade-union shorter-hours' rally held near Haymarket Square on May Day, 1976.

An active member of the Illinois Labor History Society and a regular participant in its annual Haymarket commemorations, Henry Rosemont asked that his own ashes be scattered near the martyrs' monument in Waldheim.

FR

ALBERT R. PARSONS, UNION PRINTER

To this gathering in honor of the labor heroes of the 1880s, I have been invited to speak in behalf of the local to which one of those heroes belonged: Albert R. Parsons.

Albert Parsons was a trade unionist by instinct. He was only twelve when he began as apprentice in Texas, and he subscribed at once to the union's official paper. His printing career was soon interrupted by war. He was in a Confederate uniform when only thirteen, and fought bravely for four years.

When the war ended, young Parsons agreed with those who took the Negro's emancipation in good faith, believing that the races could not get along without each other, so they should get along with each other. That philosophy was well accepted for some years, and Texas had greater racial harmony, more human brotherhood—and less crime—than it had a hundred years later. We must not ignore the fact that separate eating sections, segregated transit facilities, and other forms of Jim-Crowism came along after the Reconstruction period. Broad-visioned people like Albert Parsons pointed the true way for America. Their principles

later were trampled on by scheming demagogues, who caused the nation to lose its way. And generations of Americans have paid the sad consequences, in poverty and strife.

At age 21 Parsons was elected secretary of the Texas Senate. In the ad-

A. R. PARSONS.

ministration of President Grant he held an important post in the Treasury Department. In both these positions he served with distinction, and he appeared to be headed for a long tenure in governmental service. But he chose to return to his first love, printing, and make Chicago his home. He joined our union and was active from the first, as we can see in the old minute books. On his initiative, a Trade and Labor Assembly was formed, and he was elected again and again to its presidency—an office that meant much work and no pay. After putting in long hours in the printshop, he spent many of his evenings on union business, helped by his loyal wife and comrade, Lucy. It was a closely knit family, children and parents sharing the hardships when Parsons was blacklisted by the newspapers for supporting the great railroad strike of 1877. Like other unions, the Typographical was pitifully weak at the time, with perhaps half of its members unemployed; and Parsons himself was totally out of work for two years. He was harassed by police and by thugs. But if all this had any effect, it was only to increase his militancy and concentrate his efforts toward a shorter

36

workday. He represented the Illinois Eight-Hour League at a national labor conference in the nation's capital.

When the Federation of Trades and Labor Unions voted for an eight-hour day beginning May 1st, 1886, Parsons of course was drawn into the movement; and so were his comrades, Fischer and others. Farsighted members of the Typographical Union had been agitating the eight-hour question for years. In the first convention after the Civil War, a Chicago *Tribune* compositor proposed that the eight-hour day be inaugurated on May 1st, 1866—twenty years before Haymarket. The move was unsuccessful then, but the craft did not let the idea die. The decision to go after the eight-hour day on May Day of 1886 was made at a convention presided over by a former ITU president, William J. Hammond.

There is no need to retell the terrible miscarriage of justice that led to prison and the gallows for labor's heroic fighters. One of the saddest things about the case was that so many of their fellow workers—the very people who had the

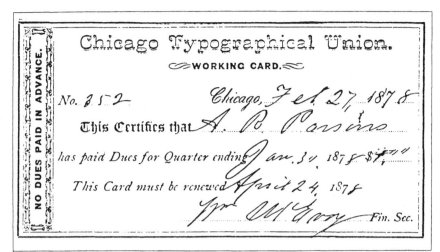

Parsons' Chicago Typographical Union No. 16 Working Card

most to gain from their sacrifices—were so quick to disown the prisoners, to shun them, so as not to be considered guilty by association. The terror was just too great; and many thousands of normally decent and kind people trembled with fear as their friends were deprived of liberty, and of life, by the hirelings of bloodthirsty Mammon. There were exceptions, to be sure; but these remained a minority till the terror had subsided and Chicagoans could speak freely again.

Since democracy is government by the majority, our great task is to ensure that the majority can make its voice heard—not silenced by terror as it was in the 1880s, or gagged by corruption as it has often been in late years.

Henry P. ROSEMONT

Regarded as the first depiction of "labor unrest" by a fine artist, Robert Koehler's powerful and dramatic image of "The Strike" was painted in 1886. It created a sensation when an engraving of it appeared in the May 1 issue of *Harper's Weekly,* which reached American homes along with news of the Chicago bomb-throwing. The German-born artist, raised in a socialist family, lived in Milwaukee and later in Minneapolis.

ALBERT PARSONS
& *THE TRAGEDY OF ECONOMIC EMPIRE*

A radical critic of domestic institutions, Albert Parsons also condemned the overseas expansion of American capitalism. In the late 1870s he detected the outward thrust of American business, driven overseas by the depression-era glut in the domestic marketplace. Responding as a proletarian internationalist, Parsons insisted that economic empire was no cure for hard times, and that it could only make things worse for the global working class.

The United States Congress gave Parsons the chance to voice his opposition to economic imperialism. In 1879, after the Panic of 1873 had precipitated the Long Depression that eventually ignited workingclass insurrections, a select committee of the House of Representatives, chaired by Pennsylvania Congressman Hendrick B. Wright, crossed the country to collect testimony on the "labor question." Congressman Wright's committee continued the work begun in 1878 by a similar committee headed by Abram Hewitt, the iron-monger and congressman from New York. In August 1879 the Wright committee arrived in Chicago. Albert Parsons soon appeared as a "volunteer witness." When asked to explain whom or what he represented, Parsons replied that he was "an active member of nearly every industrial or trade organization in this city." The committee was in for some serious testimony from a man who believed that he belonged to a citywide, a national, and even an international working class.

Parsons spoke as a national debate still raged over what had caused the depression, what could end it, and what might prevent its return. No elite consensus emerged from the 1870s variant of the debate—that would come during later crises. The middle- and upper-class proposals ranged from prescriptions for greater frugality to calls for currency expansion, land reform and more prayer. Nevertheless, one elite analysis gained more attention as the hard times persisted. In *The Roots of the Modern American Empire* (New York, 1969), William A. Williams reported that during the 1870s increasing numbers of businessmen, politicians and intellectuals came to believe that the nation suffered from "overproduction." Expanded employment—and political stability—they concluded, lay in finding new outlets for the domestic surplus in foreign markets. Some clamored for new subsidies for overseas shippers, others campaigned for an improved, trade-promoting foreign service, and many hoped to roll back British commercial power in Latin America and Asia. And some, like President Rutherford B. Hayes's Secretary of State, William M. Evarts, advised the nation that American manufacturers had to cut wages to successfully compete with European producers in foreign markets. By the end of the decade export fever had infected the business communities of even western cities like St. Louis and Chicago.

Parsons's critique of economic expansionism flowed logically from the common, workingclass argument that the nation really faced a crisis of "underconsumption," and not

a problem of "overproduction." It also closely paralleled the thinking of the Boston eight-hour day theorist, Ira Steward, whose ideas deeply impressed Parsons even before they met personally during the summer of 1879. The Eight-Hour League resolutions that Parsons submitted to the committee echo Steward's progressive vision of social history and his economic theory of the shorter workday; they even use his rather peculiar term for jobs, "days' works."

In his never-finished masterpiece, *The Political Economy of Eight Hours, or the Science of Human Progress*, Steward argued that export fever was "eminently un-American," and a form of "barbarism." The wage-cuts at home that businessmen thought necessary to compete overseas, he claimed, would further depress domestic purchasing power which, in turn, would eliminate more jobs. And he reasoned that a successful outward thrust would destroy jobs overseas, creating still more poverty in Europe that would push still more emigrants toward the already overcrowded American labor market. The final result of economic expansion, Steward was convinced, could only be "more idleness and less earnings repeated again and again, until starvation, bankruptcy and ruin is the terror of all Chrisendom (*sic*)."*

Steward and Parsons charted an alternative way out of the 1870s quagmire. The shorter workday, both men felt, would spread the available work among more hands and ease the

GRAND RAFFLE
⊹FOR A BOAT.⊹

It Was Wittled Out by A. R. PARSONS, with a Small Knife.

THIS IS FOR THE BENEFIT OF A. R. PARSONS.

TICKETS 25 CENTS.

To help raise funds, a boat whittled by the imprisoned Albert Parsons was put up for auction in New York. The picture of the boat appeared in Lucy Parsons' *Life of Albert R. Parsons*; the ticket is reproduced through the courtesy of the Tamiment Library of New York University.

stiff competition for existing jobs. Wages would then inevitably rise, and the enhanced workingclass consumption—or ''higher civilization,'' in the words of the Eight-Hour League—would create far more jobs than the export ever could.

Parsons's testimony is remarkable for its repudiation of the frontier expansionist theory of American well-being. Generations of Americans, before and after 1879, tried to evade the critical issue of the distribution of wealth by chasing after territorial or economic empire to fulfill dreams of prosperity. Albert Parsons did not. Even more remarkably, he phrased his decision to stay at home in terms of workingclass internationalism.

His testimony also provides something of a missing link in the American tradition of anti-imperialism. Philip S. Foner and Richard C. Winchester documented much of the nineteenth-century history of this tradition in *The Anti-Imperialist*

Reader, Volume I: From the Mexican War to the Election of 1900 (New York, 1984). But their story jumps from the opponents of the expansionist boomlet that immediately followed the Civil War to the critics of the imperial rampages that graced the 1890s. Parsons, and Steward, filled in the gap, condemning the essence of the expansionist impulse when it focused on overseas economies while shunning formal colonies. Moreover, although Steward's distinction between ''savage'' and ''civilized'' peoples crops up in the resolutions Parsons read, his critique of empire is not laced with the racism and nativism that infected much of the nineteenth-century anti-expansionist tradition.

Alexander YARD

* Ira Steward, ''Unemployment,'' Part 7 of *The Political Economy of Eight Hours, or The Science of Human Progress*, unpublished typescript of original manuscript, c. 1875 (?), pp. 12-13. Ira Steward Papers, Box 1, State Historical Society of Wisconsin.

ALBERT PARSONS ADDRESSES CONGRESS:
Testimony on the ''Labor Question'' (1879)

The Chairman: You mean that things from that period [of the Panic of 1873] have been growing worse?

Mr. Parsons: They have been growing continually worse until wages have got to a point in this country where (as Mr. [Abram] Hewitt informed Professor [William Graham] Sumner), in regard to those articles that we manufacture in common with other countries, the labor engaged in their manufacture is obtained at a less cost here than in the countries with which we have to compete. When that took place, and it took place two years ago in this country, we began to ship cotton cloth to England, and many other products that we are selling in foreign countries. . . . The result is that we see strikes through England, Germany, and Belgium, and the merchants and manufacturers of those countries are forcing down wages in order to recover their lost trade, which has been captured by the low-paid labor of the United States. . . . As a workingman I want to state that that has been done at the expense of the working classes—at the reduction of their life standard. . . . All wealth is the result of labor and represents precisely so many hours' labor. Therefore, in this labor question, the fight is narrowed down (because it is a fight) as to which class is going to get the benefit of these hours of labor—the employer or the employed. . . . We simply want less work and more pay, knowing that through short hours and high wages can our condition be improved. . . . We want to remove the worst disability of poverty by reducing the hours of labor; by the distributing of work that is to be done more equally among the workingmen, and consequently reducing the competition among the workingmen for the opportunity to work. By making labor scarce we will increase its value. . . . I wish to offer to the committee a set of resolutions emanating from the eight-hour league, embodying the sentiments of the trades unions of the United States, which are demanding the reduction of the day's labor to eight hours. I wish to submit these resolutions as setting forth the views of that class of men:

Resolved, That the first great event which ever occurred in the progress of industry, was a division of labor; that the progress which divides human labor is the fact that distinguishes the most of mankind from savages; that in a division of labor, the expenditures of one laborer furnish the employment or days' works for other laborers; that days' works or employments can be increased by increasing

expenditures; that the expenditures or outgoes of the laborer can only be increased by increasing his wages or income; that employment for the unemployed can only come from the larger incomes and outgoes of those who are employed; and that the only way by which the income of wage-laborers can ever be permanently increased, without reducing its purchasing power or increasing the cost of production is through a reduction of the hours of daily labor.

Resolved, That American prosperity never can develop into healthy and permanent conditions by increasing exports. . . .

Resolved, That the extraordinary increase of American exports within two or three years should be regarded with profound mortification, because they are the disgraceful result of the decreased earnings and increased poverty necessary for American laborers to undersell, discharge, and make paupers of European laborers. And the lower wages at home, necessary to capture *foreign* employments, are the lower wages necessary to destroy *home* employments.

Resolved, That the congratulations unblushingly indulged by American statesmanship over our increasing exports are sufficient evidence that it fails to comprehend the almost infinite difference between capturing the world's employments through competition, and creating new employments through a higher civilization. . . .

Resolved, That hand in hand for the great movement of eight hours must be a weekly or a frequent census and report of the world's unemployed; that eight hours or less hours will create days' works; and how many days' works must be created will be revealed when the statistics of idleness are sufficiently thorough and extended to cover the whole civilized world.

Resolved, That these two measures are not American or English or German or French, but they belong to the political economy which begins with the idea that ''Our country is the world, and our countrymen are all mankind.''

Albert R. PARSONS

From U. S. House of Representatives,
*Investigation by a Select Committee
of the House of Representatives Relative to
the General Depression in Labor and Business;
and as to Chinese Immigration*
(Washington, D.C., 1879)

39

ADOLPH FISCHER

Born in Bremen, Germany, Adolph Fischer (1858-1887) attended school there for eight and a half years. As a child he frequently accompanied his father to socialist meetings and was himself a socialist when he sailed to New York at fifteen.

Soon he was in Little Rock, Arkansas, working as an apprentice in the printing office owned by his brother, who published a weekly German paper. After he learned the printing trade in that golden age of ''tramp printers,'' Fischer set type in various cities around the country. In St. Louis, 1879, he joined the German Typographical Union, Typographia No. 3. Ten years later he married.

In June of 1883 Fischer moved to Chicago with his wife and child, and found employment at the anarchist daily Arbeiter-Zeitung. *At the time of his arrest three years later he was foreman of the composing-room.*

Fischer's radicalism had deepened appreciably over the years. Not only had he joined the anarchist movement, he had become a leading figure of the extreme left of that movement: the ''autonomist'' faction that emphasized decentralism and spontaneity. The autonomists were sharply critical of what they regarded as the inherently authoritarian character of large organizations, and especially of the centralism and reformist tendencies of trade unions. Fischer was nonetheless an active member of Chicago Typographia No. 9, an affiliate of the Central Labor Union. No. 9, however, was not only strongly anarchist-influenced, but had

in fact withdrawn from the national union in May 1884.*

from *Frank Leslie's Illustrated Weekly*

With George Engel, Fischer coedited the autonomist journal Der Anarchist, *which had for its motto: We Hate Authority. The publication was suppressed by the police after Haymarket. Fischer also took part in*

the workers' armed self-defense group, the Lehr-und-Wehr Verein.

It was Fischer who arranged for printing the Haymarket broadside, and he who inserted the line, Workingmen Arm Yourselves and Appear in Full Force!—*because, as he explained, he ''did not want the workingmen to be shot down in that meeting as on other occasions.'' When August Spies objected to the line, however, Fischer was readily convinced and the line was promptly withdrawn.*

Although he was not an orator, as were several of the other Chicago martyrs, Fischer's speech to the court was forceful and memorable:

I protest against my being sentenced to death because I have committed no crime. I was tried. . .for murder, but I was convicted of Anarchy. I protest against being sentenced to death, because I have not been found guilty of murder. However, if I am to die on account of being an Anarchist, on account of my love for liberty, fraternity and equality, I will not remonstrate.

His last words, cried out from the scaffold, were: ''Hurrah for Anarchy! This is the happiest moment of my life!''

FR

* Chicago German printers who did not secede with No. 9 reformed as Typographia No. 16. The two locals merged in 1891 as No. 9 and reaffiliated with the national union. Three years later the Typographias were chartered as autonomous locals of the International Typographical Union. On April 6, 1945, No. 9 surrendered its charter and its remaining members joined Chicago Typographical Union No. 16. In the next few years the other surviving Typographia locals also disbanded.

ANARCHISM & SOCIALISM

Many people undoubtedly long to know what the relationship between anarchism and socialism is, and whether these two doctrines have anything in common with each other. A number of persons claim that an anarchist cannot be a socialist, and a socialist not an anarchist. This is wrong.

The philosophy of socialism is a general one, and covers several subordinate teachings. To illustrate, I will cite the word ''Christianity.'' There are Catholics, Lutherans, Methodists, Baptists, Congregationalists, and various other religious sects, all of whom call themselves Christians. Although every Catholic is a Christian, it would not be correct to say that every Christian believes in Catholicism. . . .

Every anarchist is a socialist but every socialist is not necessarily an anarchist. The anarchists again are divided into two factions: the communistic anarchists and the Proudhon or middle-class anarchists. The International Working People's Association is the representative organization of the com-

munistic anarchists. Politically we are anarchists, and economically, communists or socialists.

With regard to political organization the communistic anarchists demand the abolition of political authority, the state; we deny the right of a single class or single individual

Compositor
George Bruce's Son & Co.
Type Catalog, 1882

to govern or rule another class or individual. We hold that, as long as one man is under the dictation of another, as long as one man can in any form subjugate his fellow man, and as long as the means of existence can be monopolized by a certain class or certain individual, there can be no liberty. Concerning the economical form of society, we advocate the communistic or cooperative method of production.

The term ''anarchism'' is of Greek origin and means ''without government'' or, in other words, ''without oppression.'' I only wish that every workingman would understand the proper meaning of this word. It is an absurd falsehood if the capitalists and their hired editors say that anarchism is identical with disorder and crime. On the contrary, anarchism wants to do away with the now-existing social disorder; it aims at the establishment of the real—the natural—order. I think every sensible man ought to conceive that, where ruling is existing on one hand, there must be submission on the other.

from a police photograph

He who rules is a tyrant, and he who submits is a slave. . . .

The capitalists who have taken possession of the means of production—factories, machinery, land, etc.—are the masters, and the workingmen who have to apply to the capitalists for the use of the means of production (for which they receive a small compensation in order to live), are the slaves. The interests of the capitalistic class are backed by the state (militia, sheriffs and police) while the interests of the non-possessing people are not protected. Anarchists say that there should be no class interests, but that every human being should have free access to the means of existence and that the pantries of mother earth should be accessible to all of her children. . . .

Anarchists, as well as all other thinking people, claim that in the present society a great number of people are deprived of a decent existence. We demand the reinstallation of the disinherited! Is this a crime? Is this an outrage upon society? Are we therefore dangerous criminals, whose lives should be taken in the interests of the common good of society? . . .

How will the anarchists realize their ideas? What means do they intend to employ to accomplish the realization of a free society? Much has been written and talked on this subject and, as an avowed anarchist, I will in plain terms give my individual opinion . . . "Anarchism" itself does not indicate force; on the contrary it means peace. But I believe that everybody who has studied the true character of the capitalistic form of society, and who will not deceive himself, will agree with me that now and never will the ruling classes abandon their privileges peaceably. Anarchism demands a thorough transformation of society, the total abolition of the private-property system. Now, history shows us that even reforms within the frame of the existing society have never been accomplished without the force of arms. . . .

To abolish chattel slavery in this country a long and awful war took place. Notwithstanding the fact that indemnification was offered for their losses, the slaveholders would not bestow freedom upon their slaves. Now in my judgment, he who believes that the modern slaveholders—the capitalists— would voluntarily, without being forced to do so, give up their privileges and set free their wage-slaves, are poor students. Capitalists possess too much egotism to give way to reason. Their egotism is so enormous that they even refuse to grant subordinate and insignificant concessions. . . . Would a peaceable solution of the social question be possible, the anarchists would be the first ones to rejoice over it.

As the court as well as the state's-attorney have plainly said, the verdict of death was rendered for the purpose of crushing the anarchistic and the socialistic movement. But I am satisfied that just the contrary has been accomplished by this barbarous measure. Thousands of workingmen have been led by our "conviction" to study anarchism, and if we are executed, we can ascend the scaffold with the satisfaction that by our death, we have advanced our noble cause more than we could possibly have done had we grown as old as Methuselah.

Adolph FISCHER

from Albert R. Parsons,
Anarchism: Its Philosophy and Scientific Basis, as Defined by Some of Its Apostles
(Chicago, 1887)

Reminiscences of Adolph Fischer

Although very well acquainted with Comrade Fischer for two years prior to the Haymarket tragedy, I came to know him intimately, and love him, during the eighteen months of his incarceration in Cook county jail.

He was a tower of strength, firm as a rock; looking his coming doom in the face with an unfaltering eye; awaiting it with a calmness, a cheerfulness and even a gladness that were born of real heroism. He deemed it a great privilege to die for his conviction. And yet Fischer was not tired of life or disgusted with the world. Possessing health, strength, great vitality and abundant animal spirit, with a wife and children whom he dearly loved, and hosts of warm friends, he was well equipped for happiness and to make others happy.

I shall never forget the day before I started on my lecture tour in behalf of the condemned men. It was the 14th day of November, 1886, and our comrades were condemned to die on the 3rd of December. With a heavy heart I visited the jail to say what I then feared might be a last good-bye.

Comrade Fischer took me to one side, and with his face close to the meshes of the "cage" he talked to me of his former home in St. Louis and gave me his last message to comrades whom I should find there. "Tell them," he said, "that I gladly die for my principles. Tell them that I shall not falter or hesitate; that they must not weep for me or mourn me dead, but that they must carry on the good work, and be prepared, if necessary, also to give up their lives for our great cause."

I broke down then, and tried in vain to hide my emotion, but Fischer only smiled and added, "I would not exchange places with the richest man in America."

William HOLMES

Free Society,
(Chicago, November 6, 1898)

Sketch by Art Young

ANARCHISM & FORCE

. . .Anarchism and force as such are contrary to each other. But we deny that any individual has the right to curtail the liberty and rights of others. The *oppressed* have the natural right to use force against their oppressors; or, to speak with Jefferson, force is justified as a defense of the rights of men. In accordance with this principle, the Constitution of the United States says that the right of the citizens to bear arms is inviolable. No *thinking man* will deny that the present condition of society is not bearable much longer. We stand before a radical transformation of society. Will those whom the peculiar state of society gives such enormous advantages give up their privileges peaceably? This is the question. If the anarchists would be convinced of this they would be the happiest of men. But from all observations they conclude that the privileged classes will not give way to reason, but will uphold their privileges by force, and that therefore a general conflict between the diametrical classes is inevitable. In this connection it was that the anarchists warned the people to be ready for the storm and to defend their rights.

Adolph FISCHER

Excerpts from a letter
to Henry Demarest Lloyd
and W. M. Salter,
November 4, 1887

The Typographias introduced the first printers' union label in the wake of the 8-hour strikes

LETTER TO GERMAN-AMERICAN TYPOGRAPHIA NO. 9

November 8, 1887

To the President and the Members of Typographia No. 9:

Dear Colleagues:

In view of the fact that the day on which, according to all human computation, I must ascend to the gallows is drawing close, I consider it advisable to inform you, as your colleague, of my last wishes. I would like that you, in conjunction with my family, arrange my funeral. I understand that the authorities will deliver my corpse to my family. I am indifferent as to the place of burial of my corpse, but I would request that all religious humbug be kept away from my funeral. I only mention this because I suspect that certain persons may endeavor to bring pressure in this regard, upon my wife. If a number of us will be hanged, then it would be best that we be buried together, in the bosom of Mother Earth. I have a further wish that you place in my grave our beloved red emblem, the Symbol of Equality, Freedom and Brotherhood, for which I lived, and now must die. Do not sing any sentimental songs, but, when I am lowered into my grave, sing the words of hope and freedom, such as the *Marseillaise*, etc.

Colleagues, perhaps many of you will criticize my conduct, in refusing to ask for "Mercy." Perhaps it will be said: "He should have taken this step on account of his family." Very well. I love my family, but such an application for "Mercy" would be contrary to my sense of human dignity. No scintilla of proof of any wrongdoing on my part has been forthcoming, and having done no wrong, I can not sign an appeal for Mercy. So let them proceed to murder me. However, those people who are guilty of my impending murder will some day bitterly regret their actions, and future generations will mention their names only with loathing and scorn.

In view of the great and noble cause, on behalf of which I am to die, my trip to the gallows becomes easy. In my mind's vision I already see, in the far horizon, the dawn of a better day for Humanity. The day of the Brotherhood of Man is no longer distant. In that hope and in the hope that you retain a friendly remembrance of me, I embrace you as colleagues and friends, press your hands and call to you a hearty farewell. I remain true, even unto the grave.

Yours,

Adolph FISCHER

P.S. The certainty that the workers will provide for the existence of my family and the rearing of my children gives me endless comfort and cheer.

Adolph and Johanna Fischer with their children

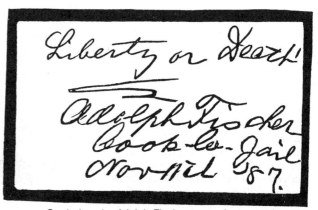

Card given by Adolph Fischer to a prison guard

42

GEORGE ENGEL

George Engel (1836-1887) was the oldest and, with Fischer and Lingg, among the most uncompromising of the Haymarket Eight. Born into a workingclass family in Cassell, Germany, Engel lost his father before turning two, and his mother a decade later. Apprenticed as a painter, he moved to Bremen, Leipzig and Rehna. In the last of these cities he married, and opened a small manufacturing enterprise, which quickly failed. In early 1873 he emigrated to Philadelphia where he labored in a sugar refinery and as a painter. A year later he was in Chicago working in a wagon factory.

According to his autobiographical sketch published in the weekly Knights of Labor,

Engel had long nurtured a fierce, if primitive, sense of class feeling before his exposure to socialist literature and meetings in Chicago. There he quickly joined the International Workingmen's Association and, after it disbanded, the Socialistic Labor Party.

At first a passionate supporter of electoral socialism, Engel's observations of the movement in Chicago led him to regard elections as rigged, and political action as certain to open labor's ranks to opportunists and factionalists. He joined the International Working People's Association in 1883 and by 1886 found even its Chicago leadership overly steeped in moderation. Engel cooperated

with Adolph Fischer in producing Der Anarchist, *an organ of the decentralist and extremely militant autonomist faction of the IWPA early that year.*

George Engel sat at home playing cards when the Haymarket bomb exploded. No evidence linked him to it. Nonetheless he died on the gallows on November 11, 1887. The following day his body, along with that of Louis Lingg, lay in state in the back room of the modest toy store the Engels had run since 1876. According to the Chicago Daily News, *10,000 people came to join his family in mourning.*

DR

HOW I BECAME AN ANARCHIST

This is the first occasion of my standing before an American court, and on this occasion it is murder of which I am accused. And for what reasons do I stand here? For what reasons am I accused of murder? The same that caused me to leave Germany—the poverty, the misery of the working classes.

And here, too, in this "free republic," in the richest country of the world, there are numerous proletarians for whom no table is set; who, as outcasts of society, stray joylessly through life. I have seen human beings gather their daily food from the garbage-heaps of the streets, to quiet therewith their gnawing hunger.

I have read of occurrences in the daily papers which proves to me that here, too, in this great "free land," people are doomed to die of starvation. This brought me to reflection, and to the question: What are the peculiar causes that could bring about such a condition of society? I then began to give our political institutions more attention than formerly. My discoveries brought to me the knowledge that the same society evils exist here that exist in German. This is the explanation of what induced me to study the social question, to become a socialist. And I proceeded with all the means at my command to make myself familiar with the new doctrine.

When, in 1878, I came here from Philadelphia, I strove to better my condition, believing it would be less difficult to establish a means of livelihood here than in Philadelphia, where I had tried in vain to make a living. But here, too, I found myself disappointed. I began to understand that it made no difference to the proletarian, whether he lived in New York, Philadelphia or Chicago.

In the factory where I worked I became acquainted with a man who pointed out to me the causes that brought about the difficult and fruitless battles of the workingmen for the means of existence. He explained to me, by the logic of scientific socialism, how mistaken I was in believing that I could make an independent living by the toil of my hands, so long as machinery, raw material, etc., were guaranteed to the capitalists as private property by the State.

That I might further enlighten my mind in regard to these facts, I purchased, with money earned by myself and family, sociological works—among them those of LaSalle, Marx and Henry George. After the

from *Frank Leslie's Illustrated Weekly*

study of these books, it became clear to me why a workingman could not decently exist in this rich country. I now began to think of ways and means to remedy this. I hit upon the ballot box—for it had been told me so often that this was the means by which workingmen could better their condition.

I took part in politics with the earnestness of a good citizen; but I was soon to find that the teachings of a "free ballot box" are a myth, and that I had again been duped. I came to the opinion that as long as workingmen are economically enslaved they cannot be politically free. It became clear to me that the working classes would never bring about a form of society guaranteeing work, bread and a happy life by means of the ballot.

Before I had lost my faith in the ballot-box, the following occurrences transpired, which proved to me that the politicians of this country were through and through corrupt. When, in the fourteenth ward, in which I lived and had the right to vote, the social-democratic party had grown to such dimensions as to make it dangerous for the republican and democratic parties, the latter forthwith united and took stand against the social-democrats. This, of course, was natural—for are not their interests identical? And as the social-democrats nevertheless elected their candidates, they were beaten out of the fruits of their victory by the corrupt schemes of the old political parties. The ballot-box was stolen and the votes so "corrected" that it became possible for the opposition to proclaim their candidates elected. The workingmen sought to obtain justice through the courts, but it was all in vain. The trial cost them fifteen hundred dollars, but their rights they never obtained.

Soon enough I found that political corruption had burrowed through the ranks of the social-democrats. I left this party and joined the International Working People's Association, that was just being organized. The members of that body have the firm conviction that the workingman can free himself from the tyranny of capitalism only through force—just as all advances of which history speaks, have been brought about through force alone. We see from the history of this country that the first colonists won their liberty only through force; that through force slavery was abolished, and just as the man who agitated against slavery in this country had to ascend to the gallows, so also must we. He who speaks for the workingman today must hang. . . .

The state's-attorney said here that "anarchy" was "on trial."

Anarchism and socialism are as much alike, in my opinion, as one egg is to another. They differ only in their tactics. The anarchists have abandoned the way of liberating humanity which socialists would take to accomplish this. I say: Believe no more in the ballot, and use all other means at your command. Because we have done so we stand arraigned here today—because we have pointed out to the people the proper way. The anarchists are being hunted and persecuted for this in every clime, but in the face of it all anarchism is gaining more and more adherents, and if you cut off our opportuni-

from a police photograph

A Few Words on GEORGE ENGEL

With [George Engel] I could only speak a few broken words; but those were sufficient to advise me of his steadfast and unfaltering conviction of the rightness of his position, and of the necessity of his meeting death for the sake of his convictions. It was hard on him; harder I have thought than upon any of the others.

I never think of him but the picture rises before my mind of George Engel and his little wife, upon whom also had fallen the frosts of many winters, as they would sit for hours upon the opposite sides of the iron grating of the jail in loving conversation, quiet and self-restrained, as the weeks and months wore on between the verdict and the execution. The scene was always to me of infinite pathos. But, as much as in the case of any other in the group, the conviction forced itself upon my mind that Engel was what he was from very necessity of his nature and his environments; and that he did what he did under an absolute persuasion that what he did was right, and was a necessity of the situation in which he found himself. I do not think any man could associate intimately with him and not reach the assurance of his absolute sincerity in all that he did and said.

Capt. William P. BLACK

from "Characteristics of the Murdered Men," Free Society *(Chicago, November 6, 1898)*

ties of open agitation, then will all the work be done secretly. If the state's-attorney thinks he can root out socialism by hanging seven of our men and condemning the other to fifteen years' servitude, he is laboring under the wrong impression. . . .

When hundreds of workingmen have been destroyed in mines in consequence of faulty preparations, for the repairing of which the owners were too stingy, the capitalistic papers have scarcely noticed it. See with what satisfaction and cruelty they make their report, when here and there workingmen have been fired upon, while striking for a few cents increase in their wages, that they might earn only a scanty subsistence.

Can anyone feel any respect for a government that accords rights only to the privileged classes, and none to the workers? We have seen but recently how the coal-barons combined to form a conspiracy to raise the price of coal, while at the same time reducing the already low wages of their men. Are they accused of conspiracy on that account? But when workingmen dare ask an increase in their wages, the militia and the police are sent out to shoot them down.

For such a government as this I can feel no respect, and I will combat them despite their power, despite their police, despite their spies.

I hate and combat, not the individual capitalist, but the system that gives him those privileges. My greatest wish is that workingmen may recognize who are their friends and who are their enemies.

As to my conviction, brought about as it was through capitalistic influence, I have not a word to say.

George ENGEL

from Albert R. Parsons, *Anarchism: Its Philosophy and Scientific Basis, as Defined by Some of Its Apostles* (Chicago, 1887)

Sketch by Art Young

Toy-dealer.

George Bruce's Son & Co.
Type Catalog, 1882

LIBERTY OR DEATH: LETTER TO GOVERNOR OGLESBY

Dear Sir,

I, George Engel, citizen of the United States and of Chicago, and condemned to death, learn that thousands of citizens petition you as the highest executive officer of the State of Illinois, to commute my sentence from death to imprisonment.

I protest emphatically against this on the following grounds: I am not aware of having violated any laws of this country. In my firm belief in the constitution which the founders of this republic bequeathed to this people, and which remains unaltered, I have exercised the right of free speech, free press, free thought and free assemblage, as guaranteed by the constitution, and have criticized the existing conditions of society, and succored my fellow citizens with my advice, which I regard as the right of every honest citizen.

The experience which I have had in this country, during the fifteen years that I have lived here, concerning the ballot and the administration of our public functionaries who have become totally corrupt, has eradicated my belief in the existence of equal rights of poor and rich; and the action of public officers, police and militia have produced the firm belief in me that these conditions can-

not last long. In accordance with this belief I have taught and advised. This I have done in good faith of the rights which we are guaranteed by the constitution, and, not being conscious of my guilt, the "powers that be" may *murder* me, but they cannot *legally punish* me.

I protest against a commutation of my sentence, and demand either liberty or death. I renounce any kind of mercy.

Respectfully,

George ENGEL

from George N. McLean,
The Rise and Fall of Anarchy
(Chicago, 1888)

George Engel speaking at an anarchist picnic

GEORGE ENGEL

Rare gentle soul, tuned like a silver bell
When struck by loving hand or kindly
*   word*
Yet keen and swift as Azrael's flaming
*   sword*
When menaced by the Christian imps
*   of hell*
On whose foul shoulders Satan's mantle
*   fell*
When legal might instead of free accord
Was in the State set up to be adored—
Whose favors legislators buy and sell.
Thou didst not humble nor deny the right
When press and pulpit howled like dogs
*   accurst,*
But calmly looked into the face of Might
And bid the dastard crew perform their
*   worst,*
Smiling in sorrow, gentleness, and grace,
Upon the superstition of thy race.

Dyer D. LUM

In Memoriam:
Chicago, November 11, 1887
(Berkeley Heights, New Jersey,
The Oriole Press, 1937)

GEORGE ENGEL.

This "playing-card"-style portrait and the engraving in the first column were featured in Haymarket Martyrs' Memorial prints produced in Germany

Mourners at Engel's Toy Store

LOUIS LINGG

Born in Schwetzingen, near Mannheim in Baden, Germany, Louis Lingg (1864-1887) enjoyed a happy childhood until his father, a lumber-worker, suffered a serious injury on his job, which led to his death three years later and brought great hardship and suffering to his family. This experience, particularly the callous indifference of his father's employer to the entire calamity, provided 13-year-old Louis with his "first impressions of the prevailing unjust social institutions"—as he noted in a short autobiography written in Cook County Jail—and implanted in his mind "a bitter hatred of existing society" which intensified as he grew older and entered "the industrial arena."

Completing his carpenters' apprenticeship in 1882, Lingg wandered for three years through Germany and Switzerland: climbing mountains, exploring the ruins of old castles, and admiring "the beauty of nature in this corner of the world," which, he remarked, was "simply indescribable." The impact that this adventure had on him is indicated by the fact that when he wrote the aforementioned sketch of his life for the weekly Knights of Labor, *he devoted fully a fourth of it to recounting these travels.*

Meanwhile, the young carpenter had become a freethinker ("a domain in which greater men than I have trod, and still greater than I will continue to walk"), joined a Lassallean socialist group in Freiburg, and taken part in socialist activity in Berne. When he met the famous propagandist-of-the-deed, August Reinsdorf, in Zurich, 1883, Louis Lingg became an anarchist.

Unwilling to fulfill what the German government regarded as his "military obligation," Lingg lived clandestinely for several months and finally decided to emigrate:

I had no desire to spend three of the best years of my youth in military service for the defense of throne, altar and money-bag, or even to satisfy the caprices of some crowned idiot in causing wholesale murders, commonly called wars.

from *Frank Leslie's Illustrated Weekly*

He arrived in New York in July 1885—just ten months before Haymarket—and went straight to Chicago, where the anarchist movement was strongest.

Lingg soon became organizer for the Chicago local of the International Carpenters' and Joiners' Union ("Every member of this society is a rabid Anarchist," said Capt. Schaack), and his fellow workers also elected him delegate to the Central Labor Union. An outspoken advocate of the policy of using "rude force to combat the ruder force of the police," he was active in his union's armed section, regularly attended rifle-practice, and learned how to make bombs. These bombs, none of them ever used, were the State's pretext for murdering a gifted young revolutionist and union organizer.

Handsome, thoughtful, intelligent, generous, well-liked by his fellow workers, popular with women and fond of children, Lingg was depicted in the press as a wild and demented monster whose sole aim in life was bloodletting and pillage. During the trial he disdained to follow the proceedings, preferring to read instead. "Tilted back in his chair," wrote one reporter, "an unlighted cigar in his mouth, he regarded the whole affair with savage scorn."*

Lingg's Address to the Court *has long been recognized as a classic of American anarchism and, together with the speeches of his fellow martyrs, has been translated into many languages.*

On the eve of his scheduled execution, Lingg killed himself with a cigar-bomb smuggled into his cell by a friend. Youngest of the Chicago martyrs, he was also the only one to die a bachelor.

Thousands of mourners filed past his open casket in the back room of Engel's toyshop on Milwaukee Avenue.

FR

* *Charles Edward Russell, in* Appleton's Magazine *(October, 1907).*

ADDRESS TO THE COURT

Court of Justice! With the same irony with which you have regarded my efforts to win, in this "free land of America," a livelihood such as humankind is worthy to enjoy, do you now, after condemning me to death, concede me the liberty of making a final speech.

I accept your concession; but it is only for the purpose of exposing the injustice, the calumnies, and the outrages which have been heaped upon me.

You have accused me of murder, and convicted me: What proof have you brought that I am guilty?

In the first place, you have brought this fellow Seliger to testify against me. Him I have helped to make bombs, and you have further proven that with the assistance of another, I took those bombs to No. 58 Clybourn avenue, but what you have not proven—even with the assistance of your bought "squealer," Seliger, who would appear to have acted such a prominent part in the affair—is that any of those bombs were taken to the haymarket.

A couple of chemists also, have been brought here as specialists, yet they could only state that the metal of which the haymarket bomb was made bore a certain resemblance to those bombs of mine, and your Mr. Ingham has vainly endeavored to deny that the bombs were

quite different. He had to admit that there was a difference of a full half inch in their diameters, although he suppressed the fact that there was also a difference of a quarter of an inch in the thickness of the shell. This is the kind of evidence upon which you have convicted me.

It is not murder, however, of which you have convicted me. The judge has stated that much only this morning in his resume of the case, and Grinnell has repeatedly asserted that we were being tried, not for murder, but for anarchy, so that the condemnation is—that I am an anarchist!

What is anarchy? This is a subject which my comrades have explained with sufficient clearness, and it is unnecessary for me to go over it again. They have told you plainly enough what our aims are. The state's attorney, however, has not given you that information. He has merely criticized and condemned, not the doctrines of anarchy, but our methods of giving them practical effect, and even here he has maintained a discreet silence as to the fact that those methods were forced upon us by the brutality of the police. Grinnell's own proffered remedy for our grievances is the ballot and combination of trades unions, and Ingham has even avowed the desirability of a six-hour movement! But the fact is, that at every

46

attempt to wield the ballot, at every endeavor to combine the efforts of workingmen, you have displayed the brutal violence of the police club, and this is why I have recommended rude force, to combat the ruder force of the police.

You have charged me with despising "law and order." What does your "law and order" amount to? Its representatives are the police, and they have thieves in their ranks. Here sits Captain Schaack. He has himself admitted to me that my hat and books have been stolen from him in his office—stolen by policemen. These are your defenders of property rights!

The detectives again, who arrested me, forced their way into my room like housebreakers, under false pretenses, giving the name of a carpenter, Lorenz, of Burlington street. They have sworn that I was alone in my room, therein perjuring themselves. You have not subpoenaed this lady, Mrs. Klein, who was present, and could have sworn that the aforesaid detectives broke into my room under false pretenses, and that their testimonies are perjured

But let us go further. In Schaack we have a captain of the police, and he also has perjured himself. He has sworn that I admitted to him being present at the Monday night meeting, whereas I distinctly informed him that I was at a carpenters' meeting at Zepf's Hall. He has sworn again that I told him that I also learned to make bombs from Herr Most's book. That also is a perjury.

Let us go still a step higher among these representatives of law and order. Grinnell and his associates have permitted perjury, and I say that they have done it knowingly. The proof has been adduced by my counsel, and with my own eyes I have seen Grinnell point out to Gilmer, eight days before he came upon the stand, the persons of the men whom he was to swear against.

While I, as I have stated above, believe in force for the sake of winning for myself and fellow-workmen a livelihood such as men ought to have, Grinnell, on the other hand, through his police and other rogues, has suborned perjury in order to murder seven men, of whom I am one.

Grinnell had the pitiful courage here in the courtroom, where I could not defend myself, to call me a coward! The scoundrel! A fellow who has leagued himself with a parcel of base, hireling knaves, to bring me to the gallows. Why? For no earthly reason save a contemptible selfishness—a desire to "rise in the world"—to "make money," forsooth.

This wretch—who, by means of the perjuries of other wretches is going to murder seven men—is the fellow who calls me "coward"! And yet you blame me for despising such "defenders of the law"— such unspeakable hypocrites!

Anarchy means no domination or authority of one man over another, yet you call that "disorder." A system which advocates no such "order" as shall require the services of rogues and thieves to defend it you call "disorder."

The Judge himself was forced to admit that the state's attorney had not been able to connect me with the bombthrowing. The latter knows how to get around it, however. He charges me with being a "conspirator." How does he prove it? Simply by declaring the International Working People's Association to be a "conspiracy." I was a member of that body, so he has the charge securely fastened on me. Excellent! Nothing is too difficult for the genius of a state's attorney!

It is hardly incumbent upon me to review the relations which I occupy to my companions in misfortune. I can say truly and openly that I am not as intimate with my fellow prisoners as I am with Captain Schaack.

The universal misery, the ravages of the capitalistic hyena have brought us together in our agitation, not as persons, but as workers in the same cause. Such is the "conspiracy" of which you have convicted me.

I protest against the conviction, against the decision of the court. I do not recognize your law, jumbled together as it is by the nobodies of bygone centuries, and I do not recognize the decision of the court. My own counsel have conclusively proven from the decisions of equally high courts that a new trial must be granted us. The state's attorney quotes three times as many decisions from perhaps still higher courts to prove the opposite, and I am convinced that if, in another trial, these decisions should be supported by twenty-one volumes, they will adduce one hundred in support of the contrary, if it is anarchists who are to be tried. And not even under such a law—a law that a schoolboy must despise—not even by such methods have they been able to "legally" convict us.

They have suborned perjury to boot.

I tell you frankly and openly, I am for force. I have already told Captain Schaack, "if they use cannons against us, we shall use dynamite against them."

I repeat that I am the enemy of the "order" of today, and I repeat that, with all my powers, so long as breath remains in me, I shall combat it. I declare again, frankly and openly, that I am in favor of using force. I have told Captain Schaack, and I stand by it, "if you cannonade us, we shall dynamite you." You laugh! Perhaps you think, "you'll throw no more bombs"; but let me assure you I die happy on the gallows, so confident am I that the hundreds and thousands to whom I have spoken will remember my words; and when you shall have hanged us, then—mark my words—they will do the bombthrowing! In this hope do I say to you: I despise you. I despise your order, your laws, your force-propped authority. Hang me for it!

Louis LINGG

from *Famous Speeches
of the Chicago Anarchists*
(Chicago, 1912)

Sketch by Art Young

47

"The Red Banner of the Carpenters' Union" (from Schaack)

IN DEFENSE OF LOUIS LINGG

Lingg. . .came from that republic sitting in the center of Europe preaching the everlasting lesson of liberty. He came here in the fall of 1885. . . . Whatever he knows of social and labor conditions in this country he learned from those about him.

He joined a carpenters' union, being himself a carpenter by trade. He attended the meetings of that union. Young, active, bright, capable, he enters the band of which they speak, and manufactures bombs. There is no law against that, gentlemen; but they claim that is a circumstance from which you must draw the conclusion of his guilt, when taken with other circumstances, for the Haymarket tragedy. . . .

The Carpenters' Union at one of its meetings resolved to devote a certain amount of money for the purpose of experimenting with dynamite. You may say that was not right, but [Lingg] was not responsible for it. There is no more reason in holding him responsible for the Haymarket affair on account of his experiments than there is to hold every other member of the Carpenters' Union for the same thing. That is how Lingg came to make bombs.

Without dynamite a bombshell is a toy. The Lingg bombs would kill nobody unless some human independent agency took hold of them. . . . And yet the State asks you to say that Lingg shall be hanged because he manufactured bombs.

This boy Lingg was dependent on others as to his impressions of our institutions. He went to Seliger's house.* Seliger is a socialist; he has been in this country for years. He is 31 years of age; Lingg is 21. And yet the great State of Illinois, through its legal representatives, bargains with William Seliger, the man of mature years, and with his wife, older even than himself, that if they will do what they can to put the noose around the neck of this boy they shall go scatheless! Ah! gentlemen, what a mockery of justice is this.

Capt. William P. BLACK

Argument for the Defense
August 13, 1886

* Lingg's residence in Chicago. The Seligers, with whom Lingg had made bombs, became witnesses for the prosecution, for which services they were well remunerated; the Chicago police paid for their transportation to Germany after the trial.

LOUIS LINGG

As social heretics condemned!
  For us, for all they dared
To lift their voices to protest!
  For us their breasts were bared!
As Leaders in grim Labor's Cause
  and speaking what we thought,
They shamed the drunken revelers
  by tales with misery fraught!

They voiced suppress'd, half-uttered
  groans of toilers in the mine;
The widow's sighs were framed to speech
  unheard at heaven's shrine;
And tears of children (they whose graves
  lie clustered round the mill)
Welled up in sorrow from their hearts
  forbidding voice be still.

The labor lords and courtly dames
  who held their revel here
Were awed to silence by their words
  and lived in quaking fear,
Till viler, meaner revelers,
  those of the drunken State,
Called on their hireling, Law, to rid
  them of the men they hate.

Still louder now the drunken State
  in giddy revel reels,
While faster through their pulsing veins
  the fatal poison steals,
Till hearts are closed and ears are sealed
  to Labor's sighs and groans,
While Hope afflicted flies to hide
  behind sepulchral stones.

But hark! our martyr's sentenced doom,
  to die a felon's death,
Is the last angel's trumpet sound!
  blown with avenging breath,
And at the State's Belshazzar-feast
  the Ghost of Lingg will rise
To vindicate his prophecy
  as Law's oppression dies!

Dyer D. LUM

In Memoriam:
Chicago, November 11, 1887
(Berkeley Heights, New Jersey,
The Oriole Press, 1937)

from a police photograph

OPEN LETTER to GOVERNOR OGLESBY

To Mr R. J. Oglesby,
Governor of Illinois:

Anent the fact that the progressive and liberty-loving portion of the American people are endeavoring to prevail upon you to interpose prerogative in my case, I feel impelled to declare, with my friend and comrade Parsons, that I demand either liberty or death.

If you are really a servant of the people according to the constitution of the country, then you will, by virtue of your office, unconditionally release me.

Referring to the general and inalienable rights of men, I have called upon the disinherited and oppressed masses to oppose the force of their oppressors—exercised by armed enforcement of infamous laws, enacted in the interest of capital—with force, in order to attain a dignified and manly existence by securing the full returns of their labor. This—and only this—is the "crime" which was proved against me, notwithstanding the employment of perjured testimony on the part of the State. And this crime is guaranteed not only as a right, but as a duty, by the American constitution, the representative of which you are supposed to be in the State of Illinois.

But if you are not the representative of the constitution, like the great majority of officeholders, a mere tool of monopolists or a specific political clique, you will not encroach upon the thirst for blood displayed by the executioner, because a mere mitigation of the verdict would be cowardice, and a proof that the ruling classes which you represent are themselves abashed at the monstrosity of my condemnation, and consequently, of their own violation of the most sacred rights of the people.

Your decision in that event will not only judge me, but also yourself and those whom you represent. Judge then!

Louis LINGG

Cook County Jail
October 30, 1887

from George N. McLean,
The Rise and Fall of Anarchy
(Chicago, 1888)

A Note on Louis Lingg

The last words of the speech of Louis Lingg showed the hatred he bore towards the system. He said: "I despise you. I despise your order, your laws, your force-propped authority. Hang me for it."

Every member of the IWW today bears the same hatred for the capitalist system.

—Industrial Worker
November 9, 1911

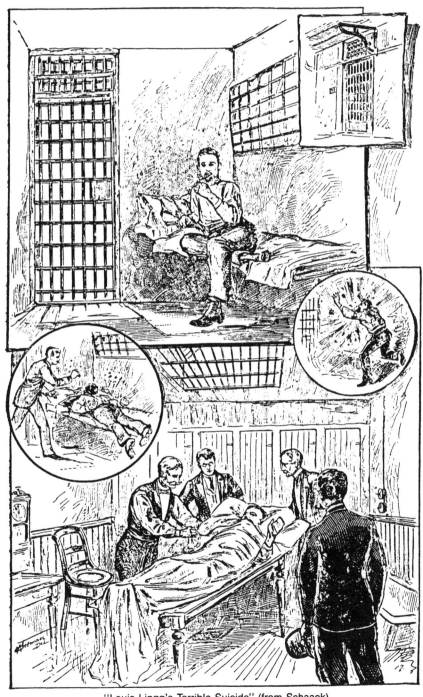

"Louis Lingg's Terrible Suicide" (from Schaack)

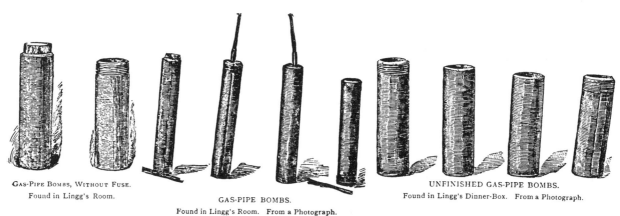

GAS-PIPE BOMBS, WITHOUT FUSE.
Found in Lingg's Room.

GAS-PIPE BOMBS.
Found in Lingg's Room. From a Photograph.

UNFINISHED GAS-PIPE BOMBS.
Found in Lingg's Dinner-Box. From a Photograph.

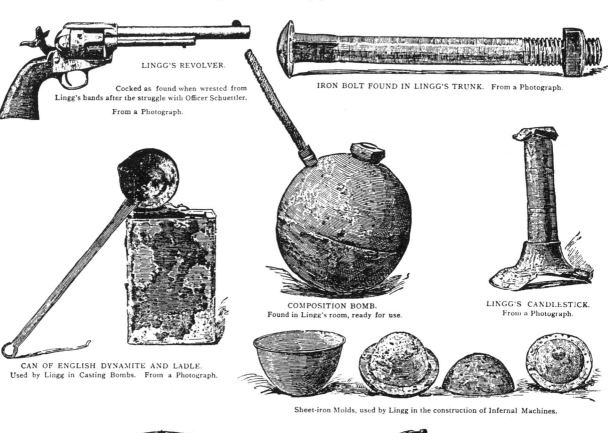

LINGG'S REVOLVER.

Cocked as found when wrested from
Lingg's hands after the struggle with Officer Schuettler.
From a Photograph.

IRON BOLT FOUND IN LINGG'S TRUNK. From a Photograph.

COMPOSITION BOMB.
Found in Lingg's room, ready for use.

LINGG'S CANDLESTICK.
From a Photograph.

CAN OF ENGLISH DYNAMITE AND LADLE.
Used by Lingg in Casting Bombs. From a Photograph.

Sheet-iron Molds, used by Lingg in the construction of Infernal Machines.

LINGG'S TRUNK.
From a Photograph.

COILS OF FUSE.
Found in the secret bottom of Lingg's Trunk.
From a Photograph.

A few of the many Lingg-related illustrations from Capt. Schaack's *Anarchy and Anarchists*

"The Most Dangerous Anarchist in All Chicago":
THE LEGEND & LEGACY OF LOUIS LINGG

In a full-length survey of labor violence published in 1913, the social-democratic writer Robert Hunter argued that while

most of the Chicago anarchists were plain workingmen, simple and kindly, at least one fanatic in the group deserves to rank with Nechayeff and Most as an irreconcilable enemy of the existing order. This was Louis Lingg.[1]

Virtually every commentator on Haymarket has agreed that Lingg somehow stood out from his comrades—that his passionately articulated extremist views, the uncompromising bitterness of his temperament, the ferocity of his disdain for the forces of "Law'n'Order" distinguished him from his co-defendants. More than any of the other Chicago martyrs, his name has provoked fearful superlatives. Cook County Sheriff Matson regarded him as "the most desperate man under his charge."[2] A New York *Post* editorial called him a "bold and desperate fanatic" and "the spark" that produced the Haymarket explosion.[3] In *The Rise and Fall of Anarchy in America*, journalist George N. McLean pronounced Lingg "one of the most arch plotters of dark and tragic history."[4] For Capt. Schaack, as he wrote in his *Anarchy and Anarchists*, the young organizer for the Carpenters' Union was "the most dangerous anarchist in all Chicago."[5]

Even among the anarchists' defenders there were many who concurred with the broad outlines of this negative estimate. Dr. Ernst Schmidt, a major figure in the Haymarket defense and amnesty campaigns, wrote later:

I never knew much about Lingg. Seeing him in jail, I took him for a surly sort of fellow, wild-eyed at times, somebody with whom you do not care to become acquainted.[6]

Not a few who were otherwise sympathetic to the defendants expressed grave doubts about Lingg, and especially about his mental health; a whole group active in the clemency drive actually hoped to prove the young man insane and thereby to overturn the verdicts.[7]

Indeed, there is evidence suggesting that several of the other martyrs themselves regarded Lingg with something less than full approbation. In an article published three days after the hangings

from the Chicago *Knights of Labor*

One peculiar feature about Lingg is his intense devotion to the cause of anarchism. In all the interviews I have had with him I have failed to make him see the error of his ways.

He has told me that he was ready to die for the cause—in fact, he says he would be only too glad to be sacrificed for the sake of the principles he advocates. And the queer part of it is that he is always self-contained and speaks as if he was in earnest.

He is the most unfathomable fellow I have ever had in charge.

Capt. Michael J. SCHAACK

from the Chicago Daily News,
May 20, 1886

the Chicago *Tribune* quoted an unnamed jail official to this effect:

Spies said that he could not understand Lingg. Schwab said that he was a puzzle. The others looked upon him as an odd compound of hardihood and unquestioned physical courage, but mentally so perverse that they never knew how to take him.[8]

One must be wary of accepting as fact such unauthenticated testimony from an unspecified informant, especially when

published in a newspaper notorious for its anti-labor bias.[9] It so happens, however, that other testimony, of indisputable veracity, lends some support to this particular bit of *Tribune* gossip. Spies, for example, is known to have described Lingg as "irresponsible" and a "monomaniac," and further stated that he had "never met as peculiar a man as he is."[10] And Michael Schwab acknowledged that he was "not on friendly terms" with Lingg.[11] However, their authenticity notwithstanding, it is impossible to give much weight to these rather modest disclaimers made long after the trial had ended. Spies' comments are from a letter written in haste immediately after bombs were alleged to have been found in Lingg's cell, a week before the executions, and Schwab's remark from an article written in the penitentiary at Joliet in 1891.

In truth, the difference between Lingg and his fellow martyrs has been enormously and bizarrely exaggerated. Had it really been true that the other defendants were merely "plain workingmen, simple and kindly," as Robert Hunter pretended; had it been true that Lingg "presents a personality utterly different from that of any of the others," as Floyd Dell argued in 1912,[12] or that "between [Lingg] and the other men on trial there was little in common," as Henry David reiterated in 1937[13] — had Lingg been so completely and drastically unlike his fellow anarchists, would not some trace of this supposedly extreme divergence have come out in the course of the trial itself, or at least much earlier in the defense campaign? Of course each of the imprisoned men differed from each of the others in a multitude of particulars, but these were differences of degree rather than of kind. Far more things united the Haymarket martyrs than divided them.

What, then, was so disturbing, so fascinating about Lingg? Affirming that he was "in many ways the most interesting of the eight defendants," Paul Avrich adds that he was "the only one among them who is definitely known to have manufactured bombs."[14] This was an unquestionably important and probably decisive factor in Lingg's notoriety. The prosecution's preposterously weak case—charging eight men with murder while having to admit that none of them had actually thrown the bomb—made it essential to play up the fact that at least *one* of the eight had had *some* connection with bombs. Attempts to prove that the actual Haymarket bomb was made by Lingg were unconvincing to all but Judge Gary and his jury, but Lingg had already been dubbed "the Bomb-Maker," and the tag stuck.

Bombings, especially dynamite bombings, were not common in America in the 1880s. Indeed, May 4, 1886 provided the first example of the fatal use of dynamite in a civil disturbance. Even today bombings and bomb-scares make shocking headlines; a hundred years ago the Haymarket explosion produced a wave of terror and panic that had no precedent.[15] It was no wonder that "Louis Lingg, the Bomb-Maker" was identified in the nation's press and pulpits as a "wild beast," "madman" and "fiend."

As if having made bombs were not bad enough, Lingg went on to ardently justify having done so, and in fact never wavered in his advocacy of revolutionary violence against what he regarded as the oppressing class. It should be emphasized that there was nothing illegal about owning dynamite or making bombs in 1886. Also worthy of emphasis is the fact that numerous articles and editorials in the *Tribune* and other big dailies had been urging massive violence—including vigilante terror, lynching and (believe it or not) arsenic-poisoning—against working people, especially tramps and strikers.[16]

The wholesale slaughter of workers during the 1877 strikes was not forgotten nine years later. In the weeks preceding Haymarket, "Black Jack" Bonfield and other police hoodlums were notoriously brutal in their frequent assaults on workers' meetings and picketlines. Largely as a result of this police brutality, all of the Haymarket anarchists were outspoken upholders of what they affirmed to be the right and even the duty of workers to defend themselves against police attack, and it is hardly surprising that a young militant such as Lingg, just out of his teens, should have become a "crack shot"

with a rifle, or that he acquainted himself with the preparation of the newfangled bombs that General Sherman and others were threatening to use against the working class.[18]

Chicago *Daily News*, May 20, 1886

The strangest man I have ever known and the least human, was Louis Lingg . . . . He was a kind of modern berserker, utterly reckless of consequences to himself, driving on in a sustaining fury of vengeance upon the whole social order.

Little of his abnormal physical strength was apparent when he was in repose. He was slightly under average height, very compactly built, with tawny hair, a face long and strong, and the most extraordinary eyes I have ever seen in a human head, steel gray, exceedingly keen, and bearing in their depths a kind of cold and hateful fire.

His hands were small and delicate; his head was large, and very well shaped; his face indicated breeding and culture. It was when he walked, as I often saw him going to and fro alone in the jail corridor, that he seemed most formidable; for then his lithe, gliding and peculiarly silent step, and the play of his muscles about the shoulders, suggested something catlike or abnormal, an impression heightened by the leonine wave of hair he wore when arrested. . . .

All in all, for a small man, he was the most terrific figure I have ever met. . . . I think that in those days few strangers observed him without a secret feeling of relief that he was on the other side of the steel bars. He was the one really dangerous man among the seven, and the only anarchist.

Charles Edward RUSSELL

Appleton's Magazine
(October, 1907)

Lingg's remorseless intransigence, epitomized in his justly famous address to the court, added appreciably to his "wild" and "desperate" reputation. "If

you cannonade us," he told Capt. Schaack, "we shall dynamite you."[19] His whole manner matched his words. "From the day [he] entered the jail," Schaack recalled,

he became surly and ugly to all the officers . . . . He held himself aloof from everybody except his fellow anarchists, and would have nothing to say to anyone except his friends or his sweetheart.[20]

He consistently refused to talk to reporters from the capitalist press. "To every question or remark," one reporter noted, "he was wont to respond with a silent stare of malignant and calculating hatred."[21]

This defiant, hostile attitude accentuated that quality remarked by everyone who came into contact with Lingg: his fervent, singleminded devotion to the anarchist movement—what his detractors were pleased to call his "fanaticism." "Sleeping or waking," wrote Schaack, "Anarchy and the most effective methods of establishing it were uppermost in his thoughts. . . . He would do anything to help along the cause."[22] A certain selflessness and generosity are the usual corollaries of such dedication, and so it was with Lingg. Schaack conceded that the young union-organizer was "scrupulously honest and conscientious in his dealings with his fellow man";[23] moreover, "in every act and word, he showed no care for himself, but he always expressed sympathy for men who had families and who were in trouble."[24] Austerity rounds out the picture: "Although he drank beer, he never drank to excess, and he frowned upon the use of bad or indecent language."[25]

Defiance, and perhaps something of a certain grim humor, also seems to have motivated his strange suicide, which in turn added yet another dimension to the Lingg legend. A man who seems always to have lived at the outer limits of life, he refused to allow the State to assign the date and mode of his death. "I will never die on the scaffold," he told his jailers, "I hate and defy you all."[26] Louis Lingg died as he lived, *against the law.*

Twenty-three years old at his death, he was by far the youngest of the martyrs—nearly thirty years younger than the oldest, George Engel, and fourteen years younger than the average age of the others. The key elements of Lingg's image as it has come down to us—

defiance of authority, passionate love of freedom, inclination toward violence, his "fanaticism" and even his suicide—all have a place under the heading of *youth*, or rather, of what thinkers as varied as Randolph Bourne and André Breton have signaled as the *genius* of youth.[27] Inspiration, revolt, audacity, refusal to compromise, the spirit of all-or-nothing—*that* is the genius of youth. A large part of what we might call the secret of Louis Lingg—the secret of the profound and enduring horror he has inspired in so many, and of the no less profound and enduring appeal he has had for others—seems to me to lie in his remarkable fidelity to this genius.

Here is an example of "poetic justice" at its wildest: Portrayed as an irredeemably evil arch-villain by the police, the press and the clergy, the young man in Cell 22 at once became a hero to rebel youth everywhere, especially to youngsters just discovering the anarchist movement. It is still widely believed that Haymarket brought the "end" of anarchism in the U.S.; the exact opposite would be closer to the truth. The martyrs themselves, admirers of old John Brown,[28] knew that the State could not put an end to a revolutionary movement by murdering any number of individuals. The Red Scare wreaked its havoc, it is true, but it also made people ask questions about America's "democracy" and "free institutions." Less than a decade after the hangings an anarchist writer, Ross Winn, affirmed that the deaths of the Chicago martyrs marked not the end but "the real *beginning* of the Anarchist propaganda in America."[29] Alexander Berkman, Emma Goldman, Voltairine de Cleyre and Kate Austin are only a few of the important figures of the next generation of anarchists who came to the movement by way of Haymarket.

In this anarchist resurgence, the special influence of Lingg was considerable. When he learned of the young anarchist's suicide, William Dean Howells declared: "All over the world people must be asking themselves, What cause is this really, for which men die so gladly, so inexorably?"[30]

At a Haymarket Memorial Meeting in 1900 Voltairine de Cleyre said: "Many a one will say with me tonight, in answer to the question, 'What made you an anarchist?'—'The hanging in Chicago.'" She made no secret of the fact that, in her eyes, Lingg was "the beautiful one, the brave defiant one. . . bravest among those who were all brave."[31]

In his *Prison Memoirs of an Anarchist* (1912), Alexander Berkman recalled a young medical student in New York "whom we playfully dubbed 'Lingg' because of his rather successful affectation of the celebrated revolutionist's physical appearance."[32] For Berkman and for Emma Goldman, Lingg was "the sublime hero among the eight. . . the beacon of our lives."[33]

> *He was curiously courteous, this man, always.*
>
> * * *
>
> *He seemed to touch the extremes of life with a wider reach than other men.*
>
> * * *
>
> *Vivid, living flashes of humor . . .made his talk inimitable.*
>
> * * *
>
> *His very method of speaking had a strange individuality about it.*
>
> * * *
>
> *Whatever the question might be, if he spoke at all, he spoke as a master.*
>
> * * *
>
> *There was an extraordinary passion in his speech, an extraordinary menace in his whole person, a flame in the deep eyes. The words of this man seemed like deeds. . . .*
>
> * * *
>
> *In spite of its clearness, his mind just touched mysticism. He felt a purpose in things—his star and fate one with the whole.*
>
> Frank HARRIS
>
> The Bomb,
> first American edition
> (New York, Mitchell Kennerly, 1909).

In 1908 Frank Harris published his novel, *The Bomb*, in which Lingg figures as the central character; the book is, in fact, the only sustained attempt at a portrait of Lingg that we have. Largely because of the fallacious suppositions on which the story is based—the prosecution's allegations that Rudolph Schnaubelt was the Haymarket bomb-thrower, and that the bomb he threw had been made by Lingg—Lucy Parsons detested it.[34] She could hardly have failed to resent, moreover, the fact that the book makes Lingg seem much more important than Albert Parsons or, for that matter, all the other martyrs combined. As John Spargo wrote in the *International Socialist Review*, "Mr. Harris makes of Lingg a great and terrible character, dwarfing all the others in intellect as well as in the bitterness of his hate."[35]

The tale is marred by irritating improbabilities—Harris goes so far as to make Lingg into an admirer of the gospels and a supporter of government-funding for the theater, absurdities for which the novelist alone is responsible, as they are unsupported by the slightest evidence—and is unsatisfactory in many other ways as well. But what concerns us here is that its portrayal of Lingg is too narrow, too one-dimensional. Preoccupied with the young anarchist's "fanaticism," Harris is too superficial, too ignorant of anarchism, and too engrossed in his own peculiar notion of "mysticism" to treat the reality of poetry and humor and dream behind that "fanaticism" with anything more than literary seasoning. His occasional flashes of real insight are unfortunately too few to relieve the rather murky effect of the story as a whole.

Nonetheless, *The Bomb* played a role—a big role—in perpetuating and advancing the Lingg legend, making it far more accessible than it had ever been before by putting it in the form of an exciting fictional narrative. Emma Goldman praised the book's "dramatic power," sold copies at her lectures around the country and advertised it in *Mother Earth*.[36] The book went through many editions here and abroad, and there can be no doubt that countless individuals have discovered "the most defiant anarchist of them all"[37] by reading it.

And so the specter of Louis Lingg has continued to haunt the successive generations of revolutionary youth. During the long period from the 1930s through the early '60s in which anarchism as an organized movement was all but eclipsed, his memory was kept alive by small groups of anarchists, by the IWW, and by an occasional out-of-the-mainstream writer such as Nelson Algren. The widespread revival of interest in anarchism in the 1960s/70s brought Lingg's image and message to the forefront once again.

Although he was not represented in the various popular anarchist anthologies edited by scholars,[38] Lingg's *Address to the Court* or excerpts from it, significant references to him, and/or his picture found their way into numerous ephemeral and "underground" publications. His presence loomed large, for example, in the anarchist calendars issued by Chicago's Solidarity Bookshop in the late sixties. In the American surrealist manifestoes that began to appear around the same time, Lingg figured as a precursor alongside such names as Charles Brockden Brown, Clark Ashton Smith and Thelonious Monk.[39]

In its most revolutionary period, which was also the period of its greatest growth and impact—1967-69—the Students for a Democratic Society

(SDS) in Chicago had a "Louis Lingg Memorial Chapter" whose members organized sizeable contingents of high-school-age rebels on antiwar demonstrations, and played a not-inconsiderable role in antidraft agitation.

On May Day, 1972, young anarchists and Wobblies attempted to set up a paper-mache statue of Lingg on the empty pedestal where the Haymarket cop statue formerly stood. But the Chicago police turned out in force to guard the pedestal and prevented the substitution from taking place.[40]

A hero to disaffected and insurgent youth, Lingg is still, for many, an object of consternation and revulsion—not only for those who recognize themselves as "Pillars of the Establishment,"

but also for reformers who insist on moderation at all costs, and even for some who think of themselves as revolutionists, but who perceive Lingg's "adventurism" as a violation of one or another "correct line." Ninety-nine years after the State drove him to suicide, he remains the most maligned and vilified of the Haymarket Eight.

Philip Foner's publication of Lingg's autobiography for the first time in book form in 1969,[41] and more recently Paul Avrich's sympathetic treatment of Lingg in *The Haymarket Tragedy* (1984), have done much to right the record, helping to divest the young martyr of the demon's mask that has been imposed on him for so long, and allowing him to assume a human form at last. But even now a friendly word for Louis Lingg is a rarity indeed. Those who recoil from the lad in fear and loathing still sound the dominant note.

It is true that the cavilings of today's Lingg-haters often sound tepid next to the blistering tirades of yesteryear. Epithets such as "madman" and "fiend" have an old-fashioned ring nowadays, and a recent commentator has preferred instead to diagnose Lingg as "partly psychopathological."[42] But the hoped-for effect remains the same: to exaggerate Lingg's differences with his fellow martyrs in such a way as to make the others look vastly superior.

That Lingg had qualities identifiable as unique is hardly more than a truism, and does nothing to drive a wedge between him and his comrades, each of whom was also unique in his way—like everybody else. In matters of anarchist theory and even of tactics Lingg was in basic agreement with his co-defendants, as he himself readily acknowledged, and which none of the others denied.[43] It is in his *sensibility* that a certain difference can be discerned. Youngest of the martyrs, he was also, and naturally enough, the boldest, the most adventurous, the most oriented toward *taking risks.* Is this to his discredit?

Lingg did not have the mellifluous eloquence or the "saintliness" of Albert Parsons, or the personable humanitarian good-will of Sam Fielden, or the wide-ranging forensic subtlety of August Spies, or the analytical pedantry of Michael Schwab, or the warmhearted militant earnestness of Oscar Neebe. In his overall uncompromising attitude he

A ferocious scorn for complacency pervades this 1917-18 canvas by German Dadaist George Grosz. Titled *Dedicated to Oskar Panizza*—in honor of the celebrated poet, playwright and one-man war against Church and State—the painting was Grosz's protest against humankind's acquiescence to authoritarian institutions.

was no doubt closer to the intransigent "autonomists," George Engel and Adolph Fischer. But Lingg had a furious serenity about him that was his alone. Is it not his *language*, brimful of the inspired insubordination and violence of youth, that distinguishes Lingg from his co-defendants more than anything else? The disquietingly disinterested vehemence with which he expressed his boundless contempt and scorn for the whole system of capitalism, cops, courts and jails, gives his *Address to the Court* a remarkable and distinctive flair, and makes it one of the most extraordinary documents in American history.

When Lingg spoke on that occasion, we are told, "he made the walls ring."[44] He expressed himself with a directness, a simplicity that makes one blink: Every word is a bullet hitting its mark. This, and several of his other pronouncements have an "absolutely modern" ring, according to the notion suggested by Rimbaud, conveying a sense of life so full of the tremors of the future that the past recedes to a dim irrelevance and the present is endurable only insofar as it approaches this future and demands no compromise. Almost in spite of himself, Louis Lingg was, after all, a kind of poet.

The courtroom speeches of the other defendants hark back to earlier martyrs—John Huss, Michael Servetus, Giordano Bruno— and are well-situated in the humanist tradition. Lingg's, with its explosive brevity and ruthless sarcasm, seems as far beyond conventional rationalist humanism as the latter is beyond ecclesiastical/monarchical superstition. His lightninglike impatience, utterly free of sentimentality, brings to mind the insatiable fury of such later masters of all-encompassing lyrical vituperation as Antonin Artaud, André Breton and Benjamin Péret.

To consider Louis Lingg in the light of surrealism helps us to perceive more clearly the dazzling prescience of his irreconcilable opposition to the structure of things-as-they-are. It is a demonstrable fact that the whole *avant-garde* cultural movement of the past century— from Symbolism through Futurism and Dadaism to Surrealism: all of which, it is it is worth recalling, began as *rebellions of youth*—owes far more to the anarchists than most critics and historians have cared to acknowledge.

This 1934 "Pell-Mell" of surrealists and precursors by Belgian poet Louis Scutenaire illustrates the surrealists' passional attraction for the extreme wing of anarchism even during the years that they were desperately trying to work in the Communist Party. Along with Marat, Hegel, Marx, Lenin, Freud, Lewis Carroll, Lautréamont, Jarry and Vaché, the montage features, in the bottom row, the celebrated anarchist "expropriator" Bonnot and six members of his gang. Scutenaire's accompanying text notes that his montage could easily have included, among others, anarchists Germaine Berton, Emile Henry, Ravachol, Sacco and Vanzetti.

And what is particularly important to emphasize here is that these currents were influenced initially not by anarchism's major theorists, but rather by the wilder propagandists-of-the-deed, dynamiters and perpetrators of *attentats*.

Surrealism especially adopted the extremist wing of anarchism as its own.[45] The first issue of *La Révolution Surréaliste* (1924) featured a full-page "Homage to Germaine Berton"—a young anarchist who had just shot and killed a notorious fascist. Celebratory surrealist references to the anarchist bomber/arsonist Ravachol and to the Bonnot Gang of anarchist expropriators (armed robbers in the eyes of the police) are common. In the *absolute* character of their rejection of capitalist society and its repressive values, and in the unheard-of violence with which they expressed this rejection, these apostles of libertarian terror presaged much of the mood and manner that was later codified in the early surrealist manifestoes, and in tracts such as *Open the Prisons! Disband the Army!* and *Revolution Now and Forever!*[46]

Louis Lingg was perhaps not the first to champion this most ardent branch of anarchist activism, but he was the first to die for it, and this, together with his youth and his thoroughgoing defiance in court and in jail—climaxed by the fact

that he died by his own hand— immediately gave him, in the eyes of young revolutionists everywhere, a larger-than-life quality of transcendant and *exemplary* valor. And because the revolt of youth is the heart and soul of all revolt, Lingg—as the incarnation and symbol of this revolt at its highest tension—inevitably illuminates the

MOTHER EARTH

Vol. IX. September, 1914 No. 7

PRICE 10 CENTS

This cover for *Mother Earth* by the American Man Ray shows that the anarchist roots of Dada and Surrealism were in fact international.

whole trajectory of revolt: yesterday, to-day and tomorrow.

For whether it knows it or not, even the most complete nonconformism still has its forerunners, its traditions, its endless ramifications. What Hegel called "the cunning of history" remains a bottomless bag of tricks, and stranger things have happened than that Louis Lingg's fiery shadow should have fallen on so many paths that were not discovered till long after his death.

Capt. Schaack and Frank Harris both refer to him as "cool," for example, and it is curious how perfectly the adjective still fits in the jazz sense. Isn't there a hint of the hipster in Lingg? We know that, while awaiting execution, he expressed a yearning to *go out and dance*; we know, too, that he did dance in his cell. If the more rebellious zootsuiters, beboppers, mods and rockers ever cared to look for ancestors, could they have found a better one than Lingg? To say so—and he is the only one of the Haymarket martyrs of whom one could possibly say it—is only to signal once again the strikingly *modern* ambience of this young man's spirit of revolt, which seems to seethe in all directions at once.

Louis Lingg's way of saying *no* proved to be full of maddening heights, sharp turns and surprises galore—a revolutionary force more volatile, more resounding, than dynamite itself.

Something of all this—something of the far-reaching implications of this total refusal—surely impinged on the consciousness of those who regarded the imprisoned Lingg as the living embodiment of all that they feared and hated most, just as it has continued to trouble so many historians and commentators who still do not know what to make of this disturbing youngster who despised everything that impeded his exalted sense of freedom and real life.

If youth's excesses seem sometimes desperate, hot-headed, impossible—foolish, in a word—still they make up the only road that leads to the only wisdom that matters. And it is the beauty and grandeur of recalcitrant youth that it *knows*, in spite of everything and no matter what, that the last laugh will be all its own.

For a hundred years, Louis Lingg has exemplified the absolute enemy of

1886 - 1.º de Mayo - 1954

Louis Lingg on the cover of *Solidaridad* (Uruguay, 1954)

LIVING GHOSTS

Not as ghost of Moloch dead,
But as ghost of Moloch living,
Speaks the State in accents dread,
Stones instead of life-bread giving;
Shall we falter, cringe, and kneel
'Neath its heavy iron heel?
On! on! drink unto the lees!
Martyrs led the way with pride,
Conqu'ring death e'en when they died:
PARSONS! FISCHER! ENGEL! SPIES!

O'er the graves of Waldheim's dead,
Where the spotless snow is falling,
Glares above them Law's dread head
Timid souls with fear appalling.
See! Take hope! To courage cling!
Yonder rises Louis Lingg!
On! on! spread unto the breeze
The red flag beneath whose fold
Stand the souls of leaders bold:
PARSONS! FISCHER! ENGEL! SPIES!

Moloch! Christ! Mahomet! State!
Sword and fagot! cell and gallows!
Hath mankind no higher fate
Than what grim oppression hallows?
Up against the foulsome thing,
Call to aid the Ghost of Lingg!
On! on! mankind dimly sees
'Neath the banner of the poor
Opening wide fair Freedom's door:
PARSONS! FISCHER! ENGEL! SPIES!

Dyer D. LUM

In Memoriam:
Chicago, November 11, 1887
(Berkeley Heights, New Jersey,
The Oriole Press, 1937)

Law'n'Order. A fighter against capitalist oppression in his teens, a class-war prisoner at 21, a suicide at 23, he remains and will long remain the exemplar *par excellence* of vital, ireducible, free-spirited youth revolt.

Franklin ROSEMONT

1. Robert Hunter. *Violence and the Labor Movement* (New York, 1913), 70. 2. "The Origin of Louis Lingg," Chicago *Tribune*, November 14, 1887. 3. Undated clipping, private collection. 4. George N. McLean. *The Rise and Fall of Anarchy in America* (Chicago, 1888), 258. 5. Michael J. Schaack. *Anarchy and Anarchists* (Chicago, 1889), 264. 6. Frederick K. Schmidt, ed. *He Chose: The Other Was a Treadmill Thing* (Santa Fe, 1968), 137. 7. Schaack, 628. 8. "The Origin of Louis Lingg," *op. cit.* 9. Elmer Gertz, "Chicago's Adult Delinquent: The *Tribune*," *Public Opinion Quarterly* (Fall 1944), 416-444; George Seldes. *Lords of the Press* (New York, 1938); John Tebbel. *An American Dynasty: The Story of the McCormicks, Medills and Pattersons* (Garden City, 1947). 10. Paul Avrich. *The Haymarket Tragedy* (Princeton, 1984), 369-70. 11. Michael Schwab, "A Convicted Anarchist's Reply to Professor Lombroso," *The Monist* (July 1891), 521. 12. Floyd Dell, "Socialism and Anarchism in Chicago," in J. Seymour Currey, *Chicago: Its History and Its Builders*, 386. 13. Henry David. *The History of the Haymarket Affair* (Second edition, New York, 1958), 271. 14. Avrich, 157. 15. *Ibid.*, 215-39. 16. Tebbel, 52-53. 17. Schaack, 264. 18. Avrich, 176. 19. "Address of Louis Lingg," *Twenty-Fifth Anniversary, Eleventh of November Memorial Edition—Famous Speeches of Our Martyrs* (Chicago, 1912), 36. 20. Schaack, 273. 21. Charles Edward Russell, "The Haymarket and Afterwards: Some Personal Recollections," *Appleton's Magazine* (Oct. 1907), 409. 22. Schaack, 256, 266. 23. *Ibid.*, 655. 24. *Ibid.*, 273. 25. *Ibid.* 26. McLean, 213. 27. Randolph Bourne. *Youth and Life* (Boston, 1913); Franklin Rosemont, ed. *What Is Surrealism: Selected Writings of Andre Breton* (New York & London, 1978), especially "Situation of Surrealism Between the Two Wars," 238. 28. Avrich, 100-101, 289; Philip S. Foner, ed. *The Autobiographies of the Haymarket Martyrs* (New York, 1969), 145; Samuel Fielden, "Comments on the Trial," *Free Society* (Nov. 9, 1902). 29. Ross Winn, quoted in Avrich, 512 (emphasis added, FR). See also C. L. James, "The Craze and Its Consequences," *Free Society* (Chicago, Oct. 27, 1901): "the sure way to encourage the growth of anarchism is to set people talking about it"; and Kate Austin, "Our Martyrs," *Free Society* (Nov. 10, 1901). 30. Quoted in Avrich, 377. 31. Voltairine de Cleyre. *The First May Day: The Haymarket Speeches, 1895-1910* (Minneapolis, 1980), 21, 7. 32. Alexander Berkman. *Prison Memoirs of an Anarchist* (New York, 1912), 8-9. 33. Emma Goldman. *Living My Life* (New York, 1931), 42; see also 31, 87. 34. *Ibid.*, 682-3. 35. John Spargo, "Literature and Art," *International Socialist Review* (June 1909), 1009. 36. Goldman, 682. 37. Schaack, 629. 38. Irving Horowitz, ed. *The Anarchists* (New York, 1964); Leonard Krimerman & Lewis Perry, eds. *Patterns of Anarchy* (Garden City, 1966); George Woodcock, ed. *The Anarchist Reader* (Glasgow, 1977). 39. *Prolegomena to a Study of the Return of the Repressed in History* (Chicago, c. 1969); *Arsenal: Surrealist Subversion* (Chicago, 1970), 15. 40. Chicago *Sun-Times*, May 2, 1972, p. 3. 41. See note 28. 42. Melvyn Dubofsky, review of *The Haymarket Tragedy* by Paul Avrich, *Labor History* (Fall 1985), 602. 43. "Address of Louis Lingg," *op. cit.*, 35. 44. McLean, 149. 45. Marguerite Bonnet. *André Breton: Naissance de l'aventure surréaliste* (Paris, 1975); Louis Leçoin. *Le Cours d'une vie* (Paris, 1965); Rosemont, *op. cit.* 46. Rosemont, *op. cit.*

Numbered plates
from *Lehr-und-Wehr-Verein* rifles

SAMUEL FIELDEN

Born in the English industrial town of Todmorden in Lancashire in 1847, Fielden experienced firsthand the "animal existence" of child laborers in the British cotton mill when he went to work in a factory at age eight. He remained in the mill until he emigrated to America in 1868 at age 21; the "horrors and barbarities" of the factory fueled his lifelong hatred of exploitation and injustice. Influenced by black American abolitionists he heard speak in Lancashire, the idealistic young mill worker learned of the "horrors of slavery" and became an enthusiastic defender of the North during the Civil War.

In reaction against the barren life of the mills, Fielden found excitement in the enthusiasm of the Wesleyan Methodist church, which he joined in 1865. The young Fielden became an "exhorter," speaking at prayer and revival meetings almost every evening. He admired the "rude eloquence" and "noble and generous lives" of the Methodist lay preachers and, shortly before he left England for America, was accepted on a trial basis as a lay preacher himself.

In America, he worked at many jobs and in many places, including a period of tramping through the South; there he learned that blacks were still held in bondage through the sharecropping system. In 1871, by now a freethinker, he settled in Chicago, where he worked in stone yards and spent much of his leisure time at the public library. Purchasing a team of horses in 1880, the brawny Fielden became a self-employed teamster hauling stone. He was a charter member of the city's first teamsters' union and a prominent member of the freethinking Chicago Liberal League.

In 1884 Fielden joined the American Group of the IWPA, becoming its treasurer.

from the Chicago *Knights of Labor*

He proved to be a popular and powerful speaker, addressing labor rallies throughout Chicago and traveling as far as St. Louis and Pittsburgh to lecture for the IWPA. With an intense and emotional speaking style derived from his youthful evangelical preaching, Fielden denounced injustice with passionate fervor.

Fielden was the final speaker at the May 4 Haymarket meeting, delivering his speech to a dwindling audience under threatening skies. Inspector Bonfield and Captain Ward hurriedly led their police to the scene as Fielden was concluding. When Ward called for the audience to disperse, Fielden attempted to reassure the police of the meeting's peaceful purpose, but as he got down from the speakers' wagon and stepped onto the sidewalk, he heard the bomb explode. As the police opened fire, Fielden was wounded in the knee.

With his comrades, Fielden was convicted of murder and sentenced to death for his writings and speeches which supposedly inspired the bombthrower. Undoubtedly, Fielden's devotion to his wife and two young children motivated his appeal to Governor Ogelesby for clemency, an appeal recommended by such well-wishers as Henry Demarest Lloyd. The day before the scheduled hanging, Oglesby commuted Fielden's death sentence to life imprisonment.

Unconditionally pardoned through the courage of Governor Altgeld in 1893, Fielden used an inheritance to purchase a ranch near Le Veta, Colorado. He lived at La Veta until his death in 1922 at age 74 and is the only one of the eight comrades not buried at Waldheim Cemetery. After his release, Fielden participated in few labor or anarchist activities, although he spoke at the November 11 commemoration in Denver in 1898 and contributed an article about the "judicial murder" to Free Society in 1902.

Blaine McKINLEY

SOCIALISM: AN AMERICAN QUESTION

What is socialism? Taking somebody else's property? That is what socialism is in the common acceptation of the term. No. But if I were to answer it as shortly and as curtly as it is answered by its enemies, I would say it is preventing somebody else from taking your property.

But socialism is equality. Socialism recognizes the fact that no man in society is responsible for what he is; that all the ills that are in society are the production of poverty; and scientific socialism says you must go to the root of the evil. There is no criminal statistician in the world but will acknowledge that all crime, when traced to its origin, is the product of poverty.

It has been said [during the trial] that it was inflammatory for me to say that the present social system degraded men until they became mere animals. Go through this city into the low lodging houses where men are huddled together into the smallest possible space, living in an infernal atmosphere of death and disease, and I will ask you to draw your silks and your broadcloths close to you when these men pass you. Do you think that these men deliberately, with a full knowledge of what they are doing, choose to become that class of animals? Not one of them. They are the products of conditions, of certain environments in which they were born, and which have impelled them resistlessly into what they are. . . .

The great masses of wealth owned by individuals in this and the Old World have been produced in exactly the same proportion as these men have been degraded—and they never could have been accumulated in any other way. I do not charge that every capitalist willfully and maliciously conspires to bring about these results; but I do charge that it has been done, and I do charge that it is a very undesirable condition of things, and I claim that socialism would cure the world of that ulcer.

These are my ideas, in short, on socialism. The ultra-patriotic sentiment of the American people—and I suppose the same comparative sentiment is felt in England and France and Germany—is that no man in this country need be poor. The class who are not poor think so. The class who are poor are beginning to think differently; that under existing conditions it is impossible that some people should not be poor.

Why is it that we have "over-production"? And why is it that our warehouses are full of goods, and our workshops have to shut up; and our workmen are turned out on the highway because there is nothing to do? What is this tending to? Let me show the change of conditions as shown in Boston in forty years. Charles Dickens, a man of acute perceptions, visited this country forty years ago, and he said that the sight of a beggar in the

make any thinking man ask if there is not something wrong somewhere?

Possibly it would be answered, "yes, a man has a right to inquire whether there is something wrong or not, but for God's sake, don't think that socialism will do it any good, or if you do we will hang you. It is all right to think, but we will punish you for your conclusions." Parsons, in his testimony, repeated what he had said at the haymarket on the night of May 4, when he stated that this was an American question, because the patriotic tricksters who have been telling the people to worship the American flag, while they quietly put their hands in their pockets and robbed them—they have said that this is merely a European question. It is an American question, and the close contact of nations cemented by the facilities of civilization, is bringing all the questions that affect one people to affect all people equally all over the world. What affects the European laborer and his employer affects the American laborer and his American employer, and the relationship is the same between the two classes.

In the winter of 1884-5 one hundred and twenty American girls of fourteen and sixteen years of age were driven from their homes by the shutting down of the Merrimac mills in Connecticut, and they were compelled to walk through the bleak New England hills and find refuge in out-houses and haystacks, and numbers of them undoubtedly found their way to lives of shame. And I say here and now that the man who can look upon suffering like this and not feel stirred to do something to change such conditions, has not got anything in his heart but the feelings of the tiger, hungry for prey.

In this city of Chicago children are working at very tender ages. Going home one very cold night in the winter of 1884, two little girls ran up to me and begged of me

streets of Boston at that time would have created as much consternation as the sight of an angel with a drawn sword.

A Boston paper in the winter of 1884-5 stated that there were some quarters in Boston where to own a stove was to be a comparative aristocrat. The poor people who lived in the neighborhood paid a certain sum of money to rent the holes on the top of the stove that belonged to the aristocrats. You see the change, and there is this comparative change in the working classes of that city, and in every large city in the Union.

It is a noted fact that within the last twenty or thirty years the farms of this country have been gradually going out of the possession of the actual cultivators, until today there is a little more than a quarter of the actual cultivators of farms in this country who are renters; and within twenty years in the states of Iowa and Illinois the mortgages on farms have increased thirty-three per cent of the actual value of the farms. Is it not enough to

to go home with them. I asked them why. They said: "A man down there has been offering us money." It was seven o'clock at night and snowing; I asked them where they had been so late. They said: "We have been working in such a store." Children, babies turned out from their mother's heart to make a living, their fathers perhaps dead—in this case they were. The civilization that will not and cannot support a widow so that she will not have to turn her children out to such temptations as that is not worth respecting, and the man who will not try to change it is no man. . . .

I tell you these things to show you that the question is an American question. . . .

Samuel FIELDEN

from Albert R. Parsons,
*Anarchism: Its Philosophy
and Scientific Basis, as Defined
by Some of Its Apostles*
(Chicago, 1887)

COMMENTS ON THE TRIAL

As the anniversary of the murder of August Spies, A. R. Parsons, Adolph Fischer, George Engel and Louis Lingg nears, it may not be amiss that one whose experience so nearly approached theirs should say a few words anent this great crime. Not that it is the only crime that has been committed by the same bloodthirsty, criminal government, upon those who have thought and said that it might behave itself a little better than it was doing; but there were some things in this affair differing in many respects from many of the foul deeds it has been guilty of. . . .

John Brown broke the laws of Virginia, to his honor be it said. Our martyrs broke no Illinois law. Judge Gary could find no law in "the books" which they had broken, and he said so. The enemy did not wait for them to break any law—they could not afford to wait for that. The murdered men were carrying on such a labor agitation as had never been known before or since. They had found them out, and the thieves saw that if they were not stopped, the whole country would be made aware of their rascalities. There is no ques-

tion that for months the clubs frequented by the businessmen of Chicago were discussing the anarchists. The newspapers were full of them; the churches frequently referred to them. It may not be susceptible of positive proof that the act with which they were charged was the outcome of the deliberation of the clubs and business organizations, the procuring of the bombthrowing and the laying of the blame upon the pestiferous agitators, thereby stopping the mouths of the men who were above all others the mouthpieces of discontent and the most feared. Certain it is that an intelligent consideration of the evidence adduced at the trial, considered in connection with the conditions prevailing previously and at the time—certain it is, I say, that this conclusion would be far more reasonable than that drawn by the jury.

We have it upon the word of Bonfield that the mayor consulted with prominent businessmen on the afternoon of May 4, and that the subject discussed was the Haymarket meeting to be held that evening. This was not divulged until after the trial. This was at least suspicious, and under the circumstances connected them with the action of the police on that night. The presumption that the whole affair was a conspiracy to get rid of undesirable fomenters of discontent is at least strengthened.

What were the circumstances surrounding the order to disperse? They were such that no one reading the evidence can draw any other conclusion than that it would have been very undesirable to the chief director of the police, Bonfield, that the meeting should disperse without trouble. It is not doubted that the meeting was peaceable; Mayor Harrison swore to that at the trial. English, the chief newspaper witness for the prosecution, swore that it was a peaceable one up to the appearance of the police; another reporter for the prosecution swore that it was more peaceable toward the close than when Mayor Harrison was present. The last speaker was drawing to a close, and had said that he would be through in a few moments, when immediately upon this there was a great bustle and hurry on the part of the police to get to the meeting before it ended. Captain Hubbard swore at the trial that he did not have time to form his men in line, but that they had to run down the street to overtake the other policemen under Bonfield who were hurrying to the meeting. These are witnesses for the State. In addition to this I might refer to the evidence of an unimpeachible witness for the defense, who swore that Bonfield told him that if it were not for the women who were at the meeting he would go down there and "clean out those damn socialists to hell."

The women had barely gone when he proceeded to put his threat into force. There is no doubt in my mind and never has been but that the determination of Bonfield was to murder the speakers; and he would have done it had not the bomb exploded as it did before the police were fairly upon the place of meeting. Owing to the interruption, confusion ensued, and Bonfield having failed, Gary and Grinnell finished the job. That this was a judicial murder is not doubted by any lawyer acquainted with the facts.

There have undoubtedly been many judicial murders before this; and perhaps some have taken consolation to themselves that if this is one, it is not the only one. There have been others—so far, so good. But this case, I make bold to say, is different from any judicial act ever perpetrated since Jeffries was sent out on his famous or infamous western circuit, in this: that, while there may have been cases of wrongful conviction and execution without the perpetrators intending to do any wrong, in this case the perpetrators went into the case with the determination to hang. The question of guilt or innocence was nothing whatever to them. Charitable persons have gone so far as to say that they might have thought the defendants were guilty in the beginning, but they could not have believed it at the end. The fact is, that the question of guilt or innocence never was thought worth considering. It was simply a question of expediency. "Damn the law! What do we care about the law! We're going to hang them!" was the way it was put by one of them more candid than the others. Another said, "I do not doubt that he is right," referring to one of the defendants, "but we have got to hang him just the same. It is necessary."

Fifteen years have passed since this diabolical crime was committed. And on the anniversary of its committal, while we who were so closely connected with them, and those who have espoused the principles for which they died, commemorate their virtuous lives and heroic deaths, it behooves us to do all we can to make the blood of our martyrs the seed which shall save the race, as they died that it should.

Samuel FIELDEN

Free Society
(November 9. 1902)

from a police photograph

Sketch by Art Young

59

A VISIT TO SAM FIELDEN

On my return from my visit to the Pima Indians of Arizona, whose traditions I had been studying, I stopped off at La Veta, Colorado, and for several days was the guest of Mrs. Lizzie M. Holmes and Mrs. Elizabeth L. Hill, the wife and sister of William Holmes, the well-known advocate of Communist-Anarchism; Mrs. Holmes being herself a vigorous and popular writer in most of the liberal papers of the day. William Holmes was a warm personal friend of the Chicago Anarchists, and on that fatal November 11th, Mrs. Holmes went with Mrs. Parsons to say a last good-bye to the condemned men, but instead of this mercy being granted, both the women were arrested, lodged in a cell, stripped and searched for explosives, and kept confined till after the execution had taken place.

Time makes strange changes and these once-dreaded people, William Holmes and his wife, are now popular and respected members of La Veta society.

But one of my chief desires in visiting La Veta was to see Sam Fielden, the sole survivor or those eight heroic if mistaken men who once stood on trial for their lives before Judge Gary.

So one lovely October morning, when the world was beautiful as Paradise and flowers even were blooming, though there had been a light fall of snow but the morning before, of which no trace now remained, Lizzie Holmes and I took the road up Indian Creek to Fielden's Ranch. It was a five-mile walk, but this pure mountain air would have made ten miles a pleasure. We were at an elevation of over 7,000 feet at the start.

As we went out of the little town we skirted the "Plaza," where still remains the adobe building in which the once noted Colonel Francisco entertained such celebrities as Fremont and Kit Carson. After that our walk was a steady but gradual rise till we came to the little ravine-like valley, almost a canyon, where Fielden has his home.

I saw him first standing by the bars, before his cabin, talking to some passing neighbor who had stopped his team for a chat—a stocky well-built man, in overalls and cap, who was regarding me keenly with two of the largest, most innocent and beautiful gray eyes I had ever seen in a man's face. Those eyes made me love him at once, they were so frank and pure, clear and clean as mountain springs, and the manly clasp of his big, horny hand finished the job.

We went to his cabin, a typical mountain house of hewn logs, beneath the shade of cottonwoods and box-elders now golden with the yellow leaves of fall, and saw his wife, a bright, active little Englishwoman, chipper as a cricket, and talked awhile and then strolled out.

What a day that was. A perfect golden day in the most perfect and golden month of the year. We went down to his little spring of pure water beside the Indian Creek, and we went up to his two little lakes on the "mesa." A hard struggle for a living here, on this arid soil, which needs irrigation to yield a crop, where drouth and frost blast, the squirrels devour the corn, the coyotes the chickens, and the cattle get "loco" on the range, but I am happy to say that Fielden seems to have got beyond the hardest primary stage, and to be fairly comfortable for a pioneer. The spot where he lives is one of almost idyllic beauty, with all its natural charms quite unspoiled by intensive "improvements." A poet, a dreamer, could hardly ask a more congenial retreat, and I almost felt tempted to wish myself his neighbor.

Fielden has a handsome, intelligent face, very English in contour, but his great gray beard, heavy curling hair, and the bushiest eyebrows ever seen over human eyes, make him look almost Russian. Kindness, goodness, pure honesty radiate from him. His voice is refined and attractive in cadence, with no Cockney faults, and his conversation intellectual, graphic, logical and finely-worded. Hermit though he is, almost, he is up-to-date on all passing questions.

J. William LLOYD

from *The Comrade*,
Vol. 3, No. 5 (Feb. 1904).

Linocut from *Solidaridad* (Uruguay)

OSCAR NEEBE

Interviewed by a northside neighbor toward the end of his life, Oscar Neebe, in poor health and nearly blind, expressed his indignation that so much of the Haymarket defense and amnesty literature had tried to convert the anarchists into "bleating lambs." He insisted that, on the contrary, his old comrades were "emphatically brave soldiers" of the Revolution. And so, it might be added, was Neebe himself.

One of the Chicago labor movement's best organizers in the 1880s, Oscar Neebe (1850-1916) was born in New York, but his parents took him to Germany as an infant and he grew up in Hesse-Cassell. The family returned to the U.S. when he was fourteen, and two years later he went to Chicago. After working for a time as a waiter and bartender, and later as ship's cook on the Great Lakes, he went back to New York and became a tinsmith's apprentice, learning the trade "to perfection in all its branches," as he wrote in a brief autobiography published in the Chicago Knights of Labor. In 1873, in Philadelphia, he met and married his wife Meta.

Although he had sympathetically listened to communist speakers in New York at the time of the Paris Commune of 1871, it was not till 1877 when, back in Chicago, he was fired for having "stood up for the right of the workmen" during the great railroad strike, that Neebe became a communist himself. Blacklisted and unable to find work at his trade, he became a yeast salesman and later, in partnership with his brother and

from a police photograph

others, formed a small yeast company, at which he made his living until his arrest.

As organizer for Chicago's anarchist-controlled Central Labor Union, Neebe organized bakers, beer-wagon drivers and brewery-workers. He also played an important role in planning and arranging workers' street-demonstrations and social affairs.

"A great friend of reading" and a particular admirer of the writings of Jefferson and Paine, Neebe was on the board of directors of the Socialistic Publishing Society which published the anarchist daily Arbeiter-Zeitung. "We socialists," he wrote, "are great believers that the laboring men should educate themselves."

Since even the prosecution admitted that the evidence against Neebe was slight, he was sentenced to only fifteen years' imprisonment. It was his belief, as he argued in his autobiography and later confirmed by information gleaned while in the penitentiary, that one of the breweries whose workers he had helped organize had paid $90,000 for his conviction.

A few months after he was sentenced, his wife Meta, in her mid-30s, died as a result of the suffering and anguish brought about by her husband's arrest, trial and imprisonment.

Pardoned along with Fielden and Schwab by Gov. Altgeld in 1893, Neebe passed the remaining years of his life in peaceful obscurity. He married a widow who had been active in the Haymarket amnesty effort and helped her run a tavern near the Chicago stockyards. He lent some support to the Populist agitation of the 1890s, turned up at the 1907 IWW convention, and for a time, according to a 1911 letter from anarchist Carl Nold, was "an ardent follower of DeLeon" of the Socialist Labor Party. But his activist days were over.

Oscar Neebe died at the age of sixty-five and was buried next to the Haymarket martyrs' monument at Waldheim.   FR

THE CRIMES I HAVE COMMITTED

I have been in the labor movement since 1875. I have seen how the police have trodden on the Constitution of this country, and crushed the labor organizations. I have seen from year to year how they were trodden down, where they were shot down, where they were "driven into their holes like rats," as Mr. Grinnell said to the jury. But they will come out! Remember that within three years before the beginning of the French Revolution, when laws had been stretched like rubber, that the rubber stretched too long, and broke—a result which cost a good many state's attorneys at that time their necks, and a good many honorable men their necks.

We socialists hope such times may never come again; we do everything in our power to prevent it by reducing the hours of labor and increasing wages. But you capitalists won't allow this to be done. You use your power to perpetuate a system by which you may make your money for yourselves and keep the wage-workers poor. You make them ignorant and miserable, and you are responsible for it. You won't let the toilers live a decent life.

* * *

Well, these are all the crimes I have committed. They found a revolver in my house, and a red flag there. I organized trade unions.

I was for reduction of the hours of labor, and the education of laboring men, and the re-establishment of the *Arbeiter-Zeitung*—the workingmen's newspaper. There is no evidence to show that I was connected with the bomb-throwing, or that I was near it, or anything of that kind. So I am only sorry, your honor—that is, if you can stop it or help it—I will ask you to do it—that is, to hang me, too; for I think it is more honorable to die suddenly than to be killed by inches. I have a family and children; and if they know their father is dead, they will bury him. They can go to the grave, and kneel down by the side of it; but they can't go to the penitentiary and see their father, who was convicted for a crime that he hasn't had anything to do with. That is all I have got to say. Your honor, I am sorry I am not to be hung with the rest of the men.

Oscar NEEBE

from Albert R. Parsons,
*Anarchism: Its Philosophy
and Scientific Basis, as Defined
by Some of Its Apostles*
(Chicago, 1887)

RESTORE THE MEANING OF MAY DAY!
An Interview with Oscar Neebe's Grandson

Oscar William Neebe was 15 when he first heard about the alleged involvement of his grandfather, Oscar Neebe, in the Haymarket Square bombing.

"My brother and I had gotten out of school early and had gone to Mexico City to visit some of my mother's relatives," Neebe, now 52, told interviewers. "My uncle couldn't believe that we had never been told of our heritage. He took us to a May Day celebration and showed us the Diego Rivera mural there honoring the Haymarket martyrs.

"History books say my grandfather was an innocent dupe because he only donated $2 to the *Arbeiter-Zeitung*, the German anarchist newspaper," Neebe continued. "But actually grandfather was more than that because he wrote for the paper and was an active socialist."

Oscar Neebe was pardoned by Gov. Altgeld in 1893 after serving seven years in the state penitentiary in Joliet.

"Grandfather's first wife died when he was in prison from what doctors said was an emotional illness caused by the tragedy. Grandfather was deeply affected by this," said O. W. Neebe.

Oscar Neebe returned to Chicago and married a widow who had been active in the campaign to secure the imprisoned anarchists' release. They had three children: Walter, Elsie and Rudolph, O. W. Neebe's father.

"My father quit school in eighth grade at 13 to support the family when grandfather died. My father was a quiet man, unaggressive. He and his sisters and brothers suffered a lot of harassment because of Haymarket, but he never changed his name, probably out of a strange kind of integrity. He never talked to me about Haymarket. But he named me after grandfather.

"There have been strange events in my life because of my heritage," Neebe added, recalling a graphic artists' convention in Aspen, Colorado, where an artist he had known for ten years in Chicago approached him. "The man was very drunk. He threw his arms around me, in tears, and confessed to me that his grandfather was the judge who had sent my grandfather to jail. He kept begging my pardon for what his family had done to mine."

O. W. Neebe went on to decry the way the United States has subverted labor history by changing May Day (May 1) to "Law Day."

"It's very stultifying. You know, almost every country in the world but ours celebrates May Day in honor of the Chicago martyrs. The young don't learn about their heritage, or labor, or what it has meant to this country."

As a member of the board of New Trier Township High School, Neebe has seen to it that "Law Day" observances featured speakers to talk about May Day and its meaning, and about the repressive use of such government forces as the police, the FBI, the CIA and the IRS.

"It's always interesting to watch students become enlightened, and to watch teachers who never gave a darn realize they are part of a system that denies access to education," Neebe said.   (1975)

Bill Garvey, Lillian Herstein, William J. Adelman and O. W. Neebe at a Haymarket Memorial Meeting in May, 1969

A VISIT WITH
OSCAR NEEBE
IN JAIL

Oscar Neebe was employed as a hospital attendant [in the penitentiary at Joliet]. He gives the impression of a vigorous character and shows much intelligence. I enjoyed a talk with him of about twenty minutes. He reported his experiences with his fellow prisoners. He had tried to exercise a moral influence upon one of them—a thief convicted for a second time, who had acted more from moral weakness than from evil intention, a case very common among criminals. We also discussed the labor problem and he grew warm on the subject, but without excess and without the least revengeful feeling. Speaking of the Haymarket meeting at which he was not present, he said that some "crank" must have thrown the bomb. . . .

A movement for the pardon of Neebe is being advocated by many influential men who have no sympathy with anarchism. It is to be hoped that the movement will be successful. . . .

Paul CARUS

The Open Court
(September 25, 1890)

Tinsmith
George Bruce's Son & Co.
Type Catalog, 1882

from the Chicago *Knights of Labor*

OSCAR NEEBE'S "LIGHTNING"

Like most of the 200-odd illustrations in Capt. Schaack's *Anarchy and Anarchists*, the engraving of "Neebe's Sword and Belt" on page 377 of that bulky volume serves a purely "decorative" function, with little bearing on arguments made in the text, except perhaps in the very general sense of conveying that anarchists are armed and should be considered dangerous. The fact that a number of other swords were seized by police in their illegal raids on alleged "anarchist strongholds" makes one wonder to what extent fencing was part of the daily life of Chicago's anarchists in the 1880s.

Elsewhere in his book Schaack alludes to Neebe's *Lehr-und-Wehr-Verein* belt—almost certainly the one depicted in the engraving—and remarks that a Colt .38 revolver was among the items belonging to Neebe that were confiscated by police. Incredibly, however, the gun inserted behind the sword in the picture is neither noted in the caption nor otherwise mentioned in the effusive detective's 698-page book.

In an interesting article,* gun historian Richard C. Marohn, M.D., has identified this gun of Neebe's as a Colt Double Action M1877, .38 cal., 3½-inch barrel, storekeeper model "Lightning"—a gun later in wide use but rare in Chicago at the time of Haymarket. Having learned that Schaack himself owned a revolver of this type (now in the collection of the Chicago Historical Society, donated by the captain's grandniece), Dr. Marohn suggests, as a "fascinating speculation," that Neebe's "Lightning," after being confiscated by police, was appropriated for his personal use by the acquisitive Schaack. As Schaack was, in fact, eventually discharged from the police force for—among other transgressions—trafficking in stolen goods, Dr. Marohn's speculation is indeed plausible.

FR

* "The Haymarket Lightning," *The Gun Report* (April, 1977).

NEEBE'S SWORD
AND BELT.

Sketch from *Guangara Libertaria*

One of many Haymarket-related lithographs produced commercially in Chicago and throughout the U.S. for sale to tourists

MICHAEL SCHWAB

Michael Schwab (1853-1898) was associate editor of the Arbeiter-Zeitung at the time of the Haymarket bombing. "He was always a reticent man," his friend and comrade William Holmes recalled in the anarchist paper Free Society (Chicago, November 6, 1898), "more a thinker and reader than a talker. And yet, in the old days, I remember how thoroughly Schwab seemed to enjoy our outings in the country, as well as our Commune celebrations and other social gatherings."

Apprenticed as a bookbinder, the orphaned Schwab differed from most of his fellow Haymarket defendants in that he became radicalized in Europe rather than in the U.S., and had already written for the radical press before landing on these shores. A Bavarian, Schwab joined the German Social Democratic Party in 1872. After a stay in Switzerland, he returned to Bavaria, from which he emigrated in 1879. He lived for a while in Milwaukee and out West before settling permanently in Chicago in 1881 or 1882. Briefly a member of the Socialistic Labor Party, he joined the IWPA as a founding member of the North Side Group.

Politically and personally close to August Spies, Schwab—like Spies—was a moderating force in the IWPA, a middle-of-the-roader on the far left. He managed the IWPA's library for a time and was the Chicago-area distributor of Johann Most's Freiheit.

from the Chicago Knights of Labor

Schwab stopped at Haymarket Square for a few minutes on the evening of the fateful May 4 meeting. He left before the speakers began in order that he might himself go to speak at a Deering Reaper Works rally. Despite the fact that he was elsewhere when the bombing occurred, he served almost seven years of a life sentence before being pardoned by Gov. Altgeld in 1893.

From his prison cell, Schwab contributed an article, "A Convicted Anarchist's Reply to Prof. Lombroso"—a refutation of the Italian criminologist's weird theory of anarchist physiognomy—to the July 1891 issue of the philosophical journal, The Monist.

The years in Joliet Penitentiary resulted in Schwab's physical and emotional deterioration; as William Holmes recalled, "he seemed like a man broken by much suffering." After his release he briefly wrote again for the Arbeiter-Zeitung, and was that paper's delegate to the Illinois State Federation of Labor's July 4, 1894 conference to formulate a new political policy. He operated a small shoe store, from which he also sold books, but the store failed and so did his health. He died from respiratory diseases contracted in prison, leaving behind a wife and four children, one of them named for Altgeld.

Schwab was buried at Waldheim near the martyrs' monument.

DR

ANARCHY ON TRIAL

To term the proceedings during the trial justice, would be a sneer. Justice has not been done. . .could not be done. If one class is arrayed against the other, it is idle and hypocritical to think about justice. Anarchy was on trial, as the state's attorney put it in his closing speech. A doctrine, an opinion hostile to brute force, hostile to our present murderous system of production and distribution. I am condemned to die for writing newspaper articles and making speeches . . .

Anarchy was on trial. Little did it matter who the persons were to be honored by the prosecution. It was the movement the blow was aimed at: It was directed against the labor movement, against socialism—for today every labor movement must, of necessity, be socialistic.

Talk about a gigantic conspiracy! A movement is not a conspiracy. All we did was done in open daylight.

There were no secrets. We prophesied in word and writing the coming of a great revolution, a change in the system of production in all industrial countries of the globe. And the change will come, and must come. Is it not absurd, as the state's attorney and his associates have done, to suppose that this social revolution—a change of such immense proportions—was to be inaugurated on or about the first of May in the city of Chicago by making war on the police? . . . .

We contend for communism and anarchy—why? If we had kept silent, stones would have cried out. Murder was committed day by day. Children were slain, women worked to death, men killed inch by inch, and these crimes are never punished by law. The great principle underlying the present system is unpaid labor. Those who amass fortunes, build palaces, and live in luxury, are doing that by virtue of unpaid labor. Being directly or indirectly the possessors of land and machinery, they dictate their terms to the workingman. He is compelled to sell his labor cheap, or to starve. The price paid him is always far below the real value. He acts under compulsion, and they call it a free contract. This infernal state of affairs keeps him poor and ignorant, an easy prey for exploitation.

* * *

Thousands of laborers in the city of Chicago live in rooms without sufficient protection from the weather, without proper ventilation, where never a stream of sunlight flows in. There are hovels where two, three and four families live in one room. How these conditions influence the health and the morals of these unfortunate sufferers, it is needless to say. And how do they live? From the ash-barrels they gather half-rotten vegetables, in the butcher shops they buy for some cents offal of meat, and these precious morsels they carry home to prepare from them their meals. The dilapidated houses in which this waits in most cases till he is compelled by the city to have them done. Is it a wonder that diseases of all kinds kill men, women and children in such places by wholesale, especially children? Is this not horrible in a so-called civilized land where there is plenty of food and riches?

* * *

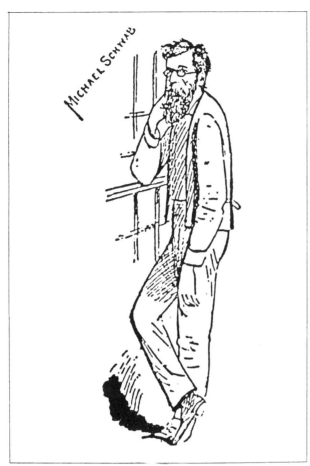

Sketch by Art Young

from a police photograph

The outcry that socialism, communism and anarchism are the creed of foreigners, is a big mistake. There are more socialists of American birth in this country than foreigners, and that is much, if we consider that nearly half of all industrial workingmen are not native Americans. There are socialistic papers in a great many States edited by Americans for Americans. The capitalistic newspapers conceal that fact very carefully.

* * *

What is anarchy?

Is it not strange that when anarchy was tried nobody ever told what anarchy was. Even when I was on the witness stand, and asked the state's attorney for a definition of anarchy, he declined to give it. But in their speeches he and his associates spoke very frequently about anarchy, and it appeared that they understood it to be something horrible—arson, rapine, murder. In so speaking, Mr. Grinnell and his associates did not speak the truth. They searched *The Alarm* and the *Arbeiter-Zeitung*, and hunted up articles written years before the month of May, 1886. In the columns of these papers it is very often stated what we, the "anarchists," understood by the term anarchy. And we are the only competent judges in this matter. As soon as the word is applied to us and our doctrine, it carries with it the meaning which we, the anarchists, saw fit to give to it.

"Anarchy" is Greek, and means, verbatim, without rulership; not being ruled. According to our vocabulary, anarchy is a state of society in which the only government is reason—a state of society in which all human beings do right for the simple reason that it is right, and hate wrong because it is wrong. In such a society, no laws, no compulsion will be necessary. The attorney of the State was wrong when he said: "Anarchy is dead." Anarchy, up to the present day, has existed only as a doctrine, and Mr. Grinnell has not the power to kill any doctrine whatever. You may call anarchy, as defined by us, an idle dream, but that dream was dreamed by Gotthold Ephraim Lessing, one of the great German poets and the most celebrated German critic of the last century. If anarchy were the thing the state's attorney makes it out to be, how could it be that such eminent scholars as Prince Kropotkin, and the greatest living geographer, Elisee Reclus, were avowed anarchists, even editors of anarchistic papers?

Anarchy is a dream, but only in the present. It will be realized. Reason will grow in spite of all obstacles. Who is the man that has the cheek to tell us that human development has already reached its culminating point? I know that our ideal will not be accomplished this or next year, but I know that it will be accomplished as near as possible, some day, in the future. It is entirely wrong to use the word anarchy as synonymous with violence. Violence is one thing and anarchy is another. In the present state of society, violence is used on all sides, and, therefore, we advocated the use of violence against violence, but against violence only, as a necessary means of defense.

* * *

The modern communist holds that labor is the fountain of all wealth and all culture and that, because useful labor only is possible by association of all mankind, the fruits of labor belong to all mankind. Even land has no value except where it can be put into use by labor. No empty lot in a city would have the least value, if labor had not built around it houses and streets, if business was not going on near that lot.

We know, further, that labor is not paid its full value; if this were the case, it would be unprofitable to employ labor and would not be done. Let one man work alone for himself, he never could grow rich, although even in such a case his knowledge would be the fruit of the work of others, the labor of generations. And because the latter is the case, the communist wants education, culture and knowledge for all. The land was common property thousands and thousands of years, and the private property system is—to speak historically—but of yesterday. And how was it introduced? Queen Elizabeth, that highly praised monster of murderous lust and brutality, for instance, had during her reign two millions of Irishmen killed in the usual way—battles, gallows, etc.—took their land and gave it to favorites. It is not for me now to give a history how the common lands in England were stolen and robbed, but it is a historical fact that it was acquired by the forefathers of the present owners by murder, arson, theft and lesser crimes. . . . The sentence: "Property is robbery" [Proudhon] is literally true. . . .

* * *

Millions of workmen are starving and leading the lives of vagabonds. Even the most ignorant wage-slave commences to think. The common misery makes it clear to them that they must combine, and they do it. The great levellers, the machines, destroyed the guild-pride of olden times. The carpenter feels that he has a common interest with the farmhand, and the printer with the hod-carrier, the German learns that his interest is that of the Negro, of the Frenchman, of the American, and in passing I would like to state that, in my opinion, it is the greatest merit of the order of the Knights of Labor to have carried out that principle in America in such an immense way. The workingmen learn that the capitalistic system, although necessary for some time, must make room for universal co-operation; that the land and means of production must pass from the hands of speculators, private individuals into the hands of the producing masses; this is communism.

* * *

Anarchism is order without government. We anarchists say that anarchism will be the natural outgrowth of universal co-operation (communism). We say that when poverty has vanished and education is the common property of the people, that then reason will reign supreme. We say that crime will belong to the past and that the misdeeds of erring brethren can be righted by other means than those of today. Most of the crimes of our days are engendered directly by the system of today, the system which creates ignorance and misery.

Art Young's sketch of Schwab and Fielden in the penitentiary at Joliet

We anarchists do believe that the time is near at hand when the working people will demand their rights. . . .

Michael SCHWAB

from Albert R. Parsons,
*Anarchism: Its Philosophy
and Scientific Basis, as Defined
by Some of Its Apostles*
(Chicago, 1887)

Sketch from *Guangara Libertaria*

A STATEMENT on the EXECUTIONS

The blind prejudice of unholy conspiracy has murdered five men, as innocent of the charges of which they were convicted as babes unborn. They were no more connected with the death of Degan than you are. . . .

I expect to be in prison the rest of my natural life and am virtually dead to the world; but the crime for which we suffer will, some day, be all cleared up. It may come in time to save Fielden and me, but state-murder done today will ever stand as a stain on the escutcheon of the country.

Michael SCHWAB

from The Word,
*edited by Ezra Heywood
(Princeton, Massachusetts,
December 1887), p. 1*

THE MAY FOURTH BROADSIDE

On May 4, 1886, around 9 a.m., Adolph Fischer went to the printing office of Wehrer & Klein and ordered 25,000 broadsides announcing a mass-meeting that night in Chicago's Haymarket Square.[1] This broadside—also called "circular," "handbill," "advertisement," "leaflet" and "flier" in the trial and in subsequent literature on the affair—is probably the most famous and certainly the most widely reproduced labor broadside in American history.

Although the author of the bilingual text of the broadside is unknown, Fischer himself is known to have inserted the bold line: "Workingmen Arm Yourselves and Appear in Full Force!"[2] Compositor August Huen set the type for the German text; who set the English text is not clear.[3]

Two hours later the first copies rolled off the press. "About 11 o'clock," August Spies stated in court, "a circular calling the Haymarket meeting was handed to me" at the *Arbeiter-Zeitung* office.[4] Spies at once made it known that he would not speak at the meeting, as Fischer had invited him to do, unless the "Workingmen Arm Yourselves. . ." line was removed from the English and German texts. He objected to the line

principally because I thought it was ridiculous to put in a phrase which would prevent people from attending the meeting. Another reason was that there was some excitement at that time, and a call for arms like that might have caused trouble between the police and the attendants of that meeting. I did not anticipate anything of the kind, but I thought it was not a proper thing to put that line in.[5]

Fischer, who had added the line because he "did not want the workingmen to be shot down in that meeting as on other occasions," was persuaded by Spies' reasoning, and the line was immediately withdrawn.[6] August Huen testified that an hour after the form had been given to the pressman the offending line was taken out.[7]

How many copies containing the line were printed is far from certain; estimates vary from "about 200" to "about 5000"[8]—the latter figure was favored by the prosecution during the Haymarket trial, where the original version of the broadside was regarded as an important part of the State's evidence proving the existence of an anarchist "conspiracy."

How many—if, indeed, any at all—of the ones containing the line were actually *distributed* is also unknown. When Fischer's friend Johann Grueneberg brought the first copies from Wehrer & Klein to the *Arbeiter-Zeitung* office, Spies said: "Well, Fischer, if those circulars are distributed, I won't speak." But then Grueneberg explained that none had yet been distributed, and that there was still time to take the line out. Spies demanded that all copies containing the line be disposed of, and he himself deleted it from the copy he gave to the compositor for publication in the *Arbeiter-Zeitung*.[9] According to William J. Adelman, "Fischer threw the 200 copies with this line into the wastebasket," from which they were later retrieved by the police.[10] Paul Avrich, however, suggests that "a few hundred. . .managed to avoid destruction and were distributed along with the rest—a circumstance that would weigh heavily at the trial."[11] At the meeting that night, the bomb was thrown.

Ninety-eight years later, in New York, we saw a copy of this "Attention Workingmen!" broadside on display, and purchased it. When we compared it with published reproductions, we noted that we had one version of at least four. Type *1a* has the German text entirely in black-letter type and also has the "Workingmen Arm Yourselves" line. *1b* has the German text in black-letter, but does not have that line. *2a* has "Massen-Versammlung" in roman type and also has the "Workingmen Arm Yourselves" line, while *2b* has "Massen-Versammlung" in roman, but does not have the line. It should be noted that all copies of *2b* that we have seen (a total of six) have a Chicago Historical Society stamp; the Kraus copy, formerly the property of Haymarket prosecutor Julius Grinnell, and which we have not seen, reportedly does not have the stamp. Tentatively, this latter copy can be called version *2b.1* and the stamped copies can be called *2b.2*.

Soon after we began our research, we discovered two more versions. *3a* appears to be identical to *1a* except there is no

The Haymarket Broadside, Type *1a* (reduced).
One of six known variants.
Type *1b* lacks the "Workingmen Arm Yourselves" line.

period after "THE EXECUTIVE COMMITTEE" and there is a comma instead of a period after "gesseln," the last word in the third line from the bottom. Type *4* has extra leading—or line-spacing—between "GREAT" and the rules beneath "Attention Workingmen!" as well as between "THE EXECUTIVE COMMITTEE" and the rules separating the English and German texts.[12]

Thus, in looking at the six versions, we were confronted not only with the question of priority (beyond the fact that copies with the "Workingmen Arm Yourselves. . ." line preceded copies without the line), but also with the need to explain the variations so far discovered. We knew that a Chicago collector, in attempting to authenticate a newly-purchased copy of *2b*, was told by a staff member of the Chicago Historical Society that his broadside was "a reprint, done around 1900." The staff member, however, does not remember identifying *any* of the broadsides as reprints. Further, there are three copies of *2b.2* in the Chicago Historical Society files that are wrapped in a typewritten note[13] that identifies them as "silk screen" reproductions, done "later than 1886." The note is undated and unsigned, and no one at the Chicago Historical Society knows who wrote it.

Thus far, very few questions had been answered, but many new ones had been posed. What follows are a few of these questions, a few hypotheses and some suggestions for further research.

The most significant questions seem to be: Are *2a* and *2b* reprints? And what are *3a* and *4*? The rumor of a "reprint . . .done around 1900" and the note about "silk screen" copies suggest that *2a* and *2b* are reprints, but there is much to be said against accepting this suggestion. First, the note carries less weight than it might have were it signed and dated. As it stands, there is an implication that the writer did not feel confident enough about the "facts" to stand by them. Indeed, this position is understandable insofar as our own inspection has led us to believe that the examples of *2b.2* are *not* silkscreen copies. The question of the thickness of the paper is obscured by the fact that most examples we have seen, *except* of *2b.2*, are backed with various materials for purposes of preservation. Thus, the question of paper thickness remains open. Further, while the anonymous note seems to refer to the particular copies of *2b.2* around which it is wrapped, in the final sentence it refers to a typographical variation present in *2a*, *2b.1* and *2b.2*, and it is not at all clear whether or not the writer thinks he or she is describing all versions of *2* or just certain copies.

The suggestion of a "reprint, done around 1900" as an explanation of various versions, also has several weaknesses. First, the source of the rumor can no longer be identified. Second, most of the proponents of the theory that version *2* is a reprint are unaware that *2a* and *2b* both appear in Capt. Schaack's book, *Anarchy and Anarchists*, published in 1889. An 1889 appearance obviously contradicts a reprint date of "around 1900." Further, if *2b* is a reprint, done later than 1886, how can the existence of *2a* be explained? This question is best answered by the hypothesis to which we personally subscribe, first published by John Kebabian in his catalog of Julius Grinnell's archives, held by H. P. Kraus.

This is the hypothesis that the broadsides were printed two-up (the black-letter and roman versions side by side), thus creating *1a* and *2a* simultaneously. When the offending line was removed *from both versions* after printing a number of copies, printing was resumed, and *2a* and *2b* were produced simultaneously. The numerous differences in typeface between *1* and *2* can be explained by the small number of characters in display fonts.

And while there is no doubt that the Haymarket broadsides have been reproduced in facsimile as souvenirs (we saw such a reprint on a fence in New York in May, 1984), the fact that version *2* exists in two forms (*a* and *b*) speaks strongly against its being a reprint. It seems to us that a leaflet might have been made of one version or another but not both. It has also been suggested that the differences in typeface between *1* and *2* speak in favor of *2a* and *2b* being reprints; but it would have been silly and expensive to reset the entire broadside (and still not come even close to an exact facsimile) when a reprint could have been made easily from a copy of *1a* or *1b*. Answering this argument, however, would be the suggestion that the reprinter did not have access to a copy of *1a* or

The Haymarket Broadside, Type *2b*.
Type *2a* has the "Workingmen Arm Yourselves" line.

1b. Against the idea of "silk screen reproductions" are the facts that this process is expensive and slow compared to other means of reproduction and, above all, that the broadsides do not appear to be silkscreens.

Broadside versions *3a* and *4* would seem to demand explanations other than those so far proposed. While a period is missing and a comma is substituted for another period, *3a* appears identical to *1a* in all other respects. The possibility exists that *3a* is an early version of *1a* corrected in press. Or perhaps, which seems to us more likely, *3a* is a later reprint of *1a*, identical except for the two points noted above. The differences between the two could be explained by *3a*'s being a proof-copy, but could also have occurred at other stages of the reproduction process. It is also possible that *3a* is a setting from the May 4th issue of the *Arbeiter-Zeitung*, since Spies is said to have handed "the leaflet to his compositor to be printed" in the paper.[14] Sadly, the microfilm of the *Arbeiter-Zeitung* at the Newberry Library, one of the few holdings that contain early 1886 issues, is missing the May issues, and we still have not been able to examine this important source.[15]

A possible explanation of version *4* is that it is a cut-and-pasted photoreproduction of *3a*, peculiarly stretched to fit a particular space in the publication in which it originally appeared. The author of this publication assures us that the publisher supplied the illustrations, but the publisher no longer has the relevant records.

The speculative nature of our ideas is obvious, but we hope it will supply at least the groundwork for future research. Before making a few suggestions for the directions such research might take, we would like to pinpoint one source of confusion. Throughout our inquiries, as we described the May 4 "Attention Workingmen!" broadside, it was assumed by many that we were talking about the May 3 "Revenge" broadside penned a day earlier by Spies. This confusion is evidently not of recent origin. Schaack, for example, notes that the "Revenge" circular was distributed at the meeting on the night of May 3, but a few pages later he speaks of the "Revenge" circular as being issued on the afternoon of May 4![16] Perhaps the source of confusion is the fact that both days' broadsides involve last minute textual alterations and August Spies.[17]

We hope this short piece will inspire a few others in the field to pursue the inquiry. Certainly the first order of business is to locate the the original broadsides *2a*, *3a* and *4*, as well as the May 4 issue(s) of the *Arbeiter-Zeitung*. Someone with more technical knowledge of paper, ink, printing and typography may be able to settle some of the questions of priority and reprinting. Hopefully, some of these will be resolved in future research.

Paul GARON and Elizabeth GARON

Notes (see "References & Sources," below):

1. Avrich, 193; McLean, 156; Schaack, 463.   2. Avrich, 193.   3. Schaack, 463.
4. *ibid.*, 512.   5. *ibid.*, 520.   6. Avrich, 193; McLean, 156.   7. Schaack, 463.
8. Adelman, 81, gives "about 200"; State's Attorney Grinnell stated "about 5000" in court (Schaack, 399). Other figures have also been proposed for the total number of broadsides printed. Schaack, 333, quotes a certain billiardmaker named Victor Clermont, who claimed to have attended that small May 3rd meeting which called for the Haymarket mass-meeting, as saying that Fischer's motion was for 10,000 copies. In court, Inspector Bonfield said: "I think 2,500 copies—25,000 or 2,500" (Schaack, 417). The figure 20,000 is also frequently mentioned (Schaack, 399; Adelman, 81). Spies testified that he believed 2,500 of the earlier "Revenge" broadside were printed, "but not more than half of them were distributed" (Schaack, 512). The May 4 broadside, however, was intended to draw people to a mass protest meeting—it was hoped that some 25,000 would attend—and it seems almost certain that far more copies would have been printed of that than of the purely informational/agitational "Revenge" broadside. In view of Fischer's active involvement with the production of the May 4 broadside, we are inclined to credit his figure of 25,000.   9. Avrich, 193.   10, Adelman, 81.
11. Avrich, 193.   12. The numbering system is our own and, we hope, will prove sensible. The locations are as follows: Copies of *1a* are at the Chicago Historical Society, Northwestern University and Kraus, and it is reproduced in Ashbaugh, Avrich and Kebabian. *1b* is at the Chicago Historical Society and is reproduced in Ashbaugh. We have not been able to locate an original of *2a*, which is reproduced in Schaack. The Chicago Historical Society and the Newberry Library have copies of *2b.2*, while Kraus has *2b.1*. *2b* is reproduced in Kebabian and Schaack. The original of *3a* is reportedly in the New York Public Library, but so far only a copy of *2b.2* has been found there. *3a* is reproduced in Nhat Hong as well as in Cahn. No original has been found of version *4* which is reproduced in Foner (1979) and Foner and Schultz. We might mention, finally, for the record, that an Italian version of the broadside, mentioned by Paul Ghio, *L'Anarchisme aux Etats-Unis* (Paris, 1901, p. 75), is nowhere else cited in the primary or secondary literature on Haymarket, and almost certainly never existed.
13. The text of this note reads as follows: "A careful examination these (*sic*) broadsides show (*sic*) them to be the result of a silk screen process; they are not printed pieces. Apparently the text was copied from an original broadside—even the peculiarities of the a's and s's were carefully observed—and reproduced on coarse paper about twice the size of those that were printed at the time of the Haymarket Riot. These copies were probably made later than 1886, for an anniversary commemoration. The only difference in the text is is the use of 'halb 8 Uhr' in place of '½8 Uhr.'"   14. Avrich, 193.   15. The Labadie Collection at the University of Michigan Library contains a Haymarket Scrapbook in which there is a newspaper reproduction of the German text of *2a*, in facsimile, with an explanatory line added at the foot. No doubt this is a reprint of *2a* and not the source of *2a*! It is probably taken from the *Sonntagspost* (Chicago) of November 6, 1927.   16. Schaack, 134, 157.   17. A compositor, Hermann Pudewa, added the heading "Revenge" to Spies' May 3 broadside text (Avrich, 190), whereas Spies himself deleted the line, "Workingmen Arm Yourselves. . ." from the May 4 broadside (Avrich, 193).

Bibliographical Note

G. T. Tanselle's "The Bibliographical Concepts of *Issue* and *State*" (PBSA, 69 [1975], 65) is helpful in drawing a terminological distinction between the *a* and the *b* versions of the broadside. Certainly the copies with the offending line removed represent a second state (instead of a second issue) if we follow Tanselle: "A state is a. . .group of copies of a printed sheet. . .which differs from other copies (within the same impression or issue) of that sheet. . .in any respect which the publisher does not wish to call to the attention of the public as representing a discrete publishing effort."

References & Sources

Adelman, William J. *Haymarket Revisited* (Chicago. 1975).
Ashbaugh, Carolyn. *Lucy Parsons: American Revolutionary* (Chicago, 1976).
Avrich, Paul. *The Haymarket Tragedy* (Princeton, 1984).
Cahn, William. *A Pictorial History of American Labor* (New York, 1972).
David, Henry. *The History of the Haymarket Affair* (New York, 1936).
Foner, Philip, ed. *The Autobiographies of the Haymarket Martyrs* (New York, 1979).
Foner, Philip, and Reinhard Schultz. *Das Andere Amerika* (Berlin, 1983).
Kebabian, John S. *The Haymarket Affair and Trial of the Chicago Anarchists, 1886* (New York, 1970).
McLean, George. *The Rise and Fall of Anarchy in America* (Chicago, 1888).
Nhat Hong. *The Anarchist Beast* (Minneapolis, n.d., c. 1970s).
Schaack, Michael J. *Anarchy and Anarchists* (Chicago, 1889).

Acknowledgments

Special thanks to Carolyn Ashbaugh, Paul Avrich, the Chicago Historical Society staff, Dr. James Conway, John S. Kebabian, Joshua Lipton at H. P. Kraus, Russell Maylone at Northwestern University Library, Bruce Nelson, the staff at the Newberry Library, Franklin Rosemont, Mia Rublowska, John Simmons, G. Thomas Tanselle and Edward C. Weber at the Labadie Collection, University of Michigan Library.

Workingmen Arm Yourselves and Appear in Full Force!
THE EXECUTIVE COMMITTEE.

The Haymarket Explosion as pictured in Capt. Schaack's book

THE BOMB-THROWER:
A New Candidate

Who threw the Haymarket bomb? To this day, a century after the explosion, the matter has not been resolved. As I noted in my book on the Chicago tragedy, the identity of the assailant has remained a mystery, and the likelihood of clearing it up beyond any shadow of doubt has faded with the passage of time.[1]

One thing, however, seems clear. The bombthrower was an anarchist. He was not a Pinkerton detective hired by business interests to wreck the eight-hour movement; nor was he an *agent provocateur* put forward by the police in order to crush the anarchists; nor yet (as Governor Altgeld believed) a disgruntled worker, unconnected with the anarchist movement, who had been beaten by the police and was bent on gaining revenge. Rather, if we may credit the testimony of Dyer Lum and Robert Reitzel, key anarchists of the Haymarket period, the perpetrator was one of their own comrades. Lum, without naming him, tells us that he was a familiar figure within the Chicago movement, a member of one of the militant German groups, who acted on his own responsibility rather than as part of a conspiracy. "Always self-reliant," in Lum's description, he disobeyed August Spies's order not to bring arms to the Haymarket meeting, preferring, as Lum puts it, "to be prepared for resistance to onslaught rather than to quietly imitate the spiritual 'lamb led to slaughter'."[2] His name, adds Lum, was known to only a tiny circle of anarchists, Lum himself among them. It was never mentioned at the trial—thus he was not one of the eight defendants, nor was he Rudolph Schnaubelt, whom the police and others identified as the bombthrower.

Who then was the Haymarket bombthrower? In my book I suggested George Schwab as a possible candidate. Schwab, a German shoemaker, had been a member of the Schlusselbein (Collarbone) Group in New York, to which only the "most desperate" anarchists belonged. But the evidence, I noted, was far from satisfactory.[3] What troubled me about Schwab, more than anything else, was that he did not come to Chicago until May 1, 1886, only three days before the explosion, whereas Lum gives the impression that the bombthrower was a longstanding member of the Chicago movement.

I should now like to put forward a new candidate. His name is George Meng. Although the evidence remains inconclusive, he meets all the necessary qualifications. There is a strong possibility, I believe, that Meng was the Haymarket bombthrower.

Why do I think so? In September 1984, shortly after my book was published, I received a letter from Dr. Adah Maurer, a psychologist in Berkeley, California. She inquired

Rudolph Schnaubelt:
The police and prosecution's candidate for bombthrower

about a German anarchist, J. P. Meng, whom I mentioned in my account of the Pittsburgh Congress of 1883, at which the International Working People's Association was founded and Johann Most issued his celebrated Pittsburgh Manifesto, the charter of the new organization. Meng was one of the delegates from Chicago, along with Albert Parsons, August Spies, Jacob Mikolanda and Balthasar Rau. Could I have gotten his initials wrong? asked Dr. Maurer. The delegate, she thought, might be her grandfather, George Meng. More important, she had reason to believe that he was the bombthrower.

My first reaction was one of skepticism. Another bombthrower letter, I thought. I checked my notes on the Pittsburgh Congress, as reported in the *Vorbote*, the Sunday edition of *Die Arbeiter-Zeitung*, the IWPA journal in Chicago. There it was in the list of delegates—J. P., not George, Meng.[4] Yet Dr. Maurer's letter stirred my interest. It had a straightforward, no-nonsense air—not the letter of a sensationalist or crackpot, but of an intelligent, level-headed individual. So, when time permitted, I went to the Tamiment Library and looked again at the *Vorbote*. Following the list of delegates was a day-by-day account of the proceedings; in it Meng's name was mentioned, this time as G., not J. P. I then turned to the previous week's issue; here it was reported that, on the opening day of the congress, the delegates elected a two-man bureau consisting of F. Ruhe of Omaha and George Meng of Chicago. At last I had his first name; it was George, as Dr. Maurer suspected. Further research—above all in Johann Most's paper, the *Freiheit*, which also contained an account of the congress—confirmed

the first initial—G., for George, Meng. J. P., in the *Vorbote*'s list of delegates, had been an error.[5]

So Dr. Maurer had been right. The delegate had indeed been her grandfather. And if she was right about this, her claim that he was the bombthrower had to be taken seriously. I wrote to her for more information. She replied as follows. George Meng was born in Bavaria around 1840 and came to America as a young man, working as a drayman on the Erie Canal before settling in Chicago. In Chicago he found work as a teamster. He married and had two daughters: Kate, born in 1868, and Louisa, born in 1871. In 1873, when Kate was five and Louisa two, their mother suddenly died. Unable to care for his children, Meng put them in an orphanage in Rochester, New York, and left them there for ten years. In 1883, having remarried, he came for them and brought them to his home, a small farm in Hegewisch, Illinois, on the outskirts of Chicago (now part of the city), from which he commuted to work.

By then Meng had become an anarchist; and in October of that year, as we have seen, he was one of the five Chicago delegates to the Pittsburgh Congress, chairing the session of Sunday, October 16, with Spies serving as secretary. A believer in armed resistance to oppression, Meng joined the North Side Group of the IWPA, one of the most militant in Chicago, whose members included Oscar Neebe, Balthasar Rau, Rudolph Schnaubelt and Louis Lingg.[6] He paraded in a red sash, believed in free education, and was a confirmed atheist who "cursed God and dared Him to strike him dead,"

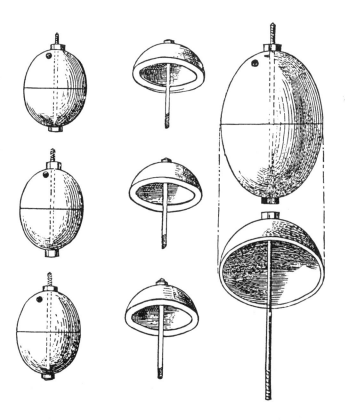

"Socialistic Bombs"
Chicago *Daily News*, January 14, 1886

72

"Peddling Bombs and Books" (from Schaack)

according to his daughter Louisa, who related this to her own daughter, Adah Maurer.[7]

Louisa, writes Dr. Maurer of her mother, "had a story inside her that she was bursting to tell."[8] Of this story, unfortunately, Louisa told her daughter only fragments. But the fragments are of great interest. One night, for example, shortly after the Haymarket incident, a man named Rudolph hid out at the Meng farm in Hegewisch. "I went out to the barn for a scuttle of coal," Louisa told her daughter, "and I saw him there when he lit his pipe." Rudolph and her father were comrades. "They talked all night in the kitchen."[9] This accords with what we know of Rudolph Schnaubelt, Meng's associate in the North Side Group, who fled Chicago on May 7, 1886, and spent the night on a farm outside the city, before heading for the Canadian border, then on to England and Argentina.

Most important, Louisa told Adah that her father had been the bombthrower. "He was the one," she repeated many times, without any elaboration. A few years later, Meng died in a saloon fire. Adah Maurer does not know the year, but it was before she herself was born (1907) and not long after the Haymrket episode. Nor, regrettably, can she provide us with a physical description of her grandfather. Thus we are unable to compare it with that of the bombthrower offered by John Bernett, the only impartial witness at the trial who claimed to have seen him (five feet nine or ten inches tall, with a mustache but probably no beard). Adah, however, imagines him as the mysterious spectator in the courtroom noted by Captain Schaack in his book on the case. The spectator, whom the police could not identify, attended the trial

regularly and talked on each occasion with some of the anarchists present, including Lucy Parsons and Lizzie Holmes. He was about forty years of age, five feet ten inches tall, 180 pounds in weight, had a round face, piercing gray eyes, and wore a short sandy beard and mustache. One day, toward the end of the proceedings, he seemed nervous and upset. Detained in the corridor by the police, he was searched for weapons, but nothing dangerous was found. He refused to answer any questions and was taken downstairs and told never to show himself in the courtroom again.[10]

Whether or not this was Adah Maurer's grandfather can only be a matter for speculation. But the rest of her story cannot be lightly dismissed. For it fits the accepted facts; it contains information—about Rudolph Schnaubelt, for instance—that is not commonly known; and it tallies with the description of the bombthrower by Dyer Lum: a German anarchist, a "self-determined" militant in the Chicago groups, a known figure in the movement (prominent enough to have been a delegate to the Pittsburgh Congress) but not one of its principal leaders and not mentioned at the trial. Dr. Maurer's story has the ring of truth, and I am inclined to believe it.

Paul AVRICH

1. Paul Avrich, *The Haymarket Tragedy*, Princeton, New Jersey, Princeton University Press, 1984, 437. 2. Dyer D. Lum, "August Spies," *Twentieth Century*, September 3, 1891; *The Alarm*, November 10, 1888. 3. Avrich, *The Haymarket Tragedy*, 444-45. 4. *Vorbote*, October 20 and 27, 1883. Cf. the *Pittsburgh Commerical Gazette*, October 14, 1883, where it is given as J. Meng. 5. *Ibid.*, October 20 and 27, 1883; *Freiheit*, October 20, 1883; Carl Nold, "Fifty Years Ago," *Man!*, January 1934. 6. Michael J. Schaack, *Anarchy and Anarchists*, Chicago, F.J. Schulte, 1889, 691. 7. Adah Maurer to Paul Avrich, October 6, 1984. 8. Adah Maurer to Paul Avrich, September 28, 1984. 9. Adah Maurer to Paul Avrich, October 6, 1984. 10. Schaack, *Anarchy and Anarchists*, 225-26.

FLOYD DELL

Born in Barry, Illinois, Floyd Dell (1887-1969) grew up in Quincy and moved with his family to Davenport, Iowa in 1903, shortly after he had joined the Socialist Party. A high-school dropout, he worked as a reporter in Davenport and later in Chicago where, as associate editor and later editor of the Friday Literary Review *of the* Evening Post, *he became a central figure in the city's short-lived "literary renaissance." He moved to New York in 1913 and the following year became associate editor of* The Masses. *When that magazine was suppressed by the U.S. government in 1917 for its opposition to the war, Dell helped edit its successor,* The Liberator.*

One of American socialism's most inspired and original essayists, Dell also wrote novels, poems and plays, as well as a notable autobiography, Homecoming *(1933). His first book,* Women as World-Builders *(1913), a collection of short sketches of Isadora Duncan, Olive Schreiner and others, revealed him to be an ardent feminist.* Were You Ever a Child? *(1919) has never been surpassed as a libertarian critique of education.* Intellectual Vagabondage *(1926) remains a key reference for understanding the development of the radical intelligentsia of the 1910s/20s.* Love in the Machine Age *(1930) was a serious radical exploration of sexual life— a rarity in those days, and uncommon even today.*

Among the first to attempt a Freud/Marx synthesis, in his fiction as well as in his essays, Dell suffered a pioneer's fate for his efforts: Marxist critics tended to find him too Freudian, while Freudians found him too Marxist. His many novels are no longer widely read, with the exception of his first, Moon-Calf *(1920), which briefly made the best-seller list, and perhaps* Jane March *(1923), which ran into trouble with the censors and was in fact withdrawn from bookstores in New York and Massachusetts. His* Love and Greenwich Village *(1926), a collection of essays, short fiction and poetry, is a classic of American bohemianism. Dell also wrote a useful study of* Upton Sinclair *(1927) and edited volumes of poems by William Blake and William Scawen Blunt, as well as the stories of his friend John Reed.*

Though he continued to regard himself as a socialist to the end of his life, Dell's participation in organized radical activity ceased in the late 1920s. His novel, The Golden Spike *(1934), was the last creative work that he published.*

"Bomb-Talking" is excerpted from an early and still valuable study, Socialism and Anarchism in Chicago, *that Dell wrote in 1912 for J. Seymour Currey's five-volume compilation,* Chicago: Its History and Its Builders.

FR

BOMB-TALKING

The Anarchists were, in part, former Socialists who had grown cynical about political methods, but who still desired what was in effect a political as well as an economic revolution: in part, they were idealists after the manner of Thoreau and Tolstoi; and for the rest they were working men who found in the Anarchist movement a voice making loudly articulate their wrongs. All of these found themselves in a movement permeated with the influence of Johann Most; not merely affected by his idealism and his eloquence, but by his teachings in regard to violence. Generally, they accepted that doctrine along with the rest; and it was possible for any of the elements of the Anarchist movement—the disgruntled Socialist, the gentle idealist, the dissatisfied workingman—to take the doctrine of violence with sufficient seriousness to act upon it. But as an actual matter of fact hardly any of them did take it in that way. So far as the movement in general was concerned, violence was a matter of talk and never a matter of action.

When the Mostian gospel first began to spread in America there were a certain number of romantic spirits who were attracted by the secrecy, the close organization and the terrorism, which were advocated and described in detail in his revolutionary handbook; and there was a certain amount of futile and rather ridiculous imitation of these things. Practical Mostism was, however, totally at variance with the revolutionary tradition already well established in America, and it died out harmlessly. The injection of such a personality as that of Louis Lingg into a group was sometimes sufficient to cause a temporary revival of this spirit. But, with such negligible exceptions, the Anarchist movement was (in spite of its discarding of political methods) a political movement; its actions were open and ordinary and legitimate. It proposed an end which was in the largest sense political, and it relied on the methods of reason and persuasion, through speeches, pamphlets, newspapers, etc., to gain adherents. Moreover, its members were for the most part what are called peaceable and law-abiding citizens. The leaders were men personally gentle, not accustomed to the use of firearms, and wholly unacquainted with the manufacture or use of the deadly explosives to which they sometimes referred with such sinister emphasis in their speeches and writings. This fact of their personal peaceableness does not necessarily extenuate these Anarchist leaders for their violent utterances; nor does the fact of the really peaceable character of the Anarchist movement remove its responsiblity for

the doctrine of violence which it sponsored. But it must be understood that these are facts. The ironic contrast between the peaceable lives of the Anarchists and their occasional violent utterances is a significant matter. The explanation of that contrast will lay bare the psychology of the period.

Bombs were talked and written about for a whole year by the Anarchists with no serious results whatever; for if one remembers that it has never been proved who threw the Haymarket bomb, and that it was certainly never traced to the Anarchists, the surprising fact appears that there is no bomb-throwing to discuss in the history of Chicago Anarchism. There is merely bomb-talking.

Why then did these men talk dynamite? It was done partly to attract attention to their real beliefs—it was a way of shocking the public into attention. So desperate a means of securing an audience is only taken by a small faction—it is the sign of weakness.

Then, too, if lawmakers and employers could be persuaded of the existence of a party ready to use violence to secure its ends, they might make concessions. So the Anarchists did not resent, and often helped to cultivate, the opinion that they were dangerous men. The newspapers to some extent co-operated with the Anarchists in building up the illusion. When news was scarce, a reporter would interview some Anarchist and print a lurid story. To amuse these reporters Spies kept on his desk at the *Arbeiter-Zeitung* office a piece of gaspipe that someone had left there. It was supposed to be a bomb; it was the only bomb that Spies had ever seen; when reporters asked, jocularly, if he had any bombs about, he pointed with a smile to this one: the same piece of gaspipe later helped to hang him. Thus the talk of dynamite was made largely in American spirit of "bluff."

But more essential than these causes was another something which may be called the Idea of dynamite. In a movement which stood for the poor and oppressed, the symbolism of dynamite, though not by any means necessarily the use of it, was bound to make a tremendous appeal. For here was a wonderful new substance which made one poor man the equal of an army: it seemed created as a sign to the oppressors of earth that their reign was not forever to endure. This symbolism of dynamite was, and not any actual interest in the use of it, that made it so frequent a topic in Anarchist speeches and writings during a certain period. It was, that is to say, a sentimental interest in dynamite.

Floyd DELL

74

GEORGE BROWN

In this essay from the November 1912 issue of Mother Earth, George Brown argues, as anarchists often did in Haymarket memorials, that the spirit of anarchism would triumph by gradually spreading throughout all areas of thought. Brown's perspective is unique, however, because he had attended the May 4 Haymarket meeting. Here he provides his eyewitness account of the police-caused "riot."

Brown was a Yorkshire-born shoemaker who worked in freethought and union causes while in England. Self-educated and an avid reader, he came to Chicago in 1886, when he was in his mid-twenties, and quickly became involved in radical activities. Blacklisted by the local shoe manufacturers for supporting the condemned Haymarket anarchists, he moved to Cincinnati and, in 1893, to Philadelphia, where he worked in a small shoe factory.

In Philadelphia he cooperated with fellow anarchists Voltairine de Cleyre, Chaim Weinberg and Joseph Cohen in the Social Science Club—a discussion and lecture group—the Radical Library, and the Modern School. A vigorous orator, Brown frequently addressed rallies for strikers and the unemployed. When a portion of Jacob Coxey's army of the unemployed marched through Philadelphia in 1894, Brown repaired their shoes. Until his death by blood poisoning in 1915, he maintained close ties with radicals within many Philadelphia unions, including the garment workers, the cigarmakers, and the shoemakers.

Blaine McKINLEY

THE POLICE RIOT: AN EYEWITNESS ACCOUNT

One Tuesday evening, about twenty-five years ago, I remained in the free library on South Clark Street, Chicago, until closing time, nine o'clock; I then walked west on Randolph Street on my way to my room, which was on Van Buren and Desplaines Street. When I reached that part of Randolph Street which is widened out to form what is called the Haymarket, I saw a crowd of people gathered around a wagon from which someone was speaking. As is my wont, I went to find out what the meeting was about. A spare dark man was speaking, and I recognized him as Albert Parsons from having heard him before on the lake front and in Knights of Labor meetings. He soon stopped talking, and a rough-looking, bearded man took his place. This was Samuel Fielden. He related how he had just left work, and indeed his clothes were soiled with the marks of his labor, which was that of hauling stone. He spoke with a rude eloquence directly in keeping with his appearance. He referred at some length to something Martin Foram, a Senator, had said about the uselessness of looking to legislation for redress for social and economic ills. He advocated what has since come to be called direct action. One of the things he said was this: "It is no use killing a capitalist; that would be but to kill a flea on a dog. What we want is to kill the dog itself, that is, capitalism."

He had talked in this strain for perhaps twenty minutes when the sky became clouded quite suddenly, and someone, I think Parsons, suggested that the meeting adjourn to Zepf's Hall, which could be seen from the wagon. Fielden said this was unnecessary, as he was about through. He started in to finish his speech when there was a movement of the crowd, which forced me back and up onto the pavement. From this position I could see over the heads of those in the street, and to my astonishment I saw a great company of police, with their revolvers drawn, rushing into the crowd which parted to make way for them. The captain commanded the meeting to disperse. Fielden leaned forward and said to the officer: "This is a peaceable meeting, and you have no right to interfere." Up to this time there had been no disorder of any kind. Now something occurred on the side of the street farthest from me, and the police captain called out, "Arrest that man," and instantly the police began firing into

the people. I thought they were firing blank cartridges, as I have seen soldiers do in English riots, but a man who stood near me was struck in the side by a policeman's bullet. I helped him to get down into the cellarway, so he might escape further injury, and then I tried to get into the saloon which was at the corner. The door was being forced also by those on the inside, and so I turned to go back past the wagon, because the firing seemed heaviest ahead. When I had just passed the wagon and reached the mouth of the little alley, something went quite high over my head which looked like a lighted cigar: in the semi-darkness only the lighted fuse showed. This was the bomb. It exploded in the midst of the police. I raised myself up as well as I could in the dense pack of the crowd, and looking past the wagon I saw a confused, writhing, squirming mass of policemen on the ground. Thinking that there were perhaps other bombs to follow, I made my way to Randolph Street again, walking east, past policemen who were firing from doorways at the fleeing citizens. I went by Canal Street to Van Buren, and then to my room. I put on my slippers, lighted a pipe, and walked along Desplaines Street, meeting the patrol wagons carrying quite other victims than those they had been harnessed up for the purpose of carrying. . . .

After twenty-five years, the things which stand out most distinctly in my mind in connection with this great historic affair are these: The great unrest of the city for some time before; the ferocious brutality of the police in dealing with it; that the police had committed many wanton murders before time; the surprising orderliness of the meeting; the fact that there was no sign of disorder until the arrival of the police and their uncalled-for interference; that the pre-arranged signal for the police to commence firing was the shouted order of Captain Ward, "Arrest that man"; that the police were shooting for at least three minutes, perhaps more, before the bomb was thrown; and then, above all, the dramatic precision with which the bomb was thrown and the exact poetic justice it wrought.

George BROWN

Excerpts from "November Memories,"
Mother Earth (November 1912)

DANCING AND PICNICKING ANARCHISTS?
The Movement Below the Martyred Leadership

Consider two advertisements buried on the third and fourth pages of *The Alarm*, the first in May 1885, the second six months later:

Grand Pic-Nic
and Summer Night's Festival
arranged by the
Central Labor Union, Chicago
on
Sunday, June 7, 1885
at Ogden's Grove
Tickets 25 cents a Person

Grand Christmas Festival
with Great Raffle of Presents
Concert, Theatre and Ball
at
Vorwarts Turner Hall,
West 12th Street,
on Saturday Evening, Dec 26 1885
Arranged for the Benefit of the Socialistic Press
Admission 25 cents a Person

It is surprising to discover that Chicago's anarchists held family picnics and went to dances because their image as unwashed, wild-eyed bomb-throwers lacks the capacity to explain the paradox. The story of the Haymarket Affair has almost completely overshadowed the history of the anarchist movement: We know all about the Eight Martyrs, we know nothing about the movement below the leaders. At its simplest, my argument here is that during the period from 1872 until 1886 the class-conscious membership of the Socialistic Labor Party (the SLP) and the International Working People's Association (the IWPA) actively cultivated a vital, militant and socialist culture inside Chicago's workingclass neighborhoods.

Some contemporary observers, like Friedrich Sorge, were impressed by the vitality and militancy of that movement:

Chicago experienced an extraordinarily energetic and effective propaganda campaign. . . . Big parades and processions were held often, and every appropriate event in public life was used to shake up the people, the workers, and to bring them to a realization of the condition and also, certainly, to frighten the philistines and politicians. The Chicago workers' festivities held in those days were wonderful events, and those held in the open drew crowds of 20,000 to 40,000 people.

With Sorge's catalog as an outline, let us look at the creation of several workingclass cultural institutions and their role in the history of Chicago's socialist and labor movements. We shall look first at anarchist dances and picnics, then at their parades, finally at the celebrations of the anniversary of the Paris Commune.

The hair-raising editorials on "Dynamite" and "Streetfighting—How to Meet the Enemy," which figured so prominently in the great trial, have not prepared us for the images of dancing or picnicking anarchists. The anarchists loved their "grand balls" and held them frequently. These were citywide events which drew on the combined membership of the IWPA's groups, on the Central Labor Union (the CLU),

and on the movement's sympathetic following. Dances were held to celebrate any kind of occasion: the Fourth of July, Christmas, Maifest, Sylvesterfest, Mardi Gras; or important anniversaries like the birth of Marx, Lassalle or Tom Paine. *The Alarm* advertised no less than five during November 1884, sponsored by the Cigar Makers' Progressive Union, the Carpteners' and Joiners' Union, the *Lehr-und-Wehr-Verein*, the Metalworkers' Union, and the IWPA itself. The hostile Chicago *Tribune* described a dance in 1885: "Every variety of step might have been witnessed yesterday. The 'Bohemian dip,' the 'German lunge,' the 'Austrian kick,' the 'Polish ramp' and the 'Scandinavian trot.' All these countries seemed to be represented, but it is safe to say that the native-born American, the Irishman and the Englishman were conspicuous by their absence." The images that repeatedly appear in contemporary accounts—of "smoothly shaven men" wearing "the well-brushed Sunday suits," "a good deal of flirtation," "the mechanic's arm. . .surrounding the waist of a German or Scandinavian damsel, while Billy Nevan's Band discoursed 'The Blue Danube'"—clash with our stereotype of Chicago's anarchists.

If the anarchists danced indoors during the cold months, they picnicked outdoors all summer. The SLP had adopted the tradition in the 1870s, but from 1881 the anarchists continued to use it. In June 1879 *The Socialist* advertised "A Grand Picnic Combined with [a] Flag Dedication and Procession [to be] Participated in by all Military Organizations, Trades Unions and other Societies." Later that month 3,000 people attended what Police Captain Michael Schaack described as "a monster picnic. . .to raise funds for an English-language paper." Chicago's socialists and anarchists always celebrated the Fourth of July and the first Monday in September.

We know more about their picnics during the summer and fall of 1885. In May the CLU arranged "A Grand Picnic" combined with "A Summer Night's Festival"; the next month *The Alarm* advertised the "Fifth [annual] Picnic arranged by the Socialistic Mannerchor of the Northside." An outing sponsored by the IWPA in July drew a crowd estimated between 2,000 and 3,000; later that month 1,000 people trekked to Indiana for the day. On Sunday, September 5, the anarchists called for a Labor Day procession from Chicago, led by "fifty young girls with a banner above them reading 'American Corps,' to Ogden's Grove, where from 3 to 4 thousand people assembled." Again in September, as if to cap off the summer, *The Alarm* advertised another "Grand Excursion to Sheffield, Indiana. . .under the auspices of the IWPA."

Dances and picnics were invariably described as "grand," and they were eagerly anticipated opportunities to flee a home or boardinghouse, to dress up, to take the children, to see friends, to hear an orchestra or choir, and to dance late into the night. Some festivals featured professional musicians, like Billy Nevans' Band or Rosenbecker's Orchestra, but most

"An Anarchist Procession" (from Schaack)

of the music came from within the movement, which sponsored at least six singing societies and several brass bands. Wright's Grove, a favorite picnic site for southwestside Bohemian anarchists, offered games and music; Ogden's Grove, on the German northwestside, had a revolving stage and a bandshell. Some of these festivals were quite elaborate and included poetry and song, recitations and speeches, games and gymnastic exhibitions, military drills and sharpshooting, in addition to agitation. German, Bohemian and Scandinavian workers could also enjoy performances of workingclass amateur theater groups which occasionally even offered original plays.

Because their picnics were located outside the city limits, the anarchists arranged processions to move from a central rallying point to the picnic grounds. These processions were an opportunity to display banners, flags, wagon-drawn tableaux, transparencies, the armed might of the organized working class, and the size of the movement. "With the smell of gin and beer, with blood-red flags and redder noses, and with banners inscribed with revolutionary mottoes, the anarchists inaugurated their grand parade and picnic yesterday," observed the *Tribune* in July 1885.

Early parades had been the objects of ridicule and derision; by the beginning of the 1880s they became fearsome. In 1879 the state legislature went so far as to ban the parades of workingclass paramilitary units without the explicit permission of the governor. The anarchists continued to march without their weapons: on the Fourth of July, on Labor Day and throughout the summer. The movement mobilized unions, singing and benevolent societies, amateur bands, the *Lehr-und-Wehr-Verein* and the IWPA's membership. These were not rag-tag marches, but ordered and orderly processions. The

Tribune described the "perfect order" of one; the equally hostile *Illinois Staats-Zeitung* judged another as "extremely peaceful." Each had an arrangements committee which appointed a chief marshall and his assistants, who were usually mounted on horseback; union flags or socialist banners identified most of the units. In August 1884, for example, *Die Chicagoer Arbeiter-Zeitung* published a "Programm der Prozession" which organized the parade into divisions, told the marchers where to rally for each, and even assigned them places within their designated units.

The largest and most impressive workingclass procession in the period before the Haymarket Affair took place in April 1886, barely two weeks before the riot. On Easter Sunday 10,000 workers assembled in Market Square and then paraded through the city's streets; their own marshalls held up traffic. A "great crowd" of as many as 25,000 more people followed the procession, which was interspersed with seven bands, all the way to the lakefront rally. The CLU, which had been founded and was then dominated by the IWPA, arranged both procession and rally, which was scheduled to inaugurate the Eight-Hour Day. The anarchist demonstration was half-again as large as the crowd assembled by the Knights of Labor only two weeks before. Most important, the anarchists were able to mobilize a larger portion of the city's immigrant and non-English-speaking working class. And it was the experience of that demonstration which led some to expect a turnout of 25,000 in the Haymarket on the night of May 4.

The quintessential anarchist festival was the annual celebration of the Paris Commune on the 18th of March. The Chicago section of the First International commemorated the first anniversary in 1872, the SLP arranged those between 1878 and

1882, and the anarchists continued the tradition at least through 1910. The first was held in the Globe Theatre with three declared objects: "the celebration of the anniversary of the establishment of Communism, the contradiction of the lies [about the Commune] circulated by the press, and to become acquainted with their fellow workingmen." The meeting was addressed in German, English and Norwegian before turning to dancing. The *Tribune* described an audience of about 400 as "composed solely of workingmen, well-dressed and well-behaved."

In the early 1870s the festival drew audiences of less than a thousand, but which steadily grew. The 1879 commemoration, which was free to use the city's largest public hall, drew the largest crowd. The *Tribune* reported "the main floor, the galleries, the platform and stand—in fact every foot of available space was covered with a dense mass of humanity; even the rafters under the roof were occupied." The *Times* set the attendance at somewhere between 20,000 and 25,000 people; a bourgeois German paper, *Der Westen*, set it at 30,000; the *Tribune* between 30,000 and 40,000; and *The Socialist* ecstatically claimed 80,000 to 100,000 participants in the two-day affair.

For almost four decades the Commune festival was an international commemoration of the Paris Comune of 1871 and the Revolution of 1848. The stage for the 1875 festival was adorned "by crayon drawings of Ferdinand Lassalle and General Blanqui"; the next year featured a living tableau of the death of General Dombrowsky. In 1879 Gabrienne Davoust, a French-born veteran of the Commune, and Dr. Ernst Schmidt, a German-born Forty-Eighter and "Friend of Karl Marx," were the featured speakers as one-hundred-thousand people [came to] celebrate . . .the first efforts for labor's emancipation." In 1880 English-born Thomas Morgan set forth "the objects and aims of the Paris workingmen in their remarkable struggle for industrial freedom." The ads for the 13th anniversary explained that "40,000 working people were slaughtered in the streeets of Paris for having dared to revolt against their capitalistic masters. American workmen should give honor to those that gave their lives that labor might be free." By 1884 the Czech groups of the IWPA in Chicago were sponsoring a "Paris Communal"; the next year their festival attracted Bohemian trade-union delegations. And in 1886 Albert Parsons, a native-born American of Puritan stock, explained that ill-health had forced "Madame Delescluz[e]. . .a participant in the Paris Commune," to cancel her appearance.

In anarchist eyes the Commune became a glorious symbol of internationalism, of solidarity, and a model for the social revolution. But for the rest of Chicago—for E. B. Washburne, who had been ambassador to France, for Marshall Field, and for Joseph Medill of the Chicago *Tribune*—the Commune remained the symbol of proletarian depravity and murder. And if the anarchists spread one message in their festivals, Washburne lectured the Chicago, Commercial, and Union League Clubs with another. The *Tribune* was shocked by "The Extra-ordinary Turnout of 'the Reds'" for the Commune festival in 1879, and its reporter explained: "It was one of those rolling, pushing, surging, crowding, unaccomodating mobs; a regular German-Scandinavian-Bohemian-American crowd. . .one of those mobs where the women are more indecent in their haste than the men. . .where the men affect total ignorance of English, and lack every essential of courtesy. In short, it was such a gathering as only a socialistic community could bring out or would tolerate."

"Banners of the Social Revolution, 1886" (from Schaack)

Precisely. These kinds of events encompassed a community in which workers could live, dance, sing, picnic and parade after work and outside the workplace—a community which tried to serve its members, from the christening of their children to their funerals, even caring for their survivors. With outdoor events in the summer, and with indoor events throughout the fall, winter and spring, the anarchist movement in late nineteenth century Chicago enjoyed a secular and class culture it had created, adapted and invented for itself.

This movement culture was not synonymous with workingclass culture; rather, movement culture was always smaller and more radical. It served as a springboard for the recruitment and maintenance of a socialist membership. While movement culture derived from the ethnic cultures within both movement and city, the two were not the same. Finally, this culture was not unique to Chicago, but could be found in several other American cities, and similar institutions and social events could be found in Germany, Britain and France.

What is important about the advertisements of dances, festivals and picnics in the anarchist press is probably not that they contradict the infamous stereotype, but rather that they illuminate the movement below the eight martyrs. The ads reveal a community of nineteenth century socialists who were committed to the working class, its organization, and its emancipation. That the anarchists failed in the aftermath of the Haymarket Affair should not blind us to their achievement. In Friedrich Sorge's words, it was "the undeniably meritorious accomplishment of the Chicago anarchists to have brought to this marvelous mixture of all nationalities and languages a certain order, to have created affinity, and to have given the movement at that time unity and goals." It would seem that the vitality, militancy and growth of that movement was at least as impressive as the prominence, eloquence and martyrdom of its leaders.

Bruce C. NELSON

Sources: The seventh chapter of my dissertation is devoted to a discussion of movement culture based on a reading of Chicago's radical press, including *Dagslyset, Der Deutsche Arbeiter, Die Chicagoer Arbeiter-Zeitung, Die Fackel, Der Vorbote, Der Illinois Volks-Zeitung, The Alarm* and *The Socialist.* See Bruce C. Nelson, "Culture and Conspiracy: A Social History of Chicago Anarchism, 1870-1900" (Ph.D. dissertation, Northern Illinois University, 1985).

OSCAR AMERINGER

In one of the few funny passages related to Haymarket, Oscar Ameringer (1870-1943) here captures both the exultant mood of the May 1 strikes and the effect of wild media reports regarding the bombing on the course of events in other cities.

Ameringer, at the time of the strike, was a teenaged Swabian immigrant furniture worker and a member of Cincinnati's Deutsche Holz Arbeiter Verein, a Knights of Labor affiliate. He would later become an important radical editor and writer in Oklahoma, Milwaukee and Illinois. His humor would earn him the title of "the Mark Twain of American socialism."

The passage below is excerpted from Ameringer's autobiography, If You Don't Weaken *(New York, 1940). For the sake of humor and simplicity it may well exaggerate the speed with which Cincinnati strikers broke ranks in the face of the coming of troops to their city. Steven Ross' recent research suggests that many Cincinnati strikers held out for days, even weeks, after the troops arrived and that over seven strikers in ten won at least partial victory in the strike settlements.*

DR

THE BAD NEWS FROM CHICAGO

It was a jolly strike. Victory was dead certain, for did not almost everybody belong to the Knights of Labor? Butchers, bakers, and candlestick makers, doctors, preachers, grocerymen and boarding-house-keepers. What could be easier? With everybody quitting work the surrender of plutocracy was a foregone conclusion. In addition, there was the union treasury. The first week "out" married men received six dollars in strike benefits—single men, three. The second week out was not so good. Married men received three dollars and single men nothing. And the third week out all were placed on a basis of American equality, everybody getting nothing.

In the meantime, something happened which took much of the original starch out of strikers and sympathizers alike.

I was standing on the picketline when an express wagon drove up unloading bundles of papers. Soon newsboys were rending the air with the ominous cries: "Anarchist bombthrowers kill one hundred policemen in Haymarket in Chicago—Anarchist bombthrowers kill one hundred policemen in Haymarket in Chicago—Anarchist—"

Things were getting serious. Many of us had called ourselves anarchists without, I am sure, being able to distinguish between arnica and anarchy.

The bad news from Chicago fell like an exceedingly cold blanket on us strikers. To our erstwhile friends and sympathizers the news was the clarion for speedy evaporation. Some of our weaker fellow Knights broke ranks. The army of the social revolution was visibly melting away. The police grew more numerous and ill-mannered. And so did the tempers of our diminishing irreconcilables.

I was standing opposite the main entrance of the furniture factory, warming half a brick under my coat-tail, when one of the erring brothers came along. If he had been content with entering the building, I might still be a poor but deserving factory hand. However, before entering, he stuck out his tongue and made a long nose at me, whereupon I let fly my half brick.

Had the erring brother been an American versed in the art of baseball, he would have caught the brick and hurled it back at me, or would have sidestepped the missile. However, being a low Dutchman, he closed both eyes, stooped down and met the brick head on.

It was a lucky strike. I was proud of it and no doubt would have gloated over the body of the fallen foe had not two policemen appeared on the run, making it advisable for me to seek more genial surroundings.

Owing to that and other overt acts, my name became emblazoned on the blacklists of Cincinnati's employers, so much so that when the strike was finally broken I experienced no trouble living up to the obligation I had assumed when joining the Knights of Labor to the effect that I would not return to work in that or any other furniture factory until our just demand, the eight-hour day plus a twenty-per-cent increase in wages, was granted.

Oscar AMERINGER

Vol. XXI.— No. 5.   MAY, 1886. $3.00 PER ANNUM.

SOCIALISTIC MOVEMENTS IN ENGLAND AND THE UNITED STATES.

SOCIALISM is neither a new craze, as some of its opponents assert, nor a new revelation, as some of its apostles would have us believe. It is, if not as old as the hills, or even as old as mankind, at least as old as civilization.

So soon as any group of men in remote ages, outgrowing the limits of family life, learnt the expediency of living together in friendship, the need arose of rules for social organization and mutual subjection to the common

SOCIALISTIC MOVEMENTS.— A LABOR STRIKE IN THE UNITED STATES.

A labor demonstration pictured on the front page of *Frank Leslie's Popular Monthly* (May 1886).

"An Injury to One is the Concern of All":
THE KNIGHTS OF LABOR
in the Haymarket Era

The dramatic explosion of the Haymarket bomb, the martyrdom of four anarchist leaders, and the enduring passions of partisans on both sides have identified the Haymarket Affair with Chicago's anarchist movement in the mind of the public. Though this makes for compelling popular history, it is only part of the story.

The full meaning of the Haymarket Affair becomes apparent only when set in the perspective of labor's Great Upheaval of the mid-1880s. In this labor upsurge working men and women from every trade, of every skill-level, and of all nationalities and races streamed into labor organizations by the tens of thousands, expressed insistent demands for shorter hours, higher wages and a permanent voice in determining their working conditions, and adopted new methods of labor solidarity to win these demands.

The labor organization that was most closely identified with this Great Upheaval in the minds of working people was the Knights of Labor. With its well-known motto, "an injury to one is the concern of all," the Knights epitomized the theory and spirit of class solidarity. The characteristic form of the Knights—mixed local assemblies drawing together workers of all trades—offered an organizational alternative to existing craft unionism. Finally, the Knights were the first labor organization to take on and defeat one of the major Gilded Age Robber Barons by employing, and thus popularizing, the new weapon of the sympathy strike.

The 1886 report of the Illinois Bureau of Labor Statistics found that the "Order" in Chicago had mushroomed from 1,900 in July 1885 to 27,000 a year later. The Knights were still outnumbered by trade unionists: 30,000 were affiliated with the moderate Trade and Labor Assembly, and between 10,000 and 16,000 with the anarchist-led Central Labor Union. However, by October 1886 the Bureau estimated that the Knights had more than doubled their membership while that of the trade unions had stabilized. Even these figures, suggesting a rough parity, can be misleading, for the Knights' strength was among factory-hands concentrated in large-scale industry: the packinghouses, Pullman works, tanneries, boot-and-shoe factories, and the agricultural implements industry. Thus, during the Great Upheaval the Knights controlled a strategic position in the city's working class and, not surprisingly, faced the brunt of capital's counterattack after Haymarket.

How the Knights in Chicago grew into the most important expression of labor's Great Upheaval is best explained by the intersection of two important historical processes in the mid-1880s. The first was the industrial transformation of both the workplace and the economy as a whole beginning in the 1870s. The second was a political crisis resulting from the growing dissatisfaction of the business elite with the conduct of the local Democratic administration.

The origins of the crisis of the 1880s lay in the great railroad strikes and riots of 1877. The unprecedented class violence of that strike left thirty workmen dead and over two-hundred wounded, and sharply polarized classes in the city. According to socialist George Schilling the strike "was the calcium light that illumined the skies of our social and industrial life, and revealed the pinched faces of the workers and the opulence, arrogance and unscrupulousness of the rich." Immediately following the strike's defeat unionists met in secret conclave to found the first local assembly of the Knights of Labor in Chicago. Meanwhile, German-speaking trade unionists coalesced behind the Workingmen's Party of the United States (soon renamed Socialistic Labor Party).

Due to the weakness of the trade unions and the timidity of the Knights, hegemony over Chicago's labor movement quickly passed to the socialists. As the decade drew to a close it appeared to many observers that the SLP was destined to become the major political expression of the new workingclass culture emerging in Chicago's shops, factories, neighborhoods and ethnic communities. Yet, in a stunning turnabout, the Democratic Party, under the charismatic leadership of Mayor Carter Harrison, almost completely supplanted the socialists as the political leaders of Chicago workingmen in the early 1880s.

In part, Harrison's success stemmed from his ability to appeal directly to the foreign-born working class by defending their leisure customs against anti-saloon reformers. But Harrison was also the first Chicago mayor to appeal to the labor movement. From the start he assiduously courted the socialists, appointing their leaders to local offices in the Department of Health and supporting socialist-sponsored legislation, notably the ordinances authorizing factory and tenement-house inspection by the city. When trade unions and the Knights grew more influential, Harrison appointed their officers also to health inspectorships.

Chicago labor received more tangible aid from Harrison during strikes. In the Irish neighborhood of Bridgeport Harrison appointed a pro-labor police-lieutenant whose non-intervention during the strikes of Irish rolling-mill workers and iron-ore shovelers enabled them to win signal victories. During every major strike in the early 1880s the Trade and Labor Assembly, whose leaders were also Knights, sent delegations to City Hall to procure support from the mayor and police superintendant. They were seldom disappointed. Frustrated employers increasingly turned to private Pinkerton guards in place of the police. In spring 1885 the iron-molders union defeated Cyrus McCormick in a strike dur-

were those of the skilled nailers, boxmakers and McCormick iron-molders, all resisting the effects of mechanization. The case of the McCormick molders is particularly important to our story becasuse of the violent conflict stemming from this strike led directly to the anarchists' "Revenge" circular and the follow-up circular calling for the May 4 meeting at Haymarket Square. Following his capitulation in 1885, McCormick decided to replace his skilled men with pneumatic molding machines. In February, 1886 the remaining workmen, who were organized in the United Metal Workers Union and the Knights of Labor, walked out to demand the rehiring of the fired molders and an advance in wages for unskilled workers. When McCormick declared his intention of reopening the plant using non-union labor, Bonfield assembled a specially picked squad of 350 police to guard the scabs. No Pinkertons were necessary this time.

The defeat of the McCormick strikers and the boxmakers as well, both at the hands of Bonfield, prompted many skilled workers—the bulk of the labor movement—to reevaluate their exclusive craft-union approach and ultimately their political alliance with the Democratic Party. At the same time an alternative strategy for labor was being posed by the Knights of Labor. Several months earlier the Knights had won an unprecedented victory over Jay Gould's Wabash Railroad. In March, 1886 the Knights began another national railroad strike against Gould. Also in March, Chicago Knights won a boycott victory over the shoe manufacturers on the issue of contract prison-labor. All at once the Knights appeared to offer an effective vehicle for a new labor solidarity capable of winning demands independent of changes in the political climate.

This point was made obvious when the Knights' District Assembly representing Chicago's industrial southside proclaimed boycotts of McCormick and the boxmaking firm of Henry Maxwell, thus breaking with the cautious national policy enunciated by Grand Master Workman Terence V. Powderly. At this point workingmen began streaming into the Knights. On March 27 the *Tribune* reported that Chicago Knights were growing at the rate of a thousand per week. Between March 20 and July 1886 the local Order grew from 10,000 to 27,000 members. In short, it was the boycott and the promise of comprehensive class unity that sparked labor's Great Upheaval. Once workers were organized in the Knights and trade unions, and once this newfound solidarity unleashed a feeling of class-assertiveness, local workingmen turned *en masse* to the eight-hour movement, which culminated in the strike of approximately 60,000 Chicago workers on May 1.

Led by Powderly, the Knights of Labor established a well-deserved reputation for opposition to the militant tactics of the anarchists. Immediately following the Haymarket bombing the Chicago *Knights of Labor* levelled a vituperative blast at the anarchists, claiming that they and their sympathizers "should be summarily dealt with. They are entitled to no more consideration than wild beasts." But when the injustice of the trial became patently clear, and when faced with a massive lockout of Knights' packinghouse workers, rank-and-file Knights gravitated toward a new leadership which defended the rights of the anarchists as victims of an anti-labor conspiracy. These new Knights' leaders also pioneered the for-

ing which the most conspicuous action of the police was their arrest of four Pinkertons for shooting into a crowd of 500 strikers which had stopped a busload of scabs. In sum, Carter Harrison had temporarily reversed the class polarization of the 1870s by engineering a social compact between workingmen and the local political order at the expense of industrial employers.

In the year before Haymarket, Harrison's policies for ensuring social peace in the city came under virulent attack from the city's business elite. Systematic overproduction, which had caused the long 1870s depression, recurred in 1883-85. Yet the fear of a repeat of the 1877 uprising and the *laissez-faire* approach of the local police toward strikes, prevented employers from reducing wages.

In response, employers adopted a two-pronged approach. Within the workplace they stepped up the introduction of labor-saving machinery to replace highly-paid unionized skilled labor. In the political arena they pressured Mayor Harrison to change his police policy. In October, 1885 Harrison appointed John Bonfield as police inspector. Bonfield's policy toward strikes—summarized by his slogan: "The club today saves the bullet tomorrow"—was first demonstrated in his brutal suppression of the 1885 streetcar workers' strike.

The ramifications of the Bonfield approach became fully apparent in February, 1886. Less than three months before Haymarket the only strikes of any consequence in the city

mation of the United Labor Party, a coalition of labor reformers, trade unionists and socialists which nominated a slate of predominantly Knights' candidates in fall 1886. So pervasive was the disaffection of workingmen with the Democratic Party that in the Spring 1887 elections Harrison declined nomination, and the Democrats—bereft of their labor constituency—took refuge in a fusion ticket under Republican auspices.

From their peak in membership, influence and prestige in the fall of 1886 the Knights fell into precipitous decline the following year. Of the 116 new local assemblies established in 1886, sixty-one percent had lapsed by 1887, and eighty percent were gone by 1888. The turning-point came in the disastrous defeat sustained by the Order in the fall 1886 packinghouse workers' strike. Powderly intervened to order the men back to work when negotiators were on the verge of a compromise settlement. Powderly later argued that sanctioning the walkout would have encouraged an epidemic of strikes and dragged the Order into certain disaster. As a result of this and other similar actions by Knights' national leaders, many local members left the labor movement in disgust. Trade-union-oriented members concluded that a leadership responsible to a variety of trades was not fit to make decisions for workers of one particular trade. These workers also left the Order but reaffiliated with the national unions of their trades and with the American Federation of Labor.

Though Powderly blundered in the timing of his directive, he cannot be blamed for the packinghouse workers' defeat, or for the decline of the Knights. Unskilled workers did not yet have the discipline or resources to win union recognition. Skilled workers soon learned that solidarity with the unskilled was not generally necessary to win their demands. A viable national labor organization uniting skilled craftsmen with unskilled workers in basic industry would have to wait until the 1930s.

Yet labor activists salvaged something important out of the wreck of the Knights. By the 1890s, AFL craft unions adopted the Knights' methods of the boycott and sympathy strike, thus affording groups such as the machinists and building-workers the power to exercise a limited control over their industrial work-environment. In this way what had once been a class goal was preserved, though harnessed to more limited and particularistic ends.

In 1905 Ed Nockels, secretary of the Chicago Federation of Labor, expressed the high regard felt by later unionists for the ideals of the Knights:

The truth expounded by the Knights of Labor and adopted by the American Federation of Labor, in effect that the "injury to one is the concern of all," seems more true today than when first announced, and upon this principle rests all the progress of our upward, forward march, and if the self-sacrificing men and women of our country did not accept and place all their hopes and aspirations upon this principle, slavery would still be extant in this country, not alone among the blacks, but among the whites.

Richard SCHNEIROV

Note: This essay summarizes themes discussed in the author's Ph.D. dissertation, "The Knights of Labor in the Chicago Labor Movement and in Municipal Politics, 1877-1887" (Northern Illinois University, 1984).

"Underground Rifle Practice: A Meeting of the *Lehr-und-Wehr-Verein*" (from Schaack)

Workers at Chicago's Horn Brothers Furniture Company on the eve of the May First Eight-Hour Strike
(photo courtesy of the Chicago Historical Society)

THE INTERNATIONAL WORKING PEOPLE'S ASSOCIATION

The International Working People's Association came to prominence in 1886 when August Spies, Albert Parsons, and six other leaders stood trial for the murder of policemen at Chicago's Haymarket. Until then the IWPA was hardly known outside the German-speaking districts of Chicago, Cincinnati, and other large cities, but it took a leading role in the campaign for the eight-hour day, alongside the infant American Federation of Labor and local assemblies of the Knights of Labor, the most renowned labor organization of its day.

Unlike these rivals, the IWPA wasted no time either with AFL-style union rules or with the Knights' ballot-box reforms. It made no secret of its wish to abolish the capitalist system by means of radical education and revolutionary organization, supplemented with the new "science of dynamite." Its doctrine was a patchwork of Marxist economics, Bakuninist anarchism, and the ideals of liberty, equality, and fraternity drawn from the French and American revolutions.

These ideas found fertile soil in the America of the Robber Barons. Boss Tweed of New York's infamous Tammany Hall set the pace in auctioning political favors to the highest bidder. National party politics became a spoils system, which reform movements like the Greenback-Labor Party were powerless to overturn. Meanwhile, unscrupulous industrialists like Jay Gould put down worker discontent by giving their striking workers a "rifle diet" while bragging they could "hire half the working class to shoot the other half."

Frustrated with the meager results of reform politics and outraged at the violent repression of the railroad strikes of 1877, small sections of the Socialistic Labor Party began to debate the *Bewaffnungsfrage* (arming question) and to organise rifle clubs on the model of the German *Lehr-und Wehr-Vereine* (learning and fighting unions). While the top leadership of the SLP held fast to an electoral alliance with the Greenback-Labor Party and ordered its members out of these clubs, an infusion of German immigrants seeking refuge from Bismarck's anti-socialist laws gave an added push to the dissident SLP sections who favored arming and rejected the ballot as anything more than a forum for propaganda.

Meanwhile, a semi-secret congress of anarchists convened in London in 1881 to found the International Working People's Association, an anarchist revival of the defunct First International. This new "Black International" proved attractive to those American socialists who began calling themselves Social Revolutionaries as a sign of their rejection of capitalism and the government that supported it. With the arrival of Johann Most and his *Freiheit* in New York, the Social Revolutionaries got a gifted propagandist whose international fame and incendiary ideas enabled him to overshadow the parlor anarchist Benjamin Tucker, editor of *Liberty,* a Boston journal espousing extreme individualism. Since

Most had scarcely any more influence outside the parlor, the IWPA would have remained an isolated anarchist sect were it not for labor agitators like Parsons and Spies.

These Chicago radicals were as much at home addressing a crowd of strikers outside Cyrus McCormick's factory gates as they were drafting a revolutionary manifesto. They joined forces with Most at the Pittsburgh Congress of the IWPA in 1883, putting the organization on a solid footing and giving it a revolutionary program, the "Pittsburgh Manifesto."

However, to Most's consternation, the Chicago radicals set about organizing trade unions. Meeting success among skilled workers hard-pressed by mechanization, they helped organize unions of cigarmakers, cabinetmakers, and metalworkers, among others, and brought them one by one into a new Chicago Central Labor Union, which soon surpassed the older Amalgamated Trades and Labor Assembly. They believed in unionism as both the means to the future socialist society and the living example of what a truly cooperative commonwealth would be like. In this, they anticipated syndicalist philosophy and the revolutionary unionism of the Industrial Workers of the World.

Whatever their differences over trade unionism, all elements of the IWPA were united in their contempt for the limited results of electoral politics. Through the columns of *The Alarm, Freiheit,* and the *Arbeiter-Zeitung*, they rarely lost an opportunity to shower scorn on civil service reform, tariff reduction, and other piecemeal changes, mocking the ballot as "that sum total of all humbugs!" This undeniably kept them free of middle-class manipulation and temptations of the spoils system, but it also undoubtedly cost them the support of many workers who regarded the ballot as nothing less than a sacred trust.

The same is true of their unflinching acceptance of the tactic of physical force. Although the individual right to bear arms and vigilantism were time-honored American traditions, armed resistance to legal authority did not strike so responsive a chord. Thus the social revolutionaries put themselves out on a limb with rhetorical provocations like Lucy Parsons' notorious advice to tramps—"learn the use of dynamite!" In a similar vein, *The Alarm* drew the lesson from a violent miners' strike in Ohio's Hocking Valley that workers would no longer rely upon passive resistance: "Force, and force only, can liberate them from the despotic rule of a lot of miserable, fiendish loafers, and they are going to use it!" In their defense, Social Revolutionaries believed they were only giving as good as they got. Pinkertons, Coal and Iron Police, and the state militias proved on numerous occasions that they did, indeed, know how to dish out a "rifle diet."

Recognizing the unpopularity of their views serves to make their prominence in the struggles of the 1880s all the more significant. For they assuredly made a contribution second to none to the great Eight-Hour strike, particularly in the storm center of Chicago. Initially, the IWPA was as strongly opposed to the eight-hour agitation as Terence Powderly, reform-minded head of the Knights of Labor (though, of course, for the opposite reason). At the onset of depression in 1884, the IWPA solution to the problem of unemployment was to organize the unemployed, supplemented by Lucy Parsons' celebrated advice to tramps. Chicago anarchists used

their influence in trade unions to detach them from hours and wages demands, and as late as October, 1885, referred to eight-hour devotees as "our more backward brethren." Not surprisingly, New Yorkers behind Most were unswerving in their denunciation of palliative measures.

But as the eight-hour fire spread some sections had second thoughts, and after further work with the unemployed, including a mock Thanksgiving Day parade of tramps, the circle around Lucy and Albert Parsons decided to try and catch up to the mass movement. Trade union anarchists in Cincinnati and St. Louis were embarking on the same course.

This change of heart among the Social Revolutionaries was vital to the cause. They contributed their considerable propaganda and agitation skills, not insignificant in a movement whose energy came from a torrent of handbills, newspaper articles, mass rallies, inspiring speeches, and angry marches. These tactics produced a rally of some 25,000 people in Chicago the week before May 1, at which Albert Parsons set the eight-hours question in the context of class struggle. Repeating a formula popularized by the Eight Hour League, he divided the working day into two parts: one when the worker created value equivalent to his cost of living, the other when he created the boss's profits. Therefore, Parsons went on, "Reduced hours would melt the wages or profit system out of existence and usher in the cooperative or free-labor system." Of course he hastened to add that the change was not going to be peaceful: "The capitalists of the world will force the workers into armed rebellion."

The fruit of these agitations ripened the first week in May. Contemporary estimates made by *Bradstreet's* and subsequent investigations conducted by the Bureau of Labor concur that something on the order of 200,000 workers struck for a shorter day. While most intense in the fast-growing industrial cities of the middle west—Chicago contributed the largest contingent (80,000) and Cincinnati, Milwaukee and St. Louis were quite active—the strikes also hit the Mid-Atlantic coast. A generation of German and Irish immigrants just coming into its own combined forces with Yankee supporters. Red and black flags mingled with red, white and blue. And the sum of these was the general strike, the single most important American contribution to the international workers' movement in the decade.

It is in the nature of the insurrectionary temper that it can not long sustain itself. When it fails to achieve immediate revolutionary objectives, disappointed hopes quickly turn to bitterness and cynicism. It blazes forth brilliantly, and then is gone. Such was the meteoric course followed by the IWPA. As the general strike disintegrated into a collection of local skirmishes, the conditions that enabled a handful of militants to play a vanguard role vanished, affected in some measure by the rise in employment levels.

The fate of the IWPA itself was sealed by the Haymarket affair. There was a general round-up of anarchists conducted with such wanton disregard for the civilized forms of law that the Mayor of Chicago said such an operation in England would have made Victoria's throne tremble. Although *The Alarm* reappeared for a time, the top leadership of the organization languished in prison, sympathizers were scared off, funds were hard to come by, and by November many anarchists abandoned principle to participate in the United Labor Party campaign.

The last significant action of the IWPA was a national lecture tour by Lucy Parsons. Although small circles around Most, Tucker and others survived, anarchism lost its mass base and retreated to the company of literati and the strategy of propaganda of the deed. It was a long way from the mass strike to the brilliant speechmaking of Emma Goldman and and the lone *attentat* of Alexander Berkman.

The campaign to save the the Chicago anarchists drew significant support from trade unionists around the country. Unionists in New York called for mass demonstrations to prevent the executions, the American Federation of Labor resolved in favor of mercy, and Samuel Gompers joined a delegation to Illinois Governor Oglesby to make a last-minute appeal. But the main task of organizing the defense was taken up by socialists. Careful to distinguish their doctrines from the anarchists, Socialistic Labor Party sections sponsored rallies and agitated in central labor unions. They sponsored an American tour of Wilhelm Liebknecht, Eleanor Marx, and her husband Edward Aveling in the fall of 1886. In their report of this tour, *The Working-Class Movement in America*, Eleanor Marx wrote, "Should these men be murdered, we may say of their executioners what my father said of those who massacred the people of Paris, 'They are already nailed to that eternal pillory from which all the prayers of their priests will not avail to redeem them.'"

She was right. The vengeful Chicago businessmen like Marshall Field who insisted on carrying out the executions were never forgiven, while their victims, after the fashion of John Brown, were venerated in death as they had not been in life. Although the teachings of the anarchists on the ballot and violent revolution were rejected by most workers, their martyrdom came as a result of the class-conscious movement they had helped create. Through their prominent participation in the general strike, the anarchists won a position of undeniable importance, and when the officialdom that had opposed the strike saw to it that they were put to death, that was enough for most labor activists to conclude that the execution of a militant minority was an attack on the larger movement.

What made the Haymarket anarchists key leaders of the American movement in the 1880s is the same thing that made them heroes in the decades to come: self-sacrificing devotion to the cause of the working people. So it is only fitting that their martyrdom became one of the unifying myths that gave American workers their collective identity.

Alan DAWLEY

CHICAGO LEHR-UND-WEHR-VEREIN

The Chicago Lehr-und-Wehr-Verein *(Instruction and Protection Society) was one of the largest workers' militias in U.S. history. Chartered by the state of Illinois in 1875, the LWV promised that its members would learn the "laws and political economy, and shall also be instructed in military and gymnastic*

exercises." The police violence during the Great Strike of 1877 in Chicago fueled LWV growth and by 1879 about 500 militia members had joined the organization. The Verein *sought to attract all nationalities and therefore conducted drill in English. Its membership nonetheless remained a largely German immigrant one even after the formation of the similar* Jagerverein, *exclusively for German workers.*

With the issue of police violence so vivid, with arms cheaply available and with traditions of ethnic and neighborhood militias strongly established in Illinois, the LWV might have grown even more substantially. However, in 1878 the Socialistic Labor Party attempted to bar its members from joining the militia. By so doing the SLP somewhat weakened the Verein *and provoked a split in its own ranks. More critically, in 1878-79 the Chicago press reacted to LWV parades with an outpouring of hysterical articles alleging that a communist coup was at hand. In 1879, the Illinois legislature passed a new militia act strengthening the state's official forces and banning any "unauthorized body of men with arms" who "associate themselves together as a military company. . .or drill or parade with arms in any city. . .without license of the Governor." The bill was directed at the LWV and the most important test cases involving the constitutionality of the law centered on the* Verein *members. By 1881, with the decision in* Presser v. Illinois, *the ability of the state to prosecute participants in LWV activities was clearly established.*

In the years leading up to Haymarket the LWV continued to exist, though it is prob-

able that some of its military activities were forced underground. The Verein *exercised great, though not direct, influence on the Haymarket events. Parsons recalled in his autobiography that the militia bill repressing the LWV solidified his growing dissatisfaction with political action. August Spies was a leading* Verein *member and Adolph Fischer went to the gallows wearing a belt-buckle featuring the letters "L.u.W.V." Indeed, the* Lehr-und-Wehr-Verein *might be considered the first attempt, and the IWPA the second, by some Chicago workers to react to police and Pinkerton violence and to develop the potential for self-defense during strikes.*

DR

A group of *Lehr-und-Wehr-Verein* in Chicago

THE CZECH ANARCHISTS IN CHICAGO

In 1879 social-democrats held in Prague a secret meeting which became known in the annals of the party as the St. Margaret's Congress. (St. Margaret was the name of a hall in Prague.) Convoked without a permit, the Congress was dispersed by the police and a number of the leaders arrested and thrown into prison.

Once on the police blacklist, the more prominent of the socialists found existence in Bohemia unendurable. So they removed to other parts of the empire, not a few leaving it altogether. Some went to Budapest; others escaped to Switzerland; still others chose as their future homes great industrial centers in Europe and America: Paris, London, New York, Chicago. . . .

The fact cannot be denied that Johann Most found ardent sympathizers among those Czech social-democrats who were dissatisfied with the orthodox, scholarly socialism of Marx and Lassalle, and who clamored for deeds. Literature and party newspapers prove this irrefutably. The protagonists of revolutionary socialism were, with a few exceptions, workmen, but workmen of the more intelligent and well-paid class—furriers, tailors, machinists, typesetters—who had learned their trade or worked at it in large cities. The earning power of these craftsmen was comparatively high; in intelligence they towered far above the unskilled agricultural and domestic labor from the non-industrial districts of Kutna Hora, Tabor, Pisek. Association with men and women of other races lent these men that air of cosmopolitanism which is the envy of the provincial. . . .

Almost all, if not all, were versed in German. This enabled them to read German-language newspapers, and associate freely with German comrades. Those who had been employed in Paris brought with them to America a smattering of French. The members of the small London colony learned English. . . .

Proselytism by means of the press reached its high-water mark between 1885 and 1890. . . . [Among] the busiest publishers were the Czech groups of the International Workingmen's Union of Chicago (Ceske skupiny Mezinarodni Delnicke Jednoty v Chicagu): Series, *Epistles of Revolution*. . . .

The advent in New York of Norbert Zoula, a silversmith from Prague, is chronicled in 1883. Zoula spent a year and a half in an Austrian prison awaiting trial; after finishing a sentence of ten months, he repaired to Switzerland, from which country he em-

Hynek Djemek

R A I D S !

About 2 o'clock yesterday morning about half a dozen police from the Hinman Street station raided the building in which the Budoucnost *used to be printed, No. 616 Centre Avenue. Three men were captured: Avers Djemek, Bohemian, 30 years old; Hynek Djemek, brother of Avers, aged 25 and a tailor by trade; and Frank Nowak, 29, Bohemian and a locksmith by trade.*

Avers Djemek was connected with the Budoucnost *and was also drillmaster of a company of Bohemian anarchists. The police captured a mold for bombs made of two bricks, half a dozen bottles containing mysterious concoctions, several boxes of cartridges, checkbooks, files of the* Budoucnost, *a large red bag, and two revolvers belonging to Avers. There were also piles of anarchistic books and papers, among the former an* Epistoly Revoluci *by Prince Krapotkine.*

Chicago Tribune
(May 9, 1886)

Frank Nowak

igrated here. After a comparatively short stay in New York, he proceeded to Chicago to edit in that city the *Budoucnost* (Future), "organ of anarchists of the Czecho-Slovak language." His associates in the management of the paper were Joseph Pondelicek, Jacob Mikolanda, Joseph B. Pecka. The vigorous police censorship which followed the Chicago Haymarket outbreak forced this journal, like many other anarchist papers, to suspend. The year the *Budoucnost* sang its swan song, Zoula died in California of tuberculosis. . . .

Joseph Boleslav Pecka, molder by trade, made his appearance in Chicago in 1884. As the recording secretary of St. Margaret's Congress, he brought upon himself in the motherland the anger of the police. For this with thirty other comrades he was put into prison. His "portion" was eighteen months and he served his term in full. Having been active in Vienna as collaborator of the *Delnicke Listy* (Workingman's News), he needed no urging to do his share in the press propaganda of the party in America. He died in Chicago in 1897, in his forty-eighth year. Two years after his death, comrades published his *Sebrane Basne* (Collected Songs). Pecka's style as a journalist was vigorous and clear. The *Collected Songs* (92 pages) are the revolutionary rhapsodies of the downtrodden proletarian.

Jacob Mikolanda, a baker, migrated in 1882 or 1883. He became connected with the Chicago *Budoucnost*, and when this radical paper was forced to the wall, he wrote for the *Pravo Lidu* (People's Rights), a weekly of more moderate tone than the *Budoucnost*. For alleged complicity in the Haymarket affair Mikolanda was sent to the workhouse for six months. His death occurred in Cleveland. . . .

Vaclav Kudlata, said to have been a student of theology in Bohemia, delivered in 1897 a lecture "on the occasion of the tenth anniversary of the death of the Chicago Martyrs," which was that year printed in pamphlet form under the heading *After Ten Years*. Another brochure by Kudlata is entitled *Half-hearted and Whole Liberalism* (1897). Kudlata died in 1917, at Elizabeth, New Jersey.

Thomas CAPEK

from Thomas Capek,
The Czechs (Bohemians) in America
(New York, Houghton Mifflin, 1920)

MAY 5, 1886.

Wisconsin National Guardsmen assembled at the Edward P. Allis Reliance Works in Milwaukee
(photo courtesy of State Historical Society of Wisconsin)

THE POLISH-AMERICAN MARTYRS
of the First May Day

On May First, 1886, about 7,000 workers struck in Milwaukee, most of them building tradesmen, cigar makers, and brewery workers. About 5,000 laborers also joined the walkout, most of them Polish immigrants.[1] But all eyes were turned on Sunday, May 2, since the Milwaukee *Journal* had predicted on April 30: "The eight-hour demonstration on Sunday will be the largest affair of the kind ever held in Milwaukee." It also reported that militia companies, including four companies of infantry, the artillery battery and the Light Horse squadron, had been put on alert, and that the police would be out in full force on that day.[2] If this was intended to frighten the workers of the city, it failed miserably. A great parade on Sunday, May 2, breathed additional life into the eight-hour movement. Sponsored by the General Labor Union, it featured a parade of workers—German, Polish, and native-Americans—through the principal streets of Milwaukee to the Milwaukee Gardens, where a picnic was to be held.

The parade was highlighted by banners in English, German, and Polish, proclaiming:

The workman does not beg, he demands.
Where is the Eight-Hour League? She works for ten hours.
Far better to fight and die than live and be conquered.
The Republic shall have no ruler, not even King Mammon.
Humbug, your name is Robert [Schilling].
Capital is the product of labor, not its master.
Eight Hours! Our password and battle-cry.[3]

On Monday, May 3, according to the Commissioner of Labor and Industrial Statistics, "the agitation took quite a different aspect."[4] Thousands of laborers in the breweries and the building trades went on strike for the eight-hour day without any reduction in wages, and a great crowd marched from factory to factory, shutting down everything in its path and swelling in numbers as it proceeded. "About 1,500 trades union men, mostly Polish," reported the Milwaukee *Jour-*

88

nal, "marched out of the shops of the Milwaukee & St. Paul Railroad and compelled the men to quit work."[5] Having closed the West Milwaukee railroad shop so that the 1,400 men employed there had to quit work, the same group, reinforced by new recruits, proceeded to the Reliance Works of Edward P. Allis & Co. There the crowd was met by a stream of water, but wet as they were, the demonstrators forced the company to close down operations, and the plant was emptied. In closing the plant, Allis charged that

. . .this afternoon a band of Polish laborers marched from the West Milwaukee shops (which they had closed) to my works, and with brandished clubs endeavored to force an entrance. Although the mob of men with clubs marched directly before the eyes of the police at the South Side Station, not a policeman moved to keep them from attack.[6]

Even the Milwaukee *Journal*, when it found time to cease bemoaning the dangers Milwaukee faced from "foreign agitators, especially those from Poland," conceded that there was so much resentment among the members of the Knights of Labor at the Reliance Works because of the intimidatory tactics used by Allis that it did not require much persuasion to get them to quit work and join the eight-hour demonstration, especially since the Polish laborers who headed the crowd were themselves members of the Polish Assembly of the Knight of Labor.[7] Incidentally, when the Milwaukee *Journal* referred to the fact that "about 1,500 trades union men, mostly Polish," had led the march, it meant that they were members of the Polish Assembly of the Knights of Labor in Milwaukee. It acknowledged that this Assembly viewed Powderly's circular denouncing the eight-hour movement with "disgust and anger."[8]

By the end of May 3, 14,000 workers were on strike in Milwaukee, and victory seemed to be in the offing. The master masons and bricklayers granted a 20 percent wage increase and allowed their men to work eight or ten hours, as they preferred; the Filer-Stowell foundry granted eight hours, and Best Brewing both reduced hours to eight and increased wages. No fewer than 5,000 workers had had to quit work as a result of the persuasive tactics of the eight-hour demonstrators, led by Polish members of the Knights of Labor.[9]

On Tuesday, May 4, the marchers assembled in the vicinity of the St. Stanislaus Polish Church, the headquarters of the Knights of Labor's Polish Assembly, and moved out, this time to the North Chicago Rolling Mill in Bay View, shouting as they went, "On to the mills!" "Eight hours!" and "Everybody must strike!" As some 3,000 people, again under the leadership of the Polish laborers, marched up to the rolling mill company, they were confronted by three companies of militia drawn up before the works. One of the companies was the Kosciusko Guards, composed exclusively of middle-class Poles. Speaking for the crowd, a Mr. Bonsell, Master Workman of the Knights of Labor Polish Assembly, urged the managers of the Rolling Mill Company to grant the eight-hour day with full pay. The response came swiftly—no eight-hour day![10]

Meanwhile, news arrived that another procession, led by the Central Labor Union, had shut down foundries and bakeries in the central part of the city. The crowd before the mill surged forward, but even though the soldiers fired volleys in the air, according to the Commissioner of Labor and Industrial Statistics, there was "no violence to the mills."[11]

The climax of the struggle in Milwaukee came early on May 5, on the morning after the bomb had exploded in Chicago's Haymarket Square. Milwaukee's mayor issued a proclamation calling upon all "citizens not to gather in crowds upon the streets or other public places in the city, but as far as possible, to remain in and about their homes and several places of business." He also called upon all owners of factories, mills and shops to request aid from the authorities if they needed it to prevent their production from being interrupted. The Knights of Labor Assembly of Bay View did not criticize the mayor, but offered to "volunteer our services, should occasion arise, to act as special police for the protection of life and property"—but on condition that "the military be immediately withdrawn."[12] Not only was the offer ignored, but the Milwaukee *Journal* advised the Knights of Labor that they could make their best contribution by instantly expelling "the revolutionary Knights of Labor Polish Assembly" and publicly denouncing the "firebrand members" of that Assembly.[13]

Meanwhile, Wisconsin Governor Rusk, who had been warned by Milwaukee employers that "our whole civilization and independence" now hinged on what was likely to happen at the North Chicago Rolling Mill in Bay View, called up additional soldiers and sent them to the mill.[14] Despite threats and intimidation, the crowd gathered once again in the vicinity of the St. Stanislaus Polish Church and made their way to the rolling mill, determined to shut it down. The leaders of the procession assured reporters for the Milwaukee *Journal* "that they had no intention of making an attack on the militia or the company property, and simply wished to show that they had not been intimidated by the presence of the militia."[15] Led by the Polish Knights of Labor, they marched to the mill in orderly fashion. At the head of the procession marched a Polish laborer carrying a red-white-and-blue banner with a clock set at eight-o'clock in the middle. They carried clubs, iron bars, broken scythes, stones, and probably a few guns. According to Wisconsin National Guard General King, Governor Rusk was telephoned and gave the order, "Fire on them!"[16]

As the crowd approached the mill, Major George P. Traeumer, the commander of the militia, gave what even the Milwaukee *Journal* conceded was an "inaudible warning to stop," and then ordered the militia to fire. Two companies discharged a single volley, firing point-blank into the demonstrators. The headlines in the Milwaukee *Journal* blared:

"THEY SHOOT."
NO BLANK CARTRIDGES
BUT SHOTS TO KILL.

The report began: "Lincoln Avenue, the boundary line between the south end of the city and Bay View, was sprinkled with the blood of Polish rioters at 9 o'clock this morning." One of the two companies which had fired, it continued, was the Kosciusko Guards, but it had "killed or injured no one." As the dead and wounded were being carried away, reported the *Journal*, "pieces of the jaw and several teeth of one of the victims were gathered up by bystanders whose conversation showed they were countrymen of the Polish agitator.''[17] Underneath the report came the listing:

THE KILLED.

Michael Ruchakis, a laborer, aged 40, shot through the breast and expired shortly afterward. He resided on Garden Street, near the city limits. He was married, but had no children.

Francis Kunkel, aged 69 years, who lived in a little shanty on South Bay Street, was shot through the heart while feeding the chickens in his yard. He was a laborer, but had not been working for four years, owing to rheumatism. He leaves a widow and five children.

Johann Maszka, a laborer, aged 24 years, was shot through the bowels, the ball going clear through him. He died in great agony at his house, No. 700 Fourth Avenue. He leaves a widow and one child.

Martin Jankowis, a laborer, aged 25 years, was shot through the chest, the ball entering in front and passing out in the rear. Extreme unction was administered to the dying man by Father Lewandski at No. 768 Eighth Avenue.

THE WOUNDED.

Albert Erdmann, aged 19, shot through the abdomen and cannot live. He resides at No. 676 Windlake Avenue.

Casimir Dudek, of Seymour, aged 30, was shot in the left cheek and arm. Half of his lower jaw was carried away by two bullets. He is not expected to live. Father Guizki administered extreme unction on the marsh where the man was shot.

Frank Nowatzak, aged 13 years, a schoolboy; was shot sideways through the upper abdomen by a stray bullet. He lives at No. 485 Maple Street. Cannot live.

Johann Osinski, aged 28 years, lives at No. 700 Grove Street. He was shot in the right shoulder while stooping down behind an embankment. His wound is not serious.

Fred Goldbeck, a section hand on the Milwaukee and St. Paul Railroad, was shot through both thighs with one bullet. He lives at No. 696 Railroad Street. The wound is not dangerous.

Later that same day, the *Journal* added the following to the list:

Unknown man, Polish, apparently a laborer, 22 or 23 years old. Shot through the abdomen. He ran some distance and was found by the roadside, 150 yards from where the line stood when it received the fire of the troops.

Unknown man, about 30 years old, apparently a Polish laborer, shot through the arm.[19]

The following day, the *Journal* announced: ''Two more of the Polish victims of yesterday's battle died today, and three others will probably die before morning.'' Without even a decent pause or a separate paragraph, the newspaper went on: ''From all parts of the State messages have come commending Gov. Rusk for the promptitude with which he acted.''[20]

The final count of victims of the bloody massacre stood at eight Polish laborers and one German laborer dead![21]

''The shooting came so sudden that it simply astonished us,'' a Polish worker who managed to escape told the reporter for the Milwaukee *Journal*, who went on to acknowledge:

All in the Polish community were indignant over what they term the unprovoked murder of their countrymen. Nearly every Pole who would open his mouth said that the matter wouldn't be allowed to rest where it was. The women were even more wild in their threats than the men. Some went from house to house, calling on both sexes to take revenge for the massacre. With the exception of one or two, all of the victims resided in the Fourteenth Ward, which is almost exclusively inhabited by Polish.[22]

The coroner's jury which investigated the massacre not only did not condemn the militia for firing upon an unarmed crowd which had done nothing to provoke the troops (it called it ''an unpleasant duty''), but it praised the officers in command for having ''acted in a humane manner in ordering the firing to cease'' after the first volley! Moreover, the jury indicted not the soldiers and their officers for their cold-blooded murders, but almost fifty workers and their leaders, charging them with ''riot and conspiracy'' or ''riot and unlawful assembly.'' In a number of cases, these men were sentenced to six to nine months' hard labor. Among them were Polish workers such as John Gabrielski, Joseph Wachiechowski, Frank Datura, Joseph Andreszewski, John Kcypczinski and Jacob Datka.[23]

Although angry crowds continued to storm about Milwaukee throughout the afternoon of the massacre, work resumed at most factories the next day on a ten-hour basis. But in the general employers' counter-offensive which followed the events in Chicago and Milwaukee, Polish workers in the latter city bore the brunt of the attacks. On May 9, 1886, the Milwaukee *Journal* reported that ''the Polish laborers employed in the Milwaukee and St. Paul railway shops were being discharged and their places would be filled by men of other nationalities.'' About three hundred Polish laborers had been notified ''that their services would not again be required. The same order has gone into effect on section work, and a section foreman refused to allow about 100 Polish laborers to go to work on the cut in the lower Fourth Ward, where the track is being put through from the new depot to the Prairie du Chien yard.'' Elsewhere, too, it reported, Polish laborers ''will not be re-employed. These are the men who took part in the demonstrations for the eight-hour day.'' The Central Labor Union sadly conceded that it could do little for these workers, since ''never before have employers inquired so anxiously about the political opinions of their employees, and the Polish laborers are all considered to be very radical.''[24]

Perhaps the most outrageous aspect of the post-massacre developments was the action of employers in presenting gifts of cash to the militia companies that had killed the Polish laborers. Even the Milwaukee *Journal* felt that this was going too far, and, in an editorial entitled ''Mistaken Generosity,'' it stated sanctimoniously that the men had only done their duty, adding: ''The sentiment which rewards simple performance of duty with gifts and lavish praise and flummery, belongs to the monarchs, who create favorites that they make slaves. It has no fitting place in the government of a free people.''[25]

Philip S. FONER

1. Wisconsin Bureau of Labor and Industrial Statistics, *Biennial Reports for 1885-1886*, 319. Hereinafter referred to as *Wis. BLS*.   2. Milwaukee *Journal*, April 30, 1886. 3. *Wis. BLS*, 326-27.   4. *Ibid.*, 328.   5. Milwaukee *Journal*, May 3, 1886. 6. *Wis. BLS*, 330.   7. Milwaukee *Journal*, May 3, 1886.   8. *Ibid.*, May 4, 1886. 9. *Ibid.*   10. *Ibid.*, May 5, 1886; *Wis. BLS*, 332.   11. *Wis. BLS*, 332. 12. *Ibid.*, 332-34.   13. Milwaukee *Journal*, May 5, 1886.   14. *Ibid.*   15. *Ibid.* 16. Thomas W. Gavett, *Development of the Labor Movement in Milwaukee*, Madison and Milwaukee, Wiconsin, 1965, 64.   17. Milwaukee *Journal*, May 5, 6, 1886. 18. *Ibid.*, *May 6, 1886.19. Ibid.*   20. *Ibid.*, May 7, 1886.   21. *Wis. BLS*, 340-41. The names listed here are basically the same as those which published in the Milwaukee *Journal*, although the spelling varies somewhat.   22. Milwaukee *Journal*, May 6-7, 1886. 23. *Wis. BLS*, 341-42.   24. Milwaukee *Journal*, May 9, 10, June 7, 1886. 25. *Ibid.*, May 10, 1886.

An engraved memorial to the Haymarket Martyrs, probably antedating the monument at Waldheim

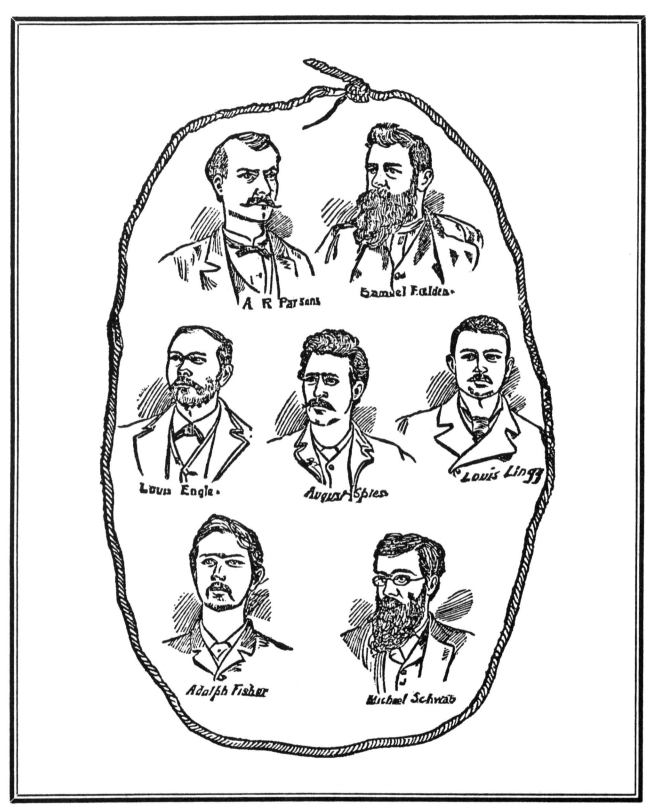

Images of the Chicago anarchists abounded in the popular commercial press. Most of them were crudely drawn, and they often had morbid overtones of the impending executions, as in this full-page illustration from *The Lives, Crime and Conviction of the Eight Chicago Anarchists and Bomb Throwers*, a sensationalistic and anonymous piece of hack-work published by G. S. Baldwin of Chicago just after the trial. The book featured a lurid anti-anarchist cartoon on the cover, drawn by *Daily News* illustrator Art Young—a cartoon Young lived to regret—but the author of the interior illustrations is unknown.

STRANGE LEGACIES:
The Black International & Black America

Legal lynchings. The very term so many have rightly applied to the executions of the Haymarket martyrs ought to remind us that the judicial murders of Parsons, Engel, Spies and Fischer occurred alongside the lynchings and burnings of thousands of Black Americans in post-Civil War America. Just as the terror against Afro-Americans had a class dimension—with for example, rises in Populist activism leading to increases in lynchings[1]—so too did racism have an impact on the fate of the Haymarket prisoners. This article briefly explores the connections between lynchings legal and otherwise and asks why neither Black nor anarchist activists saw their destinies as intertwined.

The ties of race and class surrounding principals in the Haymarket affair were laced early with irony. The first involvement of IWPA leaders Lucy and Albert Parsons in freedom struggles centered on efforts toward the liberation of Black folk in Reconstruction Texas. Albert edited a Radical Republican newspaper there in 1867 and 1868 and took a bullet in the leg for his attempts to register Black voters. Lucy, probably of African, American Indian and Mexican ancestry and likely born a slave, was also a Radical and later remembered witnessing Klan horrors in the Waco area, scene of mass murders and gang rapes of Afro-Americans in the postbellum years.[2] Albert, a Confederate veteran and brother of a rebel general, made an unlikely Radical Republican and husband to an ex-slave.[3] He apparently kept up some friendly contacts with ex-confederates as late as 1880 when he visited Alexander Stephens, who had been vice-president of the Confederacy, and learned that Stephens had come to embrace "communism" and "agrarianism."[4] Lucy, either during her radical youth or after moving to Chicago in 1873, began what was to be her lifelong practice of denying any Black ancestry.[5]

Among those who would defend the men charged with the Haymarket bombing were many whose longstanding commitment to Black freedom would insure that the case would be placed in the context of broader struggles for human freedom, but again there were ironies and ambiguities. Defense lawyer William P. Black was a Union army hero, and the racially egalitarian participants in defense efforts included the author William Dean Howells, the labor editor John Swinton, the freethinker and orator Robert Ingersoll, Lyman Trumbull, Lincoln's former law partner, and John Brown Jr., who recalled that his celebrated father was a communist as well as a fighter against slavery.* Dyer D. Lum, the first post-

Haymarket editor of *The Alarm*, was a descendant of the Tappan family of antebellum abolitionist crusaders.[6] On the other hand, the Grinnell family, with its illustrious abolitionist past, furnished the prosecutor during the trials; nor did the anti-slavery roots of Terence Powderly keep the Knights of Labor leader from endorsing the class-based brutality which followed Haymarket.[7]

If an antislavery heritage proved compatible with both prosecution and defense of those accused of the Haymarket bombing, racist ideas unambiguously hurt the anarchists' cause. The press, noting that most of the defendants were immigrants, branded them as "the offscourings of Europe," as "foreign savages" and as "the lowest stratum found in humanity's formation."[8] The widely popularized works of the Italian criminologist Cesare Lombroso took these characterizations a step further by fleshing out an *hereditary anarchist type*, marked by a deformed head, discolored skin, facial asymmetry, large sinuses and more.[9]

Hermann Raster, the editor of the *Illinois Staats Zeitung* and himself an immigrant, rejected the identification of the defendants with "foreign stock" but still proposed to treat anarchists as a type which could be placed within the framework of American racism. Writing to Illinois Governor Richard Oglesby to urge that the defendants be hanged as

This cartoon appeared in the New York *Daily Graphic* a week before the Haymarket hangings. Among much else, it illustrates the conflation of racist and anti-anarchist imagery in the popular press.

---

* The Haymarket martyrs frequently compared themselves to John Brown, as did commentators on their trial and executions. A jailer, observing a calm Adolph Fischer before his hanging noted, "He will die a second John Brown," while *Liberty* asked, "The labor movement has had its Harpers' Ferry; when will come the emancipation proclamation?" Samuel Fielden, looking back on the case in 1902, issued a caveat: "Neither was the case of John Brown a parallel case. John Brown broke the laws of Virginia, to his honor be it said. Our martyrs broke no law." See Henry David, *The History of the Haymarket Affair* (New York, 1963), 386 and 393; Lucy Parsons, ed. *The Life of Albert R. Parsons* (Chicago, 1903), xxxvi; *Free Society* (November 9, 1901).

Frederick Douglass

scheduled, Raster argued, "General Sheridan is credited with the remark 'Good Indians? pshaw! There is no *good* Indian but dead ones.' Say anarchists in place of Indians and I subscribe to the sentiments with both hands."[10]

Lucy's race was an issue during the time of the trial and the *Waco Daily Press* headline before Albert's execution read: "BEAST PARSONS. His Sneaking Snarl From Some Moral Morass in Which He Hides. Miscegenationist, Murderer, Moral Outlaw, For whom the Gallows Wait."[11]

Chicago press accounts portrayed Lucy as an animal and the Parsons' children as "anarchist sucklings." Hate mail to Lucy ranted, "Your parentage was engendered in the jungle along with the hyena."[12] In Lucy's case racism directly applied and, in the cases of all the Haymarket defendants, the biologistic assumptions and acceptance of brutality characteristic of late nineteenth-century race-hatred conditioned the treatment accorded to the anarchists.

Nonetheless, only in response to the most outrageous acts of racist terror did the IWPA hesitantly and inadequately address the issue of Black freedom. Lucy Parsons' "The Negro. Let Him Leave Politics to the Politican and Prayers to the Preacher" was the fuller of only two pre-Haymarket *Alarm* articles on the issue. In it, Lucy reacted to a series of lynchings which took the lives of thirteen Blacks in the Carrollton, Mississippi area. Writing a month before Haymarket, she advised Afro-Americans, "You are not absolutely defenseless. For the torch of the incendiary, which has been known to show murderers and tyrants the danger line, beyond which they may not venture with impunity cannot be wrested from you." At the time Lucy had little sense of racial oppression,

however. She absolutely denied that "outrages" were "heaped upon the Negro because he is black." "Not at all," she wrote. "It is because he is poor. It is because he is dependent."[13]

Albert, meanwhile, wrote frequently on the comparison between chattel and wage slavery, but without attention to the role of racism. His words sometimes suggested a hatred of Black slavery, as in an 1884 riposte against Jefferson Davis' contention that Africans' benefitted from being enslaved to Southern Christians: "How thankful the slave must have been to be rescued from a barbarian master and sold to a Christian one." However, Parsons generally accepted Davis' contention that wage slavery was a more efficient way to exploit Black workers than chattel slavery, and saw no special problems for Black workers arising from the heritage of slavery.[14]

In 1892, under Lucy's editorship, *Freedom* would return to the race issue during the period of the greatest wave of lynchings in U.S. history, with protests which allowed that racism and the heritage of slavery were central to anti-Black violence. But, remarkably, the staunchest advocates of revolutionary self-defense in late nineteenth century America had little to say with regard to defense of Black Americans, lynched during these years throughout the South and in Illinois as well.[15]

And, despite interest in self-defense among Black activists, anarchism had little impact among Afro-Americans. The postitions taken by T. Thomas Fortune, "the most noted man" in Afro-American journalism at the time are suggestive of the gulf between even a militant, pro-labor Black editor and the anarchists.[16] Fortune, editor of the *New York Freeman* had since 1884 developed an increasingly apt critique of racial and class relations in the U.S. and the world. He

Frank Ferrell and Terence V. Powderly

94

used ideas from Marx and from Henry George to argue for Black-white labor unity and was an enthusiastic supporter of the Knights of Labor even as he lambasted racism within that organization. Fortune also advocated Black self-defense, sometimes in language not less explosive than that of Lucy Parsons. Writing in the *A.M.E. Church Review* in January, 1886, he began with a discussion of the "essential element in which the Afro-American character was most deficient . . .the *dynamite element*"—a trait which "resists an injury promptly." On another occasion he offered a stategy for ending Southern terror against Blacks: "The only way to stop it is for colored men to retaliate by the use of the torch and dagger."[17] When the May 1, 1886 strikes began, Fortune wrote of them as part of a long conflict inspired by "the capitalist, landowner and hereditary aristocrat against the larger masses of society. . .the disinherited proletariat of the world."[18]

Nonetheless, in the wake of Haymarket, Fortune did not comment on the arrests in Chicago, editorializing instead on behalf of tax-reform as a solution to the "pernicious aggregation of capital in the hands of a limited number of men," and castigating strikes for higher wages and shorter hours as "absurd."[19] Four months later he would reprint a significant editorial from the *Detroit Plaindealer*, a Black weekly:

In the North men are condemned to suffer the extreme penalty of the law for urging men on by anarchistic utterances to the destruction of life and property. In the South they murder and outrage a people and yet go escaped of justice.[20]

Fortune added that "the Anarchists are hunted down and punished by the officers of the State," who ignore outrages in the South.[20] Elsewhere in the *Freeman*, the Chicago correspondent praised the "great verdict" handed down against the Haymarket defendants.[21]

The Black press was not alone in making the parallel between the anarchists and lynchers rather than between the anarchists and those threatened by and resisting lynchings. Adolf Hepner's lukewarm 1888 defense of the IWPAers still jailed, written on behalf of the Socialistic Labor Party, took a similar tack but with monumental racial insensitivity. Referring to lynching as, in theory at least, a kind of "people's justice," Hepner held that ". . .if lynching shall go unpunished it would seem that the Haymarket affair at the 4th of May should not be an object of complaint." He added, in an interesting aside, "I regret that the *influence which the American usage of lynching had in the culture of anarchist tactics* was not once considered. . .and presented as an extenuation."[22]

So long as it did not aggressively champion the anti-racist principles briefly articulated in its 1883 Pittsburgh Manifesto, the IWPA had little hope of making a case for Blacks to group the IWPA with the opponents and victims of lynching rather than with the advocates of the kind of mob law which so often victimized Afro-Americans. Indeed, in all likelihood no amount of propaganda would have done the trick. Even on the Left, as Hepner's statements illustrate, there were few whose sense of racial egalitarianism would have made Blacks trust in the results of "[white] people's justice" undertaken through direct action. Throughout the late nineteenth century Blacks and Chinese were far more often the victims of

T. Thomas Fortune

such direct action than were capitalists. Moreover, an odd anarchist like Dyer D. Lum could write—not publicly but in an 1893 letter to Voltairine de Cleyre*—that he would have joined in burning a Black Southerner at the stake:

I would have carried the wood myself if I had been there. 'Awful'!!!!!!! Yes, and so was the offense, of which every week some similar proceeding at the hands of niggers—to shoot him would only have made a county sensation. Burning him made the flesh of every nigger brute in the South to creep.[24]

It was one thing to trust in the judgment of Lucy Parsons in undertaking direct action and choosing a target, and quite another to trust in Dyer Lum's or that of countless other white Americans. Through the early twentieth century, anarchism and lynch law were to be equated, by Teddy Roosevelt, among others, and anarchists seldom found a wholly effective response.[25]

When reports of Black anarchist activity in Boston surfaced in 1892, Frederick Douglass argued, "If the Southern outrages on the Colored race continue the Negro will become a chemist." But he could not envision Black-anarchist

* It might be mentioned that, when he wrote this letter, Lum had for some time, and for many reasons, been estranged from most of his former anarchist associates, and Lucy Parsons in particular. Employed as Samuel Gompers' personal secretary, he had renounced communism and declared himself for "individualism"; he was also addicted to morphine. A few weeks after writing this letter, he died in his bed in a hotel near the Bowery in New York. See Carolyn Ashbaugh, *Lucy Parsons: American Revolutionary* (Chicago, 1976), 187; Voltairine de Cleyre, "Dyer D. Lum," in Dyer D. Lum, *In Memoriam: Chicago, November 11, 1887* (Berkeley Heights, 1937).

cooperation, only that "Anarchists have not a monopoly on bomb-making, and the Negro will learn." Similarly, the *Boston Republican*'s sympathetic editorial treating the use of "dynamite, the dagger or the bomb," by fellow Blacks who were deprived of other recourse, added, "We do not encourage dynamiters and bomb-throwers where no cause exists for indulging in such a warfare, as is the case of the Chicago anarchists a few years ago."[25] Besieged by foes on all sides, it is perhaps understandable that a Lucy Parsons would not choose to add her Black heritage to the list of reasons she was despised or that a T. Thomas Fortune would not add defense of the Haymarket defendants to his formidable task. The history of Haymarket and Black America was one of close connections, never made.

Dave ROEDIGER

1. James M. Inverarity, "Populism and Lynching in Louisiana, 1889-1896," *American Sociological Review*, (April, 1976), esp. 264-69. See also Norrece Jones, "Lynching as a Form of Economic Repression," *Pan-Africanist*, 9 (January, 1982), 32-44. 2. Carolyn Ashbaugh, *Lucy Parsons: American Revolutionary* (Chicago, 1976), 13-15, 64-66, 86, 99-100, 267-68, 274. 3. Paul Avrich, *The Haymarket Tragedy* (Princeton, 1984), 6-19; 42-43. 4. Lucy E. Parsons, ed. *Life of Albert R. Parsons* (Chicago, 1903), 65-67. 5. Ashbaugh, 267-68. 6. Henry David, *The History of the Haymarket Affair* (New York, 1963), 360-61; Sender Garlin, *John Swinton: American Radical* (New York, 1976), 3; Avrich, 250-51, 281-82, 425, 429-30; Louis Ruchames, ed. "John Brown, Jr. and the Haymarket Martyrs," *Massachusetts Review*, 5 (Summer, 1964), 765-8; Moncure Daniel Conway, *Autobiography*, 2v. (Boston and New York, 1904), 1: 308-09; "Dyer D. Lum to Mr. dear Labadie" (February 6, 1889), Labadie Collection, University of Michigan Labrary—Ann Arbor. 7. Ashbaugh, 91-94, 117-25 and 272, n. 11. 8. Quoted in Avrich, 219. 9. Samuel Yellen, *American Labor Struggles* (New York 1936), 68-9. 10. "Herman Raster to Richard James Oglesby" (November 7, 1887). Oglesby Papers, Illinois State Historical Library in Springfield. Emphasis original. 11. Ashbaugh, 99-100 and, for the headline, 86. 12. "'Rattler' to Mrs. Lucy Parsons" (January 28, 1889), typescript in Carolyn Ashbaugh Papers, Charles H. Kerr Company Archives, the Newberry Library, Chicago; Ashbaugh, 60. 13. *The Alarm* (April 3, 1886), emphasis in original; Philip S. Foner *American Socialism and Black Americans* (Westport, 1977), 79-80. 14. Parsons, ed. *Life of Parsons*, xiii,16; *The Alarm* (October 11, 1884). 15. Foner, *Black Americans and American Socialism*, 78-82; Jones, "Lynching," *passim*; Hepner, *Immoral and Unconstitutional: Our Accessoryship Laws* (New York, 1888), 18; Parsons, ed. *Life of Parsons*, 66 and 138. 16. Emma Thornbrough, *T. Thomas Fortune: Militant Journalist* (Chicago, 1972), 95; Jean M. Allman and David R. Roediger, "The Early Editorial Career of Timothy Thomas Fortune", *Afro-Americans in New York Life and History*, 6 (July, 1982), 39-52; Philip S. Foner, *Organized Labor and the Black Worker, 1619-1973* (New York, 1974), 51-52. 17. Fortune, "Civil Rights and Social Privileges", *AME Church Review*, 2 (January, 1886), esp 119; *New York Freeman* (December 6, 1884 and July 4, 1885). 18. *New York Freeman* (May 1, June 19 and December 4, 1886); Allman and Roediger, "Fortune," 49-50. 19. *New York Freeman* (May 8, 1886). 20. *New York Freeman* (September 11, 1886). 21. *New York Freeman* (August 28, 1886). 22. Hepner, *Immoral and Unconstitutional*, 18, emphasis in original. 23. David, 96. 24. As cited in Ashbaugh, 187. On leftwing racism generally, see Foner, *Black Americans and American Socialism*, *passim*. 25. Foner, *Black Americans and American Socialism*, 80ff.

This fine engraving of Albert Parsons, based on Art Young's sketch originally published in the Chicago *Daily News*, was included by Lucy Parsons in her biography, *The Life of Albert R. Parsons* (Chicago, 1889)

FROM
CONFEDERATE
TO
RADICAL

In 1868 I founded and edited a weekly newspaper in Waco, named the *Spectator*. In it I advocated, with General Longstreet, the acceptance, in good faith, of the terms of surrender, and supported the thirteenth, fourteenth, and fifteenth constitutional amendments and the reconstruction measures securing the political rights of the colored people. (I was strongly influenced in taking this step out of respect and love for the memory of dear old "Aunt Easter," then dead, and formerly a slave and house-servant of my brother's family, she having been my constant associate and practically raised me, with great kindness and a mother's love.) I became a Republican, and, of course, had to go into politics. I incurred thereby the hate and contumely of many of my former army comrades, neighbors, and the Ku Klux Klan. My political career was full of excitement and danger. I took the stump to vindicate my convictions. The lately enfranchised slaves over a large section of country came to know and idolize me as their friend and defender, while on the other hand I was regarded as a political heretic and traitor by many of my former associates.

Albert PARSONS

from Lucy E. Parsons,
Life of Albert R. Parsons
(Chicago, 1889).

WOMEN IN THE HAYMARKET EVENTS

A remarkable group of people led the Chicago workers' movement of the 1880s. Perhaps most astonishing is that these people accorded men and women equality, and women filled prominent positions of leadership, during an era in which women were generally viewed as culturally and biologically inferior to men. In a country which has failed to adopt the Equal Rights Amendment in the 1980s, the International Working People's Association a century ago — in 1883 — directed two of its six major points to equality between the sexes: "*Fourth*—organization of education on a secular, scientific and equal basis for both sexes. *Fifth*—Equal rights for all without distinction to sex or race."

The women within the IWPA lived up to these expectations of equality. Lucy Parsons and Lizzie Holmes stand out as leaders in the International Working People's Association in Chicago prior to the Haymarket police riot. These two women frequently contributed to radical publications and worked to organize the sewing-women for the eight-hour day in 1886. Lizzie Holmes was the assistant editor of the *Alarm*, of which Albert Parsons was editor. Lucy Parsons and Lizzie Holmes led the march on the new Chicago Board of Trade (better known to them as the Board of Thieves) on April 28, 1885. Lucy Parsons was well known as a forceful and articulate speaker as well as writer. A third female comrade, Sarah E. Ames, would play an important role in Haymarket events and would become head of Women's Knights of Labor Assembly 1789. That these leaders were female may have contributed to the authorities' decision not to include them in the indictments and frameups following Haymarket. But their sex did not prevent them from playing crucial roles in the anarchist movement. Nor did it exempt them from other forms of police brutality and harassment.

The movement was a "family affair," with picnics and socials arranged for all, including small children. The political beliefs of the activists were woven into the fabric of their lives and the lives of their families. The Schnaubelt family, including Maria Schnaubelt Schwab,

her sister Ida and perhaps their mother Rebecca, were activists. Lizzie Holmes' mother Hannah J. Hunt and her sister Lillie D. White both wrote for the radical paper *Lucifer*, published in Kansas by Moses Harman. Lizzie and her sister led an organizing effort in the sewing shop where they worked.

On the evening of May 4, 1886, Lucy Parsons and Lizzie Holmes were planning strategy for the sewing women's organizing drive, when an individual arrived at their meeting at the *Alarm* office to request Albert Parsons' presence as a speaker at Haymarket Square. They adjourned their meeting, and the three

adults with Lucy and Albert's two small children proceeded to Haymarket Square.

The five of them were in Zepf's Hall when the bomb was thrown and the police opened fire on the crowd. Knowing that something dreadful had occurred, Lizzie urged Albert to leave the city that night and to assess the situation and safety of his return at a distance. Lucy went home with the children, while Lizzie accompanied Albert to the train station and bought his ticket. Albert went to Geneva, Illinois to William and Lizzie Holmes' house, and Lizzie returned to the Parsons'

Lucy E. Parsons

Lizzie Swank Holmes

Maria Schwab visiting her husband

Gretchen Spies

apartment in the city to spend the night with Lucy.

The next morning, Lucy Parsons and Lizzie Holmes hurried to the *Alarm* and *Arbeiter-Zeitung* offices, determined that the next issue of *The Alarm* should come out denouncing the latest police atrocity. The police raided the newspaper office at least three times that morning, and by noon, August Spies, Michael Schwab, Adolph Fischer, Gerhard Lizius, Oscar Neebe, Chris Spies, Lucy Parsons, Lizzie Holmes, and Maria Schwab had all been arrested at the office. The police released Lucy, hoping she would lead them to Albert; they arrested her two more times that day. Sarah Ames was arrested that evening with Lucy, but they were released. Lucy immediately sent out circulars to all IWPA sections, informing them that the *Alarm* and *Arbeiter-Zeitung* had been suppressed, that many comrades were in jail, and that money was desperately needed.

The authorities held Lizzie Holmes in jail until her arraignment on May 6, when her brother paid the $500 bail. Lizzie retained a woman attorney from Milwaukee, Kate Kane. Lucy Parsons took charge of the situation for the radicals at the arraignment of Lizzie Holmes and Adolph Fischer. The charges against Lizzie Holmes were eventually dropped.

Meanwhile, in Geneva, Illinois, William Holmes and Albert Parsons read the news from Chicago. William dissuaded Albert from returning to Chicago immediately. Albert believed that in all likelihood Lucy had already sacrificed her life for the cause. He expected to fight on the barricades at any moment. Eventually, however, he was persuaded to leave the state and seek a more secure refuge. With Lizzie Holmes in jail, it was only a matter of time before Holmes' residence would be searched.

Albert Parsons communicated with Lucy through William Holmes from his hiding place in Wisconsin and asked her to consult with the defense attorneys as to their opinion about whether he should return. Lucy met twice with the attorneys to discuss Albert's offer to return. William P. Black, chief counsel, was enthusiastic. He was certain Parsons' appearance would help the case and would be a dramatic statement of

Parsons' innocence. Black was confident that an acquittal would be obtained; he vastly underestimated the powers arrayed against Parsons. Lucy communicated with Albert to come, and his return was set for June 21, 1886, the opening day of the trial. Albert went to Sarah Ames' house when he arrived in Chicago, where Lucy joined him for a few hours before they went to court for his surrender.

Lucy Parsons, Lizzie Holmes, Sarah Ames and family members of the other defendants attended the trial daily. Among the many women who attended the trial was young Nina Van Zandt, a recent Vassar graduate. Though she perhaps attended out of curiosity at first, she came to have great respect and empathy for the men on trial and for their idealism.

Lucy Parsons' article ''To Tramps'' was introduced by the prosecution as evidence against the defendants. Lizzie Holmes took the witness stand to defend her own article ''Notice To Tramps'' which appeared in *The Alarm* April 26, 1886, and to state what happened the night of May 4, 1886. Captain Schaack threatened to arrest the two most notorious women, Lizzie Holmes and Lucy Parsons. Their dedicated work did not go unnoticed by the police.

On August 20, the jury returned a guilty verdict against all eight men. Seven were sentenced to death and the eighth, Oscar Neebe, to 15 years in prison. The women heard the verdict. Maria Schwab fainted into Lucy Parsons' and Sarah Ames' arms. Christine Spies, August Spies' mother, and his sister Gretchen comforted each other. Kate Kane, the lawyer from Milwaukee, was with the defendants' families.

Following the condemned men's speeches in court on October 7-9, 1886, execution was set for December 3, 1886. Lucy Parsons left immediately on a tour of the east to bring the message of her and her comrades' movement to the people and to raise money for the appeals. She reached an estimated 200,000 persons in 16 states. In Chicago, other women carried on the work. Sixteen-year-old Mary Engel, George Engel's daughter, was especially active in promoting the radical cause.

Public opinion began to shift in favor of the condemned men, and Lucy Parsons' speaking efforts were no small part of that change. She pleaded the innocence of her comrades to the murder charge, yet defended their revolutionary goals in uncompromising terms. She parodied the capitalist press when she spoke in New Haven. "You may have expected me to belch forth great flames of dynamite and stand before you with bombs in my hands. If you are disappointed, you have only the capitalist press to thank for it." She was encouraged by the Yale students who braved a heavy rainstorm to attend her talk, and who remained to ask questions after the lecture.

Audiences were impressed by Lucy's intellect, her sincerity and her low musical voice which commanded attention. Her tall dark figure, her black dress, her piercing black eyes and her eloquence left a lasting impression on her listeners, many of whom wrote letters on her comrades' behalf and contributed money and time to the defense.

On Thanksgiving Day, the Chief Justice of the Illinois Supreme Court granted a stay of execution. Back in Chicago, Lucy Parsons spoke at a gala socialist celebration. The radicals had reason to celebrate; they believed their comrades had hope. After Thanksgiving, Lucy traveled to St. Louis, Kansas City and Omaha. In March she went east again and was jailed in Columbus, Ohio, when she attempted to speak. Her arrest made national headlines. A woman supporter, Mrs. Lyndall, was the only visitor permitted to see her; she brought Lucy her meals, thereby sparing her from the jail menu of bread and water and salt.

As avenues of recourse for the prisoners were exhausted, Lucy and Albert Parsons remained adamant that there would be no appeal for mercy. After the Illinois Supreme Court denied the appeal for a new trial in September, 1887, the executions were set for November 11, 1887. The last resort was a campaign of appeals to the governor. For over a year Lucy had said she could not accept a justice which spared her husband and killed her other comrades; Lucy and Albert refused to join in the appeals for clemency.

Lucy did, however, continue her appeal to the people on the streets of Chicago. She sold copies of General Matthew M. Trumball's *Was It A Fair Trial?* for a nickel each. She distributed copies of Albert Parsons' tract, *An Appeal to the People of America*.

Meanwhile, other women were active in laying the case before the governor. On November 9, 1887, two days before the scheduled executions, Maria Schwab, Johanna Fischer, Christine Spies, Gretchen Spies, Mary Engel, Elise Friedel (Louis Lingg's friend), and Hortensia Black, wife of chief counsel for defense, William P. Black, were among the women closely associated with the case who made the trip to Springfield to beseech the governor for clemency for the men. The Amnesty Association was represented in Springfield by a man and a woman—its president, Lucien S. Oliver and the spiritualist/reformer, Cora L. V. Richmond.

Letters in support of the condemned men came from outstanding women from around the world: from Eleanor Marx, who had visited the prisoners; from South African novelist Olive Schreiner; from Annie Besant of the National Secular Society in England; from Charlotte Wilson of the Freedom Group in England, associated with Peter Kropotkin; and from Dr. Mary Herma Aiken of Grinnell, Iowa, who organized a small section of the International Working People's Association there.

Governor Oglesby commuted the sentences of Schwab and Fielden to life imprisonment; he let stand the death sentences of August Spies, Albert Parsons, Adolph Fischer, George Engel and Louis Lingg. Lucy Parsons and Lizzie and William Holmes went to the jail on the evening of November 10, after the governor had announced his decision, for a final visit with Albert. They were not admitted, but a deputy sheriff told Lucy she could see Albert at 8:30 am the following morning.

November 11, 1887, dawned icy and blustery in Chicago. Lucy, Lizzie and the two children went to the jail. Instead of allowing them to see Albert, the police played games with them, sending them from one corner of the block to the next, promising that someone at the next corner could authorize their entrance. The children were turning blue with cold, shivering and crying. Finally, the police refused Lucy's last request that the children alone be permitted to see their father. In desperation, she attempted to cross the police line. The

Mary Engel

Sarah Ames

Elise Friedel

99

Visiting hours at Cook County Jail:
Albert and Lucy E. Parsons
with their daughter Lulu Eda

four were arrested and taken to the Chicago Avenue station where they were all stripped and searched for bombs. They were held in cells while the men were executed. Just after noon the matron came to tell them, "It's all over." Lizzie could not see Lucy, but could hear "her low, despairing moans." Friends who came to try to see them were turned away; William Holmes was threatened with arrest if he lingered in the vicinity. At 3 pm, the women and children were finally released. Nina Van Zandt Spies and her mother had also been rudely turned away by the police that day when they attempted to visit August Spies for the last time.

Lucy broke down completely when Albert's body was brought home to her apartment. The women who had been with her through the eighteen-month ordeal were with her to offer what little comfort they could. Sarah Ames and Lizzie Holmes stayed with her through the day. Mrs. Fielden held and comforted Albert Jr. and Lulu. Scenes of grief were taking place at the homes of August Spies, Adolph Fischer and George Engel.

There was one last thing Lucy wanted to do for Albert. She got the embroidered red flag which she had carried at the Board of Trade demonstration, carefully folded and braided it, and fastened it lovingly across his body. The mayor had decreed that no red flags would fly in the wind in this funeral procession, but Lucy determined that this red flag would be in the procession and would be with Albert in his grave.

In the first carriage behind Albert's coffin were Lucy Parsons, Lizzie Holmes, Sarah Ames, and Mrs. Fielden. An estimated 125,000 people solemnly lined the streets of Chicago in quiet tribute to the men who had died.

In these last awful months, Lucy Parsons, with the help of Lizzie and William Holmes, worked to publish *Anarchism: Its Philosophy and Scientific*

Children selling literature
at an anarchist picnic

Nina Van Zandt Spies

Basis by Albert R. Parsons, which appeared in December, 1887. The printer delivered 300 copies before the rest were confiscated by the police.

Women were dedicated and successful organizers for the International Working People's Association and the Knights of Labor before Haymarket. They contributed tremendously to the campaign for justice for their comrades and to keeping the Haymarket case and the social injustices of the age before the public long after the executions.

Carolyn ASHBAUGH

Lucy Parsons trying to make her way through the crowd outside Cook County Jail
to see her husband Albert on the morning of the execution
Chicago *Herald*, November 12, 1887

ANARCHISTS & THE WILD WEST

Eight of the Chicago anarchists were found guilty of murder August 20, seven to be hanged, and one imprisoned for life. The hostile Apaches, including Geronimo, surrendered to General Miles September 4, on Skeleton Canyon, about sixty-five miles southeast of Fort Bowie, Arizona.
—Harper's New Monthly Magazine
(November 1886)

The 1880s, which saw the emergence of a vital workingclass anarchist movement in America's eastern and midwestern urban centers, also witnessed the triumph of "Law'n'Order" in the Far West. Mere coincidence of chronology, as headlines of the decade announced the deaths of such already-legendary gunmen as Billy the Kid, Johnny Ringo, Jesse James and Doc Holliday—this last died in his bed just three days before the Chicago Martyrs went to the gallows—made it all the easier for the advance-guard of yellow journalism, the proprietors of wax museums and other sensation-mongering upholders of official middle-class morality to dishonestly lump together anarchists and outlaws in an amorphous amalgam of "bad guys."

More than a year before Haymarket, Prof. Richard T. Ely, distinguished head of the Department of Political Economy at Johns Hopkins University, had set the tone for this type of malicious misrepresentation in his article, "Recent American Socialism":

If it were known that one thousand men, like the notorious train robbers, the James' boys, were in small groups scattered over the United States, would not every conservative and peace-loving householder be filled with alarm, and reasonably so? Yet here [he is discussing anarchists and the IWPA] we have more than ten times that number educated to think robbery, arson, and murder justifiable, nay, even righteous. . . .

The paragraph containing these lines was reprinted "without the change of a word" in Ely's influential study, *The Labor Movement in the United States* (1886). The book adds a footnote suggesting that "there has already been a partial realization of the fears" expressed in the article, and referring specifically to the "Chicago massacre."

Geronimo:
Another "Enemy of the State" in Haymarket Days

During the Haymarket trial, the prosecution helped promote the same confusion, as when Assistant State's Attorney Walker spoke of Adolph Fischer "traveling in the streets of Chicago with an armament [a knife] worse than any Western outlaw."

In truth, the anarchists, who were striving to build a new society free of exploitation and autocracy, had as little in common with the West's homicidal maniacs and quick-on-the-draw card-sharps as they had with politicians and police. Sensationalist focus on "outlaws," moreover, served to deflect attention from the frontier's own labor radicals, many of whom were in touch with the Chicago anarchists. In 1885 a Christian missionary was quoted as saying that "You can hardly find a group of ranch-men or miners from Colorado to the Pacific who will not have on their tongue's end. . .the infidel ribaldry of Robert Ingersoll [and] the socialistic theories of Karl Marx."[1] The real-life cowboy radical was never allowed to enter popular mythology, but the purely fictional anarchist-as-western-desperado stuck around for quite a while. As late as 1904, at the St. Louis Exposition, portraits of the Haymarket Eight were included in a "gallery of notorious criminals," along with "highwaymen, murderers, robbers" and other assorted cutthroats and crooks.[2]

The decade 1880-1890 also saw another and far more resounding phase of the "taming of the West'—the definitive military "pacification" (which generally meant extermination) of the Native American population. Between the surrender of Sitting Bull in 1883 and the massacre at Wounded Knee seven years later occurred the last great Indian uprising: the valiant campaign of the Chiricahua Apaches in the Southwest, led by Geronimo. For eighteen months in 1885-86, thirty-five Apache men and eight boys, with 101 women and children to care for, outfought and outwitted 5000 U.S. army troops and countless armed civilians. For most of 1886, Apaches and anarchists were almost equivalent bugaboos in American newspapers and pictorial weeklies. Many an editor and not a few cartoonists and wits alluded to outbreaks of "savagery" in Arizona and Chicago.

If the anarchists had little or no interest in western hoodlums, they tended to be passionately sympathetic to the Indians, as the editorial below, from *The Alarm*, amply testifies. Though unsigned, it was probably written by the editor-in-chief, Albert R. Parsons, and in any case can be taken as representative of his views. Its hostility to the government and its solidarity with the native peoples contrast vividly with the racist/chauvinist policies of most American newspapers then and now. Such radical views, however, were in line with long-established tradition in the U.S. workers' movement. As far back as Andrew Jackson's notorious "Indian Removal" horror of the 1830s, the best-known spokesperson for American labor, George Henry Evans, editor of the movement's most influential paper, *The Working Man's Advocate*, affirmed that the states had "no more right to jurisdiction over the territory of the Cherokees than we have to be King of France."[3] Nearly fifty years later Wendell Phillips, the celebrated abolitionist who, after 1865, gave his energies to the cause of radical labor (Karl Marx proudly claimed him as a member of the First International), devoted one of his last pamphlets to denouncing "the system of injustice, oppression and robbery which the Government calls its 'Indian policy.'"[4]

Albert Parsons referred to America's genocidal war against Indians in a sketch of the history of American capitalism in his posthumously published *Anarchism: Its Philosophy and Scientific*

Basis (Chicago, 1887). Other Chicago anarchists were also interested in the "Indian Question." Lucy Parsons, herself of Native American descent, took up the subject in her lectures. Adolph Fischer, in a brief autobiography published in the weekly *Knights of Labor* in Chicago, turned an anecdote about the Oglala Sioux chief Red Cloud into a parable of capitalist exploitation. Most interesting of all, August Spies actually lived for several months with the Chippewas in Canada.[5]

Significantly, Spies in his *Autobiography* cited, as one of three works that influenced him most, Lewis Henry Morgan's *Ancient Society* (1877), a pioneering and revolutionary anthropological study largely concerned with the Iroquois and other native peoples. Widely hailed a generation later as one of America's greatest contributions to socialist thought, this book was not well known in the 1880s.

Doubtless Spies, like such European radicals as Marx, Engels and Kropotkin, admired Morgan's discussions of the primal peoples' non-governmental (that is, anarchist) and communist societies. Morgan's conclusion, that future society would entail "a revival, in a higher plane, of the liberty, equality and fraternity" enjoyed by "primitive" peoples, became a cornerstone of communist theory. Perhaps it also sheds some light on the Chicago anarchists' solidarity with their Native American allies in the long and bitter struggle against Capitalism and the State.

F.R.

1. Rev. E. P. Goodwin, cited in David Brion Davis, *The Fear of Conspiracy* (Ithaca, 1971), 175. 2. Henry David. *The History of the Haymarket Affair* (New York, 1958), 529. 3. New York *Sentinel*, March 19, 1832. 4. Quoted in Robert Winston Mardock, *The Reformers and the American Indian* (Columbia, Mo., 1971), 179. 5. Paul Avrich. *The Haymarket Tragedy* (Princeton, 1984), 121.

THE INDIANS:
An Editorial from Albert Parsons' *Alarm*

Hiram Price, commissioner of Indian affairs, has made his annual report to the secretary of the interior. The commissioner says that more Indians are living in houses and fewer in teepees than a year ago; more are cultivating the soil and fewer following the chase, and there are more in the mechanical shops, and several hundred and more Indian children in the schools. In the near future it is fair to presume that the Indian will be able to care for himself, and be no longer a burden on the government.

With regard to the cost of the Indian service, the commissioner says:

The Indians actually get, of the money appropriated to feed and clothe them, only about seven dollars per annum per capita, or a fraction less than two cents a day for each Indian. The appropriation is too small, if it is expected to transform the Indians into peaceable, industrious and self-supporting citizens in any reasonable time. Among the items for which more liberal appropriations should be made is for pay of police, pay of additional farmers, and pay of the officers who compose the courts of Indian offenses. More liberality in paying Indian agents, and assisting such Indians as show a disposition to help themselves, would be true economy.

The commissioner says the needs of the Indians require that the Indian appropriation bill be passed early in the Congress session. The misfortunes of the Piegan, Blackfeet and other Indians, he says, are due to the disappearance of game, and their inability to support themselves for the present by agriculture. They will have to depend almost wholly on the government for food for several years. These Indians, with proper assistance, will in a few years own teams and have land under cultivation, which, with a few cattle, will be sufficient to make most of them independent.

What a commentary the above report is upon our boasted civilization. What a jargon of meaningless assertions. The Indian has been "civilized" out of existence and exterminated from the continent by the demon of "personal property." Originally a docile race, full of pride, spirit, kindness and honor, they were betrayed, then kidnapped and sold into slavery by the early settlers of the Atlantic coast. Their lands appropriated by "law," the surveyor's chain reaching from ocean to ocean, driven from the soil, disinherited, robbed and murdered by the piracy of capitalism, this once noble but now degraded, debauched and almost extinct race have become the "national wards" of their profit-mongering civilizers. Under the aegis of "mine and thine," barbarism became so cruelly refined that man prospers best and only when he exterminates his fellow man. Left to themselves, left to the exercise of free will and personal liberty— *anarchy*—the red man would be alive and prospering today, dwelling in peace and fellowship with his Caucasian brothers. But "personal ownership" requires masters and slaves, and the Indian through a ceaseless struggle of more than three centuries has always preferred death to the latter.

from *The Alarm*,
8 November 1884

THE MAKING OF HONORE JAXON

It should come as no surprise to readers of this book that the Chicago anarchists admired the Indians for their egalitarian way of life, were outraged at their fate, and applauded their struggles. Consider their reaction to the Riel Rebellion, as it was called—one of the great Indian rebellions in the history of North America.

In March, 1885, the Metis—the mixed-blood French-Indians of the Canadian Northwest—rose in armed rebellion against the Canadian State in defense of their land rights. Led by Louis Riel, a skillful politician and a charismatic visionary, they proclaimed their independence from the British Empire, with the intention of establishing a republic in the Northwest for themselves and the other Indians of the area. Immediately, *The Alarm* broadcast the sympathy and solidarity the anarchists felt for the Metis:

They are struggling to retain their homes, of which the statute laws and the chicanery of modern capitalism seeks to dispossess them. May their trusted rifles and steady aim make the robbers bite the dust.

Alas, the Metis were crushed in blood on the battlefield. Louis Riel was tried for treason and hanged on November 16, 1885. Six days later, the American Group of the Chicago International Working People's Association held a memorial meeting in his honor. August Spies, Samuel Fielden, Albert Parsons and others spoke of their admiration and love for Riel. He was their brother, "a martyr to human freedom," slain by "social order."[1]

The Chicago anarchists had many martyrs to attend to. As time passed, it was likely that Louis Riel would retreat to the back of their minds. A most improbable thing happened, however, to keep Riel and the cause of the Metis at the center of their attention. Through a series of fantastic and fateful events, Riel's secretary joined their ranks at the beginning of 1886. He was William Henry Jackson, soon to be known as Honore Joseph Jaxon. A remarkable man, his passion in life was the rights of the Indians, although he himself was white. He and his new comrades were worthy of each other.

As Jackson settled into Chicago, he became a popular leader in the labor movement. In a position to influence the workers about him, he was an insistent voice urging them to extend their solidarity across the color line to the Indians. The atmosphere of the times made many workers receptive to his message. The bitter labor wars of the late nineteenth century coincided with the last of the Indian wars, such as the Riel Rebellion. The established press and respectable opinion-makers expressed their contempt for strikers, trade unionists and radical workers by comparing them to Indians. All of them were viewed as savages who threatened American Civilization. Treated and feeling like outcasts, it is not surprising that many workers had a certain amount of sympathy for the Indians as fellow outcasts. Appealing to this sentiment, and building on it, Jackson won a warm response and support for his cause. His success is testimony to the extraordinary radicalization of American workers in the 1880s and the important role of the anarchists in that process.

William Henry Jackson (1861-1952) was born and raised a Protestant in Ontario, where French Canadians were des-

pised, let alone the Indians. In 1882 he moved to the Northwest. It was there, in the next two years, that he overcame the bigotry of his background while coming to know the Indians about him. He was attracted to their way of life: It was "incomparably nearer to God than that of any average man taken from. . .what we call civilization." He admired them because they lived "free from selfishness, and from the grasping for property and riches as among the whites." His most intimate associations were among the Metis and he came under the sway of Louis Riel. "The oppression of the aboriginal has been the crying sin of the white race in America and they have at last found a voice." Jackson was a talented linguist and a university-educated man; with his skills and passions, Riel took him on as his secretary in 1884. Early the next year Riel revealed himself as the prophet of a new religion and propelled his people into armed rebellion. Jackson faced the ultimate test of his new-found devotion to the Indians. But a man of his qualities could not have done otherwise: He accepted Riel as his prophet and followed him to the end. As a result, along with Riel, he was tried for treason. In his case, he was declared insane and locked away.[2]

In November, 1885, Jackson escaped from the lunatic asylum and fled to the United States on foot. As he made his way through North Dakota, Minnesota and Wisconsin, he arranged public meetings where he defended the right of the Indians to a republic in the Northwest, to be achieved by the force of arms if necessary. The general public received him, as he described years later, with

the anti-social disposition which I had of course discovered in the American bourgeoisie, from the moment of my escape into this "land

Louis Riel

of the free". . .the pious disapproval. . .of a movement which had disregarded sacred "rights of property" created by a "civilized" government for the guidance of a "savage" people. . . .

He was soon to find out, however, that there were other Americans who did not hold the rights of property in such sacred regard.[3]

In January, 1886, Jackson arrived in Eau Claire, Wisconsin. Here, the lumber magnates of the town refused him the use of the YMCA hall. A Knights of Labor Assembly came to the rescue: It invited him to address a public meeting under its auspices and to set forth, as he put it,

the true inwardness of the Metis struggle, and the why and how of its relationship to the struggle of the working people of the United States against the uncrowned masters of this alleged republic and "commonwealth."

Jackson was thankful for their offer and he did his best to oblige them. The Knights were pleased: They admitted him to membership and issued him a traveling card to facilitate his speaking tour.[4]

C. L. James, Eau Claire's resident anarchist and a contributor to *The Alarm*, attended the lecture and approached Jackson afterward. James was a dignified, well-dressed gentleman and Jackson expected another dose of "the anti-social disposition" of "the American bourgeoisie":

I, of course, braced myself for the expected onslaught; and it may therefore be imagined with what a corresponding degree of astonishment I found myself listening to a criticism that I had not been quite radical enough! I had come to preach, but waked up to find myself invited to membership in the more outspoken congregation of Rabbi James!

It was a "delicious surprise." James recognized a man after his own heart and he invited Jackson to stay with him while

William Henry Jackson / Honore Joseph Jaxon

he rested up and recuperated after his exhausting and trying experiences of the past year. Jackson eagerly accepted what proved to be "a very delightful hospitality in his home." As he got to know James, he was impressed with his "breadth of view." "Rabbi" James talked with him about anarchism and a host of other topics, ranging from the guerrilla tactics the Metis might use in the future to "a bird's-eye view of the various phases of the economic struggle" in the United States. By the time Jackson was ready to move on, James had given him "an invaluable advance understanding of new struggles into which I was shortly to be plunged." James also did him another favor: He sent him on his way with a letter of introduction to Albert Parsons and other anarchists in Chicago. So it was that early in February, armed with a Knights of Labor traveling card and an inside track to the most dynamic group of revolutionaries in the United States, Jackson made Chicago his next stop.[5]

Chicago, 1886! Prepared by "Rabbi" James, Jackson threw himself into the whirl of events sweeping the city. Almost the first thing he did was to join the American Group of the IWPA. *The Alarm* records him at a meeting of the American Group as early as February 20. Needing an income, he deposited his card with a Knights of Labor carpenter assembly and went to work in the trade. Then he set about organizing the "Anniversary Celebration of the Recent Northwestern Declaration of Independence." He rented the Central Music Hall for March 16th. Advertising himself as the secretary to Louis Riel and a spokesman for "The Provisional Government of the Northwest," he promised an address that night titled "Why We Fought; How We Fought; Why We Shall Fight Again." His experience with the Knights of Labor in Eau Claire fresh in his mind, he made the rounds of all the Knights' assemblies in Chicago seeking financial support and endorsements. At this very moment, thousands of working people were rushing to join the Knights in Chicago. The motto of the Order—'An Injury to One is the Concern of All'—was resounding throughout the city. No doubt Jackson quoted it meeting after meeting, inspiring the aroused workers of Chicago to a concern for the Indians of faraway Northwestern Canada. They did not let him down: He received a number of endorsements and enough money to cover his expenses.[6]

Jackson gave a defiant address as he promised. The resulting stir and the involvement of the Knights of Labor in the affair led some conservative Knights to worry about Jackson's connection with the Order. One wrote to Terence Powderly, the head of the Knights, voicing their fears. They were afraid that Jackson's defense of the Riel Rebellion and "his shotgun policy" might compromise the Order with the public. The letter did not mention Jackson's anarchism. If the conservative Knights had known about it at the time, they would have been even more upset.[7]

The Chicago anarchists were proud of their new comrade. His advocacy of the shotgun added a needed American dimension to their cult of dynamite. Like C. L. James in Eau Claire, they knew a comrade when they saw one and they made him feel at home in Chicago. In the months before Haymarket, when the anarchists were at the height of their influence and the city was in the midst of a great social upheaval, how could a man like Jackson not have felt at home in Chicago? Although he talked of traveling to Detroit and cities further east to continue his agitation for the Indians of the Northwest, he decided to stay put instead. Here was his chance to help make a revolution along with his anarchist comrades. Here was his chance to participate in his second revolution—his second, no less, in two years!

The oppposition to Jackson within the Knights of Labor was overwhelmed and drowned out by the explosive growth of the labor movement. And Jackson knew how to resonate with the rising tide of protest: A forceful speaker, a fiery leaflet-writer, an able organizer, he quickly became a popular figure. He learned German soon after arriving in Chicago, which put him on speaking terms with the largest and most radical group of workers in the city. Within his own Knights of Labor assembly, he was elected an officer. For a period of time in the late spring and summer, he was the secretary of the United Carpenters Committee, the umbrella grouping of all the carpenters' assemblies and unions in Chicago. It was while serving in this position that he directed a strike that became one of the legends of Chicago labor history. It was after Haymarket, when the employers were on the offensive, yet the strike was successful. It preserved the eight-hour-day for certain groups of carpenters. Not long after the strike was over, the Chicago *Tribune*, with its characteristic scorn, noted the appreciation the carpenters felt for Jackson: "Among the ignorant class. . .he has become little less than a demi-god."[8]

The strike was famous not only because it was one of the few successful strikes in Chicago in the months after Haymarket. It was famous because of the strategy Jackson used to cope with the difficult situation. With his experiences and interest in guerrilla warfare, Jackson devised a paramilitary strategy that won the day. It is not known if he encouraged the strikers to think of themselves as Indian guerrilla fighters when he sent them out to do battle with the scabs. He probably did. Is it going too far beyond the evidence to suggest that the men were inspired by this image? Whatever was on their minds at the time, the carpenters and other Chicago trade unionists learned an important lesson from Jackson's winning strategy. After 1886, union-sponsored organized violence became common in Chicago. This was the legacy of the Riel Rebellion for the Chicago labor movement: Long after its goals were forgotten, its "shotgun policy" lived on. For years thereafter, Jackson himself was known as "the Father of Labor Slugging," an honor that did not please him.[9]

There is almost no documentation, unfortunately, on Jackson's activities as an anarchist once he decided to settle in Chicago. *The Alarm* would have been the best source, but it was one of the victims of the Haymarket bomb. There is evidence that Jackson was active, and even prominent, in the defense work for the Haymarket defendants. After the verdict was announced on August 20, George Schilling recruited him as the secretary of a new defense committee and as one of six labor leaders to sign an appeal for funds for a new trial. Jackson also visited the Haymarket defendants in jail. During the final days before November 11, 1887, he pleaded with Albert Parsons to appeal for clemency to try to save his life.

Jackson had intense personal reasons for his plea: His Metis comrades were dead on the battlefield or scattered to the winds; Louis Riel was dead; he didn't know if he could bear to mourn for any more martyrs.[10]

Like all his anarchist comrades after November 11, 1887, Jackson faced an uncertain future. He had to take stock of his life. Within the short space of two years, he had suffered overwhelming losses. Deeply devoted to the memory of all the people he had lost, he searched for a way to honor them. Ever since he had been Louis Riel's secretary, his devotion to the Indians and his shame at their treatment in the hands of whites had made him regret that he was a white man. Taunted by whites as an "Indian-lover" and a "traitor" to his race, an idea had slowly taken shape in his mind: He would not only identify with the Indians, and be identified with them—he would become one himself. Once he took the step, it would not be hard to convince people that he actually was an Indian; his straight black hair and his swarthy complexion would do the trick. What better way to honor Riel and the Metis than by transforming himself into an Indian? During the turbulent days of 1886-87, Jackson had been too busy to do anything but dream about becoming an Indian. The idea remained tucked away in the back of his mind. But November 11, 1887 released him to give it full and careful consideration. That terrible day also gave him the incentive to do what he had only dreamed of doing before. The Haymarket Martyrs had died because of their love for freedom. He would honor them as well by liberating himself from the bondage of his white skin. And so, as the culmination of his life with the Metis and the Chicago anarchists, William Henry Jackson crossed the color line and started passing as a Metis. In 1889, to round off his new identity, he changed his name to Honore Joseph Jaxon.[11]

This is not the place to give an account of what Honore Jaxon did with his life. In brief: For the next thirty years he lived in Chicago, where he flourished as a Metis, a spokesman for the Indians, an anarchist, a trade union activist, and a crusader for an endless number of radical causes. Just to list all the organizations he served as secretary would take a page or more. A free man, thriving on voluntary poverty, his personality blossomed in the rich soil of freedom: He became one of the great eccentrics of his time. In 1919 he moved to the East Coast. He died in poverty in New York City in 1952, his passion for justice and the Indians burning brightly to the end.

Steven SAPOLSKY

1. *The Alarm* (Chicago), April 18, 1885; October 31, 1885; November 28, 1885.
2. Donald B. Smith, "William Henry Jackson: Riel's Secretary," *The Beaver* (Spring 1981), 10-19; Donald B. Smith, "Honore Joseph Jaxon: A Man Who Lived for Others," *Saskatchewan History* Vol. 34, No. 3 (Autumn 1981), 81-101. Many thanks to Prof. Smith for sending me copies of his articles and for sharing his enthusiasm for Jackson/Jaxon with me. Unless indicated otherwise, all information in my essay comes from his articles.   3. Honore J. Jaxon, "A Reminiscence of Charlie James," *Mother Earth*, Vol. 6, No. 5 (July 1911), 144-146.   4. *Ibid.*   5. *Ibid.*   6. *The Alarm*, March 6, 1886; William H. Jackson, "Why We Fought; How We Fought; Why We Shall Fight Again," Terence Powderly Papers, Microfilming Corporation of America, reel 14; W. H. Riley to T. V. Powderly, March 30, 1886, Powderly Papers, reel 14. Many thanks to Bryan Palmer for sending me copies of these documents. 7. W. H. Riley to T. V. Powderly, March 30, 1886, Powderly Papers, reel 14.
8. "The Versatile Jaxon," *The Saturday Evening Post*, June 1, 1907, page 17; Richard S. Schneirov, "The Knights of Labor in the Chicago Labor Movement and in Municipal Politics, 1877-1887," Ph.D., Northern Illinois University, 1984, 449-451.; Lloyd Lewis and Henry Justin Smith. *Chicago, The History of Its Reputation* (N.Y., Harcourt, Brace, 1929), 168-169.   9. *Ibid.*   10. *The Labor Enquirer* (Denver), September 11, 1886; Carolyn Ashbaugh. *Lucy Parsons, American Revolutionary* (Chicago, Charles H. Kerr, 1976), 168.   11. The impact of November 11, 1887 on Jackson is my hypothesis. It feels right to me, but I have no specific evidence to back it up.

I Martiri dell'Anarchia.

CHICAGO, 11 Novembre 1887.

"THE MARTYRS OF ANARCHY"

Reproduced as hand-colored lithographs ("suitable for framing"), as post cards, and on the covers of countless periodicals, pictures like this one from Italy were the late nineteenth and early twentieth century anarchist movement's ironic equivalent of religionists' "holy cards," saints' pictures and other devotional images.

THE HAYMARKET ATHEISTS

*Mrs. Swank, Mrs. Parsons, Mrs Schwab and Mrs. Ames
were also arrested. . . .The authorities are making a point
against them that they do not believe in God.*
—Letter in the *Detroit Labor Leaf*,
May 12, 1886[1]

"Neither God Nor Master" is one of those short, self-evident slogans which early anarchism made its own. Like Bakunin's magnificent challenge to humankind ("God or Human Freedom; now, let all choose") it spelled out the only relevant alternatives with a starkness and rigor that still rings truer than the automatic equivocations our own times seem to prefer.[2] Not accidentally, the Haymarket Anarchists were also the Haymarket Atheists, actively opposed to the religious recruitment and indoctrination of the workers. Their prominent affiliation with the International Working People's Association—co-founded by Johann Most, an anarchist equally well known for his militant atheism—involved them in a movement whose program and slogans were diametrically opposed to the Christian social ethic of their day.[3]

The IWPA's *Pittsburgh Manifesto* of 1883, adopted unanimously by the delegates—including Albert Parsons and August Spies—stated that "The Church finally seeks to make complete idiots out of the mass, and to make them forego the paradise on earth by promising them a fictitious heaven." Prof. Richard T. Ely, writing in the *Christian Union* the following year, expressed his horror that the IWPA anarchists attacked religion "with what may be considered practical unanimity," and that "the onslaught. . . is made in language of unparalleled coarseness and shocking impiety."[4] The Chicago anarchists would certainly have agreed with their arch-enemy Capt. Schaack that "Christianity and Anarchy are entirely opposite. . . . Religion and Anarchy. . .do not and never will go together."[5]

Philosophically, the Haymarket Eight were atheists in the Stratonician sense—that is, they folded their arms and placed the burden of proof on the theists.[6] Whether they averred positive atheism like Michael Schwab, or agnosticism like Samuel Fielden or, like George Engel, spoke from an unambiguous world-view that was from top to bottom incompatible with any notion of a transcendental deity, they concurred in this: No one spoke to them as god. Or as master. As far as they were concerned, there was no Supreme Pinkerton to impede the social revolution.

Although their anti-religious agitation apparently resulted in police harassment of Chicago anarchists, historians of the Haymarket Affair have not explicitly assessed the impact of this question on the arrests, verdict and sentences.[7] They have shown, however, that voices from the freethought and secular movements offered early, courageous and long-lasting support to the radicals during the trial and clemency drive. D. M.Bennett's widely-read freethought journal, *The Truth-Seeker*—in sharp contrast to the brutal hostility of all but the tiniest minority of America's religious press, and to the silence or reserve of mainstream political and even labor publications—denounced the Haymarket verdict and executions in no uncertain terms as "judicial murder." It editorialized, correctly, that within five years this view would be almost universally accepted.[8]

From Valley Falls, Kansas, *Lucifer*, an unorthodox libertarian/freethought journal, challenged the Haymarket legal proceedings with a lengthy investigative study by Gen. M. M. Trumbull, and quickly condemned the subsequent executions.[9] Still another freethought publication, *The Social Science Review* of New York, declared after the executions that it was "time for everybody to be anarchists, so far as that government is concerned," referring to the state apparatus in Chicago and Illinois.[10] In London, England, workingclass secularist clubs counting many thousands of members joined the movement for clemency for the condemned men, along with prominent skeptics such as playwright George Bernard Shaw, and Annie Besant of the National Secular Society.[11]

Of all freethinkers sympathetic to the cause of justice for the Haymarket atheists, former Illinois Attorney General Robert Ingersoll was the most famous. However, his very fame—or notoriety—as an outspoken infidel threatened to make his support counter-productive; he himself expressed the fear that if he entered the case in a legal capacity, as he was belatedly invited to do, it would jeopardize the condemned men's last chance for a reversal of their sentences. Ingersoll speculated that the philistine gendarmes of the press and the churches would cry with glee: "We have got the whole brood together now, Atheists and Anarchists."[12]

A rising young activist in the freethought movement who was actually drawn to revolutionary anarchism by the Haymarket events was Voltairine de Cleyre. As a poet and intellectual rebel, she was so impressed by the valor of the godless Chicago martyrs that she took up their ideas—advancing, as Paul Avrich points out in his biographical study, from rejection of religious domination to rejection of *all* domination, including that of state authority and private economic power.[13]

The extensive printed record of the Chicago anarchists' words and writings in the last months of their lives enables us to assess the views of the individual defendants on the question of God and religion.[14]

Albert Parsons expressed himself most definitively when he replied to a query in the Chicago *Tribune* (November 4, 1887): "There is but one God—Humanity. Any other kind of religion is a mockery, a delusion and a snare." Parsons had found the meaning of his life and death in exposing the deceptions, and fighting the anti-human injustices, of the capitalist system. In his long speech at the end of the trial he lashed out at "the Christian ministry" whom he included among "those pious frauds who profess their faith in the power of God, while they employ the police, the militia and and other armed hirelings to enforce their man-made laws and maintain their power over their fellow man." On the morning of his hanging he was visited by an uninvited Methodist minister in his death-cell, but he dismissed the man with gospel allusions to the "generation of vipers" and "whited sepulchres."[15]

August Spies, the learned and eloquent editor of the Chicago *Arbeiter-Zeitung*, often expressed his attitude by ironically contrasting the lofty Christian ideals of the capitalist "Board-of-Trade men" with their sordid actions: murder of workers, extortion, exploitation of women and children, perjury, political corruption, etc. He equated these wealthy fomentors of the Haymarket frame-up with the usurers that Luther demanded be "quartered and wheeled. . .persecuted, cursed and beheaded."[16] With his neat verbal caricatures Spies turned the tables both ways, proving the dreaded anarchists to be infinitely less bloodthirsty than capitalists and Christians. He was wholly sincere in his admiration for heterodox Christian rebels such as John Huss and Thomas Muenzer, but he admired their rebellion and not their theology. Reading Spies' statements and writings, one cannot help but conclude that, for him, the social revolution began in the early revolts of the long-past Reformation era, "Against Pope and Master."

Adolph Fischer, who faced the scaffold on November 11, 1887 along with Parsons, Spies and Engel, took up the matter of religion rather bluntly in his autobiography in the Chicago *Knights of Labor*. His point was to show how religion actually functions as the "opium of the people." Not expressly using that metaphorical phrase, or even referring to Marx, he nevertheless reinforced the well-known argument. "Let us investigate the matter," his discussion begins.

From their earliest childhood the working men are being prepared for their destiny like dancing bears brought up for the profession

---

A LETTER ON RELIGION

Cook County Bastille, Cell No. 29
Chicago, November 3, 1887

Editor of the *Tribune*:

In your issue of today on the "People's Page," and column headed "Voice of the People," a correspondent asks: "To settle a dispute please state what religion Anarchist Parsons has, or has he any religion?" To which you reply, "No."

To settle a dispute concerning my religious belief, which will doubtless arise after my judicial assassination, when it will be beyond my power to speak, I desire to say to your inquirer, and to all others, that religion in the sense now understood and practiced by those who profess it is merely a blind faith of the honestly superstitious, or a cloak of designing knaves.

If there is a Supreme Being, or Almighty God, who rules the universe, the sphere as well as the actions of puny men, then why do those who profess allegiance to Him cast aside and violate His laws and impeach His integrity and insult His beneficency by erecting man-made governments and enacting man-made laws, and use the bloody weapons of war to prop up and maintain these man-made laws and Government?

My religion—if it can be called such—is *viz.*: Who so lives right dies right; there is but one God—Humanity. Any other kind of religion is a mockery, a delusion, and a snare.

Respectfully,

Albert R. PARSONS

Chicago *Tribune*
November 4, 1887

---

by his master. In the schools and churches they are told it is the will of God that there should be rich and poor people.

Fischer goes on to sketch his view of faith in a god: It is a deceitful means employed by rulers and the wealthy to soften and justify the disinheriting of humankind and its consequent enslavement.[17]

German immigrants like Fischer, Engel and Lingg, from the impoverished working class of a nation where religious conformity was widely enforced by law, were in a good position to evaluate the accuracy of that much-quoted aphorism of Marx. Even Oscar Neebe, who was sentenced to only fifteen years for the horrible heresy of organizing working people, viewed religion in much the same way as the other seven defendants. Yet in his way, Neebe also added something different, perhaps echoing the IWPA *Manifesto*, hinting at the idea of exchanging the present-day capitalistic hell for a "Paradise Now." He tells us that

As a boy, already many contradicting thoughts came over me. I read Thomas Paine and I made up my mind that a God who was almighty and would allow so many cruel and terrible acts to be performed in his name, could not be a just and good one, and became a freethinker, but although a freethinker, I went to church, and when I heard the preacher describe how beautiful heaven was, I thought why not have heaven now on earth. Hell we had already. I saw the sparkling eyes of the devoted, and how many poor, deluded workmen would think by the description of heaven which is for the poor; how his oppressor and slavedriver would be punished in hell and roasted, and all that for ever and ever. This delusion of the workmen and promising of the glories of heaven is performed so that the poor workman should not think for himself, think that he might have heaven on earth, if he only wanted. . .In my 20th year I had cut myself off from all religious sects.[18]

George Engel did not dwell on such things in his statements or writings available to us. No doubt he experienced something similar in his own childhood and youth, but from all appearances it could have gone in one ear and out the other. These ideological obstacles were not located geometrically on the straight line of proletarian class struggle that he saw immediately ahead:

Some day, not twenty-five years from now, the war will break out. There is no doubt about that in my mind. Therefore all workingmen should unite and prepare for the last war, whose outcome will be the end forever of all war, and will bring peace and happiness to all mankind.[19]

Atheistic, agnostic or areligious, George Engel's mind was too concentrated on other things to be concerned with theological frivolities. As Capt. Schaack put it, Engel, "like all anarchists. . .had no use for clergymen or the church, Sisters of Charity or anything else that had a tinge of religion in it. He called them all hypocrites and frauds."[20]

In contrast, Michael Schwab seems to have had a strong recollection of early religious indoctrination: "I was a religious fanatic at the age of ten to twelve." This was because his teachers in his Bavarian homeland had convinced him that, as he explains it, all great thinkers and kings and emperors of the past were believers—and surely they could not all have erred. Soon, however, at age thirteen, Schwab began to doubt this argument when he observed the drunken irreverence of a priest driven to bored distraction by a religious outing on which he was escorting a group of first communicants, Schwab among them. This priest, who was later to become

"An Anarchist Sunday School: Teaching Unbelief and Lawlessness" (from Schaack)

Bishop of Spier, and who published a book on papal infallibility, was one of the earliest destabilizers of Schwab's faith. "My faith dwindled and dwindled and when I was sixteen, instead of being a Roman Catholic, I was an atheist—that is, my faith was simply the belief in a personal God, and some years later I did not even believe in that."[21]

The religious ethos known to Samuel Fielden as a Lancashire millhand from childhood through early manhood was English workingclass Methodism, something very different from the *gemutlich* foibles of entrenched southern German Catholicism. Methodism offered young Fielden a kind of serious moral and ideological struggle early in his life, as well as the example of selfless commitment given by the unpaid workingclass preachers who held the regional church structure together. He eventually rejected religious explanations altogether and exchanged Methodism for the more lucid struggle of proletarian anarcho-socialism. Nevertheless, he retained a respect, convincingly expressed, for his early religious co-workers and teachers.[22] Even after he had espoused anarchism and freethought, Fielden was able to meet with religionists and disagree with them without the least trace of anti-clerical rancor. Of a meeting with the evangelist Dwight Moody, he writes:

We parted at the door with the best feeling toward each other. I am only sorry to say that my opponent has persisted in following the wrong path to this day. I am truly sorry for him. I only wish that we both turn to the right before it is everlastingly too late.[23]

Fielden's respect for certain preachers is understandable as an instance of the kind of sympathy that can exist between those who are passionately driven to communicate with, and to *move*, others—to move, that is, their minds, spirits and wills. There is nothing patronizing in it. As a corollary to this affinity, Sam Fielden, as much an anarchist as any, plainly felt no need to silence the preacher, his "opponent," as he put it. Wrong though his teachings may be, the preacher with his text and his unaided voice stands at equal risk within his own realm of personal freedom. It is only when political links with ruling-class authority implicate the religionist in the oppression of workers that he becomes an opponent, in the political sense, of those struggling for their liberation. It is hard to imagine that the tele-electronic religious capitalisms

A VISIT TO AN ANARCHIST SUNDAY SCHOOL

One Sunday afternoon in the late winter [1889] a reporter took me to visit a so-called anarchist Sunday School, several of which were to be found on the northwest side of the city. The young man in charge was of the German student type, and his face flushed with enthusiasm as he led the children singing one of Koerner's poems. The newspaperman, who did not understand German, asked me what abominable stuff they were singing, but he seemed dissatisfied with my translation of the simple words and darkly intimated that they were "deep ones," and had probably "fooled" me. When I replied that Koerner was an ardent German poet whose songs inspired his countrymen to resist the aggressions of Napoleon, and that his bound poems were found in the most respectable libraries, he looked at me rather askance and I then and there had my first intimation that to treat a Chicago man, who is called an anarchist, as you would treat any other citizen, is to lay yourself open to deep suspicion.

Jane ADDAMS

From Twenty Years at Hull-House *(1910).*

109

of today would be sent off with the same kind of respect that Sam Fielden extended to Mr. Moody and the pious workmen of his youth.

Of all the eight Haymarket defendants, Louis Lingg was the most viscerally feared and admired. ''There are many perhaps who may be curious,'' he wrote in the last paragraph of his brief autobiography, ''to learn something of my non-religious convictions.'' Explaining that he grew up in a liberal jurisdiction during Bismarck's policy of curtailing church influence in state institutions, he concludes that he

can thank luck that our schoolteachers inculcated substantial knowledge instead of belief in something about which nobody knew anything and united learning could explain nothing. Accordingly, though used to deplore the fact that taxes on labor prevailed, I rejoiced in the conviction that penalties on thought had ceased. I availed myself of the situation and was naturally a freethinker, a domain in which greater men than I have trod, and still greater than they will continue to walk.[24]

Lingg's terse words bring us to the end of this summary of the non- and anti-religious opinions of the Haymarket anarchists. For most of them, other citations could be provided, introducing additional themes and nuances. But the foregoing presentation suffices to demonstrate that these men seriously reflected on their real experiences with the religious establishment of their time. They did not receive a readymade plastic atheism in an ill-fitting package from some lugubrious Eighteenth Century Enlightenment, as some conservative critic might like to pretend. The Chicago anarchists were neither dogmatic nor unjustly biased against any individual doctrines or sects.

It should also be noted that some of these atheist radicals read and publicly quoted the Bible, and particularly the new testament, consciously honoring the age-old revolutionary verses and slogans of justice contained therein.[25] Albert Parsons, for example, closed his autobiography with a passage from the Epistle of James (V:1-5)—the very text that was the favorite of the anarcho-communistic Ranters in the English Civil War of the seventeenth century:

Go to, now, ye rich men, weep and howl for your miseries that shall come upon you. Your riches are corrupted and your garments are moth-eaten. Your gold and silver is cankered; and the rust of them shall be witness against you; and shall eat your flesh as it were fire. Ye have heaped treasures together for the last days.

There was neither sarcasm nor capitulation in such recourse to the sacred texts. For their words had long been the medium for an ancient truth, the *truth that makes us free* by uniting and inspiring humankind in struggle, and the collective name of that truth is not religion but *poetry*. To the terrain of poetry the anarchist frame of mind is uniquely adapted; and indeed, the Chicago martyrs quoted the revolutionary and romantic poets—Heine, Freiligrath, Herwegh, Shakespeare, Whittier, Morris and many others—much more than the Bible.[26] This freer moral orientation unquestionably helped them to understand the true significance of their fate.

For the five condemned defendants had no more factually positive knowledge about the great unknown they were facing than the most guilt-ridden religionist possessed. Yet they greeted it not with the fear and self-flaying renunciation of the penitent, but with songs, poems, slogans of liberty and, in Louis Lingg's case, a defiant act of voluntary embrace.[27] Here, in the personification of the Christian's most unassimilable horror, Death, they found no punishing bogie but a new challenge to their experience, courage and love of freedom.

Joseph JABLONSKI

LOS MARTIRES 1886
DE CHICAGO 1986

from *Guangara Libertaria*

1. Quoted in Henry David, *The History of the Haymarket Affair* (New York, 1958), 225. 2. According to Bakunin, ''He who desires to worship God must harbor no childish illusions about the matter, but bravely renounce his liberty and humanity'' (*God and the State*). 3. David, *Affair*, chapters 3-5; Paul Avrich, *The Haymarket Tragedy* (Princeton, 1984), chapters 5-7. For Johann Most, see his *The God Pestilence* (Tucson, 1983), and Fred Woodworth's introduction thereto. 4. ''Recent Phases of Socialism in the U.S.,'' quoted in David Brion Davis, ed., *The Fear of Conspiracy* (Ithaca, 1971), 165-6. 5. Michael J. Schaack, *Anarchy and Anarchists* (Chicago, 1889), 674. 6. Antony Flew, *A Dictionary of Philosophy*, 340. 7. Criticism in this regard may have been anticipated by the prosecution, since a self-styled freethinker was included on the jury. See Lucy Parsons, ed., *Famous Speeches* (Chicago, 1912), 108. 8. David, *Affair*, 400, 407. 9. Hal D. Sears, *The Sex Radicals* (Columbia, 1977), 137, 138. 10. David, *Affair*, 471. 11. *Ibid.*, 426. 12. *Ibid.*, 395; Avrich, *Tragedy*, 299. 13. Paul Avrich, *An American Anarchist: The Life of Voltairine de Cleyre* (Princeton, 1978). 14. See especially Philip S. Foner, ed, *The Autobiographies of the Haymarket Martyrs* (New York, 1969). See also Lucy Parsons, ed., *Famous Speeches*; Albert R. Parsons, *Anarchism: Its Philosophy and Scientific Basis* (Chicago, 1887); and Lucy Parsons, ed., *The Life of Albert R. Parsons* (Chicago, 1889). 15. Avrich, *Tragedy*, 387. 16. August Spies, *Autobiography, His Speech in Court and General Notes* (Chicago, 1887). 17. Foner, *Autobiographies*, 77-78. 18. *Ibid.*, 165-6. 19. *Ibid.*, 98. 20. Schaack, 283. 21. Foner, *Autobiographies*, 100-104. 22. *Ibid.*, 145-7. 23. *Ibid.*, 150. 24. *Ibid.*, 177-8. 25. See Shmuel Eisenstadt, *The Prophets: Their Times and Their Social Ideas* (New York, 1971). 26. Avrich, *Tragedy*, 137. 27. *Ibid.*, 381-93.

PART II:
DEFENSE & AMNESTY

"The First Martyrs of the General Strike": a Haymarket Martyrs' Memorial Card from Spain

ERNST SCHMIDT

Born in a small town near Bamberg, Germany, Ernst Schmidt (1830-1900) received a Jesuit education but quickly acquired a taste for proscribed, "blasphemous" authors—Feuerbach, Borne, Heine—and came under the influence of a grand-uncle who in his youth had been a close friend of Jean-Paul Marat, and who inspired young Schmidt with radical ideas.

As a young medical student Schmidt took an active part in the insurrectionary activity of 1848. Finding life in Germany unbearable after the reaction, he and his young wife Teresa decided to emigrate to the U.S. In 1857 they arrived in Chicago, where they found many friends who had been "48'ers." The following year Schmidt became active in the abolitionists' "Underground Railroad" and met John Brown.

After campaigning for Lincoln in 1860 he moved to St. Louis where he met Mikhail Bakunin at Tony Faust's Beer Cellar and served as surgeon in the Union Army during the Civil War. Returning to Chicago, he taught at Chicago Medical College. In 1864 he was elected coroner on the Republican ticket, but soon resigned. He co-founded the socialist newspaper Vorbote *in 1873, ran for mayor as a socialist six years later, and hosted Johann Most on the occasion of his visit in 1882.*

Schmidt played a major role in the Haymarket defense and amnesty campaigns, and was a featured speaker at the unveiling of the monument to the martyrs at Waldheim in 1893.

A man of extraordinary culture, a classical scholar, fluent in Hebrew, Greek and Latin, Dr. Schmidt in his last years translated poems by Longfellow, Poe and Edward Markham into German. Among the many speakers at his funeral were former governor Altgeld and Clarence Darrow.

FR

THE DEFENSE & AMNESTY CAMPAIGNS

Immediately after hearing that the labor agitators had been taken into custody and indicted for the murder of Policeman Degan, I decided to do what I could to give these men a fair trial. I called on as many of my friends as I could contact for help. Their response was magnificent, but no public hall was to be had for our meeting. The owners of rooms and saloons suitable for this purpose were so afraid of the police that they all refused me. I then decided to hold the meeting in my office in the *Staats-Zeitung* building, where more than a hundred men crowded into the room on a hot May afternoon. Over $500 was contributed that afternoon toward the defense of the men awaiting trial.

As president and treasurer of the newly formed defense organization, I sent out a brief appeal to liberal-minded humanitarians of all creeds inviting their contributions to aid the prisoners. The appeal was also widely reproduced in the liberal and labor press. It had its intended effect. . . .

No efforts on my part would have succeeded [in this project] without the constant support and encouragement of George Schilling. He accomplished the seemingly impossible in securing documents for the use of our attorneys in appealing the case to the Supreme Courts of the United States and the State of Illinois. His many friends among labor leaders donated handsomely to our fund.

In a short time, contributions began to pour in, all in small amounts and from such distant places as Upsala, Sweden; Bombay, India; Tokyo, Japan; and San Francisco, California, each contribution being accompanied with a letter of sympathy and encouragement. Money was sent from every state and every territory of the Union. Sometimes as little as 10 cents was contributed by men poor as the woman in the Bible who gave her mite. Small articles of jewelry were sent by others who had no money. One of these articles, a small scarf-pin sent by a man in the Michigan woods, was raffled off at a picnic for $200. About $8000 was raised in Chicago, of which nearly half was collected at picnics, dances and lotteries. . . .

[On September 14, 1887, the Supreme Court of Illinois affirmed the judgment of

George Schilling

the lower court.] An attempt was then made by Captain Black and Mr. Salomon, assisted by Roger A. Pryor, J. Randolph Tucker and General Benjamin F. Butler, all lawyers of national reputation, to secure a review of the case by the Supreme Court of the United States. This court, however, on November 2, 1887, declined to issue a writ of error.

In thus affirming the judgment of the lower court, no regard was taken of the fact that the trial-record showed many procedural errors. The judge, for instance, had repeatedly made remarks during the trial that bristled with malevolent insinuations tending to influence the minds of the jurors against the defendants.

All but two members of the committee felt that we were wasting money in making an attempt to secure clemency for the prisoners by taking the case to the Supreme Court of the country. Spies and Parsons were constantly begging us to turn over whatever money still remained on hand to the women who they were certain would soon be widows.

The two members favoring taking the case to the higher courts were Frank Stauber and I, although we too feared the appeals would fail. Stauber had learned about American political malfeasance a few years earlier when, having been duly elected alderman in the Fourteenth Ward of Chicago on the Socialist Labor Party ticket, he had had to wait a full year to be seated before the Republican Party's attempt to defraud him of his victory was finally nullified.

But had we not taken the matter to the courts for review, our friends and the sympathizers with the cause of labor would have said that we had delivered their leaders to the hangman without even trying to save them and that the Justices of the Supreme Court of the United States would certainly have shown mercy. Stauber and I believed the attempt should be made if only to expose jurisprudence in America for what it is—neither better nor worse than in the old capitalistic countries of Europe which we had abandoned in the hope of finding a land where justice prevails for all classes of society.

Springfield and Washington having acted as expected, there was nothing left but to make an appeal for executive clemency. All this required money and our funds were running low.

I made another appeal for funds and the response was beyond expectations. We wanted to present Governor Richard Oglesby of Illinois with definite proof of a universally sincere desire for his executive clemency. And we got it! Huge stacks of petitions asking for leniency began piling up in Springfield and Chicago, signed by thousands of organized workingmen of America, England, Germany and France; also by members of the French Chamber of Deputies and of the Paris Municipal Council. Among individual petitioners were the prominent British freethinker Annie Besant, George Bernard Shaw, William Morris and countless others who felt that a monstrous atrocity was about to take place. . . .

The manner in which the trunk [containing all of the petitions for clemency] was received at the governor's made it clear that the authorities regarded anything connected with me as highly suspicious. True, it was a shabby-looking old box, large enough to hold a good-sized bomb, and to make it worse, I had scratched out my name and address and in its place had written Oglesby's. Anyone examining the label could see that it had originally borne my name.

The trunk was not taken indoors at Springfield. Instead, it was removed most carefully to a shed in the farthest corner of the grounds, where it would have remained if the Chicago delegation had not asked for it on their arrival in Springfield on Tuesday, three days before the date set for the execution.

I did not go to the capital with the delegation because I was convinced that nothing would make a politician turn his back on his wealthy sponsors, most of whom, with the notable exception of Charles Farwell and a few others, were for hanging. Then, too, I knew my own temperament so well that I feared I would be unable to preserve my composure in the governor's presence. By airing my feelings and bitterness over the outrageous conduct of the trial, I could easily jeopardize any chance the prisoners might still have of winning Oglesby's favor.

Amnesty Association Headquarters
(Chicago *Tribune*, November 10, 1887)

Capt. William P. Black
Chief Counsel for the Defense
(from McLean)

A TRIBUTE
to
ERNST SCHMIDT

Ernst Schmidt always fought against injustice. A fearless abolitionist of Negro slavery before the Civil War, he was equally loud in denouncing the injustice of enslaving white factory-workers afterwards. . . .

Citizens of the middle class constantly tried to claim him as their own, enticing him with their choicest political plums. All these and more he refused, declaring that he would always remain with those who have no portion in the happiness of this world. This is what makes the man so great, what marks him from the others: that he felt with the people, laughed with them, cried with them and, not seldom, dried the tears of the poor. . . .

Never self-seeking, he rejected all recognition. By helping to found the Socialist Labor Party and by coming out for the principles of socialism, he raised the workingman in his moral consciousness and strengthened his will to fight for his rights at a time when to be a socialist was not only unpopular but highly dangerous.

Always bold and forthright in declaring himself, never a hedger or a hypocrite, at Pittsburgh in the early '80s he openly admitted that he felt more in common with radical socialists than with his "blue stocking" comrades of the party.

John Peter ALTGELD

Memorial Services for Dr. Schmidt,
North Side Turner Hall,
September 1, 1900

My unpopularity in Springfield and in the homes of wealthy coupon-clippers on Prairie Avenue is readily understandable. Had I not had the insolence to defend the prisoners against the wishes of these men? Also, our defense committee had not only succeeded in delaying the execution but had made it necessary for the opposition to increase appreciably their payments to State's Attorney Grinnell for the consummation of such underhanded dealings as it took to block our efforts toward obtaining executive clemency for the condemned men.

* * *

I felt my confidence in America's future slipping away. If this murder of innocent men could happen once it could happen again. My trust that this great nation would never sink to the level of the European police-states that I had known as a youth was ebbing fast. Even Bismarck, the so-called Iron Chancellor, exclaimed on hearing of this strangulation of justice: "No, we never could have managed that in Germany."

* * *

On the morning of the burial of the four labor martyrs, a large crowd of men and women were gathered at the cemetery to pay their last respects. The poplars around the graves were rapidly giving up their last few leaves to the chilly November wind. The mourners turned up their coat collars. . . .

A few words to the unfortunate widows and children, and I turned to look again at the graves, thinking, "Some day you will be vindicated, but the stain on American jurisprudence can never be erased."

Ernst SCHMIDT

from Frederick Schmidt, ed.
He Chose: The Other Was A Treadmill Thing
(Tucson, 1968)

Signing amnesty petitions
(Chicago *Daily News*, November 7, 1887)

113

THE CHICAGO ANARCHISTS OF 1886:

Adolph Fischer	Louis Lingg	August Spies
Michael Schwab	Lucy E. Parsons	Samuel Fielden
Albert R. Parsons		Oscar Neebe

from William D. Bancroft, *McKinley, Garfield, Lincoln: Their Lives, Their Deeds, Their Deaths, With a Record of Notable Assassinations and A History of Anarchy* (Chicago and New York, 1901)

HAYMARKET WIDOWS

The Haymarket trial and its aftermath brought tragedy and grief into the lives of women whose husbands, brothers, sons and comrades were imprisoned and executed. These family members and friends of the men who stood trial for a murder which none of them committed suffered immeasurable loss. Although the personal tribulations of many of these women have not been recorded, it is clear that they all suffered the emotional loss of a partner, close relative or friend, as well as the financial loss of that person's income.

The workers' movement helped support the widows and children of the Haymarket martyrs through the Pioneer Aid and Support Association, founded on December 15, 1887. The widows received $8 a week plus $2 each for the first two children and $1 for a third. Anarchists and sympathizers from all over the world contributed to this fund; a single rally in Havana, Cuba, raised nearly $1000 for the purpose. The Association also collected funds to erect the Haymarket Martyrs Monument at Waldheim (Forest Home) Cemetery.

But for the martyrs' female family members—Lucy Parsons, Nina van Zandt Spies, Christine Spies, Gretchen Spies, Maria Schwab, Johanna Fischer, Elise Friedel, Mrs. Engel, Mary Engel and Mrs. Fielden—life would never be the same.

Meta Neebe, wife of defendant Oscar Neebe, died during the ordeal. At her death in March 1887 she was only in her mid-thirties, and many—including her doctor—attributed her death to the stress and anxiety caused by her husband's incarceration and trial. The Chicago *Tribune* for March 13, 1887 reported that her funeral "called out more sympathy and excited more interest than any event that has occurred in the neighborhood since it was reclaimed from the prairie," and added that it was, indeed, "in some respects, the most notable funeral demonstration Chicago has ever seen."

Mrs. Fielden was described as someone who had never taken a streetcar downtown by herself prior to her husband's arrest; she had major adjustments to make during Samuel

Fielden's seven-year imprisonment. Johanna Fischer was left with three small children to support after Adolph Fischer's execution. Mary Engel and her mother lost father and husband, George Engel. Mrs. Engel continued to run her husband's toy-shop after his arrest. The Engels may have fared better economically than several of the other families, as the women were able to operate the family business.

Maria Schnaubelt Schwab, herself an active member of the International Working People's Association, would eventually lose her husband to tuberculosis contracted in the Illinois State Penitentiary at Joliet, despite Michael Schwab's pardon and release by Governor Altgeld in 1893. As a result of the Haymarket events, she did not see her brother Rudolph Schnaubelt for another thirty years, when she visited him in Argentina.

Little has been written on the later activity of the Haymarket widows, sisters and friends, but we do know that several of them remained active, in one way or another, in the anarchist movement.

In 1888 Christine Spies, August Spies' mother, published a 182-page compilation, *Reminiscenzen von Aug. Spies*. The last page announced the availability of the English-language *Autobiography of August Spies*, pub-

lished by Nina van Zandt Spies, and listed mailing addresses for two leading anarchist publications: *The Alarm* and Johann Most's *Freiheit*.

In May 1901 the Chicago anarchist weekly *Free Society* urged its readers to contribute to a fund recently started by the Central Labor Union to help support Christine Spies, who was then 70 years old. The June 16th issue reported that the paper had collected over ninety dollars for this purpose, and noted that several CLU members had volunteered to provide for her.

Lucy Parsons' paper *Freedom* ("A Revolutionary Anarchist-Communist Monthly") announced in April 1892 the marriage of the "amiable and accomplished" Gretchen Spies, "sister of our martyred comrade," to Comrade Robert Steiner, "well known throughout the country as an active worker in the cause of Labor. . .now connected with the editorial staff of the *Arbeiter-Zeitung* of this city. . . .*Freedom* wishes the newly married couple all the happiness possible in the marriage relation under present social arrangements."

Capt. Schaack, in his *Anarchy and Anarchists*, reported that detectives later noted Louis Lingg's friend Elise Friedel at "several dances," but whether these were anarchist events is not clear.

Railroad ticket for the dedication of the monument at Waldheim, 1893

115

Nina van Zandt's life changed dramatically with her interest in the Chicago trial and her marriage to the imprisoned August Spies in January, 1887. A Vassar graduate and the only child of wealthy Chicago parents, she followed the trial closely and soon realized that the defendants were honest, principled individuals dedicated to the betterment of humanity, rather than the depraved monsters guilty of heinous crimes depicted in the press. She wrote an article on the case for the Chicago *Knights of Labor*, later reprinted in her edition of August Spies' *Autobiography*, to which she also contributed a preface.

In later years Nina Spies was a colorful and familiar figure at the Hobo College and IWW meetings in Chicago, as well as at May Day and Eleventh of November commemorations. She eked out a marginal existence running a rooming-house on Halsted Street, and she took in stray dogs and cats as well as homeless persons. After Haymarket, her life ran a different course than expected of a graduate of a prestigious women's college. Her funeral in 1936 was a well-attended gathering of activists representing virtually every current of American radicalism.

The best known of the women immediately connected with the Haymarket events was the far-from-wealthy Lucy Parsons, who had made her own reputation as a persuasive and dramatic radical speaker prior to the Haymarket police riot. The Chicago police considered her "more dangerous than a thousand rioters" and broke up her meetings for thirty years after Haymarket. The execution of her husband and comrades made her more determined than ever to go on with the struggle, yet it left her with a legacy of personal tragedy and set the stage for further tragedy.

Lucy Parsons gave herself wholly to the movement and avoided discussion of her personal life. Albert Parsons' death left her a widow with two small children; poverty had already forced her to move from the apartment the family had occupied on Indiana Street to a third-floor walk-up flat on Milwaukee Avenue. As the executions approached, she worked her fingers to the bone sewing to support herself and her children, and she also worked herself to exhaustion selling pamphlets about the case and

trying to avoid police harassment. Yet she adamantly refused to encourage her husband to petition to the governor for clemency. Albert Parsons had said, "If the State of Illinois can afford to hang an innocent man, I can afford to hang." Lucy and Albert held to this position; they were devoted to truth and justice at all cost.

Lulu Eda's death two years after her father's was another devastating blow. Albert Parsons Jr. can be seen as the final casualty of Haymarket, the victim of incarceration in the Illinois Northern

Lucy E. Parsons

Hospital for the Insane from 1899 until his death from tuberculosis in 1919. His fate was in the unfolding of the Haymarket tragedy and the characters of its strong-willed participants: his martyred father, and his mother, determined to bring up a son to take his father's place in the social struggle.

Lucy Parsons' impoverishment in the years following Albert's execution and her experience with persecution and abuse for her beliefs may have in part led her into a relationship with the young anarchist Martin Lacher, a printer who helped her publish *The Life of Albert R. Parsons* in 1889. The two lived in the country with two large watchdogs to protect them. Lucy's personal life, no less than her political life, was under constant surveillance, and the protection afforded by her young comrade and the dogs may have kept the police at bay. Ironically, her relationship with Lacher ended in police court in 1891 where she

sought protection against his abuse of her as a woman and former lover.

In the years after Haymarket the Chicago police systematically denied Lucy Parsons her first-amendment rights. As soon as she began to speak at a meeting she was arrested, booked for disorderly conduct and released—an interruption long enough to disrupt the meeting program. Graham Taylor of the Chicago Commons settlement-house first met Lucy at the northside Turner Hall on November 11, 1896, nine years after the executions. The police arrested her just as she began to address the crowd of 1200 people.

When Lucy appeared at a free-floor meeting at the Commons several years later, it was unanimously voted that she should speak the following Tuesday. "Taken by surprise and not a little embarrassed," Graham Taylor related, "I offered no objection to the proposal, which I knew would be regarded as a supreme test of the freedom of the floor." As the meeting was private, Lucy was able to speak without being arrested. This meeting, near the turn of the century, was a rare occasion for Lucy Parsons to be heard in Chicago—a speech by her was indeed the supreme test of free speech!

Lucy Parsons remained an ardent revolutionist to the end of her life, and she was an important influence on innumerable later activists in the radical labor movement. In 1894 she addressed "Coxey's Army" of the unemployed on their ill-fated March on Washington. In 1905 she helped found the Industrial Workers of the World (IWW) in Chicago. Later she took part in William Z. Foster's short-lived Syndicalist League of North America, though she stayed on good terms with her Wobbly friends, and continued to write for the IWW press.

A featured speaker at the anarchist Free Society Forums in Chicago in the 1920s, she also appeared at forums and meetings organized by the IWW, the Proletarian Party and, especially in later years, the Communist Party, as well as at the bohemian Dill Pickle Club. For many years she was a familiar sight at workers' demonstrations and on Chicago street-corners, where she sold her *Life of Albert R. Parsons, Famous Speeches of the Chicago Martyrs* and other anarchist and revolutionary publications.

Especially active in labor defense, she wrote and spoke on behalf of Tom Mooney, Sacco and Vanzetti, the Gastonia and Scottsboro defendants. In one of her last public appearances, in 1941, she addressed strikers at International Harvester, successor to the old McCormick Reaper Works where the police shooting of workers had resulted in the fateful Haymarket meeting in May 1886.

Lucy Parsons and her companion George Markstall, with whom she had lived since around 1910, died in a fire at their Chicago home in March 1942. They were cremated and their ashes buried together in a grave close to the Haymarket Martyrs Monument at Waldheim.

Carolyn ASHBAUGH

LIFE OF
ALBERT R. PARSONS

Governor John P. Altgeld's
Pardon of the Anarchists
and His
Masterly Review
of
The Haymarket Riot

LUCY E. PARSONS
Publisher

3130 NORTH TROY STREET
CHICAGO, ILL.

10/20 1930

The Famous Speeches of the
Chicago Anarchists
in reply
to Why the Sentence of Death
Should not be Passed Upon
Them — Delivered in Court

PRINCIPLES OF ANARCHISM
A Lecture by
LUCY E. PARSONS

LUCY & NINA

. . .There were also a number of women, each of whom claimed the title, "Queen of the Hoboes." Among these were two elderly women who were not only queens but champions of the working class. Both were widows of Chicago anarchists of Haymarket Riot fame who were hanged November 11, 1887.

The better known of these two was Lucy Parsons, who invited me to her home and gave me a copy of her book, *The Life of Albert Parsons.* Her skin was quite clay-colored, like that of a Mexican, and I learned that she was born in El Paso and had a full-blooded Indian father. She was bent over with age, yet her hair was hardly grey at all. I got a big thrill out of hearing from her the speeches of the earlier Chicago anarchists, her husband and Louis Lingg, when they were on trial for their lives.

The other anarchist widow was Nina van Zandt Spies, a large breezy woman who wore many underskirts and walked with a cane and always had her hair flying about from under a pokey hat. Formerly she had been very beautiful, they told me. When I knew her she wore bifocal glasses and peered over them intently. She harbored many stray dogs and cats in her apartment, and the story went, until the health department interfered, she had kept a horse there, too. She had a voice that sounded aristocratic, and whenever she spoke in Bughouse Square

she thrilled audiences as she told the story of "how they murdered my dear innocent husband."

BOX-CAR BERTHA

From *Sister of the Road:*
The Autobiography of
Box-Car Bertha [Thompson]
as told to Dr. Ben L. Reitman
(New York, 1937).

A MASS MEETING & DEMONSTRATION

To Commemorate the thirteenth anniversary
of the death of

THE CHICAGO MARTYRS

WILL BE HELD ON

TUESDAY, NOVEMBER 13,

at 8 p.m., at the

WORKINGMEN'S CLUB & INSTITUTE UNION

CLERKENWELL ROAD, W.C. (NEXT TO HOLBORN TOWN HALL)

Speakers:

P. KROPOTKIN,   JOHN TURNER,
E. MALATESTA,
SIDNEY BLOOMFIELD,   W. TCHERKESOV,
T. del MARMOL,
E. SHEPHERD,   S. MAINWARING,
R. ROCKER,
I. CAPLAN,   E. LEGGATT,
F. KITZ,
W. J. NEEDES,   W. WESS.

Doors open at 7.30. Commence at 8.

ALL ARE WELCOME!

We sing their praise because they died for humanity.

English handbill, 1900

A SHOUT OF PROTEST
(Haymarket Defense Song)

In Chicago stand convicted
  Seven of nature's noblest men,
Jailed because they have predicted
  What was truth and clear to them;
Giving to the rich a warning
  That their end is drawing near,
Telling of a coming dawning
  Of a future bright and clear.

CHORUS
Let us save our noble brothers!
  Raise your voices loud and high!
Noble men who lived for others,
  Cannot, will not, must not die!

Foully tried by judge and jury,
  Victims of rich soundrels' hate,
Devilish capitalistic fury
  Would for such reserve the fate
Of Jesus Christ and other martyrs;
  Bloody-minded tyrants they,
Wolves, hyenas, murdering Tartars
  Worse than any beast of prey.

Shout aloud: Stop this foul murder!
  Let it ring throughout the land!
Tell the brutal Judge Magruder
  That we will no longer stand
Foul injustice to our brothers—
  Making liberty a lie—
Noble men who starved for others
  Cannot, will not, must not die!

Arthur CHEESEWRIGHT

Chicago *Labor Enquirer*
October 19, 1887

THE MIDDLE-CLASS REACTION

The plutocrats know by experiment how easily our middle class can have their good sense and reasoning faculties utterly stampeded by terror. This was proven to a demonstration by the Chicago Anarchy episode. The monopolist saw in that untoward event an opportunity to deal organized labor a crushing blow. The eight-hour day was almost gained, and capitalism knew that this victory for the workingman would be but the first of a series of triumphant battles that might ultimate in the industrial emancipation of the toiler. The near fruition of the laborers' weary hope was blasted by the Haymarket bomb. The plutocrats marked the chance and swiftly seized it. For weeks and months the monopoly press of the country kept up one long screech of horror. The comfortably-circumstanced middle-class people of all sections were simply convulsed with terror. Their craze of fear made them incapable of weighing evidence or giving anything like a just estimation of the actual situation. Their trembling souls were dominated by one awful thought: "The anarchists are here; law, order, government and Christian civilation are liable to be swept from the land by a wave of fire and blood. Save us at any price! Give us a despotism if you can do no better, but save us, whatever you do."

If in the spring of 1886 a bold and ambitious military man had been in the Presidential chair, instead of Grover Cleveland, he could have made himself dictator of the nation and afterward emperor without the slightest opposition on the part of the middle class. For months after the Haymarket affair a Russian "white terror" was in possession of a great metropolis of the American republic. The police of Chicago became as supreme and irresponsible as those of St. Petersburg. The prisons were choked with suspects arrested without warrant, and the victim who asked for a trial in vain. The homes of the poor were invaded by squads of lawless detectives, and the constitutional right of the American citizen to keep and bear arms was arbitrarily taken away. The ordinary force of spies, informers, shadowers and detectives was increased to an enormous extent, and the bankers and millionaires raised a large fund for the employment of a special corps of sleuths, spotters and doggers to keep ceaseless watch on every man known to be a reformer. It was a rich harvest time for the criminal and dissolute scoundrels composing the only class that will hire out as spies. These despicable wretches must earn their money, so they turned in lying reports that were greedily believed by their masters. The tyrant Czar's terrible third section held saturnalia on American soil, and Liberty shud-

dered. Peaceful meetings of workingmen were broken up by the policeman's club and whosoever dared to protest was brutally beaten and dragged off to a cell. Free speech was throttled and freedom under the law ceased to be a living fact. . . .

Thousands of thoughtful Americans who were in Chicago during the anarchist craze received a moral shock from which they can never recover until this republic is planted anew on the old foundations of democratic liberty. That masque of despotism had its dread hour, and the hideous nighmare vanished, but ere it departed the most precious faith of many a patriotic soul had withered under its blighting shadow. Men who had sealed an inherited love for the republic in many a battle, and by the side of many a comrade's grave, felt the first doubt come to their exultant belief in the all-sufficiency of their country for every trial, and with the new questioning came a bitterness that passed the bitterness of death. They saw the sacred elemental principles, which must underlie a government that is truly of the people, by the people and for the people, ignored, profaned and shamelessly violated under the influence of a blind and unreasoning terror that was sedulously propagated by the designing plutocracy, which had much to gain through it. . . .

While all the civil functions of our democratic order of society were supposed to be in full force, the arbitrary methods of the Russian police were used with brutal lawlessness. The democratic idea in human government was mocked at and spit upon, and the omnipotent middle class not only tolerated the outrage but approved it, so that it stands today as an unquestioned precedent; and when the next "wild scare" comes along, either through accident or by the careful planning of the plutocracy, the middle class will without a murmur see a city, or a state, or the whole country, pass into the hands of a despotism as savage as that of Persia. Let them be once assured that they are not going to be hurt by it, and that their precious property and sources of income will be doubly secure by a plutocratic "white terror" with its summary arrests and dragonnades, and they will acquiesce in the destruction of every sacred tradition of the republic. This they will do if their action during the Chicago anarchy craze has any value as indicating their future course under similar circumstances. That national tragedy gave the republic the most shattering blow that it ever received.

Lester C. HUBBARD

from *The Coming Climax*
in the Destinies of America
(Chicago: Charles H. Kerr. 1891)

Chicago *Daily News*, May 5, 1886

HAYMARKET
AND THE JEWS

Sigmund Zeisler

Moses Salomon

The Haymarket affair blew many things sky-high, not the least of which was the faith of the workers, including the Jewish workers, in the courts of our country. The case had wide national and international repercussions.

On this anniversary, it is instructive to outline the impact of this major event in American history on the Jewish population at that time.

The first May Day demonstration, May 1, 1886, in the form of strikes for the eight-hour day, had been held in many cities of the United States. In Chicago alone, 40,000 had struck. The main slogan was the demand for the eight-hour day. The employers were alarmed and prepared for action. On May 3, the police fired on strikers demonstrating against scabs at the McCormick Harvester plant, killing four workers and wounding many more. On May 4, a meeting to protest the police attack was held in Chicago. As the peaceable meeting was ending, and the workers were beginning to disperse, again the police attacked in full force. A bomb exploded.

To this day no one knows who threw that bomb in Haymarket Square, Chicago, that caused the death of seven policemen and four workers and wounded scores of others. But since June 26, 1893, when Illinois Governor John Peter Altgeld issued his great document pardoning the three living defendants, the world has known there was a frame-up of workers involved. Three academic historians summed up the case in one sentence in 1940: "The verdict was the product of public hysteria, a prejudiced judge, perjured evidence, and a strange theory of conspiracy."[1]

COURAGEOUS LAWYERS

The commercial press, which had all along been fighting the movement for the eight-hour day out of which grew the Haymarket meeting, now howled for the blood of the "anarchists," as they called the revolutionary trade unionists or Anarcho-Syndicalists who were heading that movement in Chicago. A pious echo of this incitement was voiced by Rev. Isaac M. Wise in *The American Israelite* in Cincinnati on May 14 when he warned anarchists and socialists that "Judge Lynch is a tremendous expounder of the law."

In such an atmosphere not a criminal lawyer in Chicago would take up the legal defense of the eight indicted and it fell to four courageous civil lawyers to assume this role. First to step into the situation was the firm of Salomon & Zeisler. The senior partner, Moses Salomon, was only 28 and was then the counsel for the Central Labor Union of Chicago, led by the Anarcho-Syndicalists, which asked him to take the case. His partner, Sigmund Zeisler, was only 26 but had already lectured in Roman Law at the Northwestern University Law School. To add weight to the defense battery, they succeeded in enlisting two eminent men, Captain W.P. Black and William A. Foster.

Opening the case for the defense before a fraudulently selected jury and a biased Judge Joseph E. Gary, Moses Salomon in vain urged the jury to evaluate the evidence strictly on the charge of murder and not to allow themselves "to convict any of these defendants either because he may be an Anarchist or a Socialist." Following him, Sigmund Zeisler explained that a social revolution could not be "made," that it "is a thing which develops itself, but no single man, nor a dozen of men can control the inauguration of a revolution," and that the charge of conspiracy, when leveled against people who publicly proclaimed their views, was fantastic.[2]

The battle of the defense lawyers was in vain. The jury, which included a relative of one of the slain policemen, brought in a sentence of death for seven and 15 years for the eighth. The unexpected brutality of the sentence, while it was ferociously applauded by the general press, shocked elements among the workers and liberals into opposition.

"This verdict is a crime against the workers," declared *Di Nu-Yorker Idishe Folkzeitung* on August 20, 1886. Yet, while the conservative *Idishe Gazetten*, *The Jewish Reformer* and *The Jewish Messenger* in New York supported the prosecution and the verdict, *The American Israelite* apparently thought the lynching had gone too far. On September 3, 1886, Rev. Wise came out in opposition to the death sentence because of "an extenuating point, viz: Those men may be true in their pretensions, that they acted for the benefit of their fellow-men, from convictions which are undoubtedly false and unreasonable, but not criminal, *per se*."

THE AMNESTY MOVEMENT

While the State Supreme Court was confirming the verdict and the federal Supreme Court was characteristically refusing to review the case, the amnesty movement against the execution grew to immense proportions. At first even the organized workers, except for the left wing, had been paralyzed by the furious red-baiting attack. Terence V. Powderly, head of the 700,000-strong Knights of Labor, forbade Knights to take part in the defense—lest they be called anarchists and socialists. But these orders from on top soon began to be flouted by the workers in the labor assemblies. In New York, the large District Assembly 49 combined with the Central Labor Union to form a joint committee of 25 for a campaign of petitions and mass meetings. On this Committee

119

Samuel Gompers, Gregory Weinstein, M. Weiner and Louis Weiss were active.

As the execution date, November 11, 1887, approached, the the expanding clemency movement led hundreds of thousands to express themselves for clemency. Among the Jews who spoke up were Rev. Sabato Morais in Philadelphia, Rev. Emil G. Hirsh in Chicago, and Felix Adler in New York. The *Idishe Folkzeitung* of October 14, 1887 lists the names of Jews in Carmel, N.J., who had raised $10 for the defense fund, in contributions of 15, 25, and 50 cents. While *The Jewish Exponent* in Philadelphia on November 4 was opposing "leniency" and fearing "an evil precedent" if the hangings did not go through as scheduled, the petition campaign grew.

In Chicago during the last week, 41,000 signatures were obtained from people of all classes and beliefs, among them Julius Stern, a past president of the Chicago Law Institute. At the governor's clemency hearing in Springfield, Samuel Gompers, offically as president of the American Federation of Labor, was among those who argued for clemency.[3] But the governor was more responsive to the voice of Marshall Field than to that of the petitioners. He commuted the sentences of two to life imprisonment; four were hanged, and a fifth committed suicide to beat the hanging. The crack of broken necks was heard around the world.

EFFECT ON THE JEWISH MASSES

The Jewish immigrant masses were profoundly stirred by these horrible events in a land to which they had come in search of equality, freedom and justice. The activity of the Jews among the anarchists influenced thousands, through an organization of Jewish anarchists founded in October 1886, *Pioneren der Freiheit* (Pioneers of Freedom). Jews who had no interest in anarchism as such rallied to defend the Haymarket martyrs against injustice. A few became confirmed and organized anarchists, becoming, as S. Yanovsky puts it, "a profound hater of all that went under the name of justice, law and legality."

One of the classic Yiddish proletarian poets, David Edelshtat (1866-1892), was stirred to the depths. He was only 20 when the trial took place, a Russian-speaking intellectual more interested in events in Russia than in the United States. The Haymarket Affair "Americanized" Edelshtat, turning his heart and mind to the masses about him. He plunged into the defense activity, and was himself arrested for his pains. When he began to write poetry in Yiddish for the anarchist press, he had a new social content and the ring of passion. Yet it was not until almost two years after the execution that he composed his first poem on the Haymarket, *"Ver Varen Zai?"* ("Who Were They"—published in translation in *Jewish Life*, Nov. 1954.) Around anniversary time in 1890, Edelshtat published poems on August Spies and Albert Parsons, who had been hanged, and Louis Lingg, the suicide, and a fourth one, "The 11th of November." In 1891 he wrote "The 11th in a Strange City" and the year after that he began to translate some of Parsons' own poetry. Edelshtat did not live to see the pardon of the three imprisoned, in 1893.[4]

When Governor Altgeld finally issued his pardon on June 26, 1893, carefully analyzing the misconduct of the prosecutor, the jury, the judge and the witnesses, the commercial press

WHO WERE THEY?

They would not sleep in shame, like all the rest,
Nor could they either slaves or swindlers be.
They spoke the free and open truth. Till death
They fought for human rights and liberty.
They carried in their breasts the scarlet flame
Of Truth, sweet radiance that freedom casts.
They bid us speak in Truth's unsullied name,
And summoned us to man's unfinished tasks.
They never gave consent to those decrees
Which only blind the people, and enslave.
They ripped apart the laws of tyranny,
To laws of nature recognition gave.
They broke a window through in mankind's hated
Prison-house of black obscurity,
And freely let the sunlight permeate
The pallid world of human slavery.
Usurpers paled and tyrants shook in fright;
The slave was waking, tearing at his chain,
Had understood at last his human right,
"Liberty or death!" his fierce refrain.
But when the cruel, man-devouring class
Had barely heard the Truth thus spoken free,
It seized its bloodstained knife in deadly grasp
And plunged into this monstrous butchery.
Oh brothers! They have killed our champions, who
Were leading us through strife to victory.
Oh baseness vile! how brilliantly have you
Prevailed, in this, the nineteenth century!
How powerless the people stood, and mute—
So like a child! Not one bold hand to thwart
The rope, to stop the tyrant's hangman-brute!
Oh masses! Where your reason? Where your heart?
In Waldheim now, man's freedom-thinkers rest.
And still are heard, from that eternal site,
The savage hangman's roaring epithets,
Which rouse the world of slaves to freedom's fight.

They ask no hymns of praise, no monument
Of marble, bloodied by the slave's own hand,
Their sole request is man's enlightenment,
The fight for human rights their one demand.
Unite, oh people! Learn your strength! Awake!—
And heed the wish that echoes from their graves.
Throw off your yoke! And crush the vicious snakes
Which poisoned you and turned you into slaves!

David EDELSHTAT

Cincinnati, Ohio,
23 September 1889
(Translated by Max Rosenfeld)

was almost unanimous in its vituperation of this signal act of justice. *The American Hebrew*, in an editoral on July 7 entitled "A Flagrant Wrong," parroted the outcries about the "murderous butchers" who had been hanged, denounced "this gross blunder " of Altgeld's and adjudged that he had covered himself "with contumely and contempt." No wonder there was fury at this act of belated justice! As the Yiddish *Arbeiter-Zeitung*, official organ of the United Hebrew Trades, wrote on June 30: "The capitalist class has, by one of its own governors, been acknowledged as a gang of low-down murderers!"

Although the terrorization spread by reaction intimidated many workers, the resistance, expressing itself in the amnesty campaign, strengthened the class-conscious elements among the workers. Less than a year after the hangings, new organizational victories were achieved.

Morris U. SCHAPPES

from *Jewish Life*
(now *Jewish Currents*),
November 1956

[1]Harry J. Carman, Henry David, Paul N. Guthrie, *The Path I Trod: The Autobiography of Terence V. Powderly*, Columbia University Press, New York, p. 159, note; the best treatments of the case are: Henry David, *The History of the Haymarket Affair*, New York, 1936; Harry Barnard, *Eagle Forgotten, The Life of John Peter Altgeld*, New York, 1938; Alan Calmer, *Labor Agitator: The Story of Albert R. Parsons*, New York, 1937; and of special interest because it is by one of the defense lawyers, Sigmund Zeisler, "Reminiscences of the Anarchist Case," *Illinois Law Review*, Nov. 1926, p. 224-250.
[2]Dyer D. Lum, *A Concise History of the Great Trial of the Chicago Anarchists in 1886*, Chicago, 1886, p. 103; David, work cited, pp. 303-304.
[3]Gregory Weinstein, *The Ardent Eighties and After*, New York, 3rd ed., 1947, opp. p. 203; David, work cited, p. 430, 431, 451; Samuel Gompers, *Seventy Years of Life and Labor*, New York, 1924, vol. 2, pp. 174-181.

WILLIAM P. BLACK

William Perkins Black (1842-1916) risked one of Chicago's most promising legal and political careers to defend those accused in the wake of the Haymarket explosion.

Kentucky-born, Black helped organize the 37th Illinois Infantry during the Civil War. His heroism at the Battle of Pea Ridge won him a Congressional Medal of Honor before his twentieth birthday. After the war he settled in Chicago and became a successful lawyer, a charter member of the city's Bar Association and a partner in a prestigious firm. A Democrat after a flirtation with Liberal Republicanism, Black came within an eyelash of election to Congress in 1882.

The decision to defend the Haymarket prisoners did not come easily to Black. Visited by Dr. Ernst Schmidt and defense attorneys Sigmund Zeisler and Moses Salomon, he promised at first only to help find suitable counsel. Failing to do so, Black asked Judge Murray F. Tuley if he should undertake the defense. Black knew it would entail "an almost total sacrifice of. . .business" and "possibly of. . .future prospects" to do so. Tuley allowed that such an assessment "underestimated" the cost. Still Black agreed to serve, in what Zeisler termed an "act of heroism."

Black's able and aggressive defense—Edward and Eleanor Marx Aveling called him a "magnificent advocate" of the accused—failed to prevent convictions, though it was probably instrumental in saving the lives of three of the defendants. For his efforts, and especially because he and his wife Hortensia wrote and spoke of their admiration for and friendship with the accused, Black won the hatred of Judge Gary, who singled him out for abuse in his 1893 reminiscences of the trial. Black also saw his corporate clients drift away and his income decline by two-thirds. Despite all this, he remained active as a Populist Democrat, a free-silver supporter and, above all, a civil libertarian.

DR

EULOGY AT WALDHEIM

I am not here this afternoon, dear friends, to speak to you any special word concerning the cause for which these men lived, nor concerning the manner of their taking off; but to speak to you rather of themselves, to tell you their love for the cause which commanded their services, was sealed at last by their lives, not grudgingly, but given with unstinted measure for the sake of those they loved. You know, many of you, who have read the press, how grandly they passed out of this life that is seen into the perfect and glorious life that is beyond the reach of misjudgment, of resentment, or of pain.

As the years go by, of whose record the story of their services will form a splendid part, they will come to be better known, to be loved, to be revered. I am not here to talk of their violent end as of an ignominious death. We are not beside the caskets of felons consigned to an inglorious tomb. We are here by the bodies of men who were sublime in their self-sacrifice, and for whom the gibbet assumed the glory of a cross. They moved to their appointed death slow-paced and strong—no faltering, no trembling, no turning back. . . .

To such men death had, and could have, no terrors, and their execution, which was self-immolation, could have no touch of shame. Whatever else may be said of these dead, it will not be denied that they were loyal and true to the convictions which had taken captive, years ago, their hearts, and to what they believed to be the welfare of the people, whom they loved.

I must not keep you long, and yet there is one thing that I specially want to say, because doubtless in this great throng there stand many who misapprehended their position and their views. They were called Anarchists. They were painted and presented to the world as men loving violence, riot, and bloodshed for their own sake; as men full of an unextinguishable and causeless hatred against existing order. Nothing could be further from the truth. They were men who loved peace, men of gentle instincts, men of gracious tenderness of heart, loved by those who knew them, trusted by those who came to understand the loyalty and purity of their lives. And the Anarchy of which they spoke and taught—what was it, but an attempt to answer the question, "After the revolution, what?" They believed—ah! I would that there were no grounds for this belief—that there was that of wrong and hardship in the existing order which pointed to conflict, because they believed that greed and selfishness would not surrender, of their own volition, unto righteousness. But their creed had to do with the tomorrow of the possible revolution, and the whole of their thought and their philosophy, as Anarchists, was the establishment of an order of society that should be symbolized in the words, "order without force." Is it practicable? I know not.

I know that it is not practical now; but I know also that through the ages poets, philosophers, and Christians, under the inspiration of love and beneficence, have thought of the day to come when righteousness shall reign in the earth, and when sin and selfishness should come to an end. We look forward to that day, we hope for it, and with such a hope in our hearts can we not bring the judgement of charity to bear upon any mistakes of policy or action that may have been made by any of those who, acknowledging the sublime and glorious hope in their hearts, have rushed forward to meet it?

We are not here this afternoon to weep, we are not here to mourn over our dead. We are here to pay, by our presence and our words, the tribute of our appreciation and the witness of our love. For I loved these men. I knew them not until I came to know them in the time of their sore travail and anguish. As months went by, and I found in the lives of these with whom I talked the witness of their love for the people, of their patience, gentleness, and courage, my heart was taken captive in their cause. . . .

Capt. William P. BLACK

from Lucy E. Parsons,
The Life of Albert R. Parsons
(Chicago, 1889).

VOL. XX.—No. 495.   NEW YORK, SEPTEMBER 1, 1886.   PRICE, TEN CTS.

KEPPLER & SCHWARZMANN, Publishers.   TRADE MARK REGISTERED 1878.   PUCK BUILDING, Cor. Houston & Mulberry Sts.

ENTERED AT THE POST OFFICE AT NEW YORK, AND ADMITTED FOR TRANSMISSION THROUGH THE MAILS AT SECOND CLASS RATES.

THE ONLY MOURNER—THE ANARCHIST EDITOR.

Cartoon by Frederick Burr Opper (1886)

JOSEPH A. LABADIE (1850-1933)

At the time of the Haymarket affair, Joseph A. Labadie was 36 years old, one of Michigan's foremost labor organizers and activists and, for the past three years, an extremely vocal philosophical anarchist. Although the condemned men espoused communistic anarchism and preached violence as a necessary part of the coming revolution, and Labadie represented individualistic anarchism and anticipated the transformation of society peacefully through education, he did not hesitate to defend the prisoners from the start. The violence at Haymarket, as he saw it, was caused by "authority" attempting to suppress free speech.

Labadie was at that time principal contributor to the Detroit *Labor Leaf*, one of the few labor papers to oppose the anti-radical hysteria. "I do wish the labor papers would stop distributing the nasty puke the capitalist papers have seen fit to cover their dirty sheets with," he wrote two weeks after Haymarket. August Spies, writing from jail four months later, told Labadie it was "gratifying to see that in the general stampede of cowardly retreat there are at least some voices who boldly and fearlessly proclaim The Truth."

Labadie visited the seven condemned men in jail in Chicago in October 1887, on his way to the Minneapolis Knights of Labor convention, and again on his return, shaking hands with them by putting his little finger through the iron grating.

Labadie returned from the convention bitterly opposed to Terence Powderly, leader of the Knights, for his refusal to support clemency for the Haymarket anarchists and for his "autocratic" methods. In 1889, he became allied with Samuel Gompers and helped found the Michigan Federation of Labor, a state affiliate of the American Federation of Labor, serving as its first president.

Jo Labadie was born April 18, 1850, in Paw Paw, Michigan, of French-Canadian stock. His great-great grandmother was a full-blooded Ojibway Indian. His childhood was spent in the woods among local Indians, his father serving as an interpreter between them and the Jesuits.

With little formal education, Labadie began as a printer's assistant at the age of 16 and first became involved with the labor movement two years later when he joined a printers' union in Kalamazoo. By 1872 he was an active propagandist for state socialist groups. He ran unsuccessfully for mayor of Detroit on the Greenback-Labor ticket in 1878, and later held national office in the Socialist Labor Party.

In 1878 he organized the Michigan Knights of Labor and two years later was a prime mover in creating the Detroit Council of Trades and Labor Unions. He was appointed Deputy Commissioner when the Michigan Bureau of Labor Statistics was formed in 1884 and helped to prepare its first two reports.

He turned to anarchism in 1883 through reading Benjamin Tucker's *Liberty*, and contributed to that journal until it ceased publication in 1908. He also wrote for a multitude of other periodicals, both "capitalist" and radical, throughout his long life, employing a lively, lucid and witty style.

A widely popular figure in Detroit despite his dissident views, Labadie was a carefully-groomed man of great personal charm and magnetism. A benefactor gave him, in 1912, some land in the country where he spent his later years printing tracts and his own poetry, hand-bound in wallpaper scraps with ribbon ties, and given free to anyone who "didn't have the price."

His son Laurance followed in his father's footsteps as an individualist anarchist of note.

In 1911, he gave his collection of some 5,000 items of labor and radical materials spanning four decades to the University of Michigan, where it formed the nucleus of the Labadie Collection, today ranking as one of the foremost repositories of social protest literature in the world.

Carlotta ANDERSON

"CRANKY NOTIONS" ON HAYMARKET

Excerpts from Jo Labadie's "Cranky Notions" column in the Detroit Labor Leaf.

May 12, 1886: It is to be hoped that readers of this paper will suspend judgment in the matter of the troubles in Milwaukee and Chicago until the newspapers get cooled off a little. I was going to say until they regained their reason, but the average newspaper cannot regain what it never lost. The reporters have pretty generally worked themselves up into a terrible state of frenzy, and lies and ignorance come from their pens as slime from a mad dog's mouth. You want to believe but a small fraction of what you read in the newspapers.

May 19, 1886: The Detroit *Tribune* wants the government to stop carrying the Chicago *Alarm* and *Arbeiter Zeitung* and Most's *Freiheit* in the mails. I disagree very materially with many things I have seen in the *Alarm* and as I do not read German, I cannot say whether I agree with the other papers or not. . .but. . .it does seem to me that. . .if the United States government will not carry their mail for them, it certainly should relieve them of the taxes for. . .the postal budget and let them start a post office of their own. But the United States government will not do that. It is run on the same brutal, ignorant and malicious principle as are the editorial columns of the *Tribune*. . . . Force is the only argument this kind of cattle can understand.

June 16, 1886: There has been a good deal of "mush" sentiment expressed over the dynamite affair in Chicago. Whether it was the right thing to use dynamite at that time or not I do not propose to discuss, but I do believe that when any body of men goes to break up any kind of meeting they should go at the peril of their lives. If it is necessary to use dynamite to protect the right of free meetings, free press and free speech, then the sooner we learn its manufacture and use the better it will be for the toilers of the world. Anything is better than a beastly submission to wrong and injustice.

August 25, 1886: In an interview with a newspaper reporter in Chicago Saturday, Capt. Schaack, of the police force, said: "I tell you the anarchist business in Chicago has only commenced, and before it is through with we will have them all in jail, hung, or driven out of the city.'' I have never been an advocate of dynamite as a means of pushing forward the social movement, but I have no hesitation in saying that, being forewarned of the intention of this savage beast, all those who are striving for better social and industrial conditions should put themselves in such a position to successfully resist the unwarranted and brutal acts of this monster and his brood. . . . There is no doubt in my mind that the ruling class is urging on a premature and violent revolution, with the hope of crushing the labor movement at its present stage of development. . . .

October 13, 1886: And so the Chicago ''anarchists'' must hang by the neck until they are dead, must they? Well, it will only be the logical result of ''law and order'' government, if they do. And yet you must not forget that government is intended (!) for the protection of life and property. I am not at all surprised at the results so far, and will be very much surprised if the lives of these brave men are saved. But it is a foolish thing for the authorities to do, to hang these men, if they really mean to stop the radical and violent revolutionary movement. These men dead are a hundred times more dangerous than living to the existing order of things. Their death will not prevent the manufacture and use of dynamite as a defensive and aggressive weapon against constituted authorities, but will have the opposite effect, the effect of making the desperate still more desperate, and will drive those who now believe in peaceful methods to the use of violent methods. . . . Men who have learned the iniquities of the present social system are not to be terrified by even the most cruel acts of the powers that be. Let this judicial fool [Judge Gary] but take a look Russiaward and see how men and women can suffer and die for justice. But this advice is futile. Authority is always blinded by its own power, and the only logic it comprehends is physical force.

From the Report of Joseph A. Labadie, Delegate to the General Assembly, Knights of Labor, Minneapolis, 1887, to Detroit District Assembly 50, November 14, 1887,

Joseph A. Labadie

after his return from the convention and three days after the Haymarket executions:

The most earnest and exciting matters considered [at the convention] were the resolution asking executive clemency for the Chicago anarchists and the disclosures of maladministration made by Barry and Bailey. . . . Only 55 out of a total 173 dared to raise their voices in behalf of men unjustly tried and convicted.

Most of the speakers admitted that the anarchists had not had a fair trial nor had they been justly convicted, yet they thought they were not justified in committing the Order to asking the governor of Illinois to prevent their exercution. . . . The most illogical, cowardly, brutal and violent speech made came from the general master workman [Powderly] himself. I hold him as much responsible for the murder committed in Chicago last Friday as any one connected with that most unfortunate affair. He threatened that if the resolution passed, there would never be held another session of the General Assembly, and declared that no matter what action the General Assembly took he would not be bound by it. He warned the convention if it passed the resolution he would go out on the public platform and denounce the men under sentence of death. He can now contemplate what a heroic part he played in that great tragedy. He can now take what consolation he can in knowing that he helped to hang better men than he ever was or ever can be. If it is an act of heroism to attack men who stand upon the scaffold with ropes around their necks, then is Mr. Powderly a hero? And yet this is the man whose feelings overcame him and caused him to shed tears when some of his friends presented him with a crayon portrait of himself. . . .

Whether or not I can remain with you, and enjoy the pleasant associations I have formed during my connection with the labor movement and this Order in this city, future developments will decide. Mr. Powderly says an anarchist cannot be a Knight of Labor. The G. A. [General Assembly] seemed to take that view of the case, too, and whether I shall quietly take my leave of you or put you to the test of expelling me for having ideas not altogether in harmony with the majority, I will determine before long. . . .

(Note: *Labadie left the Order soon after the Minneapolis convention.*)

Compiled by Carlotta ANDERSON

JOSEPH R. BUCHANAN

One of the foremost labor organizers and editors of his time, Joseph R. Buchanan (1851-1924) was a printer by trade, a longtime member of Denver Typographical Union No. 49 (and its delegate to the 1882 ITU convention), later of Chicago Typographical Union No. 16. He was also on the executive board of the Knights of Labor until 1887, when he was expelled because of numerous differences he had with General Master Workman Powderly.

Buchanan was also a prominent figure in Burnette G. Haskell's International Work-

men's Association, the ''Red International'' (not to be confused with the International Working People's Association to which the Chicago anarchists belonged), and his paper, the Denver Labor Enquirer—one of the most influential labor papers in the country—served as the IWA's official organ.

From the start Buchanan's Enquirer was a vigorous voice in defense of the Haymarket prisoners; its issue of May 17, 1886, for example, included Lucy Parsons' summary of the May 4th events and the ensuing police terror. When he moved to Chicago early in 1887, he started a new paper, the Chicago Labor Enquirer, a weekly (sometimes twice-

weekly) that continued to tell the truth about Haymarket, and thus to defend the imprisoned men; Parsons and Spies were frequent contributors. Buchanan was also active in other phases of the Haymarket defense, and was one of those who called on Gov. Oglesby during the last-minute appeal for clemency.

Joe Buchanan was one of Albert Parsons' pallbearers, and master of ceremonies at the martyrs' funeral. His brief account, reprinted here, is excerpted from his exceptionally valuable memoir, The Story of a Labor Agitator (1903).

FR

The Haymarket Funeral Proceeding Along Milwaukee Avenue (from *The Pictorial West*, December 1887)

From left to right on top: The Spies Residence   Engel's Store   Fischer's Home   Parsons' Flat

Fred Muller's   Viewing the Remains

THE HAYMARKET FUNERAL

The bodies of the executed men, and that of Louis Lingg, the suicide, were laid in the temporary vault, at Waldheim Cemetery, on Sunday, November 13. The funeral cortege was said to be the largest ever seen in Chicago. The five hearses were followed by thousands of mourners, and the newspapers estimated the vast crowds that lined the streets through which the procession passed at nearly two hundred thousand. As one of Albert Parsons's pall-bearers I marched through three miles of crowded streets that day, and upon every one of the thousands of faces I saw about me there was a look of sorrow. I noticed that some of the policemen bared and bowed their heads as the hearses passed them.

The police department had issued an order prohibiting the carrying of banners or flags of any kind. With a single exception the order was obeyed. Just as the procession began to move down Milwaukee Avenue a veteran of the Civil War stepped quickly in front of the first rank and unfurled a small American flag. The old veteran was not molested by the police; he carried the flag to the end of the march.

At the cemetery short addresses were made by Capt. Black, Thomas J. Morgan and others, and chants were rendered by several of Chicago's singing-societies.

On Sunday, December 18, the caskets containing the mortal remains of "the boys" were placed, side by side, in an underground vault which had been built in Waldheim to receive them. A vast concourse of people assembled to participate in and witness these final ceremonies. After reaching the cemetery I was requested by the committee to preside. I accepted the honor, making a short speech in opening the exercises. Addresses were made by Captain William P. Black, Paul Grottkau and Albert Currlin. Captain Black's address was the most eloquent and most impressive funeral oration I have ever read or heard.

Joseph R. BUCHANAN

From Joseph R. Buchanan,
The Story of a Labor Agitator
(New York, 1903)

Anarchy in the mass media in the 1880s

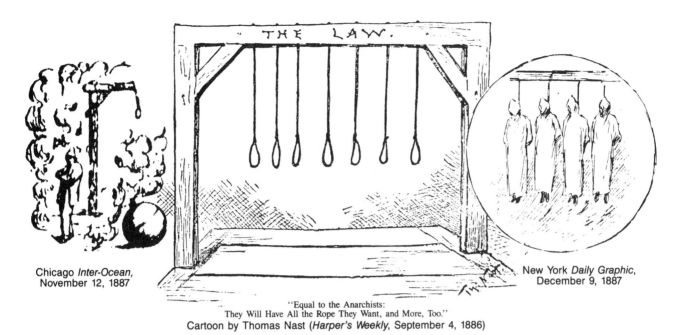

Chicago *Inter-Ocean*,
November 12, 1887

New York *Daily Graphic*,
December 9, 1887

"Equal to the Anarchists:
They Will Have All the Rope They Want, and More, Too."
Cartoon by Thomas Nast (*Harper's Weekly*, September 4, 1886)

YEAR OF THE HANGMAN'S NOOSE

The smoke from the Haymarket bomb had hardly settled when U.S. newspapers, almost as if on cue, began to clamor for the deaths of the Chicago anarchists. The very next day, May 5, 1886, a *Daily News* editorial outlined what would become the prosecution's central—albeit legally unprecedented—argument:

The bomb that did such deadly work last night must have been prepared with the knowledge and consent of the anarchist leaders. The man who hurled the missile must have been appointed by those persons who represent the law-breakers. The act was a murderous one. Under the law all parties advocating and abetting the deed are guilty of the crime. Responsibility must rest upon the self-avowed heads of the socialistic bodies.

In other words, because someone—no one knows who—threw a bomb, the most radical leaders of the labor movement should be made to sacrifice their lives.

A firestorm of hate swirled out of Chicago. The drive to hang the anarchists became all-pervasive, and commanded prime space in the mainstream press for months—until November 1887, when four anarchists indeed went to the gallows.

1886: The year in which the Statue of Liberty went up in New York, was also the year in which the hangman's noose became America's national icon.

The passions of another time are hard to recreate, even in our minds. The accompanying illustrations are a small sampling of popular iconography spawned by the Haymarket affair. Garishly illustrated newsweeklies like *Frank Leslie's*, display ads and drawings in the daily papers, sensational "potboiler" books like *The Chicago Riot* by *Daily News* reporter Paul C. Hull and Capt. Schaack's later deluxe coffee-table compendium: These provide clues to what Americans found of interest in the immediate aftermath of Haymarket.

Many Haymarket "artifacts" not reproduced here are also revealing in their way. Brass bomb tokens were sold, prob-

ably to raise funds for the police statue. An Atlantic & Pacific Tea Company ad in the *Tribune* featured the word EXPLODING three times in capitals and large type. Stereopticon slides of the "riot" were marketed. Anarchists were portrayed in wax museums, and starred as villains in detective stories. A "panorama" created by Chicago Alderman Sheridan was shown at the Dime Museum, along with Big Winnie Johnson, an unfortunate overweight black woman from Kentucky. But the predominant image was the gallows with dangling nooses.

Interestingly, many of those closest to the Haymarket prisoners adopted the gallows-and-noose as their own symbol of defiance. From the Christian's cross to the unrepaired shoe taken up as a campaign emblem by Adlai Stevenson's supporters in the 1950s, examples of such symbolic appropriation are not rare in history. Lucy Parsons and other defenders of the anarchists wore gold and silver jewelers' miniatures of the scaffold on their clothing, no doubt at least in part as a riposte to newspaper editors who were constantly goading the courts to hang *all* anarchists, socialists and "agitators" in general. Wearers of the device formed an "Order of the Gallows."

Significantly, too, the popular press of the time reveals that, along with its consuming fascination with the gallows and paraphernalia of death, the American public was also eager to know what the anarchists looked like. Many different likenesses of the defendants appeared in the press, and primitive portraits were evidently sold on the street.

The images assembled here—and others scattered throughout this *Scrapbook*—convey something of the press and public appetite for trivia in 1886-87, and of their obsession with bombs, explosions, the anarchist-as-monster, and above all with hangings, gallows, violence, revenge and death.

Theodore WATTS

VOL. XXI.—No. 527.   NEW YORK, APRIL 13, 1887.   PRICE, TEN CENTS.

KEPPLER & SCHWARZMANN, Publishers.   TRADE MARK REGISTERED 1878.   PUCK BUILDING, Cor. Houston & Mulberry Sts.

ENTERED AT THE POST OFFICE AT NEW YORK, AND ADMITTED FOR TRANSMISSION THROUGH THE MAILS AT SECOND CLASS RATES.

"What fools these Mortals be!"
MIDSUMMER-NIGHTS DREAM

Puck

ORDER REIGNS IN CHICAGO!
She Strangles the Vipers She Has Nourished Too Long.

Chicago strangles anarchists as well as Carter Harrison's Democrats in this 1887 cartoon.

128

"MY MEN SHOOT WELL":
Theodore Roosevelt and the Urban Frontier

In January 1886 Theodore Roosevelt delivered a lecture in which he shared with a New York audience his utter contempt for Indians:

I don't go so far as to think that the only good Indians are the dead Indians, but I believe nine out of every ten are, and I shouldn't like to inquire too closely into the case of the tenth. The most vicious cowboy has more moral principle than the average Indian.

That spring, back with the cowboys on his ranch in the Dakota Badlands, he reacted to news of the Haymarket explosion with his own well-known outburst:

My men are hard-working, laboring men, who work longer hours for no greater wages than most of the strikers; but they are Americans through and through. I believe nothing would give them greater pleasure than a chance with rifles at one of the mobs. When we get the papers. . .they become more furiously angry and excited than I do. I wish I had them with me and a fair show at ten times our number of rioters. My men shoot well and fear very little.

And two years later he wrote that "the day that the anarchists were hung in Chicago, my men joined with the rest of the neighborhood in burning them in effigy."

In an excellent chapter on the "Red Scare" in *The Haymarket Tragedy* (1984), Paul Avrich quotes a portion of TR's bloodthirsty outburst as an instance of the public indignation "goaded by an hysterical press." It was surely that, but why were TR and all the other good citizens so ready for the goading? So prone to what William Dean Howells called "those spasms of paroxysmal righteousness to which our Anglo-Saxon race is peculiarly subject"? So ready to believe anarchists "entitled to no more consideration than wild beasts"? To hunt them "like wolves"? To embrace "Judge Lynch"? To believe with the St. Louis *Globe-Democrat* that "There are no good anarchists except dead anarchists"? A foray into Roosevelt's life and works may provide answers that will help complement Avrich's analysis.

The only good Indian and/or anarchist was a dead Indian and/or anarchist, for in the lexicon of the day they were metaphorically reversible "savages," red and white, wilderness (so called) and urban. Thus the Indian-hating in the cowboy-aristocrat's lecture in New York City smoothly resurfaced in the red-baiting and exterminatory rhetoric of his letter from the Dakota Territory.

Shortly Roosevelt made explicit the theoretical underpinnings of his views in *The Winning of the West* (1889-1896), a multivolume study that reduced American history to an endless game of Cowboys and Indians. The Cowboys' forebears earned his supreme acclaim for the "conquest of this continent"—an achievement of great "race importance"—and for the attendant killing and subjugation of the "original red lords of the land":

Whether the whites won the land by treaty, by armed conquest, or, as was actually the case, by a mixture of both, mattered comparatively little so long as the land was won. It was all-important that it should be won for the benefit of civilization and in the interests of mankind.

Even the Sand Creek Massacre, in which Colonel J.M. Chivington's irregulars murdered 450 Cheyenne men, women and children, was, in spite of certain details, "on the whole as righteous and beneficial a deed as ever took place on the frontier."

To keep what had been won through racial war on the land frontier from being lost through class war on the urban, it followed, was no less all-important. But with the closing of the era of "free" land, the western safety-valve had plugged and backed up human scum; however white, to menace "civilization"—or more precisely control of the cities by the corporate and professional elite. Just as Indians (and blacks) had been chastised and made properly subordinate, so now immigrant workers, agitators, anarchists, tramps, and other members of the "dangerous classes" had to be put down. Hence Roosevelt aimed his invective at "renegades" who betrayed their class by taking the part of strikers—they were the counterparts of the "foolish sentimentalists" who took the part of the "squalid savages"—and constantly exhorted his own and the middle class to take decisive action, not to lose "the hard fighting virtues," to be worthy members of "the great masterful races," to play "a man's part among men" by sharing his own bottomless passion for killing. And hence he had wished to give his cowboys—those properly subservient "Americans through and through"—the fringe benefit of pleasure through "a chance with rifles" at largely unarmed assemblies of poor people. Beyond doubt he would have justified that too as, "on the whole, as righteous and beneficial a deed as ever took place" on the urban frontier.

Roosevelt was not showing off one of his charming idiosyncrasies when he applied the exterminatory language of Indian-hating to industrial and urban conflicts. In his insightful *The Fatal Environment* (1985), Richard Slotkin shows that other influential members of TR's class responded to the upheavals of the Civil War, Reconstruction, economic depression, and especially the great railroad strike of 1877 with a concerted effort to merge the categories of race and class through a metaphorical depiction of "Strikers as Savages." Illustratively, in the *New York World* Manton Marbles habitually tied labor troubles to Indian troubles. In *The Nation* E. L. Gotkin, whose views dovetailed with Roosevelt's at vital points, spoke of "savage whites" and "savage Indians" in one breath. Since only capitalism had raised "man above the beasts," according to Gotkin, strikers, anarchists, and other enemies of capitalism had become fit stand-ins for the "merciless Indian savages" of old, and like them, beasts that sought to return man to "the woods and caves."

But a metaphor is a metaphor. For all their efforts to distance themselves from those *The Nation* called "this mass of envious discontent," Gotkin, TR, and other members of the white elite could never make that distance racial—even *Harper's* reluctantly acknowledged strikers as members of "the dominant race upon this continent" and as such never subject to wars of extermination, removal, reservations. To be sure, in times of public hysteria such as that following Haymarket, labor organizers, socialists, anarchists and other radicals could be hunted "like wolves" and tried before "Judge Lynch," a.k.a. Judge Gary. But when the hysteria ebbed, the enormity of the stakes made those in "the dominant race" restive about their own safety and well-being. No matter what the Haymarket defendants had been accused of, said John Peter Altgeld in justifying his pardon of the three survivors, "they were entitled to a fair trial, and no greater damage could possibly threaten our institutions than to have the courts of justice run wild or give way to popular clamor." Predictably Roosevelt joined in the attack on the governor's pardon by denouncing Altgeld as another renegade "friend of the lawless classes," but cooler heads came to recognize that treating Indians as beasts was one thing and treating white citizens as such by denying their fundamental rights was another.

Class was not race and anarchists were not Indians. Still, the concerted effort to apply Indian-hating directly to urban strife helps explain the intensity and virulence of the Haymarket Red Scare and those that followed, and helps account for the violence of American labor wars—all the Homesteads and Pullmans, Everetts and Centralias. And perhaps Theodore Roosevelt was not entirely wide of the mark, after all, for Indians and anarchists have indeed shared a commitment to personal freedom and an opposition to the oppression and imperial expansion the cowboy-aristocrat championed. Anyway, I find fitting Paul Avrich's account of Rudolph Schnaubelt, the only Haymarket defendant to escape, crossing over into Canada on foot and, "after wandering in the woods, he was given food and shelter by friendly Indians."

Richard DRINNON

THE ROAD TO FORT SHERIDAN

The Haymarket bomb, the trial and execution, and the sudden interest in a worldwide celebration of May Day—all these things were to have a profound effect on the city of Chicago.

Many members of the elite Union League Club in Chicago were horrified by the growth of labor unions and the Haymarket bomb. Sidney Corning Eastman, a prominent attorney, after walking along the lakefront and listening to one of the rallies of the workers, issued an "Open Letter to the Union League Club." This open letter was eventually printed up as a 21-page pamphlet and distributed to all members of the club. It stated that because of all these foreign groups in Chicago and their agitation, we must have a revival of American Patriotism. Members of the club felt that these foreigners *must* follow the American way, and who personified that more than George Washington? George Pullman, Marshall Field and other members agreed to lobby for the annual celebration of Washington's Birthday. They said that to perpetuate "the ideals of loyalty which were personified in Washington by an annual tribute to his character as a man and his service as a military leader and president" would exercise an elevating influence upon the life of the community.

It is ironic that the labor movement struck back by deciding to use Washington's Birthday in 1889 as a kick-off to their new "Eight-Hour Day Movement" set for May 1890. But the businessmen of Chicago wanted more than just Washington's Birthday: They wanted military protection as a check on labor agitation in the city. Marshall Field, a member of both the Commercial Club and the Union League Club, rose before the Commercial Club and made one of his rare speeches. Field argued that there should be a regiment of soldiers near Chicago "instead of a thousand miles away, like Fort Laramie or Fort Riley."

John V. Farwell, another prominent Chicagoan, explained the need for the fort proposed by Marshall Field by saying that "the theory was that if they had some troops nearby, it would act as a preventive and prevent a lot of riots occuring in Chicago because the soldiers could get there so quickly."

With both Field and Farwell in back of such a proposal, the Commercial Club and many members of the Union League Club personally raised money to buy 632 acres of ground thirty miles north of Chicago at Highland, Illinois. In October of 1887 the land was presented to the United States Army with the understanding that troops would be permanently stationed there. The fort was soon expanded to 725 acres and named Fort Highland until the death of General Philip Sheridan, who had been a close friend of Marshall Field and George Pullman. The Fort was then renamed Fort Sheridan, and it took as its motto the phrase, "Essential to Freedom Since 1887."

Later, a military highway, Sheridan Road, would connect the fort to the city so that troops could be moved quickly from the fort to Chicago. Armories were later built in ethnic and industrial neighborhoods to house the troops during times of strikes and demonstrations. Many of the rich members of the Union League Club and the Commercial Club built palatial mansions along the North Shore near Fort Sheridan, leaving their older mansions along Rush Street, Prairie Avenue and Ashland Avenue. Never again would they have to live in fear as they had during the Railroad Strike of 1877. Never again could someone like Albert and Lucy Parsons lead a "Poor People's March" up their street demanding food and jobs as they had on Thanksgiving Day 1884.

William J. ADELMAN

Haymarket Revisited
(Chicago, 1976)

A HAYMARKET FILM?

The high drama of 1886 has yet to find its film-maker. The brochure reproduced on the facing page advertises an early attempt in that direction, that of the Wild Irons Eight Hours Pioneers Association, an offshoot of the Haymarket Pioneer Aid and Support Association, to produce an epic film based on the eight-hour struggle. The promotional literature promised a "pathbreaking" movie with a score slated to be "a compendium of the airs and songs of all nations." But the post-World-War-I project never came to fruition. Records of the effort are in the Labadie Collection at the University of Michigan, from which the illustration here is reprinted with permission.

DR

"My American countrymen let me speak, oh——"
"Our silence in the grave will speak louder than the voices you are strangling now."

Listen, workers, to the voices of the dead!
They are speaking to you, you!

Give heed! Learn from the Past to
make life a blessing for the living!

WILD IRONS

An epos in pictures, on the struggle of toilers to obtain a day
of EIGHT HOURS FOR WORK
of EIGHT HOURS FOR REST and

EIGHT HOURS FOR PLEASURE AND-EDUCATION

Abbreviated synopsis and scenario, adopted to the novel of same
title, WILD IRONS, by Theobald Trust. Music by Franz Beidl

W.E. Trautmann, 585 N. Lake ave. Pasadena

Copyrighted for Protection, production and Exhibition, by the

WILD IRONS EIGHT HOURS PIONEERS ASSOCIATION

to be incorporated as Stock Corporation, Limited

All rights to novel reserved by author and his legal successors

THE DAY WILL COME WHEN OUR SILENCE WILL BE MORE
POWERFUL THAN THE VOICES YOU ARE THROTTLING TO DAY

The Monument of Labor's Strangled Pioneers. Chicago, Ill.

THE OLD AND THE NEW

1886: "There, young man, see if you can beat that record."

Shipwrecks, an earthquake, municipal political corruption, the Statue of Liberty and boxing (the original Jack Dempsey's upcoming bout with Charley Mitchell was big sports news in May, 1886) figure in this New York *Daily Graphic* cover cartoon for December 31, 1886. But the accent is clearly on the "Labor Question," as signified by images pertaining to the Chicago anarchists, Johann Most, the Henry George mayoralty campaign, the streetcar drivers' strike and other manifestations of class conflict.

HAYMARKET AND THE FEDERATION OF LABOR

One of the ramifications of the Haymarket affair was its effect on trade union leaders who were attempting to create a national federation of labor during the 1880s. Many of them, like Carpenters' leader P. J. McGuire, had been members of local assemblies of the Knights of Labor but had resisted interference in their trade affairs by higher-level Knights' officers. Some helped to found the Federation of Organized Trades and Labor Unions of the United States and Canada (FOTLU) in 1881, an organization McGuire felt preserved "the industrial autonomy and distinctive character of each trade and labor union, and without doing violence to their feelings and traditions, blends them all in one harmonious whole. . . ."[1]

The men who founded the FOTLU for the most part did not know each other well. Mark Crawford recalled riding a train headed for a Terre Haute meeting in May 1881 preliminary to establishing the FOTLU. Crawford was a leader in the Chicago Trades and Labor Assembly at the time, as well as an organizer of the Illinois State Federation of Labor; he would become secretary-treasurer of the International Typographical Union in 1882. He rode with a stranger of whose identity he was unaware until they both registered at the same hotel. The man was Lyman Brant, president of the Detroit Trade and Labor Council and at the time corresponding secretary of the International Typographical Union. "I mention this incident," Crawford offered, "to show how little we knew of the men who gathered at this meeting."[2]

Similarly, when the founding convention of FOTLU met in Pittsburgh in November, a local newspaper found the Pittsburgh delegates worrying about the Easterners who would be attending. One of the more prevalent and, in retrospect, more bizarre rumors at the time was that the socialists of the East were prepared to seize control of the convention for their leader. Reflecting the extent of their misinformation, the Westerners believed that the leader of the socialists was none other than cigarmaker Samuel Gompers, a man who was already earning a reputation in New York City as one of the socialists' staunchest foes.[3]

During FOTLU's five years, a collection of trade union leaders became a community. FOTLU's eight-hour movement contributed to this process. The movement originated in a proposal by McGuire to the FOTLU's 1882 convention. In the tradition of manly assertiveness that was part of the culture of the shop floor of many trades, McGuire proposed achieving a universal eight-hour day without the enactment of laws "which go on our statute books never to be enforced." He hoped to see "an enactment of the workmen themselves, that on a given day they will agree to work no longer than eight hours per day and to enforce that rule themselves."[4]

At the FOTLU's 1884 convention the delegates designated May 1, 1886, as the date after which eight hours would constitute a legal day's work. The call proved enormously popular, helping to galvanize thousands of workers who joined trade unions or KOL assemblies for the first time or formed totally new organizations of their own. Amid parades and demonstrations on May 1, 1886, some 350,000 workers struck for the shorter workday.

Even as the eight-hour campaign culminated, FOTLU was proving to be no match for the KOL, whose burgeoning growth gave it 700,000 members by 1886. The FOTLU never emerged as anything but a weak federation, composed of less than a dozen national trade unions and a smaller number of city central labor bodies at any given time; it was basically an underfunded political lobby with no salaried officers. With the Knights' growth came a multiplication of jurisdictional conflicts with the national trade unions, whose independent interests the FOTLU was supposed to protect. Faced with this challenge, trade union leaders began to consider replacing the FOTLU with a stronger organization.

They did so in an atmosphere charged with conservative reaction to the Haymarket affair. The coincidence of Haymarket with the eight-hour demonstrations encouraged employers, the press and public opinion to link anarchism with unionism as common threats to public order. When trade unionists met in Philadelphia at the end of May to deal with encroachments by the Knights of Labor, they were already on the defensive. Perhaps that is why Gompers remembered so vividly the conservative appearance of the delegates: "Practically every man wore a silk hat and a Prince Albert coat," he recalled. "Each was a dignified and self-respecting journeyman who took pride in his trade and his workmanship."[5]

When a larger group met in December 1886 in Columbus, Ohio, to create a strong American Federation of Labor (AFL) in place of the FOTLU, Grafton Pierce of the Ohio State Trades and Labor Assembly set the tone in his welcoming address:

The members of trade unions are not lawless. Their intelligence has long taught them that a resort to violence—to arson, murder and an indiscriminate destruction of property—is not only opposed to the principles of good government and personal rights, but is the surest way of forfeiting the respect and support of the community.

Samuel Gompers, soon to be the new organization's first president, declared that "trade unions were conservators of the public peace. By them the vicious and ignorant are held in check, and society, the people and property are kept in safety."[6]

Despite drawing a sharp distinction between themselves and the Haymarket anarchists, these trade unionists tended to defend them, Gompers avowing for the delegates that the trade unions believed in "independent manhood, the right of free speech and free assemblage."[7] Many of those who listened had only a month or so earlier marched in parades and massed in great meetings in workingclass political campaigns that invoked the spirit of the American Revolution. Some had been part of New York's great October torchlight parade for Henry George. In announcing that event in *John Swinton's Paper*, Gompers and typographers' leader William McCabe had described its participants as motivated by "the same spirit which gave birth to the Declaration of Independence" and believing that "the principles and institutions inherited by the citizens of America from the sages and heroes of the Revolution will, when applied to the vexed problems of the day, promote the general welfare and secure life, liberty and happiness to the individual."[8]

The spirit of aroused republican citizenship was the logical complement to the spirit of manly assertiveness in the late nineteenth century American workplace. Underlying both were expectations of what workers ought to be able to achieve for themselves by peaceable means in a true republic. When Gompers, who took a leading role in the Henry George campaign, found himself and all George's supporters branded "anarchists" by the eventual victor, Abram Hewitt, he responded both as outraged worker and outraged citizen:

> If we are always stigmatized as Anarchists when we do anything to better our condition. . .by and by we shall consider that there is no harm in anarchy. If, when we resist employers reducing our wages below a living basis, we are called Anarchists, we shall know that anarchy is not wrong. If they tell us to appeal to the ballot-box and when we do so they call us Anarchists, then anarchy is not wrong. . .We have yet left to us certain inalienable rights.[9]

In the year after Haymarket Gompers joined other leaders in a campaign of meetings and petitions ending with a visit to Illinois Governor Richard Oglesby in November 1887. He told the governor that the AFL was opposed to anarchy and committed to "legal, peaceable, and honorable means and methods," but implored him to spare the anarchists. If the state punished men for exercising their rights to free speech and free assemblage, Gompers warned, it would make them martyrs in the eyes of the workers and give credibility to their violent methods.[10]

The drive to free the three Haymarket defendants who survived 1887 continued for six more years, culminating in Governor John P. Altgeld's pardon in 1893. As the daily press attacked the governor for his apostasy, Gompers urged Chicago labor leaders to honor Altgeld by inviting him to address their labor day celebration. It was a symbolic gesture that would not have been wasted on the workers of the day. The press and the capitalist class were "howling down a man for a just act," Gompers observed. It was important for the "organized intelligent masses of labor" to rally one more time, to give "grateful acknowledgement" to Altgeld's "manly, just and honorable action."[11]

Stuart Bruce KAUFMAN

1. *Carpenter*, Dec. 1882.   2. Crawford, "Large Oaks from Little Acorns Grow," *American Federationist*, 27 (Feb. 1920): 145.   3. *Pittsburgh Commercial Gazette*, Nov. 16, 1881.   4. *Carpenter*, Jan. 1883.   5. *Seventy Years of Life and Labor: An Autobiography* (2 vols., 1925), I: 257.   6. *New York Tribune*, Dec. 8, 1886.   7. *Ibid.*   8. *John Swinton's Paper*, Oct. 31, 1886.   9. *New York World*, Oct. 30, 1886.   10. *Chicago Tribune*, Nov. 10, 1887.   11. Gompers to T. J. Elderkin, July 20, 1893, Samuel Gompers Letterbooks, reel 7, vol. 9, p. 298, Library of Congress.

WHY THE AFL DEFENDED THE CHICAGO ANARCHISTS

Reports of proceedings in the anarchists' trial before Judge Gary came through the daily press and other avenues and it was a shocking story of official prejudice and clumsily disguised effort to punish men for identification with anarchy. The labor movement has ever had its radical wing of those who despair of practical constructive methods or who have become embittered by injustice. Though the more evenly balanced rank and file does not approve of the radical wing, yet they cannot safely abandon the radicals to the vengeance of the common enemy. As the Haymarket bomb in Chicago destroyed our eight-hour movement, we trade unionists had no reason to sympathize with the cause of the anarchists as such. However, labor must do its best to maintain justice for the radicals or find itself denied the rights of free men.

Because there was no direct evidence showing that these men were guilty of throwing the bombs, there were numbers of men who believed that clemency should be exercised by commutation of sentence from death to imprisonment. I opposed capital punishment, not only because I thought that the execution of these men was unwise and unjust, but I have always been, as I now am, opposed to the taking of life whether by an individual, a group, or the aggregation of individuals as expressed by the state.

About the seventh or eighth of November, 1887, I was sitting in my small office back of [Cigarmakers'] Union No. 144 when Ed King and James Lynch (of the Carpenters) came to me and asked me whether I would not go to Springfield to make a plea before Governor Oglesby for commutation of the sentence. The time had been set for the hearing in the Governor's office and it was either to decide to go at once or else lose the opportunity of making the plea.

They presented to me the idea that because of my being well and favorably known and that I was regarded as a conservative man, my plea would help. Without further ado I closed my office door, and without any belongings other than those which I wore I went directly to the train and with them to Springfield.

The hearing was in the Governor's chamber and was under the leadership of George Schilling of Chicago. Very earnest pleas were made.

There were in the group representatives of trade unionists, farmers, the Legislature, women's organizations, and nearly every social group.

* * *

I remember speaking coolly and calmly, and I pleaded as strongly as I could for the exercise of the Governor's clemency, at least to grant a reprieve to the men for a considerable time so that an opportunity might be had to establish their innocence, if they were innocent. At the close of my statement Governor Oglesby arose to greet me, and thanked me and added that my appeal made the strongest impression upon his mind. However, all the appeals were of no avail, for the Governor declined to stay the execution. The men were executed on November 11, 1887.

* * *

In 1895, in connection with my trip to Cardiff, Wales, as a Federation fraternal delegate to the British Trades Union, I visited a number of cities on the Continent, and in nearly every labor hall there were pictures of Parsons, Spies, Lingg, etc., and with an inscription: "Labor's Martyrs to American Capitalism." During my later visits to the labor offices on the European Continent, I have seen the same pictures still there.

Samuel GOMPERS

From *Seventy Years of Life and Labor*
(New York, 1925)

LOW POINTS

The Haymarket affair caused a wide variety of leaders to dive into the mire of anti-communist and anti-immigrant hysteria; newspaper owners, politicians, police, preachers and social scientists all got in the mud together. But two figures came, by remarkably similar scenarios, to occupy places deeper in the muck than almost anyone. They were Henry George and Terence Powderly.

George and Powderly sank so low largely by virtue of the fact that both dove swampward from the heights of social reform. George's land- and tax-reform theories, popularized in his widely-circulated *Progress and Poverty*, made him a logical leader for the United Labor Party, an independent political mobilization by workers which gathered strength in the wake of Haymarket. As the ULP's mayoral candidate in 1886 in New York City, George drew almost a third of the vote in a hotly contested three-cornered race. Powderly, a Pennsylvania machinist, had become Grand Master Workman of the Knights of Labor in 1879 and had presided over the astronomical growth of that union which had as many as 700,000 members by 1886. He was Scranton's mayor from 1878 through 1882. Both George and Powderly also had built impressive records in the Irish nationalist movement. And each had a direct reason to support the Haymarket defendants. For George, such a defense effort would have been on behalf of persons whose trials had galvanized support for the ULP, especially in Chicago, where Lucy Parsons was a leading ULP supporter. For Powderly to rally to Albert Parsons' defense would have been to come to the aid of a fellow Knight— indeed, of the first Knights of Labor member in Chicago.

That both George and Powderly admitted that the Haymarket defendants had received an unfair trial before refusing to petition to save the lives of the convicted men illuminates the tragic descent of the two leaders during the months following the bombing. George, for example, wrote in January 1887 that "Spies and his associates were convicted by a jury chosen in a manner so shamelessly illegal that it would be charitable to accuse the judge of incompetency." Six months later he still could ask a supporter of the defense efforts to "assure the boys in jail that I am in full sympathy with them, and they can count on me to do all in my power to set them free." But during the crucial weeks before the executions, George refused to sign clemency petitions. Henry David has suggested that George was motivated by a combination of a desire to avoid controversy during his campaign for Secretary of State of New York and a need to score points against socialist rivals in the ULP by smearing them as advocates of violence by virtue of their Haymarket defense work. Whatever the reason, George's October 8, 1887 statement on the case in the *New York Standard* set a wretched standard for opportunism and political quick change artistry:

There is no ground for asking for executive clemency in behalf of the Chicago Anarchists as a matter of right. An unlawful and murderous deed was committed in Chicago, the penalty of which, by the laws of the State of Illinois, is death. Seven men[1] were tried on the charge of being accessory to the crime, and, after a long trial, were convicted. The case was appealed to the supreme court of the State of Illinois, and that body, composed of seven judges, removed both in time and place, from the excitement which may have been supposed to have affected public opinion in Chicago during

Well-known public figures in their day, George is shown here in a Sam Loyd puzzle, and Powderly in a clothing manufacturer's advertising card.

135

the first trial, have, after an elaborate examination of the evidence and the law, unanimously confirmed this sentence.

Although Powderly opposed defense efforts from early on, arguing in October, 1886 that the labor movement owed only a "debt of hatred" to the IWPA, he allowed in January 1887 that "the men who are under sentence of death. . .were too hastily judged," that "passion has as much to do with the conviction as reason," and that a new trial was required. Nonetheless, Powderly continued to oppose efforts to place the Knights of Labor on record as favoring defense of the convicted. His most bitter opposition to even a mild resolution in behalf of the men facing execution came at the October 1887 convention of the Knights. But Powderly had probably reached his nadir three months before in private testimony given before Denver Knights of Labor[2] who questioned his course in certain strikes and in refusing to defend the Haymarket prisoners. The testimony, later published in the *Pittsburgh Dispatch*, featured sharp questioning by Burnette Haskell. After Powderly repeatedly held that acts of strike violence attributed to the Knights were in fact committed by police and company agents, Haskell masterfully asked why the Grand Master Workman considered it unlikely that similar forces were responsible for the Haymarket bombing. Powderly replied that he personally had secret proof, furnished by Albert Parsons' brother, that the accused were murderers. Since Powderly refused to furnish any evidence, it is likely

that many agreed with Joe Buchanan, a Denver labor editor, who observed that Powderly had concocted "a lie out of whole cloth." But such wild charges, like his October 1887 accusations that anarchists were trying to kill him, cannot have failed to undercut some working class support for the Haymarket defendants. That Powderly was willing to go to terrible lengths to accomplish just such a goal is perhaps best illustrated by his reply when Haskell asked why he had not defended Lucy Parsons' right to speak when she was arrested in Columbus, Ohio, in March 1887. Powderly managed to mix race-baiting, sexism and taunts against "free love" in answering that he did not defend Albert Parsons' wife "because she is not his wife; because they only live together, and are not married and because it is not my business to look after any woman of bad reputation, white or negro, who tramps around the country as she does."

Dave ROEDIGER

1. Of course, *eight* persons were in fact tried. The factual error rather calls into question George's later contention that his thorough study of the Illinois Supreme Court's opinion caused him to change his position regarding the case. George did send a weakly worded private letter to the governor of Illinois five days before the execution advising commutation to the sentence so not to make martyred heroes of the condemned.
2. The testimony was taken on July 15, 1887 and is available at the State Historical Society of Wisconsin at Madison. It is skillfully discussed in Carolyn Ashbaugh, *Lucy Parsons: American Revolutionary* (Chicago 1976), 123-25. A clipping from the *Pittsburgh Dispatch* containing part of the testimony is included in Reel 23 of the microfilm edition of the Terence V. Powderly Papers, available from Catholic University.

N.Y. CENTRAL LABOR UNION & DISTRICT 49

One of the high spots in labor's defense of the Haymarket prisoners came on September 16, 1887 when the powerful New York Central Labor Union, probably the strongest city central body in the nation and the one most influenced by socialism, joined Knights of Labor District 49 in endorsing the stirring joint statement reprinted below. Not only did District 49, the most influential and second largest Knights assembly, defy its organization's national leadership to join in the call, but it also put aside its longstanding, if sporadic, conflicts with New York craft unions to work in common cause. Thus, among the fourteen individual signers were Samuel Gompers, head of the AFL; Master Workman James Quinn of District 49; Frank Ferrell, the most prominent black leader in the Knights of Labor; and United Labor Party leader Henry Emrich. At the October 20 mass meeting called for in the document, as many as 4000 New Yorkers braved a heavy storm to hear Gompers, Quinn and socialist Carpenters' Union leader P. J. McGuire speak on the behalf of the Haymarket prisoners.

DR

APPEAL TO THE WORKING CLASS

You are aware of the decision rendered by the Supreme Court of Illinois confirming the verdict of the lower court . . . and fixing the day of execution of the prisoners on November 11th of this year.

As citizens who stand united on the broad platform of human rights and equal justice to all, irrespective of political or social opinions, we now appeal to you to do all in your power to secure a modification of the above-mentioned decision.

Liberty, free speech and justice impartially and fearlessly meted out to friend and foe, are the only safe-guards and the primary conditions of a peaceable social development in this country.

Under the misguiding and corrupting influence of prejudice and class-hatred, those men have been condemned without any con-

clusive evidence, as accessories to a crime, the principals of which, as well as the motive which may have actuated the same, are unknown.

The execution of this sentence would be a disgrace to the honor of our nation, and would strengthen the very doctrines it is ostensibly directed against.

The undersigned appeal, therefore, to you as representatives of Organized Labor, the foremost champions of our rights and liberties, to immediately take such steps as may save our country from the disgrace of an act that can be considered in no other light than as a judicial murder, prompted by the basest and most un-American motives. . . .

Leaving to you to decide as to the most efficient method to be adopted, we would suggest that a call should be issued by all

the representative labor organizations of this country for a great public demonstration to be held simultaneously in this [New York] and in all other cities of the Union on or about the 20th of October. . . .

Yours in the cause of
Justice and Humanity,

Samuel GOMPERS,   Jas. E. QUINN,
Martin A. HANLY,   Frank FERRELL
Edward KING,   Everett GLACKIN,
Henry EMRICH,   Tom O'REILLY,
John D. DUNN,   Geo. H. McVEY,
A.G. JOHNSON, Jr.,   Matthew BARR,
Fred HALLER,   and Michael J. KELLY.

September 16, 1887

An anti-Most cartoon by Thomas Nast (*Harper's Weekly*, May 29, 1886)

JOHANN MOST

Johann Most, the "Voice of Terror," as he has been labeled by a not-very-well-informed biographer[1] —the man who "came to symbolize all that terrified and alarmed respectable American society"[2] and who according to the press, "should have been hanged with the others" in November 1887—was born in Augsburg (Bavaria) in 1846. At the time of the Haymarket tragedy he had been in politics for twenty years, having entered the labor movement in 1867.

An orator of rare capacities, Most first became known to a wider public in 1870 as a defendant in the first high-treason trial against labor leaders in Austria, where he had been one of the speakers on the platform of the largest demonstration yet known in Vienna for free speech and workers' political rights. Condemned to five years imprisonment (later reduced to three), he was soon pardoned under a new government— and subsequently banished from the country. Returning to Germany, he became the most popular Social Democrat besides August Bebel, thanks to his extraordinary gifts both as speaker and writer, and was famous and loved for his humor (a rare quality among socialists), his polemical genius, and his capacity to popularize difficult ideas.

Most's aim was "the emancipation of the workers," following no specific political catechism—in this regard being as eclectic as most German socialists at the time. While he was the first to attempt a popularization of Marx's *Capital*,[3] he was by no means a Marxist, and did the same for other political authors whom he regarded as important as Marx in the critique of capitalist society.[4] As a socialist, he was politically a moderate, remarkably prepared to compromise, and did not believe in violent methods. Like all his contemporaries in the German labor movement, he believed that a revolution was inevitable, but in a more or less distant future. What made him different—besides his ability to bring problems to the point and to condense them into witty formulae— was his unusual loyalty to the workers he represented, and the readiness with which he followed their moods as he experienced them in his meetings.[5] He was pushed to extremes but did not lead to them, and was from the beginning prepared to accept and bear the responsibility for them—a by no means typical attitude on the part of labor politicians, who preferred to blame him for his "susceptibility." And what further distinguished him from other prominent socialists (and later also anarchists) was his willingness to accept dissenting views and opinions, and to publish them in the papers he edited.[6]

Like most other Social Democrats in Germany at the time, Most strongly denounced the attempts on the life of the German emperor in 1878 (something he later preferred to forget); he changed his views in this regard only when driven into exile by Bismarck's antisocialist law. This change occurred only after 1880 when he was in London, under the influence

Revolutionäre

Kriegswissenschaft.

Ein Handbüchlein zur Anleitung betreffend
Gebrauches und Herstellung von Nitro-
Glycerin, Dynamit, Schießbaumwolle,
Knallquecksilber, Bomben, Brand-
sätzen, Giften u. s. w., u. s. w.

Von

Johann Most.

New York.
Druck und Verlag des Internationalen Zeitungs-Vereins,
167 William Street.

Cover of Most's *Science of Revolutionary Warfare*

Johann Most

of Russian revolutionaries and people like Edouard Vaillant and Andreas Scheu, his old friend and co-defendant of 1870 in Vienna. Above all, the assassination of Alexander II in March 1881 started his almost mystical belief in dynamite and its effectiveness in the class struggle. He applauded the assassination in a notorious article titled "At Last!," which earned him nineteen months imprisonment.[7]

On his release, in October 1882, he found it impossible to publish the *Freiheit* in Europe and decided to transfer it—and himself—to New York. He thought the U.S. would be only a temporary residence; his main interests remained in Europe where he expected a revolution, especially in Germany, in the not-too-distant future.

To help this revolution come about, Most tried to help set up a number of plots; he shipped dynamite and published recipes explaining how to produce it in *Freiheit* and in his notorious pamphlet, *The Science of Revolutionary Warfare*; he supplied funds to "emissaries" who were prepared to commit "propaganda-of-the-deed." He reasoned that the workers, oppressed as they were, needed only some successful examples of how to rid themselves of oppressors in order to take courage and start to revolt.

All this was without any result. The self-declared heroes disappeared with the money, and the only actual "deeds" that Most had anything to do with were either utterly futile (the bombing of the Frankfurt police headquarters by a Bohemian anarchist, Josef Richetsky, who afterward came to the U.S. and vanished from the scene), or had motives quite different from "propaganda of the deed" (the killing of a leading Frankfurt policeman by an anarchist seeking revenge for two years imprisonment).[8] By 1886 Most seems to have given up this sort of business, either through disillusionment or because German anarchists had found ways to organize the provisioning of dynamite for themselves—without any results, by the way. In any case, all dealings of this sort were given up by the first half of 1887.

Despite all the misery, despite all the injustice and oppression, and despite all efforts, nowhere could Most detect anything that could be interpreted as the first movements of a revolution. But he did not give up hope, and he continued to do what he thought was important: to encourage revolt and revolution—that is, to make workers realize that they are oppressed and exploited *and* that they are able to defend themselves and to change these conditions if they only have the courage to do so. He used ever stronger words to get "the water boiling" and to build up more steam for the inevitable eruption. At the same time he renounced all efforts that he imagined could result in letting off some of the "steam" necessary for starting the revolution. From the beginning he fought what he called the "Eight-Hour Fraud," fearing that such reform could eventually relieve the "revolutionary tension." On this he disagreed completely with several of his friends in Chicago, but he stuck to this opinion all his life.

Haymarket, the trial and the hanging—the latter of which he regarded as impossible to the last minute—made him definitively revise his position and drop his indiscriminate call for "actions." Imprisoned for an inflammatory speech delivered in New York on April 28, 1886, he was not available for the trial in Chicago, where he would certainly have had

138

a good chance of being sentenced to death and hanged with the others. He spent a year in Blackwell's Island, until June 1887. As soon as he was released, he called again for action—but this time it was for action to free the eight imprisoned friends: propaganda in favor of the defendants, bringing the pressure of public opinion to bear on the judiciary, trying everything possible to prevent the hanging. The results must have been anything but encouraging to him, yet still he believed to the very end that the authorities would not "dare" to hang any of the convicted Chicago anarchists.

Long after November 1887, Most tried hard to conceal his resignation, and to find ways to encourage not only his readers and followers, but himself as well. Thus he wrote in early 1888:

Most governments, by their blind rage, have made it impossible for the enemies of the existing order to count their numbers. They have to operate almost underground. Were that not so, we could certainly state today that in the year that has just finished the contingents of the social revolution must have gained by hundreds of thousands.

But he had to defend himself immediately: "Perhaps we have not advanced further in the last year just because we were too optimistic."[9]

From this point on he refused to reprint his manual of "Revolutionary Warfare"[10] and advised his readers not to speak publicly about arming and weapons.[11] He appealed for tolerance among revolutionists, spoke against the anarchist movement's splitting up into different schools of thought or even into sects, and began to advocate what a little later—first in Spain and then in other European countries—would be called "anarchism without labels." As a matter of course, he was severely attacked for such tolerance. Perhaps more important in this context, he repeatedly set out the conditions for the revolutionary use of violence, for individual acts:

There is no greater error than to believe that we, as anarchists, need only to commit *any* deed, no matter *when*, *where* and against *whom*. To have a propaganda effect, every deed needs to be *popular*; it must meet with approval by an important part of the proletariat. If that is not the case, or if it actually meets with the *dis*approval of the very part of the population it is intended to inspire. . .anarchism makes itself unpopular and hated. Instead of winning new adherents, many will withdraw.[12]

Most did not see America and the workers in America ripe for deeds which would lead to revolts and revolution—and said so again and again. But he was heard only when he applied this to an actual deed and criticized it: in August 1892 when, in an article titled "Reflections on an *Attentat*," he criticized Alexander Berkman's attempted assassination of H. C. Frick. This served to deepen the already existing breach in the anarchist movement, and further estranged many comrades from the increasingly bitter Most.

After 1887 he never again called undiscriminatingly for "action," or asked for "deeds"—except those that involved the distribution of *Freiheit* and other radical literature. All the more "drastic" articles to appear in *Freiheit* in later years were reprints of much older material: It was a fifty-year-old article on tyrannicide by Karl Heinzen that, in 1901—at the time of the McKinley assassination—resulted in Most's being sent to yet another year at Blackwell's Island.[13]

Would his chances of staying out of prison been any greater had he been even more clever and reprinted some nice little

excerpts on the right to rebellion from John Locke's *Treatises on Government*—published in 1689?

Heiner BECKER

1. Frederic Trautmann. *The Voice of Terror: A Biography of John Most* (Westport, 1980).
2. Paul Avrich. *The Haymarket Tragedy* (Princeton, 1984),
3. Johann Most. *Kapital und Arbeit. Ein Populaerer Auszug aus* Das Kapital *von Karl Marx* (Chemnitz, 1873); second edition, revised by Marx and Engels (Chemnitz, 1876). An American translation of the second edition by Otto Weydemeyer was published under the title, *Extracts from the* Capital *of Karl Marx* (Hoboken, 1878).
4. Johann Most, "Ein Philosophe." Serialized in the *Berliner Freie Presse* (September-October, 1876). This will be included in a collection of Most's writings to be published in 1986.
5. A typical example is the famous metal-workers' strike in Chemnitz (Saxony), in October 1871, which Most tried to prevent, foreseeing its failure. But once the workers had started the strike, and the workers asked him—as the ablest speaker available—to represent them, he agreed; he also accepted the blame for its failure.
6. Contrary to accusations made against him by his opponents, and often repeated since, this can easily be demonstrated by perusing the various papers he edited.
7. Sixteen months' hard labor plus three months before the final verdict. On this, and on another important trial in 1882, see Bernard Porter, "The *Freiheit* Prosecutions, 1881-1882," *The Historical Journal*, 23 (1980), 833-856.
8. For killing the policeman an anarchist named Julius Lieske was tried and beheaded in 1885; the actual killer, however—as the police soon learned—was another anarchist, a Bohemian named August Peschman. Some of the surviving evidence has been used by Volker Eichler, *Sozialistische Arbeiterbewegung in Frankfurt am Main, 1878-1895* (Frankfurt am Main, 1983).
9. "Beim Jahreswechsel," *Freiheit* 10: 1 (January 1, 1888).; "Missverstaendnisse," *ibid.*, 10: 3 (January 14, 1888).
10. "Die Agitation," *ibid.*, 10: 8 (February 18, 1888).
11. "Bewaffnung und Aufklaerung," *ibid.*, 10: 6 (February 4, 1888).
12. In a more or less explicit form, again and again between 1888 and 1892—and after. The quotation here is from *Freiheit*, 14: 17 (April 23, 1892), "Herzenserguesse," Most's first statement after his release from his second imprisonment on Blackwell's Island (for his speech following the Haymarket executions).
13. "Mord contra Mord," *Freiheit* (September 7, 1901), the day of the assassination.

Linocut of Johann Most, bookbinder, by D. Chun (from *Man!*)

FREEDOM

A JOURNAL OF ANARCHIST SOCIALISM.

VOL. 3.—No. 26.   NOVEMBER, 1888.   MONTHLY ; ONE PENNY.

THE CHICAGO MARTYRS.

WHEN this number of *Freedom* appears, we shall be on the eve of an

Parsons and Spies did their best to prevent a bloody conflict which would have led to the defeat of the workers. It is proved, on the other hand, that the chief of the Chicago police wished to have an armed conflict and thought "to make short work" of some 3000 Socialists if he

Started in October 1886 and still published today, the English anarchist paper *Freedom*, with which Peter Kropotkin was closely associated, played an important role in Haymarket defense agitation in the British Isles.

PETER KROPOTKIN

Peter Kropotkin (1842-1921) transcended his origins in the Russian nobility and became perhaps the premier anarchist-communist thinker of the late nineteenth and early twentieth centuries.

Born in Moscow and descended from the princes of Kiev, Kropotkin seemed destined to apply his enormous talents to a military career. He instead joined an Amur Cossack regiment which employed him not as a commander but as an explorer in Siberia and elsewhere. Frustrated by corruption and bureaucracy in the military, Kropotkin quit

to devote himself to a career in geography and geology. His Siberian, Finnish and Swedish researches led to his being offered the coveted secretaryship of the Russian Geographic Society before his thirtieth birthday. He declined the post in order to concentrate on the revolutionary activities which would dominate the last half-century of his life.

Kropotkin's revolutionary theory combines eloquence, scientific criticism and playfulness to an unparalleled degree. He was, as Emma Goldman observed, "recognized by friend and foe as one of the greatest minds

. . .of the nineteenth century." He is also a strikingly modern writer, notwithstanding all the utopian nostalgia and high romanticism which pervade his work. In such classics as An Appeal to the Young, Memoirs of a Revolutionist, Mutual Aid, The Conquest of Bread *and* Fields, Factories and Workshops, *Kropotkin considers how the people of the world might best feed and house themselves, how science might serve humankind, how rural and peasant traditions might enrich a new society, and how freedom and socialism might prosper together.*

DR

BEFORE THE STORM:

Excerpts from a Speech Delivered by Peter Kropotkin at the Farewell Meeting for Lucy Parsons After Her Speaking Tour of England & Scotland in 1888

Dear friend, tell to our American comrades that their heroes did not die in vain.

There is not a single city worth naming in Spain where the bloody anniversary [the Eleventh of November] was not commemorated by enthusiastic crowds of workers. Not one in Italy. Not one in Germany where the names of Parsons, Spies, Engel, Schwab, Fischer, Lingg, Neebe and Fielden were not invoked by workers who met in small groups, as they were not allowed to hold big meetings.

The commemoration of the Chicago martyrs has almost acquired the same importance as the commemoration of the Paris Commune.

Many have already died for the grand cause of Freedom, but none of the martyrs of Freedom have been so enthusiastically adopted by the workers as *their* martyrs. And I will tell you why.

The workmen know that our Chicago brethren were thoroughly *honest.* Not one single black spot could be detected in their lives, even by their enemies. Not one single black spot! Mark that, young men and women who come to join the socialist movement. The masses *are* honest and they ask the same from those who come to help them in their work. While a black past goes for nothing in the ranks of the politicians, the workers ask from their combatants to be pure of any reproach, to live in accordance with the grand principles they are preaching.

They were honest all their lives through, these martyrs of the labor cause, and once they had joined the anarchist movement, they gave

themselves to it, not by halves, but entirely, body and heart together.

And—they had no ambition. They were anarchists and understood when they became socialists, that it was not that they might climb themselves upon the shoulders of their fellow workers. They did not ask from the masses a place in Parliament, in a Municipality, or on a School Board. They sought no power over the others, no place in the ranks of the ruling classes. They asked nothing but the right to fight in the ranks, at the post of danger. And there they died.

Only such men could die as they have died, without making the slightest concession to the enemy, loudly proclaiming their anarchist principles before the judges who said that anarchy is on trial, amidst the lawyers who whispered: "Renounce anarchy, and you will be saved."

They proclaimed their principles during the terrible year spent on the threshold of death; they proclaimed them on the scaffold, and they hailed the day on which they died for those principles as the happiest of their lives.

Such men *can* inspire the generations to come with the noblest feelings. And so they do, and will do. The idea which lives in such men will never die—it will conquer.

Peter KROPOTKIN

from *Freedom*,
(London, December 1888)

CITIZEN TRAIN DEFENDS THE ANARCHISTS

Of all the men and women who came to the defense of the Haymarket anarchists, none was more unusual or more colorful than George Francis Train (1829-1904). Renowned in his own lifetime as America's greatest eccentric, he led a life of unparalleled diversity and adventure, and had an extraordinary effect on his time.

Orphaned at four, the Boston-born Train enjoyed a real-life "rags-to-riches" career, although he added many unique touches of his own that never figured in any Horatio Alger tale. Arguably the nineteenth century's foremost transportation genius, he revolutionized several branches of the industry and more or less single-handedly invented others. His clipper ships, most notably the famous *Flying Cloud*, were the fastest and most beautiful of all time. Second to none in developing the transcontinental railroad, he initiated the Credit Mobilier which financed it, and later he went on to build street-railways in Britain. A prolific journalist, he wrote some twenty-five books and pamphlets on a wide range of subjects. He was a major promoter of Irish immigration to the U.S., the founder of Omaha, Nebraska, and the inventor of the pencil with attached eraser as well as of the perforated stamp. He was also a great traveler: His 1870 voyage around the world in eighty days inspired Jules Verne's celebrated novel on that theme.

Largely as a result of the California gold rush, and the later gold rush in Australia, Train, with his extensive shipping interests, became a millionaire. He went to live for a time in Australia, where revolutionary miners offered him the presidency of the republic they hoped to establish in what turned out to be an ill-fated effort to declare their independence from England. Although Train declined the honor, it was clear that he was already recognized as a man of progressive and even radical views.

His wealth notwithstanding, Train grew more radical as the years went by. An atheist in his childhood ("I could not see the necessity of God. . .religion never appealed to my intelligence or to my emotions"), as an adult he rejected the conservatism of his business associates. Although his wife was a close relative of Jefferson Davis, Train—in England during the Civil War—was a vigorous supporter of the Union cause; his speeches and publications were an important factor in educating British workers on the war issues, and in blocking British government support for the Confederacy. His abilities as an agitator did not go unnoticed by those in power. For years, he wrote later, "five or six governments kept their spies shadowing me in Europe and America."

George Francis Train

After the war, Train's radicalism blossomed in all directions. Seeing no reason why ideas—or indeed, life itself—should lag behind technology, he took up virtually all the advanced ideas of his day. He funded the feminist paper, *Revolution*, edited by Susan B. Anthony and Elizabeth Cady Stanton; identified himself with the First International; took an active part in the Marseilles Commune; supported the independence of Ireland; became a vegetarian; and, in 1872, went to jail for defending free-love advocate Victoria Woodhull against "obscenity" charges leveled against her by that bookburning Puritan, Anthony Comstock. This was neither Train's first time behind bars, nor his last; he later boasted that he had been imprisoned fifteen times without ever having committed a crime.

Train's eccentricities, already in evidence in earlier years, became pronounced in the 1870s. Styling himself the "Great American Crank" and even "the greatest man in the world," he went about in a bright red sash (indicating his passion for communism), and sported a green umbrella and lavender gloves. After running for President in 1872, he declared himself a candidate for dictator, intending to establish "a pure autocracy of love." Asked by a reporter if, as dictator, he would occupy the White House, he replied that he preferred to rule the universe from the park bench that he regarded as his headquarters.

Eventually, his fabulous wealth long since exhausted, he withdrew from public life altogether. Believing that contact with adults was injurious to evolutionary development, he spoke only with children, birds and squirrels, with whom he shared the peanuts which were his principal food.

What brought Train out of his self-imposed seclusion from adult society was the Haymarket affair. In a lecture on the trial on September 18, 1887, he declared that if seven men had to hang, the American people would do much better to hang the seven judges of the Illinois Supreme Court rather than the anarchists. He sent a wire to the imprisoned men, expressing his willingness to lecture on their behalf and asking them if they thought his doing so would help the cause. When Parsons and his comrades said yes, Train left immediately for Chicago.

Speaking in the city's Princess Skating Rink, Train threatened: "You hang those seven men if you dare, and I will head twenty million workingmen to cut the throats of everybody in Chicago!" He asked: "How can you convict men of being accessories to a crime for which there is no principal?" And again: "What do they want to hang these men for? Are they afraid of them?"

As a result of this address, Train was barred from further speech-making in

Chicago, and the paper he had started, *The Psycho-Anarchist*, was also suppressed. These latest incidents in a seemingly unending series of violations of fundamental democratic rights prompted Albert Parsons' letter to Train, reprinted here. When the venerable sage of the *Flying Cloud* sent a basket of fruit to each of the prisoners, he received another salutation from Adolph Fischer, also included here.

In an interview after the executions, Train expressed his belief that Louis Lingg was not a suicide, but had been killed by jail authorities. He also avowed his refusal to live in a country guilty of the judicial murder of the anarchists,

and announced that he was leaving for Canada, where he did in fact live for a time.

In 1890 he traveled round the world again ("I go round the world every twenty years, to let it know I am still alive"), and three years later made a splash at the World's Columbian Exposition in Chicago. Radical to the end, he had encouraging words for Coxey's Army and the Populist movement, and denounced U.S. imperialism during the Spanish-American War.

Train's 100,000-word autobiography, published in 1902, is dedicated "To the Children and to the children's children in this and all lands, who love and

believe in me because they know I love and believe in them."

Penelope ROSEMONT

SOURCES

Avrich, Paul. *The Haymarket Tragedy* (Princeton, 1984).
David, Henry. *The History of the Haymarket Affair* (New York, 1958).
Mitchell, Edward P. *Memoirs of an Editor* (New York, 1924).
Potts, E. Daniel and Annette. *A Yankee Merchant in Gold Rush Australia* (Melbourne, 1970).
Riegel, Robert. *American Feminists* (Lawrence, Kansas, 1968).
Seitz, Don C. *Uncommon Americans* (Indianapolis, 1925).
Thornton, Willis. *The Nine Lives of Citizen Train* (New York, 1948).
Train, George Francis. *My Life in Many States and in Foreign Lands* (New York, 1902).
Wallace, Irving. *The Square Pegs* (New York, 1957).

George Francis Train and John Brown Jr. both sent baskets of fruit to the Haymarket prisoners.
(Chicago *Daily News*, November 9, 1887)

ONWARD! CITIZEN TRAIN!

Prison Cell 29,
Chicago, Ill.
Oct. 14, 1887

Citizen George Francis Train,
Champion of Free Speech,
Free Press and Public Assemblage:

Despotism of America's money-mongers again demonstrated. They deny the right of the people to assemble to hear you speak to them. Free speech! They will not allow the people to buy or read the Psycho-Anarchist. Free press! They interdict the right of the people to assemble and petition for redress of grievances. Right of assembly!

United States constitution nullified by Supreme Court's decision. Revolution!

The people clubbed, arrested, imprisoned, shot and hung in violation of law and constitution at behest of America's monopolists.

Free speech, free press, and right to assemble cost seven years' bloody revolution of 1776. But degenerate Americans style those who maintain the Declaration of Independence as anarchists. Jefferson, Adams, Hancock, Washington, Franklin,

Paine, Henry and other revolutionary sires they ridicule as "fools," "cranks," etc. America's plutocrats of 1887 sneer at these things.

Police censorship over press, speech and assemblage! Russia, Spain, Italy, France—abashed! Working-women's union prohibited by Chicago police from singing the [Marseillaise] at social entertainments!

Tyrants forge missing link. Chain complete. America joins "International Brotherhood of Man." Proletariat of every clime and tongue, from Moscow, Berlin, Vienna, Madrid, London and Paris to Chicago, join refrain and sing the [Marseillaise]. . . .

Onward! Citizen Train! Freedom shall not perish! Let the welkin ring, and from land to land labor's innumerable hosts proclaim— "Liberty! Fraternity! Equality!" Salut!

A. R. PARSONS
Proletar.

Anarchism: Its Philosophy
and Scientific Basis
(Chicago, 1887)

LONG LIVE CRANKS!

Citizen George Francis Train:

I thank you for the basket of fruit you were kind enough to send. I noticed that the daily papers refer to you as the "champion crank." Don't mind that! What is a crank, anyway? As much as I know there is not a specific definition of the word, but I do know that all men who are in advance of their age go under the category "crank." Socrates, Christ, Huss, Luther, Galileo, Rousseau, Paine, Jefferson, Franklin, Phillips, and last but not least, old John Brown, and many other more or less known apostles of progress have been considered "cranks" by their contemporaries because they held ideas which were contrary to and in advance of the customary social, political, religious, or scientific arrangements of things. But for these "cranks" civilization would be in its infancy yet. Therefore, long live the "cranks." With hearty greetings, sir, I subscribe myself,

Adolph FISCHER

from The Alarm,
January 14, 1888

A LETTER FROM JOHN BROWN, JR.

To Franklin B. Sanborn

Put-in-Bay Island Lake Erie
Ottawa Co. Ohio, Nov. 11th 1887

My Dear Friend,

I mailed letters to you yesterday, but owing to a gale from the northwest the Steamer Jay Cooke which carries the mail did not leave her dock. . . .

Today, I suppose, those Anarchists at Chicago must meet the demands of Illinois justice. Owing to the storm, have no late papers.

Last Sunday, I devoted the day to preparing for shipment to each of those men a basket of Catawba grapes as a token of my sympathy for them and their cause,—removal of the great burdens borne by the working, dependant class. I have socialistic tendencies, though my notions are not so well defined, for I have never met a "Socialist," to my knowledge, nor have I read much of any thing pertaining to their doctrines. Father's favorite theme was that of the *Community plan of cooperative industry*, in which all should labor for the Common good; "having all things in common" as did the disciples of Jesus in his day. This also has been, and still is, my Communistic or Socialistic faith. I cannot be an Anarchist, as I understand the meaning of the term Anarchy.—Would not resort to dynamite until I had exhausted all other means when

"forbearance had ceased to be a virtue."

I expect to lose many friends in consequence of my small token of sympathy for those men, who have, according to the measure of their light and honest convictions, been *faithful to their highest ideas*. It will make no difference with me if such should be the result; for I have in this matter, been faithful to my highest sense of duty.

As a part of my last "Sabbath days journey," I wrote to each of those men a letter to accompany my gifts of the grapes, of which letter, the following is a *true copy.*

Put-in-Bay Island Lake Erie,
Ottawa Co. Ohio, 7th Nov. 1887

Brother:

I send you by to day's Boat, a basket of Catawba grapes, pre-paid through, as per Express receipts enclosed. These grapes, I beg you to accept as a slight token of my sympathy for you, and for the cause which you represent.

Four days before his execution, my Father wrote to a friend, the following.

"Charlestown, Va., Jail,
Nov. 28th 1859

It is a great comfort to feel assured that I am permitted to die for a cause,—not merely to pay the debt of nature, as all must.

John Brown"

That a like assurance may be a comfort to you, is the earnest desire of
Ever yours, for the cause of the faithful, honest laborer.—
John Brown, Jr.

To August Spies.
(Chicago Jail,)
Care, Sheriff of Cook County,
Chicago, Illinois.

If my letter to those men should not be published, or if published should appear in any other words than the foregoing, you will do me a favor to publish in such a way as you choose.

It is nearly daylight once more, and I will go the P.O. for the gale is not now so heavy and the Boat will probably leave this morning. Have much more to write you, but will resume another time.

All well, and would, I know, join me in sending regards to yourself and family, were they not still asleep.

Faithfully yours,
John Brown, Jr.

F. B. Sanborn, Esq.,
Concord,
Mass.

from Louis Ruchames, ed.,
"John Brown Jr. and the Haymarket Martyrs,"
Massachusetts Review
(Summer 1964)

. . .AND ONE FROM A SOUTH CAROLINA LAWYER

I thank you for sending me the various papers concerning the eight condemned socialists. All were read with avidity, but especially the autobiography of Mr. Spies. The woodcut likeness of him was wonderfully good. It carried me back to the courtroom in Chicago, where I used to look at and admire his noble face and head. The picture, of course, could not give the kindly look of his eyes. I now take a deeper interest in him than ever. I am sure he is a good man, with a pure and childlike heart. When I think of him I find myself unwittingly humming the words of Coleridge:

He prayeth best who loveth best
All things both great and small;
For the dear God who loveth us
He made and loveth all.

You will readily see the appropriateness of the lines.

If I lived in your city it would certainly be impossible for me to prevent my appearing in court on behalf of Mr. Spies and his fellow prisoners. I am sorry Carolina is so far from Chicago. I know in my heart these men are entitled to a new trial. It will be a

scandal to civilization and to christianity if they are refused one; and I should like to show a supreme court the reasons for the faith that is in me. This has nothing to do with the guilt or innocence of the prisoners—although I really consider that Spies and his co-prisoners had nothing to do with the Haymarket riot. But apart from their guilt or innocence, I still assert that Judge Gary's charge to the jury is enough in itself to justify the supreme court, nay, to compel it to grant a new trial. I sincerely trust that Captain Black and his associate counsel will quit them like men and and be strong. Lawyers, if they but knew it and remembered it, are the champions of liberty. The bar has for centuries been the bulwark of our rights. The prisoners' counsel should rise to the great occasion in defiance of public opinion—man's greatest tyrant—happily, like most tyrants, a great coward, and easily routed.

I authorize you to subscribe my name to the protest and the petition. But I am lawyer enough to put small hope in petitions and protests. My confidence is in the justice of

the case, in their right to a new trial, which should be a fair trial. Will you kindly send me a complete copy of the speeches, and any newspapers that detail the various steps in the progress of the case?

Let me say to you as you persevere in your good work of demanding justice for these men, God speed you! In the words of Goethe:

The future hides in it
Darkness and sorrow;
We press still through,
Naught that abides in it
Daunting us. Onward!

Col. William Christie BENET

Abbeville, South Carolina
November 20, 1886

[The foregoing letter appeared in the Chicago Knights of Labor, *December 4, 1886, and was reprinted in* The Autobiography of August Spies, *published by Nina van Zandt Spies in 1887. A note on Colonel Benet describes him as an "eminent lawyer. . .president of the South Carolina Club. . . [and] one of the two lay delegates from his state to the recent Episcopal Convention held in Chicago."]*

· LABOUR'S · MAY · DAY ·
DEDICATED · TO · THE · WORKERS · OF · THE · WORLD ·

Drawing by Walter Crane

SPIRIT'S PROGRESS:
Radical Mediums in the Haymarket Era

*The history of the world is the history
of the struggle for Freedom.*
—Cora L. V. Richmond

The black-coated orator turns and faces a group of stylishly-dressed bourgeois on a Sunday-evening outing. He luridly denounces the reign of their class over North America; their dispossession of the original native inhabitants; their reduction of the nominally-free working class to a state of virtual bondage and real starvation; their ugly, pretentious "Christian" civilization, which is but a hypocritical mask for every cruel and ridiculous infamy whose consequences their ill-gotten wealth can buy their way out of. He invokes the specter of the late rising of the Paris Commune: The wealthy and powerful Americans are now drinking the blood of the slaughtered communards. Soon this ruling class will disappear in the whirlwind of vengeance that their greed and stupidity have released.

If it had been uttered in Chicago at the same time (*circa* 1885-86), this speech could easily have earned its author a long visit to the police station, and possibly, if the orator had been a labor organizer or a member of the IWPA, a place in the prisoners' dock at the Haymarket trial. The speech was made, however, not in Chicago but in the Shaker settlement of Mt. Lebanon, New York, by Shaker Chief Elder Frederick W. Evans (1808-1893), and was reported by Elie Reclus in the French review *Societe Nouvelle* (1886). Reclus, an anarchist and brother of the Communard Elisee Reclus, had been visiting Shaker communities in the U.S. and wished to inform his countrymen of the radical social views of Evans and his friends.

Hardly an isolated outburst, the speech sums up the determined progress of Shakerism, especially in the eastern states, toward social revolutionary perspectives. A new concept had emerged in the thinking of Elder Evans and his close associate, Elder Daniel Fraser (1804-1889), regarding the relations be-

tween their "United Society of Believers in Christ's Second Appearing" and the outside world: The communist associations of Shaker believers must be supplemented by a socialist political economy in the United States. Only this could now bestow on the landless millions and urban toilers the benefits that the believers still enjoyed on their rural communes.

They were, of course, challenged by more conservative Shakers for this

Frederick W. Evans

departure, especially since it involved an uncomfortable effort to propagandize in the most controversial arena of modern life. But the astuteness shown by the radical elders is unmistakable in view of the convulsive changes taking place in U.S. society—beginning with post-Civil-War industrialization and reaching a plateau of widespread and violent class conflict in the railroad strikes of 1877.

This new Shaker radicalization bears out, in an interesting way, the confidence Friedrich Engels had shown in Shaker communism in an early essay

(1844) in which he described Shaker society and cited it as proof of the viability of communism:

The first people to set up a society on the basis of community of goods in America, indeed in the whole world, were the so-called Shakers. . . .Amongst these people no one is obliged to work against his will. . . .They have no poor-houses or infirmaries, having not a single person poor or destitute. . . .all their needs are met and they need fear no want. In their ten towns there is not a single gendarme or police officer, no judge, lawyer or soldier, no prison or penitentiary; and yet there is proper order in all their affairs. The laws of the land are not for them and as far as they are concerned could just as well be abolished and nobody would notice any difference. . . .They enjoy . . .the most absolute community of goods and have no trade and no money among themselves.

Engels would have found this early judgment confirmed if he had chanced to read, in the New York *Tribune* of December 26, 1886, Elder Daniel Fraser's polemics against the Roman Catholic Archbishop and the press of New York City on the question of socialism and the proper measures for the relief of the oppressed workers:

The wild conduct and talk of some of the toilers is merely due to aggravations and long-continued repressions. The press of Christendom today is repressive in the interest of those who trample on the toiler, and are "snatching from his grasp the fruit of his labors."

Fraser discredited his opponents' bad-faith arguments against socialism and went on to indict "modern Christian Civilization, which leaves in the city of New York 200,000 helpless women the victims of destructive competition." This sally occurred in the heat of the ongoing Haymarket controversy and Henry George's campaign for mayor of New York, which the Shakers were supporting.

The Shakers, of course, were dedicated pacifists. However, as Fraser's remarks indicate, they could not bring themselves to criticize workers who sometimes struck back at their oppressors in their own defense. Writing to

145

Elder Evans of the need to refortify Shaker principles of pure justice to all, Fraser took a fatalistic view of the consequences of this moralistically-based radicalism:

Because in the nature of things, all revelation is to disturb, to unsettle, to supplant, to overthrow. *Behold, I create all things new* is a most revolutionary utterance . . . .The ideas and thoughts of the Abolitionists disturbed more than one continent. The vast amount of property de-stroyed during the great rebellion was due to resisting the unfoldment of the moral law. The awful destruction of human life was also due to that cause. On the afternoon of the last day of the battles of Gettysburg, within about forty minutes two thousand able-bodied men bit the dust.

Fraser is here effectively trying to convey an idea of the magnitude of, and responsibility for, the dire consequences of resisting the promptings of the Spirit which is calling men and women toward righteousness—by which he meant both the strict purity of the Shaker life and the strictest social justice, which was encompassed only by the equal and universal ownership of land and the means of production.

In view of the attitude of the radical elders, we can easily imagine them speaking out in principled support of the Haymarket defense and clemency efforts. But such action is not evident, and when the total situation of the Shaker societies in the late 1880s is taken into account, it is no longer very imaginable. For the ideas of the radical elders had critics within Shakerdom, crucially in the western settlements in Ohio and Kentucky where conservatism prevailed. Internal ruptures and a negative

effect on the United Society's already declining recruitment were the least of the troubles Evans and Fraser would have invited had they allowed their opinions on the labor question to override their concerns for the organization to which they had devoted fifty years of their lives.

Nevertheless, the stance taken by the radical elders on the social and labor crises and the immanence of socialism in the 1880s is an important measure of the depth to which consciousness of these crises had penetrated. It further reduces the alleged historical isolation of the immigrant-led radical tendencies by showing that the revulsion against rampant capitalism was rooted deep in the Euro-American grain through its dissenting, anti-hierarchical traditions.

That this is indeed so becomes even clearer when we consider the Shakers' relationship to the enormous Spiritualist movement of the time. Both Frederick Evans and Daniel Fraser had passed from rationalist Owenite socialism to Shaker communism through the medium of Spiritualism. Like nearly all articulate Shakers, they hailed Spiritualism as the very basis of their creed and way of life, and argued that the believers themselves had originated the modern Spiritualist movement in 1837. Elder Evans spent several months spanning late 1886 to mid-1887 in missionary travels in England with Spiritualist J. M. Peebles, who was in turn an ardent ally of the Shakers.

Indirectly, then, as participants in the wider Spiritualist current, the Shakers can be said to have been represented in

the Haymarket clemency efforts of Cora L. V. Richmond, poet/philosopher of the "Infiniverse" and leading light of the Chicago Society of Spiritualists.

Cora Richmond (1840-1923) was a nationally known Spiritualist medium, and in the 1880s she was probably the movement's most celebrated figure. In her youth she had been a protege of the renowned Spiritualist publicist Thomas Gales Forster, the author of the popular treatise, *What Is Spiritualism?* who had served for a time as vice-president of the largest trade union in the country, the National Typographical Union. Over the years Cora Richmond's zeal for social reform brought her into the ranks of the abolitionist and woman's-rights movements, and later into the movement in defense of American Indians; she also had ties to nonresistance-advocate Adin Ballou and his Hopedale community in Massachusetts.

One of the most prominent figures in the Haymarket Amnesty Committee, Cora Richmond was co-leader of the delegation who went to Springfield and pleaded with Gov. Oglesby on behalf of the anarchists during the last hours of the lives of Parsons, Spies, Engel and Fischer.

An inspired medium and public speaker since the age of fourteen, Cora Richmond had addressed countless audiences and moved many thousands of hearers. Her plea to Gov. Oglesby that day in Springfield was regarded as impressive by all who heard it. As Henry David wrote many years later, "she utilized every device to touch the Governor's heart, and left the eyes of her auditors tear-stained." Her very presence in the amnesty campaign and her tireless efforts for the cause had helped greatly to swell the number who signed petitions and wrote letters to the Governor urging clemency.

But how did her views on social problems and the radical labor movement compare with those we have already heard from the radical Shaker elders? The similarities are striking, both in timing and content.

The Weekly Discourse for March 14, 1886 contains her address titled "The Lesson of the Hour." Here is an example of what Cora Richmond was saying to her fellow Spiritualists as the eight-hour movement in Chicago and else-

Shakers dancing the Square Order Shuffle

146

where moved toward the great strike projected for May First:

When we were asked one year ago, ''Will not the temperance question be the next subject of political agitation?'' we answered ''No: The imminent question of the hour is the relation between capital and labor,'' and now it is upon you, the whole flood-tides have been let loose, and that which has been pending for ten years over the whole world is now exerting its influence and power.

The context she uses—''for ten years over the whole world''—has tacit reference to the Paris Commune and the nationwide labor insurrections in the U.S. in 1877.

She goes on to address the widespread fear of revolution, turning like Fraser to the example of the antislavery struggle and the Civil War to gain some measure of perspective and balance:

At the time of the existence of slavery in the Southern states and in Santo Domingo there were those who feared insurrection, who mightily trembled when they went to their rooms to sleep, lest the slaves should rise up and murder them in the night. For what? For their freedom, because they were enslaved, but the slaves did nothing of the kind. It was the Masters who rose up, and *it was slavery that slew itself.*

Again like the Shaker radicals, Cora Richmond attributed the impetus behind social upheaval to a spiritual force relentlessly trying to realize itself in human life and society. She referred to it as a *moral force,* that thought that is gradually rising in the world, that people and not things constitute the rights of men; that life and labor and the enjoyment of them and the happiness that ensues from the privileges of civilization belong to those who win them by their daily toil.

She hailed the left-wing abolitionists, and especially Wendell Phillips, for taking up the cause of the wage-slaves after the demise of plantation-slavery, and invoked a coming time

when it will be impossible for a man to be the possessor of a million dollars, when it will be a monstrosity for him to declare himself a millionaire, when the moral sentiment of the people will no more permit this individual augmentation of wealth than it now permits the holding of slaves. . . .

In October of 1886 she was writing in *The Weekly Discourse* on ''The Handwriting on the Wall,'' the signs of the times pointing to momentous changes in society:

The powers of Mammon, of human selfishness are doomed, whether in the individual or in society, or in corporations or in governments, or in crowns or in kingdoms.

Beneath the moralistic wording, we find here a theory of social revolution as resulting from the development of irresistible spiritual forces. Violence comes about only because the capitalists, along with ''church, state, society, business. . .who are partaking of this feast,'' resort to armed force to prevent the unfolding of a new and higher order of life conceived by the awakened workers.

These sentiments accord very well not only with those of the radical Shakers.

Cora L. V. Richmond

but also with those expressed by August Spies in his brilliant counter-indictment leveled at the court that convicted him and the seven other defendants in the Haymarket case. Said Spies:

If anyone is to be blamed for the coming revolution it is the ruling class who steadily refuse to make concessions as reforms become necessary; who maintain that they can call a halt to progress, and dictate a standstill to the eternal forces of which they themselves are but the whimsical creation.

Indeed, this is no more than what all the Haymarket prisoners averred. They believed in force for legitimate self-defense, violence in the service of pre-existing life over which society's laws have no authority. When the capitalists revolutionized society by forcibly making it into an engine for their own exclusive profit and enjoyment, they

forced the proletariat to arms, and ever since then the workers have had every right to make the revolution their own, and to seek the total downfall of the ruling class.

These interesting parallels do much to demonstrate how, in the 1880s, a revolutionary class-struggle perspective was still putting forth new variants in the most unexpected places. Or were these, perhaps, only eccentric episodes without any real substance or basis? After all, the Shakers were supposed to *separate* themselves from the world when they entered the millennial life of the United Society of Believers; and Spiritualist mediums, Shaker or secular, withdrew even further into a *state of trance* or deep reverie in pursuit of their oracles of disembodied guidance. In a sense, one could hardly be more quietist.

Yet I would argue that the withdrawal, when genuine, demonstrably helped free their thought-patterns of capitalist/christian ideological hegemony. And that with that *cleansing* was released a certain dynamic of thought whereby the mediumistic reverie, in liberating the man or woman from the *demands of the world,* enabled him or her to *demand the world.*

In their rigorous fidelity to the revelations of reverie—to the ''promptings of the spirit'' outside all dogma and orthodoxy—the most derided heretics of their day approached the domain of the unfettered imagination cherished by the ''accursed'' poets. Indeed, it could be argued that they had far more in common with authentic poetry than with any kind of religion. While ninety-nine and nine-tenths percent of this country's clergymen joined in the clamor for the Haymarket anarchists' death (let it not be forgotten that the clergy had also, with very few exceptions, supported black slavery till the end) leading Shakers and Spiritualists stood on the side of the working class in revolt. If in one sense Shaker/Spiritualist radicalism looks back to the Lollards, the Brethren of the Free Spirit and the Rosicrucians, so too, in another sense, it looks ahead to the surrealists—those protagonists of ''pure psychic automatism'' who insisted that ''the Dream too must have its Bastille Day!'' and who, steadfastly devoted to the cause of ''Poetry, Freedom and Love," situated themselves unreservedly "in the service of the Revolution."

As we have seen, the world the Shakers and Spiritualists demanded was not a self-centered and exploitative property-world abstracted from the relational matrix of humanity by the impersonal logic of privatism, power and competition. Rather, their world reflected the anarchist-communist dream of a free society, and was full of umbilical linkages with brothers and sisters, comrades-in-arms, spirits of the departed, Mother Earth and the Dance of Life.

In Haymarket days, the dialectic of their millennial dream and repressive reality reached an almost explosive tension, and it is not surprising that the Shaker and Spiritualist movements, as such, proved unable to survive the epoch. The project that Cora Richmond defined—opening magic and spiritual powers to the comprehension of all— would henceforth be taken up in very different ways by people with very different underlying assumptions.

But the fact remains that these movements' outstanding spokespersons were among the freest spirits of their age. Their lives and works will long remain worthy objects of inquiry and reflection, not least because their whole experience is still full of valuable lessons for true seekers in an age that has rediscovered alienation and anguish, and is just beginning to discover something of what Lautreamont meant by "poetry made by all."

Many age-old problems of individual conscience, social transformation, and the complex interplay between the two, can still be illuminated by the trance-poets of bygone utopias. Seen against the background of Haymarket, the radical Spiritualism of Frederick Evans, Daniel Fraser and Cora Richmond affords us a glimpse of the remarkable process of *solitude giving birth to solidarity.*

Joseph JABLONSKI

SOURCES:

Andrews, Edward Deming. *The People Called Shakers* (New York, 1953).
Barrett, Harrison D. *Life Work of Mrs. Cora L. V. Richmond* (Chicago, 1895).
David, Henry. *The History of the Haymarket Affair* (New York, 1936).
Desroche, Henri. *The American Shakers, from Neo-Christianity to Pre-Socialism* (Amherst).
Engels, Frederick. "Description of Recently Founded Communist Colonies Still in Existence" (written mid-Oct. 1844), in Marx & Engels, *Collected Works*, Vol. 4 (Moscow, 1975).
Evans, Frederick W. *Autobiography of a Shaker* (New York, 1973).
Holloway, Mark. *Heavens on Earth: Utopian Communities in America, 1680-1880* (New York, 1966).
Jablonski, Joseph. "Millennial Soundings: Chiliasts, Cathari & Mystical Feminism in the American Grain," *Free Spirits: Annals of the Insurgent Imagination* (San Francisco, 1983).
Melcher, Marguerite. *The Shaker Adventure* (Princeton, 1941).
Nordhoff, Charles. *The Communistic Societies of the United States* (New York, 1966).
Richmond, Cora L. V. *Psychosophy* (Chicago, 1915).
—. *Weekly Discourses* (Chicago, 1886).
Spies, August. "Address of August Spies," in Lucy E. Parsons, *Famous Speeches of the Eight Chicago Anarchists* (New York, 1969).

Note: Cora L. V. Richmond married several times. Originally Cora Daniels, she was also Cora Hatch and Cora Tappan before she became Cora Richmond.

ROBERT HERRICK

Born in Cambridge, Massachusetts and educated at Harvard, Robert Herrick (1868-1938) taught literature at the University of Chicago from 1893 to 1923. The Memoirs of an American Citizen (1905), one of the most significant reflections of Haymarket in fiction, is generally regarded as his most important and most readable novel. Notwithstanding the tone of New England moralism that runs through the book, its mixture of angry realism and sentimentality prefigures later "Chicago novels" by such writers as Frank Norris and Theodore Dreiser.

The lasting impact of Haymarket on Herrick is discernible in his response to the execution of Sacco and Vanzetti in 1927, which he denounced as the result of "the intolerant egotism of a dominant class. . . .The shoemaker and the fish-peddler, who had the temerity in these United States to avow their belief in anarchy and to dream of another and better form of society, paid for their naivete with their lives. For over seven years they proclaimed to the world from prison how completely America has renounced the traditional role of devotion to Justice. . . ."

FR

THE MORNING AFTER THE FOURTH OF MAY

The morning after the fourth of May the city was sizzling with excitement. From what the papers said you might think there was an anarchist or two skulking in every alley in Chicago with a basket of bombs under his arm. The men on the street seemed to rub their eyes and stare up at the buildings in surprise to find them standing. There was every kind of rumor flying about: some had it that the police had unearthed a general conspiracy to dynamite the city; others that the bomb throwers had been found and were locked up. It was all a parcel of lies, of course, but the people were crazy to be lied to, and the police, having nothing better, fed them lies. At the yards, men were standing about in little groups discussing the rumors; they seemed really afraid to go into the buildings.

* * *

From the start it seemed plain that the state could not show who threw the fatal bomb, nor who made it, nor anything about it; the best the state could do would be to prove conspiracy. The only connection the lawyers could establish between those eight men and the mischief of that night was a lot of loose talk. His Honor made the law—afterward he boasted of it—as he went along. He showed us what sedition was, and that was all we needed to know. Then we could administer the lesson. Now that eighteen years have passed that looks to me like mighty dangerous law.

Robert HERRICK

from *The Memoirs of an American Citizen* (Chicago, 1905)

EZRA HEYWOOD & THE CHICAGO MARTYRS

Ezra Heywood (1829-1893) was an individualist anarchist active in the abolitionist, labor reform, and free-love movements. He lived most of his life in Princeton, Massachusetts, together with his companion of twenty-eight years, Angela Tilton Heywood. The Heywoods organized a number of reform organizations, including the American and New England Labor Reform Leagues, and the New England Free Love League.

Ezra Heywood published a newspaper, *The Word* (1872-93), which was a leading outlet for individualist anarchist thought in the nineteenth century. He also operated the Co-Operative Publishing Company, which published and distributed a wide range of social reform pamphlets, including several by Heywood himself on labor reform, free love, temperance and free speech. His best-known pamphlet was *Cupid's Yokes*, a tract that argued for self-government and denounced marriage. The Victorian enforcer of virtue, Anthony Comstock, arrested Heywood in 1877 for selling it. But Heywood only became more aggressive in his assertion of woman's rights, including her right to birth control. Comstock had Heywood arrested five times on various obscenity charges. Two of these arrests resulted in prison terms. The second term, from 1890 till 1892, broke Heywood's health; he died within a year of his release.

Individualist anarchism was a social and political philosophy that flourished in the second half of the nineteenth century. Its exponents emphasized individual sovereignty and thus opposed the invasive authority of the state and the church. They argued that no social institution had the right to place limits on individual autonomy or to enforce obedience to a particular set of rules. Many individualist anarchists viewed themselves as defenders of the ideas of self-rule which Thomas Jefferson had enunciated in the Declaration of Independence.[1]

The individualist anarchists shared certain fundamental principles. Most placed primary emphasis on economic issues. They believed that men and women had the right to own what they produced with their own labor. A free and unregulated society of autonomous individuals would achieve a natural state of harmony, based on voluntarism. Under capitalism, the state and various monopolies controlled society and prevented the free workings of the marketplace, where people could freely produce and barter. The individualist anarchists bitterly denounced not only capitalism, but also state socialism, which they felt would sustain tyranny

Ezra Heywood

simply by changing the identity of the rulers.

The individualist anarchists failed to make a substantial impact among American workers for various reasons. Most did not toil in factories in the expanding cities; rather, they tended to be farmers, lawyers, printers, editors and small manufacturers, often living in rural areas, as was the case with Heywood. Language barriers and cultural differences were other factors separating the individualists from working people.

Another group of nineteenth-century anarchists, mostly foreign-born, played a far more significant role in working-class agitation. These urban laborers, who called themselves social revolutionaries, were based in the major in-

dustrial cities with large workingclass immigrant populations. Committed to issues of class struggle, these activists were, according to historian Paul Avrich, "socialists of a distinctive type, anti-statist, anti-parliamentarian, and anti-reformist. . ."[2] In contrast, the individualist anarchists traced their roots to Jefferson and the Transcendentalists, and celebrated the yeoman farmer and the artisan. Still, these groups had certain ideas in common, including a concern for individual liberty, a belief in free association, and the conviction that society would change only when individuals had transformed themselves. Both groups opposed the state and private monopolies.

However, there were serious disagreements. The social revolutionaries believed in revolutionary unionism and sought an anarchist society in which industry would be organized for the public good. The individualists could not endorse the notion that social cooperation and respect for the individual could be equal components in a radical program. They did not support the forcible redistribution of wealth and property, and were hostile to large-scale organizations. The anarchists did agree among themselves that if the state socialist system were adopted, it would end, in the words of the individualist anarchist Benjamin Tucker, in a "state religion, to the expense of which all must contribute, and at the altar of which all must kneel."[3]

The individualist anarchists also parted ways with the social revolutionaries in that most of the individualists eschewed the language of class struggle and any advocacy of violence. Ezra Heywood took a more complicated position on the question of violence in social change. During the Civil War, Heywood had broken with the overwhelming majority of abolitionists over their support of the war effort. He had argued then that a movement which sought individual freedom and self-rule could not endorse violence against another person, holding that such violence was the ultimate denial of self-rule. However, reacting to years of hardship of the depression of 1873-77, and specifically in reaction to the great strike of 1877, Heywood chose to qualify significantly his pacifism. He drew a qualitative distinction between the violence of the oppressor and the violence of the oppressed. He termed the strikers of 1877 lawful belligerents engaged in justifiable defense action to protect their natural rights. Heywood had begun to understand the sources of frustration and anger that often led to threatened or actual violence among American workers in this period.[4] Heywood's flexibility on this issue allowed him to be more supportive of the social revolutionaries than were other individualist anarchists.

Moreover, for Heywood and many other nineteenth-century anarchists, distinctions between the individualists and the social revolutionaries, and even between socialism and anarchism, were not at all as sharply defined as they would later become. Heywood was especially adverse to drawing fine distinctions. While the term "anarchism" was neither common nor clearly defined in Heywood's time, there is no doubt that he considered himself an anarchist. Writing in 1880, he declared that individualist anarchism was rooted in the American democratic tradition:

. . .Democracy, as taught by Paine, Jefferson, Franklin and Adams, collective order that recognizes and *guarantees* Personal Liberty, this is Anarchy, natural order, fruitful association, private and public felicity.

Like the social revolutionaries, Heywood at different times defined himself as an anarchist as well as a "socialist," a term often used in this period as a generic word for radicalism. Heywood taught classes in socialism which focused on his particular concerns: labor reform and free love. Socialism, for Heywood, respected the claims of all and invaded no one's rights.[5]

Of all the individualist anarchists, Heywood was most willing to support a broad range of groups. In 1872, he praised the International Working Men's Association. In 1877 he published a manifesto in *The Word*, written by nineteen Italian anarchists in prison. Heywood was the first person in the U.S. to print an English translation of the writings of the collectivist anarchist Michael Bakunin; in the 1880s he printed Bakunin's "The Gospel of Nihilism" in *The Word*. During the 1880s, Heywood's paper printed several speeches and letters of Johann Most, probably the most notorious of the social revolutionaries.[6]

Heywood was keenly aware that in the 1880s economic and social injustices

Josephine Tilton

Josephine Tilton:
Message to the Martyrs

Josephine Tilton, Ezra Heywood's sister-in-law, was a lifelong supporter of Heywood and his anarchist activity. An abolitionist in pre-Civil-War years, she was later a committed labor reformer and free-love advocate. For years she was one of the most zealous promoters of *The Word* and the Co-Operative Publishing Company's pamphlets.

In an editorial in Benjamin Tucker's *Liberty* immediately after the judicial murder of the Haymarket anarchists, Tucker cited Josephine Tilton's message to the martyrs:

"Not good-bye, but hail brothers!" telegraphed Josephine Tilton to Albert Parsons on the morning of the fatal day. *"From the gallows trap the march shall be taken up. I will listen for the beating of the drum!*

"The drum-tap has sounded; the forlorn hope has charged; the needed breach has been opened; myriads are falling into line; if we will but make the most of the opportunity so dearly purchased, victory will be ours.

"It shall be; it must be. . . ."

Martin BLATT

were growing, as was the repressive power of the state, and that workers were justifiably becoming impatient. He wrote in 1885:

. . .What John Brown was to slaveholders, dynamiters are to coercive authority—the stern reply of downtrodden Life to insatiate Death. . . . The issue is Right or Dynamite. . .

He believed that society must be radically altered quickly or face the righteous anger of the exploited. Still, he held that "war with its fierce brood of measures is evil. . ."[7]

Heywood warmly supported the Haymarket anarchists while they languished in prison awaiting their fate. He compared their approaching martyrdom with the martyrdom of John Brown. "Spies & Co.," he declared,

have a thousandfold more influence today than they would have had if never arrested ast all; if released, they will soon become ordinary men; if hanged, their souls will "march on" in ever-growing power.

On March 26, 1887, Heywood spent an hour in jail visiting with the Chicago anarchists, and also met with the wives of Fielden, Parsons and Spies. He editorialized that the Chicago anarchists were "noble men. . .guilty of serving Labor, Liberty, and Justice too well."[8]

After the executions, Heywood dedicated a major portion of the December 1887 issue of *The Word* to the Haymarket martyrs:

Far beyond ordinary gentlemen, Spies & Co. had intelligent hands, serviceable brain and heroic heart. [They were] agnostics in religion, Equitists in faithful work, sinking self in Moral Order, mounting the scaffold with serene, ecstatic fortitude. . . . Enriched by their Thought, luminous in their martyr Service, labor literature has in their mental work [a] precious heritage![8]

Martin BLATT

1. For detailed treatments of the individualist anarchists, see James J. Martin, *Men Against the State: The Expositors of Individualist Anarchism in America, 1827-1908* (Colorado Springs, 1970); William O. Reichert, *Partisans of Freedom: A Study in American Anarchism* (Bowling Green, 1978); and Rudolf Rocker, *Pioneers of American Freedom* (Los Angeles, 1949). 2. The best book on the social revolutionaries is Paul Avrich, *The Haymarket Tragedy* (Princeton, NJ., 1984). 3. Benjamin R. Tucker, *State Socialism and Anarchism* (Colorado Springs, 1972). 15. 4. See Ezra Heywood, *The Great Strike: Its Relations to Labor, Property and Government* (Princeton, MA., 1878). 5. Charles Shively, "Introduction," Stephen Pearl Andrews, *The Science of Society* (Weston, 1970), 21; *Lucifer* (April 3, 1891), 3; *The Word* (February 1880), 2. 6. *The Word* (May 1872), 3; (July 1877) 2; (April 1880), 1. I am grateful to Paul Avrich for the information that Heywood was the first to publish Bakunin in English in the U.S. 7. *The Word* (February 1885), 2. 8. *Ibid.*, Sept. 1886, 2; April 1887, 2; Dec. 1887, 1 and 2.

JOSEF DIETZGEN

When the Red and the Black are again united, thrones may well tremble.
—Otto von Bismarck

An important socialist theorist whose writings exerted considerable influence on the workers' movement in the late nineteenth and early twentieth centuries, Joseph (or Josef) Dietzgen (1828-1888) was a tanner by trade, born near Cologne, Germany.[1] Because of his revolutionary activity in 1848, he fled to the U.S. the following year. He wandered from the Hudson to the Mississippi and from Wisconsin to the Gulf, learning English on the way.

He went back to Germany in 1851, but eight years later emigrated again and set up a tannery in Montgomery, Alabama. The lynching of some of his friends who shared pro-northern (and/or anti-slavery) views caused him to return to the Rhine. For several years he lived in Russia where he wrote his first and most famous book, *The Nature of Human Brain-Work* (1869).

By the early 1870s Dietzgen was already a prominent figure in the German socialist movement. Karl Marx who, according to some reports, visited him at his home in Siegburg, praised him in his preface to the second edition of the first volume of *Capital*, and at the Hague congress of the First International introduced him to the other delegates with the words: "Here is our philosopher."

Frederick Engels also saluted the "workingman philosopher" in his *Essay on Feuerbach*, and credited him with the independent discovery of materialist dialectics.

Dietzgen came to the U.S. a third time in June 1884. After living for a time in New Jersey, he moved to Chicago in March 1886. A visit to August Spies, whom he found "very friendly," encouraged him to start writing for the *Arbeiter-Zeitung*, which he continued to do for the rest of his life. Meanwhile, he had been invited by the National Executive Committee of the Socialistic Labor Party in New York to write articles on the Chicago situation. When he sent them a report on the Haymarket events, however, the SLP leaders—who were already denouncing the anarchists and proclaiming the respectability of socialism—refused to publish it.

Opposed to the SLP's divisive attitude, Dietzgen did his best to effect solidarity between the two currents of the revolutionary workers' movement. He criticized the "narrow souls" of the SLP for believing that anyone who spoke in favor of the anarchists was a "traitor to our special cause,"[2] and continued to argue that "the difference between anarchists and socialists should not be exaggerated."[3] In his response to the SLP, published in the *Arbeiter-Zeitung*, Marx's old friend went so far as to call *himself* an anarchist.

J.F.H.

Lettering and sketch by J. F. Horrabin
(*Plebs*, December 1928)

ANARCHISTS & SOCIALISTS

For my part, I lay little stress on the distinction, whether a man is an anarchist or a socialist, because it seems to me that too much weight is attributed to this difference.

While the anarchists may have mad and brainless individuals in their ranks, the socialists have an abundance of cowards. For this reason I care as much for one as the other.

The majority in both camps are still in great need of education, and this will bring about a reconciliation in time.
April 20, 1886

* * *

The terms anarchist, socialist, communist should be so "mixed" together, that no muddlehead could tell which is which. Language serves not only the purpose of distinguishing things but also of uniting them—for it is dialectic.
June 9, 1886

* * *

I am still satisfied with my approach to the anarchists and am convinced that I have accomplished some good by it.
April 9, 1888

Joseph DIETZGEN

Excerpts from letters in
Briefe an Sorge,
English translation in the
Charles H. Kerr Company Archives,
Newberry Library, Chicago

On the motion of the imprisoned August Spies, and to the horror of many of his Marxist associates, Dietzgen was unanimously elected editor-in-chief of the three papers issued by the anarchist-run Socialistic Publishing Society: the daily *Arbeiter-Zeitung* and two weeklies, the *Vorbote* and the *Fackel*. Under his editorship, he wrote with pleasure, "Spies and Schwab are collaborating diligently"—their articles smuggled out of their cells by visitors—"and that makes my office very easy."[4]

In a letter to their mutual friend Friedrich Sorge, Engels objected to Dietzgen's anarchism, but added that "the moment may excuse this" and reaffirmed his confidence in the old philosopher who, he felt, was "on the right track." Engels was far more critical of the "fine gang. . .at the head of the [SLP] in New York," whose paper, the *Sozialist*, he regarded as "a model of what a paper should not be."[5]

In Chicago, while working on the anarchist press, Dietzgen wrote his *Excursions of a Socialist into the Domain of Epistemology* and *The Positive Outcome of Philosophy*, both published in Germany. In the early 1900s these were included together with the earlier *Brain-Work* volume and several other essays in two volumes of Dietzgen's writings published by Charles H. Kerr. Every IWW and Socialist Party hall, and many a trade-union library, had these books, which were reprinted several times (*Positive Outcome* was issued in a revised translation by W. W. Craik on the occasion of the Dietzgen Centenary in 1928), and enjoyed a circulation well beyond the borders of the U.S.[6]

It was reported that in the homes of South Wales miners during the 1920s, Dietzgen's works were prominently featured and "treated with reverence" as sacred texts.[7] Indeed, according to one observer, virtually an entire generation of Welsh miners seem to have regarded Dietzgen as "literally the greatest philosopher who ever lived."[8]

In Britain as in the U.S., his works played a significant role in the movement for workers' education. "For a worker who seeks to take part in the self-emancipation of his class," Dietzgen had said, "the prime necessity is to cease allowing himself to be taught by others and to teach himself instead."

The influence of his "cosmic-monistic" dialectical philosophy is discernible, in a general way, in the works of a number of very different revolutionary theorists, including V. I. Lenin who, though not uncritical of Dietzgen, conceded that there is "much that is great" in his work and argued that "in order to reach understanding, workers must read Dietzgen"; Mary E. Marcy, editor of the *International Socialist Review* and one of America's most brilliant and popular socialist pamphleteers; and the

Yugoslav surrealists Koca Popovic and Marko Ristic.[9]

There are some, however, for whom Dietzgen's writings loomed so large that they could properly be called Dietzgenists. These include German-born paleontologist Ernest Untermann, translator of Volumes II and III of *Capital*, and author of *Science and Revolution* and other works; the Dutch astronomer and council-communist Anton Pannekoek; William W. Craik, co-founder of England's Central Labour College; Fred Casey, British author of *Thinking: An Introduction to Its History and Science*; and John Keracher, a Scotsman, author of *The Head-Fixing Industry* and other pamphlets, a founding member of the Communist Party of the U.S., and for many years the central figure of the Proletarian Party.

Dietzgen's farflung influence was entirely posthumous, however, for he died two years after Haymarket. At home enjoying a cigar after a stroll in Lincoln Park, he was engaged in a "vivacious and excited" discussion of the "imminent collapse of capitalist production" when he suddenly stopped in mid-sentence, his hand uplifted—dead of "paralysis of the heart."

He was buried at Waldheim on April 17, 1888, a few feet away from the Haymarket martyrs.

FR

NOTES

1. Eugene Dietzgen, "Joseph Dietzgen: A Sketch of His Life," in Joseph Dietzgen, *Some of the Philosophical Essays* (Chicago, 1906). Unless otherwise noted, biographical details and quotations in the present article are from this source.   2. *Briefe an Sorge* (Friedrich Sorge's correspondence), letter from Joseph Dietzgen Nov. 8, 1886. Typescript of English translation in the Charles H. Kerr Company Archives, the Newberry Library, Chicago.   3. *Ibid.*, May 17, 1886.   4. *Ibid.*, Oct. 10, 1887.   5. Karl Marx and Frederick Engels, *Letters to Americans, 1848-1895* (New York, 1953), 61.   6. *The Charles H. Kerr Company: A Hundred Years of Socialist Publishing*, catalog of the Kerr Archives (Chicago, 1985), 32.   7. Jonathan Ree, *Proletarian Philosophers: Problems in Socialist Culture in Britain, 1900-1940* (Oxford, 1984), 37.   8. *Ibid.*, 23.   9. For these and the authors noted in the next paragraph see the list of "Other Sources" below.

OTHER SOURCES

Fred Casey, "Josef Dietzgen," *The Plebs* (London, Dec. 1928).

W. W. Craik. *Central Labour College, 1909-29: A Chapter in the History of Adult Working-Class Education* (London, 1964).

John Keracher, "Josef Dietzgen: His Life and Work," *The Proletarian* (Chicago, Dec. 1928).

V. I. Lenin. *Materialism and Empiriocriticism*, in *Collected Works*, Vol. 14 (Moscow, 1968).

Mary E. Marcy. *You Have No Country! Workers' Struggle Against War* (Chicago, 1984).

Frank P. Murphy, "Dietzgen Recalled on Anniversary of Burial in Waldheim," *Industrial Worker* (Chicago, April 17, 1937).

Anton Pannekoek. *Lenin as Philosopher* (New York, 1948).

—: "The Standpoint and Significance of Josef Dietzgen's Philosophical Works," Introduction to Joseph Dietzgen, *The Positive Outcome of Philosophy* (Chicago, 1928).

Koca Popovic and Marko Ristic. *Nacrt Za Jednu Fenomenologiju Iracionalnog* (Belgrade, 1931).

Untermann, Ernest, "A Pioneer of Proletarian Socialist Science," *International Socialist Review* (Chicago, April 1906).

ELEANOR MARX

The youngest daughter of Karl Marx, and the only one to become a public figure in her own right, Eleanor "Tussy" Marx (1855-1898) was born in England where she spent nearly all her life. A tireless activist in the British workers' movement, she organized the first women's branch of the National Union of Gasworkers and General Labourers, served on its Executive Committee for several years, and played an important role in many strikes as well as in eight-hour-day agitation. With William Morris and H. M. Hyndman she was one of the most renowned socialists in late-nineteenth-century England, and a popular speaker at radical workers' meetings.

From September to December 1886 she and her common-law husband Edward Aveling were in the U.S. on an extensive speaking tour. From New York and Rhode Island to Minnesota and Kansas, they addressed large workingclass audiences in dozens of

cities. Defense of the Haymarket Eight was a regular feature of their speeches.

Arriving in Chicago on November 5—they stayed five days—the Tribune *and other*

dailies called for their arrest as "incendiaries" and suggested that they might share the fate of the condemned anarchists. Their talk that evening drew a crowd of 3,500.

Three days later in nearby Aurora, at the Turners' Hall, Eleanor delivered the speech excerpted here to an overflow audience.

During her Chicago sojourn she also visited the anarchists at Cook County Jail. Back in England she continued to be an energetic campaigner for amnesty.

Eleanor Marx co-authored with Aveling a number of pamphlets, including The Woman Question *(1887),* The Working Class Movement in America *(1887, later expanded), and* Shelley's Socialism *(1888). She also helped prepare for publication a number of writings by her father and by Frederick Engels, and translated plays by Ibsen, Gustave Flaubert's* Madame Bovary, *and Lissagaray's classic* History of the Commune of 1871.

Her strife-filled relationship with the obstreperous and egotistical Aveling led her to take her own life at the age of 43.   FR

IN DEFENSE OF THE CHICAGO ANARCHISTS

If I were speaking anywhere else or at any other time than the present, I should go straight to my subject, which is to make clear to you what we mean by socialism, but in this town, and at this time, I should feel myself a coward, I should feel I was neglecting a manifest duty, if I did not refer to a matter which I am sure is present in the minds and hearts of all here tonight; which is present in the minds and hearts of all honest men and women. I mean, of course, to the anarchist trial—it is called a trial—and the condemnation to death of seven men.

Now I do not hesitate to say most emphatically and explicitly that if that sentence is carried out, it will be one of the most infamous legal murders that has ever been perpetrated. The execution of these men would be neither more nor less than murder. I am no anarchist, but I feel all the more that I am bound to say this. Nor do I make such a statement on socialistic or anarchistic authority alone. Why, only this morning, in the Chicago *Tribune*, you will

find the statement that "they hang anarchists in Chicago." That is, they are going to hang these men not as murderers, but as anarchists. That is the very confession we wanted. Not we, but our opponents, say this—that seven men are to be done to death not for what they have done, but for what they have said and believe.

That cowardly and infamous sentence will *not* be carried out. The votes cast by the working class will put a stop to that, at least so I believe. Should these men be murdered, we may say of the executioners what my father said of those who massacred the people of Paris: "They are already nailed to that eternal pillory from which all the prayers of their priests will not avail to redeem them."

Eleanor MARX

Speech delivered in Aurora, Illinois, November 1886, as printed in the Chicago *Knights of Labor* (December, 1886)

THE END OF DANIEL DELEON'S ACADEMIC CAREER

During the last decade of the nineteenth century, probably no individual influenced the radical wing of the American labor movement more than did Daniel DeLeon. While many an organizer would fall prey to the ideology of liberal capitalism, DeLeon and the Socialist Labor Party became early labor stalwarts against reformism, racism and imperialism.[1]

Born December 14, 1852 in the Dutch colony of Curaçao (off the coast of Venezuela), DeLeon received his secondary and university education in Germany and the Netherlands.[2] Within a few years of returning home, he migrated to New York. Shortly after his arrival in 1872, he began his first known political work —serving as an associate editor of a Cuban exile newspaper.[3]

DeLeon attended the Columbia College School of Law from 1876 until he graduated in 1878. When Columbia created a prize lectureship in Political Science, the faculty nominated him as its best candidate for the three-year appointment beginning in 1883.[4] Such an honor was an excellent start for a comfortable, liberal academic life. Married in 1882, DeLeon's first wife Sarah gave birth to their son Solon in 1883. DeLeon's political sympathies at that point in his life were clearly indicated when he named his second son Grover Cleveland DeLeon in 1886.[5]

But the next few years were tumultuous. Columbia renewed his three-year appointment in 1886, the year of the Haymarket events. DeLeon was so moved by the victory of striking New York streetcar-workers and so repulsed by the contemptuous sneers of his academic colleagues that he offerred his services to single-taxer Henry George, then running for Mayor of New York City.[6] Actions such as supporting strikers and speaking for Henry George did not sit well with the higher echelons of Columbia College. The President of the College introduced a motion to the Board of Trustees to dismiss DeLeon from the faculty, and even though it was not passed, it made clear that the future of his academic career was dubious at best.[7]

Of course, the Haymarket persecution was far more politically explosive than the New York strike. The defendants gained support from around the country and a large rally was held lin New York City's Cooper Union. DeLeon had supported the joint resolution of the Knights of Labor and New York Central Labor Union on behalf of the Haymarket defendants.[8] But his Cooper Union speech on October 20, 1887 was a sharp break from genteel mugwump Republican and single-tax milieus from which he was emerging. Sharing the platform with Samuel Gompers, who would soon become his bitter foe, DeLeon's condemnation of the death sentences did not foreshadow his revolutionary future as much as it reflected the legal training of his past: "I come here deliberately and for the good name of our beloved country that its proud record shall not be bloodstained by a judicial crime as the one contemplated in Chicago."[9]

At that time, DeLeon's personal life was in as much turmoil as his political life. Earlier that year, his wife had died giving birth to stillborn twins. This, combined with the impending doom of his academic future, could well have contributed to DeLeon's willingness to abandon his political past. His enthusiasm for single-taxism was waning by 1887; he joined the Knights of Labor the following year, and by 1889, was a new member of the Nationalist movement inspired by Edward Bellamy's utopian novel, *Looking Backward*.

As a member of the single-tax United Labor Party and the Nationalist clubs, DeLeon came into close contact with Lucien Sanial and other members of the Socialist Labor Party.[10] By 1890, his new workingclass-oriented socialist views were reflected in a commemoration of the Haymarket defendants published in the SLP's *Workmen's Advocate*:

If, then, the Chicago martyrs were innocent, why were they executed?. . . . They were executed by a murderous plutocracy because they were felt to be the champions of the outraged proletariat, because by their words they threatened to prevent the capitalist conspiracy from cowing the working people and keeping them in tame subjection grinding out profits and voting like cattle for the Democratic and Republican parties—the parties of their exploiters.

It was for that reason that the thankful proletariat now commemorated the death of their champions; and for the further reason that, owing to the manhood, the abnegation, the fortitude of those champions in their great trial, the great labor movement, so far from having been nipped in the bud in accordance with the plan of capitalism, had received a tremendous impetus.[11]

DeLeon joined the SLP in 1890 and the following year the Party asked him to become editor of its newly-established paper, *The People*. For a quarter century, DeLeon would use this post to assail reformism and defend his militant version of socialist unionism.[12]

Happening as they did at a critical time in his evolution from liberalism, the injustices of Haymarket had a profound

Daniel DeLeon in 1904

153

effect on DeLeon. But Haymarket was forgotten by his official Socialist Labor Party biographers. Olive Johnson does not mention Haymarket at all in her first-hand account of working with DeLeon; nor does Arnold Peterson in his biography.[13] In the decades following DeLeon's death the SLP drifted into a legalistic, almost pacifistic hope that socialism would be accomplished by voting capitalism out of existence. As they emphasized the legalistic side of DeLeon's socialist industrial unionism, his official heirs may have been somewhat embarrassed by his enthusiastic support for the Haymarket martyrs.

Don FITZ

1. H. H. Quint. *The Forging of American Socialism: Origins of the Modern Movement* (Columbia, S.C., 1953), 142-145.　2. David Hereshoff. *The Origins of American Marxism* (New York, 1967), 108.　3. G. L. Seretan. *Daniel DeLeon: The Odyssey of an American Marxist* (Cambridge, 1979), 6, 9.　4. *Ibid.*, 6.　5. Hereshoff, 108.　6. Olive Johnson, "Daniel DeLeon—Our Comrade," in *Daniel DeLeon: The Man and His Work—A Symposium* (New York, 1920), 88-91.　7. Seretan, 15-16.　8. Carl Reeve. *The Life and Times of Daniel DeLeon* (New York, 1972), 18-19.　9. Henry David. *The History of the Haymarket Affair* (New York, 1936), 412.　10. Seretan, 44.　11. *Ibid.*, 38.　12. Reeve, 40-41.　13. Olive Johnson, *op. cit.*; see also the biography by Carl Reeve.

The Chicago Martyrs on the Gallows at Cook County Jail

FREEDOM IN AMERICA

Where is thy home, O Freedom? Have they set
Thine image up upon a rock to greet
All comers shaking from their wandering feet
The dust of the old world bondage, to forget
The tyrannies of fraud and force, nor fret,
Where men are equal, slavish chain unmeet;
Nor bitter bread of discontent to eat,
Here, where all races of the earth are met?

America! beneath thy banded flag
Of old it was thy boast that men were free,
To think, to speak, to meet, to come, to go.
What up to Labour's sons who would not see
Fair Freedom but a mask—a hollow show?

Walter CRANE

from Commonweal,
October 15, 1887.

154

EDWARD BELLAMY

Written in the dazzling light of the Haymarket events, Edward Bellamy's Looking Backward (1888), a science-fiction romance that is also a penetrating critique of capitalism, was the most widely read and influential book of the late nineteenth century.

An immediate best-seller, the novel inspired a movement: More than 150 "Bellamy Clubs" were formed across the country, largely middle-class in composition at first, but with far more labor connections than historians have recognized. According to Sam Gompers, for example, Bellamyists organized the first Labor Press Association in the U.S. Eugene Debs, Daniel DeLeon, Charlotte Perkins Gilman and Austin Lewis all took part in the Bellamy movement. Leading Wobblies such as Elizabeth Gurley Flynn and Covington Hall acknowledged Bellamy's influence on their own intellectual formation, as did socialist publisher Charles H. Kerr and the founder of the Newspaper Guild, Heywood Broun.

Edward Bellamy (1850-1898) was born and lived most of his life in the small milltown of Chicopee Falls, Massachusetts. His early novels and tales reveal his enduring interest in psychical research, dreams, erotic passion and interplanetary travel: William Dean Howells praised his "romantic imagination surpassed only by that of Hawthorne." Hints of his later social concerns abound in these early works—The Duke of Stockbridge, for instance, "A Romance of Shays' Rebellion," sympathetically portrays the 1786 debtor-farmers' insurrection.

Bellamy's radical development, moreover, did not stop with Looking Backward. At least in part because of libertarian socialist criticism by William Morris and others, most of the statist aspects of that book are absent from its less-well-known sequel, Equality

(1897). His weekly paper, The New Nation, (1891-94) shows that Bellamy, in the last years of his life, increasingly identified himself with the cause of radical labor. "The political republic," he insisted, "can only be preserved by making it an industrial republic." He wrote in support of the shorter-hours movement and the Homestead strikers. He was an impassioned opponent of the two dominant political parties, which he regarded as virtually identical tools of the monopolists. He called May Day "the most significant and important anniversary of the year," arguing that whereas other holidays were retrospective and concern the past, "labor's May Day is prospective and portends the future."

To a surprising extent Bellamy's radicalism eludes traditional categories and has a peculiarly modern ring: In addition to supporting workers' struggles he championed radical feminism, expressed deep concern for wilderness preservation, and denounced genocide against the Eskimos as well as the "slaughter and destruction of whales."

While the American press responded to the 1890s wave of anarchist attentats in Europe with xenophobic tirades reminiscent of the Haymarket red scare, Bellamy penned the following editorial for The New Nation. Lucy Parsons reprinted it in the June 1892 issue of her paper, Freedom ("A Revolutionary Anarchist-Communist Monthly"), with a prefatory note calling it "a correct and intelligent version of the situation across the waters. . .in such striking contrast to what our capitalistic press would have us believe . . . . Mr. Bellamy's deductions and conclusions meet with our hearty endorsement."

The following year Bellamy hailed Gov. Altgeld's pardon of the surviving Haymarket prisoners, remarking that "it ought to have been done long ago," and urging "editors, orators and other public instructors to post themselves upon the facts of these famous Chicago trials. They are going to be more and more talked about. . . ."

FR

THE LESSON OF THE ANARCHIST OUTRAGES IN EUROPE

The European anarchists seem to have entered upon a concerted campaign of insurrection and dynamite. In Spain desperately revolutionary outbreaks by armed bands, and in France a series of terrific dynamite explosions, destructive of life and property, have created an extraordinary panic. In Italy, Germany and Austria the police are taking precautions against similar outbreaks by wholesale arrests of suspected anarchists, and in England great alarm is felt over the discovery of extensive conspiracies for blowing up buildings and public persons in that country.

In the plentiful newspaper discussion of these events, there is a singular lack of illuminating comment. The average editor seems to be completely mystified by the phenomenon of the anarchist. He finds him a sort of unaccountable moral monster, a malefactor animated by none of the usual impulses of law-breakers. Here is a person who commits the most shocking crimes apparently without personal motive. Money or gain he certainly is not after. Neither can he be said to be seeking notoriety, for the only condition of safety for the dynamiter is the concealment of his identity as far as possible even from his comrades. His only motive evidently is that which he avows, namely, an implacable and unquenchable enmity to the entire social order and all that represents it.

Now that a man might criticize society in some of its details and even occasionally urge specific reforms, is comprehensible enough to the average newspaper editor. In fact he sometimes gently criticizes public abuses himself and very sharply indeed when they can be plausibly laid to the opposite political party; but how a rational being can work himself up to such a state of frenzy against the whole social structure as to be perfectly willing to risk his life if he can but strike one blow at it or its official representatives, quite passes his understanding and the only way he can account for the anarchist is by calling him "a wild beast."

This is not scientific. Men are not wild beasts and when they act like them, we should seek the explanation in special conditions, and particularly when considerable elements of the population, as in Spain, Italy and France, seem infected with the same seeming madness.

The analysis of the conditions which produce anarchy is not, it seems to us, at all difficult. A very moderate exercise of imagination ought to enable any one to comprehend how the Frenchmen, Spaniards and Italians who are stirring up this trouble abroad, come to feel as they do toward society.

Suppose yourself born of working parents in the mining districts of Belgium or France, or from starving peasants in Italy or Spain, growing up among conditions of squalor and wretchednes, constant want and unremitting toil, utterly without hope of better things. Imagine yourself looking up from the social mire in which you grovel, at the world of the rich and well-to-do above you, living gaily, idly and luxuriously upon the product of your labor. Suppose yourself to have been taught from bitter experience to see in the government nothing but the jailer of the social dungeon you are confined in, the tool and instrument of your oppressors. By the time you had brooded over the situation through the years of youth and early manhood and found your despair multiplied by the misery of a dependent family, would you not very possibly begin to regard the whole social, industrial and political structure as nothing but an enormous prison which you could only hope to escape from by tearing it down?

Surely no one who knows from observation what is the condition of the lower classes in Europe can wonder that it turns men into "wild beasts." The wonder to us is that the masses are not all anarchists, and indeed a terribly large and fast-increasing proportion of them are. The despatches represent Paris in a panic over the dynamite explosions. That means gay Paris, rich Paris, shopkeeping Paris. There is another Paris living in cellars, in the tenement, in the factory and in the street, which is smiling grimly, a Paris that would be quite willing to take its chances with the other half in a general explosion.

Is there any warning for America in the terrible social situation in Europe to which these dynamite explosions call attention? Indeed there is a most urgent warning, though our contemporaries seem quite unanimous in ignoring it. The degradation of the masses, the misery of the poor, the hopeless industrial serfdom of the workers, the ostentation, luxury and cruelty of wealth, which have bred anarchism in Europe, are fast reproducing themselves here. As yet the anarchists among us are chiefly men who were formed by European conditions. But we shall not much longer need to im-

port our anarchists. They are breeding by millions from native stock in the slums of our great cities. If the ripening of that crop is not forestalled and prevented by the institution of radical industrial and social reforms within ten years, we shall by that time quite generally be busy dodging dynamite bombs.

Does anybody think a standing army will be an antidote to anarchy? France has the biggest in the world, and does not find it so. The fact is, and the European kings know it, the larger an army is, the more popular in basis and in sympathy it must become, and the more difficult will it be in any proposed social struggle to turn it against the masses from which it is drawn.

The fact cannot be too urgently impressed upon thinking men that if a radical industrial reform is to be peacefully effected in America there is no time to lose. In the first half of the this decade we have an opportunity which, not embraced, will soon pass away.

For this nation now is the accepted time, now is the day of salvation.

Edward BELLAMY

from *The New Time,*
May 7, 1892

WILLIAM DEAN HOWELLS

William Dean Howells (1837-1920) risked his considerable fame as a novelist, critic, and editor to challenge the Haymarket executions, which he characterized as "the greatest wrong that ever threatened our fame as a nation." Born into an Ohio family influenced by abolitionism, Swedenborgianism and Quakerism, Howells had already achieved some notoriety as a poet when his 1860 campaign biography of Lincoln helped him secure a consular position in Venice. After the Civil War, Howells edited Atlantic Monthly *and wrote a series of well-crafted realistic novels. The best of these,* A Modern Instance *(1882) and* The Rise of Silas

Lapham *(1886), contributed to the reputation Howells placed on the line in the Haymarket defense. The searing* A Hazard of New Fortunes *(1890) and the visionary utopian* Traveler for Altruria *(1894) reflect something of the influence that the Haymarket events, and social conflicts generally, had on Howells' work, which increasingly came to advocate a kind of Christian socialism. Like his friend Mark Twain, Howells sharply criticized American imperialism in the early twentieth century. Equally active as an anti-racist, Howells was a founder of the National Association for the Advancement of Colored People.*

DR

"THE JUDGMENT OF HISTORY":
Letter to the New York Tribune

As I have petitioned the Governor of Illinois to commute the death penalty of the anarchists to imprisonment and have also personally written him in their behalf, I ask your leave to express here the hope that those who are inclined to do either will not lose faith in themselves because the Supreme Court has denied the condemned a writ of error. That court simply affirmed the legality of the forms under which the Chicago court proceeded; . . .and it by no means approved the principle of punishing them because of their frantic opinions, for a crime which they were not shown to have committed. The justice or injustice of their sentence was not before the highest tribunal of our law, and unhappily could not be got there. That question must remain for history, which judges the judgment of courts, to deal with, and I,

for one, cannot doubt what the judgment of history will be.

But the worst still is for a very few days reparable; the men sentenced to death are still alive, and their lives may be finally saved through the clemency of the Governor, whose prerogative is now the supreme law in their case. I conjure all those who believe that it would be either injustice or impolicy to put them to death to join in urging him by petition, by letter or through the press and from the pulpit and the platform to use his power, in the only direction where it can never be misused, for the mitigation of their punishment.

William Dean HOWELLS

Letter to the Editor,
New York *Tribune*
(November 6, 1887)

Heading of leaflet issued by the Chicago Trade and Labor Assembly, 1893

THE FRIENDSHIP OF BERT STEWART & HENRY DEMAREST LLOYD:
A Personal Vignette

The social crisis of the mid-1880s, of which the Haymarket Affair was the most striking manifestation, had its counterpart in the numerous crises of identity felt by many of the individuals who participated in the events of this era. It is rare enough for historians to obtain an intimate glimpse into the lives of working people and their leaders; it is even rarer for these open windows to shed illumination on the critical events of history. Such is the case with the warm and fruitful friendship, originating in the 1880s, of Henry Demarest Lloyd, one of America's leading reform intellectuals, and Bert Stewart, a factory worker, member of the Knights of Labor, and labor journalist.

What first stands out in the backgrounds of Lloyd and Stewart are their dissimilarities. By the time Lloyd had graduated from Columbia Law School, he had been assimilated into the educated, well-to-do New York gentry of the late 1860s. Young Lloyd combined a reforming idealism with a conventional faith in the beneficent march of commerce and science as expressed in the immutable laws of orthodox political economy. On the recommendation of Columbia President Barnard, he became an organizer in the American Free Trade League, a reform group supported by elite merchants.

By 1872 the brilliant and well-connected Lloyd had become a liberal Republican journalist attacking the spoils system and tariff-fostered monopolies. On the defeat of Liberal candidate Horace Greeley by U.S. Grant, Lloyd became disillusioned with politics as a vehicle of reform and turned to journalism. He came to Chicago in 1872 to work for the free-trade *Tribune*, for which he served successively as literary editor, financial editor and, from 1880 to 1884, as chief editorial writer. During this time he married into the family of William Bross, part-owner of the paper and one of Chicago's leading citizens. By the 1880s Lloyd and his wife Jesse owned enough *Tribune* stock to be independently wealthy and to move easily in the social circles of Chicago's "better sort."

Bert Stewart, by contrast, grew up on a farm in Logan County, Illinois. From the age of seven the onset of a lifelong affliction of stuttering practically barred him from attending school. Stewart still managed to read the Latin classics as a child and to memorize large portions of Shakespeare and the English romantic poets. Until age twenty he farmed in the summer and studied in the winter. Leaving the farm Stewart drifted from job to job: editor, private secretary, house-painter, packer, drayman and factory laborer. In 1879 he married Lettie Fox, attracted by her love of poetry and literature; but he still lacked regular employment and a living wage to support his family.

By the early 1880s both Lloyd and Stewart were facing personal crises stemming from the labor upheaval of the period—crises which each helped the other resolve. Following the 1877 strikes Lloyd increasingly recognized the irrelevance of formalistic economic theory to social and ethical problems. In his editorials he questioned laissez-faire dogma through his advocacy of national arbitration of railroad disputes. In the early 1880s he suggested federally-set railroad rates, and his work has been credited with paving the way for passage of the Interstate Commerce Act of 1886. Meanwhile, Lloyd popularized his critique of monopoly to a national audience in widely read articles in the *North American Review* between 1881 and 1884.

In 1884 Stewart was a laborer in the Decatur Coffin Factory when he read Lloyd's "Making Bread Dear" and "Lords of Industry." He wrote to Lloyd thanking him for demonstrating that poverty need not be blamed on the poor. A month later in the dead of winter the coffin factory shut down for forty days, throwing Stewart out of work with his wife on the verge of childbirth. In his enforced leisure Stewart read Bureau of Labor reports from different states and prepared seven articles, several of which he sent to Lloyd. Though he was unable to get them published, Lloyd wrote to Stewart encouraging him "not to give up the ship."

Two years later Stewart again wrote Lloyd, recalling "how nearly I was to that door of despair upon which is engraven 'all hope abandon, ye who enter here.'" When he received Lloyd's confidence-building response, he wrote back, "I carried your letter until it was worn out. We lived through the forty days and I went to work, and worked nights studying and reading." During this period Stewart founded a workingman's club in Decatur, which eventually catapulted him to labor's nominee for city clerk. Blacklisted for his efforts, he joined the Knights of Labor in 1885 and in July began editing the Decatur *Labor Bulletin*. In September Republican Governor Richard Oglesby, a friend of Lloyd's, appointed Stewart, also a Republican, as a commissioner of the state Bureau of Labor Statistics. After this, wrote Stewart, "quite a number of journals then recognized me and asked for articles; many of them paid me for them. I was enabled to buy a little house."

By mid-1886 events thrust Stewart to the forefront of the labor movement in Chicago. George Detwiler and George Sceets, publishers of the *Knights of Labor*, the labor paper with the largest circulation in the city, had reacted to the Haymarket bomb by editorializing that the anarchists "were entitled to no more consideration than wild beasts." In early December 1886 growing outrage within the Chicago labor movement at the unfair trial received by the accused led these men to abandon the paper. The new owners brought in Bert Stewart as editor. Hearing of this, Lloyd wrote him: "Detwiler says you are very 'radical.' I like that especially. It is about time that somebody got radical on the side that has been radically plundered."

Handbill, 1890

Stewart began his tenure with a series of eloquent editorials portraying the verdict in the "anarchist case" as an assault on workers' rights of free speech and free assembly. He also criticized national Knights chief Terence V. Powderly when he enjoined local Knights from aiding the accused in any way. All the while, Stewart was performing a large portion of the practical work in the preparation of the voluminous 1886 report of the Illinois Bureau of Labor Statistics. In the ensuing spring Stewart threw himself wholeheartedly into the local election campaign of the United Labor Party, a coalition of Knights, trade unionists and socialists.

In his stay as editor of the paper Stewart came face to face' with his internal dilemma: how to reconcile his outrage and his passionate hatred of class injustice with his striving for cool intellect and for learning. In a long letter to Lloyd baring his soul-searching he compared the labor struggle of the 1880s to the Protestant Reformation:

No doubt, Erasmus, with his mighty brain did something to bring about the reformation. . .but Luther, the fiery, vindictive, passionate Luther. . .brought about the Reformation. He had not much brains and very little heart; but one idea, one purpose had burned its way into his life, and with it he burned every one that came near him, and set the whole human stubble of Europe on fire. . . .

No one realizes more painfully than I the danger contingent upon redressing industrial wrongs by means of those who are wronged. Passion may be kindled by an orator who thereby creates a mob he cannot control. Much better that the labor problem be solved for the working people than by them. From above it can come like the peaceful sleep that follows the convulsive fit, forcing itself up from below, the crust of our social fabric will be cracked asunder and the lava of human blood will flow. But God help us; when I talk to the so-called statesmen and men of brains I am told the subject is too intricate for solutions, and that the remedy lies in being temperate. My dear Mr. Lloyd, I have seen *my* babies cry for bread, I have seen *my* wife lie sick and hungry in a cold house; I searched from early morn until driven in by the darkness in search of work; I have taken in and done washing to get wherewith[al] to feed *my hungry children*. I have got down on my knees and begged for work and was *kicked in the breast* and kicked out of the shop for asking for work, I never touched a drop of whiskey in my life, I never spent a cent of money in my life for liquor or tobacco in any form, yet I have suffered this much, and as I am not yet thirty years old God knows what may be in store for me. Having had the *Labor Question* thus burned into my very life, do you wonder that I get mad and say mean things, and call men liars when they say that if "workingmen would quit drinking whiskey there would be no labor question." I may be vindictive, I try to keep cool; b[ut] the ashes of memory smolder and burn though I strive to forgive and forget. You tell me that I must be wise, I wish to be. I would knowingly injure none. While recognizing no vested rights, no special grants, I pray heaven keep me ever [from] touching with tongue or pen the natural rights, the real rights of any human soul.

With the defeat of the United Labor Party Stewart turned toward intellect and away from the revolt born of desperation that he was on the verge of endorsing. When ownership of the paper passed into unfriendly hands he resigned as editor. By the end of the year he had accepted a post as special agent with the U.S. Bureau of Labor. Until this point both Democrats and Republicans had courted Stewart, hoping to use his name to win the support of independent labor voters in Illinois. According to one Democratic politician, referring to Stewart: "I doubt if any other man in Illinois enjoys organized labor's confidence to the same degree."

For Stewart, Lloyd had served as an intellectual and political father. As the young Knight wrote in 1887: "There is no man on earth today except my father whose disapprobation would have so depressing effect on me as yours.'' Lloyd's talks with Stewart at his home in Winnetka, and his easing of Stewart's path into government, saved him from the embitterment which could have resulted from labor's defeats in 1887. In 1893 Stewart wrote Lloyd that he had buried his ''outrage.'' Though his conclusions would still be ''radical,'' his ''manner of stating them'' would henceforth be ''mild.''

Stewart's self-reconciliation enabled him to do yeoman service for the Department of Labor. During the 1910s he was chief statistician for the U.S. Children's Bureau. From 1920 to 1932 he headed the U.S. Bureau of Labor Statistics and contributed important studies of the early nineteenth century labor movement which are still of use to scholars. The end of Stewart's career demonstrated that his primary commitments had not dimmed. During Herbert Hoover's 1932 reelection campaign the embattled President announced that unemployment was falling. Stewart then held a press conference to release figures proving precisely the opposite. For his indiscreet honesty Stewart was forced into retirement.

In the life of Henry Demarest Lloyd the Haymarket period was also the major turning-point. Under pressure from *Tribune* publisher Joseph Medill to moderate his attacks on monopoly, Lloyd resigned his position. Then, depressed at abandoning his life career, he suffered a nervous breakdown in September 1885. After an extended period of recovery, Lloyd returned to Chicago a month after Haymarket. Soon, he threw himself into the campaign for clemency for the convicted anarchists. When Governor Oglesby commuted the sentences of Samuel Fielden and Michael Schwab, Lloyd was accorded the honor of delivering the message to them.

Three months later Lloyd returned to print for the first time since his breakdown with a passionate reply to Judge Gary, the Haymarket judge, in which he defended trade unionism as America's greatest hope. The Trade and Labor Assembly circulated 50,000 copies of the article, and henceforth Lloyd became Chicago labor's most respected spokesman. It was also the final break with his patrician past. Well-to-do friends refused to see him, he was dropped from clubs, and snubbed on the street.

Meanwhile, under the influence of William Salter of the Ethical Culture Society, Lloyd began the study of idealist philosophy, attempting a synthesis of Emersonian individualism with the imperatives of welfare democracy. His solution, ''The New Conscience,'' first delivered as a talk

Henry Demarest Lloyd

in February 1888, set forth a moral basis for his indictment of the wage system. Lloyd had completed his personal transformation from an aloof journalistic critic to independent reformer devoted to the cause of workingmen. His new commitment was expressed in his oft-repeated epigram: ''The workingman is often wrong, but his is always the right side.''

Though the personal journeys of Lloyd and Stewart were in opposite directions, the basic conflict each faced was the same. Both were idealists and American individualists schooled in Emerson and the early-nineteenth-century romantic poets. Thrown together by the labor upheaval of the 1880s, each underwent an intense personal struggle to reconcile older American values of liberty and equality with the harsh realities of industrial capitalism. Though both rejected Marxian ''scientific socialism,'' each contributed to the new synthesis of individualism and collectivism that emerged in this period.

Richard SCHNEIROV

Sources: Bert Stewart Papers, Southern Historical Collection, University of North Carolina; Henry Demarest Lloyd Papers, Wisconsin State Historical Society; *Knights of Labor* (Chicago), 1886-87; Chester McArthur Destler, *Henry Demarest Lloyd and the Empire of Reform* (Philadelphia: University of Pennsylvania Press).

Henry Demarest Lloyd addressing Milwaukee streetcar strikers in the rain   (Chicago *Chronicle*, June 14, 1896)

Anarchist editors such as Moses Harman, Jo Labadie, Johann Most, Albert Parsons and August Spies exerted considerable influence, but this lithograph's suggestion that they directed the entire labor movement is clearly an exaggeration.

THE KANSAS RESPONSE

For much of the twentieth century, the state of Kansas has suffered the reputation of being a conservative bastion, yet during the 1880s, through the Populist movement of the following decade, and even until the anti-radical repression of World War I, it was a dramatic laboratory of social experimentation, free thought and wild political insurgency. The Haymarket Affair was widely used by Republicans to attack all progressives; correspondingly, Haymarket served as a kind of social template for the radicals, and their responses to it are instructive in their vitality, sense of history and political courage.

In his capacity as a labor organizer, Albert Parsons toured Kansas, Nebraska and Missouri in the summer of 1885. On July 4 he spoke to a crowd of some 3,000 in Ottawa, Kansas on the topics of political economy, socialism and the present struggle against capitalism.[1] He found himself in a turbulent atmosphere, as the Knights of Labor had won a strike against the Union Pacific, and were in the process of winning another on the Southwest lines of Jay Gould, which ran through the state.[2] He also addressed large meetings in Topeka, Omaha, Kansas City and St. Joseph. After the Topeka talk he reported:

The capitalistic papers denounced us the next day, and threatened your humble speaker with lynching, but it is far more probable that the workingmen of Topeka would lynch the capitalists of Topeka than to allow themselves to be mobbed by them.

In St. Joseph,

the conservative workingmen, who profess to have faith in the curative powers of the ballot-box, strikes, arbitration, etc., were loud in their denunciations of the revolutionary Socialists, and they were at great pains to have the public understand that the Knights of Labor was an organization which had nothing to do with these "Communists."

But Parsons claimed to have drawn the largest number of people to such a gathering in the city's history. It is evident, however, that there was a local faction of the Knights opposed to his views. Parsons proceeded to the "Little Balkans" coal region of southeast Kansas, and addressed miners in Scammonville, Weir City and Pittsburg. He saw unemployed men traveling "on the wayside everywhere," and in the market-square of Kansas City he spoke to a mass meeting, "mostly 'tramps.'" Summing up his month's tour of the region, he estimated that he had reached "fully 20,000 wage slaves," and concluded:

The working people thirst for the truths of Socialism and welcome their utterance with shouts of delight. It only lacks organization and preparation, and the time for social revolt is at hand. Their miseries have been unendurable, and their necessities will soon compel them to act, whether they are prepared or not. Let us then redouble our efforts and make ready for the inevitable. Let us strain every nerve to awaken the people to the dangers of the coming storm between the propertied and the propertyless classes of America. To this work let our lives be devoted. Vive la Revolution Sociale!

Thus Albert Parsons had first-hand knowledge of Kansas' militant workers, and they of him.

The following spring of 1886 was marked by an enormous national agitation for the eight-hour day. In addition the second or "Great" Southwest railroad strike was a central element in the social drama of those months. Under the able leadership of a socialist, Martin Irons, the Knights of Labor confidently hoped to better their conditions, and when a shop-worker and fellow Knight was discharged by the Texas & Pacific at Marshall, Texas, all the Knights on the Gould lines struck in early March.[3] Workers killed steam-engines in numerous places, prompting a severe reaction by state and local officials. Governor John A. Martin of Kansas called out the National Guard to protect non-striking workers running the trains, and soon the strike was completely broken. Hundreds of workers were dismissed and blacklisted, and the failure of the strike greatly contributed to the subsequent decline of the Knights of Labor.[4]

In the aftermath of the Haymarket explosion, William Holmes, who sheltered Albert Parsons from the police, suggested that he make his way to Kansas.[5] Parsons, however, opted for nearby Wisconsin. Out in Valley Falls, Kansas, fellow anarchist Moses Harman was writing his first response to the whole affair. Harman, a survivor of the Civil War period in Missouri, had settled in this small town in the northeastern part of the state, to commence the publication of his remarkable newspaper, *Lucifer the Light Bearer*.[6] A freethinker and proponent of advanced views on sexual matters, Harman was inclined to pacifist notions, and his first response to Haymarket was one of outright hostility:

Again has the cause of labor—the cause of Freedom and of justice—been betrayed and crucified in the house of its professed friends. The so-called Socialists—the self-styled Anarchists of Chicago, have precipitated a "reign of terror" in that city. While calling themselves Anarchists their acts prove them to be the exact opposite. Instead of Anarchists they have shown themselves to be Archists of the most rabid and dangerous kind. If we must submit to Archism—to despotism—we much prefer that such despotism shou'd take the form of an organized government, even though that government be administered in the interests of a band of robbers—rather than that we shou'd fall into the hands of an unorganized despotism and mob—such as wrecked buildings and destroyed life in Chicago a few days ago. The time for the rightful use of the dynamite bomb in America has not yet arrived, and it is sincerely hoped will never arrive.[7]

In the next week's issue of the paper, Harman was more cautious, and wrote of considering "the causes that led to the murderous affray," concluding: "From all we can learn it would now seem that free speech is on trial in Chicago, as well as the Socialistic strikers."[8] News of the atmosphere of hysteria and repression in Chicago undoubtedly prompted Harman to consider the whole matter more deeply. He was much concerned to shore up his position: "Our Anarchism was learned in the school of Franklin, Jefferson and Paine—not in that of Robespierre and Marat," and again called for the "peaceful dethronement of capital from its usurped seat of power, and the enthronement of labor in its stead."[9] Within two months he was supporting a call for legal defense for the Chicago radicals.[10]

Harman had some reason to be circumspect during those days, for other radicals in Kansas were receiving harsh treatment. Harry Vrooman, a student at Washburn University, had met Albert Parsons in Topeka in 1885.[11] Vrooman had been attacked as a dynamiter and member of the Red International by the Topeka *Commonwealth* shortly afterward, and in an eloquent letter he declared that he did indeed believe in dynamite, but in the form of radical ideas and education.[12] During the summer and fall of 1886, Harry's brother Walter was refused permission to speak in Ottawa, where Parsons had addressed thousands just a year before; in Kansas City and St. Joseph, he was arrested, but he wrote of one speech he was able to deliver: "I began to thump the crowd over the head with the golden rule, carve their vitals with the sword of the spirit, and depress the minds of some with weighty truths from holy writ." Young Walter's Socialism was apparently of the Congregational kind, but still Red enough to impress the authorities. At an outdoor rally in Pittsburgh, Pennsylvania on May 9, 1887, Walter Vrooman was again arrested for having provoked a fight among his listeners by declaring that "in the light of the miscarriage of justice in the trial of the Haymarket anarchists the American flag had been reduced to a mere rag on a stick." He was fined $25 and costs on a charge of disorderly conduct.[13]

During the summer of 1887, it became apparent across the nation that the Chicago anarchists were in real peril of their lives, and consequently liberals and radicals rallied to their support. In Topeka a young attorney named G. C. Clemens had been active in politics, and he took up their case in a

Moses Harman

pamphlet titled *A Common-Sense View of the Anarchist Case, with Some Points Apparently Unnoticed by Others, By a Western Home-Spun Country Lawyer.*[14] Contrary to the claims of its title, the pamphlet, while cogent in noting many holes in the case of the prosecution, offered little that had not been written elsewhere before, except for a bizarre claim that the Pope was somehow behind the impending executions, because "American policeman are almost to a man Irish Catholics." Clemens concluded that the real charge against the Chicago men was for thinking: ". . .the idea of metaphysical crime was evolved." In Kanas and throughout the subsequent history of the United States, such crimes of intellect have figured prominently in the repression of radicalism.

Clemens did not restrict his activities to writing pamphlets, but spoke several times during the summer in behalf of the condemned men, and also against police brutality in Topeka itself. He was the author of a broadside boldly headed "DAMNABLE! POLICE INFAMIES OF A SINGLE WEEK," addressed to "Lovers of Liberty." This spoke of "a dozen workingmen arrested 'on suspicion' and sent to the rockpile twenty-five days without trial or evidence," as well as similar incidents, and concluded with a call to a rally, seeking the abolition of the Police Court and jail: "Let thousands come and join in this demand. Any man that stays away deserves to be bossed, bullied, choked and locked up, as he will be when his turn comes."[15]

Meanwhile, down in Winfield, Henry and Leopold Vincent established a newspaper, *The American Nonconformist and Kansas Industrial Liberator*, transferring it from its beginnings in Iowa. The Vincents were allied with the Union Labor Party and the Knights of Labor. On the front page of their issue of November 4, 1887 they printed a story about Lucy Parsons being refused entry into a hall she had rented in Jersey City, whereupon the crowd broke down the doors and went in anyway, and she gave her talk. Just below the story was a bit of homespun humor:

"So you are an anarchist, are you?"
"Pray sir, what is an anarchist?"
"An anarchist is—er, yes, a—dang my buttons! I did know once, but shot if it isn't gone from me; an anarchist is, blow'd if I *do* know and that's all about it."
"It is an abolitionist, isn't it?"
"Yes, yes, that's it, an abolitionist, that's it."
"Well, an abolitionist is a pretty good sort of a fellow."
"Let's have none of your sass."

With the execution of the Chicago men scheduled a week away, the moment was not especially humorous; indeed, on an inside page of the same issue was printed a bold headline: "CITIZENS! LOOK INTO THIS THING! AND IN ANY EVENT DEFEAT IT!" The partriarch of the Vincent clan, James Vincent Sr., had written an open letter to Judge Gary "by an Old Time Abolitionist," and as the Chicago newspapers did not print it, it appeared in distant Winfield. After comparing the condemned men to Archimedes and Christ, the elder Vincent wrote:

You talk of putting down anarchy and socialism! I freely admit I know but very little of these systems, but from what I have learned, their foundation principle seems to me to be the old abolition principles. That is the principle I was trained in. I worked under it under such men as Clarkson, Wilberforce, Geo. Thompson, and later with

Garrison, Pillsbury, Phillips, Sumner, Gerrett Smith, Lovejoy, John Brown and that class who "loved their fellow men." And if the old abolition doctrine is the doctrine of those so-called anarchists and socialists, get ready your noose Judge Gary, but I am for giving them all the help I can. I used to help the black slaves at the risk of fine and imprisonment. I am as ready to help both black and white slaves to-day, with death staring me in the face, in their efforts to shake off the worse yoke of bondage to corporate oppressions, than the yoke of chattel slavery was. So far from putting down anarchy, you will make anarchists. Once more.

It was undoubtedly with a recollection of many daring raids by the abolitionists that the Chicago police took unprecedented security measures at the time of the executions.

After the executions, newspapers and other observers widely noted comparisons with John Brown, one of the heroes of Kansas history.[16] The *Labor Chieftain* of Topeka, affiliated with the Knights of Labor, wrote: "They were hung legally, perhaps, and so was John Brown. But it took four years of war, millions of treasure, unnumbered lives, and heart-broken wives and mothers, and fatherless children to correct this grievous 'legal' error."[17] In *Lucifer* Moses Harman expressed similar views:

The proslavery monopolists demanded the blood of John Brown and his comrades, believing that by this means they could "stamp out" abolitionism in the United States. The result was that they stamped out their own "peculiar institution." The monopolists of to-day demand the execution of Spies, Parsons, Fielden, et al., believing that by this means they can stamp out the great popular uprising against the despotism of corporate capital. Their success will probably equal that of their illustrious predecessors.[18]

Harman expressed his horror at the fact that the hanged men had died slowly by strangulation, but prefaced his comments by an odd and flinty note:

Many of our Labor and Socialistic exchanges are coming to us heavily dressed in mourning in honor of the murdered men of Chicago. While heartily sympathising with the spirit which prompts this manifestation of respect for the worthy dead, we do not reverse our column rules, for the reason that we regard public mourning as a vain ostentation. Especially do we deprecate the profuse display of somber black, as calculated to add needless gloom and pain to the fact and scenes of death. Then, also, the habit imposes a grievous burden upon the poor, who generally think they must vie with the wealthy in the outward acknowledgment and assertion of their grief.[19]

Ever opposed to Puritanism and doctrinaire religion in all its forms, Harman had in any case come far from his initial condemnation of the Chicago comrades.

Down in Winfield, the conflict arising in part from Haymarket was taking a particularly tense and divisive form. All along, as we have seen, *The Nonconformist* defended the anarchists, if not in all of their positions, at least in their legal rights and progressive purposes: "It is charged that the *Nonconformist* above all other journals is an 'anarchist sympathizer.' The reason for that is that it has been recognized as the most powerful organ in Kansas in opening the eyes of the people to the situation the country is in."[20] Among those who thus charged them was the redoubtable Edwin P. Greer, who published the *Courier*, also in Winfield; he proclaimed that theories "smacking of anarchism" were dangerous: "It is the duty of every citizen to at once and em-

phatically stamp out this treason in our midst."[21] Eleven months later Greer was able to commence his plan of achieving exactly this result, when on October 4, 1888 he published an expose of the Vincent brothers' involvement in a secret organization called the National Order of Videttes, a kind of shadow directorate of the Union Labor Party. Papers including a coded constitution, oaths of office and ritual of the Videttes had been given to Greer by George W. Poorman, a printer who had been fired from *The Nonconformist*. On October 18 further revelations about the Videttes were published by the *Courier*, this time from one C. A. Henrie, another turn-coat printer who had met Albert Parsons in Topeka in 1885. All around Kansas the Republican newspapers reprinted the *Courier* articles.

And then occurred one of the most remarkable and mysterious incidents in Kansas history. In the town of Coffeyville, about 100 miles from Winfield, a railway express package addressed to the latter town exploded, seriously injuring two women. Both the name of the sender and that of the addressee were fictitious. The *Courier* charged "Evidences of Anarchism in Kansas are Increasing," but the Vincents alleged a Republican plot to frame them, as had occurred in Chicago. An election was coming up in a few days, and the whole amazing controversy affected the outcome in favor of the Republicans. Three years later a joint legislative investigation produced mountains of "evidence" on both sides, but the sender of the explosive package was never identified

G. C. Clemens

163

Henry Vincent

(similarly with the Haymarket bomber).[22] The whole affair of the Coffeyville Explosion warrants a place in what Paul Avrich has called the "Cult of Dynamite" which was such a striking feature of the era.[23]

The Union Labor Party disappeared soon after the election of 1888, but the Vincents and other Kansas radicals became just as dedicated to the Farmers Alliance and the People's Party which immediately succeeded it. A recent history has called the Populists "the largest democratic mass movement in American history."[24] Anything like even a brief summary of this movement is beyond the scope of this essay, but it is *apropos* to note that during that period the issues which Haymarket raised were very much alive in Kansas. For example, out in Medicine Lodge, the City Marshall of the town, a former rancher by the name of Jerry Simpson, had decided to run for Congress on the Alliance ticket. During the summer of 1890, the campaign heated up considerably; the Republican *Cresset* of August 1 charged:

Religiously, this man is an infidel, but tries to keep this from the public, knowing that it is an unpopular belief. He also claims that the state of Illinois was in error when it hung the Chicago anarchists; that if they desired to wave the red flag they could, for to him it was as good as the stars and stripes.

In its issue of August 22, the *Cresset* reprinted from the Wichita *Journal* a "story" of Jerry's arrival in that city:

Simpson's reputation as an anarchist preceded him to Wichita and a committee composed of Bob Coates, Frank Smith and J. R. Brown was appointed to search the gentleman and take from him any dynamite bombs that might be lurking about his person.

After this precaution Rufe Cone advanced, and welcomed the visitor, and through force of habit started with him for the county jail, but was recalled to his senses by a dig in the ribs by F. F.

McMechan and the line of march was changed, and the visitor was escorted to a convenient watering place where he was sized up by all the boys. A *Journal* reporter saw him, and fell into a dead faint at the sight.

Jerry Simpson is a man who looks as though he had not been out of the woods ten days. He is uncultivated, uneducated and almost uncivilized in appearance. If he is an anarchist and a true believer in the red flag his looks do not deceive him, if not, he should sue himself for slander and malicious libel.

In response, the *Barber County Index* stated tersely: "The *Index* flatly denies that Mr. Simpson is an anarchist or an atheist."[25] By the end of September it was apparent that Simpson's forces were going to make a strong showing, for on the 27th of that month, there was an enormous parade of some 400 wagons through Medicine Lodge, flying banners such as "Death to Trusts," "Abolition of National Banks" and "Brother laborers, the power is with us." Simpson addressed a joyous crowd of perhaps 4,000, and the *Index* resounded: "If there was anarchy in that welcome, God pity this country!"[26] Simpson won the election in a landslide, and became famous as the "Sockless Socrates of Kansas."

Governor Altgeld's pardon of the surviving Haymarket prisoners on June 26, 1893 provoked another spate of controversy. The conservative Topeka *Daily Capital* commented sourly: "Several democratic voters are added to the strength of that party by Gov. Altgeld's pardon of the Haymarket anarchists."[27] Such a statement was heavily sarcastic in view of the subsequent end of Altgeld's political career. On the other hand, one of the leading Populist journals printed a long essay by the persistent G. C. Clemens, titled "Anarchism as Anarchists Understand It."[28] Clemens began with the local context:

For daring to be true to our convictions, and because in the hour of their triumphant supremacy we dared accuse as murderers certain decorous, Mammon-inspired Chicago assassins, some of us in Kansas have for seven years endured all the vilifications of which malicious ignorance and hired libel are capable.

He reviewed the case, and noted that thousands of people had just attended the dedication of the martyrs' monument in Waldheim Cemetery. Furthermore, Clemens considered the international context: "The persecution of these men by American capitalism was identical in its motive with the persecution of the socialists by Bismarck." Waxing eloquent, he declared that "the crime of these men was in preaching no more than the Omaha platform affirms," and soared yet further: "Anarchism is the philosophy of peace—of universal brotherhood. The much cursed red flag merely symbolizes the sentiment that God has made of one blood all the nations of the earth." Concluding claimed: "I trust I have succeeded in showing that anarchism, whether foolish or wise, is at least neither un-American nor wicked; that it rests upon the Declaration of Independence and the Sermon on the Mount," then returned to his first theme: "May I not hope that after this exposition of our creed, our hope and our aim, we 'Kansas anarchists' may enjoy a cessation of libelous attacks to which hitherto we have been subjected?"

This remarkable summation was shortly answered in the columns of the same paper by one Eugene B. Sandfort of Winfield, who objected that the Chicago men were members of the nefarious International, were dedicated to dynamite and violence as a way of life, and that furthermore Clemens had insulted the framers of the moderate Omaha platform by comparing them to anarchists.[29] Clemens responded in the same issue that the International had not had a political platform of dynamite, and finished the dispute thus:

"Anarchism has an extensive literature. The writings of its expounders are accessible to all who choose to read them. They are, as a rule, the works of ripe scholars who were masters of style. They are not dreary reading, and no man can rise from their perusal without feeling his nobler impulses stirred.

Naming a long list of famous radicals such as Proudhon, Prince Krafatkin *(sic)*, Emerson, Thoreau and Edmund Burke (the latter surely a strange inclusion), he then recommended Albert Parsons' book on the subject, saying that its purchase would help his widow and orphan to live: "I shall be delighted to help any convicted sinner to obtain anarchist books, including the New Testament, of which I find a most lamentable ignorance prevailing among anarchism's bitter foes."

Next year, in June of 1894, Clemens was involved in advising the movement of homeless workers gathering and passing through Kansas on their way to Washington as part of Coxey's Army.[30] Soon afterward he moved toward socialism, heading the state ticket in 1900.[31] Unrepentant to the end, G. C. Clemens was one of the most intellectual and articulate of all the Kansas radicals.

In the first part of the twentieth century, a kind of dreary calm descended over the great midwest of the United States. Vachel Lindsay bitterly expressed it in his unforgettable poem "Eagle Forgotten" in which his hero Gov. Altgeld had "gone to join the ironies with old John Brown." In 1911, Emma Goldman visited Kansas, and later commented:

The State of Kansas, like Massachusetts, lives on past glory. Had it not given John Brown to the cause of the slaves? Had not the rebel voice of Moses Harman sounded there? Had it not been the stronghold of free thought? Whatever its historic claim to progress, Kansas now gave no sign of it. The Church and Prohibition had evidently performed the last rites at the interment of liberalism. Lack of interest in ideas, smugness and self-complacency characterized most cities of the State of Kansas.[32]

Emma did speak at the university in Lawrence, and the tone of her comments suggests regret that she simply had not had more invitations. While there is certainly something to what she says about the triumph of Puritanism as a general rule, during this same period her comrade Alexander Berkman was telling of his life to young Meridel LeSueur in a Fort Scott kitchen; the Socialist Party still had locals in some 140 Kansas towns; and one of the greatest freethought publishing ventures of all time, the Little Blue Books of E. Haldeman-Julius, was about to be launched in Girard.[33] The radical and anti-war prisoners in Leavenworth's federal penitentiary managed to stage a wild and fervent May Day demonstration within its walls in 1918.[34] And thus ended a phase in the early history of Kansas radicalism, arising in part from its connections with and responses to the Haymarket Affair.

Fred WHITEHEAD

Jerry Simpson

Paul Avrich, *The Haymarket Tragedy* (Princeton, 1984), 243.   6. Hal D. Sears, *The Sex Radicals: Free Love in High Victorian America* (Lawrence, 1977) is an outstanding study of Harman and his circle; his discussion of Harman's response to Haymarket is on 137-139.   7. *Lucifer*, May 7, 1886. Harman's printed date gave the year as 286 E.M., which stood for the Era of Man, beginning with the year of Giordano Bruno's execution in 1600.   8. *Lucifer*, May 14, 1886.   9. *Lucifer*, May 21, 1886.   10. *Lucifer*, June 25, 1886.   11. *Life of Albert Parsons*, 30.   12. Ross E. Paulson, *Radicalism & Reform: The Vrooman Family and American Social Thought, 1837-1937* (Louisville, 1968), 42-47.   13. Paulson, 49-56.   14. Michael J. Brodhead and O. Gene Clanton, "G. C. Clemens: the Sociable Socialist," *Kansas Historical Quarterly*, Vol. 41 (1974), 475-502. I am grateful to Professor Clanton for first drawing my attention to Clemens' connection with Haymarket. Clanton gives the place of publication of the pamphlet as Enterprise, Kansas, and the date as 1887, but the copy in the Kansas State Historical Society lacks this information.   15. Copy in the collection of the Kansas State Historical Society, bearing Clemens' signature and the date of August 7, 1887.   16. Avrich, 405, 410-411, and see index under "John Brown" for additional references to the influence of his example on the whole historical and cultural milieu of the 1880s radicals.   17. *Labor Chieftain*, November 18, 1887.   18. *Lucifer*, November 11, 1887.   19. *Lucifer*, November 18, 1887.   20. *American Nonconformist*, November 17, 1887.   21. Quoted in Harold Piehler, "Henry Vincent: Kansas Populist and Radical Reform Journalist," *Kansas History*, Vol. 2, No. 2 (1979), 14-25.   22. *Proceedings of the Joint Committee of the Legislature of the State of Kansas, Appointed at the Session of 1891, to investigate the Explosion Which Occured at Coffeyville, Kansas, October 18, 1888* (Topeka, 1891), compiles 647 pages of documents, newspaper reports, editorials, maps, testimony concerning the explosion, Parsons' 1885 visit to Topeka, C. A. Henrie's expulsion from the Knights of Labor, etc. See also Piehler; Sears, 139-143; and James C. Malin, *A Concern About Humanity: Notes on Reform, 1872-1912 at the National and Kansas Levels of Thought* (Lawrence, 1964,) 155-165.   23. Avrich, Chapter 12. On the front page of each edition of Denver's *Labor Enquirer*, the reader could find quoted, instead of a stock market summary, the current price of dynamite; see Joseph R. Buchanan, *The Story of a Labor Agitator* (New York, 1903), 68-69.   24. Lawrence Goodwyn, *The Populist Movement in America* (Oxford, 1978), vii. The standard work on Kansas is O. Gene Clanton, *Kansas Population: Ideas and Men* (Lawrence, 1969).   25. *Barber County Index*, August 27, 1890.   26. *Barber County Index*, October 1, 1890. For a contemporary, if rather sentimental biography, see Annie L. Diggs, *The Story of Jerry Simpson* (Wichita, 1908). Simpson was a member of the Knights of Labor, as indicated by the record of his fraternal visits to the Local Assembly of nearby Kiowa; minute book in the Stockade Museum of Medicine Lodge.   27. *Daily Capital*, June 27, 1983.   28. *Advocate*, July 5, 1893.   29. *Advocate*, July 19, 1893.   30. *Daily Capital*, June 1, 1894; *State Journal*, June 1, 1894; *Pratt County Union*, June 7, 1894.   31. Brodhead and Clanton, 497-502.   32. *Living My Life* (Salt Lake City, 1982) 477-78.   33. Meridel Le Sueur, *Crusaders: The Radical Legacy of Marion and Arthur LeSueur, with a new introduction by the author* (St. Paul, 1984) xxi; introduction by LeSueur to the Salt Lake City edition of Goldman's autobiography; ditto list of Socialist Party locals in Kansas during 1915, in my personal possession; Mark Scott, "The Little Blue Books in the War on Bigotry and Bunk," *Kansas History*, Vol. 1 (1978), 155-76.   34. Susan Kling, "A Most Unusual May Day Celebration," *Daily World* (New York), April 27, 1978.

1. *Life of Albert Parsons* (Chicago, 1889), 26-34. In this volume the Ottawa speech is dated July of 1884, but from the context it is almost certainly a misprint for 1885.   2. Philip S. Foner, *History of the Labor Movement in the United States*, Vol. 2, 2nd ed. (New York, 1975), 50-53.   3. Foner, 83-86; Ruth A. Allen, *The Great Southwest Strike* (Austin, 1942) is the standard work.   4. Foner, 86-92; Allen printed photographs of the grave of Martin Irons at Bruceville, Texas, over which the Missouri Federation of Labor erected a monument. See also *Mother Jones Speaks: Collected Writings and Speeches*, ed. Philip S. Foner (New York, 1983), 280-81, 312, for her memories of Irons, her visit to his grave, and her campaign for the monument.   5.

Robert Green

THE TRUE STORY BEHIND THE
HAYMARKET POLICE STATUE

For many years, visitors to Chicago's historic Haymarket Square saw only a statue to honor the Chicago Police Department. This was truly ironic because of the true story of what happened that May 4th evening in 1886. Foreign visitors to Chicago were particularly upset when they viewed this monument, and they were shocked by both the inappropriateness of its subject matter and the words on the back of its base: "Dedicated by Chicago. . . to her Defenders in the Riot of May 4, 1886." Why was this statue ever erected here and by whom? What has been its fate over the years?

Mayor Carter Harrison during the trial would criticize the Chicago Police Department for marching against the workers after he had told them not to do this. Governor John Peter Altgeld, in his 1893 pardon of the Haymarket Martyrs, would point out one incident after another of earlier examples of police brutality. Yet, the Chicago *Tribune* and anti-labor businessmen who were against the Eight-Hour-Day Movement, felt the need to rewrite history through the erection of a statue to the police.

There is a great deal of evidence to prove that the police had actually behaved in a cowardly fashion when the bomb exploded. Many of them ran into a building on the west side of Desplaines and hid until everything was over. Later, policemen like Inspector "Black Jack" Bonfield and Captain Schaack, who had testified against the workers during the Haymarket Trial, were thrown off the police force in disgrace. Yet, in spite of all these facts, the Chicago *Tribune* would, on January 19, 1888, urge the public to donate to a monument fund and announce they would offer a $100 prize for the best design.

The *Tribune* then began to raise the $5,000 to $7,000 that they felt would be needed to cover the cost. However, by November 23, 1888, after ten months of campaigning for funds, only $150 had been collected. Chicagoans seemed reluctant to contribute to "the popular subscription fund" of the *Tribune*. Finally, some large donations came from anti-union businessmen from Rockford, Aurora and other communities surrounding Chicago. The "Committee of Twenty-Five" was formed. This committee was headed by R.T. Crane. It was in front of his factory, the Crane Plumbing Company, that the Haymarket meeting had taken place. The businessmen of this committee were members of the Union League Club, and the Union League took it upon themselves to raise the balance needed. Eventually, over $10,000 was raised. The statue cost $10,000 when it was finally completed. According to the minutes of the Union League Club, several hundred dollars was still left, and there were several very heated discussions about how this balance should be used, but supposedly they never arrived at a solution.

A total of 168 designs were submitted to a Citizen's Committee formed by the *Tribune* to select the winning design that would receive the $100 prize. The selection of the winning design took place at the Union League Club on

September 23, 1888. It was submitted by Charles F. Batcheider of St. Paul, Minnesota, a newspaper reporter who had worked in Chicago. His design showed a sketch of a policeman with his arm raised. The second prize design was very similar to the base that the police statue would later be mounted on, with the Seal of the State of Illinois and lamps on each side.

The sculptor, John Gelert, who had also executed a statue of General Grant for the City of Chicago, was selected to bring Batcheider's design to reality. After receiving the commission, Gelert left the Union League Club at Jackson and Dearborn; reaching the intersection of Clark and Madison Streets, he saw a policeman named Thomas F. Birmingham, directing traffic. Gelert immediately asked this big Irish cop to be his model. He told the *Tribune* on December 14, 1888, that he used as his model a "robust patrolman" that he chose because "in his countenance, which is frank, kind, and resolute, he (Gelert) was able to catch those ideal qualities of the guardian of the peace instead of the more unpleasant ones of mere strength and insensibility." However, there is a story that when the "Committee of Twenty-Five" observed the clay model they were horrified that the statue looked Irish. They wished a Protestant, Anglo-Saxon-looking policeman. Gelert refused to change the figure, but he also used other models, since Birmingham was often drunk and unable to pose.

The statue was finally dedicated on Memorial Day, 1889, with about 2,000 people present. It was a rainy spring day and 176 policemen took part in the ceremony, the same number that had marched up Desplaines Street three years earlier. The 17-year-old son of Mathias Degan unveiled the statue, and Mayor Cregier spoke the following words:

May it stand here unblemished so long as the metropolis shall endure to say to the millions who come upon it: This is a free and lawful country with plenty of room for the people of all the earth who choose to come here to breathe the free air and to obey these laws, but not an inch of room or an hour to dwell here for those who come for any other purpose.

In the years to come the police statue and Thomas F. Birminghan would both have many problems. Birmingham was paraded around the Columbian Exposition of 1893 as the symbol of the perfect policeman, but in 1898, and again in 1899, he was brought before the Civil Service Commission for violation of Rules 58, 67, and 73, which meant that Birmingham had been working with criminals and selling stolen merchandise for his own gain. Eventually, he was thrown off the police force, and according to Emma Goldman, he died in County Hospital after having been a drunk and a petty thief on Skid Row for several years.

The statue also encountered its share of problems. Supposedly on May 24, 1890, a discovery was made of "unmistakable traces" of an attempt to blow it up. In May of 1903, the crest of the City and State were stolen from the base. In 1927, on the 41st anniversary of the Haymarket meeting, a streetcar driver named O'Neil drove his streetcar full speed and jumped the track, knocking it off the base, because he said he was sick of seeing that policeman with his arm raised.

In 1928, the statue was repaired and moved to Union Park. Later it was moved around the park several times as the streets were widened or moved. It finally ended up on Jackson Boulevard, facing the statue of Mayor Carter Harrison, who had, ironically, testified against the police.

In 1956, the statue was moved to a special platform built during the construction of the Kennedy Expressway. The Haymarket Businessmen's Association sponsored the moving of the statue, hoping it would promote tourism. On May 5, 1965, as a result of the efforts of the Chicago Police Department and several police associations, the monument was designated a historic landmark by the City Council.

On May 4, 1968, the statue was defaced with black paint after an incident in the Civic Center with the police during a demonstration against the Vietnam War.

On October 6, 1969, the statue was blown up, supposedly by the Weatherman Faction of the Students for a Democratic Society (SDS). Mayor Daley promised to replace it, and Wally Phillips, a disc-jockey, helped raise the money. Sculptor Mario Spampinato was hired to restore Gelert's statue. The new statue was unveiled May 4, 1970.

Leading fomentors of Chicago's anti-anarchist hysteria in the wake of Haymarket, police officers Bonfield, Ward and Schaack were removed from the police force in 1889 for various criminal offenses.

The statue was again blown up on October 6, 1970, and again Spampinato restored it. There was talk of putting a plastic dome over it or making many statues out of fiberglass and replacing them as each new one was blown up, but Mayor Daley wished it restored in the original material. The mayor ordered round-the-clock security that cost the city $67,440 a year.

In February, 1972, the statue was removed from its base and placed in the Lobby of the Central Police Headquarters at 11th and State Streets, a suggestion made earlier by the Illinois Labor History Society in a letter to Mayor Daley. Even the Chicago Landmarks' Commission had stated that the police deserved a statue, but it did not belong in Haymarket Square.

In 1976, the statue was moved from the Central Police Headquarters to the New Police Academy at 1300 W. Jackson, and placed in a courtyard in the middle of this steel and glass structure. No longer visible to the public, it is now safe from any future bombings.

The base of the statue is still in Haymarket Square, but by 1985, the Seal of the State of Illinois had been removed, as well as the plaque containing the names of the seven policemen that had died. Many groups have covered the stone base with graffiti proclaiming a number of causes. One group has boasted they will have all of the stone base removed by the Centennial of the Haymarket Affair.

As the Centennial of Haymarket approached, plans were launched for a Labor Park in Haymarket Square. A press conference announcing this was held on November 12, 1985, the anniversary of the funeral of the Haymarket Martyrs.

A petition-drive was started by the Haymarket Centennial Committee and the Illinois Labor History Society. Letters were written to Edmund Kelly, Superintendent of the Chicago Park District, requesting that they purchase the empty lots at the Northwest corner of Randolph and Desplaines as a site for a park and monument.

This new monument would be a fitting one, dedicated to the struggle of workers not only for the Eight-Hour-Day, but for freedom of speech and assembly, the rights of minority groups, and the right of all workers to have free democratic trade unions.

William J. ADELMAN

This satirical proposal for a monument to the police was attributed by the Chicago *Tribune* to none other than Johann Most.

VOL. 27 NO. 667   JULY 28 1894   PRICE 10 CENTS

Judge

ENTERED AT THE POST OFFICE AT NEW YORK AS SECOND CLASS MATTER. COPYRIGHT 1894. BY THE JUDGE PUBLISHING CO. TITLE REGISTERED AS A TRADE MARK.

ANARCHY

A DANGEROUS LEADER.

By voting Democratic last election Illinois placed herself under the guidance of an Anarchist.

One of many cartoons portraying Governor Altgeld as an anarchist

Irving Abrams, last surviving member of the Pioneer Aid and Support Association, speaking at an Illinois Labor History Society Haymarket Memorial Meeting, May 1971

THE HAYMARKET MONUMENT AT WALDHEIM

The beautiful monument at the martyrs' grave in Waldheim Cemetery was designed by the sculptor, Albert Weinert. Justice is represented by a woman placing a laurel wreath on the head of a fallen worker. She is marching into the future, ready to draw the sword if she must, to win a better life for the generations to come.

The sculptor was inspired to use the theme because the Haymarket martyrs had sung the "Marseillaise," the French national anthem written at the time of the French Revolution. One of the verses of the song describes the scene depicted in the monument.

The bodies of Spies, Parsons, Engel, Fischer and Lingg were placed in a simple temporary vault in 1887 as everyone listened to their attorney, William Black, give his eulogy just as the sun was setting.

In the years between 1887 and 1893, Lucy Parsons worked hard to set up the Pioneer Aid and Support Association to provide for the widows and orphans of those who were executed as well as the dependents of those who were still in Joliet penitentiary. This society also supported publications on the Haymarket case, as well as appeals for the freeing of those still in jail. It was the Pioneer Aid and Support Association that erected this monument, especially important after the erection of the Police Monument in Haymarket Square.

When this monument to the martyrs was dedicated a vast parade was held in downtown Chicago, with a ceremony at the cemetery on Sunday, June 25, 1893. Marching in this parade were over 3,000 people including singing societies, Turners, trade unionists, and musical organizations. Thousands of people watched the 1893 parade as it went up Market Street (now South Wacker Drive), then east to Wells and south to Harrison where five special trains, again at the Grand Central Station, were waiting to carry the throng to Waldheim. The Chicago *Tribune*, usually conservative in its estimates of crowds, reported that over 8,000 people went out to the cemetery after the parade. The Columbian Exposition was taking place at this time and there were visitors in Chicago from all over the world, many of whom went to Waldheim that day.

The thousands who arrived at the cemetery found that an interesting program had been planned with speeches in English, German, Bohemian and Polish. There were floral tributes from unions in England, France and Belgium. The monument was draped in red, and the speakers' platform was decorated with the crimson banner of the Architectural Ironworkers Union No. 2, the blue flag of the Brewery Workers Union, the red banners of the International Mannerchor and of the Workingmen' Clubs, and the Stars and Stripes.

A VISIT to WALDHEIM

The first thing I did after I arrived [in Chicago. 1913] was to visit the big German cemetery at Waldheim, where the Chicago martyrs lie buried. The simple monument over their grave is most impressive, the figure of Liberty with the laurel wreath, and the year 1887. And these last words of August Spies on the pedestal: "The day will come when our silence will be more powerful than the voices you are throttling today."

For more than twenty years I had in various countries joined in the annual memorials held on November 11th for these men at whose grave I stood now. There is no question that they were condemned unjustly, that they were the victims of a judicial murder, put to death not for any crime, but for their beliefs, which they upheld courageously before their judges. . . .

I stood for a long time, thinking, silently, beside their grave. Nearby there was a fresh grave, with grass and wild flowers growing over it. It was the resting place of Voltairine de Cleyre, who had died in Chicago on June 6th, 1912, at the age of 46. A remarkable woman, a rare spirit. . . .

Rudolf ROCKER

from Rudolf Rocker,
The London Years
(London, 1956)

The "Red Squad" of the Chicago Police Department was there, and the *Tribune* reported that "detectives from the Chicago force mingled with the throngs and a photographer quietly took several views of those around the platform."

The program began with the sculptor, Weinert, presenting the statue to the President of the Pioneer Aid and Support Association. Fetzner's Orchestra played the "Marseillaise," and the monument was unveiled by Albert Parsons Jr., then 14 years of age. The Humboldt Singing Society sang an old Lutheran hymn, "Wake Up," and then Dr. Ernst Schmidt spoke.

Seventy-eight years later, on Sunday, May 2, 1971, the ceremony was repeated as Irving Abrams, a Chicago attorney and the last surviving member of the Pioneer Aid and Support Association, presented the deed to the monument to the Illinois Labor History Society, in the presence of Mark Neebe, a great grandson of Oscar Neebe. A student from Concordia Teachers' College Choir of the nearby German Lutheran school in River Forest sang "Wake Up" and the "Marseillaise." Joseph Jacobs, the labor attorney, again read from Dr. Schmidt's 1893 address.

Each year, on the Sunday closest to May 4th, members of the Illinois Labor History Society and other organizations gather at the monument. Red roses, carried at the funeral in 1887 and placed at the monument's base at the original dedication of the monument in 1893, have become a symbol of these men who died for freedom of speech and assembly.

Other organizations place wreaths at the monument on November 11th each year, "Black Friday," the day that Parsons, Engel, Fischer and Spies were executed. At the base of the statue are the last words spoken by August Spies.

William J. ADELMAN

from William J. Adelman,
Haymarket Revisited
(Illinois Labor History Society)

A May Day button
from 1936

Shorter Hours button, 1978

FROM NOVEMBER 11, 1887 TO JUNE 26, 1893

On November 11, in a city that had been turned into an armed camp in expectation of radical outbreaks, four men were hanged by the neck until they were dead. But the case would not die. Parsons, Spies, Engel and Fischer became heroes. Fielden, Schwab and Neebe were increasingly regarded as men unjustly in prison. Parsons' last words on the gallows had been: "Let the voice of the people be heard!" He got his wish at once. His funeral procession was viewed by at least a quarter of a million, one person of every four in Chicago. The site of the graves in Waldheim Cemetery became almost a holy spot. Memorial meetings were held there annually.

The unflagging movement to get Schwab, Fielden and Neebe released from jail was fed in many ways. In 1888 and in 1889 there were charges of bribery against the Chicago police, and Chief of Police Ebersold, Inspector Bonfield and Captain Schaack were all suspended from the force. The trade unions in Chicago built up their strength, and in 1889 the Illinois Federation of Labor dared for the first time to declare that the Haymarket defendants had not received a fair trail. A new era of free speech began in Chicago, and Lyman Gage presided every Sunday evening over public meetings at which all shades of opinion were expressed.

Each succeeding governor of Illinois was petitioned repeatedly to release the Haymarket prisoners from prison. But none did so. And then, in 1892, John Peter Altgeld was elected governor. . . .

Although Altgeld had not made any campaign promises to free the Haymarket prisoners, his election brought new hope to the Amnesty Association and stimulated it to increased effort. But Altgeld was very ill after the campaign ended, so ill that his doctors forbade him to go to Springfield for his inauguration on January 10. He went anyway. During the ceremony the air in the overheated Capitol was stifling, but Altgeld did not remove his overcoat. At the reception afterward he nearly fainted and was forced to leave. After ten days in bed he was ordered by his doctors to go south for a rest. This time he followed orders. . . .

Clarence Darrow had told Altgeld that release of the Haymarket prisoners should be his first act as governor. Altgeld said no, that many other things had to be done first, but that after he had time to study the case he would act. Within ten days after the inauguration he asked the sheriff of Cook County to send him the files about Haymarket, and he also got the transcript from the state supreme court in Springfield. Altgeld speculated about freeing only Neebe

and reducing the sentences of Fielden and Schwab from life imprisonment to a fixed term that would expire sometime in the future. "But he doubted," Schilling recalled later, "whether any man could continue to live in Illinois and pardon all three."

The Altgeld statue in Chicago's Lincoln Park.

Darrow could not see it that way. He thought that Governot Oglesby's earlier commutation of the sentences of Fielden and Schwab from execution to life imprisonment, and especially the many petitions for mercy from well known men, would protect Altgeld from censure. Darrow did not miss a chance to urge the pardon on the Governor, but always Altgeld evaded him. Darrow began to be rent by doubts. Had he been mistaken in Altgeld? Was the man lacking in courage? Had he no feelings for justice? Darrow could bear it no longer, and he went to Altgeld—the massive lawyer towering over the slight Governor—and told him that his friends could see no excuse for delays. It should be done at once.

Altgeld spoke precisely: "Go tell your friends that when I am ready I will act. I don't know how I will act, but I will do what I think is right."

Darrow showed his irritation and disappointment, and Altgeld spoke again.

"We have been friends for a long time. You seem impatient; of course, I know how

you feel; I don't want to offend you or lose your friendship, but this responsibility is mine, and I shall shoulder it. I have not yet examined the record. I have no opinion about it. It is a big job. When I do examine it, I will do what I believe to be right, no matter what that is. But don't deceive yourself: If I conclude to pardon those men it will not meet with the approval that you expect; let me tell you that from that day I will be a dead man politically."

Darrow returned to his friends and reported that it was hopeless to discuss the case with Altgeld again. There was nothing to do but wait. . . .

On Sunday, June 25 [1893], eight thousand gathered at Waldheim Cemetery in Chicago to dedicate a monument to the Haymarket martyrs. The monument portrayed a workingman dying while a heroic bronze figure of Justice put a laurel wreath on his head.

The next morning, very early, Brand Whitlock was summoned to the Governor's office. Altgeld's secretary told him to immediately make out pardons for the three Haymarket prisoners. "And do it yourself, and don't say anything about it to anybody."

Whitlock was stunned. In a daze he went to the office of the secretary of state where he worked, and got out three large sheets of imitation parchment. In the still deserted office he made out the pardons for Oscar Neebe, Samuel Fielden and Michael Schwab. Impressing them with the Great Seal of the State, he took them to Altgeld.

The governor was having trouble with the secretary of state, Buck Hinrichsen. Altgeld told him, "I am going to pardon Fielden, Schwab and Neebe this morning. I thought you might like to sign the papers in person rather than have your signature affixed by your chief clerk."

Hinrichsen thought that, since he was chairman of the Democratic state committee and this act was sure to affect the party's fortunes, Altgeld had broken the news "rather carelessly." Altgeld looked at him curiously. Hinrichsen asked, "Do you think it policy to pardon them?" Without waiting for an answer he added that he did not think it was.

Altgeld hammered his desk with his clenched hand and exclaimed: "It is right." The pardons were signed. . . .

On the table was a high pile of proofs of the message in which the Governor explained his reasons for the pardons. The proofs were released to the newspapers that same day.

Ray GINGER

from *Altgeld's America* (Chicago, 1958).

PART III.
THE HERITAGE

- A · GARLAND · FOR · MAY · DAY · 1895 ·
- · DEDICATED · TO · THE · WORKERS · BY · WALTER · CRANE ·

Vol. I, No. 3   MAY, 1919   Whole Number 3

The One Big Union Monthly

INDUSTRIAL FREEDOM

THE SPIRIT OF THE FIRST OF MAY.

PRICE: 15 CENTS

Best known for his celebrated ''Mr. Block'' comic strip that inspired one of Joe Hill's most popular songs, German-American cartoonist Ernest Riebe contributed numerous drawings to the Wobbly press, including this rapturous vision of May Day.

174

THE FACTS ON MAY DAY

May Day, May First—World Labor Day in most of the world—has its roots in North America, in the New England winters and Appalachian springs that made May 1 the appropriate time for building trade unions to negotiate their new terms of employment or else strike. It became a world labor holiday for the first time in 1890 on the urging of Samuel Gompers, President of the American Federation of Labor. (You can find his account of it in his *Seventy Years of Life and Labor*, Vol. I, pages 295-297.) He had sent Howard McGregor of the Seamen to the founding congress of the Second Labor and Socialist International, at the 1889 Bastille Day centenary in Paris, to urge demonstrations for the eight-hour day in all countries on May 1, 1890. The AFL was committed to strike action for that demand; making it a worldwide demand undercut the employer argument that to grant the shorter workday would send jobs to other countries. That congress had already decided that some date should be set for international demonstrations before McGregor got there, and so set the date as May 1 at Gompers' request. (Details can be found in Sidney Fine's account in *The Historian*, XVI, Spring 1954, pages 121-134).

Twenty-three years before that first World Labor Day, on May 1, 1867, there was a massive parade for the eight-hour day in Chicago, and that year, on the urging of Illinois Attorney-General Robert Ingersoll, an eight-hour law was enacted, but it had little effect. People still worked ten hours for the same pay, only now it was figured on an hourly basis instead of at the old daily rate.

How did that first World Labor Day go in 1890? *The Nation* of May 29, 1890 gave extensive coverage. It explained: "There was no intention of violence but only that on this day laborers all over the world should feel the unity of their class as a bond superior to all others, and should give peaceable expression to that feeling in taking a holiday and demonstrating." The article depicts the fear in the upper class of what a worldwide labor demonstration might do. Yet in Vienna it was a joyous holiday and in Berlin, despite police interference, there was a parade of 20,000. The British workers waited until Sunday, but they had two thousand in a London parade.

The May First 1890 world labor day celebration had been planned for that one year only, but it created such enthusiasm that it has endured worldwide except in the land whose cold winters and late springs gave it birth.

On May Days our thoughts go back prior to 1890 to the Haymarket bomb of May 4, 1886, and perhaps that is why in the U.S. that date is officially Law Day. In 1884 the Federation of Organized Trades and Labor Unions of the United States and Canada had resolved on widely spread strikes for the eight-hour day to take place on May 1, 1886. The response won the eight-hour day in many places—it was already the rule for U.S. government employees—and elsewhere cut ten-hour days to nine, and eleven-hour days to ten, despite opposition by Knights of Labor conservatives as well as by radicals who denounced it as reformism. It was generally viewed as a success, and that fall the organization

that had called it reorganized as the American Federation of Labor. But the struggles of May 1886 are usually remembered for the Haymarket incident where a bomb was thrown by some unknown person for some unknown purpose at a protest meeting in Chicago's Haymarket area. It had been called to publicize police brutality against strikers, and was breaking up as rain started, when police approached to attack it. The bomb fell between police and attendants at the meeting, killing some of both, and had the crowd not been retreating it would have killed them, not the police. Yet it was those who spoke at the meeting who got hanged.

Why is Labor Day observed in the U.S. in September but on May 1 in the rest of the world? Labor Day was first observed on Tuesday, September 5, 1882 to welcome the Knights of Labor convention in New York with a parade and a picnic. (See Jonathan Grossman's account in *Labor History*, Fall 1973.) That was a success repeated on Wednesday, September 5, 1883, and thereafter on the first Monday of September. It was a good time for a picnic halfway between the Fourth of July and Thanksgiving, and in those pre-TV days a good time for politicians to start their campaigns. Several states adopted it as a holiday in 1887, and in 1894 the U.S. Congress adopted it for federal employees without debate, so no reason was given. But considering the tense labor struggles of 1894, the thought may well have been to avoid a labor holiday with the rest of the world on May One, lest that occasion lead to thoughts of what world labor solidarity might accomplish.

Fred THOMPSON

Cartoon by I. Swenson (*Industrial Worker*, 1921)

"The New Master of the Democratic Party."
An anti-Altgeld cartoon
(from *Leslie's Weekly*)

THE EAGLE THAT IS FORGOTTEN

(John P. Altgeld. Born December 30, 1847; died March 12, 1902)

Sleep softly . . . eagle forgotten . . . under the stone.
Time has its way with you there, and the clay has its own.

"We have buried him now," thought your foes, and in secret rejoiced.
They made a brave show of their mourning, their hatred unvoiced.
They had snarled at you, barked at you, foamed at you day after day,
Now you were ended. They praised you . . . and laid you away.

The others that mourned you in silence and terror and truth,
The widow bereft of her crust, and the boy without youth,
The mocked and the scorned and the wounded, the lame and the poor
That should have remembered forever . . . remember no more.

Where are those lovers of yours, on what name do they call,
The lost, that in armies wept over your funeral pall?
They call on the names of a hundred high-valiant ones,
A hundred white eagles have risen, the sons of your sons;
The zeal in their wings is a zeal that your dreaming began,
The valor that wore out your soul in the service of man.

Sleep softly . . . eagle forgotten . . . under the stone,
Time has its way with you there, and the clay has its own.
Sleep on, O brave-hearted, O wise man, that kindled the flame—
To live in mankind is far more than to live in a name,
To live in mankind, far, far more . . . than to live in a name.

Vachel LINDSAY

VACHEL LINDSAY

Vachel Lindsay (1879-1931), one of American poetry's outstanding eccentrics, was highly popular in his lifetime, known especially for his booming recitations and his practice of tramping around the countryside trading poems door-to-door for fresh fruit and sandwiches.

Obsessed with his home-town of Springfield, Illinois, as well as with with Johnny Appleseed, motion pictures, Egyptian hieroglyphics and Poe, he elaborated a crotchety mysticism all his own ("the gospel of beauty," "the higher vaudeville"), which also included elements of Swedenborgian and Campbellite theology, populism, temperance and the Single Tax. Increasingly despondent in his later years, at least in part because of his unrequited love for the poet

Sara Teasdale, he finally took his own life by drinking a bottle of Lysol.

Lindsay deserves to be better-remembered, not only for his impressive body of poetry but also for his haunting cartoons and his pioneering appreciation of the poetic/mythic potential of film (*The Art of the Motion Picture*, 1915).

"The Eagle. . ." is probably his best known poem. His other titles include "Abraham Lincoln Walks at Midnight," "Bryan, Bryan, Bryan, Bryan" (an evocation of the 1896 presidential campaign), "The Golden Whales of California," "The Kallyope Yell" and "Why I Voted the Socialist Ticket."

FR

WHERE ARE THE VOICES?

Where are those loud voices
That rang thru the land in its towns and cities,
In its hop fields and lumber camps,
In its textile mills and steel mills,
In its wheat fields and its waterfronts,
Voices so loud that entire police forces would
*   attend their rallies*
To give riot-gun ovations and billy-club caresses?
. . .

Where are the voices of the stout-hearted
*   Haymarket Germans*
Who in Chicago had started a tide
No army of pinkertons and finkertons could hold back
And paid for with their lives to bring
The extra hours of leisure time
That working fools like you and me now enjoy?

*   . . .*

Those are the voices of men and women
Who seek no refuge in gray-flannel-suited anonymity
Or khaki-colored respectability
Or chromium-plated mediocrity.
Those are the voices of the inheritors
Of a million years' struggle
From primeval quadruped to quixotic biped
And neither Roman arenas
Nor medieval floggings,
Inquisitional torture chambers,
Guillotines,
Firing squads,
Electric chairs
Nor congressional investigations
Can still those voices
For those are the voices only Freedom can silence!

Carlos CORTEZ

RADICAL WOMEN:
The Haymarket Tradition

The Haymarket police riot and the ensuing miscarriage of justice in Chicago affected everyone interested in progressive social change. The influence of these events on several generations of women radicals has been enormous and persistent.

Jessie Bross Lloyd, whose father William Bross was one of the owners of the Chicago *Tribune* and a former lieutenant-governor of Illinois, was disinherited from an estimated $5-million fortune because of her and her husband Henry Demarest Lloyd's efforts on behalf of the anarchists. Undaunted, in later years she participated in anti-imperialist agitation and assisted her husband's "muckraking" efforts.

Although Hortensia Black, wife of the anarchists' chief defense counsel William P. Black, had initially opposed his taking the case, she became intimately involved in it and in the clemency movement. She and her husband endured a lowered standard of living after the trial as well as ostracism by former friends. The Blacks suffered a great emotional loss at the deaths and imprisonment of the men they had come to respect and love.

When Jane Addams and Julia Lathrop established Hull House in 1889, the pall of Haymarket still lay over the city. More than once it served the interests of city officials and/or the police to link the settlement-workers with the "terrorist" doctrines of 1886, as for example in 1901 when Jane Addams arranged for Abraham Isaak, editor of the anarchist journal *Free Society*, and his family to be released from jail during the "anarchist scare" following the assassination of President McKinley. Again in 1915 the police accused Jane Addams of anarchism after she secured the release of Lucy Parsons, Fanya Baron and other female "hunger demonstrators" from jail.

If the repercussions of Haymarket affected women such as these, whose social and political views were comparatively moderate, one can imagine the effect the events had on women who

were already active in the anarchist movement in pre-Haymarket days, and who had personally known and worked closely with the Chicago Martyrs.

Sarah E. Ames, an important figure in the Chicago IWPA's American Group and leader of the Knights of Labor Women's Assembly 1789, played an appreciable role in the Haymarket defense and amnesty campaigns. Her *Open Letter to Judge Joseph E. Gary* (1893) is a detailed and sharply-worded refutation of a magazine article in which the "Hanging Judge" tried to justify the Haymarket trial and executions.

Lucy E. Parsons

Another leading figure in the Chicago IWPA, Lizzie Swank Holmes, continued active in the movement for many years, focusing much of her attention on the more philosophical issues of American anarchism. Later she helped form the Ladies' Federal Labor Union and the Illinois Women's Alliance. She contributed commemorative articles about her martyred comrades to many publications, frequently describing the profound effect which Haymarket had had on her life. The hardest task, she wrote in *Free Society* ten years after the executions, was "learning how to live without them; of taking up the burden of life again. . . . Many a true comrade came through the ordeal changed and broken, never to be again what he had been."

Haymarket brought untold suffering and hardship, but it also brought many newcomers into the anarchist movement, among them two women who became well-known and highly articulate spokespersons for the poor and oppressed: Emma Goldman and Voltairine de Cleyre.

In 1886, a woman socialist speaker, Johanna Greie, confirmed Emma Goldman's belief that the Haymarket defendants were innocent. Devastated by the executions, Emma resolved to devote her own life to the cause for which they had sacrificed theirs. She wrote of her "awakening":

I had a distinct sensation that something new and wonderful had been born in my soul. A great ideal, a burning faith, a determination to dedicate myself to the memory of my martyred comrades, to make their cause my own, to make known to the world their beautiful lives and heroic deaths,

In a few years Emma Goldman was the best-known anarchist in America, an outspoken advocate of free speech, sexual freedom and birth control, and a popularizer of the modern drama.

Beginning as a lecturer in the freethought and secular movements, Voltairine de Cleyre became an anarchist in 1888 as a direct consequence of Haymarket. One of American anarchism's finest prose-stylists, she was also a poet; her "Light Upon Waldheim" is a powerful tribute to the Chicago Martyrs. A collection of her November Eleventh commemorative addresses was published in 1980 as "a classic of anarchist literature."

Emma Goldman and Voltairine de Cleyre are both buried in Waldheim Cemetery, close to the Haymarket Martyrs' monument.

A less well-known but no less articulate and courageous woman who came to anarchism as a result of Haymarket was Kate Austin, whose articles and letters from her backwoods farm in the Ozarks were a regular feature of many anarchist periodicals in the 1890s and early 1900s.

Emma Goldman, Voltairine de Cleyre and Kate Austin became anarchists in the immediate aftermath of Haymarket and continued to promote the message of the Chicago Martyrs for the rest of their lives. Esther Dolgoff is a woman anarchist of a later generation who has directly carried on what we might call the "Haymarket Tradition." Active for many years in the old Libertarian League in New York, and a regular contributor to its journal, *Views & Comments*, she has also translated many important anarchist writings into English, most notably Joseph Cohen's history of the Jewish anarchist movement in the United States. Today Esther still writes for several anarchist publications as well as for the IWW paper, the *Industrial Worker*.

Many other women were radicalized by the Haymarket events without necessarily becoming anarchists. Indeed, virtually every female radical labor activist since Haymarket—whether anarchist, IWW, socialist, communist or just plain radical—has found lasting inspiration in the strength and courage of the Haymarket Martyrs.

Mary Harris "Mother" Jones devoted a chapter of her famous *Autobiography* to "The Haymarket Tragedy." "Although I never endorsed the philosophy of anarchism," she wrote, "I often attended the meetings on the lake shore [in Chicago in the 1880s], listening to what these teachers of a new order had to say to the workers." And the "Miners' Angel" concluded:

In the cemetery of Waldheim, the dead were buried. But with them was not buried their cause. The struggle for the eight-hour day, for more human conditions and relations between man and man lived on, and still lives on.

Many women radicals of the next generation—women *and* men—were brought close to Haymarket by personal encounters with Lucy Parsons. In her autobiography, *The Rebel Girl*, Elizabeth Gurley Flynn warmly recalled meeting Lucy at the 1907 IWW convention in Chicago. Many years later, when Lucy died, Flynn wrote a tribute to her for the *Daily Worker*.

Vera Buch Weisbord—also an IWW member and later a Communist; a key figure in the textile-mill strikes in Gastonia, North Carolina, in 1929; and in more recent years an independent radical—recalls hearing Lucy Parsons speak at a meeting. "I sat very close to the front so that I had a good view," she says. "I can't remember what she said, but it was eloquent." Vera further recalls Lucy's "warm, outgoing personality."

Vicky Starr—organizer for the Packinghouse Workers and later of the University of Chicago clerical staff, and more recently a star of the documentary film, *Union Maids*—also has warm recollections of meeting Lucy Parsons. Tears came to her eyes as she grasped Lucy's hand in solidarity, linking past, present and future. As she looked into the old woman's eyes she saw there the source of her strength and courage. For women activists of the Great Depression years, Lucy was the living embodiment of the Haymarket spirit.

These activists, in turn, helped bring the Haymarket legacy into the new women's movement that began to emerge in the 1960s. Across the country, women's centers began displaying posters of Lucy Parsons and Emma Goldman. Women whose destinies were directly linked to Haymarket became heroines of a whole new generation of radical women.

Carolyn ASHBAUGH

VOLTAIRINE DE CLEYRE

Named for Voltaire by her freethinker father, Voltairine de Cleyre (1866-1912) endured an impoverished midwestern childhood before her father converted to Catholicism and sent her to a Canadian convent, where she spent her teenage years. This experience, which she later invariably referred to as nightmarish, left her a militant atheist, and for many years she was one of the American freethought movement's star lecturers. She was briefly a socialist after encountering Clarence Darrow in 1887, but the example of the Haymarket martyrs soon inspired her to take up their cause.

As poet, pamphleteer and inexhaustible agitator, de Cleyre quickly became an important force in international anarchism. Her friends included Kropotkin, Malatesta, *Louise Michel. Emma Goldman called her the "most gifted and brilliant anarchist woman America ever produced."*

Translator of Yiddish poets and publicist for the Mexican Revolution (she was Chicago correspondent for Ricardo Flores Magon's paper, Regeneracion*), de Cleyre was also an ardent feminist and, in her last years, an enthusiastic supporter of the IWW, whose members turned out in large numbers at her funeral. She is buried at Waldheim close to the martyrs who so decisively influenced the course of her life.*

A collection of her poems, essays and short stories was published after her death by the Mother Earth Publishing Company in New York, but the greater part of her literary work remains scattered in numerous ephemeral anarchist and freethought publications.

FR

LIGHT UPON WALDHEIM

(The figure on the monument over the grave of the Chicago martyrs in Waldheim Cemetery is a warrior woman, dropping with her left hand a crown upon the forehead of a fallen man just past his agony, and with her right drawing a dagger from her bosom.)

Light upon Waldheim! And the earth is gray;
A bitter wind is driving from the north;
The stone is cold, and strange cold whispers say:
"What do ye here with Death? Go forth! Go forth!"

Is this thy word, O Mother, with stern eyes,
Crowning thy dead with stone-caressing touch?
May we not weep o'er him that martyred lies,
Slain in our name, for that he loved us much?

May we not linger till the day is broad?
Nay, none are stirring in this stinging dawn—
None but poor wretches that make no moan to God:
What use are these, O thou with dagger drawn?

"Go forth, go forth! Stand not to weep for these,
Till, weakened with your weeping, like the snow
Ye melt, dissolving in a coward peace!"
Light upon Waldheim! Brother, let us go!

Voltairine de CLEYRE

London, October, 1897

178

LIZZIE HOLMES

No friend of the martyrs worked harder to keep their memory fresh than Lizzie Holmes, who made almost annual tributes to the men whose vision and comradeship continued to burn within her. In this memorial essay from a November 1899 issue of Free Society, *she defines the revolutionary and his function.*

Born in 1850 into a freethinking family, Lizzie Holmes moved to Chicago in 1877, after the death of her first husband, to learn more about the labor movement. She worked as a music teacher and as a seamstress; the latter employment led to her pioneering efforts in the Working Women's Union to organize sewing women and to publicize the wretched conditions they faced. At first a member of the Socialistic Labor Party, she turned to anarchism in 1883.

Two years later she married the English-born anarchist William Holmes. The Holmeses worked closely with Albert and Lucy Parsons in Chicago's American Group of the International Working People's Association. Lizzie served as assistant editor of The Alarm, *and the day before the Haymarket meeting she led a march of 300-400 working women demanding the eight-hour day. When the authorities suppressed* The Alarm *Lizzie was one of those arrested; in 1887 Dyer D. Lum revived the paper and appointed Lizzie as associate editor.*

Tireless in support of the martyrs, she was also active in the Knights of Labor and helped form the Ladies' Federal Labor Union (1888) under the auspices of the AFL. In the mid-1890s William and Lizzie Holmes moved to Colorado, living in La Veta, where Samuel Fielden was a neighbor, and in Denver. Still later they went to Farmington, New Mexico; there Lizzie died in 1926. Until about 1908 she contributed regularly to anarchist papers, especially Free Society, *and wrote for a variety of labor journals, including* The Industrial Advocate, *edited by her husband, and the AFL's* American Federationist. *Her syndicated articles for the Associated Labor Press appeared in labor papers across the country.*

Throughout her life, Lizzie Holmes believed that women and workers could achieve justice only in a society built on the principles for which the anarchist martyrs had died.

Blaine McKINLEY

REVOLUTIONISTS

Our martyred comrades were revolutionists. They never denied it and they worked, hoped and died for it. It was part of their lives, a religion, in a sense, and they carried it to that last moment when Fischer cried, ''This is the happiest moment of my life!''

But a revolutionist is not to be comprehended by the common mind which thinks as it is told to think; and he is more than *we* are wont to believe. He is pictured as a caricature of rage and rebellion. He is more likely to tower above our heads, calm, thoughtful, courageous, realizing better than we, the danger, yet patiently, bravely awaiting it. He is more than a reformer, more than a well-wisher of humanity. He does not hope—he *wills*.

He sees a vision of society as it should be, thrown up against the sky of the future, and all his mighty energies are bent upon making it a reality. The terrors facing him do not count; the immediate perils are small compared to centuries of anguish stretching behind him, and the marvelous possibilities glowing in the future. Compromises, palliatives, peace measures, are but obstacles in the way of a true adjustment of human relations. He is standing upon a mountain-top, and he knows before we do what is coming.

He does not love violence and bloodshed; his great heart is breaking over the sufferings of the poor; he cannot endure that this shall go on forever, and in his prophetic brain, he knows—*it will not!*

But the world does not need such men, it is said. ''A revolutionist is about nine parts crank and one part criminal,'' comes from a very lenient critic; and he adds, ''Evolution is the silent force at work, and our impatience, our violence, our unhappiness over sad conditions do not hasten or retard the general progess. Why not make the best of things and so add to the stock of happiness by being happy ourselves?''

But evolution is made up of growth and sudden changes, and painful births, and deaths of the old. It is not all gentle unfoldment in the warm, sleepy sunshine. Pain and struggle and irresistible energy are elements in evolution. The destroyer is a part of the process of up-building, and we need not fear it.

> *''Whate'er of good the old time had*
> *Is living still.''*

That fiercely, desperately, earnest soul who is ready to die that the truth may be uncovered from the weight of thousands of years, is a necessary factor in development. We dread his disturbing influence; so do we dread the furious storm which clears and purifies the air, but it must come.

It is not in us all to be revolutionists. Many of us are not made of that stuff which can rise above the present, troublous danger and live and die for a coming glory. We have not that terrible courage which demands justice though the heavens fall. It is not necessary, perhaps. Planners and builders are wanted; cheery souls who can conserve the possibilities of happiness until all can enjoy them, sweet natures who will live beautifully, as we all wish to do sometimes, and who preserve the ideal. The art of living must not be forgotten while we are struggling for the opportunities to learn it; the poetry of life must be cherished by someone, while others are fighting for a place for it.

It is not easy to make happiness, to keep bright and cheery and brave under conditions which tend to kill the spirit; and they, too, are heroic who can always do this. But let them never belittle the grand, great natures who can do what is also essential, and which they cannot do.

The world worships its successful fighters, and questions little why they fought. The slain and the vanquished are reviled rebels, though their cause was the noblest; one lauded victor must have climbed over the bodies of many martyrs—and they are forgotten. Our comrades are as yet among the vanquished; it depends on us to rescue their names from obloquy, and to keep bright the cause for which they died. The love of life was strong in their young, ardent natures, yet they shrank not from the sacrifice. Their devotion was an inevitable part of evolution; quiet work, endurance, patience, hopefulness, the simple *living* of those principles we love, are also necessary. But—ah, let us never forget the men who could rise to heights we perhaps never could, or blame them for being the lofty souls they were. The martyrs of the race have been its saviors.

Lizzie M. HOLMES

from *Free Society,*
(November 2, 1899)

EMMA GOLDMAN

Born in Kovno, Russia in 1869, Emma Goldman became America's best-known anarchist. "Red" Emma arrived in the U.S. in 1886 and became prominent in the 1890s, first as a protegee of Johann Most and then through working for the release of Alexander Berkman from imprisonment for his attempted assination of industrialist Henry Clay Frick. In 1906 she began her famous anarchist journal Mother Earth, *which she financed by cross-country lecture tours. The Wilson government deported her to Russia in 1919 for her anti-war and anti-draft activities. Disillusioned with Bolshevik authoritarianism, Goldman left Russia in 1921. Until her death in 1940, she resided in England, France and Canada, devoting her last years to enlisting support for the heroic Spanish anarchists.*

Goldman's popularity today owes much to her interest in the modern drama as a social statement, and her faith in unfettered personal freedom brought her to the attention of middle-class progressives as well as traditional audiences of workers.

While she broadened her audiences and her message, Goldman did not abandon the workers' struggle, although she operated outside union structures. On her tours, Goldman often collected strike funds. An advocate of direct action, she supported the IWW by joining their free speech fights and raising money for their strikes in Lawrence and Paterson. She stood by the McNamara brothers, even after their "confession"—part of a complicated attempt at "plea-bargaining" arranged by their attorney, Clarence Darrow—that they had bombed the Los Angeles Times *building in 1910, and stood by Tom Mooney when many radicals accepted his guilt.*

In her 1931 autobiography Goldman attributed her anarchist awakening to her emotional reaction to the judical murder of November 11, 1887. She had followed the trial and subsequent events closely, and the martyrdom convinced her to dedicate herself to the martyrs' cause. As she desired, she is buried near the martyrs in Waldheim Cemetery. The following excerpt is from "The Crime of the 11th of November," Mother Earth, *November 1911.*

Blaine McKINLEY

THE CRIME OF NOVEMBER ELEVENTH

Our comrades in Chicago knew what to expect in a court whose course was directed by the privileged classes. They knew that the high dignitaries of plutocracy and power clamored for the conviction and death of the Anarchists; and that the police as well as the court were determined to meet the demand for a fair trial with deaf ears and with brutal fists.

In choking our comrades to death, the authorities hoped to nip in the bud the spirit of resistance among the workers, and to eradicate Anarchy. But they erred miserably. Ideas can never be killed.

When the Russian revolutionist, Soloviov, mounted the scaffold, he said: "I die today, but our cause will never die." The oppressors of mankind, much against their will, are being forced to recognize this truth as an irrefutable fact.

The memory of the heroic death of Parsons, Spies, Lingg, Engel and Fischer stirs anew our admiration and love for them; filling us with a yearning for a fate equally sublime as theirs. Our souls rise in deep indignation against their executioners; but hideous as their murder was, it yet gives birth to all that is good, strong and beautiful in our beings. Their memory inspires us to raise the torch of rebellion, to spread its glowing light from horizon to horizon, that the people may be gripped to their very depths, and cry out against the wanton crime.

That martyrs of liberty grow in their graves, that they become more dangerous in the stillness of their deaths than as living champions, that they remain immortal, must

This bas-relief portrait of Emma Goldman appears on her monument at Waldheim, close to the Haymarket Martyrs' Monument

be a terrible truth to the enemies of freedom. Yet the vital lesson they will never learn.

While the memory of despots and tyrants, of statesmen and warriors is maintained only though artifical and arbitrary means, that of the pioneers and advance-guards of humanity perpetuates itself from generation to generation, serving as an impetus to lofty ideas and efforts, pointing the way to great and daring deeds. The thought of them has inspired the best and the bravest of mankind and has urged them on to hold high the banner for which their comrades had given their lives. Not so the cursed memories of the Neros, the Napoleons, the Bismarcks, the Shermans, the Stolypins and their kind. It is productive only of hatred and strife, brutality and greed.

Our great dead, buried at Waldheim, in the Communard grave at Pere Lachaise and at the black wall of Montjuich, are the greatest educators of mankind. They need no system; their sublime example helps to awaken enthusiasm, fortitude and zeal.

Our great dead, from the scaffold and the block, the rifle shots and the electric chair, who sent their last greetings to Liberty, are not dead; they live with us always, unto all eternity. Thus the people learn to know the men and women who have perished for the emancipation and liberation of all. Not a single one of the great legion has lost his life in vain. Their thoughts and deeds supply the leaven by means of which will rise a new and a beautiful world.

Emma GOLDMAN

Mother Earth
November, 1911

NINA VAN ZANDT SPIES

One of the strangest and most colorful episodes in the Haymarket affair was the marriage by proxy of wealthy debutante Nina van Zandt to the imprisoned August Spies.

Rose Sara Nina Stuart Clarke van Zandt, daughter and heiress of the chief chemist of the James Kirk soap company, attended Miss Grant's Finishing School and graduated from Vassar in 1883. Like many "society ladies" of the day, she and her mother decided to "take in" the anarchists' trial one summer afternoon, for amusement. What started out as a fashionable escapade, however, soon led to her making the anarchists' cause her own, as she recounts in the text reprinted here.

Because of her marriage to Spies she was reviled in the press, persecuted by neighbors, and deprived of a $400,000 inheritance from her aunt. The future owner and czar of the Chicago Tribune, Robert R. McCormick, who lived near her, recalled that in the 1880s everyone was "deadly afraid" of the widow Spies.

In 1891 she married an Italian lawyer, but they were later divorced. For many years she ran a rooming-house in Chicago; aside from providing cheap lodging for working people, she also took in numerous stray animals.

An active radical to the end of her life, Nina Spies was especially close to the IWW, who arranged her funeral and her burial at Waldheim, near the Haymarket martyrs' monument, in 1936. Her Wobbly and anarchist friends were indignant, however, when they learned that she had willed some $3000 not to the revolutionary movement but to a home for stray cats and dogs.

FR

MY MARRIAGE TO AUGUST SPIES

I did not know any of the accused when, during the comedy called trial, I entered the courtroom. Having received what information I had concerning the prisoners from the newspapers, I was expecting to see a rare collection of stupid, vicious, and criminal-looking men. I was greatly surprised to find that several of them, so far from corresponding with this description, had intelligent, kindly and good faces. I became interested. I soon found that the officers of the court and the entire police and detective force were bent upon the conviction of these men—not because of any crime of theirs, but because of their connection with the labor movement.

Animated by a feeling of horror produced by what I saw and heard, and no less by a feeling of justice, I determined to range myself on the side of the persecuted. Desirous of proffering my sympathies and of discovering how I could serve those rendered helpless, I visited, in company with my mother, the close, dark prison where they were spending the hot summer months. . . . My sympathy with the persecuted and lawlessly adjudicated prisoners soon changed into a feeling of amity for Mr Spies when I became personally acquainted with him. And from this feeling of friendship gradually developed a strong affection.

As a mere friend, many obstacles were put in my way when visiting the jail. To enjoy the privileges of a relative, to which our mutual affection entitled me, we became affianced. But I was informed that only *wives* were allowed the privilege of seeing their husbands outside of the regular visiting days; and it was also intimated that under the new jail regulations I would not be permitted to visit the prisoners any more at all. It was clear to me that my efforts in behalf of the prisoners, in behalf of *justice*, were disagreeable to a certain class interested in their extermination—a feeling only intensified by my social standing and connections. It was clear to me that they sought to exclude me from all communication with the prisoners and my affianced. Upon this discovery, we decided to become husband and wife by law.

As my parents were favorable to our union, it was an affair that concerned no more nor less than two (2) persons. But a mob of newspapermen, respectable *roues* many of them, howled and raved when our proposed marriage became known. Had I committed every crime denominated in our criminal code, these "chivalrous, gallant American gentlemen" could not have vilified and denounced me more than they did. Had I been "some obscure, foreign girl" not a word would have been said in condemnation of the marriage. But an American girl from "respectable ancestry and standing" following the voice of her heart—which course alone I hold to be moral—instead of the sound of dollars! "That's unprecedented, scandalous—the girl must be silly! must have read trash novels!"

Had I married an old, invalid *debauche* with great riches, those "moral" gentlemen who assail me now would have lauded me to the skies, and many of my Christian sisters and brethren would have said to their sons and daughters: "Very commendable! A very sen-

sible girl!'' and those who knew me personally—"I have always thought her *so* sweet!''

I prefer the censure of these "moral" people—who, it seems, cannot comprehend a love made doubly strong by a similarity of mental tastes and pursuits, as ours is—to their approval. I am equally proud of the friends that I have made—persons who can understand a pure and unselfish love.

Nina van Zandt SPIES

Chicago, January 27, 1887

from the Preface to
August Spies' Autobiography
(Chicago, 1887)

Nina van Zandt Spies

181

KATE AUSTIN

Kate Austin (1864-1902) was a radical feminist-anarchist Ozark housewife who lived with her husband Sam and their five children on a remote farm in southwest Missouri. She represented a strain of home-grown American radicalism far more common in late nineteenth century rural America than later generations would suppose. Her politics, and her career as a radical propagandist, fused elements of stubborn yeoman independence, popular free-thought, green-back-laborite economics, free-love feminism, European anarchism, and doctrines of evolutionary progress.

Austin's radicalism had its roots in family tradition and cornbelt experience. Her father was a freethinker. She grew up in LaSalle County, Illinois, a hotbed of rural radicalism. She matured and married in central Iowa, where the Austins, like several thousand other settlers, lost their farms in

a vast public land swindle. The Haymarket tragedy of 1886-87 confirmed everything family tradition and personal experience had taught Kate Austin about plutocratic capital and oppressive government. She channeled her revulsion at the trials and executions into propaganda work; Haymarket became both the symbol and catalyst of grassroots rebellion. At first she spread revolutionary doctrines by word of mouth and private letter. Later, after the Austins moved to Missouri in 1890, she began to publish a torrent of radical essays that earned her an international reputation. She deeply impressed Emma Goldman, who included a moving account of her visit to the Austin farm in Living My Life. *Kate Austin had hardly reached full voice as a propagandist when she succumbed to respiratory disease at the age of thirty-eight. Even her brief radical career, however, amply demonstrated how deeply the shock waves from Haymarket had penetrated into popular culture.*

HOWARD S. MILLER

"SOWING THE WIND"

Inclosed find twenty-five cents for your little paper. I have already received several copies; it is sharp and to the point. All radicals should stand together to the extent of subscribing for a paper that is not afraid to call things by their right names. A year ago I read in a private letter, from one who claimed to know whereof he spoke, and was a member of a secret group, that there were 100,000 well armed and well drilled Socialists in the United States. He belonged to a company of militia in Kansas, and an officer and several others used to meet at night and drill, in the Armory, 'till they received arms, from where he did not know (only the officer knew that). But finally the officer removed, and finally resigned, and lost track of his comrades. I hope this is true. The time is not far distant when arms and military knowledge will be necessary. Peaceable propaganda if possible, if not, then take the advice of Louis Lingg and "meet force with force."

May you prosper in your good work, and help keep green the memory of our "martyrs of Chicago." You have an elephant on your hands in the shape of ignorance. Here many believe that the earth is flat, and do not know whether Chicago is in Illinois or Ohio. Still there is a native good sense and honesty among them that would lead the majority to stand on the side of the people in case of trouble. I find everywhere an inborn hatred for the rich and aristocrats; it

seems to be in the air. In time of revolt this spirit is the one that will bring destruction on many an innocent head; not the clear, fine reasoning powers of Harman or Debs, who would only seek justice and mercy for all. The "powers that be" do not realize that when they strangle and imprison men of heart and brain, and go on dehumanizing the masses, they are sowing the wind and will reap a whirlwind of blood and destruction. In the French Revolution the one idea of the frenzied people was to exterminate the whole race of aristocrats, root and branch. In the Nat Turner rebellion in Virginia, in 1831, the slaves' one idea was to exterminate the whites, and 55 women and babes were hacked to pieces by 40 slaves in their wild break for freedom. Such lessons are never forgotten by thoughtful students.

I am a farmer's wife. We have always worked early and late for a bare living, and, in this "land of free schools," got but little education.

Hopefully yours for liberty,

KATE AUSTIN

Caplinger's Mill, Mo.

Firebrand
(Sept. 1, 1895)

Stamps issued by the 50th Haymarket Commemoration Committee (Chicago, 1937)

LUCY E. PARSONS

One of the most impressive figures in American labor history, Lucy Ella Parsons (1853-1942) was of Black, Mexican and Indian descent, and probably born into slavery in Texas. Virtually nothing is known of her early life. Around 1869-70 she met Albert R. Parsons, who became her husband. In the winter of 1873-74 the young couple moved to Chicago, where they soon were involved in radical activity.

Before the decade was over Lucy Parsons had started writing for The Socialist, organ of the Socialistic Labor Party, and also had begun an outstanding career as labor orator that spanned some sixty years. An early woman member of the Knights of Labor, a writer for The Alarm and other radical papers, a prominent figure on Thanksgiving Day demonstrations and other workers' events, she was one of the best-known labor agitators in Chicago from the 1880s on.

No one worked harder for the Haymarket defense than Lucy Parsons. Indeed, for the rest of her life she did more than any other single person to keep the memory of the Chicago martyrs alive. She published Albert R. Parsons' compilation, Anarchism: Its Principles and Scientific Basic (1887); The Life of Albert R. Parsons (1889), a collection of writings by and about her husband; and several editions of the martyrs' Famous Speeches.

It would be utterly false, however, to accuse Lucy Parsons of "living in the past"—as did the snobbish editors of Notable American Women, who refused her a place in their multivolume reference-work. Lucy Parsons was, on the contrary, an inexhaustible and influential revolutionary activist. She spoke in scores of cities all over the country, on such subjects as anarchism, industrial unionism, the French Revolution and labor defense. She wrote countless articles on a wide range of subjects for anarchist, Knights of Labor, IWW and Communist publications. She edited two anarchist papers of her own: Freedom (1891-2) and The Liberator (1905-6). She helped found the IWW in 1905. She took part in every labor defense effort from pre-Haymarket days till her death. She was arrested innumerable times for the crime of public speaking; the Chicago police, especially, feared and persecuted her as they have never feared and persecuted anyone before or since.

"Wild and dark and beautiful, like those roses one finds growing in the woods, alone and splendid"—as Howard Fast described her in his novel, The American (1946)—Lucy Parsons was a marvelous inspiration to three generations of American radicals and unionists. Her ashes, and those of her companion George Markstall, are buried at Waldheim next to the martyrs' monument.

FR

THE VOICE OF THE PEOPLE WILL YET BE HEARD

The twentieth anniversary of the 11th of November, which has just been observed in Chicago, was a great success from many standpoints, notably among which was the increased number of young people who took part in it. . . .

As these years speed by, our comrades' lives will be better understood; their great work for the uplifting of humanity understood and appreciated. This has been the case of the martyrs of all ages. . . .

"'The Voice of the People' will yet be heard.

The Demonstrator
November 20, 1907

* * *

It is now 18 months since I published the [*Famous Speeches of the Haymarket Martyrs*]. In that time I have traveled from Los Angeles, *via* Vancouver, B.C., to New York city, twice. I have devoted my entire energies to visiting Locals of the AF of L. From those Locals I have received most courteous treatment everywhere. I have credentials from some of the best known central bodies in this country, including the Central Federated Union of New York city. I am continually rapping at the doors of Locals, being admitted and selling the speeches. The result is that I have sold 10,000 copies and am just going to place my order with the printer for the sixth edition, making 12,000.

I regard these speeches as the greatest piece of propaganda literature extant; and when circulated among organized labor are bound to bear fruit.

The Agitator
December, 15, 1911

* * *

The Haymarket meeting is referred to historically as "The Haymarket Anarchists' Riot." There was no riot at the Haymarket except a police riot. Mayor Harrison attended the Haymarket meeting, and took the stand at the anarchist trial for the defense, not for the state.

The great strike of May 1886 was an historical event of great importance, inasmuch as it was. . .the first time that the workers themselves had attempted to get a shorter workday by united, simul-

taneous action. . . . This strike was the first in the nature of Direct Action on a large scale. . . .

Of course the eight-hour day is as antiquated as the craft unions themselves. Today we should be agitating for a five-hour workday.

The Industrial Worker
May 1, 1912

* * *

The Eleventh of November has become a day of international importance, cherished in the hearts of all true lovers of Liberty as a day of martyrdom. On that day was offered to the gallows-tree martyrs as true to their ideal as ever were sacrificed in any age. . . .

Our comrades were not murdered by the state because they had any connection with the bombthrowing, but because they were ac-

Lucy Parsons addressing anarchist picnickers
(from Schaack)

183

tive in organizing the wage-slaves. The capitalist class didn't want to find the bombthrower; this class foolishly believed that by putting to death the active spirits of the labor movement of the time, it could frighten the working class back to slavery.

The Agitator
November 1, 1912

* * *

Parsons, Spies, Lingg, Fischer and Engel: Although all that is mortal of you is laid beneath that beautiful monument in Waldheim Cemetery, *you are not dead.* You are just beginning to live in the hearts of all true lovers of liberty. For now, after forty years that you are gone, thousands who were then unborn are eager to learn of your lives and heroic martyrdom, and as the years lengthen the brighter will shine your names, and the more you will come to be appreciated and loved.

Those who so foully murdered you, under the forms of law—lynch law—in a court of supposed justice, are forgotten.

Rest, comrades, rest. All the tomorrows are yours!

The Labor Defender
November 1926

* * *

Once again on November 11 a memorial meeting will be held to commemorate the death of the Chicago Haymarket martyrs. 1937 is the fiftieth anniversary, and this meeting bids fair to be more widely observed than any of the forty-nine previous ones. . . .

On that gloomy morning of November 11, 1887, I took our two little children to jail to bid my beloved husband farewell. I found the jail roped off with heavy cables. Policemen with pistols walked in the inclosure.

I asked them to allow us to go to our loved one before they murdered him. They said nothing.

Then I said, "Let these children bid their father good-bye; let them receive his blessing. They can do no harm."

In a few minutes a patrol-wagon drove up and we were locked up in a police station while the hellish deed was done.

Oh, Misery, I have drunk thy cup of sorrow to its dregs, but I am still a rebel.

The One Big Union Monthly
November 1937

Lucy E. PARSONS

JIM CONNELL

The most famous of the labor songs inspired by the Haymarket executions was written in Britain rather than the United States. Indeed when Jim Connell (18??-1929) wrote "The Red Flag" in 1889 he was on a London train. But, according to his reminiscences in 1920, Haymarket was on his mind as he wrote, along with the struggles of the Irish Land League, of Russian nihilists and of London dockers. Connell, self-described as a "sheep-farmer, dock labourer, navvy, railwayman, draper, lawyer (of a sort), and all the time a poacher," penned one of history's two or three most beloved labor songs on that train. "The Red Flag" became, and remains, the anthem of the British Labour Party. First published in the U.S. in the Industrial Workers of the World's *Industrial Union Bulletin* in 1908, it has found inclusion in various editions of the Wobbly songbook.

DR

Mike Konopacki

THE RED FLAG

The People's flag is deepest red,
It shrouded oft our martyred dead;
And ere their limbs grew stiff and cold
Their life-blood dyed its every fold.

Chorus:

Then raise the scarlet standard high
Beneath its folds, we'll live and die,
Though cowards flinch and traitors sneer,
We'll keep the red flag flying here.

Look 'round! the Frenchman loves its blaze,
The sturdy German chants its praise;
In Moscow's vaults, its hymns are sung,
Chicago swells its surging song.

It waved above our infant might
When all ahead seemed dark as night;
It witnessed many a deed and vow,
We will not change its color now.

It suits today the meek and base
Whose minds are fixed on pelf and place;
To cringe beneath the rich man's frown,
And haul that sacred emblem down.

With heads uncovered, swear we all,
To bear it onward till we fall;
Come dungeons dark, or gallows grim,
This song shall be our parting hymn!

Jim CONNELL

EUGENE V. DEBS

Eugene V. Debs (1855-1926) was the best-known and perhaps the best-loved socialist in U.S. history. Born in Terre Haute, Indiana, he began working on the railroad at fifteen and quickly became a local officer of the Brotherhood of Locomotive Firemen. By the 1880s he edited that craft union's national journal and was a noteworthy Democratic Party politician in Terre Haute. In the eventful years after 1892 Debs broke with craft unionism and led the industrially organized American Railway Union during its mushrooming growth before it was broken during repression caused by its role in the Pullman strike of 1894. Briefly a Populist, Debs became a socialist after the jail term which resulted from his leadership of that strike. On the very day he was released from jail, he visited the Haymarket monument at Waldheim to pay respects to the martyrs. He helped to found the Social Democratic Party in 1897, the Socialist Party in 1901 and the Industrial Workers of the World in 1905.

Debs was the Socialist presidential candidate five times. During the last of these candidacies, in 1920, he ran from the Atlanta Federal Penitentiary, where he had been jailed for his opposition to World War I.

"The Martyred Apostles of Labor" originally appeared in the February 1898 issue of The New Time, *published by Charles H. Kerr. It was later reprinted in* Debs: His Life, Writings and Speeches *(Charles H. Kerr, 1908), from which the excerpts here are reproduced.*

DR

THE MARTYRED APOSTLES OF LABOR

The century now closing is luminous with great achievements. In every department of human endeavor marvelous progress has been made. By the magic of the machine which sprang from the inventive genius of man, wealth has been created in fabulous abundance. But, alas, this wealth, instead of blessing the race, has been the means of enslaving it. The few have come in possession of all, and the many have been reduced to the extremity of living by permission.

A few have had the courage to protest. To silence these so that the dead-level of slavery could be maintained has been the demand and command of capital-blown power. Press and pulpit responded with alacrity. All the forces of society were directed against these pioneers of industrial liberty, these brave defenders of oppressed humanity—and against them the crime of the century has been committed.

Albert R. Parsons, August Spies, George Engel, Adolph Fischer, Louis Lingg, Samuel Fielden, Michael Schwab and Oscar Neebe paid the cruel penalty in prison cell and on the gallows.

They were the first martyrs in the cause of industrial freedom, and one of the supreme duties of our civilization, if indeed we may boast of having been redeemed from savagery, is to rescue their names from calumny and do justice to their memory.

The crime with which these men were charged was never proven against them. The trial which resulted in their conviction was not only a disgrace to all judicial procedure but a foul, black indelible and damning stigma upon the nation.

It was a trial organized and conducted to convict—a conspiracy to murder innocent men, and hence had not one redeeming feature.

It was a plot, satanic in all its conception, to wreak vengeance upon defenseless men, who, being found guilty of the crime charged in the indictment, were found guilty of exercising the inalienable right of free speech in the interest of the toiling and groaning masses, and thus they became the first martyrs to a cause which, fertilized by their blood, has grown in strength and sweep and influence from the day they yielded up their lives and liberty in its defense.

As the years go by and the history of that infamous trial is read and considered by men of thought, who are capable of wrenching themselves from the grasp of prejudice and giving reason its rightful supremacy, the stronger the conviction becomes that the present generation of workingmen should erect an enduring memorial to the men who had the courage to denounce and oppose wage-slavery and seek for methods of emancipation.

The vision of the judicially murdered men was prescient. They saw the dark and hideous shadow of coming events. They spoke words of warning, not too soon, not too emphatic, not too trumpet-toned—for even in 1886, when the Haymarket meetings were held, the capitalistic grasp was upon the throats of workingmen and its fetters were upon their limbs. . . .

The men who were judicially murdered in Chicago in 1887, in the name of the great State of Illinois, were the avant couriers of a better day. They were called anarchists, but at their trial it was not proven that they had committed any crime or violated any law. They had protested against unjust laws and their brutal administration. They stood between oppressor and oppressed, and they dared, in a free (?) country, to exercise the divine right of free speech; and the records of their trial, as if written with an "iron pen and lead in the rock forever," proclaim the truth of the declaration.

I would rescue their names from slander. The slanderers of the dead are the oppressors of the living. . .The stigma fixed upon their names by an outrageous trial can be forever obliterated and their fame be made to shine with resplendent glory on the pages of history.

Until the time shall come, as come it will, when the parks of Chicago shall be adorned with their statues, and with holy acclaim, men, women and children, pointing to these monuments as testimonials of gratitude, shall honor the men who dared to be true to humanity and paid the penalty of their heroism with their lives, the preliminary work of setting forth their virtues devolves upon those who are capable of gratitude to men who suffered death that they might live.

Eugene V. DEBS

from Debs: His Life, Writings and Speeches
(Chicago, Charles H. Kerr, 1908)

Eugene V. Debs' campaign button, 1920

185

JAY FOX

Throughout his long and varied radical career, Jay Fox—a tall, soft-spoken Chicagoan born in 1870—found his inspiration in the commitment and example of Parsons, Spies and their comrades. Fox was wounded at 16 by the police at the May 3, 1886 demonstrations outside the McCormick Reaper plant. The next year he marched in the martyrs' funeral procession to Waldheim Cemetery. When Chicago police rounded up anarchists after President McKinley's assassination in 1901, Fox was among those jailed.

At various times Fox belonged to the Knights of Labor, the Blacksmiths' Union, and the American Railway Union. In 1905 he attended the founding convention of the IWW as an unaffiliated woodworker; later he vigorously supported IWW policies of industrial unionism and direct action.

In 1910 Fox moved to the anarchist colony at Home, Washington where he lived,

except briefly in 1913, as the most prominent citizen until he died in 1961. Between 1910 and 1912 he edited Home's news-

paper, The Agitator, *which advocated the IWW and anarchism.*

Fox soon aligned himself with William Z. Foster, and when Foster broke with the IWW to form the Syndicalist League of North America, Fox followed. The Agitator re-emerged in 1913 as the short-lived The Syndicalist *under the auspices of Foster's League. After Foster moved into the Communist party, Fox contributed several articles during the 1920s to the Communist magazines* Labor Herald *and* Workers Monthly.

In the following essay from the anarchist paper Free Society *in 1897, Fox describes that year's November 11 memorial meeting in Chicago. L. S. Oliver, whom Fox mentions, had been president of the Amnesty Association seeking reprieves for the condemned martyrs and later contributed frequently to anarchist papers.*

Blaine McKINLEY

MARTYRS' DAY IN CHICAGO

Chicago is a "famous" city in many respects, the most noteworthy of which is her adoration for the god Mammon. So immersed is she in her devotion to this heinous joss that she has committed the most diabolical crime in the history of America to appease his envious wrath. It is now ten years since she offered up the precious lives of Spies, Parsons, Lingg, Fischer and Engel, as a sacrifice upon the crimson altar of that infernal deity.

On the morning of Nov. 11, 1887, the black flag was raised over the Cook county jail and those noble heroes marched boldly upon the scaffold without a halt in their steps, stood manfully upon the fatal trap and without a quiver in their mighty voices, in clear, ringing tones bid defiance to the tyrants, and a last fond farewell to their friends, passed into eternal martyrdom, happy in the thought that the cause they were dying for, and to which their powerful talents had been devoted, would be espoused by others, who would carry on, as fearlessly as they, the mighty battle for human freedom. Those men feared not to die; death to them was as nothing when compared with the falsehood and injustice that surrounded them and their fellow men. They knew no danger in the sight of misery and woe.

That the producers of the country were being fleeced of the product of their toil, and were dying in their hovel for want of food and raiment, and were ignorant of the causes of their misery and want, was what urged these brave fellows on to the work they had undertaken—that of educating the toilers. But they learned that education in this free (?) country that had not the sanction of the masters was forbidden; that only such knowledge as passed the close scrutiny of the modern slave-owners was permitted to reach the white slave. The exploiting class say what shall constitute the education of the fleeced mass, and woe unto any who infringe their decrees. Education is as dangerous to their interests as it was to that of the chattel slave-owner forty years ago, when it was a crime to educate a negro. It wasn't a capital offense, however, to teach the black slave, but it is now, to teach the wage slave, as the memory of our valiant comrades testifies. They were teaching the people the true definition of liberty, in whose name the flunkies and priests of Mammon have been practicing the most infamous of tyrannies for the last 100 years in this country. They taught that liberty consisted not in the freedom by which one set of men can exploit the labor of another, but in the equal and free opportunity of all men to exploit

nature, unencumbered by any artificial restraints, under whatever disguise they might appear; that the liberty dealt out according to law was a mockery, a delusion, a snare that held the unthinking worker in the most abject slavery, whilst believing himself free; that liberty admits of no restriction, and that any attempts at regulating or measuring it by law or authority, whether intentional or not, are but aims at its destruction; that where law and authority are supreme, hypocrisy, injustice and tyranny prevail; that where liberty is, no law, authority, or any of their concomitant evils can prevail; that liberty and authority can not exist in any one place at the same time; that where one is, the other is not, and cannot be.

It was for teaching these grand truths that they were hung, becoming martyrs to the cause of liberty and humanity; in memory of which martyrdom thousands of wage slaves who have grasped the force and import of their teachings assembled in two of the largest halls in the city on the evening of Nov. 11 and paid fitting tribute to their memory. The exercises proper began in the morning, when representatives of trades unions and other advanced organizations, visited the resting place of our martyrs, and deposited their offering of flowers upon their graves, a solemn duty indeed. Many and large were the floral decorations; I will describe but one. It represented a large wheel out of which five spokes had been broken, typical of the five heroes who had been torn from the masses, who are constructing a gigantic wheel that when once started upon its revolution will crush every tyrant on the earth. No demonstration was held at the tomb, owing to the cemetery authorities admitting but a limited number to the grounds. At Turner Hall the people began to assemble as early as 7 o'clock. The decorations consisted of the several large red banners of the trades unions and other appropriate mottoes, one a painting of a gallows with four nooses dangling from it, and underneath, the inscription "Murdered but not dead." Another gave the last words of the immortal Spies. "There will be a time when our silence will be more powerful than the voices you strangle today." And surely there were none present but fully realized that that time had come.

The vast hall was thronged almost to suffocation by men and women who toil, their calm and determined faces bearing testimony that they fully comprehended the gravity of the occasion, and when Prof. Meinken's orchestra opened with a funeral march a look of deep sorrow overspread their pallid countenances.

L. S. Oliver was the principal English speaker. His utterances were well received. In reviewing the history of the trial he arraigned the judge and police in the most scathing language. Dwelling at some length upon the principles advocated by our dead comrades he showed that Anarchy was not a foreign importation, but that it grew and flourished wherever tyranny and oppression reigned, and that the best indication of the tyranny, injustice and hypocrisy of the American rulers was the fact that vast numbers of the oppressed class are arraying themselves on the side of liberty, equality and fraternity as propagated by the Anarchists. ''Law,'' said he, ''is a name for all the tyrannies of the human mind.''

Emma Goldman spoke in German. Her speech aroused our German comrades to a high pitch of enthusiasm. The vigorous and determined manner in which she condemned the wrongs of society, and the clear, defiant ring of her eloquent voice could not fail to arouse even the most apathetic.

''Our Martyrs' Hymn,'' to the air of ''Annie Laurie,'' written especially for the occasion by Mrs. Shirlie Woodman, was sung with much effect by Mrs. V. Kinsella, the audience, which had been supplied with printed copies, joining.

L. S. Oliver delivered an original poem entitled ''My Murdered Comrades.''

The allied German singing societies gave some beautiful vocal selections, as did the ladies' chorus.

Prof. Meinken and orchestra displayed perfect musical training in the several appropriate selections they rendered.

The meeting closed at 12 o'clock with the singing of the ''Marseillaise'' by the audience.

Our Bohemian comrades held a large and enthusiastic meeting in another section of the city. Thus the tenth anniversary has passed into history as the largest and most successful yet held. The silence of the dead is being heard.

JAY FOX

Free Society
(December 5, 1897)

JAMES P. CANNON

James P. Cannon (1890-1974) was for forty years the foremost Trotskyist leader in the United States. Born to an Irish-American socialist family in Rosedale, Kansas, Cannon joined the Socialist Party in 1908 and the Industrial Workers of the World three years later. Cannon, who had worked in Kansas City's meatpacking industry even before he reached his teens, became an effective traveling organizer in the IWW. He left the Wobblies in 1917 when, stirred by the Russian Revolution, he decided to concentrate his work inside the pro-Bolshevik wing of the Socialist Party. He became a member of the Communist Labor Party in 1919 and was elected to the Central Committee of the United Communist Party in 1920. The following year he became a Central Committee member of the Workers' (Communist) Party. A major Communist Party leader in the twenties, Cannon headed International Labor Defense from 1925 to 1928 and served for a time on the Presidium of the Communist International.

The Communist Party expelled Cannon for Trotskyism in 1928 and shortly thereafter he cofounded the Communist League of America, a Trotskyist organization whose newspaper, The Militant, *he edited. In 1938, he helped to found both the Socialist Workers Party in the United States and the Fourth International. He served thirteen months in prison for his opposition to World War II. National Secretary of the Socialist Workers Party through 1953, Cannon later became National Chairman of that group.*

Cannon was a prolific writer, with Socialism on Trial *and* The First Ten Years of American Communism *among his most important books. However, his reminiscences of Lucy Parsons, published here for the first time, are informed less by his scholarship than his unique place as the early Communist leader who, as Theodore Draper has observed, ''more than anyone else . . . embodied the free-swinging Western tradition of the IWW.''*

DR

REMEMBERING LUCY PARSONS

I first got acquainted with [Lucy Parsons'] operations I guess along about 1917 when I was living in Kansas City. I got hold of—I don't know exactly how I got hold of—one of those pamphlets, *Speeches of the Haymarket Martyrs*. And it fascinated me. And I got hold of [*The Life of Albert Parsons*]. . . . I was told by many people that she went around from union to union telling her story and selling these pamphlets and books, and that was already thirty years after the event, after the martyrdom. And I think she was mainly responsible, as far as I know, for keeping the memory of her husband alive.

We admired her, a great lady—admired the speeches and the books and the men involved. So it was natural when I got the opportunity with our magazine *Labor Defender* to restore their memory, I leaped at it. I always felt good about that. I doubt whether the new radical movement knows as much about the Haymarket martyrs as they should. We relied so much on that magazine [*The Labor Defender*]. . . . It had a bigger circulation than the [Communist] Party press. And then our conference [the 1927 International Labor Defense Conference in New York] featuring it. And she [Lucy Parsons] was the guest of honor. . . . But we never talked Party.

I never talked Party to her. I just assumed she was an anarchist and that didn't affect my willingness to cooperate with her—nor her with me, apparently.

My favorite character. . .I guess, in American labor history, is Albert Parsons. Has been since I first read about him.

My meetings with [Lucy] were always in our [ILD] office . . .in Chicago. We started the ILD in 1925, and we moved to New York in the fall of 1927.

I knew [Ralph] Chaplin very well. We worked very closely. He was a member of the Executive Board of the International Labor Defense. He was in ILD from the start. He was one who helped start it. . . . In his [autobiography]. . .he refers to a meeting at the IWW hall celebrating something, and Lucy Parsons and the widow of Spies spoke. He said it was the first time they had spoken to each other for thirty years or so. . . . They met and shook hands.

James P. CANNON

from an interview
with Carolyn Ashbaugh

187

The November 11, 1905 issue of *The Liberator*, Lucy Parsons' anarchist/IWW newspaper

The Impact of Haymarket on the Founding of the IWW:
THE ANARCHISM OF THOMAS J. HAGERTY

William D. Haywood, who chaired the IWW's founding convention, considered Haymarket the decisive event that shaped his convictions and commitment to labor radicalism. In his teens at the time, Haywood learned of the bombing from newspapers and was deeply affected by what he read. He talked incessantly about the event with his friend Pat Reynolds, a member of the Knights of Labor with whom he had gained his first lessons in unionism. He kept "trying to fathom in my own mind the reasons for the explosion," Haywood wrote in his autobiography. "Were the strikers responsible? Why were the police in Haymarket Square?" And he wondered why the authorities were so set on hanging these men called anarchists. "The last words of August Spies," Haywood later remembered, "kept running through my mind: 'There will come a time when our silence will be more powerful than the voices you are strangling today.' It was a turning point in my life."[1]

Others attending the founding convention had participated in the 1886 eight-hour movement. During the convention some of these delegates articulated links between the Haymarket anarchists and the form of industrial unionism being initiated at the convention. Al Klemensic, who represented the Colorado Journeymen Tailors' Union, powerfully invoked the memory of the Chicago anarchists in his speech to the delegates:

I have seen men hanged for the truth in this very city, in this very place (applause). Industrial unionism at that time had begun to shake capitalism to its very foundations, and the judges and plutocrats in this country decided to hang the men with the hope of hanging industrial unionism at the same time. But let me tell you that industrial unionism is here in this very city again to declare its right and demand its right (applause). The voices that plutocracy thought to silence when it tried to hang unionism are heard again, and we are here today to reorganize the work they started twenty years ago (applause).[2]

Toward the end of the fifth day of the convention an announcement was made that a delegation would visit the graves of the Haymarket martyrs.[3]

The convention proceedings indicate that the IWW's founding delegates were conscious of the continuity between their efforts and the earlier struggles of the Haymarket anarchists. However, the importance of the Chicago anarchists as forerunners, as well as the role of delegates who had participated in or had been directly affected by the eight-hour movement of the 1880s, have been ignored in the numerous studies devoted to the history of the IWW. Paul F. Brissenden, whose pioneering study provides the most thorough investigation of the IWW's formative period, considered the influence of the Chicago anarchists to have been outweighed by the effects of the tragedy:

The labor movement lay stunned after its brief flirtation with anarchy. The union men drew away from the anarchist agitators, and taking their information from the capitalist press only, concluded that socialism and anarchism were the same thing, and would, if tolerated, lead the movement to ruin and disaster.[4]

Viewing the Haymarket tragedy as an unquestionable setback for the labor and socialist movements, Brissenden regarded the Chicago anarchists' experience as little more than a remote and roundabout prefiguration of the IWW. Drawing heavily on the work of the social-democrat Robert Hunter for his interpretation, Brissenden concluded that

these riots [*sic*] really gave French unionists the idea of the general strike and thus helped to give form, first, to modern French syndicalism, and second, both by relay back to this side of the Atlantic and directly by its influence in this country, to American syndicalism in the form of the IWW.[5]

Though aware of an anarchist presence at the IWW's founding convention, Brissenden made no effort to search for continuities linking these delegates to the eight-hour agitation of the 1880s. He merely identified the anarchists who participated in the convention as a small constituent element among the doctrinal types represented. He did not consider anarchist efforts in the IWW to be noteworthy until the third convention. Subsequent accounts have similarly failed to trace the links between the Haymarket anarchists and the founders of the IWW, apart from an occasional passing reference to Lucy Parsons' presence at the 1905 convention.

Historians rediscovering the IWW in the 1950s and '60s did not question the meager role Brissenden assigned to anarchists in the formation of the industrial union movement. For the most part these studies elaborated on factional disputes between "reformist" and "doctrinaire" elements in the Socialist Party and the Socialist Labor Party, treating these as the major determinants of the first convention's outcome. One recent interpretive study of the IWW has gone so far as to insist that the anarchists present at the founding convention amounted to mere remnants of the old Chicago group, and that they exerted no real influence.[6]

The conflict between the Socialist Party and the Socialist Labor Party, however, did not alone shape the the principles of industrial unionism adopted by the IWW. Rather, the decisive conflict that influenced and shaped the founding of the IWW was between the political Marxism of the two socialist parties on the one hand, and on the other, the syndicalism of such revolutionary socialists as William E. Trautmann, and the anarchism of Thomas J. Hagerty, Lucy Parsons and other delegates who had participated in the 1880s eight-hour movement or were influenced by the ideas and actions of the Haymarket martyrs.[7]

Among the anarchists active in the industrial union movement, Thomas J. Hagerty was an especially vital participant. He played an instrumental role in the January conference that led to the IWW's formation, and became a major architect of its industrial union principles. Having helped draft the 1905 *Industrial Union Manifesto*, he was also the principal author of the IWW's Preamble, which drew some of its essential principles from the Haymarket anarchists' "Chicago Idea."

Hagerty's association with the emerging industrial union movement began through his contact with the Western Federa-

"One Ray of Thy Light, O Sun! One Stroke of Thy Arm, O Labor!

SPIES: "There will come a time when our Silence will be more powerful than the voices you strangle today."
PARSONS: Let the voice of the People be heard."

Industrial Worker, 1909

tion of Miners and the American Labor Union in New Mexico sometime around 1902. During the summer of that year he toured the mining camps of Colorado with Eugene V. Debs, recruiting members for the ALU and the Socialist Party. In 1903 Hagerty traveled throughout the country lecturing under SP auspices.[8]

His approach to socialism, however, soon led to increasing conflicts with the SP's right wing. Critical of the Party's gradualist policy, Hagerty spoke against its strategy of parliamentary reform, and against what William Z. Foster would later call ''boring from within'' AFL unions, as effective methods of achieving the cooperative commonwealth. A speech to San Francisco socialists ended his brief career as an SP publicist. In this speech Hagerty denounced the Party's reliance on political action as a means of attaining workingclass emancipation. ''We must have revolution,'' he is reported to have said, ''peaceful if possible but, to tell the truth, we care not how we get it.'' After the chairman broke his gavel attempting to bring the meeting to a close, angry SP'ers rushed the platform, forcing Hagerty to stop speaking. Outraged by news of the speech, the prominent Socialist Victor Berger wrote, ''There is no room in our party. . .for

Hagerty. [He] ought to do as anarchists do, and renounce all participation in politics.''[9]

Hagerty's revolutionary conception of socialism had been formed not only through his participation in the earlier eight-hour movement, but also through his contact with individualist anarchists and by his reading of Benjamin Tucker's paper, *Liberty.* A letter of Hagerty's to Joseph Labadie, dated March 1889, reveals his commitment to the cause of the Haymarket anarchists:

I have been inactive in the cause since the murder of our brave comrades. for one year prior to that sad event, I gave my intire time to collecting money to help defray the expenses of their trial, and to visiting the various trades unions to create a favorable opinion and expression on their behalf.

In his letter, Hagerty responded to an idea of Labadie's for the publication of a book or pamphlet containing articles on anarchism. ''I fully agree,'' Hagerty wrote,

. . .that the time has arrived when the few men who understand and indorce the principle of Anarchy should step to the front and give reasons for their advocacy of a doctrine which is regarded with horrible forebodings of danger to society. . . .

190

Unsure whether he could meet Labadie's request for an article on the subject, but resolved to publicly affirm his anarchism despite any repercussions, Hagerty added that

I have little confidence in my ability to present my ideas of a true anarchistic condition of Society in as concise and plain a manner as the nature of your requirements might demand; as I have not had time to read any books bearing on the subject and would have to rely upon what little information I have received through the columns of *Liberty* as well as my own inherent knowledge of Justice and Liberty. . . . I have "no scruples that will stand in the way" of my doing all that lays in my power to present our cause in its clearest light, and although it may bring great pecuniary and other losses to me should I publically proclaim the faith that is in me, yet I always stand ready to make any sacrifice for a cause which I know to be right and Just.[10]

Forming alliances with revolutionary socialists and trade unionists, Hagerty became one of the earliest advocates of industrial unionism. As editor of the *American Labor Union Journal* between 1902 and 1904, he advocated a form of industrial unionism derived in part from ideas advanced by the Chicago anarchists as well as those of the more recent French anarcho-syndicalists:

The workers must so organize in proportion to capitalist concentration in industry irrespective of trade or tool, that, when they shall have acquired a sufficient class-conscious majority in every industry, they may be able to take over and collectively administer the machineries of production and distribution in the co-operative commonwealth.[11]

Hagerty later developed these ideas into a motion adopted at the January conference that laid the foundations for the IWW's inaugural convention. This motion, written into the *Industrial Union Manifesto*, proclaimed that the new movement "be established as an economic organization of the working class without affiliation to any political party." Hagerty was responsible for reintroducing this revolutionary industrial-unionist principle into the intellectual atmosphere of the time.[12]

Hagerty's original draft of the Preamble did not include a role for a political party; rather, it emphasized the importance of the union as the center and foundation of revolutionary struggle:

Between these two classes [working class and employing class] a struggle must go on until all the workers come together on the industrial field, and take and hold that which they produce through an economic organization of the working class.[12]

Meeting with Eugene V. Debs at his home in Terre Haute, Hagerty and William E. Trautmann discussed this critical sentence of the Preamble. Following their explanation, Debs remarked that "had a such a program, such an idea been known, [the American Railway Union] wouldn't have turned into a political organization, the ARU would have made the nucleus of an organization. . .for the management of the industries in the industrial commonwealth."[13]

Concerned that the program presented by Hagerty and Trautmann would eclipse all others, Debs questioned his visitors on the role of the political party in the new movement. Hagerty and Trautmann argued that the new movement represented a concerted effort not to repeat the mistakes that led to the collapse of the ARU. The new movement, they explained, sought to avoid the mistake of combining

in the economic organization the functions of the political parties necessary to exist until the political state and political government will be supplanted by the agencies to be organized within the industrial organizations of the working class.

They conceded that for a while two parties would claim to represent the interests of the working class and that such a condition carried the potential of impeding the progress of the movement. For this reason, they argued, the non-political and non-parliamentarian socialist would be crucial to the formative stages of the organization.

Shortly before the convention opened, their plan and strategy met with opposition from the SLP's Daniel DeLeon. In a meeting with Hagerty and Trautmann, DeLeon insisted that the Preamble was unacceptable without the insertion of the following clause: "and on the political field without affiliation with any political party." Given the rivalries between the two socialist parties and the need for a basis of unification of syndicalism and socialism, Hagerty and Trautmann tentatively accepted the insertion of DeLeon's clause.[14]

During the convention, however, a lengthy debate ensued over this clause. Hagerty elaborated on the meaning of the political clause, pointing out that it did not state for what purpose workers would unite on the political field, and that this seemed pointless, since the workers were to gain what they produced through an economic organization. Defending his original intent, Hagerty argued that politics had nothing to do with political parties. Pointing to Russian workers then engaged in politics through revolutionary struggle, he argued that the working class did not need a political party to gain its freedom. "The ballot box," Hagerty said, concluding his speech

is simply a capitalist concession. Dropping pieces of paper into a hole in a box never did achieve emancipation for the working class, and to my mind never will.[15]

The amended clause was ratified by the delegates but did not end the debate on the role of the political party in the revolutionary industrial union movement. In 1908 the clause was completely rewritten reflecting Hagerty's original intent:

Between these two classes a struggle must go on until the workers of the world organize as a class, take possession of the earth and the machinery of production and abolish the wage system.

Commenting on the 1908 Preamble, Samuel Yellen wrote in his *American Labor Struggles* : "In principle the IWW resembled the 'Chicago Idea' anarchists of 1886, but advanced beyond them to syndicalism." More than merely resembling the "Chicago Idea," the IWW's principles of revolutionary industrial unionism were the direct result of the conscious efforts of anarchists like Thomas J. Hagerty who continued to affirm, in the face of great adversity, the principles for which the Haymarket anarchists gave their lives.

Sal SALERNO

1. William D. Haywood. *Bill Haywood's Book* (New York, 1929), 31.   2. *The Founding Convention of the IWW* (New York, 1969), 128.   3. *Ibid.*, 216.   4. Paul F. Brissenden. *The IWW: A Study of American Syndicalism* (New York, 1957), 39.   5. *Ibid.*, 40.   6. Joseph R. Conlin. *Bread and Roses Too: Studies of the Wobblies* (Westport, 1969), 43.   7. Don K. McKee. "Daniel DeLeon: A Reappraisal," *Labor History* (Fall 1960), 291-295.   8. Gary M. Fink, ed. *Biographical Dictionary of American Labor* (Westport, 1974), 139.   9. Robert E. Doherty. "Thomas J. Hagerty, the Church, and Socialism," *Labor History* (Winter 1962), 51-52.   10. Thomas Hagerty to Jo Labadie (March 1889). Joseph A. Labadie Papers, Labadie Collection, University of Michigan Library. Thanks to Ronald Creagh who called my attention to this impoprtant document.   12. Mckee, 280.   13. William E. Trautmann, "A Brief History of the Industrial Union Manifesto," *Industrial Union Bulletin* (August 8, 1908).   14. *Ibid.*   15. *Founding Convention*, 152.

Anarchist Alexander Berkman speaking at an IWW meeting in New York's Union Square, 1914.

The sign reads: They who die for A Cause NEVER Die. Their Spirit Walks Abroad

"IN NOVEMBER WE REMEMBER"

The IWW & the Commemoration of Haymarket

No labor organization in the U.S. has more profoundly or more consistently identified itself with the traditions of Haymarket than the Industrial Workers of the World. The active participation of several veterans of 1880s Chicago anarchism in the IWW's founding convention in 1905 helped implant something of the Haymarket spirit in the new union right from the start. An early IWW historian noted that Lucy Parsons' presence at the first convention was ''a constant reminder to the delegates of the Haymarket tragedy, which had ended the first great drive for a revolutionary unionism, in this same city of Chicago, nearly a generation before.''[1]

Lucy Parsons' impact on labor radicals in general and Wobblies in particular was in fact immense. IWW organizer Art Boose acknowledged that he might have turned out to be a ''scissorbill'' had he not encountered Lucy, and many others surely could have said the same.[2]

In the IWW's historical books and pamphlets—such as the Historical Catechism of American Unionism, The Blood-Stained Trail *and* Nuroiso, Oppi ja Tyo/Youth, Learning and Labor *(a bilingual Finnish-English textbook used in children's classes at the IWW Work People's College in Duluth) —Haymarket figured prominently as a milestone in the struggle for workingclass emancipation in the U.S.*

The One Big Union's feeling of kinship for the Haymarket anarchists became yet more poignant when, in the course of their own

''conspiracy trial'' during World War I, Ralph Chaplin and others were locked up in the very cells of Cook County Jail that had once confined Parsons, Spies, Fischer, Engel, Fielden, Neebe and Schwab.

IWW "silent agitator" stickerette
by Ralph Chaplin

Especially interesting is the way in which the Wobblies incorporated the Haymarket martyrs into their own extensive proletarian martyrology—Joe Hill, the Everett Massacre, Wesley Everest and others—as vividly portrayed in the text reprinted here by the well-remembered Charles Velsek, an old-time Wob

who was one of the mainstays of the Chicago Branch till his death in 1979.

As Fellow Worker Velsek noted, IWW Branches and Locals held November meetings to commemorate Haymarket as well as other ''victims of class war.'' These nonsectarian gatherings generally featured speakers representing a broad spectrum of radical workers' organizations. Lucy Parsons and Nina Spies often attended, along with Irving Abrams of the Pioneer Aid and Support Association, Boris Yelensky and Maximiliano Olay of the anarchist Free Society Group, John Keracher of the Proletarian Party, Hugo Oehler of the Revolutionary Workers' League, as well as representatives of the Socialist Party, the Communist League of America and other groups.

Such memorial meetings—together with the songs, poems, articles and cartoons on the ''In November We Remember'' theme, which to this day are a feature in November issues of the Industrial Worker—*helped, as one Wobbly writer put it, ''to give a sense of continuity to the struggle of the workers, not only from year to year but from generation to generation.''[3]*

FR

1. Harold Lord Varney, ''The Story of the IWW,'' Chapter 4, *One Big Union Monthly* (Chicago, June 1919), 39. 2. Carolyn Ashbaugh, *Lucy Parsons: American Revolutionary* (Chicago, 1976), 195-6. 3. Albert Hanson, ''Chicago Honors All Labor Martyrs at Big Memorial Meeting,'' *Industrial Worker* (Chicago, November 16, 1935), 3.

IWW COMMEMORATES LABOR'S MARTYRS

On November 11, 1887, Parsons, Spies, Fischer and Engel were hanged at the County Jail in the City of Chicago. The four men were convicted of complicity in the so-called Haymarket Riot, which occured on May 4, 1886. The four men were entirely innocent of the charges placed against them. They were railroaded, not because of what happened on May 4, 1886, but because they dared to advocate the eight-hour day and to help the workers of the McCormick Reaper Works in trying to secure it.

On November 15, 1915, Joe Hill, rebel songster and organizer, was legally murdered by a firing squad, at Salt Lake City, Utah. Joe Hill was active in organizing the workers of the Utah Construction Company. For this he was framed and charged with murder, and shot, although innocent. His last words were, ''Don't mourn, but organize.''

On November 5, 1916, Felix Baran, Hugo Gerlot, Gustav Johnson, Abraham Rabinowitz and John Looney lost their lives aboard the steamer ''Verona,'' which was carrying the free- speech fighters to Everett, Washington. Without reason or cause, the ''Verona'' was fired upon by deputies under the orders of drunken Sheriff McRae.

On November 11, 1919, Wesley Everest met his death, after being unsexed by a member of a fiendish mob. He died after attempting to protect the IWW Hall at Centralia, Washington.

On November 21, 1927, six coal-miners were killed and a score wounded, when state police opened fire, without warning, on several hundred miners who were peacefully picketing the Columbine Mine in Northern Colorado. The pickets were unarmed.

These are only a few of those who have lost their lives in the month of November, so that you and I could get a little more out of life. The Class War continues. We will carry on where they left off.

Meetings to honor these and other November Martyrs, have been arranged in Seattle, Washington and Chicago, Illinois. . . .

All IWW Branches and General Defense Locals are asked by the General Executive Board to hold similar meetings.

Charles VELSEK

Chairman,
General Executive Board

Industrial Worker,
November 2, 1935.

> *''Wherever you find injustice,*
> *the proper form of politeness is attack.''*
> —T-Bone Slim

193

RALPH CHAPLIN

Revolutionist, poet, songwriter, graphic artist and cartoonist, Ralph Chaplin (1887-1961) grew up in Chicago, with short intervals in Dodge City, Kansas and on a farm in Panora, Iowa. While still in his teens he became a commercial artist and joined the Socialist Party. For many years he was the Charles H. Kerr Company's chief graphic artist, designing and illustrating books and pamphlets by such writers as Edward Bellamy, James Connolly, Clarence Darrow, Mary E. Marcy and Upton Sinclair, as well as doing covers and interior artwork for the International Socialist Review. *He did a series of posters used in the Mexican Revolution, and also designed the Kerr Company's* Socialist Playing Cards, *for which Mary Marcy wrote humorous jingles.*

Chaplin joined the IWW in 1913 and quickly became one of its most prominent figures. He edited and wrote extensively for the IWW papers Solidarity *and the* Industrial Worker;

became one of the union's best and most prolific cartoonists; contributed numerous songs, including "Solidarity Forever," to the Little Red Song Book; *designed many IWW "silent agitator" stickerettes; and wrote several important IWW books and pamphlets, including* The Centralia Conspiracy *(1920) and* The General Strike *(1933). Many of his poems are collected in* When the Leaves Come Out *(1917) and* Bars and Shadows *(1919; expanded edition, 1923).*

One of the 101 Wobblies indicted and convicted in Chicago for opposing World War I, Chaplin spent over four years in Leavenworth Penitentiary. The long confinement took its toll on his morale, but he continued to be active in the IWW and labor defense for many years. His autobiography, Wobbly: The Rough and Tumble Story of an American Radical *(1948), reflects his later conservatism, but remains one of the most valuable IWW memoirs.*

FR

LIFE IN COOK COUNTY JAIL

There were raids and raids and raids all over the country on the fifth of September, 1917. Department of Justice agents swarmed down upon every IWW union and branch office in the nation. In each case, federal agents entered private homes or union halls without warrants in search of incriminating evidence. Tons of seized material, including union ledgers, records, files of correspondence, and office equipment poured into the Federal Building in Chicago from all parts of the country. Scanning newspaper reports of the raids, Bill Haywood remarked drily, "I always thought it was against the law to force American citizens to give testimony against themselves."

The raids were supposed to be a surprise, but everybody knew about them in advance. I was at the Western Newspaper Union plant that day getting *Solidarity* to press. Since noon I had been taking a ribbing about "incandescent copy" from the printers. The linotypers were asking for "asbestos gloves." Pressmen complained that "the forms were steaming."

"Let him alone!" the shop foreman commented. "He made this issue hot because he knows it's the last he'll get out for a long time."

"Don't worry," I told them. "Before very long some of you fellows may be setting up this week's editorial for history books."

"Yeah," said the foreman, "and Bill Haywood and yourself will be reading them in the cooler."

"Lots of history has been made that way too," I reminded him.

Newspapers on the streetcorners were competing with sensational headlines: "Federal Agents Raid Reds—I.W.W. Leaders Face Retribution!—Nationwide Dragnet for Wobblies."

* * *

The federal men ransacked our little apartment from one end to the other. They played every phonograph record on the old Victrola and opened our many books separately, fluttering the pages to shake out any loose secret documents. They rolled up carpets, seeking incriminating "charts and diagrams." They took the pictures off the walls and searched every drawer and file for "revolutionary plots and plans."

They discovered a *Ladies Home Journal* dress pattern, still in its envelope, which the investigators opened up and spread out on

the dining-room table. One of them pointed to the perforations and said something in an undertone to the other two. "Surely you don't want that!" Edith [Chaplin's wife] said.

"I'm sorry, but the United States Government will have to decide," the special agent answered.

* * *

An indictment on five counts was returned against one hundred and sixty-six of us on September 28. All who were associated with Bill Haywood at the general headquarters of the IWW in Chicago were included. Each of us was charged specifically with having committed "ten thousand crimes." Every minute was an hour as we waited at the general office to be arrested. Just to pass the time I roughed out a cartoon. It pictured a worker behind prison bars. Underneath was the slogan: "We're in here for you, you're out there for us." The defense committee would be needing that soon. We waited and waited. "This is going on all over the country today," remarked Bill.

* * *

Darkness had fallen outside, and there was a cold drizzle of rain. The patrol wagons were being loaded with agonizing slowness. There were sharp orders, an occasional curse, and the clank of handcuffs as men were shoved through the "paddy wagon" door by burly policemen. . . . Across the street, above a cheap movie theater, an electric sign announced: "Special Feature—The Menace of the IWW." In big red letters another line, "The Red Viper," came on and off spasmodically.

* * *

Day and night the jailhouse noise and stench were indescribable . . . . At the far end of the bullpen, almost hidden in shadows, were the primary beams of the gallows from which the Haymarket men had been hanged in 1887. That was the year I was born. That was the year May Day was born—and the movement to establish the eight-hour day!

Week by week our numbers were augmented by IWW prisoners from other states. Although charged with "conspiracy," few of

194

us had ever met before. Our side of the cell block was rapidly filling up. Rumor had it that the entire wing was being cleared for our accomodation. We were now caged in the same cells in which Parsons, Spies, Lingg, Fischer and Engel—the "Haymarket Martyrs"—had awaited execution thirty years previously. And, later on, Debs had lived in one of them.

Every night I would lie awake, listening to faint sounds of Elevated and streetcar traffic. . . .

* * *

One sleepless night I lay looking at the dirty whitewashed wall back of my bunk. On it had been scribbled the names, initials and monikers of previous occupants of the cell. I had been thinking of Edith and Vonnie [the Chaplins' young son], of the Haymarket martyrs, of Joe Hill and Frank Little, and of Lindrum, a convicted murderer who was shortly to be hanged. While listening to the sounds of the indifferent world that came in through the bars from the darkness outside, the rhythm of a poem started to beat inside my skull. I found room on the wall to write down the stanzas as they came to me. It was my first prison poem, "Mourn Not the Dead":

> Mourn not the dead that in the cool earth lie—
>   Dust unto dust—
> The calm sweet earth that mothers all who die,
>   As all men must;
> Mourn not your captive comrades who must dwell—
>   Too strong to strive—
> Each in his steel-bound coffin of a cell,
>   Buried alive;
> But rather mourn the apathetic throng—
>   The cowed and meek—
> Who see the world's great anguish and its wrong
>   And dare not speak!

Ralph CHAPLIN

from *Wobbly: The Rough-and-Trouble Story of an American Radical* (Chicago, 1948)

FELLOW WORKERS:

Remember!

WE ARE IN HERE FOR YOU; YOU ARE OUT THERE FOR US

Stickerette drawn by Ralph Chaplin in Cook County Jail, based on a drawing by Australian IWW cartoonist Dino

---

FOUR HEROES

Radicals have their heroes just like scissorbills have theirs.
You hear of several mushroom millionaires
Every day; their names adorn the front page
Of your favorite newspaper quite often.
Let them wear their pants a little longer
Or their skirts a little shorter,
The news is put on the ass. press at once.

Well, I'm not going to bother about such silly folk;
I'm going to sing of real men, four of them.
None of them was a hero to his valet
For the simple reason that he never had one.

Well, the hero of my youth was AUGUST SPIES,
I'd like to have met him; he died for a cause,
The cause of freedom—and died game.
He helped me to form good tastes,
For real men and women, instead of wax figures.

JOE HILL came next; I liked the way he died
With a song on his lips
And a message of cheer to his comrades.
He died like a man; shot by coward bullets.

FRANK LITTLE soon followed him: a true martyr.
Little was a consistent pacifist;
Rather than acclaim slaughter god,
He went a willing victim to the trestle.

Never was a bridge more honored
Than when it sustained his bruised body
Suspended on a ruffian rope.

Last comes WESLEY EVEREST, who died fighting;
His is the most dramatic figure of them all.
I like the way he returned shot for shot,
Until his gun clogged from heat.
He had been taught to murder for pelf,
And he wiped out that stain by killing for self,
And in defense of the sacred right of asylum.
No wonder his heroic stand roused the fury of the hellhounds
To heights of insane froth.
His example is a great inspiration;
His death a noble martyrdom;
His blood shed in freedom's cause
Is already breeding defenders.
A sacrifice like his proves, more than words,
That slavery is doomed
To sudden and ignoble death.

Robin DUNBAR

The One Big Union Monthly
(September, 1920)

HAYMARKET MEMORIAL MEETINGS.

In commemoration of the 25th anniversary of the death of August Spies, Albert R. Parson, Louis Lingg, Adolph Fisher and George Engel, who were murdered by the corrupt judiciary of the employing class in Chicago, November 11, 1887, there will be meetings held throughout the world by the revolutionists.

In Chicago the meeting will be held under the joint auspices of the Industrial Workers of the World, the Mexican Liberal Defense League Bohemian Labor organizations, and of the Jewish, Lettish, Bohemian and Italian groups. The meeting will be called at 2 p. m., on Sunday, November 10, at Pilsen Auditorium, 1657 Blue Island avenue. The speakers will be William D. Haywood, Annibal Ferero, Jan Tesar and William Nathanson. There is no charge for admission.

In San Francisco, Cal., at 8 o'clock on the night of November 11, there will be a memorial meeting in Jefferson Square hall, 925 Golden Gate avenue. The speakers will be Austin Lewis, Ed Nolan, Thos. J. Mooney, E. B. Morton and Selig Schulberg, with Hugo Ernst as chairman. The admission is free. A collection will taken and the entire proceeds forwarded to the defense of the sixty-four lumber-jacks whom hirelings of the lumber trust are trying to judicially strangle.

Industrial Worker, Nov. 7, 1912

Pashtanika in the *One Big Union Monthly*

RED NOVEMBER,
BLACK NOVEMBER

Red November, black November.
Bleak November, black and red;
Hallowed month of Labor's martyrs,
Labor's heroes, Labor's dead.
Labor's hope and wrath and sorrow—
Red the promise, black the threat;
Who are we not to remember?
Who are we to dare forget!

Black and red the colors blended,
Black and red the pledge we made;
Red, until the fight is ended,
Black, until the debt is paid.
Wesley Everest and Al. Parsons
With Joe Hill and all the rest.
Who are we not to remember?
Who are we to dare forget!

Ralph CHAPLIN

ELIZABETH
GURLEY FLYNN

Elizabeth Gurley Flynn (1890-1964) was among the greatest of twentieth century labor speakers and organizers. Born in New Hampshire to an Irish family active in union, socialist and anti-colonial struggles, Flynn joined the Industrial Workers of the World in 1907. A model for Joe Hill's "The Rebel Girl," Flynn stirred countless thousands of workers in IWW free-speech fights, defense campaigns and, above all, in strikes, especially those at Lawrence (1912) and Paterson (1913). In 1920 Flynn helped to found the American Civil Liberties Union. She was both a comrade and lover of the anarchist Carlo Tresca through much of the decade before 1925. Flynn later joined and helped to lead the Communist Party. During the anti-communist hysteria of the 1950s she served twenty-eight months in prison because of her political beliefs. Her writings include Sabotage (Cleveland, 1915), The Rebel Girl (New York, 1973) and My Life as a Political Prisoner (New York, 1963). Flynn's grave, appropriately enough, lies with a stone's throw of the Haymarket Martyrs' Monument in Chicago's Waldheim Cemetery.

DR

AT THE IWW CONVENTION
(CHICAGO, 1907)

The first IWW convention I attended was in Chicago in 1907—I had just passed 17 years, and was still in high school. My family and friends were hesitant about letting me go, but I was determined. . . .

At this convention I was thrilled to meet Mrs. Lucy Parsons, widow of Albert Parsons, who had been executed 20 years before in the yard of the Cook County Jail in the heart of Chicago. While he was hanged he was held a prisoner in the Clark Street Station House, not far from where we were then meeting. I met Oscar Neebe, one of Parsons' co-defendants and the imprisoned martyr of the eight-hour-day struggle who was pardoned by Governor Altgeld. I remember Mrs. Parsons speaking warmly to the young people, warning us of the seriousness of the struggles ahead that could lead to jail and death before victory was won. For years she traveled from city to city, knocking on the doors of local unions and telling the story of the Chicago trial. Her husband had said "Clear our names!" and she made this her lifelong mission.

Elizabeth Gurley FLYNN

from *The Rebel Girl:*
An Autobiography
(New York, 1973)

The working class and the employing class have nothing in common.
—IWW Preamble

196

Martyr's Widow Heads Haymarket Memorial Move

CHICAGO.—Mrs. Lucy Parsons, widow of Albert Parsons, one of the five innocent men executed in the famous Haymarket case in 1887 in the fight for the 8-hour day, will head a committee of unionists sponsoring a gigantic memorial to the Haymarket martyrs Nov. 11, 50th anniversary of their execution.

A mountain of flowers and laurel wreaths will be placed at the foot of the Haymarket memorial monument in Waldheim cemetery here, where the martyrs lie buried.

Industrial Worker (Oct. 9. 1937)

"Don't mourn—organize!"
                              —Joe Hill

I. W. W.

Sons of the sansculottes,
Savage, erect, disdainful,
Proud of their pariah estate,
They return to the civilization that has cast them out,
Hate for hate and blow for blow.
Society denied them all life's sweet, soft, comfortable
        things,
And so society raised up unto itself its destroyers.

Reckless of the jails, of the policemen's clubs, of the
        lynching parties made up of frightened good
        citizens,
Cheerfully accepting the anathema of all reputable peo-
        ple and lovers of law and order,
They laugh aloud and sing out of their little red book
Blasphemous ribaldries against all the gods and all the
        masters.
(Beware, gods and masters, of rebels who laugh and
        sing!)
Onward to the conquest of earth these outlaws press,
Pausing by the corpses of their martyrs only long
        enough
To utter, grim-lipped, "We remember."

                              Donald C. CROCKER

Industrial Pioneer (Nov. 1924)

Songs! Songs!

To Fan the Flames of Discontent
SONGS OF JOY!
SONGS OF SORROW!
SONGS OF SARCASM!
Songs of the Miseries That Are.
Songs of the Happiness To Be.
Songs that strip capitalism bare;
show the shams of civilization; mock
at the masters' morals; scorn the
smug respectability of the satisfied
class; and drown in one glad burst
of passion the profit patriotism of
the Plunderbund.

SONGS! SONGS!
I. W. W. SONG BOOKS.
10c each, $5.00 per hundred, $35.00
per thousand, cash in advance. Order of the "Industrial Worker," Box
2129, Spokane, Wash.

IN MEMORY OF THE HAYMARKET LABOR MARTYRS

CHICAGO, Ill.—On November 11 Chicago will commemorate the fiftieth anniversary of the death of the Haymarket martyrs. With many unions, including the I.W. W., and other organizations participating, a memorial meeting will be held on that date at Amalgamated Center, 333 S. Ashland Blvd. The meeting begins at 8 p. m.
                    Industrial Worker (Nov. 13, 1937)

ON THE IWW TRIAL

In the opening words of his statement why sentence of death should not be pronounced on him, August Spies, one of the Chicago martyrs of 1887, quoted the speech of a Venetian doge, uttered six centuries ago:

I stand here as the representative of one class, and speak to you, the representatives of another class. My defense is your accusation; the cause of my alleged crime your history.

                              John REED

"The IWW in Court,"
The Liberator
(New York, 1918)

One Big Union Monthly (Nov. 1920)

HARRY KELLY

Harry Kelly, born in 1871 in St. Charles, Missouri, strove tirelessly for labor and anarchist causes. As a young man he worked as a printer and was active in the St. Louis local of the International Typographical Union. While in Boston in 1894, he became an anarchist after wandering by chance into a lecture by the English anarchist Charles W. Mowbray.

Living in England from 1898 to 1904, Kelly became part of the Freedom Group, grew friendly with Kropotkin, and actively participated in the local printers' union. After he returned to the United States, Kelly contributed regularly to Emma Goldman's Mother Earth; his articles repeatedly stressed the need for anarchists to cooperate closely with unions and to stay in touch with workers and the unemployed.

The slightly built Kelly impressed all who knew him with his warmth and generosity, his calm and friendly personality, and his capacity for practical detail. One associate accurately called him "a practical idealist," for Kelly always emphasized that anarchism must be lived in everyday life.

In 1910 Kelly helped found the Francisco Ferrer Association, which was created to form Modern Schools in America patterned after those set up by the martyred Spanish educator. Kelly's zeal for creating anarchist communities and schools prompted him to take the lead in establishing libertarian colonies and Modern Schools at Stelton, New Jersey (1915) and Lake Mohegan, New York (1923). His practical skills and gentle patience nurtured and maintained these institutions, which Kelly viewed as important for developing an anarchist way of life.

Throughout the 1920s and 1930s, Kelly continued to contribute to anarchist periodicals. He died in 1953 and is buried in Waldheim, near the Haymarket martyrs. In the following article from Mother Earth, Kelly finds some small measure of progress since 1887 and notes that the Chicago martyrs were the first to die for anarchism.

Blaine McKINLEY

THE MARTYRS OF CHICAGO

Moloch, like the past twenty-three years, has claimed many victims, martyrs of a noble ideal. Some, whose names are inscribed in the temple of fame and who rank as immortals; others, nameless and unknown, who lie in forgotten corners or, like those of '71, who sleep beneath the walls of *Pere Lachaise*. They are all dear to us, and we pay our tribute to known and unknown with equal power. We single out the martyrs of Chicago, not because they died more courageously than Ferrer or suffered greater tortures than the martyrs of Montjuich, or Passanante, Spiridonava, and a thousand others. It because they were the first to die for Anarchism, and at their death a new movement blazed forth with all the brilliancy of a new star.

"Liberty! I say with a sigh, men are perhaps not worthy of thee! Equality! they would desire thee, but they cannot reach thee!" Thus Turgot, and when we think of the ever-growing line of martyrs sacrificed to these ideals we are inclined to agree with that sentiment. But to do so would be to ignore the duality of man and to forget that if society numbers amongst its members those who scoff at equality and would assassinate liberty, it also has those who die for those principles. Engels has pointed out, in cryptic fashion, that each society has within it the seeds of its own destruction. Men like Parsons, Spies, Engel, Fischer and Lingg are the seeds that will destroy ours.

If it be said that the story of Chicago's shame and tragedy has been told these three and twenty years until there is no more to be said, let us admit it. Yet, let us not forget, however, that the story loses none of its truth or potency for being told again. A new generation has grown since 1887, and that new generation must be told again and again the debt the American labor movement and all liberty-loving people owe the men of '87.

When representatives of labor are able to meet those who lay claim to coal mines, railroads, and other forms of industry, and say to them, "Your profits have been thus and so during a period of years, but our wages have remained stationary; now we demand our share"—it implies a partnership. True, it is an unequal and unjust one, the producer getting but a minor share of his own product. But that assertion and recognition of ownership is a healthy sign, and such consciousness is in a large measure the fruit of the agitation to which the Chicago men devoted their lives and sanctified by their death.

New York IWPA emblem
(from Most's *Freiheit*)

If the labor movement owes much to them, they also owe much to it: it was there they received the inspiration which bore them through the heat of battle to the very end. The force and strength of their propaganda illustrate the weakness of ours. To disassociate oneself from the people—with all their faults and foibles—is to lose one's inspiration; for when a truth becomes an abstraction, its real value is lost. As part and parcel of the labor movement the Chicago martyrs made the cause of labor their own; no concession wrung from the exploiter was disdained: it meant one barricade less before storming the final ramparts.

With twenty-three years to look back upon and the eight-hour day all but universal among the organized workers of America, we can say that Chicago Anarchists saw as clearly as we see that those issues touch but the fringe of the real question. They took them up because labor demanded a little more leisure for itself, a slightly higher standard of comfort. A rallying cry for labor, the eight-hour movement united men of every creed, race and color, in a common cause: those who would strangle a Ferrer, and those who recognize in him a great teacher. In our time it has been impossible to convict Moyer, Haywood and Pettibone, just as it will be impossible to send to jail Gompers and Mitchell, who flaunt and deride the United States courts on questions of labor. We do no injustice to Moyer, Haywood and Pettibone when we say that, weak as the evidence was against them, it was a hundred times more conclusive than that on which our comrades were done to death. We insist upon their guiltlessness at this late day, not because we are opposed to resisting oppression by every and all means in our power or because we believe that the Chicago martyrs thought otherwise. Policemen are but men, and if in their lust for power or upon the grounds of self-interest, they seek to prohibit protests against their own brutality, the people should defend themselves. Believing this, and further believing that our Chicago comrades thought as we do, we declare them murdered for an act which—according to the evidence—they neither committed nor abetted.

To measure the influence of their propaganda by their lives and death is impossible. That it has been great, there is no question; that it will continue to grow and inspire men, we do not doubt. "By their works ye shall know them." By their works we know these men and knowing them, we love and honor them for the enemies they made.

Harry KELLY

Mother Earth,
(November 1910)

WILLIAM Z. FOSTER

William Z. Foster (1881-1961) was probably responsible for more workers joining trade unions than any other American active in the first quarter of the twentieth century. In later years he became a major leader of the Communist Party.

Born in Taunton, Massachusetts to an Irish immigrant father active in Fenian politics and a Scotch-English Catholic mother, Foster spent most ·of his youth in the poor and rough Skitereen section of Philadelphia. Beginning to work at the age of ten, he picked up a variety of trades as an itinerant. He also acquired an early interest in politics, supporting the presidential candidacy of William Jennings Bryan in 1896. Shortly after a three-year membership in the Industrial Workers of the World, Foster founded the Syndicalist League of North America in 1912. The latter organization, of which Lucy Parsons was for a time a member, shared the IWW's distrust of electoral politics but differed in that it hoped to transform the existing American Federation of Labor unions into revolutionary organizations by "boring from within" them. As a member of the Brotherhood of Railway Carmen, Foster initiated the successful 1917 campaign to organize packinghouse workers into a federated Stockyards Labor Council. The prestige of this organization drive led to his appointment as secretary to the AFL's Committee to Organize Iron and Steel Workers and to his leadership of the massive, heroic, but ultimately unsuccessful, steel strike of 1919.

Foster visited the Soviet Union in the wake of that strike and joined the Communist Party in the U. S. in 1922. He was three times a presidential candidate on the Communist ticket. Jailed for his militant activities in unemployed organizations, he was released just in time to campaign for the presidency in 1932. He also served as general secretary of the party. A prolific writer and especially effective pamphleteer, Foster's most important works include Syndicalism *(1912, with Earl Ford),* The Great Steel Strike and Its Lessons *(1920),* Pages from a Worker's Life *(1939) and* The Negro People in American History *(1954). His grave lies a short distance from the Haymarket Monument in Waldheim Cemetery.*

The vignette below is reprinted with permission from Arthur Zipser, ed., More Pages from a Worker's Life *(New York: American Institute for Marxist Studies, 1979). For more information on Lucy Parsons and Tom Mooney, see Carolyn Ashbaugh's contributions to this* Haymarket Scrapbook.   DR

With Lucy Parsons & Tom Mooney

The first time I met Tom Mooney was under rather peculiar and embarrassing circumstances. It took place in Chicago in 1913. I was national secretary of the Syndicalist League of North America. Mooney, already a well-known revolutionary worker of San Francisco, was a member of our organization, but I had never met him personally. However, Tom was elected a delegate from his local union to the Molders' convention in Milwaukee and, on his way there, stopped over at Chicago to visit me. We both later went on to Milwaukee, where we worked together at forming a Syndicalist group inside the Molders' union.

I lived at the rooming house conducted by Lucy Parsons, widow of Albert R. Parsons, one of the Haymarket martyrs. The night Mooney arrived at our place it happened that we had a bit of a gathering there. Present were several S.L. of N.A. members and a half dozen Wobblies from various cities, delegates to the Industrial Workers of the World (IWW) convention which was then being held in Chicago.

All of us were much impressed with the personality of Tom Mooney. In those days he was a fine, handsome, powerful, upstanding figure, full of spirit and vitality. He already had a growing reputation as a militant fighter. But little did we dream of the tragic fate that was in store for him.

We had a pleasant evening together and, as always among revolutionaries, our talk centered around the problems of the labor movement. The main subject of our discussion was the question of boring-from-within the trade unions. Mooney and the rest of us S.L. of N.A. members strongly favored the policy of working inside the conservative labor organizations, while the Wobblies all aggressively defended the traditional left-wing policy of dual unionism.

We had had several hours of discussion and all the IWW's and nearly all of the S.L. of N.A. members had gone home,

Advertisement from the *Labor Herald,* official organ of William Z. Foster's Trade Union Educational League in the 1920s

when suddenly Lucy Parsons broke in upon us with very disconcerting news. Her watch had disappeared, a beautiful gold watch given to her by her husband on the eve of his execution. She said it was simply nowhere to be found in the apartment. Lucy, naturally enough, was heartbroken over the loss of her precious keepsake.

What had become of the watch? Tom and the rest of us puzzled over the matter. It was impossible to believe that anyone present that evening had stolen it. Nevertheless the watch was gone, utterly vanished, nor could all our search of the premises dig up the invaluable heirloom. Unpleasant though the task was, there was nothing to do but to check up on all who had been at our gathering and this unpleasant job was done. I took the matter up with the S.L. of N.A. and Lucy Parsons went to the IWW delegates. We told them of the great sentimental value of the watch and begged its return at all costs if anyone had taken it. But nobody admitted knowing anything of the timepiece.

Two or three days passed, the watch remained unfound and Lucy was griefstricken. But one day she came to the S.L. of N.A. rooms, which adjoined her place, all radiant and happy, the watch in her hand. It seems that that morning on going to the wood-box on the outdoor porch (the flat being stove-heated), she had lifted up a stick of kindling wood and there, under it, was lying Albert R. Parsons' gold watch, quite unharmed.

We were all overjoyed at the happy outcome. But the whole business became still more inexplicable, for the strange circumstance of the watch's finding was added to the mystery of its disappearance. Had the watch simply been mislaid by Lucy herself, or had somebody stolen it, not knowing its significance, and then returned it upon our pleading? We never learned the answer.

William Z. FOSTER

from William Z. Foster, *More Pages from a Workers' Life* (New York, 1979)

AMMON HENNACY

Ammon Hennacy (1893-1970) grew up on an Ohio farm once owned by the Coppac brothers, martyred associates of John Brown in his raid on Harpers Ferry. A portrait of Brown graced the Hennacy family parlor and both of Ammon's parents supported the Populist movement. Ammon joined both the Ohio Socialist Party and the Industrial Workers of the World in 1910.

Seven years later, jailed in Atlanta Federal Prison for conspiracy to resist the draft, Hennacy was converted to anarchism, partly through contacts with Alexander Berkman. During that same jail term he also became a Christian, though, as he later put it, "not a very orthodox one, spelling God with a small g and two o's."

Throughout his long career as a "Tolstoyan anarchist Christian," Hennacy, as one historian of Catholic radicalism has recently observed, "enjoyed preaching pacifism and religion to revolutionary anarchists and anarchism and revolution to Christians and pacifists." Humorously allowing that revolutionary pacifism was like "wanting to eat the chicken without killing it," Hennacy nonetheless preached and practiced nonviolent revolution with remarkable persistence and consistency.

Hennacy heard Dorothy Day and Peter Maurin speak at the Catholic Worker House of Hospitality in Milwaukee in 1937 and then began to frequent Worker events. At the time of the meeting described below, Hennacy was neither a Catholic nor a Catholic Worker member, but, in part as a result of his admiration for the movement's adherence to pacifist principles during World War II, he did join the Catholic Workers in the postwar years.

Hennacy resisted war taxes during the World War and the early Cold War by taking a job as a migrant day-laborer in the Southwest from 1944 through 1950. In effect, he was a tax-resister through voluntary poverty. As a Catholic Worker, especially between 1952 and 1962, he was an inventive, enduring and flamboyant direct-actionist and pacifist. His leadership of the campaigns against compulsory air-raid drills was particularly important in reviving anarcho-pacifism in the U.S.

Hennacy left the Catholic Worker movement in 1962 and opened his own "House of Hospitality" in Salt Lake City. Not too surprisingly, given the balancing of peace and revolution which characterized his life's work, he named it for Joe Hill.

DR

A HAYMARKET ANNIVERSARY IN MILWAUKEE

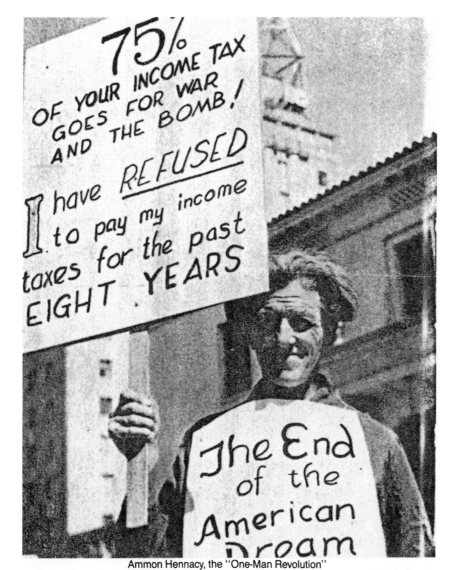

Ammon Hennacy, the "One-Man Revolution"

Nov. 11, 1937 was the 50th Anniversary of the hanging of the Haymarket Martyrs. I was able to get Lucy Parsons, the wife of Albert Parsons, one of the martyrs, to speak on Nov. 19th at a Memorial meeting. Fred Basset Blair, Communist leader, also spoke. I told him if he praised Russia I would tell on him, so he kept to the subject. Martin Cyborowski of the CIO also spoke, as did Prof. Philip Persons of the University of Wisconsin Extension. I was Chairman.

Sponsors of the meeting, which was well attended, included my good friend Henry L. Nunn of Nunn-Busch Shoe Co., a Tolstoian and advocate of 52 paydays a year for his workers, even in the depression. He was much more radical than his employees; a fine man, strict vegetarian and a Christian outside of any church. One of his prized possessions is a picture of Tolstoy carved on a piece of bark by Tolstoy himself and given to a visitor, who upon his death gave it to Mr Nunn. Socialist and union leaders of Milwaukee and several pacifists among the clergy were also sponsors. The ushers of the meeting were the young Catholic Workers. The diocesan paper did not like this united front of the CW with anarchists and Communists but the CW youngsters stood their ground and distributed a pink leaflet giving the CW position on labor.

Ammon HENNACY

from *The Book of Ammon*
(Salt Lake City, 1965)

> *Say what ye will, the strike is good;*
> *It clears things long misunderstood. . . .*
> *The strike tears off the mask of things,*
> *To mass and class the issue brings.*
> —Covington Hall

ART YOUNG

The only notable artist who sketched the Haymarket martyrs from life, Art Young (1866-1943) was born near Orangeville, Illinois and grew up in rural Wisconsin, where his discovery of Gustave Dore's illustrations for Dante's Inferno inspired him to take up drawing. Already cartooning in his teens, by 1887 he was in Chicago sketching baseball games and train-wrecks—as well as anarchist prisoners—for the Daily News.

Two years later he went to Paris where he lived on the same street as Jean Baptiste Corot and Oscar Wilde, and studied art under the arch-conservative painter Bouguereau. Apolitical in his youth, he grew more radical as he grew older. He became a socialist in his thirties and ran for the New York Senate on the SP ticket. A regular contributor to The Masses, he was a mainstay of Greenwich Village radicalism for many years. Best-remembered today for his radical political cartoons—which are in fact his best work—he also did numerous "gag" panels, caricatures and "serious" sketches of people, buildings and trees. Even before World War I his work was featured in such mainstream periodicals as Life and Puck as well as IWW and socialist publications. From 1919 to 1921 he edited his own remarkable radical humor magazine, Good Morning.

Because of his powerful antiwar cartoons and his active opposition to the draft, Young was indicted in 1918 for "conspiracy against the government in time of war." Once again, as he had done thirty-one years earlier, he sketched the defendants in a "conspiracy" trial. But this time he was able to include himself and a characteristic bit of humor: a self-portrait titled "Art Young on Trial for His Life" shows him asleep and snoring. After two trials in which the juries could not reach a verdict, the charges were dropped.

FR

SOME IMPRESSIONS OF A CALLOW YOUTH

One of my important assignments as a newspaper artist in Chicago was "The Trial of the Chicago Anarchists." . . .In the courtroom where they were tried I made sketches of the judge, the jury, the attorneys for the defense and the State and one afternoon spent some time studying the faces and general appearance of the defendants in their cells at the Cook County jail.

The history of this trial is too well known to write at length about it, but I am here giving a few impressions of one callow youth who looked on when assigned to a task—thinking not so much of justice or injustice as of drawing pictures.

My memory of Louis Lingg is distinct because the sun was shining in his cell as I sketched him. He was a handsome boy, sitting proudly and looking directly toward me as much to say, "Go ahead, nothing matters." He might have been thinking of something—a desperate something that he resorted to a few days later when, reaching over from his cot where he was lying, he drew a lighted candle toward him and touched the fuse of a small cylinder-shaped bomb that he held between his teeth. . . .

August Spies, editor of the *Arbeiter Zeitung*, was proud and cynical. . .Once a reporter asked Spies if he believed in free love. He answered: "Yes, as opposed to bought love."

Parsons looked like a country editor, sitting in his cell, at the side of a table on which were many books and papers.

On the day of the execution of Spies, Parsons, Engel and Fischer, November 11th, 1887, my friend William Schmedtgen, of the art department of the *Daily News*, was assigned to witness the hanging. Perhaps the editor thought I was too young for the final scene. I saw Schmedtgen put a revolver in his pocket as he started out on the assignment. The very air was surcharged with fear, for a rumor had penetrated the homes and offices of Chicago that sympathizers with the anarchists would shoot millionaires and blow up the city if their comrades were executed. Many people had taken trains for other cities and suburban towns.

The city was silent, so silent it seemed numb and lifeless. About five o'clock, as if in exultation, the evening papers were shouted from the throats of running newsboys: "All about the Anarchists Hung!"

The next day the city of Chicago was still intact.

Those who hurried out of town came back.

On My Way
(New York, 1928)

The speaking and writing of these men called anarchists (although some of them were Marxian economists) in behalf of the unity of labor and the eight-hour day was ended. But now the eight-hour day is taken for granted. Organization of labor goes on, and every year meetings are held in many parts of the world in commemoration of these martyrs who fell victims to that worst mob of all—respectable legalized vengeance.

Art YOUNG

Art Young: Sketches of the Haymarket anarchists at Cook County Jail
(Chicago *Daily News*, 1887)

Cover of a dime novel, August 7, 1886

A BOMB-TOTING, LONG-HAIRED, WILD-EYED FIEND:
The Image of the Anarchist in Popular Culture

*It is only by the whole that
one can judge the details.*
—Fabre d'Olivet

Historically, actual bombings attributable to anarchists are very few in number. Long before the "roaring twenties" it was clear that most illegal dynamitings were the work of racketeers and extortionists, and that in any case politically- or labor-motivated dynamiters tended to be, not anarchists at all, but rather protagonists of one or another nationalist cause, or conservative AFL trade-unionists who were church-going Catholics and supporters of the Democratic Party.

In the comics, however, and in the whole field of popular imagery, bombs are to anarchists what the red-white-and-blue top-hat and suit are to Uncle Sam: an aspect of their identity so indispensable that without them they would hardly be recognizable. Everyone knows the ridiculous and unsavory image: Besides the one or more bombs clutched in his hands or protruding from his pockets, the stereotype anarchist usually is furnished with a variety of other weapons, including daggers and revolvers, and is further identifiable by his evident aversion for barbershops, bathtubs and fine clothes, as well as by his eyes, fixed as they almost always are in a distracted stare that one associates with lunatics.

This cartoon version of The Anarchist is an enduring legacy of Haymarket. It portrays the self-proclaimed enemies of the State exactly as middle-class editors and prosecuting attorneys wanted them portrayed during the first American Red Scare: as poor, ugly, unwashed, animal-like, mentally deranged and dangerously violent foreigners.

The premier examples, which established the basic image once and for all, appeared in newspapers and magazines the same month that the famous bomb was thrown. The fact that none of the Haymarket anarchists even vaguely resembled the stereotype did not matter in the least. All that mattered was that 1) a bomb had been thrown, and 2) anarchists had been charged with the crime.

The quaint image grew out of an anti-anarchist tradition which is actually much older than anarchism itself. "Anarchy" as a pejorative term has been traced back as far as 1539,[1] but the first person to proclaim himself an anarchist was Pierre-Joseph Proudhon, in 1840, and he seems to have originally adopted the label largely out of his predilection for paradox and scandal. There were earlier anarchists and quasi-anarchists, of course—including people as different from each other as the Englishman William Godwin (1756-1836), the Frenchman D. A. F. de Sade (1740-1814), and the American Josiah Warren (1798-1874)—but they did not use the word.

Long before Haymarket, American readers had had ample opportunity to encounter attacks on anarchy in popular literature. The republic was barely ten years old when, in 1786, a group of "Hartford Wits" brought out *The Anarchiad*, a ponderous rhymed satire with the anarchy-is-chaos theme, aimed at the poor farmers who had just taken taken part in Shays' Rebellion. This early propaganda was by no means leveled only or even primarily at those who opposed all government; more often than not, "anarchy" was merely a convenient term of abuse used by advocates of one form of government against proponents of other forms. In an early American best-seller, Judge Hugh Henry Brackenridge denounced "the horrors of that dreadful state of anarchy, with crop after crop of atrocities"; he was referring to the Jacobin dictatorship during the French Revolution.[2]

Underlying these early expressions of hostility to anarchy is the age-old statist notion that government is all that stands between humankind and the total war of each against all. Ignorant of the non-statist and communal-property forms of many "primitive" societies, ideologists of government the more easily convinced themselves that society without government would automatically and immediately revert to bloody chaos. Such a view implied, in turn, that anyone who dared to question the usefulness of government must necessarily be mad.

That our cartoon anarchist is mad is suggested by his shaggy hair and overall raggedy appearance, though these are also meant to connote poverty and ill-breeding. The cartoon anarchist's eyes, however, leave no doubt that he is a creature utterly bereft of reason.

The "wild-eyed" expression is well-known in the history of art. Readily accessible pre-Haymarket versions of it include a curious self-portrait of Gustave Courbet's from 1843-44, and Gustave Dore's impression of Coleridge's *Ancient Mariner*. Pictorially it is a variant of the sorcerers' and necromancers' "evil eye," known to us through Renaissance paintings and engravings of witches, demons, devils and tormenteds souls in Hell, as well as by later offshoots of this popular iconography, especially the illustrations for the early Gothic romances. The cartoon anarchist is, in fact, a direct albeit proletarianized descendant of the Gothic/Byronic villain. Like the sinister Schedoni in Ann Radcliffe's *The Italian* (1797), and like the somber rogues in Byron's long poems, *The Corsair* (1813) and *Lara* (1814), the cartoon anarchist has unforgettable eyes and an unsmiling, malevolent, horror-inspiring demeanor; like them, too, he is a monster of energy equipped with obsessive singlemindedness, an abiding hatred for society and its conventions, and an endless capacity for evildoing.

If the cartoonist's image of The Anarchist can be traced back to more or less traditional prejudices against "anarchy" and to Gothic and "shilling shocker" villains, its more immediate sources lie in the mainstream press reaction to insurgent labor after the Civil War. Anti-anarchist propaganda in the 1880s, even before Haymarket, emphasized that anarchists almost by definition were foreigners, and violence-prone to a terrifying degree. Journalist J. W. Buel, in a book on Russian Nihilism published in St. Louis in 1883, pointed out that "anarchists. . .like violent maniacs, strike in obedience to a distracted mind, having the one desire to kill, ruin or subvert."[3] Two years later the Christian missionary Josiah Strong, in an influential racist, xenophobic and imperialist tract, did his best to scare his conservative readers out of their wits by alluding to the radicals' interest in dynamite and arguing that

there never was a time in the history of the world when an enemy of society could work such mighty mischief as today. . . . We are preparing conditions which make possible a Reign of Terror that would beggar the scenes of the French Revolution.[4]

At around the same time Prof. Richard T. Ely of Johns Hopkins University was issuing panicky warnings of his own:

There are those who, when extensive and riotous strikes occur again, will remember the teachings which are entering into their flesh and blood, yes, into their very soul, and will take their muskets and their dynamite, and "descend into the streets," and, thinking the great day has arrived, will cast about right and left, and seek to demolish, to annihilate all the forces and resources of wealth and civilization.[5]

Each of the various components of the stereotype anarchist was thus ready to hand well before May 4, 1886. All that was needed was a sensational pretext—the Haymarket bomb provided it—to fuse them all together, definitively, into a single repulsive image made-to-order for front-page promotion of police and vigilante terror against militant workers and their organizations.

Anti-Most cartoon by Thomas Nast
(*Harper's Weekly*, May 22, 1886)

The Chicago martyrs themselves had virtually nothing in common with the stereotype beyond the facts that some of them wore beards, that they were mostly foreign-born and far from prosperous, and that they had openly supported the right of workers to defend themselves against police violence—and hence could easily be portrayed as violent themselves. Not one of them, however, is known ever to have committed a violent deed; on the contrary, examples of their sociability and even gentleness are abundant. There is not the slightest evidence, moreover, that any of them were mentally unbalanced. All were neat and clean in appearance; their speeches and letters were articulate and thoughtful. Throughout the entire ordeal they bore themselves with remarkable dignity and forebearance. Even in the newspaper and police sketches of the prisoners, which attempted to present them at their worst—those in Capt. Schaack's book, for example—it seems hardly possible that anyone not already hopelessly biased could see any trace of a depraved monster. Wealthy young socialite Nina van Zandt wrote that she

entered the court, for the first time, expecting to see a fiendish-looking wretch in each one of the chairs set for the prisoners, but prejudiced as I was, I could not detect an ill-looking man amongst them; several had noble faces.[6]

It is true that, in the months and especially the weeks preceding Haymarket, there were well-armed gangs of law-breaking thugs roaming the streets of Chicago—trigger-happy hoodlums who were notorious for their wanton use of violence; who regularly and for no apparent reason broke up orderly meetings of peaceable and unarmed citizens; who forced their way into men's homes, stole their property and abused their wives and children; who beat up innocent people and shot them and killed them without cause. These were not gangs of anarchists, however, but of policemen, and their leaders were the very ones who directed the anti-anarchist hysteria: Bonfield, Ward and Schaack.

This irony was not lost on the Haymarket prisoners. While the anarchists, who had hurt no one and had broken no law, were being portrayed as bloodthirsty criminal maniacs—as "a newly-discovered species of cannibal," as August Spies put it[7]—the police, who were known to have committed endless acts of brutality and even murder, were feted as heroes of the hour. The stereotype anarchist was thus not a mere caricature but a *complete inversion of the truth*: To the extent that the image was meant to portray mindless and excessive brutality, it fitted the anarchists not at all, but rather their bitterest enemies, the police. "*You* are an 'anarchist,' as you understand it," defendant Oscar Neebe said to Capt. Schaack in court; and then, addressing the judge and the rest of the prosecution, he added: "You are *all* 'anarchists,' in this sense of the word."[8]

That the guardians of the capitalist State should use, as the symbol of their most feared enemy, an image that embodies the essence of the capitalist State itself, suggests that George Orwell's 1984 "newspeak" is not so new after all, and that it even predates Hitler's "Big Lie" by nearly half a century. This is not the place to examine the interrelationship of capitalism and schizophrenia, but let us note in passing that it is perhaps not *only* a coincidence that the famous tale of

Dr. Jekyll and Mr. Hyde was published in that fateful year of 1886.

Significantly, when Bonfield, Ward and Schaack were removed from the police force a few years after Haymarket—for trafficking in stolen goods and receiving payoffs from prostitutes—the result was not an admission on the part of newspaper editors that they might have erred in the Haymarket case, but rather a whole new wave of anti-anarchist editorials and cartoons: The firing of the crooked policemen was viewed by many as "Anarchy Triumphant." When Gov. Altgeld pardoned the three surviving Haymarket prisoners in 1893—with a message that fully vindicated all the defendants and excoriated Bonfield as "the man who is really responsible for the death of the the the police officers"[9] at Haymarket—editors and cartoonists attacked *him*, the Governor of Illinois, as a bomb-toting, wild-eyed anarchist, and continued to do so almost to the end of his life.

The fact that the Chicago martyrs had next to nothing in common with the stereotype anarchist did not prevent the press and prosecution from pretending otherwise. Had the affair not ended so tragically, people would have laughed at the State's Attorney's ridiculous efforts to portray these courageous and excellent labor organizers as ogres and ghouls in league with Satan. Louis Lingg especially was forced into the stereotype simply because he had made bombs—indeed, boasted of it—and conducted himself throughout the police interrogations and trial with supreme intransigence. Public attention inevitably focused on the 21-year-old firebrand, and police as well as journalistic accounts adjusted their descriptions of him to the readymade image of what an anarchist was supposed to look and act like. When Capt. Schaack, in his *Anarchy and Anarchists* (1889) wrote that

Lingg's teeth gnashed with rage, and his eyes fairly bulged from their sockets with savage scorn. The arch-Anarchist looked the picture of desperation. . . .

or again, nearly 400 pages later in the same book:

His face became almost livid with rage, his eyes fairly snapped fire, and he fumed in his cage like an imprisoned beast of prey. He was speechless with anger, and every motion betrayed an energy of passion that was fearful to behold.

—he offered not only some exquisite examples of a policeman's purple prose, but precisely the sort of frightful caricature that everybody already expected and recognized.

Of other real-life anarchists who were to one degree or another "incorporated" into the stereotype, Johann Most is not only the most obvious but also the most important, and has been identified as such by Paul Avrich.[10] "The most vilified social militant of his time," as Avrich has called him, the renowned agitator was the author of a German-language *Science of Revolutionary Warfare* (a manual on the use of explosives and other weapons for urban guerrillas) and editor of the incendiary paper *Freiheit* (*Freedom*). The daily papers featured him as a terrifying homicidal zealot—an insane monster of destruction hell-bent on indiscriminate and wholesale arson, bomb-throwing and bloody murder. Countless German workers who knew and admired the "Rabelais of the Proletariat," and who loved his rousing songs and biting wit, would hardly have recognized the capitalists' caricature

of their venerable comrade who had been twice elected to the Reichstag before he came to the U.S. in 1882.

By a strange and amusing coincidence, an engraved portrait of Most was included in the May 1886 issue of *Frank Leslie's Popular Monthly*, which was already on the stands when the Haymarket bomb was thrown. The picture of Most is sensitive, dignified and plainly captioned: "John Most, Socialist Leader." The accompanying article explained that "There is no risk of Anarchical Socialism ever becoming a serious danger among us." Later the same month, the old German anarchist was being portrayed very differently throughout the land. Thomas Nast, the most famous American cartoonist of the nineteenth century, did a whole series of anti-Most cartoons for *Harper's Weekly*, featuring Most as a dissheveled, pistol-waving, bomb-carrying lunatic—and a coward to boot.

German-born Thomas Nast (1840-1902) was a prolific cartoonist; his work spans over four decades. Best-remembered today for his many cartoons attacking Boss Tweed's Ring of corrupt Tammany Hall politicians in New York, he is also credited with devising the classic image of Santa Claus. It was Nast, more than anyone else, who established the cartoonist's stereotype anarchist.

Nast's anarchist was a variation of a more general anti-labor cartoon-image—often labeled "Knights of Labor" but sometimes simply "Agitator"—that was already familiar when the news-bulletins from Chicago suggested the anarchist as a far more serviceable scapegoat. Nast, who had been doing anti-labor cartoons at least since early 1871, had to change his

BETWEEN TWO FIRES:
Employer: "If you don't go to work, I must fill your place."
Anarchist: "If you go to work, I'll make it hot for you."

An early version of the stereotype by Thomas Nast
(*Harper's Weekly*, May 22, 1886)

ANARCHY TRIUMPHANT.

MAY 4
1886

FEB 6
1889

WARD.
STANTON
BONFIELD
SCHAACK

REMOVED
By
Roche

"The Mayor Playing into the Hands of Officer Degan's Murderers."

One newspaper's response to the firing of crooked policemen
(Chicago *Herald*, February 8, 1889)

representative Knight/Agitator only slightly to make it serve anti-anarchist purposes. His anarchists, except when Most was the model, tended to be physically much thinner than his Knights, and they had, of course, a wilder look in their eyes. But their overall seedy and malicious character remained intact. It is interesting to note that with the advent of the cartoon anarchist, the Knights of Labor disappeared from stage-center in the world of cartoons.

In the four months from mid-May to mid-September 1886 Nast contributed nearly a dozen anti-anarchist cartoons to *Harper's Weekly.* They show that his hatred for anarchism was as obvious and as total as his ignorance of it. His anarchists do little more than trample on the American flag, throw bombs and carry placards reading "Kill the Police!" and "Burn the Town!" For Nast, anarchists were thoroughly dehumanized devils who deserved nothing but death at the hands of the Law; several of his grisly cartoons feature a gallows equipped with nooses. The inglorious career of the stereotype anarchist was well on its way.

Many hundreds, probably thousands of anti-anarchist cartoons followed. All through the Haymarket trial and all through the ensuing defense, clemency and amnesty campaigns these monotonous editorial drawings bombarded the American public, demanding death for the Haymarket prisoners, death and/or deportation of other anarchists, and assorted repressive measures against labor radicals in general.

A product of America's first red scare, the cartoon anarchist has turned up at every subsequent red scare as well as at every major and many a minor labor struggle. Altgeld's pardon provoked a deluge in 1893 and so did the Pullman Strike the following year. Coxey's Army of the unemployed and Bryan's campaign for the presidency in '96 brought forth yet another wave, as did the series of anarchist *attentats* in France in the 1890s, and Leon Czolgosz's assassination of President McKinley in 1901.

The great labor defense cases—the McNamaras, Mooney and Billings, Sacco and Vanzetti and others—showed that the bomb-toting cartoon character was always available for active duty in the anti-labor press. He rarely wore a label identifying himself as an anarchist: He didn't *have* to—everybody *knew* who he *really* was, no matter what label he might be hiding under at the moment. The same old stereotype—long hair, bushy beard, wild eyes, bombs and all—often passed as an IWW member or militant trade-unionist in the 1910s and early '20s, and later as a Communist.

From time to time his nationality changed. From Haymarket through the early 1900s he was almost always a beer-drinking German, like most of the Haymarket Eight, and like those fearful monsters, Most and Altgeld. After 1905, and especially after 1917 he appeared more and more frequently as a Russian. During World War I, however, he went back to being German again, now working hard for the Kaiser and receiving large payments from the suspiciously wealthy I-Won't-Works.

Very early on the cartoon anarchist branched out into other areas of literary and artistic life. In the very year of the Haymarket police riot he made his debut in the dime-novel, to which he returned again and again. Just to make sure that readers got the point, the full-color cover of *The Red Flag; or, The Anarchists of Chicago*, No. 192 of *The New York Detective Library*, featured *two* red flags and *five* bombs, one of them exploding. We are informed that, at an anarchist meeting described in the book, "the men in the audience were unkempt and wild-looking," and that "there was not a native American among them." As if we didn't know!

In *Belle Boyd, the Girl Detective: A Story of Chicago and the West* (1891), the lead character, with the help of a local street-urchin named Billy the Waif, triumphs over terrible Red Mag, her dog Death and a whole gang of ruthless dynamiters.

An issue of *Old Sleuth Weekly* titled *The War of the Reds; or, Trailing the Bomb Throwers* (1911), introduces us to a vicious gang of Russian anarchists led by a blackmailing hypnotist, Alceste Valieres. Attractive and wealthy young Honora Gannett was briefly a member, but she assures the Old Sleuth that she had been *forced* to join:

I met [Alceste] at one of the Settlement houses. . .where I used to have a girls' class. His socialistic patter first amused me and then interested me—and before I knew it, I found that when I was near him, I could have no thoughts of my own.

If this sounds merely idiotic and puerile, it should not be forgotten that for many years the Chicago police regarded Jane Addams' Hull-House as a hotbed of anarchy.

One of the most prolific dime-novelists, the one-time soldier of fortune Prentiss Ingraham—best-known for a two-volume tale of the pirate Jean Lafitte that he plagiarized from his own father—devoted several of his Buffalo Bill tales to combating the anarchist menace.

Anarchists, in fact—the editorial cartoon variety—remained stock villains in dime-novels as long as dime-novels were published, and long before their demise our wild-eyed hellions had secured a niche for themselves in other genres of popular literature.

Retaining all the standard features of the graphic original, the literary version of the cartoon anarchist added an important element—*conspiracy*—which of course had been at the core of the Haymarket prosecution, but which had been difficult to convey by means of drawing.

Here is a curious phenomenon: Having given themselves a horrible scare when a single bomb went off in May 1886, and having eagerly and gullibly swallowed the prosecution's fiction of a "conspiracy" to account for it, American readers avidly sought more and more fiction that told of hundreds and thousands of infinitely more destructive bombs being hurled by throngs of anarchists involved in gigantic worldwide conspiracies of incredible complexity. In the 1890s and early 1900s there appeared several novels featuring anarchist-led invasions of vast armies of dynamiters equipped with huge flying-machines specially designed for total war.[11]

The classic of this type is undoubtedly *Hartmann the Anarchist; or, The Doom of the Great City* by E. Douglas Fawcett (London, 1893). The reader knows right off that Hartmann is an anarchist for he is a "bushy-bearded man with straight piercing glance" and of "cruel hardness." No one could be surprised to learn that he became an anarchist because he wanted to revenge himself on the human race "which produced and then wearied" him. His followers' faces, of course, are "filthy with grime and brutal to a degree." One comrade affirms: "I live for the roar of dynamite." The plan of Hartmann's aerial invasion of England is thus summarized: "During the tempests of bombs, the anarchists below will fire the streets in all directions, rouse up the public, and let loose pandemonium upon earth." The object? You guessed it: "to wreck civilization."[12]

The Angel of the Revolution: A Tale of Coming Terror by the once-popular English science-fiction writer George Griffith (London, 1894) is a *Hartmann*-like tale but nearly twice as long and painted on a wider canvas. It is of interest chiefly because it builds on the suspicion shared by Bonfield and Schaack, and later taken up by J. Edgar Hoover and the John Birch Society: that the Red Conspiracy is in fact vastly larger and more inclusive than most people have been willing to admit:

. . .that which is known to the outside world as the Terror is an international secret society underlying and directing the operations of the various bodies known as Nihilists, Anarchists, Socialists—in fact, all those organizations which have for their object the reform or destruction, by peaceful or violent means, of Society as it is at present constituted.

Yep—the Women's Christian Temperance Union was never anything but a front for the *Lehr-und-Wehr-Verein*.

A real literary curiosity is *The Electric Thief* by Neil Wynn Williams (Boston, 1906), in which we meet a Russian anarchist with "dark," "brilliant" and "piercing" eyes who dir-

THE PESTILENCE THAT WALKETH IN DARKNESS AND THE DESTRUCTION THAT WASTETH AT NOONDAY.

RECORD

ASSAULTS ON WOMEN.

ASSAULT ON CORPSE

ATTEMPT TO BLOW UP HOTEL ALEXANDRIA.

ATTEMPT TO DYNAMITE HALL OF RECORDS.

This cartoon appeared in the labor-hating Los Angeles *Times* in 1910. Soon afterward, a mysterious explosion destroyed the *Times* building.

ects a "remarkable, widely-spread conspiracy" to steal—good grief!—*electricity!*—and on a massive scale, too, "by means of accumulators." The idea was to gather immense quantities of the stuff and then to begin "selling it below market price in the large towns," using the income for "propagation of the anarchistic cause by emissary and document." With the aid of a huge underground electromagnet and cleverly-used microphones, these dastardly fiends bring London to an economic and political standstill by staging *sound-riots*: "As the atmosphere grew more and more loaded with vibrations, scores of human brains proved unable to stand the strain and horror of this strange siege by sound." This does seem a lot like the world we live in today, doesn't it?—except that it is not the anarchists who have the microphones.

Over the years, anarchist villains continued skulking their way into virtually every category of popular literature. They can even be found as bit-players in books whose titles offer not the slightest hint that bomb-throwing terrorists are hiding within. *Under the Ocean to the South Pole; or, The Strange Cruise of the Submarine Wonder* by a ghost-writer under the house-name Roy Rockwood (1907), part of The Great Marvel Series of "Good Books for Boys," includes a sub-plot in which the two lead characters are mistaken for the sons of an English anarchist who had blown up a hotel "in an attempt to assassinate Lord Peckham." The mystery of the "Boy

Anarchists'' is cleared up only in the last two pages of the book.

Anarchists are not common in boys' and girls' series books, however, probably because the moralists who assumed control of such publications from the start would have regarded anything to do with anarchism as unsuitable for juvenile readers. The dime-novel had given us The Boy Student Nihilist in the late nineteenth century, but anyone who proposed a ''Boy Anarchist Series'' to the syndicate that owns Nancy Drew and the Hardy Boys would have been lucky to get off with a sternly-worded rejection-slip and a friendly visit or two from the FBI.

The immense field of pulp-fiction—direct successor to the dime-novel—featured anarchist bad guys aplenty, but they added little to the stereotype and in fact actually diluted it considerably. Pulp anarchists increasingly tended to be interchangeable with any and all other villains, less interested in attacking capitalists and destroying government than in pilfering diamonds and robbing banks. Probably in part because of the formulistic character of so much of this writing, the original anti-radical propaganda motivation for including such characters in fiction was sometimes discernible only in the barest undertones. A pulp-writer who dashed off full-length novels at the rate of one or two or even more a month, and whose hero had just vanquished—in one story after another—river pirates, counterfeiters, jewel thieves, opium smugglers, a mad scientist, cattle-rustlers, kidnapers and train-robbers, would almost inevitably introduce an anarchist bomb-thrower or two into one of his stories, sooner or later, just for variety, and without necessarily taking the trouble to sermonize, as had so many of the dime-novelists, about the divine goodness of government, the eternal nobility of the police, and the hideous evils perpetrated by the demons of ''mutual aid.''

Satan's Death Blast by Grant Stockbridge, published in the pulp magazine *The Spider* in June 1934, has many of the trappings of cartoon-anarchist terrorism. It features a gang led by a criminal mastermind known as The Devil who has at

Uncle Sam: ''You are all right, my friend, but who is that behind your back?''
Cartoon by Rollin Kirby in the New York *Evening Sun*

his disposal a supply of tiny electronically-controlled super-bombs, prepared from a substance distilled from electric eels by German chemists working in subterranean laboratories. ''Police stations, electric plants, radio and telephone exchanges'' were ''blown into the dust! . . .the city was being looted, house by house, bank by bank. . . . A mad mob, filled with the mania of destruction, infuriated against all civilized authority.'' Here is a lurid tale firmly and unmistakably in the tradition of *Hartmann the Anarchist*. However, apart from a single reference to the fact that ''absolute anarchy reigned'' after one of the bombings, the book contains not even a hint of the *ism* cherished by all those bearded, long-haired, bedraggled and wild-eyed characters we have come to know so well.

The fact is that while the stereotype anarchist has endured in the world of cartoons, where traditional symbolic representation is a recognized and even indispensable convention, it proved to be only a transient in literature. Even before the end of World War I, fiction-writers who wanted to write about labor violence or revolutionary conspiracies had begun to call their villains Wobblies—as in the case of Zane Grey's vicious tale, *The Desert of Wheat* (1919)—and of course, increasingly as the years went by, Bolsheviki and Communists. The stories had much in common with the old anti-anarchist novels; they were xenophobic, anti-radical, and filled with a lot of superpatriotic rhetoric. But the anarchist, as such, was retired from the role of leading monster in favor of newer-style radicals who were, at least for the time being, better news-makers.

A much later example of anti-anarchist fiction—a sleazy science-fiction paperback, *Anarchaos* by Curt Clark (1967)—shows how thoroughly incomprehension and hatred of anarchism can be set forth without recourse to the old stereotype. Set on a planet whose founding colonists relied on Bakunin's writings ''as the core of their social philosophy,'' *Anarchaos*

ANARCHIST HORRORS
in the
WAX MUSEUM

. . .I knew about anarchists, because of the execution of the Haymarket martyrs when I was ten years old. In the ''chamber of horrors'' of the Eden Musee, a place of wax-works, I saw a group representing these desperados sitting around a table making bombs. I swallowed these bombs whole, and shuddered at the thought of depraved persons who inhabited the back rooms of saloons, jeered at God, practiced free love, and conspired to blow up the Government. In short, I believed in 1889 what ninety-five percent of America believes in 1932.

Upton SINCLAIR

from *American Outpost:*
A Book of Reminiscences
Pasadena, The Author, 1932

introduces us to an entire population of "anarchists" who, in the absence of Law and Authority, seem to spend most of their time enslaving and murdering each other. The chief interest of the book lies in the naive clarity with which it reveals the absurd horror to which the authoritarian fear of freedom inevitably leads. At the end of the story the anti-anarchist hero actually becomes a mad bomber, no less. He places bombs all over the planet, hoping thereby not only to kill as many anarchists as possible, but also to destroy their transportation and communication systems. The fact that countless innocent people were to perish in these bombings phases our hater of anarchy not at all: "Tourists might be slaughtered, missionaries and merchants might be slaughtered, engineers and prospectors and all honest work-men might be slashed and hacked. . .but now something was going to happen"—that is, the forces of interplanetary government would have to step in and impose state power on this unpleasant population, or whatever fraction of it managed to survive the anti-anarchist's devastation.[13] The book is a kind of unintentional parable of U.S. foreign policy in the Third World.

In literature the anarchist stereotype held on for about thirty years; his film career was considerably shorter. Around 1907-08 he had the starring role—a typically crazed, sloven-ly, drunken, wild-eyed, foreign-looking agitator inciting the mob to violence—in a series of anti-labor propaganda shorts produced by open-shop employers: *Lulu's Anarchists, The Riot, Gus the Anarchist, The Dynamiters, The Murderous Anarchist* and *Dough and Dynamite*.[14] A writer for the Cleveland *Citizen* suspected that "behind this class of pic-tures, if the veil is removed, would be the National Associa-tion of Manufacturers." The brevity of these films preclud-ed the outrageous plots and incredible adventures that gave at least a semblance of substance to the dime novels. Apart from their significance as ridiculous anti-labor documents, these early examples of the anarchist in cinema are of slight interest.

Some fifteen years later, however, Buster Keaton's classic two-reeler, *Cops* (1922), included a marvelous sequence which must be counted as one of the most memorable episodes involving the anarchist stereotype in any medium: In the course of a police parade, an anarchist hurls a large, round, black bomb at the cops, but it falls short and lands next to Keaton who, however, fails to notice it. After several suspenseful seconds, Keaton sees the bomb at last, whereupon he nonchalantly lights his cigarette with it. Then, as if it were a burnt match, he tosses the bomb aside—at the police!

This hilarious moment from Keaton's *Cops* highlights a ramification of the anarchist stereotype we have not yet con-sidered: *humor*. The early anti-anarchist cartoons by Nast and others presumably were meant to be funny, and may well have provoked an occasional chuckle from railroad magnates, bank presidents, Pinkertons and others who shared their view of the world. But such graphic effusions, so narrowly didactic and malevolently shrill, really belong—at best—to the do-main of wit or sarcasm, for they are utterly devoid of the *elevating*, *liberating* and *rebellious* qualities that theorists from Hegel through Freud to Breton invariably have attributed to genuine humor.[15]

Keaton's *Cops* demonstrates an important point: that the humorists' use of the anarchist stereotype differs appreciably and in some cases totally from its editorial/propagandistic use. The anarchist in *Cops* is neither frightening nor other-wise repulsive because the humor of the situation transcends such conformist reactions. Moreover, Keaton, the hero of the film, proceeds (innocently enough) to carry out the stereotype anarchist's deed—and thus in a sense becomes an anarchist stereotype himself, or at least an accomplice thereof: very much so in the eyes of the cops, hundreds of whom spend the rest of the film pursuing him every which way.

Cops is in fact a wildly *anti*-cop film: a glorification of the freedom of the individual against the forces of institu-tional repression symbolized by the police. And it would not be an exaggeration to affirm that all of Buster Keaton's films—indeed, all the great film comedies—are pervaded by much the same spirit. In the films of Charlie Chaplin, Fatty Arbuckle, Ben Turpin, Harry Langdon, Laurel & Hardy, the Marx Brothers, the Three Stooges—and in the early Bugs Bunny and Woody Woodpecker cartoons—cops, bureaucrats, government figures and military officers seem to exist primarily to be kicked in the pants, knocked down, hit in the face with pies, and in countless other ways heckled, abused and made fun of. When Antonin Artaud hailed the Marx Brothers' *Monkey Business* as "a hymn to anarchy and wholehearted revolt,"[16] he hit on one of the most striking signs of the times: that, from the days that we now call the "golden age" of film comedy, the silver screen has bristled with elements of an authentically anarchist attitude.[17]

The anarchist intrusion into American humor did not start in films, however, but in the columns of the daily newspapers,

---

ALICE IN JUSTICE-LAND

"Who are these poor unfortunates in this miserable bullpen?" asked Alice, a sympathetic tear in her eye.

"They are guilty of free speech," said the White Knight.

"Please don't tease me," said Alice. *"Persons cannot be charged with free speech."*

"Who said anything about charging them with free speech?" demanded the White Knight. *"They aren't charged with anything of the sort. Free speech is only what they're guilty of."*

* * *

"Oh," said Alice, just a little exasperated, *"let's change the subject. "Who is that man sitting in the solitary confine-ment cell?"*

"That," said the White Knight, *"is a Dangerous Criminal."*

"Oh, a murderer."

"Certainly not. More dangerous than a murderer. He is a Thinker."

* * *

"The whole system," said Alice, *"is silly."*

"Nothing of the kind," said the White Knight. . . . *"The whole thing in a nutshell is this:*

"It's much easier to convict a man of something he didn't do than it is to prove that what he really was doing was a crime."

Jake FALSTAFF

from Jake Falstaff (Herman Fetzer),
Alice in Justice-Land
(New York, 1929)

An episode from
George Herriman's strip,
The Family Upstairs
(1910).

"The Anarchist Pro-Football Quarterback," in *Mad Magazine*, mid-1960s (artist: George Woodbridge; writer: Frank Jacobs)

where so much of the best—as well as the worst—writing of the late nineteenth century first saw the light of day.

Finley Peter Dunne, in his "Mr. Dooley" column in the Chicago *Evening Post* for September 25, 1897, told of listening to socialist streetcorner-speakers who advocated the use of "dinnymite." "I'm not afraid," says Mr. Dooley,

Th' American rivolutionist is th' most peaceful man on earth. He's as law-abidin', as ca'm an' as good-natured as anny livin' man. Did ye iver hear iv wan iv thim torch an' bomb lads swingin' a torch or peggin' a bomb? Not wan. Afther they're through th' little song an' dance on Sundah afthernoon they go home an' play with th' babies.

In another column from the same period, titled "On Anarchists" and reprinted in *Mr. Dooley in Peace and War* (1899), "Mr. Dooley" concluded a fable with the moral "arnychists is sewer-gas"—*i.e.*, that anarchists are not the cause but the result of social conditions.[18]

George Washington Peck, a union printer who became Governor of Wisconsin, introduced anarchists into several of his popular "Peck's Bad Boy" series, which grew out of a column originally run in his own paper, *Peck's Sun*. When the Bad Boy and his Pa visit Switzerland in *Peck's Bad Boy Abroad* (1904), they quickly run into the familiar stereotype: "There are more anarchists in Geneva than anything else, and they look hairy and wild-eyed, and they plot to kill kings and drink beer out of two-quart jars." The Bad Boy's Pa thinks it would be a "good joke" to pass himself off as a fugitive wanted for attempting "to assassinate someone," so the Bad Boy promptly starts a rumor that his Pa was

wanted for attempting to blow up the president of the United States by selling him baled hay soaked in a solution of dynamite and nitroglycerine. . . . It wasn't two hours before long-haired people were inviting dad to dinners, and the same night he was taken to a den where a lot of anarchists were reveling, and dad reveled till almost morning. When he came back to the hotel he said his hosts got all the money he had with him, through some game he didn't understand, but he understood it was to go into a fund to support deserving anarchists and dynamiters.

In *Peck's Bad Boy in an Airship* (1908) Pa is again suspected of being an anarchist, "and since the assassination of the king and crown prince of Portugal the police had overhauled his baggage in his room several times. . . ." Later the Bad Boy sets off a firecracker. "The police came in to. . .find the anarchist who threw the bomb," and a good time was had by all.

Ambrose Bierce's specific references to anarchists and socialists are neither numerous nor humorous, but his sharpest barbs were directed against government, politicians, religion, business, law, the police, the military. In view of his prestige as a master-humorist in his later years, it seems certain that his *Devil's Dictionary*, started in 1869 and continued at intervals through the first decade of this century, contributed significantly to the diffusion of generally nonconformist and particularly antiauthoritarian sentiments. Notwithstanding Bierce's peculiar pseudo-aristocratic cynicism, many of his definitions would not have been out of place in *The Alarm* or the *Arbeiter-Zeitung*:

Arrest: Formally to detain one accused of unusualness.
Arrested: Caught criming without the money to satisfy the policeman.
Commerce: A kind of transaction in which A plunders from B the goods of C, and for compensation B picks the pocket of D of money belonging to E.

Jury: A number of persons appointed by a court to assist the attorneys in preventing law from degenerating into justice.
Trial: A formal inquiry designed to prove and put upon the record the blameless character of judges, advocates and jurors. . . .

A later newspaper humorist, Don Marquis, went so far as to have his most famous character, Archy the cockroach, declare himself an anarchist. In one story the six-legged libertarian sets out to foment an insects' revolution. Silly? Of course! But it was a kind of silliness unthinkable in the 1880s.

Marquis' *Archy's Life of Mehitabel* (1929), in which the roach's anarchist agitation plays a role, was illustrated by George Herriman, whose sublime *Krazy Kat* is widely regarded as the greatest comic strip of all time.[19] Comic-strip artists quickly followed their humor-columnist colleagues in perceiving the endless possibilities of the stereotype anarchist in "gag" situations. Herriman, Harry Hershfield and Gus Mager are only a few of the Old Masters of the comic page who appropriated the old editorial cartoon character for new and very different purposes of their own. Even Frederick Burr Opper, who did some cold-blooded anti-anarchist editorial cartoons from the late '80s through the '90s, in later years—as he saw the monopolists strangle what little was left of America's democratic institutions—came to view radicals less maliciously while portraying "plutocracy" with all the savage humor at his disposal.[20]

The humor of "Mr. Dooley," Peck, Bierce—and of Herriman and other comic-strip artists—extracted the poison from the established anarchist stereotype. Their anarchists are still long-haired and wild-eyed, and they still carry bombs, but they tend to be funny rather than fiendish. More importantly, by allowing these funny anarchists to encounter funny cops and funny capitalists, humorists and comic-strip artists helped to expose the hypocrisy and meanness—and especially the ridiculousness—of so much of the prevailing "constituted authority."

The fact that an anarchist, or at least an anarchic, humor has flourished in the popular media does not mean, of course, that the creators of this humor have been anarchists, or even sympathizers with anarchism. Indeed, a few outstanding comedians have actually avowed reactionary views: W. C. Fields and Jonathan Winters are examples. But what is important is that their consciously retrograde attitudes rarely affect the quality of their humor, as such, which in fact retains the provocatively emancipatory essence of humor at its best. One of the most humorous things about the dialectics of humor is that it proceeds without, and often in spite of, the conscious intentions of the humorist.

That humor—as a broad social phenomenon—should increasingly provide refuge for genuinely anarchist ideas and aspirations is not really surprising when one considers the inevitable instability of repressive ideology in the modern world. Throughout this century in most countries, and especially in the U.S., anarchism has not been "taken seriously"—as a movement, a body of ideas, a critique of society, a way of life—except by rare individuals and small, widely scattered groups. Precisely because it has *not* been taken seriously by the leading authorities on seriousness, it has often found its best transmission-belt to a larger public in uproarious humor.

Anarchik at work: Cartoon by Roberto Ambrosoli

Anarchik's merry adventures in applied anti-authoritarianism have in turn inspired many cartoonists in many countries to develop similar characters of their own.

Today, we might say, following Hegel's *Phenomenology*, that the old stereotype is no longer the slave of another, doomed to stoical submission to a reified reality, but has mastered its one-time masters and surged forth anew as an image of living freedom.

Humor in the service of revolution! The appropriation of the anarchist stereotype by anarchists and other radicals who have unleashed it against the very world-view that originally nurtured it, is surely a glimmer of the Haymarket martyrs' revenge at last. Against the *esprit de serieux* with which the administrative apparatus of contemporary wage-slavery attempts to delude itself and everyone else that its reign is safe and sound, Ambrosoli and other anarchist and radical cartoonists have demonstrated once again, in their own way, that a burst of laughter has the unsettling effect of—*dynamite!*

Franklin ROSEMONT

1. Nhat Hong, *The Anarchist Beast* (Minneapolis, c. 1978).   2. Hugh Henry Brackenridge, *Modern Chivalry* (Philadelphia, 1857), 61. Part I of this work was completed by 1797.   3. J. W. Buel, *Russian Nihilism and Exile Life in Siberia* (St. Louis, 1883), 186.   4. Josiah Strong, *Our Country: Its Possible Future and Present Crisis*, quoted in David Brion Davis, *The Fear of Conspiracy* (Cornell, 1971), 174-5. 5. Richard T. Ely, *The Labor Movement in the U.S.* (1886), 291.   6. Nina van Zandt, in *August Spies' Autobiography* (Chicago, 1887), 85.   7. *August Spies' Autobiography* (Chicago, 1887).   8. Oscar Neebe, in Albert R. Parsons, *Anarchism* (Chicago, 1887), 73.   9. John P. Altgeld, *Reasons for Pardoning the Haymarket Anarchists* (Chicago, 1986), 46.   10. Paul Avrich, *The Haymarket Tragedy* (Princeton, 1984), 61. 11. Johann Most's *Science of Revolutionary Warfare* had predicted "that airships would one day be able to drop dynamite on military parades attended by emperors and kings." Avrich, 165.   12. *Hartmann the Anarchist* was reprinted in the magazine *Forgotten Fantasy* in June and August 1971. An introductory note by the editror stated that "many of the ideas expressed by Hartmann. . .could be taken straight from the revolutionary speeches and writings of today's radicals."   13. Much science-fiction, however, is implicitly anarchist. See John Pilgrim, "Science Fiction and Anarchism," *Anarchy* (London, Dec. 1963).   14. Philip S. Foner, "A Martyr to His Cause: The Scenario of the First Labor Film in the U.S.," *Labor History*, Winter 1983, 103.   15. G. W. F. Hegel, *Aesthetics* (Oxford, 1975), 607-9; Sigmund Freud, "Humor," in *Character and Culture* (New York, 1963), 263-69; André Breton, *What Is Surrealism?* (New York and London, 1978), 80, 154, 188-96.   16. Antonin Artaud, "The Marx Brothers," in Franklin Rosemont, ed., *Surrealism and Its Popular Accomplices* (San Francisco, 1980), 48.   17. On anarchist elements in cinema see Ado Kyrou, *Le Surréalisme au cinema* (Paris, 1963); Robert Benayoun, *Le Dessin animé apres Walt Disney* (Paris, 1961); Franklin Rosemont, "Buster Keaton," "Homage to Tex Avery," 'Bugs Bunny," etc., in *Surrealism and Its Popular Accomplices*. Alan Lovell's *Anarchist Cinema* (London, *Peace News*, c. 1967) strangely ignores comedy.   18. The comments of "Mr. Dooley" on anarchism were appreciated by anarchists; see the letter from *Freedom* (London) quoted in *Free Society* (Chicago, Oct. 20, 1901).   19. "George Herriman," in *Surrealism and Its Popular Accomplices*.   20. See "A Cartoonist of the People," *Wilshire's Magazine* (Oct. 1902); B. O. Flower, "Frederick Opper: A Cartoonist of Democracy," *The Arena* (June 1905; and the introduction to *Mr. Block: 24 IWW Cartoons* (Chicago, 1984).   21. See Dave Wagner, "Donald Duck: An Interview," *Radical America*, VII, 1, 1973; Franklin Rosemont, "Carl Barks/Uncle Scrooge," *Surrealism and Its Popular Accomplices*.   22. A fine portfolio of Roberto Ambrosoli's Anarchik cartoons, with an article by Ambrosoli, was featured in the summer 1985 issue of the anarchist review *MA!*, published in Geneva.

Predictably, the worldwide reawakening of social radicalism that began in the 1960s revived the old anarchist stereotype—directed now against "campus anarchy," "black ghetto anarchy" and a sickeningly ill-defined "terrorism." But this time there was—lo!—something new under the sun. It is no secret that the "new radicalism" in its initial heyday reflected a profoundly radical libertarian tendency; not accidentally, the anarchist movement also enjoyed its greatest resurgence in decades during the same years. It is well known, too, that one of the principal ways in which the New Left differed from the Old was in the degree to which it drew its inspiration from popular culture—and from humor above all. Many "new radicals" owed as much to Tex Avery, Harpo Marx, Ernie Kovacs and *Little Lulu* as to any social theorist, and not a few found their appreciation of Karl Marx's *Capital* heightened and deepened by Carl Barks' studies of the world's richest duck.[21]

In such conditions, it might have been anticipated that the old editorial cartoonists' anti-anarchist, anti-labor, anti-radical stereotype was destined to change. What actually happened, however, was even funnier and better: The old image was seized *by radicals* and turned against the upholders of Law'n'Order.

The Italian anarchist Roberto Ambrosoli was the first to adapt the old stereotype for specifically anarchist purposes. His character Anarchik—bearded, long-haired, wild-eyed, bomb-toting and delightful—appeared in the mid-1960s, and has flourished ever since, not only in Italian anarchist periodicals but in radical publications all over the world.

Roberto Ambrosoli: Anarchik poses the question

212

MOTHER JONES & HAYMARKET IN MEXICO

Mary "Mother" Jones (1830?-1930) is the foremost labor support activist yet to agitate on American soil. Born in Ireland, she grew up in Canada. By the time of the Civil War, she had worked as a school teacher in Michigan and a dressmaker in Chicago. Her six-year marriage to Iron Molders' Union militant George Jones ended tragically in 1867 when he and the couple's four small children died in a Memphis cholera epidemic. In the 1870s, while working again as a Chicago dressmaker, Mother Jones began to support vigorously the activities of the Knights of Labor and other unions. For a half-century after 1877, she toured the strike-torn areas of the U.S.—speaking, picketing and organizing, especially among miners and on the behalf of child laborers. She suffered arrest many times, even in her eighties. In 1905 she was a founding member of the Industrial Workers of the World.

Mother Jones was in Chicago in 1886 and participated in the eight-hour movement, including the May 1, 1886 demonstrations on behalf of the eight-hour strikers. In her classic *Autobiography of Mother Jones* (Charles H. Kerr, 1925) she recalled her attendance at prestrike meetings organized by the IWPA but added that she "never endorsed the philosophy of the anarchists." Jones' connections to Mexican workers also illuminate the passage reprinted below.

An ardent advocate of the Mexican Revolution, Jones went to Mexico in 1911 to celebrate the overthrow of the Diaz dictator-

ship and to initiate ultimately abortive attempts to organize Mexican miners. She was a supporter and friend of the Mexican revolutionary Pancho Villa. Shortly before writing the passages reprinted here, Jones spoke at the Third Congress of the Pan-American Federation of Labor in Mexico City.

Her visit came less than a year after the accession to power of the "millionaire

socialist" regime of Alvaro Obregon in Mexico. As part of the quite fragmentary liberalizations undertaken by Obergon, May Day became a national holiday in Mexico, with part of the legislation setting it aside for celebration reading:

It is true that the killing of the workers in Chicago in Chicago for demanding the eight-hour day should not be a day of "fiestas," it should more appropriately be a day of sorrow. Considering, however, that social progress has always been paid for with blood, the First of May should be the cause of pride not only for the proletariat of the United States but of the whole world and a holiday for labor.*

The letter excepted excerpted here, containing a description of May Day in Mexico in 1921, was directed from Mexico City to John Fitzpatrick and Edward Nockels, the president and the secretary of the Chicago Federation of Labor; it is dated 16 May 1921. The original is in the John Hunter Walker Collection at University of Illinois Library and is reprinted in Philip S. Foner, ed. *Mother Jones Speaks* (New York: Monad Press, 1983), 649-51.

DR

*Quoted in Witter Bynner, *Journey with Genius: Recollections and Reflections Concerning the D. H. Lawrences* (New York, 1951), 71-72. Bynner also vividly describes tributes to the Haymarket martyrs in Mexico's 1923 May Day festivities. See Chapter 12, passim.

LETTER TO THE CHICAGO FEDERATION OF LABOR

*Mexico City,
May 16, 1921*

My Dear friends:

Your very beautiful telegram of May the first reached me on May second. I don't know of anything I received in years that so deeply affected me for the time being. I hope you do not think or have the impression that I was unappreciative for your humane consideration of me in a far off city. I have no words to convey to you and your associated in the great struggle for justice the deep appreciation that I feel.

My reason for not acknowledging your message at once was that I was not well, but I am just beginning to get back my old fighting

Inscription on a large public monument dedicated to "Los Martires de Chicago" in Matehuala, Mexico, "erected by the organized workers" of that city in 1925. The phrase regarding the "capitalist hyena" is taken from Louis Lingg's *Address to the Court.*

qualities. On the day your message arrived, I was down in Orizaba, a strictly manufacturing town. I addressed a large meeting there with several diputados, or congressmen also. It was the most remarkable meeting I addressed in years; the spirit was so marvellously fine. The town was thoroughly organized and the spirit they possessed was an inspiration. One got new hope for the future. They had a union band with the finest music I ever heard in a labor display. The building was a municipal building, very large, tendered by the public officials to the labor movement. There was no uniformed police there, either at the entrance or inside of the building. This was something marvellously new to me, because with us in the United States, in the great American Republic, you know the outside and the inside would have been multiplied by the uniformed representatives of the high class burglars. The meeting continued until nearly twelve o'clock. Not one human soul left the hall. All were deeply interested to my surprise, a flag representing the murder of the so-called anarchists in Chicago of '86 came marching in side by side with the national banner. Everyone of you would have been put in jail for the next ten years if that occurred in Chicago. The congressmen, most all of them, referred to it in their speeches, the briute [tribute] paid to that banner as it entered that hall was the most remarkable demonstration I had witnessed in all my years in the industrial conflict. The next morning as the train pulled in and stopped on its way to Mexico City, the workers came out of the shop and jumped on the train and no one could keep them off. They came in and urged me to come back again. I promised them to do so. . .

MOTHER JONES

Lithographs of the Haymarket Martyrs were produced in dozens of countries and in amazing variety. Some were of austere design; others were imaginative extravaganzas—like this wild vision topped by the cloven-hooved vampire of Monopoly.

JOSE MARTI AND HAYMARKET

In an article entitled "The First of May, 1886," published in *El Partido Liberal* of Mexico City, Jose Marti, Cuban revolutionist and poet, who was then a New York correspondent for the Latin American press,[1] wrote: "Enormous events take place in Chicago, but rebellion exists throughout the nation." Marti explained that the eight-hour movement which sparked the May Day demonstrations throughout the United States and especially in Chicago, was part of a struggle between capital and labor which "has been in preparation for years." It was a "just struggle," for "Things are not right when an honest and intelligent man who has worked tenaciously and humbly all his life does not have at the end a loaf of bread. . . ."[2]

Although Marti sympathized with the eight-hour movement and supported the strikes for the shorter working day on May 1, 1886, he was extremely hostile at first to the Chicago anarchists who were on trial for their lives because of their supposed involvement in the explosion on May 4, 1886 at Haymarket Square. In his first report on the Haymarket tragedy, published in *La Nacion* of Buenos Aires, Marti wrote:

Who can do more, the reasonable workers with their eyes fixed upon an absolute social reorganization, proposing to move toward it by making, through their united vote, laws which will permit them to achieve their objectives without violence? Or those who, with the power of an anger accumulated century after century in the despotic lands of Europe, have come from there with a hate factory in every heart—men who want to achieve social reorganization by means of crime, fires, theft, fraud, assassination, and scorn for all morality, law, and order?[3]

Marti could understand that in Germany workers might be forced to resort to violence:

There the worker does not have a free vote, a free press, does not have his hand holding the shield; there the worker does not elect deputies and senators and judges, and the President as he does here; there he does not have laws to guide him, so he leaps over the men who bar his way; there violence is just because he is not permitted justice.[4]

But he had no sympathy for men like those on trial in Chicago who

advised the use of remedies dreamed up in countries where the sufferers have neither a vote nor a word—here where the most unhappy have in their mouths the freedom of speech to denounce the wrongs, and in their hands [the means] to vote [for those] responsible for passing the laws that will overturn those wrongs. . . .[5]

The anarchists had taken advantage of "a just revolt by the working people throughout the country to improve their conditions." But workers had no sympathy for the anarchists, and no one had voiced any criticism of the guilty verdict and the sentencing of seven of the eight anarchists to death.[6]

But Jose Marti was shedding many of his earlier conceptions about the struggle between capital and labor in the United States, and his attitude toward the Chicago anarchists began to change. Discussing the view, which he himself had advanced, that there was no need for revolutionary violence in American social conflicts, he wrote on April 4, 1887:

"Look to the law for righting your wrongs!" said the political parties to the workers in censuring them for their attempts at violence or anarchy, but as soon as the workers organized themselves into a party to look to the law for help, they were called anarchists and revolutionaries.[7]

Marti never condoned the use of bombs and dynamite as a means of achieving social change. But in an article written for the Latin American press on the funeral of the Haymarket martyrs, he pointed out that "Chicago's anarchist forces" were motivated by "the purest sense of compassion exalted to the point of folly by the spectacle of irreparable misery, and annointed by the hope of just and lofty times." He now asked:

Well, what did they want (since it was clear to their eyes that a man lives under abject despotism) other than to fulfill the obligations counseled by the Declaration of Independence in overthrowing that despotism and substituting for it a free association of communities that exchange among themselves their products of equal value, governing themselves by mutual agreement and without war, and educating themselves in accord with knowledge having no distinctions of race, creed, or sex.[8]

Previously Marti had written of Albert R. Parsons and his wife Lucy Parsons with bitter anger, but now he described him as "one who believed in humanity," and he noted that "the grief of the working people" stabbed the hearts of Parsons and his wife "like a dagger." Of Lucy Parsons' speeches, he wrote:

Such was the impact of a rugged and flaming attack that the anguish of the downtrodden was said never to have been depicted so eloquently. Her eyes flashed lightning, her words shot bullets, she clenched her fists; but when speaking of the sorrows of an impoverished mother, her voice took on an immense softness and the tears flowed.[9]

The lack of justice received by the Haymarket defendants aroused Marti's wrath. "The trial?" he wrote:

The witnesses are the police themselves and four bought anarchists, one of them an admitted perjurer. . . . The trial? The seven were condemned to death by hanging, and Neebe to the penitentiary, by virtue of a special charge of conspiring to homicide, a charge in no way proved true.

Even though not a single shred of evidence was presented to prove that any of the eight condemned men had actually thrown the bomb, "the entire press from New York to San Francisco falsifies the trial, pictures these men as harmful beasts, puts images of policemen blown apart by the bomb on everyone's breakfast tables," and said nothing about the fact that the jury was packed and the judge prejudiced against the defendants.[10]

In the face of "the cruelty and stupidity of the trial," Marti insisted that "those seven men must not die." He condemned the Supreme Court for its decision, "unworthy of the whole affair,"[11] confirming the death sentence, and paid tribute to those who were organizing protests against the impending executions and calling upon the Governor of Illinois to prevent the death sentences form being carried out.[12]

While the Haymarket Affair was not alone, as some Marti scholars claim, responsible for the radicalization of the great Cuban revolutionary leader,[13] it definitely helped him understand how the United States was changing and becoming more and more dominated by powerful industrial and financial forces. In his article on the funeral of the Haymarket martyrs, he wrote: "Because of its unconscionable cult of wealth, and lacking any of the shackles of tradition, this Republic has fallen into monarchical inequality, injustice, and violence." While Marti did not embrace the socialist cause and its ideology, he showed in this article an understanding of the need for a revolutionary party to defend the interests of the working class. The article makes abundantly clear his abandonment of his total hostility to the condemned Chicago anarchists and his respect for their courage and devotion to their principles, as well as his understanding of the role of the state, and especially the courts, in defending the interests of the business power over the interests of the working class.[14]

Philip S. FONER

1. For the discussion of Marti's career as a journalist in New York and a selection of his journalistic writings, see Philip S. Foner, editor, *Inside the Monster: Writings on the United States and American Imperialism by Jose Marti* (New York, 1975). Most of the translations from the Spanish are by Elinor Randall.   2. Reprinted in Phillip S. Foner, editor, *Our America: Writings on Latin America and the Struggle for Cuban Independence by Jose Marti*, (New York, 1977), 63-64. The translation is by Elinor Randall.   3. See Henry David, *The History of the Haymarket Affair*, (New York, 1936); Paul Avrich, *The Haymarket Tragedy*, (Princeton 1984); Philip S. Foner, editor, *Autobiographies of the Haymarket Martyrs*, (New York, 1970); Philip S. Foner, *History of the Labor Movement in the United States* (New York, 1955) 2: 105-15.   4. *La Nacion*, (Buenos Aires, June 26, 1886). Translation by Elinor Randall.   5. *La Nacion*, (Buenos Aires, July 2, 1886).Translation by Elinor Randall.   6. *La Nacion*, (Buenos Aires, October 21, 1886). Translation by Elinor Randall.   7. *Ibid.*   8. *La Nacion*, (Buenos Aires, January 1, 1888). Translation by Elinor Randall.   9. *Ibid.*   10. *Ibid.*   11. *Ibid.*   12. *Ibid.*   13. *Ibid.*   14. Antonio Martinez Belloy, *Ideas sociales y economicas de Jose Marti*, (La Habana, 1940), 159-60. For a criticism of this view see John M. Kirk, *Jose Marti: Mentor of the Cuban Nation*, (Tampa, 1983), 168.   15. Juan Marinello, "El Pensamiento de Marti y Nuestra Revolucion," *Cuban Socialista*, (January 1966, 16-24; Philip S. Foner, *Inside the Monster*, 39.

HAYMARKET

Sunrise to sunset bondage, that was our portion,
we rose to refute it: 8 hours of labor,
8 to rest from labor and 8 for the pleasantries,
solace, enlightenment, with friend or in family.
We asked for the kettle and the lamp at evening,
a chair in the corner, a pipe and the homage
of simple affection. We struck for an hour of sun:
6 workers . . . murdered . . . by the Harvester Trust.
Out to the Haymarket! proclaim against murder.
Into the mass of workers protesting,
the burst of a bomb, four workers slain—
by McCormick the Reaper!

Don now the robe and the periwig,
master of provocation, Pinkerton of prey,
the law is the nuance of murder.
Slander the murdered, libel the dead,
burden your guilt on the innocent dead,
sort out the men who asked for an hour of sun,
call them "barbarians," you who have murdered,
bind them, imprison men of the people,
send to the gallows, remember that May!

Voices well, cordial their resonance,
far is it heard, returning the May song,
memorial answer: There is no lapse,
only replenishment, urging new motion,
gathering impetus, further momentum,
fury well-ordered, securely ascendant.
Green are the Haymarket graves.

Masters of provocation, Pinkertons of prey,
O "Board of Trade men, merchant princes,
railroad kings and factory lords,"
balance your ledgers and take your rewards,
these are the days of liquidation!

Harry Alan POTAMKIN

LAST JUROR PASSES AWAY

Theodore Denker, said to be the last member of the jury that tried and found guilty the Haymarket Square Anarchists, has died from the strain of the case, which so affected him that he lost his mind.

Of the jury that heard the case of the Anarchists, every member, Denker last of all, has met death under peculiar circumstances. Denker was confined in the State Insane Asylum at Elgin ever since the trial, excepting for short infrequent intervals when he was permitted to return home. His death occurred at the asylum.

Denker was forty-seven years old and lived at 214 East 63rd Street, where his wife conducts a restaurant. The notoriety to which the members of the jury and everybody connected with the case was subjected at the time of the trial was so great that Mrs. Denker has tried to conceal the fact that her husband was a member of the jury.

Denker was objected to at the trial on the ground that he might be prejudiced, as he was of the same nationality as the defendants. He was finally accepted, however, as the eleventh juror. Soon after the trial and execution of the anarchists Denker began to act strangely and his mind gave way. He was adjudged insane and taken to the asylum.

Death was due, according to the coroner's physician, to softening of the brain.

Chicago American,
April 13, 1904

FROM HAYMARKET SQUARE TO TRAFALGAR SQUARE:
WILLIAM MORRIS & *COMMONWEAL*

In an article entitled "Free Speech in America," in *Commonweal*, 8th October, 1887, William Morris wrote of the Haymarket events:

. . .it will be a disgrace to the British workmen, whatever their politics may be, if they do not express themselves clearly and emphatically on this attack on the liberties which the United States have been supposed to guard so jealously, but which it would seem are but a one-sided affair after all.

In making this call to his readers—mostly members, like himself, of the Socialist League—Morris did not hesitate to do as he preached. Moreover, in one major article after another, he sought to link the experiences of the American worker, in particular the active socialist or anarchist, with those of his counterpart in Britain; and to demonstrate a similarity of response by the police, judiciary and press to any protest action which took place. To him, the clear cause of the antagonism was commercialism in the shape of the "money-lord."

From its inception, Morris had seen to it that the Socialist League and its paper, *The Commonweal*, had strong international links, and during the Chicago events regular "Letters" were sent from, first, William Holmes, on the happenings around 4th May 1886, then later from Henry F. Charles. Morris's son-in-law, H. Halliday Sparling also supplied news, as did Edward Aveling. The regular column by Eleanor Marx-Aveling, *Record of the International Movement*, turned at this time to American news, and this team supplied strong evidence of the suspect and unconvincing evidence of "witnesses," the bias of the courts and above all of the despicable role of the press as the lackey of capitalism. Examples were quoted, as when the Chicago *Times* called for the closure of all pubic halls to socialists and the suppression of their doctrines, emphasizing the foreignness of the "guilty" anarchists: "It is the descendants of this mixture of Scythian, Hun and devil who have invaded the peaceful shores of the Republic." To this, Sparling retorted (*Commonweal*, 29 May 1886), that the foreigner and "stranger within the gates" is always blamed when people turn turbulent. "The bourgeois press. . .as here, recognises that its 'freedom' only lasts as long as it will rant, crouch, whine and snivel at the bidding of the money-bag."

It was clear to the *Commonweal* correspondents that "the police had come to fight, and fight they would." After the bombthrowing, reports claimed consistently that "socialists are hunted like wolves, simply because they are socialists," every bit as malignantly as in the Germany or Russia of that time— and only fellow socialists had condemned it; the trade unions of Chicago had not done so. Overoptimistically, Edward Aveling was reporting a "complete change" in public opinion by January 1887, predicting a retrial and acquittal. Later that year, Charles instanced the prevention of a meeting taking place by prohibiting the use of the Union Hill Skating Rink, North Hudson County, New Jersey, by Local Assembly 1864 of the Knights of Labor and a small section of the Socialistic Labor Party which was to have protested against the "judicial murder" of the anarchists. By such means, Charles and the others were saying, free speech was being denied in the United States.

In article after leading article, Morris linked the fight for free speech in America with the struggle going on in the British Isles. As early as 15th May 1886 he wrote of Chicago: "Long since was it well known that the first opportunity would be taken by the authorities for a display (if possible, a *use*) of force against a Socialist meeting." Then, prophetically, the day before Bloody Sunday,* he wrote of the shopkeepers of Trafalgar Square that they were very angry at the gatherings of the unemployed and the speeches being regularly made there:

Perhaps they will go further, and imitate their brethren on the other side of the Atlantic, and get another Pinkerton army here; they will find that very inconvenient no doubt; but it will have the disadvantage of war—in the long run the knocks wouldn't be all on one side.

As with the Union Skating Rink, so with the Cleveland Hall in London, which was closed by the police after it had been advertised as the venue of a protest meeting, in October 1887, in support of "The Condemned Anarchists." In the event, this meeting *was* held—crowded, international —at the Communist Club, Tottenham Street, with Morris in the chair. Repression tried its hand even in "quiet Thames country," when the village hall at Buscott was closed by the squire to prevent Morris talking on socialism and the disturbances in London. The meeting went ahead at the rectory!

Morris queried why Socialist League meetings were only now being attacked and harassed by the police, when they had been meeting in now "traditional" open-air spots and halls for some eighteen months. He put it down to the "susceptibilities of the rich" and recommended to Sir Charles Warren, who was acting as though London were in a state of siege, to peruse the Illinois Conspiracy Law (given in *Commonweal*, 19th November 1887), for ". . .it will simplify matters considerably for him if he can get it passed by the English legislature; it assuredly will aid him in the cold-blooded and brutal work in which he is engaged, which is his function."

Morris's own function, as didactic editor and now seasoned campaigner, led him to doubt whether the trial of the Chicago anarchists would be a fair one, in view of his experience of English ones. There were a number of those to judge by: one in particular bore resemblances to the Chicago events, namely that in Norwich where, rather like Parsons and Fielden, two Leaguers, who were not in the meeting initially where a riot followed, were called to it when someone asked for a socialist speaker. Mowbray and Henderson both received sentences of hard labor when arrested. Morris remarked, as he did of the Chicago victims: "comrades are being punished not for rioting but for being socialists." Of the Chicago trial, he wrote: ". . .truly revolutionary soldiers do always fight with a rope round their necks. For the rest no thoughtful and honest man, whether he be Socialist or not. . .will doubt that it was impossible that these men should have a fair trial.'' As he said later of the Trafalgar Square outrage, a confrontation had been necessary in order to find a victim ''whatever the evidence might be.''

The momentum of the campaign was sustained in branches of the Socialist League, where resolutions of protest were passed and collections made to help the families of the executed anarchists. A new feature began in January 1888, clearly inspired by events in Chicago: A *Revolutionary Calendar* was compiled by the League's Librarian and Propaganda Secretary, David Nicoll, a young anarchist. Drawing on events such as the execution of Louis XVI and the death of Herzen, it included a longish article on Thoreau. *Commonweal* had carried biographies of all the condemned anarchists in the weeks after November 1887, and the League produced a special pamphlet, *The Chicago Martyrs*, containing the men's speeches, a record of the trial and portraits.

These sold very well at League branch meetings and public meetings throughout 1888.

Undoubtedly, the culmination of the campaign was the joint anniversary meetings of November 1888, advertised as early as August, promising the presence of Mrs. Lucy Parsons and linking together *Chicago Martyrs and Bloody Sunday* (to the disapproval of such as the Fabian Mrs. Annie Besant). Mrs. Parsons was addressed at a Meat Tea at St. Paul's Churchyard Cafe to open proceedings, and major meetings were held during that and the following weekend: in Hyde Park, Victoria Park and the Wornum Hall. Morris chaired the latter, and speakers included many Leaguers who had been in the recent fray. Most notable perhaps was Prince Peter Kropotkin, the anarchist, for whom Morris shared a mutual respect and warm affection. Mrs. Parsons went on to tour and speak at commemorative meetings in London (including those at the International Club and the Autonomie Club, where she spoke on ''The Labour Movement in America''); and in Glasgow, Edinburgh, Norwich and Ipswich. Her portrait appeared as a supplement to the 10th November *Commonweal*; collections were taken at League branch meetings to help finance her trip and the tour was largely organised by the League.

There is little doubt that the Chicago affair helped increase the popularity of anarchism in Britain for a time at least, largely because of people's revulsion for the ruthless actions of the authorities there. It is also true that in the long run, Morris lost control of both the Socialist League and *Commonweal* to the anarchist members, with a number of whom he had worked amicably for several years—such men as Frank Kitz, Joseph Lane and David Nicoll. Morris's own views led him to sympathise with theirs to some extent: he had no time for over-centralised State Socialism; he loathed the huge impersonality of modern industrial cities, preferring a small unit of society (''the commune or ward or parish'') for its basis. Moreover, his anti-parliamentary views together with his internationalism had led him to break with Hyndman and the Democratic Federation.

Soon, however, he rejected what he regarded as the destructivism and negativism of the anarchists, under the impact of which all Socialist League cohesion fell. There were signs that the agitation, education and organisation of the growing Labour movement was making progress; the vote and the industrial struggle now seemed valid: first steps on a long road. Even so, the American struggle was a significant episode and Morris recognized its worth to the full, in the fight against ''that spirit of cold cruelty, heartless and careless at once, which is one of the most noticeable characteristics of American commercialism'' (*Commonweal*, 24 September 1887).

Beryl RUEHL

CHICAGO MURDERS

AND

BLOODY SUNDAY.

''Let the voice of the people be heard.''—*Parsons.*

A MEETING

To Celebrate the Anniversary of above events

WILL BE HELD ON

MONDAY EVENING, NOVEMBER 11TH,

AT

SOUTH PLACE INSTITUTE

South Place, Moorgate Street, Finsbury.

The following comrades will speak:—James Blackwell, Frank Kitz, Peter Kropotkin, C. W. Mowbray, Wm. Morris, D. J. Nicoll, H. H. Sparling, John Turner and Lothrop Withington.

Eleanor Aveling, G. Brocher, F. Fregenbaum, Dr. Merlino and S. Stepniak have also been invited.

Revolutionary songs will be sung during the evening, including the '' Marseillaise,'' ''Carmagnole,'' ''Linnell's Death Song,'' '' When the People have their Own Again,'' and '' Annie Laurie.''

By order of the Committee,

THE SOCIALIST LEAGUE.

13, Farringdon Road, E.C.

And 24 Great Queen Street, Lincoln's Inn Fields, W.

A leaflet from 1889

* *Bloody Sunday*: 13th November 1887, just two days after the four Chicago anarchists were executed, police charged a crowd largely of unemployed in Trafalgar Square in London, protesting Coercion. Three hundred were arrested. Three died as a result of injuries. Morris himself—who had twice been arrested, in 1885 and 1886—was present in Trafalgar Square on Bloody Sunday, with the contingent for Clerkenwell Green, in the East End. The incident, which shocked many who were not socialists, is regarded as the major instance of police brutality in the British struggle for free speech.

An early Danish portrait of the Haymarket Martyrs

BETWEEN CLASS SOLIDARITY AND POLITICAL CRITICISM:
The Danish Social-Democracy & the Chicago Murders

The Danish labor movement was founded in 1871 as a section of the International Working Men's Association, and soon achieved a relatively high degree of popularity. From the outset in its political work it combined political and trade union efforts, which brought it into the proximity of Marxist positions; these were extended on the basis of the internationalism of the movement which, in turn, rested on the experience of major parts of the working class.

Many of the trade unions established between 1871 and 1876 did not survive the recession of the late 1870s, but those that did survive were almost exclusively social-democratic. The liberal, charitable, Conservative and Christian associations which existed or were established in the following years did not gain any real influence in the working class.

The organizational crisis of the social-democratic Danish labor movement was overcome in the early 1880s, but a dispute concerning political theory arose within the movement. There had of course been differing attitudes in the movement concerning the correct way to establish socialism. It must also be taken for granted that members had differing ideas as to what socialism was. However, the discussions of the 1870s had had as a result that the movement rejected a dogmatic Lassalleanism, *i.e.*, it maintained a combination of trade union and political struggle. The third aspect of the struggle—the theoretical—was also taken up: The *Social-Demokraten* published important contributions toward an understanding of the practical struggle, including articles by Wilhelm Liebknecht, August Bebel and Karl Marx.[1] In the 1870s the political course was not as clear as these names might seem to suggest, but it was hardly a coincidence that the Danish delegate to the International Working Men's Association congress in The Hague, 1872, supported Marx.

Around 1880-81, however, oppositional ideas made themselves felt within the movement, criticizing the moderate leadership which the movement had had since 1878. This opposition was "revolutionary"—that is, it rejected party work, trade-union work, participation in parliamentary elections, and had as its only tactical option the armament of the working class, or rather of its "revolutionary vanguard." In other words, it was essentially of a "putschistic" nature.

The opposition had traditions behind it, and it also had successors after having withered away in the course of 1881. But the immediate outcome was that the moderate leadership of the party and the press had been replaced by people who were better-educated theoretically, and had a more profound understanding of the link between theoretical and practical work. The discussion had also resulted in a rejection of anarchism—or what was considered anarchism, with its "putschistic" tactics.

In the following years the new political line in the Social-Democracy triumphed. Party and trade-union membership increased substantially, circulation of the labor press multiplied, two members of parliament were elected and the initial volumes of a "Socialist Library" were published, including translations of the first two volumes of Marx's *Capital*, in 1886 and 1888. During these years the movement had developed a coherent theory and practice largely identical to that of Social-Democracies elsewhere. Nevertheless, there continued to exist a radical opposition within the party, which surfaced at the 1888 party conference and was expelled by the end of the following year.

The daily newspaper *Social-Demokraten* followed developments in the labor movements of other countries carefully, publishing long articles as well as innumerable short notes which together supplied quite an exhaustive description. Articles were often translated from U.S. newspapers, such as the Chicago *Vorbote* and the *New Yorker Volks-Zeitung*. On May 5, 1886 there was a lengthy note concerning the U.S. strikes and demonstrations for the eight-hour day. It was emphasized that the socialist elements in these demonstrations had been especially pronounced in Chicago.[2] On the following day came the report of the Haymarket massacre.

The paper's first reports on Haymarket were based on telegrams received from Reuters and the Danish news-agency, Ritzau. The editors made clear, however, that they did not give much credence to these telegrams: "Both Reuters and Ritzau have a tendency to make the workers responsible for all the crimes engendered by the capitalist system." Nevertheless, the paper also pointed out that Chicago was a stronghold of American anarchism, and that the difference "between dynamiters and Social-Democracy" must be kept in mind.

The following days brought more information concerning the fight for the eight-hour day and the Chicago struggle in

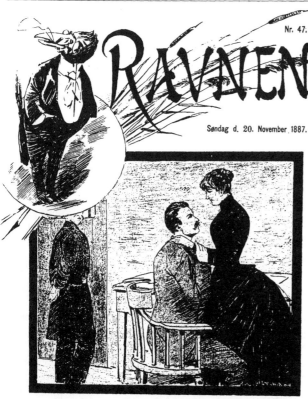

Nr. 47.

RAVNEN

Søndag d. 20. November 1887.

August Spies og hans Hustru i Fængslet.

Cover of the Danish socialists' satirical weekly *Ravnen*, featuring August and Nina van Zandt Spies

particular. On May 8 *Social-Demokraten* pointed out that it had been the Chicago police who had attacked the workers, and that the workers had only defended themselves. In a May 9 editorial on "The Labor Movement in Chicago," the general development of the city was described, and the experience of the working class there compared with equivalent experience in Denmark. Two days later the Berlin *Volkszeitung* was quoted as having the opinion that socialist workers do not fight in the way in which the Chicago anarchists had apparently fought. In the following days still further information was brought in, but little distinction was made between atrocity stories and real news.

In a series of letters written by Wilhelm Liebknecht for *Social-Demokraten*, he touched on the Chicago events (May 13). Liebknecht dissociated himself politically from Johann Most and the anarchists in general. He assumed, however, that their strength had been overestimated, and he was convinced that the anarchists were not strong among the working classes.

Subsequent issues published a number of notes on the development of the eight-hour struggle, criticism of the Knights of Labor for its stance in the railway strike, news of Johann Most's arrest and release, and even an article by Most, from the *Freiheit*.

Not until May 21 did *Social-Demokraten* analyze the "Chicago Unrest" in an editorial. This editorial began by making clear that the bloodshed in Chicago was mainly due to the behavior of the police, who had been recruited from among the worst hoods of the city and were consequently characterized by extreme brutality. It was further argued that the police had had no just cause for interfering with the Haymarket meeting; that it had been "unconstitutional" for them to have done so; that there was no proof whatever that any worker had thrown the bomb; and that the workers, at the meeting, were "defending their completely legitimate rights." The editorial also insisted that the Chicago anarchists—who in contradistinction to Most had joined the eight-hour movement—were completely justified in propagating their opinions. In the view of *Social-Demokraten*, the Haymarket events had been given such prominence in the press in order to "compromise the eight-hour-day movement as much as possible."

Social-Demokraten also published an exhaustive report from Chicago (byline J.B.), that included a detailed factual description of the course of events. Gradually, Danish Social-Democrats were able to gain a reasonable impression of the police attack and the external circumstances leading to it. To this was added the first account of the workers arrested, and the incident was now directly linked to the eight-hour struggle. In a supplementary article on the following day (translated from the German weekly *Der Sozialdemokrat*) the tactics of Powderly and the Knights of Labor were criticized, and the growing trade union movement praised, although the writer did criticize what he regarded as its insufficient understanding of the political struggle. Furthermore, arguments in favor of Johann Most were put forward—without, however, retracting the criticism leveled against him and anarchism (*Social-Demokraten*, June 24 and 25).

In July, three long articles were published on the labor movement in the U.S., translated from American party papers, particularly the *New Yorker Volks-Zeitung*. But these articles dealt solely with the eight-hour struggle and wage strikes. In an August article, *Social-Demokraten* stated that "the North American republic finds itself in the middle of a class struggle between proletariat and bourgeoisie." The paper continued its coverage of this struggle by means of a lecture by Dr. Ernst Schmidt, a German-born Chicago socialist who had insisted on the necessity of working politically for the liberation of the working class (August 25). This line of thought was continued in succeeding reports on various initiatives toward the establishment of a labor party; however, Henry George's candidacy in the New York mayoral election was viewed with a certain amount of skepticism.

Only on the 25th of September did the paper report the protests against "The Blood Judgments of Chicago." According to the paper, the protest movement implied that the workers of the U.S. were joining ranks for a class movement irrespective of ethnic and political position. Similarly, a Knights of Labor resolution in favor of the sentenced anarchists was welcomed (October 30). In a polemic with the Danish Conservative newspaper *Berlingske Tidende*, the *Social-Demokraten* stated that workers had been aroused "by the cruel sentences" in Chicago, and had now started to work for an independent political party founded on socialist ideas, according to *Berlingske Tidende* itself.

After the American elections on November 2nd, the paper published several reports concerning the good results, indicating that in addition to the German workers, the Anglo-American workers also were now joining the new socialist party. In the December 14th issue the paper further drew the conclusion that

When comparing the *terror* of the American bourgeoisie over the *election results* on the 2nd of November with the *joy* of the American bourgeoisie over the *Chicago May-bombs*, it must become clear also to less clear-thinking people *which tactics* the proletariat has to follow in order to destroy the supremacy of capitalism. . . . Those workers who have hitherto believed in the *dynamite cliches* have had the scales removed from their eyes, and when Liebknecht spoke to a mass meeting largely consisting of former "anarchists" on the 5th of November his words of reconciliation were received with *unanimous* and *enthusiastic* applause. . . . The fact of the matter is: In America there has never existed an anarchist party. . .the program which the the Chicago convicts have supported before the jury is— apart from some cliches—the *socialist program*.

Already prior to this analysis the paper had severely attacked the biased judgment of the Chicago court (November 11). Nevertheless, it kept criticizing the anarchists in strong terms—to some extent even in a libelous manner (December 14)—for being caught in police traps which they could not avoid because of their phraseology (January 5, 1887).

Until September 1887 *Social-Demokraten* did not report anything concerning the sentenced Chicago workers, but it did print a number of articles and reports on developments in the U.S. which, in the paper's annual survey (January 7, 1887), were evaluated as moving in the right direction. But in the September 17th edition the paper tersely stated that the death sentences had been confirmed. A month later (October 16) it published a long excerpt from August Spies' *Autobi-*

ography. Starting with the November 5th issue, reports were published almost daily—concerning protest resolutions, refutations of the court's impartiality, and criticism of the trial procedure.

After the executions, *Social-Demokraten* published short biographies of all the convicted men, as well as other pertinent reports and documents. Between November 27, 1887 and January 3, 1888 the paper published—on the front page—the Chicago prisoners' last statements in court, together with excerpts from their autobiographies (including that of Louis Lingg).[3]

In its survey of the development of the international labor movement, *Social-Demokraten* (January 7, 1888) naturally took up the U.S. and stated that

the most important event of the year was the execution of the Chicago anarchist leaders. This event has widened the gulf between capitalists and workers even more. It will be the task of American socialism to win the proletariat for a more dignified and efficacious way of struggling than the one favored by the anarchists. . . .

Gerd CALLESEN

1. Gerd Callesen and John Logue, eds. *Social-Demokraten and Internationalism: The Copenhagen Social-Democratic Newspaper's Coverage of International Labor Affairs, 1871-1958* (Kent, Ohio, 1979).   2. Even though a Danish/Norwegian-language socialist weekly, *Den Nye Tid*, was published in Chicago from 1878 to ? (the paper has not yet been found in any library), the socialist movement was very weak among Danish-American workers in the 1880s. See Jens Bjerre Danielsen, "The Early Danish Immigrant Socialist Press," in Dirk Hoerderr, ed. *Essays on the Scandinavian-North American Radical Press, 1880s-1930s* (Bremen, 1984), 56-76.   3. The Danish social-democracy also published an illustrated satirical weekly, *Ravnen*, which, on November 20, 1887, published an issue with colored drawings of the convicted anarchists. This number was published in three large issues in the course of a very few days—and the drawings were included as free extras in the following number.

Ringing the workers' May Day liberty bell: Cover of *La Nigra Flago*, periodical of the Japanese Anarchist Federation (*circa* 1920s)

ACRACIA

REVISTA SOCIOLÓGICA

Publicación mensual de treinta y dos páginas, á **una peseta** trimestre, y más el exceso de franqueo en el extranjero

Noviembre de 1887

Año II   N.º 23

La correspondencia administrativa y de redacción dirijase á Bienvenido Rius, San Olegario, 2, pral.; **Barcelona**

La razón ha de ceder hoy el puesto al sentimiento. No podemos hoy razonar con nuestros amigos lectores; hemos de expresar la indignación que nos causa ver á nuestros hermanos pendientes de la horca ó condenados á cadena perpetua ó temporal. Hemos de exhalar nuestra protesta contra el crimen perpetrado por la República. Hemos de consignar el hecho de que esa institución hipócrita que, manchada con sangre de liberales y envilecida con la riqueza de la explotación y la usura, sumerge en espantosa miseria á los productores y lleva al patíbulo á los apóstoles de la libertad. Una vez más el capitalismo dominante ha puesto de manifiesto que en la lucha por la justicia, los intereses propenden única y exclusivamente á su conservación y cortan por lo sano hollando todo pacto y toda ley. No cabe dudar ya que la dificultad única que el progreso ha de arrollar para seguir su marcha es el principio de autoridad; porque mientras exista, el que mande ó los que manden, de su propia esencia y de la necesaria pasividad de los mandados, sacarán fuerzas para cumplir su obra de tiranía. Autoridad y obediencia son términos incompatibles con la dignidad humana, sea cualquiera el régimen político y la diferente manera en que se halle establecido cómo unos hombres deben mandar y cómo otros deben obedecer. La horca de Chicago es nuestro irrebatible argumento. Accionistas de grandes compañías cuyas acciones se cotizan con grandes beneficios y trabajadores reducidos á la más esquilmada reducción de la mano de obra ó al paro forzoso, todos viven bajo el falso nivel de una constitución democrática, y el resultado, ya lo veis, es un atropello sin precedente, porque no tiene la excusa de la barbarie del absolutismo, no se justifica por la pasión del fanatismo de secta, no puede dispensarse por la excitación revolucionaria; es un atropello cometido á sangre fría en nombre de la ley, en nombre de la libertad, en nombre de la República. Con este motivo ACRACIA dedica esta página como un cariñoso recuerdo á los mártires de Chicago, como una protesta contra la República-verdugo y como una lección á los trabajadores.

SPIES

PARSONS

FISCHER

ENGEL

LINGG

SCHWAB

FIELDEN

NEEBE

Spanish anarchist typographical workers designed this unique homage to
"Los Martires de Chicago" in November 1887

THE ORIGINS OF MAY DAY IN SPAIN:

The Haymarket Tragedy and Its Impact,
1886-1890

The intense labor agitation associated with the campaign for the eight-hour day in the United States created an immense stir, not only in America, but in Europe as well. This was apparent during the latter part of the 1880s and especially following the celebrated Haymarket Affair of 1886, when thousands of European workers and those who were sympathetic to their cause held massive demonstrations to protest first the trial and then the execution of the Chicago anarchists. The repercussions of these events were felt for many years afterward; the most notable being the celebration of May 1st as an international workers' holiday. Of all the European countries, it was in Spain that the eight-hour campaign in America and the affair of the Chicago anarchists were to have the profoundest effects on the development of the working classes. This was largely because of the important position anarchism (and to a lesser extent socialism) held among the workers. Precisely how "May Day" and the Haymarket tragedy affected the Spanish labor movement in the period 1886-1890 is the subject of this paper.

THE EIGHT-HOUR CAMPAIGN AND THE ORIGINS OF MAY DAY IN SPAIN

With the founding of the Spanish section of the First International in 1868, anarchism became the principal intellectual and organizing force of both the agricultural and industrial proletariat.[1]

The workers do not understand that they have initiated this movement in order to reach a state in which it is normal within an eight hour day to earn a salary with which one can attend in a dignified manner the necessities of civilized man, this is a true utopia; they propose to conduct war against the privileges of the bourgeoisie, to produce disturbances, to begin the revolutionary period that has as its end the abolishment of wages.[2]

Like their American comrades, the Spanish anarchists came to regard May Day as an occasion for staging violent protests—usually in the form of a revolutionary general strike—which could be used by the workers not only to achieve their demands for improved working conditions but also to demonstrate their power in the class war against the bourgeoisie. The anarchists, then, attached a revolutionary significance to the campaign for an eight-hour day and the celebration of May Day, and as we shall see, this distinguished them from the socialists and other reformist-minded sections of the Spanish working classes who placed their faith in legal action as a way of furthering workers' interests.

THE CHICAGO MARTYRS AND THE CELEBRATION OF NOVEMBER ELEVENTH

Following the notorious Haymarket affair of May 1886, the eight-hour movement in America became the focus of labor groups and radicals around the world. The incident itself represented, in the words of the historian Paul Avrich, "the culmination of a decade of strikes and agitation" in this campaign. As the details of the affair are well known there is no need to recount them here. Suffice it to say that although the Haymarket bomb explosion alone created quite a sensation—especially among the middle-classes—what primarily disturbed the international working classes was the gross miscarriage of justice carried out against the eight Chicago anarchists who were held responsible for the bombing. On November 11, 1887, against a background of worldwide protests, the State of Illinois put to death Fischer, Engel, Parsons and Spies.

In Spain the deaths of the Chicago anarchists had a two-fold significance. On one level, their executions served to reinforce the revolutionary connotations of May Day, for the four men were generally identified as martyrs of the eight-hour movement. Yet, quite apart from their association with May Day, the Chicago martyrs themselves became a symbol of inspiration for Spanish workers of all schools of thought.

For the anarchists, the hangings illustrated graphically what they had long argued in their antistatist credo, namely, that the state was by nature repressive—whether it was the autocratic kind found in Russia or the democratic republic (*republica modelo*), the United States: \

Authority and obedience are terms that are incompatible with human dignity; no matter what kind of political regime it may be and in whatever manner it may have been established, some men are obliged to rule and others are obliged to obey them. The scaffold of Chicago is our irrefutable argument of this.[3]

But the executions in Chicago did more than just provide the anarchists with a pretext for asserting the validity of their doctrine. Perhaps more significantly, the incident had the immediate effect of inflaming the tempers of the Spanish anarchists, thereby giving fresh impetus to their revolutionary movement. Obviously outraged by what had happened, the anarchists declared their determination to avenge the "legal murders" of their comrades, who were now being referred to as the "Chicago Martyrs." Even moderate libertarians, like the highly respected intellectual Ricardo Mella, were moved to make incendiary speeches. In one of his widely-read pamphlets, Mella proclaimed defiantly that "the terrible tragedy of Chicago was the bloody harbinger of the definitive triumph of the proletariat," and in workingclass clubs and meeting halls (*ateneos* and *centros obreros*) everywhere these sentiments were echoed again and again by those who cried "Eternal praise to the Chicago Martyrs! Long live Anarchy! Long live the Social Revolution!"[4]

By the next year, the date "November Eleventh" had acquired the status of a workers' holiday and it was commonly

La Anarquia (Madrid), November 11, 1891
honoring "Los Martires de Chicago"

recognized as being as important an event as the commemoration of the Paris Commune.[5] Reporting in the London anarchist journal *Freedom*, a Spanish correspondent explained its significance in the following way: "This date [November 11th] is in Spain a workers' holy day, and also an occasion for Anarchist demonstrations and propaganda. In all of the great cities, and in many country towns, the people commemorate the death of the noble workers, whose martyrdom instead of degrading them, glorified the instrument, at the same time that they view with horror the disgusting and untimely social institutions which now exist..."[6] The ceremonies of the "holy day" were usually held in the evening, when, after having worked a full day, the workers would gather at their trade union local or town hall. The walls of these meeting places were decorated with brightly colored red and black banners that encircled large portraits (*retratos*) of the Chicago Martyrs as well as other venerated figures of the socialist movement such as Pierre J. Proudhon and Michael Bakunin. Following several brief introductory speeches about the significance of the date, the meeting was given over to readings of prose and poetry pieces dedicated to the memory of all those who had fallen victim to state persecution. Although a somber atmosphere prevailed over these proceedings, toward the end of the meeting the solemn mood was abruptly broken when the audience rose to its feet and burst into spirited songs and verses espousing the glory of the Chicago Martyrs and the emancipation of man by man.[7]

Despite the fact that the anarchist trade union organization, *Federacion de Trabajadores de la Region Espanola* (FTRE), was gradually breaking up in the period 1886-1888, the Chicago Martyrs continued to arouse considerable interest among the anarchists until the early 1890s. The revolutionary spirit engendered by the Haymarket tragedy was kept alive not just by the annual memorials referred to above but in a variety of ways. For example, the anarchists raised money to be sent to the families of the Chicago Martyrs, devoted whole issues of their periodicals to the subject of the Haymarket affair, and even gave their affinity groups such names as "The Martyrs of Chicago" and "The Eleventh of November"—the latter of which paid tribute to their American comrades in 1889 by organizing what turned out to be the largest and perhaps most significant workingclass cultural event to take place in Spain during the nineteenth century, the Second Socialist Literary Competition (*Segundo Certamen Socialista*).

Around this time many anarchists began voicing their concern that May Day itself was rapidly losing its revolutionary origins. This was happening, according to them, because it was being converted by the socialists into "...a day of ritual, of cults and idolatry..."[8]

MAY DAY AND THE SECOND INTERNATIONAL

At the founding Congress of the Second International held in Paris in July 1889, it was decided to follow the American example and adopt May 1st as an international workers' holiday. As far as the socialists were concerned, May Day was meant to serve several purposes—not only was it a way of demonstrating the solidarity and political effectiveness of the international workingclass movement, it was, above all, a way of giving dramatic expression to their resolve to reduce the working day by law to eight hours. The Spanish delegate Pablo Iglesias spoke for many others when he stated that May Day should be recognized as a universal public manifestation by all those who suffered under the yoke of "the oppressing classes." He went on to declare:

For that reason, because it affirms the class struggle so powerfully and announces to the proletarians a certain triumph, the May 1st demonstration is more than an action full of pomp and beauty—it is an action that is supremely useful to the working class.[9]

For all their apparent enthusiasm for staging May Day demonstrations, the socialists could not agree on the specific form of action that was to be taken on this day.[10] Some, like the Austrians and the majority of the French delegation, advocated a complete stoppage of work on May Day in order to display the economic leverage that lay behind workers' demands. On the other hand, the Germans, who represented the largest and best organized section of the Second International, did not share this view, and therefore they refused to pledge themselves to any tactic which implied strike action. Lacking a consensus on how May Day was to be celebrated, the Congress finally adopted a resolution which left this decision to the the respective socialist parties:

The workers of the various countries will have to accomplish the manifestation under the conditions imposed on them by the particular situation in each country.[11]

224

Interestingly enough, the debates surrounding this issue were brought up again at the 1891 Brussels and 1893 Zurich Congresses. Those who stressed the necessity of stopping all work on May Day argued that this was in keeping with the revolutionary spirit of the holiday, whereas the Germans, whose votes ultimately determined the outcome of the question, persisted in their opposition to the strike tactic. Thus, by the end of 1893, the Second International was, at least temporarily, forced to abandon the idea of using May Day as a manifestation of the solidarity among the international working classes.[12]

MAY DAY AND SPANISH SOCIALISM

In order to understand the impact May Day had on Spanish socialism, one has to bear in mind several facts about the early development of the movement. Since its foundation in 1879, the Socialist Party (*Partido Socialista Obrero Espanol, PSOE*) had endured a miserable existence. The party's efforts to attract a following among the workers had met with little success except within certain unions, like the Typographers Union in Madrid — which was predominantly Marxist — and the reformist labor groups in Barcelona, principally the textile association *Tres Clases de Vapor* (TCV). During the 1880s the socialists passed through a phase which one historian has likened to "crossing the desert." The only promising developments of the period came in March 1886, when the PSOE began publishing its own mouthpiece, *El Socialista*, and in August 1888, when a trade union branch of the party, the *Union General de Trabajadores* (UGT), was established in the industrial region of Catalonia.

The early evolution of socialist ideology was a crucial factor in determining the position socialism held among the working classes. Deeply influenced by the French Marxists, the Spanish socialists maintained a doctrinaire view of their relationship to other labor groups. On a practical level, this entailed eschewing political alliances with the bourgeoisie on the one hand, and rejecting the ultrarevolutionary tactics of the anarchists on the other. Thanks to this dogmatic ideological stance, the socialists remained, during the first part of the Restoration (1875-1899), isolated from the mainstream of the labor movement.

It therefore followed that their May Day demonstrations had to be conducted according to the principles of socialism. Because they were unswervingly committed to political methods, the socialists seriously questioned the efficacy of using strikes and other economic weapons as a means of advancing the social revolution. Their goal was to achieve control of the local and national governments through electoral organization and propaganda. As regards May Day, this meant that the socialists favored the idea of holding strikes as long as their overall aim was strictly limited to improving working conditions (*las huelgas parciales*). They would have none of the anarchist concept of the insurrectionary general strike (*la huelga general*).

As the first socialist-sponsored May Day drew nearer, it became increasingly evident to the socialist leadership that they could not coordinate the demonstrations in the different regions. Socialist strength and influence was, as we have seen, negligible in most areas, and even in Madrid, the headquarters

of the PSOE, there was no mass base for the movement. However, in Barcelona, where the UGT had been founded, socialism was more advanced. In fact, ever since the mid-1880s the socialists there had come out in favor of the eight-hour day, and had even supported the anarchist-inspired Internal Commission of Eight Hours created in 1886.

Given the uneven development of their movement and given their uncertainty of how both the workers and the bourgeoisie would react to their call for May Day demonstrations, the Spanish socialists decided to hold their first May Day events on two different days, May 1st in Barcelona and May 4th in Madrid.[13] Both occasions reflected the cautious attitude adopted by the socialist leaders. Antonio Garcia Quejido, the popular head of the UGT, led the demonstration in Barcelona, while the leading lights of the PSOE, Pablo Iglesias and Matias Gomez Latorre, presided over the one in Madrid.[14]

The May Day activities of the socialists in Barcelona were overshadowed by a paralyzing general strike which had been called by the anarchists. Refusing to involve themselves in the strike — which dragged on for another four days — the socialists proceeded with their own demonstration. They convoked a meeting in the Tivoli Theater, after which an estimated twenty thousand workers marched to the office of the Governor General to present him with a petition of workers' demands. Then, without a hint of disturbance, the socialist procession broke up and the workers returned to their homes.

A journal from Catalonia, May Day, 1893

Portraits—or *retratos*—of "Los Martires de Chicago" were long popular among Spanish workers and were often sold for a few *pesetas* at Haymarket memorial meetings held every year on November Eleventh. This one is from Barcelona, 1890.

In contrast to Barcelona, May Day events in Madrid took place in a relatively tranquil atmosphere. There some two thousand workers assembled at the gardens located in the Buen Retiro where they listened quietly to speeches delivered at the Liceo Reus. When this meeting concluded they, along with several thousand others, marched to the Council of the Presidency where they presented the liberal Prime Minister Sagasta with a list of their demands.[15]

Elsewhere in Spain, May Day celebrations were of little consequence, except in the Basque city of Bilbao where a demonstration touched off an impressive strike. Although during the 1880s socialist ideas were only beginning to penetrate the mining districts of the north, by 1890 it was becoming increasingly apparent that socialism had found echo among the militant miners. This was abundantly manifested in Bilbao following the demonstration held on May 4th. In response to the miners' show of solidarity, the owner of the *La Orconera* mine dismissed all of the workers belonging to the socialist group called *La Arboleda*. On the 12th, miners from several pits replied by going out on strike, demanding not only the reinstatement of the fired workers, but also improved living conditions (for the mine owners were responsible for building the shoddy barracks in which the miners and their families lived) and the reduction of the workday from between 12 and 14 hours to ten. By the 15th, over 15,000 miners and approximately 12,000 other workers from the neighboring towns and villages (*e.g.*, carpenters, cabinet-makers and marblecutters) had joined the strike. At this point, however, government troops were called in to crush their resistance, and as a result, the strike movement collapsed.[16]

It is noteworthy that the Bilbao strike had not been planned by the socialists, and, more important, it was clearly an example of the general strike tactic which in principle had been rejected outright by the leadership. Nevertheless, the propaganda value of the strike was not lost on figures like Pablo Iglesias who joined others in declaring it an important socialist victory. He pointed out, for instance, that as a result of the miners' action their workday was reduced to ten hours and their abysmal dwellings ("cuarteles") were declared by the authorities to be unfit for habitation. With respect to the socialist movement, the strike itself was to have lasting significance; for, more than any other single event of the period, it served as an impetus for the growth of socialism in the Basque region.

THE LEGACY OF MAY DAY

Although occasionally interrupted by a strike like the one in Bilbao, the nonrevolutionary pattern of activity established at the socialists' May Day demonstrations of 1890 remained unbroken in the coming years. Because it was bound up with the issue of the eight-hour day, May Day had provided both the socialists and the anarchists with a potentially powerful rallying point for their respective movements. In another sense, though, it was also true that the introduction of May Day, far from promoting solidarity among the diverse groups of Spanish workers, simply threw into sharper relief the ideological boundaries that were dividing them into opposing camps.

226

The issue of the revolutionary general strike represented the biggest obstacle in the process of reconciliation between the anarchists and socialists. The socialists, while willing to admit that limited strikes served to radicalize the workers and thus foster solidarity among them, never tired of preaching about the shortcomings of the general strike tactic, calling it the product of "woolly thinking" (*un pensamiento descabellado*). Yet, ironically, one violent or highly disruptive strike—such as the one that occurred in Bilbao—probably did more to advance the socialist cause than did years of carefully orchestrated and pacific demonstrations held on May Day.

Even though the anarchists never lost their faith in the *huelga general* as a means of generating revolutionary solidarity among the workers, after 1892 it became increasingly difficult for them to mount large-scale strikes on May Day. This was partly due to increased government repression of the anarchist movement and partly because the anarchists themselves were abandoning the trade unions and instead were turning more and more towards individual acts of violence or "propaganda by the deed" to oppose the ruling classes. Thus, while the emotional force and symbolic significance of May Day demonstrations were never wholly dispelled for the anarchists, by the mid-1890s they had ceased regarding them as effective vehicles for obtaining workers' rights.

George ESENWEIN

[1] On the history of the International in Spain see especially, Anselmo Lorenzo, *El Proletariado Militante*, (Madrid, 1974); Max Nettlau, *Bakunin y la Alianza en España*, (Buenos Aires, 1925); and Josep Termes, *Anarchismo y syndicalismo en España*, (Barcelona, 1927). [2] *Acracia*, October 1886, 110. [3] *Acracia*, November 1887, 377. [4] *La Solidaridad*, 9 December 1888. It should be pointed out that the "Martyrs" included not only those who had died—liked Louis Lingg who committed suicide while awaiting his execution—but also Samuel Fielden, Oscar Neebe and Michael Schwab, all of whom were later pardoned. [5] Peter Kropotkin made a similar observation in *Freedom*, December 1888; cited in Henry David, *History of the Haymarket Affair* (New York, 1958), 534 and Paul Avrich, *The Haymarket Tragedy* (Princeton, 1984), 412. [6] *Freedom*, January 1890. [7] *La Alarma*, 22 November 1889. [8] Ricardo Mella, "La tragedia de Chicago," in *Cuestiones Sociales* (Valencia, 1912), 271. This originally appeared in the anthology of the *Segundo Certamen Socialista* in 1889. See also, *El Productor*, issues for May and June, 1890. [9] Quoted in Maurice Dommanget, *Histoire du Premier Mai* (Paris, 1972) 415. [10] See James Joll, *The Second International* (New York, 1966), 48-65. [11] Quoted in G.D.H. Cole, *History of Socialist Thought: The Second International, 1889-1914*, Vol. III, Part I, (London, 1956) 9. [12] Phil H. Goodstein, *The Theory of the General Strike from the French Revolution to Poland* (New York, 1984), 110-114. [13] Although at the Paris Congress it was decided to hold May Day manifestations on the 1st, In Great Britain and in parts of Spain demonstrations were held on the 4th (Sunday). In Great Britain this practice reflected the trade unions' desire to avoid both violent confrontations with the authorities and any stoppage of work. [14] Detailed accounts of the 1890 May Day celebrations can be found in *El Socialista* and the anarchist paper *El Productor*. [15] Among other things, they asked for the eight-hour day, the abolishment of night work for women and workers less than eighteen years of age and the prohibition of labor for children under fourteen years old. [16] On the Bilbao strike see, Great Britain, Royal Commission on Labour, *Foreign Reports*, Vol. VII, 1893-1894; and Eugenio Lasa Ayestaran, "Socialismo en Viscaya: La huelga general de Mayo de 1890," in *Tiempo de Historia*, June 1975.

Sources: The best secondary works on the subject of May Day, the Haymarket affair and Spanish anarchism are: Diego Abad de Santillan, *Contribucion a la historia del movimiento obrero español*, Vol. I (Mexico, 1962); Jose Alvarez Junco, *La Ideologica politica del anarquismo español, 1868-1910* (Madrid, 1976); Juan Hernandez Les, "En los inicios del primero de mayo—La cuestion de las ocho horas," in *Tiempo de Historia*, May 1977; Lily Litvak, *Musa Libertaria* (Barcelona, 1981); Max Nettlau, *La Premiere Internationale en Espagne, 1868-1888* (Dordrecht, 1969); Rafael Nunez Florencio, *El terrorismo anarquista, 1888-1909* (Madrid, 1983). On the socialists see: Janvier Aisa (with V.M. Arberloa), *Historia de la Union General de Trabajadores* (Madrid, 1975); Jose Andres Gallego, "La UGT No Nacio Socialista," in *Historia 16*, May 1979; Juan Pablo Fusi, *Politica obrero en el pais vasco* (Madrid, 1975); Miguel Izard, *Revolucio industrial i obrerisme: Les "Tres Clases de Vapor" a Catalaunya* (Barcelona, 1970); Juan Jose Morato, *El partido socialista obrero* (Madrid, 1918 and 1976); Manuel Perez Ledesma, "El Primo de Mayo de 1890. Los Origenes de Una Celebracion," in *Tiempo de Historia*, May 1976; also his "La Union General de Trabajadores: socialismo y reformismo," in *Estudios de Historia Social*, January-June 1979; and chapter vii of his *El movimiento obrero en la historia de España* (Madrid, 1972). Works cited in the footnotes are not repeated here. Instead I have included a brief survey of the literature that deals specifically with the themes of the essay.

KENNETH REXROTH

Protagonist of a short-lived Dadaist group in 1920s Chicago, poet/painter/essayist Kenneth Rexroth (1905-1982) was also for a time a member of the IWW, and to the end of his life he maintained links both to cultural "avant-gardism" and to the libertarian Left. His friends and acquaintances included Mary E. Marcy, Sacco and Vanzetti, Isadora Duncan, Tristan Tzara, Sherwood Anderson, Dylan Thomas, Charlie Parker and many other well-known radicals, poets and artists. His translations of Pierre Reverdy and of Chinese and Japanese poets are highly esteemed. His Autobiographical Novel *(1964) is not a novel at all but a valuable, minutiae-filled memoir.*

The poem reprinted here originally appeared in the first issue of Holley Cantine's Retort, *an anarchist "Quarterly of Social Philosophy and the Arts," Winter, 1942.*

FR

AGAIN AT WALDHEIM

"Rain upon Waldheim"
—Voltairine de Cleyre
on the Haymarket martyrs

*How heavy the heart is now, and every heart
Save only the word drunk, power drunk
Hard capsules of the doomed. How distraught
Those things of pride, the wills nourished in the fat
Years, fed in the kindly twilight of the books
In gold and brown, the voices that had little
To live for, crying for something to die for.
The philosophers of history,
Of dim wit and foolish memory,
The giggling concubines of catastrophe—
Who forget so much—Boethius' calm death,
More's sweet speech, Rosa's broken body—
Or you, tough, stubby recalcitrant
Of Fate.*

     *Now in Waldheim where the rain
Has fallen careless and unthinking
For all an evil century's youth,
Where now the banks of dark roses lie,
What memory lasts, Emma, of you,
Or of the intrepid comrades of your grave,
Of Piotr, of "mutual aid,"
Against the iron clad flame throwing
Course of time?*

      *Your stakes were on the turn
Of a card whose face you knew you would not see.
You knew that nothing could ever be
More desperate than truth; and when every voice
Was cowed, you spoke against the coalitions
For the duration of the emergency—
In the permanent emergency
You spoke for the irrefutable
Coalition of the blood of men.*

Kenneth REXROTH

Drawing by Alfredo Monros

WALDHEIM

At Waldheim Cemetery,
before the monument to
the Chicago Martyrs

The Idea is in mourning,
shrouded is the Idea.
Gravestones of the graveyard
in shapes of sorrow,
attentive and eternal sentries
guard in solemn vigil,
lives at one time cut short;
dreams that got lost. . . .

Federico ARCOS

November 11, 1962

228

PRIMO MAGGIO:
Haymarket as Seen by Italian Anarchists in America

During the many ''pic-nics'' that were held in America by the Italian anarchists, after the food had been eaten, after the propaganda had been ''made,'' after the money had been raised ''pro vittime politiche'' (for political prisoners), there inevitably came the moment when someone would begin to sing old anarchist songs. And always during this musical interlude there came a moment when the soft beginning strains of Verdi's great operatic chorus, ''Va, pensiero, sull'ali dorate'' (Go, thought, upon wings of gold), known by heart to most Italians, would slowly rise and swell to their majestic close, with everyone standing and singing the words as fullthroatedly as possible. Verdi's powerful and moving music, written originally as a lament of the Hebrews by the river Jordan for a home of their own, had been reset to new words by the anarchist poet Pietro Gori, to honor *Primo Maggio*—May Day. It was to such deeply felt occasions, celebrating anarchist dreams of the future and remembering anarchist martyrs of the past, that Bartolomeo Vanzetti looked back upon, shortly before his own execution, as he translated the final stanza of Gori's verses for an American friend:

> *Give flowers to the rebels failed*
> *With glances revealed to the aurora*
> *To the gayard that struggles and works*
> *To the vagrant poet that dies*

It was thus, through the compelling music and image of *Primo Maggio*, that many Italians first came to hear about the Haymarket martyrs, the ''failed rebels,'' and it is by tracing the image of *Primo Maggio* within the Italian movement in America that we can get a sense of the impact that the Haymarket affair had upon it and the nature of the emotions that it aroused.

At the time of the Haymarket incident there was no substantial anarchist movement among the Italians in America. In 1888 the first Italian-language journal, *L'Anarchico*, struggled through six issues in New York City before disappearing. Not for several years, till the enormous migration of the 1890s, would a vital anarchist presence spring up among the Italians in America. This was largely created by many of the important figures of Italian anarchism—Merlino, Gori, Ciancabilla, Malatesta, Galleani—who had been driven into exile by the fierce political persecution of the Italian govern-

ment. Some of this persecution was caused, ironically enough, by the government's reaction to May Day demonstrations, held throughout Italy in support of the Haymarket anarchists. The violent intervention of the Italian police in one of these first May Day demonstrations in Rome, 1891, led to the death of an anarchist and intensified repressive measures against the entire movement.

Francesco Saverio Merlino—lawyer, journalist, anarchist theorist—was among the first of these anarchists to find his way to America. In 1892 he helped to found *Il Grido degli Oppressi* in New York City, and it was in its pages, November 10, 1892, that he wrote the first substantial account of the Haymarket affair in the Italian anarchist press. Merlino's factual, unrhetorical version was coupled with short biographies of the eight Haymarket anarchists. In his analysis of the event he concluded that the men had been killed not for the sake of justice but to sustain the existing social system. Haymarket was still too current an event to have acquired the great symbolic force that it was soon to gain within the Italian movement

This began several years later, in 1895, with the arrival of Pietro Gori. Gori's energy was prodigious. He helped to found *La Question Sociale* in Paterson, New Jersey, the first Italian-language anarchist journal of significant circulation. In little more than a year's time he gave over four hundred conferences, speeches, dramatic readings across America from Boston to San Francisco. His magnetic presence attracted many new adherents to the Italian anarchist movement and turned it into one of appreciable size.

During the course of all this activity Gori also found time to write a poem, ''Undici Novembre,'' dated Chicago, November 11, 1895, which dealt directly—if rather romantically—with the Haymarket executions. But it was a short dramatic sketch that he had written several years before (1890) in an Italian prison, which proved to be one of the major reasons that May Day became so well known among the Italians. The one-act *Primo Maggio* (first published in Philadelphia, 1895), which began and ended with Verdi's chorus, ''Va, pensiero. . .'' reset to Gori's words, was a tremendous popular success that Gori himself often acted in. This short symbolic drama was about the necessity of leaving the past behind, of leaving the old world, even of leaving one's home and family, to seek a new land over the horizon where peace, justice, and light are to be found. It struck a warmly responsive chord among the many emigrants who had left Italy seeking such a land in America. In turn, the injustice, the bitter, cruel struggle of everyday American life that many had found instead, led many who saw Gori's playlet to discover anarchism.

Several years after Gori had returned to Italy, in 1899, Giuseppe Ciancabilla became the editor of *La Question Sociale*. Ciancabilla, initially a socialist, but disillusioned by that movement's lack of militancy, had been converted to the cause of revolutionary anarchism during the course of an interview he had conducted with Errico Malatesta. For Ciancabilla *Primo Maggio* became, in his journalism and his poetry, a call to action, a symbolic banner, but a banner that one carried into battle. His writtings about *Primo Maggio*, of *Maggio Tragico* as he sometimes referred to it, rarely contained specific references to the historical event itself, but talked passionately about sacred vengeance, the hour of justice, the final victory.

When Ciancabilla was succeeded by his erstwhile mentor, Errico Malatesta, as editor, the prose (and masthead) of *La Questione Sociale* became much less florid and rhetorical. Malatesta, in the United States for less than one year, does not seem to have written anything about the Haymarket affair while here, though he did write on it much later in Italy while editor of *Umanita Nova*.

Interestingly enough, Malatesta was the only figure within the Italian movement who had any personal connection with the Haymarket affair itself—albeit a very slight one—and it was perhaps because of this that he did not write about the case while in America. It was on his advice that in 1887 Rudolph Schnaubelt, the lone indicted Haymarket anarchist to elude the grasp of the authorities, slipped away to Argentina (where Malatesta was living at that time) to live the rest of his life in peaceful obscurity. One can only speculate whether Malatesta ever met him there and discussed the case.

At any rate, during the period of Malatesta's involvement with *La Questione Sociale* (1899-1900), the journal, whenever it discussed Haymarket, reflected his simple direct style, not overly celebratory or exhortatory, but clear, reasoned calls for practical action.

The separating of *Primo Maggio* from its historical circumstances (the then-revolutionary demand for an eight-hour working day), and its change into a more symbolic event was an ever-present tendency that troubled many anarchists—and one to which the anarchists themselves were not immune. They did not want the memory of Haymarket to be turned into a mere occasion for speeches, banquets, dances and drinking; they did not want it turned into a legal holiday (*La Festa del Lavoro*/Labor Day) as some socialists wanted to do; they did not want to describe it with images borrowed from religion (*La Pasqua dei Lavoratori*/the Workers' Easter) as even some anarchists did. They insisted that it should be a day of real solidarity with the dispossessed, a day of unyielding militancy, such as the May 1886 strike had been.

It was Luigi Galleani, Malatesta's successor at *La Questione Sociale* for the years 1901-1902, who would fuse the

THE FIRST OF MAY

Come O May! The people await you
Their hearts longing for freedom await you
Sweet Easter of those who work
Come and shine in the glory of the sun

Sing a hymn of winged hopes
To the great greenness that brings
*   the fruit to ripeness*
To the great flowering Ideal
Within which the shining future trembles

> *O phalanxes of slaves, run away from*
> *The worksites, the parched workshops,*
> *Flee from the fields, from the*
> *   swelling seas*
> *Put aside never-ending toil*

Let us raise our calloused hands
Let us join together in a growing force
We want to redeem our world
Tyrannized by both sloth and gold

Youth, griefs, yearnings
Springtimes of secret fascinations
Green May of humankind
Give your courage and your faith
*   to our hearts*

> *Give flowers to the rebels who failed*
> *Their sight fixed upon the break of dawn*
> *To the bold rebel who fights and works*
> *To the far-seeing poet who sings*
> *   and dies*

Pietro GORI

factual and symbolic aspects of Haymarket in the most compelling fashion of all. Galleani, during his nineteen years in America (1901-1919), helped to create the largest and most militant part of the Italian-American movement, and in the pages of the new journal that he founded, *Cronaca Sovversiva* (1903-1919), he referred to *Primo Maggio* time and time again. In his inspirational style Galleani used it constantly as a touchstone for the condition of the movement. When the movement was full of life and fighting spirit, it became *Maggio pieno di sole* (May bursting with sun), *Maggio di fiori* (flowering May), *Maggio proletario* (proletarian May). When the movement was hesitant or cowardly or betrayed, it was *Maggio scellerato* (cruel, villainous May), *Maggio grifagno* (rapacious May), or—most terrible of all—*Maggio caino* (the May of Cain), when worker fought worker. When anarchist militants were injured or killed, it was *Maggio di sangue* (bloody May) and *Maggio di passione* (the passion of May).

Galleani always referred to the Haymarket incident itself, and to the martyrs, with the greatest admiration. He especially noted Louis Lingg's desperate courage in cheating his executioners, August Spies' militancy in calling for force to meet force, and the noble solidarity of Albert Parsons—that *rara avis* among native-born American radicals, a genuine revolutionary—in rejoining his comrades during the trial.

Galleani firmly believed that the world of *Primo Maggio* could have become a reality if the unknown militant who had resisted the action of the police and thrown the bomb had not been alone. Those who heard the fire and eloquence of Galleani's words would carry the memory with them all of their lives, even when some had later come to question the reality of his vision.

In Chicago, *L'Allarme*, a paper which included many admirers of Galleani among its founders, chose to begin publication in November 1915, in homage to the Haymarket martyrs. Emblazoned across the front page of the first issue were a translation of the message of the May 3rd "Revenge" circular: "Abbiate cuore, schiavi, insorgete!" (Take heart, slaves, and arise!).

At the peak of its militancy the Italian movement was dealt a series of heavy blows that began with the advent of World War I. The "Red Scare" of 1919-1920, the failure of the social revolution to materialize in post-World War Italy, and the subsequent rise of fascism, added to its desperate circumstances. Its journals were suppressed, its militants deported or driven underground, and tragically, the movement produced two of its own "failed rebels," Sacco and Vanzetti. Their trial became the great political trial of the twentieth century in America, as Haymarket had been the great political trial of the nineteenth century.

Under the heading "Il Mio Ultimo Primo Maggio," Sacco and Vanzetti, several months before their execution, on April 30, 1927, bid their farewell to May Day in the pages of *L'Adunata dei Refrattari*, the journal which had replaced *Cronaca Sovversiva*. As militant and as unyielding as the Haymarket martyrs, Vanzetti ended with the words, "E al bel sole di Maggio io lancio il mio Evviva all'anarchia e alla rivoluzione sociale" ("To the beautiful shining sun of May 1, shout 'Long live anarchy and the social revolution'"). Sacco took this occasion to pay tribute to a friend and comrade of his youth who had been killed during a strike while just

several paces from him; he spoke of "fulgido Maggio invendicate" (shining May which has not yet been avenged).

After the execution of Sacco and Vanzetti, *Primo Maggio* became, in the pages of *L'Adunata* and of Carlo Tresca's *Il Martello,* the occasion for raising the banner of anti-fascism against Mussolini and Franco. The names of Gino Lucetti, Anteo Zamboni, Michele Schirru, Angelo Sbardellotto, and others who had tried to strike down fascism were often joined with those of the Haymarket martyrs on May Day in America's Little Italies.

But more and more May Day was becoming a symbolic occasion rather than a day of militant protest and agitation. *L'Adunata* noted that a 300-member chorus of socialists were singing but not marching, that the communists were staging their protest in Union Square, but only after receiving permits from the police commissioner. It was a trend, however, that was not to be reversed, not even among the anarchists. The revolutionary demands of the Haymarket anarchists, their unyielding militancy now often seemed old-fashioned and out-of-place to many radicals. The voices of the Haymarket martyrs would not be heard clearly again until the demonstrations of the sixties. By this time, however, because of age and declining numbers, the Italian-American movement was quietly winding down to a close. But among those who were left, the call of Haymarket, of the "Revenge" circular and of the martyrs' speeches which had so stirred them when they were young, was still remembered: "Abbiate cuore, schiavi, insorgete" (Take heart, slaves, and arise!)—and they continued to believe that other generations would heed its message and create the world of which *Primo Maggio* sang.

Robert D'ATTILIO

L'ALLARME

✦ CONTRO OGNI FORMA DI AUTORITA' E DI SFRUTTAMENTO ✦

ANNO I.   CHICAGO, ILL. 1 NOVEMBRE 1915.   NUMERO 1

| Un gruppo di anarchici sente il bisogno di propagare e diffondere l'anarchismo nelle masse lavoratrici, in mezzo a tutti coloro che in questa societa' capitalistica si sentono a disagio, e pubblica questo foglio. | **ABBIATE CUORE, SCHIAVI: INSORGETE!**

1887   **11 NOVEMBRE**   1915 |

ANARCHY.

Neither GOD nor LAW nor PROPERTY:

-BUT-

LIBERTY—EQUALITY—FRATERNITY.

No. 1.   November, 1891.   Monthly, 1d.

11 NOVEMBER.

In 1886 in Chicago, U.S.A., a scoundrel named Bonfield (chief of police) made an attack with troops on an open-air meeting of working men, after the Mayor, who presided, had left, & some person, still unknown, threw a bomb, as part of a plot of Bonfield's. For this several anarchists & other labor agitators were arrested; although it was not only proved but admitted by Bonfield & the Government that they had nothing to do with it in any way, they were sentenced to death, & hanged on 11th Nove1887, & then a law was passed to legalise this murder. Bonfield was embezzling trust money, & he & Schaak, his lawyer, lived by levying blackmail on whores. So he invented this plot to make himself popular with the capitalists & keep his crimes

from being looked into but only succeeded for 3 or 4 years.

These capitalists were afraid of the teachings of our comrades, who urged the people to be no longer robbed & enslaved; but the day of reckoning might not have come in their time. What they feared at once was loss of money through even such slight things as the 8-hour movement, which our comrades were agitating for so as to give work to 20,000 unemployed; so these men were not even hanged for being anarchists, but purely as common labor agitators, for the purpose of frightening the mass of the people into being submissive. In the same way capitalists here try to act, & State officers; like Bonfield, help them.

The workers should remember, that private property must always come to the same thing, & that the State will always in the long run

The first page of the first issue of J. A. Andrews' *Anarchy* (Australia, 1891)

232

THE HAYMARKET AFFAIR "DOWN UNDER"

*I believe that the day is not far distant
when the dreamers of the world
will reap their reward.*
—Ernie Lane

The first reports of the Haymarket Affair to arrive in Australia were published in the commercial press on 6 and 7 May 1886. On 10 May, an editorial appeared in the *Advertiser* (Adelaide) whose "neutrality" clearly sided against the anarchists. Eager to explain that it would be an

injustice to the cause of labor to represent the riot and bloodshed. . . as the natural and legitimate outcome of the system of combination which labor has in late times adopted as its great hope against the absolute dictation of capital,

the editorial argued further that

the violent measures into which those engaged in a movement, lawful and laudable in itself have been betrayed, have not infrequently alienated public sympathy and thrown back for a long time the cause that those measures were intended to forward.

By publishing the first reports of Haymarket to reach these shores, the capitalist press was able to print lies with impunity. It was also able to prescribe the pros and cons of the Haymarket debate: The dividing line was set. Those who denounced the anarchists for using violence (whether they did nor not) on one side; those who knew that the guilt lay elsewhere, on the other.

Only the radical press would present the truth about Haymarket. "What has happened in Chicago," wrote Harry Weber in defense of the anarchists,

was simply the action of the capitalist class against the working class. If the capitalist class had given the true report of the whole affair and shown their actions in their base nakedness, it would not have been more mean, more brutal than it has been. But they have not to do so; they have falsified every account given from their side—they have acted deliberately with a firm intent to blind the people, to keep the truth from them, by threatening and bribing—by all means possible.

Among the most staunch defenders of the Chicago anarchists were those who met at the meeting rooms of the Australian Secular Association on the first of May, 1886, and called into existence the Melbourne Anarchist Club. At the meeting were Fred Upham, the brothers David and Will Andrade, and three others.

Little could the organizers have predicted the significance of this date in the light of the events that were soon to follow. All had been active in the Free Thought initiative "down under," but they formed the MAC in rebellion against the organized Free Thought of the ASA, and particularly against its president, Joseph Symes. President and chief lecturer of the Association since his arrival from England in 1884, Symes was also editor of its journal, *The Liberator*. Early in 1886, Will Andrade accused Symes of being inconsistent. He argued in debate that Symes' actions in defying the government were not consistent with his support for the procedure of changing laws through the ballot box. Will Andrade insisted that "the people at present put barriers to their own freedom by having governments. Anarchy was what the

world needed and progress could only be attained by individual freedom."

The members of the Melbourne Anarchist Club distrusted all institutions which were not voluntary. In their prospectus they stated that their objects were "to expose and oppose that colossal swindle, Government," and "to advocate, and seek to achieve, the abolition of all monopolies and despotisms which destroy the Freedom of the Individual and which thereby check social progress and prosperity." Among these "despotisms" were the police who were already showing themselves to be far from impartial defenders of "law and order."

The means by which these "despotisms" would be "abolished" was also hotly discussed. In a debate on "Individual Liberty" reported in *The Liberator* on 25 April 1886, David Andrade spoke unequivocally:

Social liberty can only be realised by granting individual liberty. And if it cannot be got by peaceable means, through the obstruction of physical force, physical force must be employed to secure it. Dynamite is one of the best friends of toiling humanity.

Cover of *The Republican* (Sydney, February 8, 1888)

233

J. A. Andrews

Not everyone agreed with Andrade's view that violence, individual or organized, was a valid means to obtain social liberty. After the fourth of May, 1886, however, the reality of Haymarket would stamp its own distinctive mark on the thoughts and actions of a whole generation—and beyond—of Australian labor activists.

In the face of unprecedented processions of unemployed across the country, and no doubt influenced by the news, not only of Haymarket, but also of mass demonstrations in London, Symes wrote in *The Liberator* on 16 May 1886:

Newspapers may write down the poor, soldiers may be called out to shoot the agitators, advanced or anarchic newspapers may be seized. . .what then? Their sufferings will add fuel to the fire and only hasten on the final victory.

Influenced by other reformist members of the ASA, and also by his concern for a "respectable" parliamentary career, Symes moved quickly to dissociate the ASA from the MAC and also from support of the Chicago anarchists. Symes began to support the equation, already popularized in the capitalist press, that anarchism equals physical violence. Following on from this dubious position, it was quite easy for Symes to proclaim that the Chicago anarchists deserved all they got. And he did so, many times.

On the wild side of politics, defense of the Chicago anarchists moved on apace. It was quite clear to all principled labor activists that Parsons, Spies and their comrades were innocent, and that in fact it was the police, as representatives and defenders of Capital, who were the guilty party. In the April 1887 issue of *Honesty*, the journal of the MAC, an unsigned editorial refers to "the base intrigue of the authorities as they stained [with blood] that memorable meeting held in Chicago last May."

The same editorial cites

a healthy spirit of discontent growing up amongst the workers of the whole civilised world—not simply the discontent which growls without seeking a remedy—but a truly healthy discontent which, not satisfied with useless complainings, seeks to trace the cause of social evils and takes action to remove them.

In the eyes of the Melbourne anarchists, this global discontent provided the background of the Haymarket Affair, just as it made clear to many workers that the Chicago anarchists were not enemies of liberty, but its truest defenders. Workers, the MAC was convinced, knew who the enemy was: They knew the facts about the murderous cops, and not only abstractly, in the form of "exotic" news items from afar—the organized violence of the State was a daily reality for those who were the objects of what the MAC called "the shameful system of exploitation and legal butchery."

Portraits of the Haymarket anarchists were exhibited in radical meeting halls throughout Australia. Numerous defense meetings were held, indoors and out. On 27 January 1887, a special lecture on "The Chicago Anarchists' Trial" was delivered by David Andrade at an MAC public meeting, at the conclusion of which a resolution was unanimously adopted and transmitted to the Governor of Illinois, expressing sympathy for the condemned men.

The May 1887 issue of *Honesty* reported that

upwards of four-thousand pounds was collected for the defense of the Chicago anarchists, whose case was to be reheard in March. While Reuters' telegrams keep us informed upon Queen Victoria's little pleasure trips, of course [they have] nothing to say about this portentous trial, beyond giving a few falsified accounts at the outset, and leaving the Australian public to believe that the condemned men have been hanged long ago.

In November 1887 *Honesty* reported that four of the Chicago anarchists had been hanged on the eleventh of that month. David Andrade denounced the executions as

one of the foulest crimes that ever stained the bloodiest pages of American history. Four of humanity's truest friends were hanged to satisfy the vengeance of the merciless usurers who tyrannize over the American people—four of the saviors of the proletariat were crucified by the pharisees of the 19th century.

Arguments over the events of 4 May 1886 and the subsequent trial had been heated; the debate that followed the hanging of the martyrs was positively fiery. The capitalist and reformist press gleefully proclaimed that "Anarchy is dead!" In answer, and echoing both Albert Parsons' and August Spies' final words, David Andrade wrote:

But is all yet ended? Shall the voice of the people be heard? Yes, departed comrades, it shall be heard, and it shall grate in the ears of every heartless plutocrat as do the cruel exultations of joy from your murderers now grate in our own.

Anarchy is not yet dead, for humanity still lives, and yearns to taste of the glorious fruits of liberty which is now stained with your innocent blood. The time is fast approaching when your silence shall be more powerful than your strangled voices.

"Against the enemy, revendication is eternal," and your comrades shall continue to sow the seeds you have sown, until they blossom into liberty; and your murderers, who have sown the wind of their hatred, shall reap the whirlwind of an oppressed and outraged humanity. The bloody crime of the oppressors shall be revenged in the overthrow of oppression; the tyrant laws which oppress and destroy us shall be trampled under foot; and labor shall be free! The martyrs shall not die in vain!

Meetings were held regularly each year to commemorate the deaths of the martyrs. The memory of this heinous crime could not, and would not, be erased. Ernie Lane, who referred to the Haymarket Affair as "one of the most epochal events in all Labour history," wrote in his memoirs that, "it became for years the rallying centre for the revolutionary Socialist movement, a shrine where one found inspiration and hope for a better realisation of the immorality of capitalism and the inevitability of Socialism."

Apologists for the existing order could not leave well enough alone, and continually enlarged on the lies and slander that had accompanied the trial. The press reported that more lives had been lost, more bombs thrown. One report, written by Symes, accused Lingg of being in possession of "some 50 or 60 bombs." In 1888 appeared a pamphlet by a certain Felix Vivian, *The Dance of Death in the Gaolyard*, which Harry Weber called, "a repetition of all the knavish lies and calumnies spread by the newspapers during the last two years about the Chicago butchery" of 1886, and "a glorification of the fanatical murder of justice, committed November 11, 1887." Weber railed against the police whom he called "the willing tools of tyranny—the instruments of oppression—a shameless, thoughtless crowd of brigands,—the vilest, meanest, scum of human beings,—a degenerate band of criminals."

Weber continued:

Working men! In the name of humanity I call upon you to keep these facts in mind. In the name of common sense I ask you: How long shall this continue? In the name of your rights and welfare, in the name of justice, I charge you, make an end of this fearful system. Workers of the world! Inquire into these facts; bring them to your knowledge—educate yourself and your fellow workers. Agitate!! Organise!! Workers! And when you *are* organised, then—arm yourselves with common sense, arm yourselves with right and justice and break down the system of brutality, of robbery; sweep away this shameful system of exploitation and legal butchery.

This *is* the voice of Haymarket! Harry Weber may have penned these insurgent words but it was the spirit of the Chicago anarchists that armed his consciousness.

One of the most eloquent defenders of the Haymarket martyrs was J. A. Andrews, whose writings were marked by a curious blend of reason and humor. He pointed out that "If our comrades were such experts in explosives as we are told, they would not have used a *fuse-bomb* which is both dangerous to the thrower and unreliable altogether, but a percussion bomb." A gifted theorist, Andrews was also a poet, a writer of science fiction and history, and an inventor. Among his inventions was a variant of the printing technique known as "Xylography," which he used to print a small journal, *Anarchy*. Its first issue, in November 1891, was devoted to the Haymarket affair, and included a detailed expose of the shifty maneuverings of the notorious Chicago police captains, Bonfield and Schaack.

Year after year Australian revolutionaries would look to Haymarket and recall its message. "Phoebus-like, the work and aspirations of the Chicago martyrs have sprung from that dread scaffold into active life, not only in America, but throughout the length and breadth of the domains of tyrannical capitalism." So wrote Ernie Lane in an 1892 memorial, adding:

Even here in Australia, where anarchy is almost unknown, these men live before us in all their grandeur and heroism, showing us what men can and will endure for the great cause, and pointing ever onward to the goal of human happiness, *viz.*, Freedom, for which they so nobly laid down their lives.

Twenty-odd years later, when the stay-at-home patriots were sending workingmen to their destruction in the First World War, the Australian section of the Industrial Workers of the World (IWW) continued to fan the flames of discontent. The Australian IWW newspaper, *Direct Action*, on November 15, 1914, published excerpts from the speeches of Parsons, Spies, Lingg and Engel. The same issue included a scathing critique of capitalist justice, in an editorial dedicated to the Chicago martyrs.

In Australia as elsewhere, the Wobblies proved to be among the truest inheritors of the Haymarket legacy. Tom Barker, one of the best known IWW agitators "down under," summed it up well:

When the workers resent the everyday violence perpetrated upon them the horrified and sanctimonious crew and their lickspittle toadies lift their blood-stained, profit-mongering hands in air with horror. But, oh. . .my masters. Beware of what you do! Prisons, and hunger, and gallows will not save your ruling class. Nor stifling human thought. Nor limiting human actions. Organize! organize! organize! ye toilers all!

Michael VANDELAAR

Note: For a great deal of the information in this article I am indebted to Bob James and to his unpublished thesis, "Anarchists and Political Violence in Sydney and Melbourne, 1886-1896."

SPECIAL
MAY DAY ISSUE

"An Injury to One an Injury to All"

Anti-war Australian IWWs recall the Haymarket Martyrs in 1917

235

BA JIN'S BLOOD OF FREEDOM:
A Chinese Anarchist's Response to Haymarket

During the first decades of the twentieth century, Chinese anarchists played an important role in China's early revolutionary movement. Ba Jin, who was born in 1904, is the most well-known of these early socialist libertarians. His given name is Li Feigan, but his chosen pseudonym, Ba Jin (Pa Chin in the older Wade-Giles spelling), is a phonetic rendering of the names *Ba*kunin and Kropot*kin*. Ba Jin's interest in anarchism began as a youth living in Chengdu, Sichuan province, which led him to join the anarchist Equality society at the age of fifteen. These personal convictions underlie his career as a novelist and advocate of the libertarian cause.

Ba Jin's fascination with the romantic martyr-hero is reflected both in his novels and in his writings about pioneers of the worldwide anarchist movement. The intense individualism and self-sacrifice of the characters in his novels were the qualities he conveyed in his portraits of anarchist heros. Both sought to inspire the reader to identify with and emulate these pioneers of freedom. He was particularly drawn to the story of the Chicago martyrs.

One of the first anarchist tracts to inspire Ba Jin was Kropotkin's *An Appeal to the Young*, a call he was to echo in his own work. Ba Jin's upbringing in the confines of a traditional extended family and the demands of filial piety that led to his brother's tragic suicide made him denounce the strict dictates of familial authority. His best-known novel, *Family*, was the first in a trilogy titled *Turbulent Stream*. This semi-autobiographical novel was a passionate critique of the patriarchial family as a "state-in-small," an indictment he extended to China's authoritarian sociopolitical order.

Ba Jin's denunciation of Chinese society must be seen against the revolutionary upheavals and civil wars of those decades. His first novel, *Destruction*, was an account of the bloody suppression of the radical workers' movement in Shanghai in 1927, and its theme of

Ba Jin

heroic death was a call to the revolutionary struggle. Similarly, the martyr-heroes of the international anarchist movement provided the model pioneers of China's own struggle for freedom.

Ba Jin first described the Haymarket anarchists in *The Chicago Tragedy*, published in 1926. His *Pioneers of the Revolution* (1928) and *Past Anarchists* (1931) also included the story of the Chicago martyrs. This earlier work was reprinted in a separate volume, *Blood of Freedom,* issued in 1937 to commemorate the fiftieth anniversary of the Haymarket tragedy. Ba Jin appended to

去 過

THE ANARCHISTS

Compiled and edited by
Li Pei Kam

Shanghai

1931

Title-page of *Past Anarchists*
(Shanghai, 1931)

his portrait of their judicial murders his admiration of their self-sacrifice:

Humankind's freedom and courage are surely inseparable. The noble integrity of the Chicago martyrs—their sincerity, zeal valor and self-sacrifice, are what moves people most. Theirs were the perfect ethical guidance and ideals.

The lesson Ba Jin drew from their example is that true revolutionary ends can be achieved only through free individual choice. For Ba Jin, political and military strategies of revolution are inherently elitist—the end never justifies the means. Pointing to the Haymarket martyrs, he says "Ethics and ideals ought always to be united—without this unity, the unscrupulous become turncoats." Turning his comments to China, Ba Jin's denunciation of elitist theories of revolution echoes Bakunin's nineteenth-century criticism of the "new czars." "Those cowardly and deceptive opportunists—those high folk who would command and direct the course of the revolution—would only replace the old system with a new elitism." He says,

Recently some advocates of revolution adopt the strategy of sham brute force, sacrificing the masses to give rise to the leaders. This suits the careerists' quest for political power. The revolution for the freedom of the masses depends on the true, enthusiastic, and courageous strength of the masses and pioneers. Has there been an time in history when liberation hasn't come about through the conscious, courageous struggle and self-sacrifice of pioneers and the masses? Yet subsequent wise leaders hold back from disposing with political power. The 1911 Revolution and the overthrow of the Qing dynasty—wasn't this the achievement of heroic self-sacrifice?

For Ba Jin true revolution can be achieved only by voluntary individual commitment to the cause of freedom: "As the masses voluntarily come forth to courageous struggle, they can thereby guarantee the true, rapid sucess of the revolution." These ideals, he argues, are those of the Haymarket martyrs, posing a challenge and a cause to be taken up by China's own heroes:

Those who would struggle for the progress of human freedom must individually devote

236

their lives to the struggle for ideals. Comrades who strive for freedom! Step along the bloody road of the May First martyrs!

Ba Jin's own road to revolution was to be a tortured one. Though many anarchists left China following the communist revolution of 1949, Ba Jin chose to remain. His last letters to the American anarchist Agnes Inglis on the eve of the revolution express both his sympathy for the land-reform goals of the communist movement and his determination to pursue his own work. He wrote also of his preparation of another manuscript on the Chicago anarchists in which he hoped to provide the personal histories of each of the Haymarket martyrs.

As one of China's foremost novelists, Ba Jin has been alternately esteemed as an early revolutionary hero and denounced as a "petty-bourgeois anarchist." Following the "hundred flowers" movement of the mid-1950s, when intellectuals expressed their criticisms of the Communist Party, Ba Jin was among those singled out for attack. His much publicized self-criticism and rejection of anarchism have been variously described as an outright betrayal of his ideals, or a recantation such as Galileo was forced to make during the Inquisition. Similarly, although he agreed to reissue his works after expunging all references to anarchism, he openly continued to protest against political cen-

記憶有時使我痛苦，但我是靠記憶而生活。

如果不是有記憶的話，我也許會在街頭巷角茶樓酒館去兇罵別人搶錢奪利了。然

而記憶抓住了我，使我走現在的這一條路。因為在記憶中有如許多的可愛的人，為了

他們我不得不忘掉自己。

在悲哀中，有他們來安慰我；在失望中，有他們來鼓舞我；在黑暗中，有他們來

指引我。這許多年以來在這荒涼的沙漠上就只有他們是我的伴侶。

時間上他們貸是過去的了。過去卻也是多麼值得留戀的，只要她是現在與未來之

母親的時候。因為她們指引我們走向未來的不可知的道路。

我們要繼承有過去的遺產向著未來猛進。

Preface to *Past Anarchists*

sorship. The insistent individualism of the youthful rebel-heroes that remained even in his now-sanitized novels again made him a political target during the Cultural Revolution. Publicly de-

nounced, placed under house-arrest, his novels proscribed, and his home ransacked by Red Guards, Ba Jin was again to assert the right of individual conscience and to defiantly reverse the lesson that his televised denunciation at People's Stadium was intended to convey. Forced to kneel in repentance on broken glass, he cried out "You have your ideals and I have mine. You can't change this fact even if you kill me."

Ba Jin still lives in Shanghai and, in the more open years of China's recent past, has emerged as a figure of esteem. He continues to publicly assert the right to individual and intellectual freedom. It seems appropriate to conclude with Ba Jin's own testament to the Chicago martyrs, whom he saw as sharing a human covenant with China's own revolutionary heroes.

Yet we shouldn't be sad, nor should we grieve our dead. We should express our respect and vindicate our love for them. If anyone reading this feels tears welling in their eyes, they should listen to the song sung by A.R. Parsons, one of our dead, as he approached the scaffold. "Come not to my grave with your mournings. . . . Cease your sorrowful bell; I am well!"

Diane SCHERER

SOURCES: The interested reader is referred to Olga Lang's *Pa Chin and His Writings* (Harvard, 1967) and Nathan Mao's "Pa Chin's Journey in Sentiment: From Hope to Despair," *Journal of the Chinese Language Teachers Association* 11.2 (May 1976). A number of his novels are available in English translation, including *Family* (Anchor Books, 1972). Ba Jin's letters to Agnes Inglis are part of the holdings of the University of Michigan's Labadie Collection.

Les Martyrs de Chicago

Chapter title-page and illustration from Ba Jin's *Past Anarchists*

PISCATOR, BRECHT & THE HAYMARKET EPIC

In one of those curious dialectical twists of which Karl Marx was so fond, the Haymarket trial of 1886 helped change the history of the theater.

In 1924 Erwin Piscator staged and directed Alfons Paquet's *Flags*, a play about the Haymarket trial, at the Berlin Volksbuhne. This production marked the birth of the now-famous "epic" style in theater. As Piscator later noted, *Flags* was also "in a certain sense the first Marxist drama, and that production the first attempt to grasp these materialist forces and make them tangible."

Twice-wounded during the First World War, and a recent adherent of the German Communist Party (KPD), Piscator set out to revolutionize the social function of stage-design and the acting style of the German theater. That he was to succeed with the Epic Theater is a tribute to his vision as well as to the extraordinary group of artists whose collaboration he enjoyed, among them the poet/playwright Bertolt Brecht. Brecht was to call Piscator "one of the most significant theater people of all time."

The Chicago of 1886 had been one of the largest German-speaking communities in the world, and there was intense and enduring interest, in Germany, in the situation and culture of its German population.

The Berlin of the 1920s, with its huge and radical workingclass audiences, was the perfect site for a play about an incident that had fascinated and enraged all of Germany. The Haymarket trial had been clearly perceived by German socialists as an attack by American capitalists on German workers.

The trial also stigmatized Chicago, for European radicals, in a way and to a degree that no event had before or has since. The trial gave Chicago an international reputation for corruption and state-sponsored violence. Hollywood's romance with the crime-film freeze-framed Chicago's "gangster" image in the 1920s/30s, but German socialists knew that the Prohibition-era movie fantasies had a much earlier but no less bloody background in the last two decades of the nineteenth century. Histories of Haymarket and the Pullman

Strike left no doubt for writers such as Brecht, who described Chicago as a "cold hell" where workers were used up and thrown on the streets to die.

The Chicago-as-hell image already had a long history by the 1920s. Arthur Holitischer, co-founder with Piscator of

Anarchists scripted and performed dramas of the Haymarket tragedy early on, and have continued to do so, as this 1964 Argentinian anarcho-syndicalist poster indicates. From Brecht and Piscator through Ben Hecht's and Charles MacArthur's 1920s *Front Page* and choreographer/dancer Eleanor King's 1930s *Song of America* to the 1985 three-act play on Sam Fielden by San Francisco Bay Area playwright Fred Hayden, the impact of Haymarket on theater has been extensive, and awaits its historian.

Berlin's Proletarian Theater, had visited Chicago in 1910 and recorded at length his impressions of "the most dreadful city on earth," which he regarded as a "caricature" of America. "All America looks with fear at this city," he wrote. "I don't hesitate to say: Chicago is hell."

Chicago had a special fascination for Brecht, and he set much of his early work there. He summed up all his old obsessions with the city—clarified at last through his reading of Marx—in his play *St. Joan of the Stockyards*.

Piscator described the space around him, during rehearsals of *Flags*, as increasingly "empty." The consensus at the time was that the play would end his brief career in the German theater. Sensing a disaster, he offered to resign—but his offer was refused. In the last hours before the opening he reworked the play completely—and awoke next morning to find himself the talk of Berlin.

In dramatizing *Flags*, Piscator decided against "a naturalistic milieu. . .a psychological study." *Flags* was to be "like a newspaper report" that would "speak for itself." For the first time in theater, slides introduced pictures of the participants while there was action on stage. (Piscator had even wanted to use motion-picture film, but there had not been time.) Titles divided the nineteen scenes of the play and additional textual material was projected onto screens at either side of the stage. The play opened with verses about the principals in the drama, such as Judge Gary:

Calvinist psalms fill his Sunday hours
Moloch who living flesh devours.

The play's text was kept clear and factual. Critic/novelist Alfred Doblin described the dialogue as "somewhere between drama and prose fiction." The language helped "distance" the audience in a way that Brecht was later to perfect.

Flags was about class conflict: McShure, the city boss, bribes the police to plant a bomb and then to frame the Haymarket defendants. The men are tried by a jury of capitalist clerks, overseen by Gary, the Hanging Judge.

Edward Suhr's set introduced what would become a standard feature of "epic" productions: a revolving stage.

For Piscator, *Flags* was the breakthrough that changed the theater. For Brecht, it helped formulate some of the major dramaturgy of the twentieth century.

Alfred Doblin called the Epic Theater, born in the courtroom and on the gallows in Chicago in 1886-87, the "form and spirit of our time."

Warren LEMING

238

May Day, 1972: Chicago police arrive in force to prevent local anarchists and members of the Industrial Workers of the World from placing a paper-maché statue of Louis Lingg on the empty pedestal of the Haymarket police statue.

"Reckless Politics in Chicago":
NELSON ALGREN & LOUIS LINGG

One of the few "1930s authors" who never really grew old, who never bent his knee to the Old Order, and whose books are all about youth—workingclass youth and its desperate struggle for *life* against the unlivable horror of modern society—Nelson Algren characteristically invoked Haymarket martyr Louis Lingg as the epitome of a certain Chicago-style youthful recalcitrance that he found admirable and worthy of emulation.

Algren quoted the concluding words of Lingg's famous *Address to the Court*— "I despise your order, your laws, your force-propped authority. Hang me for it!"—in his *Chicago: City on the Make* (1952), again on the first page of his introduction to the 1961 edition of that book, and yet again in "Pottawattomie Ghosts," an article in the Chicago *Free Press* (October 26, 1970). In this last piece, Algren gleefully told of the most recent dynamiting of the Haymarket cop statue, which the authorities had announced would once more be rebuilt and remounted. As an alternative to this authoritarian monstrosity Algren proposed a statue of Albert Parsons, with Lingg's "challenge to the court" emblazoned on its base.

Born in Detroit of Swedish-American and German-Jewish parents, Nelson Algren (1909-1981) lived most of his life in Chicago, the setting for much of his fiction. Algren's Chicago was always the "town of the hard

and bitter strikes and the trigger-happy cops . . .where undried blood on the pavement and undried blood on the field yet remember Haymarket and Memorial Day" (*Chicago: City on the Make*).

His first novel, *Somebody in Boots* (1935), was followed by *Never Come Morning* (1942), *The Man With the Golden Arm* (1949) and *A Walk on the Wild Side* (1956). Last and greatest of Chicago's "realist" writers, Algren was also the most excessive; the black humor of many tales in *The Neon Wilderness* (1947) and *The Last Carrousel* (1975) seems closer in spirit to a kind of H. P. Lovecraft version of the Three Stooges than to most "social" fiction. In his last years he was deeply concerned with the case of the black boxer and political prisoner Rubin "Hurricane" Carter, the subject of his last novel, *The Devil's Stocking* (1983).

Already a radical in the early 1930s, for several years Algren was close to the Communist Party, but never joined it, finding in it "a certain kind of rigidity" as well as an "authoritarian attitude" that repelled him. In later years he acknowledged the word *anarchist* as a self-description, and remarked: "I would like to think I am basically against government."

Though never really an activist himself, Algren warmly supported the civil rights and antiwar movements, and the new campus

radicalism that emerged in the 1960s. Sensitive to cultural revolt as well, he disdained the "Beat" fad (he remarked that no government committee would ever ask anyone: "Are you now or have you ever been a member of the Beat Generation?"), but when surrealists at Chicago's Roosevelt University formed an "Anti-Poetry Club" in 1962, for the express purpose of harassing and denouncing the school's already existing Poetry Club, Algren declared it the best thing that had happened in Chicago in years, and invited the "anti-poets" out for beer.

In a prolonged period of political and intellectual chicken-heartedness and hypocrisy, Algren persisted in his radical nonconformism. "If the man in the gray flannel suit was getting married to Marjorie Morningstar right down the street," he was fond of saying, "I still wouldn't go to the wedding."

Of his last book he said: "I've tried to write about a man's struggle against injustice—that's the only story worth telling."

Aloof to the ruling fashions in literature and politics, Nelson Algren remained on the side of the outcasts, loyal in his own way to the defiant dream of a 21-year-old immigrant who, in May 1886, got thrown into jail for the crime that Algren called "practicing reckless politics in Chicago."

FR

CARL SANDBURG

Born of Swedish-American parents in Galesburg, Illinois, Carl Sandburg (1878-1967) attended his home-town's Lombard College, where he edited the school paper and was captain of the basketball team. In his autobiography, Always the Young Strangers *(1952), he recalled his childhood impressions of Haymarket and how deeply moved he was when he later read Altgeld's pardon message, which hastened his own development as a radical.*

For many years Sandburg worked as a reporter and writer for such papers as the Chicago Daily News *and the remarkable* Day Book. *An active member of the Socialist Party, he was a prolific contributor to the socialist press, including Mary E. Marcy's* International Socialist Review, *published by Charles H. Kerr; his poem reprinted here originally appeared in the* Review *for May 1916.*

When the U.S. entered World War I, he supported Woodrow Wilson's policies and left the socialist movement. In later years he called himself a ''pacifist between wars.''

Sandburg regarded poetry as ''a search for syllables to shoot at the barriers of the unknown and the unknowable.'' Probably the single best-known Chicago poet of the 1910s and '20s, he was the target of many attacks by critics of ''free verse'' troubled by his vigorous, homely, ''unpoetic'' imagery. But the leading advocate of free verse in the U.S., Amy Lowell, also attacked him—as a propagandist of the poor and oppressed.

His Chicago Poems *(1915),* Smoke and Steel *(1920) and* The People, Yes *(1936) were all popular in their day, and his* Collected Poems *(1951) won a Pulitizer Prize. But at least in part because of the devastating changes that have taken place in the Chicago he wrote about, his poetry has been neglected in recent years. ''All we have today of the past is the poetry of Sandburg,'' wrote Nelson Algren in 1961, ''now as remote from the Chicago of today as Wordsworth's.''*

Best-remembered today for his monumental two-part biography of Lincoln, Sandburg also wrote an important study, The Chicago Race Riots *(1919), and compiled* The American Songbag *(1927), which marks him as a forerunner of the widespread revival of interest in folk-songs that started in the 1960s.*

FR

GOVERNMENT

By Carl Sandburg

The Government—I heard about the Government and I went out to find it. I said I would look closely at it when I saw it.

Then I saw a policeman dragging a drunken man to the calaboose. It was the Government in action.

I saw a ward alderman slip into an office one morning and talk with a judge. Later in the day the judge dismissed a case against a pickpocket who was a live ward worker for the alderman. Again I saw this was the Government, doing things.

I saw militiamen level their rifles at a crowd of workingmen who were trying to get other workingmen to stay away from a shop where there was a strike on. Government in action.

Everywhere I saw that Government is a thing made of men, that Government has blood and bones, it is many mouths whispering into many ears, sending telegrams, aiming rifles, writing orders, saying yes and no.

Government dies as the men who form it die and are laid away in their graves and the new Government that comes after is human, made of heartbeats of blood, ambitions, lusts, and money running thru it all, money paid and money taken, and money covered up and spoken of with hushed voices.

A Government is just as secret and mysterious and sensitive as any human sinner carrying a load of germs, traditions and corpuscles handed down from fathers and mothers away back.

EDGAR LEE MASTERS

A major figure in the midwestern ''poetic renaissance'' of the 1910s/20s, Edgar Lee Masters (1868-1950) was also Clarence Darrow's law-partner for many years. His *Spoon River Anthology* (1915), from which ''Carl Hamblin'' is taken, consists of monologues by 244 ghosts of real and imaginary inhabitants of the southern Illinois region where he grew up. Pessimistic, mordant, overflowing with outrage at the ''human condition,'' the book was an immediate sensation. Masters wrote many other volumes of poetry as well as plays, and biographies of Lincoln, Whitman, Mark Twain and his friend Vachel Lindsay, but *Spoon River* remains by far his most memorable work.

FR

CARL HAMBLIN

The press of the Spoon River Clarion was wrecked,
And I was tarred and feathered,
For publishing this on the day the Anarchists were
*   hanged in Chicago:*
''I saw a beautiful woman with bandaged eyes
Standing on the steps of a marble temple.
Great multitudes passed in front of her,
Lifting their faces imploringly.
In her left hand she held a sword.
Sometimes striking a child, again a lunatic.
In her right hand she held a scale;
Into the scale pieces of gold were tossed
By those who dodged the strokes of the sword.
A man in a black gown read from a manuscript;
'She is no respecter of persons.'
Then a youth wearing a red cap
Leaped to her side and snatched away the bandage.
And lo, the lashes had been eaten away
From the oozy eye-lids;
The eye-balls were seared with a milky mucus;
The madness of a dying soul
Was written on her face—
But the multitude saw why she wore the bandage.''

Edgar Lee MASTERS

Joffre Stewart (far left, with newspapers and shopping bag) at a Haymarket Square May Day commemoration, 1969.

THE HOME TO MAY DAY

The Home to May Day
    for May Day
        of May Day
it is the shrine of Labor History
the Mecca of Russians
the end of the line
for the last plot of Emma Goldman
just a few yards lateral
of sculpture
in the Forest Home of
martyrs
set up in one of Kapital's plots
to smash the Anti-Political,
which act favored the Political
bias

which builds socialism
within the parameters
of Ruling Class designs

which connect
the Drake Hotel
the Merchandise Mart
and the City Hall
with tunnels
that secure the mobility
of the Second City's Ruling Class
inaccessible by the Lake
or by ways to the river
with bridges raised

against the return of the repressed
against the Spectre of Labor
sick with and of Authority
which must be destroyed
to "avenge", as it were,
the Pullman Strike,
the McCormick Strike
the Haymarket set-up
the Memorial Day Massacre
and innumerable police brutalities
resistance
to any one of which
might bring down the government
in Poland...

                    Joffre STEWART

241

IN MEMORIAM
CHICAGO HAYMARKET MARTYRS

FIFTIETH COMMEMORATION
Friday, Nov. 11, 1887 — Thursday, Nov. 11, 1937
LABOR DOES NOT FORGET ITS MARTYRS

Memorial Mass Meeting
MECCA TEMPLE
55th STREET, Near SEVENTH AVE.   NEW YORK CITY
Thursday, November 11, 1937

Judge Gary vs. The People:
POLITICAL CONSPIRACY TRIALS IN AMERICA

"We have not the bomb-thrower here. We have got the accessories, the conspirators, the individuals. . .who advised and encouraged it, and if we never knew who did it. . . still the defendants are guilty." With these words State's Attorney Julius S. Grinnell summed up his final arguement to the jury in the Haymarket trial. Judge Joseph E. Gary instructed the jury,

If these defendants or any two or more of them, conspired together with or not with any person or persons to excite the people . . . of this city . . . to take lives of other persons . . . in the pursuance of such conspiracy, and in furtherance of its objects, any of the persons so conspiring publicly, by print or speech, . . . and [if] induced by such advice or encouragement, murder was committed, then all of such conspirators are guilty of such murder, whether the person who perpetrated such murder can be identified or not.

Thus Grinnell and Gary enlarged the already nebulous domain of conspiracy theory and law.

The Haymarket defendants were not the first, nor have they been the last, labor, civil rights, or peace crusaders to be tried under the conspiracy laws of one of the United States. Conspiracy law originated in English common law and was first applied to a labor dispute in the U.S. in 1806 following the Philadelphia cordwainers' strike; the decision of the court was that the shoemakers who had entered into an agreement to strike for higher wages were guilty of criminal conspiracy.

Judge Gary's court set the precedent in conspiracy law that individual defendants did not have to know one another to be held liable for the deeds of another defendant who was deemed to be a member of the same conspiracy, and that the principal in the case—the person who actually committed the crime—did not have to be known either to the defendants or to the prosecution. Moveover, the court ruled that public acts, including speeches and writings, may constitute a conspiracy. No longer did a conspiracy necessarily take place in secrecy, behind closed doors. Conspiracy law could now be applied against any group of individuals whose publicly expressed views were inimical to the status quo.

In the United States and England, conspiracy has been a catch-all charge against persons who are frequently not indictable on more substantial charges. Conspiracy law, loosely interpreted according to the whims of the court, powerful interests, and public opinion, is widely applied against a variety of political "offenders." Hearsay evidence, inadmissable in most trials, is admissable in conspiracy trials, and guilt is largely inferred on circumstantial evidence.

In some jurisdictions, persons can be held guilty of conspiracy even when the act they conspire to commit is not illegal. The act does not have to be committed for defendants to be judged guilty in conspiracy cases. In many states, the penalty for conspiracy is more severe that the penalty for the act which the "conspirators" planned to commit. Clarence Darrow, in his long fight against conspiracy laws, used a simple example to illustrate this point. If a boy stole a piece of candy, he might be convicted of a misdemeanor; however,

if two boys conspired to steal a piece of candy, whether or not they actually stole the candy, they could be convicted of a *felony*!

Darrow condemned conspiracy law as "the modern and ancient dragnet for compassing the imprisonment and death of men the ruling class does not like." Conspiracy has proved a convenient vehicle for prosecutors to link together persons who may not ever have met one another. If two persons have separately made plans with a third person, all three may be tried together as co-conspirators and each held fully responsible for the actions of any one of the others, regardless of lack of prior knowledge or involvement in an act. August Spies summed up the unlimited liability concept of conspiracy law after bombs were discovered in Louis Lingg's jail cell. Spies ironically remarked, "If anyone holds us, or any one of us, responsible for Lingg's deeds, then I can't see why we shouldn't be held responsible for any mischief, whatsoever, in the world."

Not only did Judge Gary's court extend the realm of conspiracy, but prosecutor Grinnell and company employed a perjured witness, Harry Gilmer, to testify that he had seen Spies light the bomb and Rudolph Schnaubelt throw it. Ten persons testified to Gilmer's unreliable character, and after Gilmer's testimony had been impeached, the prosecutors did not even pretend to have established the identity of the bomb-thrower. The manufacture of evidence and paid perjurors have remained a mainstay in American political trials.

In 1894, Eugene V. Debs was jailed on charges of criminal conspiracy and violating a Federal injunction in connection with the American Railway Union's support of the Pullman strike. At the trial, the prosecutor reasoned that since Debs had authorized the strike, he could be held criminally liable for any violence or damages which occurred during the strike—whether committed by strikers, militiamen or agents

Cartoon by Jacob Burck, early 1930s

Nicola Sacco and Bartolomeo Vanzetti

of management—and despite the fact that Debs had repeatedly counseled against violence. Clarence Darrow ably defended Debs against the conspiracy charge. However, when a juror became ill, the judge continued the case. Although the defense attorneys repeatedly challenged the government to conclude the proceedings, the government chose not to reopen the case. Debs remained unconvicted on the conspiracy charge, but he was convicted of contempt in a separate trial and went to prison.

In 1906 three leaders of the Western Federation of Miners—Big Bill Haywood, Charles Moyer, and George Pettibone—were kidnapped in Colorado by Idaho authorities and illegally brought to Idaho to stand trial for the murder of the former governor. The charge was conspiracy, and the goal of the prosecutors was to put the union out of business. The only evidence against the three unionists was the testimony of a paid perjuror, Harry Orchard. Lucy Parsons, Eugene Debs and Emma Goldman were among the many who promptly raised their voices against the illegal extradition and impending trial. Clarence Darrow again performed admirably for the defense; the jury voted to acquit.

On July 22, 1916, a bomb exploded during a Preparedness Day parade in San Francisco. For several years United Railroads officials had tried to put Tom Mooney behind bars; now, with the connivance of the district attorney, they were determined to pin this bombing on Mooney. Mooney was charged with conspiracy to bomb the parade. His co-conspirators were alleged to be his wife Rena, Warren K. Billings, Edward D. Nolan and Israel Weinberg. Mooney had associated with well-known anarchists like Lucy Parsons, Alexander Berkman and Emma Goldman for several years. Israel Weinberg was an anarchist. Perhaps most significantly, Tom Mooney was the principal organizer of the streetcar-workers' strike in San Francisco that summer.

Alexander Berkman quickly and almost alone began to raise money and support for Mooney's defense. Berkman's efforts secured attorney W. Bourke Cockran's unpaid services as chief defense counsel. Although prosecutors leaked rumors to the press that the bombing plot was hatched in the offices of Berkman's *Blast*, they did not have a shred of evidence on which to arrest him. Mooney was their principal target, and they would wait to attempt to get Berkman.

Despite the efforts of the defense attorneys, Billings was quickly tried and sentenced to life in prison. Mooney was tried separately and sentenced to death. An elaborate conspiracy was fabricated by the prosecutors who paid witnesses to testify that the Mooneys and Billings had been driven down Market street by Weinberg and that Billings and another man got out of the car and planted a suitcase containing the bomb.

Although prosecution witnesses testified to the presence of Mooney and Billings at the site of the bombing just minutes prior to the explosion, an amateur photographer snapped a picture of Tom and Rena Mooney on the roof of the building in which they lived at the exact time the witness placed them blocks away. The jeweler's clock in the photograph of the Mooneys impeached the veracity of the prosecution's witness.

By the end of Weinberg's trial in October 1917, it was clear that the original prosecution witnesses had perjured themselves. Among those who appealed to the governor for a pardon for Mooney was Judge Griffin, in whose court Mooney's had been tried. Goldman and Berkman had made Mooney's death sentence an international issue. Under pressure from President Wilson, his sentence was commuted to life in prison.

In 1926, nine of the ten living jurors appealed to the governor on Mooney's behalf; the tenth stated he would like to see Tom Mooney free and would "be one of the first to take him by the hand when he is released." Still Mooney was not released from prison. In 1932 a group of United States senators wrote a report condemning the trial which had sent Mooney to prision. Powerful interests in California kept Thomas J. Mooney in prison from 1916 until 1939.

The Mooney trial was only the beginning of war-time conspiracy trials. Many of them followed the precedent set in Judge Gary's courtroom in 1886 and used radicals' speeches and published writings to establish "conspiracies."

Thirty years after the Haymarket executions, the state of Wisconsin directly used the Haymarket precedent to convict all eleven defendants in The State of Wisconsin *vs.* Peter Bianchi, Mary Nardini, *et al*. The eleven anarchists, like the Haymarket defendants, had been shown to have possessed radical literature and to hold views contrary to prevailing opinion. It was not shown that they had bombed the police station and killed ten people, including two detectives. The district attorney held that anyone possessing anarchist literature was equally guilty of the bombing as the perpetrator, although, as in the Haymarket case, the actual bombthrower was not identified.

After serving a year of their 25-year prison sentences, they asked Clarence Darrow to appeal their case. Nine of the defendants were acquitted in the new trial; Darrow went to the governor regarding the two who had been convicted a second time, and the governor pardoned them.

The passage of the Espionage Act in June 1917, and the Sedition Act in May 1918, broadened the government's authority under which radicals could be charged. Eugene V. Debs, Kate Richards O'Hare and Rose Pastor Stokes were among many socialist leaders charged and convicted under the Espionage Act.

In Centralia, Washington, thirteen Industrial Workers of the World members were charged with conspiracy to murder after defending their hall against vigilante attack. Also indicted was their attorney, Elmer Smith, who had advised them of their right to defend themselves. Elmer Smith and one other defendant were acquitted; the others were convicted and sentenced to 25 to 40 years in prison.

Charges, convictions, and imprisonment for political beliefs did not end with the end of the war. Although the Espionage and Sedition Acts offically expired at the end of the war, many states passed their own repressive acts.

After being arrested in 1920 for distributing radical literature, Nicola Sacco and Bartolomeo Vanzetti were charged with conspiracy and murder in a shoe factory payroll robbery which authorities were anxious to solve. Despite international efforts to save them, Vanzetti and Sacco were executed in 1927.

In 1929, the radical National Textile Workers Union attempted to organize millworkers in Gastonia, North Carolina. All violence which occurred during the strike was charged to strikers and strike-leaders. When a vigilante mob destroyed union headquarters, ten strikers were arrested and charged with the destruction. Strikers rebuilt a headquarters and wrote to the governor stating their intentions to defend it. When police officers attempted to invade union headquarters a few weeks later, a struggle ensued, and the chief of police was killed. No one knew who had fired the fatal shot or whether it came from the gun of an officer or the gun of a striker. However, sixteen organizers and strikers were placed on trial for conspiracy to murder. A mistrial was declared after one juror went insane.

Charges were dropped against nine defendants before the second trial, and the charges against the remaining defendants were reduced to murder in the second degree. All seven were convicted of conspiracy to murder. The Supreme Court of North Carolina upheld the conviction, citing the Haymarket case (Spies *vs*. The People, 122 ILL.1) and Commonwealth *vs*. Sacco and Vanzetti (255 Mass .369) as precedents for holding it ''competent to cross-examine as to the part they took in the distribution of publications in question'' and ''in exciting resistance to the officers and discontent with the Government.''

Again and again conspiracy laws have been invoked. The theory promulgated by Judge Gary, that the defendants may be found guilty of any heinous crime whatsoever if their speeches and writings are perceived to threaten the status quo, has come to the rescue of many a prosecutor who lacks a solid case.

In 1951, Julius and Ethel Rosenberg and Morton Sobell were convicted of conspiracy to engage in espionage. The Rosenbergs were executed, and Sobell was sentenced to 30 years in prison. As a high school student, Julius Rosenberg had first been drawn to the radical movement after hearing about the injustices done to another political prisoner, Tom Mooney. During the Cold War and McCarthy period, many Communist Party members were charged with conspiracy, tried, convicted and imprisoned.

More recently, activists against the Vietnam war have been charged with conspiracy, tried, convicted and imprisoned. Conspiracy laws were invoked against the Black Panthers in the late 1960s and early 1970s. A century after the Haymarket trial, American Indian Movement leaders and Puerto Rican nationalists languish in prison, convicted under conspiracy laws. Dr. Benjamin Spock, Rev. William Sloan Coffin, H. Rap Brown, the Berrigan brothers, Daniel Ellsberg and Anthony Russo, the Seattle Eight, the New Haven Nine, the Wilmington Ten, and the Harrisburg Seven are among the many tried during the Johnson and Nixon years. As this book goes to press Ramona Africa of the Philadelphia group, MOVE, has been found guilty of conspiracy after police bombed the group's headquarters and home.

The Chicago Conspiracy trial of 1969 in Judge Julius J. Hoffman's court was in many ways reminiscent of the Haymarket trial. Again there were eight defendants, charged with conspiracy linking their speeches and writings to acts committed by persons they did not know.

Attorney General Ramsey Clark stated that he did not believe there to be sufficient evidence against demonstrators at the 1968 Chicago Democratic Party Convention and ordered an investigation of the conduct of the Chicago police. However, Judge William J. Campbell convened a federal

NOW FOR THE 2,000,000 MARK

SHALL
MOONEY HANG?

JUSTICE   RAPED   IN   CALIFORNIA

TOM MOONEY,
Sentenced to be hanged at San Quentin Prison, Cal., although proven to be the innocent victim of the Oxman perjury plot.

NINTH
EDITION

By ROBT. MINOR

TEN CENTS
PER COPY

Published by the
TOM MOONEY MOLDERS DEFENSE COMMITTEE
P. O. Box 894   203   San Francisco, Cal.

1,000,000   COPIES   IN   CIRCULATION

grand jury and proceeded against selected leaders of the demonstrators. The case was brought to trial with the support of the Nixon Administration Justice Department under John Mitchell.

Judge Hoffman refused two statements of a hung jury and forced the jury to reach a decision. The jurors compromised by acquitting all defendants of conspiracy, acquitting John Froines and Lee Weiner of all charges, and finding David Dellinger, Rennie Davis, Tom Hayden, Abbie Hoffman and Jerry Rubin guilty of crossing state lines with intent to incite to riot. Bobby Seale's case had earlier been separated from that of the other defendants. In November 1972, an appellate court reversed the convictions and ordered a new trial. The government chose not to hold another trial and chose not to try Bobby Seale on the original charges.

The rulings in the Haymarket trial have contributed repressive legal precedents which have been used for 100 years. Had they been used prior to Haymarket, Abraham Lincoln, James Russell Lowell. Ralph Waldo Emerson and Henry David Thoreau might well have gone to jail for opposing the 1848 war against Mexico. And William Lloyd Garrison, Frederick Douglas and Wendell Phillips might well have been tried as accessories to John Brown's attack on Harpers's Ferry.

Carolyn ASHBAUGH

"Dust" Wallin: The Supreme Court Making the Awful Lawful (*One Big Union Monthly*, March 1920)

RECOLLECTIONS OF LUCY PARSONS
& the 50th Anniversary of November 11th

I first met Lucy in the 1920s in Chicago when I was delivering a talk at the Free Society Group Forum, titled "Is Anarchism Possible?" But I left Chicago around 1929 and had no direct contact with her again until 1937, when we both spoke at a meeting at Ashland Auditorium, November 11th, 1937, the fiftieth anniversary of the execution of the Haymarket martyrs.

As members of the Pioneer Aid and Support Association, which maintained the Haymarket martyrs' monument in Waldheim Cemetery, the Free Society Group was instrumental in arranging this Fiftieth Anniversary Haymarket Commemoration—at a huge mass meeting at the auditorium and the next day at the monument itself. I was invited to address the meeting, and the Association paid my expenses from the Stelton (New Jersey) Modern School where Esther and I and our two children lived.

The Secretary-Treasurer and legal counsel of the Pioneer Aid and Support Association was Irving S. Abrams. He performed all the legal work connected with the property and other bequests left by deceased widows Lucy Parsons, Nina Spies and others; he also gave free legal advice and services to comrades caught in the legal trap. Abrams was a member of the Free Society Group which, though it consisted only of a handful of comrades, was probably the most active anarchist propaganda group in the country at that time.

The history of the Free Society Group is inseparably linked to the life of its principal founder, the Russian-Jewish anarchist, Boris Yelensky. After settling in Chicago, where he became a paperhanger, Yelensky returned to Russia in July 1917 to participate in the Russian Revolution, as is graphically recounted in his full-length memoir, *In the Social Storm*, a truly revealing primary source, written in Yiddish, and which should be published in English translation. Yelensky returned to Chicago in 1923 and in that year played a big part in organizing the Free Society Group.

I recall that the chairman of the fiftieth anniversary Haymarket meeting was a fellow named Flaherty from the Painters' Union, and that one of the speakers was Gerhard Segar, a Socialist Party member of the German Reichstag who had escaped Nazi Germany in the nick of time. Lucy stepped out on the platform, bent with age, almost totally blind—but still defiant, still hurling curses at the powers-that-be, still calling for the overthrow of capitalism. We exchanged greetings, and I was almost overcome with emotion when she remembered me.

The next day I also spoke at the Haymarket monument in Waldheim Cemetery. I did not see Lucy, but I did meet Theodore Appel, who had been a close friend of Johann Most and of several of the Haymarket martyrs, with whom he actively worked in the anarchist and eight-hour-day movements. He had edited the German-language anarchist paper *Alarm* (suppressed by the U.S. government in 1916), and had presided at the tenth anniversary Haymarket commemoration, at Waldheim, on November 11th, 1897, which was addressed by, among others, Lucy Parsons and Emma Goldman.

Regardless of what Lucy thought about one thing or another, I loved her. How deeply touched I was when, in Chicago some years ago, I saw for the first time her modest little tombstone buried close to her beloved comrade-husband, Albert Parsons, and the other comrades whom she loved and mourned these many years!

There will always be a warm spot in my heart for the indomitable, fearless rebel—Lucy Parsons.

Sam DOLGOFF

Fiftieth Commemoration

Dedicated to the Memory of

AUGUST SPIES, ALBERT R. PARSONS, LOUIS LINGG, ADOLPH FISCHER, GEORGE ENGEL, MICHAEL SCHWAB, SAMUEL FIELDEN and OSCAR NEEBE

Arranged by the

50TH HAYMARKET COMMEMORATION COMMITTEE

THURSDAY, NOVEMBER 11, 1937

at AMALGAMATED CENTER, 333 S. ASHLAND BLVD.

Chicago, Illinois

COSMOPOLITAN PTG. & PUB. CO. 304 212 N. OGDEN AV., HAY. 2337

Capital and Labor Are Partners—Not Enemies

John D. Rockefeller, Jr.

IWW cartoon by "Dust" Wallin (*One Big Union Monthly*, March 1919)

THE CHARLES H. KERR COMPANY & THE HAYMARKET HERITAGE

The 1986 Haymarket Centennial is also the Centennial of the Charles H. Kerr Company, the oldest independent labor and socialist publishing house in the world.

Charles Hope Kerr (1860-1944) was born in LaGrange, Georgia, where his abolitionist parents, Illinois natives, planned to establish a clandestine school for Blacks. At the outbreak of the Civil War the family fled north *via* "Underground Railroad." In 1881 Charles graduated from the University of Wisconsin in Madison, where his father, a classical scholar who translated Plato's *Republic*, headed the Department of Classics.

Kerr had long been involved in the left wing of the Unitarian movement when he started the publishing house in Chicago in March 1886, and early Kerr Company catalogs feature books by and/or about such writers as Theodore Parker, O. B. Frothingham, George Eliot and James Russell Lowell.

Imbued as they all were with abolitionist/transcendentalist/utopian radicalism, Kerr and his co-workers could hardly have failed to recognize at once the injustice of the Haymarket case, and the intolerable horror of the Red Scare. Unfortunately, we know little of Kerr's personal activity at the time of Haymarket, apart from his work at the publishing house. However, from the fact that so many of his closest associates were important figures in the Haymarket defense and amnesty efforts, we infer that Kerr himself—a quiet and remarkably self-effacing man—was also active in the imprisoned anarchists' behalf.

We know, for example, that the Kerr Company was intimately allied at the time with

Charles H. Kerr

the Chicago Ethical Culture Society, whose leading personality, William M. Salter, had debated Albert Parsons in 1885. According to Henry David, Salter "worked tirelessly" to save the men, and his pamphlet, *What Shall Be Done With the Anarchists?*, was a significant contribution to the clemency drive. Salter was among the group who went to Springfield to plead personally with the Governor to stop what he called the Cook County hangman's "public crime."

Working closely with Salter were Kerr's future partner, B. F. Underwood, a prominent freethinker and co-editor of the philosophical journal, *The Open Court*; Henry Demarest Lloyd, who a few years later would be a Kerr Company shareholder and perhaps the greatest of the muckrakers; and Jenkin Lloyd Jones, Unitarian minister of All Soul's Church and editor of *Unity*, a weekly published by Kerr. A frequent contributor to *Unity* and one of Kerr's closest friends was another minister, James Vila Blake of Chicago's Third Unitarian Church, where a large public meeting was held to protest the impending executions.

Some of Kerr's associates in those days—Henry Demarest Lloyd was clearly an exception—doubtless took part in the Haymarket clemency drive primarily because they were opposed to capital punishment, and not because they shared the anarchists' dream of a radical social transformation. However, in December 1886 Kerr's *Unity* published the challenging open letter excerpted here, by yet another Unitarian minister, H. Tambs Lyche —a letter remarkable for its militant tone and its closing paean to the red flag, prefiguring

---

AN OPEN LETTER ON SOCIALISTS & ANARCHISTS

Dear Unity,

Will you give room for the following lines, prompted by that brute and savage howl of revenge and hatred, which today goes up from the American press against the condemned anarchists and their brethren in spirit?. . .

Let us be frank and fair!—if [the anarchists] sincerely see in the present social order the cause of the greater part of the misery and degradation of the masses and the millions, and that a new social order based upon principles of equality and brotherhood can create happiness, freedom and glory where now is only degradation —is it any more wonderful that they preach war than that Garrison did it in slavery times? The slavery and misery the socialist would free the world from is surely a hun-

dred times deeper and blacker than Negro slavery. Why then is John Brown a hero, and the bomb-throwing socialist a monster? Why? The condemned anarchists have not, of course, thrown any bombs. . . .

It is easy enough to preach patience, and peaceable means, and gradual reforms, when we sit in our armchairs, surrounded by the comforts of civilized life, seeing about us only the better side of life; but it looks very different, be sure, to him who from early morning till late at night lives in the whirl of misery, enslaving drudgery, even starvation. For men do starve here, even among us and in this nineteenth century. . . . Let us share that kind of life for a while, and we shall better understand anarchism. . . .

But the fact is these men have done much. The Haymarket meeting marks quite

a step in the progress of the world. We dare no longer be quite so blind as before to existing wrong and misery. The light from their bomb may be the signal of danger and need. . . .

And say what we will about it, there is grandeur and glory, a halo of growing light around that red flag, which today runs up in every civilized land, up above our national and partisan colors. . . . Who knows but that that red flag may wave on the breeze when the stars and stripes are long forgotten?

H. Tambs LYCHE

from Unity,
published by Charles H. Kerr,
December 4, 1886

A few of Lucy Parsons' many advertisements in the *International Socialist Review*

the Kerr Company's later dedication to revolutionary socialism.

By the end of its first decade the Charles H. Kerr Company had become the largest publisher of reform literature in the U.S. Kerr's catalogs in the 1890s reflect decidedly Populist leanings, but were broad enough to include titles by socialists, Bellamyists, single-taxers, anarchists, radical feminists, freethinkers and—starting as early as 1887—a whole series by a then-little-known lawyer named Clarence Darrow, who played such a crucial role in the movement to secure pardons for the three surviving Haymarket prisoners.

A powerful aid to the Haymarket amnesty drive was labor journalist Lester C. Hubbard's *The Coming Climax* (1891), excerpts from which are included in this *Scrapbook*. Prefaced by Charles H. Kerr himself, this was the Company's first best-seller.

After Governor John P. Altgeld pardoned Fielden, Neebe and Schwab in June 1893, links between Kerr and Haymarket continued to proliferate as a new generation of Americans whose radicalism was awakened by the 1886-87 events encountered the country's most persistent publisher of anti-Establishment literature.

Altgeld himself, later in the decade, became an enthusiastic booster of Kerr's new journal of social criticism and reform, *The New Time*; his is the first signature on a letter addressed "To All Friends of Social Reform," saluting the publication's "lofty courage" and "unselfish zeal," and urging the public to support it.

The last book Altgeld published in his lifetime, *Oratory*—which he regarded as his most important work—was brought out by Kerr in 1901. At Altgeld's death the following year, Kerr published Darrow's moving memorial address honoring the former governor who had "opened the prison doors and set the captive free."

Another supporter of *The New Time*, and co-signer of the letter "To All Friends of Social Reform," was Capt. William P. Black, who had been the Chicago anarchists' chief counsel and friend, one of the principal speakers at their funeral, and a contributor to Lucy Parsons' compilation of writings by and about her martyred husband.

Eugene V. Debs' fine tribute, "The Martyred Apostles of Labor"—excerpted elsewhere in these pages—first appeared in *The New Time* in February 1898, and was later reprinted in the large collection, *Debs: His Life, Writings and Speeches*, a volume which also included the first biography of Debs (by Stephen Marion Reynolds), published by Kerr in 1910 with an introduction by Mary E. Marcy.

The Kerr Company was reorganized as a cooperative in 1893, and six years later it became a specifically labor and socialist publishing house. In 1900 Kerr began to publish the *International Socialist Review*, widely regarded by historians as the most important socialist publication in the U.S. up to that time. Significant Haymarket echoes in the pages of the *Review* include John Spargo's notice of Frank Harris' novel, *The Bomb*; A. M. Simons' review of Lucy Parsons' *Life*

of Albert R. Parsons; numerous advertisements for the *Famous Speeches*; and many another reference or allusion. Interestingly, too, Lucy Parsons' companion, George Markstall, became a Kerr Company shareholder during the *Review*'s first decade.

Among the *Review*'s most prolific contributors were many whose lives had been significantly transformed by the extraordinary complex of events that extended from May 1886 to Altgeld's pardon seven years later—including Ralph Chaplin (a longtime member of the Kerr Board of Directors), Big Bill Haywood (who was on the *Review*'s Editorial Board), Carl Sandburg (whose pamphlet, *You and Your Job*, Kerr published in 1908), IWW organizer Elizabeth Gurley Flynn, and many others.

Another major contributor to the *Review* was the great Mother Jones, who had listened to anarchist speakers on the Chicago lakefront in pre-Haymarket days. Her classic *Autobiography*, originally published by Kerr in 1925 and many times reprinted, includes a chapter on "The Haymarket Tragedy."

Kerr also published *The Career and Conversation of John Swinton: Journalist, Orator and Economist* by Robert Waters (1902)—the first biography of Swinton, a personal friend and correspondent of Karl Marx and the only well-known American newspaperman to denounce the Haymarket frame-up right from the start.

Oscar Peterson, the Kerr Company's Secretary-Treasurer in the late 1920s and early '30s, wrote a rousing tribute to "The Chicago Haymarket Martyrs" for the December

1928 issue of *The Proletarian*, journal of the Proletarian Party. "Let us learn," he wrote, "to do but a small part of what these men did and we will have done something."

All through the hard years from the beginning of World War II to the early 1960s, when so many American radical traditions of solidarity and internationalism died as casualties of "national security," the Taft-Hartley Slave Labor Act and McCarthyist witch-hunts, the Kerr Company somehow held out against seemingly impossible odds—one of a very few tangible links with the Haymarket heritage. Kerr Board members John Keracher, who was born in Scotland; Al Wysocki, the son of Polish parents; Bohemian-born Anna Tomasek; the Sicilian Charles Barone; the Afro-American Charles Ray; German-born Frank Baumann; Scandinavian Stanley Cederlund—all now deceased—and Sam Calander, elected to the Kerr Board in 1939 and still on the Board today, were among the stubborn "keepers of the dream" who continued to take part in Eleventh of November and May Day commemorations.

It was thus entirely fitting that Irving Abrams, the last surviving member of the old Pioneer Aid and Support Association, formed in 1887 to care for the widows and children of the Haymarket martyrs, and later to care for the monument at Waldheim, should have played a key role in reactivating the Kerr Company in the early 1970s. Helping in this effort, and still active on the Kerr Board today, were Joseph Giganti, midwestern director of Sacco-Vanzetti defense in the 1920s, and organizer of several Paris Commune commemorations at which Lucy Parsons was the featured speaker; and Fred Thompson of the IWW, an alumnus of San Quentin (for "criminal syndicalism") who in 1936 made the arrangements for Nina Spies' funeral.

In 1976, the ninetieth anniversary of Haymarket, Kerr published Carolyn Ashbaugh's outstanding biography, *Lucy Parsons: American Revolutionary*.

During the last decade many people have come to the aid of the Kerr Company, either as participants in the recently-formed support-group, the "Friends of Kerr," or in other ways. Among these are many old-timers who knew Lucy Parsons or Nina Spies, or have been otherwise deeply affected by Haymarket traditions—including Sam and Esther Dolgoff, Georgia Lloyd, Henry Rosemont, Vicky Starr, Vera Buch Weisbord and O. W. Neebe, grandson of Haymarket anarchist Oscar Neebe.

The Kerr Company started off its centennial year by bringing out a new edition of Altgeld's classic pardon message, and—for the first time in book-form—*The Autobiography of Florence Kelley*, an appointee and co-worker of Altgeld's who was also a mainstay of Jane Addams' Hull House. Irving Abrams' memoirs and a selection of Voltairine de Cleyre's poems are "in the works." And now here is the *Haymarket Scrapbook*.

The Kerr Company emphasizes labor history not out of nostalgia but to advance the cause of workingclass emancipation here and now. The questions raised by Haymarket—indeed, by the entire history of the workers' movement—are still vital today. The Charles H. Kerr Publishing Company starts its second century as a living symbol that *the struggle continues.*

FR

SOURCES

Paul Avrich. *The Haymarket Tragedy* (Princeton, 1984).
Paul Buhle. "Great Moments in Agitpop: The Kerr Company's Red Lit Revival," *Village Voice Literary Supplement* (New York, September 1985).
Ralph Chaplin. *Wobbly* (Chicago, 1949).
Henry David. *The History of the Haymarket Affair* (New York, 1958).
Charles H. Kerr. *A Socialist Publishing House* (Chicago, 1904).
—. "A Working Class Publishing House," *Plebs* (London, February 1910), 33-34.
H. Tambs Lyche. "Socialists and Anarchists," *Unity* (Chicago, December 4, 1886), 177-178.
Susan Quackenbush. "*Unity*: 1878-1918," *Unity* (Chicago, March 7, 1918), 9, 10, 16.
Unity, Tenth Anniversary Number (Chicago, March 3, 1888).
Vogel, Virgil. "The Story of America's Oldest Socialist Publisher" (mimeo circular, 1978).
Books, periodicals, catalogs issued by the Charles H. Kerr Company, in the Charles H. Kerr Company Archives, Newberry Library, Chicago.
Interviews with Katharine Kerr Moore (Charles H. Kerr's daughter), Sam Calander, Joseph Giganti, Fred Thompson, and the late Al Wysocki.
And thanks to Allen Ruff of Madison, Wisconsin, who is completing a doctoral dissertation on the Charles H. Kerr Company, for information on Kerr/Haymarket connections in the early years of the firm.

"Lest We Forget: The Eight-Hour Railroad Worker of 1916."
Cartoon by Robert Minor from Alexander Berkman's *Blast*,
reprinted in the *International Socialist Review*, May 1916

NOTES ON CONTRIBUTORS

William J. Adelman is the author of *Haymarket Revisited* (1976; revised 1986) and two other labor history tour-guides: *Touring Pullman* and *Pilsen and the West Side*, all published by the Illinois Labor History Society, which he co-founded and now serves as Vice-President. Co-ordinator of the University of Illinois' Chicago Labor Education Program, he was instrumental in organizing the Haymarket Centennial Committee.

Editor of the local paper in Glen Echo, Maryland, **Carlotta Anderson** has worked as a freelance writer, journalist and researcher for *Newsweek* and the London *Daily Mail*, and is currently preparing a full-length biography of her grandfather, Joseph A. Labadie.

A veteran of the Spanish Revolution, **Federico Arcos** lives today in Canada. A collection of his poems, *Momentos*—in which "Waldheim" is included—was published by Black & Red in Detroit in 1976.

Carolyn Ashbaugh is the author of *Lucy Parsons: American Revolutionary*, published by Charles H. Kerr in 1976. Currently studying microbiology in California, she has lectured throughout the country on the subject of women and the labor movement.

One of the major historians of the international anarchist movement, **Paul Avrich** is Distinguished Professor of History at Queens College and the Graduate School, the City University of New York. His books include *The Haymarket Tragedy, An American Anarchist: The Life of Voltairine de Cleyre*, and *The Modern School: Anarchism and Education in the United States*, all published by Princeton University Press.

Heiner Becker of the International Institute of Social History in Amsterdam has recently edited and introduced an anthology of Johann Most's writings (in German) and is preparing a biography of Most. He is also actively involved in publishing projects connected with the 1986 centennial of Freedom Press in London.

Martin Blatt has edited and introduced *The Collected Works of Ezra H. Heywood* (M & S Press), and has completed a biography of Heywood to be published by the University of Illinois Press. He has worked with Boston-area unions and the Massachusetts History Workshop in organizing a centennial commemoration of the struggle for the eight-hour day.

A leading Danish labor historian whose articles have appeared in many anthologies and journals, **Gerd Callesen** is also head of the periodicals department of the Danish Labor Archives in Copenhagen.

Son of a Mexican Wobbly father and a German socialist mother, IWW poet and artist **Carlos Cortez**, born in 1923, lives in Chicago where he is a featured columnist for the *Industrial Worker*. His exhibit, *Wobbly: 80 Years of Rebel Art*—organized to commemorate the eightieth anniversary of the IWW in 1985—is currently touring the country. The full text of "Where Are the Voices?" appears in Joyce Kornbluh's *Rebel Voices: An IWW Anthology*, forthcoming from Charles H. Kerr.

One of the greatest artists active in the anarchist movement, **Flavio Costantini** lives in Rapallo, Italy. A superb album of his work, *The Art of Anarchy*, was published by Cienfuegos Press in London, 1975, with an introduction by Stuart Christie. Costantini's *Chicago, May 3rd, 1886* is available as a large full-color poster from Charles H. Kerr.

Robert D'Atillio is a historian of Italian-American anarchism currently researching the Sacco-Vanzetti case. He helped organize the the 1979 Sacco-Vanzetti Conference in Boston and co-edited its proceedings, *Sacco-Vanzetti: Developments and Reconsiderations* (Boston Public Library, 1982). He lives in Medford, Massachusetts.

Alan Dawley has taken the lead both in the writing of the "new labor history" and in making that history broadly accessible to the public. His *Class and Community: The Industrial Revolution in Lynn* won the Bancroft Prize. A member of the history faculty at Trenton

State, Dawley has served on the Editorial Board of *Labor History* and is co-editor of the excellent new popular history of U.S. labor, *Working for Democracy*.

Sam Dolgoff, now in his eighties, has been active in the anarchist movement and the IWW since the early 1920s. Author of such pamphlets as *The American Labor Movement: A New Beginning* and *The Relevance of Anarchism to Modern Society*, he also edited the anthology, *Bakunin on Anarchism* (Knopf, 1972; new edition, Black Rose, 1980), and has recently completed an autobiography. He lives in New York.

Richard Drinnon teaches at Bucknell University. His biography of Emma Goldman (*Rebel in Paradise*, 1961), his editing of her writings and those of Alexander Berkman, and his many articles in *Anarchy* and other journals mark him as a leading historian of American anarchism. His *Facing West: The Metaphysics of Indian Hating and Empire Building*, is a powerful analysis of racism, violence and American expansionism.

George Esenwein's studies of the Spanish Left have appeared in the journal *Labor History* as well as in the *Historical Dictionary of the Spanish Civil War* and the *Biographical Dictionary of Marxism*, published by Greenwood. He is currently working at the Stanford University Library and completing a doctoral dissertation on nineteenth-century Spanish anarchism.

Don Fitz is the manging editor of WD Press in St Louis and an editor of *Workers' Democracy*, an anti-authoritarian journal advocating socialist industrial unionism. He has written on a wide range of topics—including Marxist theory, organizing strategies, and the history of labor and racism in St. Louis.

Philip S. Foner is America's most prolific historian of labor, radicalism and the Black experience. Among his scores of books are *Organized Labor and the Black Worker, Mark Twain: Social Critic* and the multi-volume *History of the Labor Movement in the U.S.* Professor Emeritus at Lincoln University, Foner edited *The Autobiographies of the Haymarket Martyrs* and *Inside the Monster, On Education* and *Our America*—collections of writings by Jose Marti.

Paul and Elizabeth Garon are the proprietors of Chicago's Beasley Books, specializing in modern first editions and radical literature. Paul has been active in surrealism since 1968; his *Rana Mozelle* is available in the Surrealist Research & Development Monograph Series. He has also written a study of blues-singer *Peetie Wheatstraw: The Devil's Son-in-Law*, and the widely-acclaimed *Blues and the Poetic Spirit*, published by DaCapo.

Ray Ginger pioneered in the writing of Gilded Age history as he masterfully combined the subjects of business, labor, politics and everyday life. His biography of Eugene Debs, *The Bending Cross*, remains a classic. Among his other books are *Altgeld's America* and *The Age of Success*. A professor at Harvard, Wayne State, Brandeis and elsewhere, he edited *Business History Review* and *U.S.A.*

Robert Green's cartoons have appeared in the *Industrial Worker, Cultural Correspondence, Workers' Defense, Free Spirits*, etc., and are featured in the Radical Humor Exhibition that toured the U.S. in recent years and is now on its way through Europe. A co-founder of the Surrealist Movement in the U.S. in the mid-1960s, he is increasingly recognized as one of the greatest surrealist sculptors. A collection of his drawings and poems, *Seditious Mandibles*, was published by Black Swan Press in 1981.

Joseph Jablonski, former union shop-steward in Pennsylvania's welfare department and active in the surrealist movement since 1970, has contributed studies of Shakers and other utopians to such journals as *Free Spirits, Cultural Correspondence* and *Arsenal: Surrealist Subversion*. He has also written two books of poems, *In a Moth's Wing* and *The Dust on My Eyes is the Blood of Your Hair*, both published by Black Swan Press. He lives in Harrisburg, where he is completing an anthology of atheist and antireligious writings.

Stuart Bruce Kaufman heads the Samuel Gompers Papers Project and teaches history at the University of Maryland. His *Samuel Gompers and the Origins of the American Federation of Labor, 1848-1896* has contributed much to the historical reassessment of the early AFL and its outstanding leader.

Widely recognized as one of the best labor cartoonists in the U.S. today, **Mike Konopacki** has had cartoons published in hundreds of AFL-CIO publications as well as in independent papers such as *Labor Notes*, the *Industrial Worker* and *UE News*. A collection of his Madison *Press Connection* cartoons appeared in 1979, and a book of his more recent work is in preparation.

Actor, musician, stand-up comedian and theater historian, **Warren Leming**, formerly with Chicago's Second City, is a member of the International Bertolt Brecht Society and has lectured extensively on Brecht in recent years. He has also collaborated on a full-length video on the Haymarket affair.

Sidney Lens, Senior Editor of *The Progressive* and founder of Mobilization for Survival, has been active in the labor and socialist movements since the early 1930s. His many books include *Left, Right and Center*, *The Crisis of American Labor*, *Radicalism in America*, *The Labor Wars* and an autobiography, *Unrepentant Radical*.

Professor of American Thought and Language at Michigan State University in East Lansing, **Blaine McKinley** has written on aspects of anarchist history for the *Journal of American Culture* and *American Quarterly*.

Howard S. Miller, Professor of History at the University of Missouri in St. Louis, is the author of a wide variety of historical works on subjects ranging from science to philanthropy to the Eads Bridge. He is currently at work on a major study of Ozark Mountain anarchist Kate Austin and her relationship to traditions of rural radicalism.

Especially well known for his widely-reproduced poster of "The Garrote," Spanish painter **Alfredo Monros** has contributed extensively to libertarian publications in many countries. He lives in Canada.

Bruce Nelson is the leading expert on Chicago's radical labor movement in the late nineteenth century. His dissertation, *Culture and Conspiracy: A Social History of Chicago Anarchism, 1870-1900*, explores both the political and the social life of that movement. He is a contributor to the special Haymarket issue of *International Labor and Working Class History*. An active member of the Chicago Area Labor History Group, he has presented numerous papers on Chicago anarchism at its discussions. He is on the faculty at Northern Illinois University.

A member of the National Staff of the Students for a Democratic Society in 1967-68, **Penelope Rosemont** has contributed to such publications as *Free Spirits*, *Radical America* and *Cultural Correspondence*, as well as to surrealist journals throughout the world, and her paintings have been included in surrealist exhibitions in many countries. A collection of her poems, *Athanor*, is available from Black Swan Press. Active in Chicago Typographical Union No. 16, she has been the local's delegate to labor conferences and is the first woman to serve as director of No. 16's Credit Union.

Born and raised in Birmingham, England, where she still lives, **Beryl Ruehl** has been active in the British labor movement since childhood. A nuclear disarmament activist in the 1960s, she has also taken part in Centre 42, a movement to involve trade-unionists in the arts. After completing a degree in history at the University of Birmingham in 1974, she worked with Dorothy Thompson on a Chartist bibliography, and researched William Morris' work as editor of *Com-*

monweal. A contributor to the feminist peace studies anthology, *Over Our Dead Bodies* (Virago, 1983), she is also a poet and has taught at the Open University.

Sal Salerno recently completed a doctoral dissertation on *The Early Labor Radicalism of the IWW: A Socio-Cultural Critique*, focused on anarchist and syndicalist influences on the origins of the industrial union movement in the U.S., especially as manifested in Wobbly culture. He teaches sociology at the University of Massachusetts.

Steven Sapolsky, whose recent work appears in *International Labor and Working Class History*, teaches at the University of Pittsburgh where he is completing a meticulously researched and broadly conceived study of building trades workers in late nineteenth and early twentieth century Chicago.

An editor of the journal *Jewish Currents*, **Morris U. Schappes** has written widely in the field of Jewish labor and radical history. His *Documentary History of the Jews in the United States* is published by Schocken.

Diane Scherer, a graduate student at the University of Michigan in Ann Arbor, is writing a dissertation on Chinese anarchists and their activity in the labor movement.

Richard Schneirov, who completed his dissertation on *The Knights of Labor in Chicago* in 1984, has also co-authored *A History of the Carpenters of Chicago*, forthcoming from Southern Illinois University Press, and has contributed to such journals as *Chicago History* and *Labour / Le Travail*.

Joffre Stewart, the best-known anarcho-pacifist poet in the U.S., was born in 1925. Long before the 1960s civil rights agitation he began his one-man sit-ins protesting segregation and militarism, earning him the greatest arrest-record of any poet of his generation. Over the years he has contributed to numerous radical publications, including *A Way Out*, the *Industrial Worker* and *Peacemaker*. "The Home to May Day" is excerpted from "In Pottawattomie Country" in *Poems and Poetry by Joffre Stewart* (1982). He lives in Chicago.

Born in St. John, New Brunswick, Canada in 1900, **Fred Thompson** joined the Industrial Workers of the World in the early 1920s and shortly thereafter was convicted of "criminal syndicalism" and spent nearly four years in San Quentin. Editor of the *Industrial Worker* at various times, he has written *The IWW: Its First Fifty Years* (1955; revised and expanded, 1975), and valuable introductions to *The Autobiography of Mother Jones* and Paul Lafargue's *Right to Be Lazy*, both published by Charles H. Kerr. He lives in Chicago.

Michael Vandelaar, co-founder of the Surrealist Group in Australia and co-editor of *The Insurrectionist's Shadow*, has organized a conference on Haymarket for the centennial of the anarchist movement in Australia on May 1, 1986.

Labor historian **Theodore Watts** is the author of *The First Labor Day: Tuesday, September 5, 1882—Media Mirrors to Labor's Icons* (Phoenix Rising, 1983), an examination of popular iconography of the organized labor movement. He lives in Silver Spring, Maryland.

A Kansas native, **Fred Whitehead** is an ex-welder, poet and teacher in adult and labor-related college programs in the Kansas City area. He has published widely on workingclass history and culture, and recently organized a commemorative exhibition on the centennial of the Great Southwest Strike of 1886. A more detailed version of "The Kansas Response" appears in the journal *Kansas History*.

Alexander Yard has studied and taught at the University of Missouri at St. Louis, and Washington University, and currently teaches at St. Louis' Crossroads School. His *St. Louis in American History: Narrative Texts and Curriculum Units*, an innovative work that integrates local and national history, is scheduled to appear soon.

A HAYMARKET BIBLIOGRAPHY

BOOKS

ADAMIC, Louis. *Dynamite: The Story of Class Violence in America.* New York: Viking, 1935.

ADELMAN, William J. *Haymarket Revisited.* Chicago: Illinois Labor History Society, 1972; revised, 1986.

—. *Pilsen and the West Side: A Tour Guide.* Chicago: Illinois Labor History Society, 1983.

—. *Touring Pullman.* Chicago: Illinois Labor History Society, 1972.

ALGREN, Nelson. *Chicago: City on the Make.* Sausalito, Contact Editions, 1961.

ALTGELD, John P. *Live Questions.* Chicago, George S. Bowen, 1899.

—. *Reasons for Pardoning the Haymarket Anarchists: Fielden, Neebe and Schwab.* Introduction by Leon M. Despres. Chicago: Charles H. Kerr, 1986.

AMES, Sarah E. *An Open Letter to Judge Joseph E. Gary.* Chicago: Ames, 1893.

ANDREWS, J. A. *What Is Communism? and Other Anarchist Essays.* Prahan, Australia: Backyard Press, c. 1980.

ASHBAUGH, Carolyn. *Lucy Parsons: American Revolutionary.* Chicago: Charles H. Kerr, 1976.

AVELING, Edward and Eleanor Marx. *The Working-Class Movement in America.* London: Sonnenschein, 1890.

AVRICH, Paul. *An American Anarchist: The Life of Voltairine de Cleyre.* Princeton: Princeton University Press, 1978.

—. *The Haymarket Tragedy.* Princeton: Princeton University Press, 1984.

—. *The Modern School Movement: Anarchism and Education in the United States.* Princeton: Princeton University Press, 1980.

BARNARD, Harry. *Eagle Forgotten: The Life of John Peter Altgeld.* Indianapolis: Bobbs-Merrill, 1938.

BERKMAN, Alexander. *What Is Communist Anarchism?* Introduction by Paul Avrich. New York: Dover, 1972.

BLATT, Martin, ed. *The Collected Works of Ezra Heywood.* Weston: M & S Press, 1985.

BOYER, Richard O. and Herbert M. Morais. *Labor's Untold Story.* New York: United Electrical, Radio & Machine Workers of America, 1974.

BRECHER, Jeremy. *Strike!* San Francisco: Straight Arrow, 1972.

BROMMEL, Bernard. *Eugene V. Debs: Spokesman for Labor and Socialism.* Chicago: Charles H. Kerr, 1978.

BROWNE, Waldo R. *Altgeld of Illinois.* New York: Huebsch, 1924.

BUCHANAN, Joseph R. *The Story of a Labor Agitator.* New York: The Outlook Company, 1903.

BUHLE, Mari Jo. *Women and American Socialism.* Urbana, University of Illinois Press, 1981.

BUHLE, Paul, with Scott Molloy and Gail Sansbury. *A History of Rhode Island Working People.* Providence: Rhode Island State Federation of Labor, 1983.

— and Alan Dawley, eds. *Working for Democracy: American Workers from the Revolution to the Present.* Introduction by Herbert Gutman. Urbana: University of Illinois Press, 1985.

CAHN, William. *A Pictorial History of American Labor.* New York: Crown, 1972.

CALMER, Alan. *Labor Agitator: The Story of Albert R. Parsons.* Foreword by Lucy Parsons. New York: International, 1937.

CHAPLIN, Ralph. *Wobbly: The Rough-and-Tumble Story of an American Radical.* Chicago: University of Chicago Press, 1948.

CHRISTMAN, Henry M., ed. *The Mind and Spirit of John Peter Altgeld.* Urbana: University of Illinois Press, 1965.

de CLEYRE, Voltairine. *The First May Day: The Haymarket Speeches, 1895-1910.* Introduction by Paul Avrich. London & Minneapolis, Cienfuegos Press and Soil of Liberty, 1980.

—. *Selected Writings.* New York: Mother Earth, 1914.

COMMONS, John R. and Associates. *History of Labour in the United States.* Vols. I & II. New York: Macmillan, 1921.

COSTANTINI, Flavio. *The Art of Anarchy.* Introduction by Stuart Christie. London, Cienfuegos Press, 1975.

CURRLIN, Albert, ed. *Reminiscenzen von Aug. Spies.* Chicago: Christine Spies, 1888.

DARROW, Clarence. *The Story of My Life.* New York: Scribner's, 1932.

DAVID, Henry. *The History of the Haymarket Affair.* Second Printing with New Preface. New York: Russell & Russell, 1958.

DEBS, Eugene V. *Walls and Bars.* Chicago: Charles H. Kerr, 1973.

DELANEY, Ed and M. T. Rice. *The Bloodstained Trail: A History of Militant Labor in the U.S.* Seattle: The Industrial Worker, 1927.

DOLGOFF, Sam. *The American Labor Movement: A New Beginning.* Champaign: Resurgence, 1980.

—, ed. *Bakunin on Anarchism.* Montreal: Black Rose, 1980.

DRINNON, Richard. *Rebel in Paradise: A Biography of Emma Goldman.* Chicago: University of Chicago Press, 1961.

FAST, Howard. *The American: A Midwestern Legend.* New York: Duell, Sloan & Pearce, 1946.

FONER, Philip S., ed. *The Autobiographies of the Haymarket Martyrs.* New York: Monad Press, 1969.

—. *History of the Labor Movement in the United States.* Five volumes. New York: International, 1947-68.

FUSFELD, Daniel R. *The Rise and Repression of Radical Labor in the U.S., 1877-1918.* Chicago: Charles H. Kerr, 1980; third edition, revised, 1985.

GARLIN, Sender. *William Dean Howells and the Haymarket Era.* New York: American Institute for Marxist Studies, 1979.

GHIO, Paul. *L'Anarchisme aux Etats-Unis.* Paris: Armand Colin, 1903.

GINGER, Ray. *Altgeld's America.* New York: Funk & Wagnall's, 1958.

—. *Eugene V. Debs: A Biography.* New York: Collier, 1962.

GOLDEN, Harry. *Carl Sandburg.* New York: Crest, 1962.

GOLDMAN, Emma. *Anarchism and Other Essays.* New York: Mother Earth, 1911.

—. *Living My Life.* New York: Dover, 1970.

GUERIN, Daniel. *Anarchism.* Introduction by Noam Chomsky. New York: Monthly Review, 1970.

—. *100 Years of Labor in the USA.* London: InkLinks, 1979.

HAYWOOD, William D. *Bill Haywood's Book.* New York: International, 1958.

HARRIS, Frank. *The Bomb.* New York: Mitchell Kennerley, 1909.

HERRICK, Robert M. *The Memoirs of an American Citizen.* Cambridge: Harvard University Press, 1963.

HONG, Nhat. *The Anarchist Beast: The Anti-Anarchist Crusade in Periodical Literature, 1884-1906.* Minneapolis: Soil of Liberty, c. 1980.

HUBBARD, Lester C. *The Coming Climax.* Chicago: Charles H. Kerr, 1891.

HULL, Paul C. *The Chicago Riot.* Chicago, 1886.

HYNDMAN, H. M. *The Chicago Riots and the Class War in the U.S.* London, 1886.

IWW Songs: To Fan the Flames of Discontent. Chicago: Industrial Workers of the World, 1985.

JOLL, James. *The Anarchists.* New York: Grosset, 1966.

JONES, Mary Harris. *The Autobiography of Mother Jones.* Chicago: Charles H. Kerr, 1925; third edition, 1976.

KEBABIAN, John S. *The Haymarket Affair and the Trial of the Chicago Anarchists, 1886.* Catalog of State Prosecutor Julius Grinnell's collection. New York: H. P. Kraus, 1970.

KEDWARD, Roderick. *The Anarchists: The Men Who Shocked an Era.* New York: American Heritage, 1971.

KOGAN, Bernard R. *The Chicago Haymarket Riot: Anarchy on Trial. Selected Materials for College Research Papers.* Boston: Heath, 1959.

KORNBLUH, Joyce, ed. *Rebel Voices: An IWW Anthology.* Expanded edition. Chicago: Charles H. Kerr, 1986.

KROPOTKIN, Peter. *Kropotkin's Revolutionary Pamphlets.* Edited and introduced by Roger A. Baldwin. New York: Dover, 1970.

LANG, Olga. *Pa Chin [Ba Jin] and His Writings.* Cambridge: Harvard University Press, 1967.

LENS, Sidney. *The Labor Wars: From the Molly Maguires to the Sitdowns.* New York: Anchor, 1974.

LUM, Dyer D. *A Concise History of the Great Trial of the Chicago Anarchists in 1886.* Chicago: Socialist Publishing Co., 1887.

—: *In Memoriam: Chicago, November 11, 1887.* Introduction by Voltairine de Cleyre. Berkeley Heights, New Jersey: The Oriole Press, 1937.

MACKAY, John Henry. *The Anarchists: A Picture of Civilization at the Close of the Nineteenth Century.* Boston: Benjamin R. Tucker, 1891.

MALATESTA, Errico. *Malatesta's Anarchy.* Translated by Vernon Richards. London: Freedom Press, 1974.

McLEAN, George N. *The Rise and Fall of Anarchy in America.* Chicago: Badoux, 1888.

MOST, Johann. *Beast and Monster: Two Essays on Anarchism.* Tucson: The Match!, 1973.

—. *The God Pestilence.* Tucson: The Match!, 1983.

PARSONS, Albert R. *Anarchism: Its Philosophy and Scientific Basis, as Defined by Some of Its Apostles.* Chicago: Mrs. A. R. Parsons, 1887.

PARSONS, Lucy E., ed. *The Famous Speeches of the Eight Chicago Anarchists.* Chicago: Lucy E. Parsons, 1912.

—. *The Life of Albert R. Parsons.* Chicago: Lucy E. Parsons, 1889; new edition, 1903.

—. *The Principles of Anarchism: A Lecture.* Chicago: Lucy E. Parsons, n.d.

PIERCE, Bessie Louise. *A History of Chicago.* New York: Knopf, 1937.

Political Justice: The Haymarket Three. Middletown: Xerox Corporation, 1972.

RICHARDS, Vernon, ed. *Errico Malatesta: His Life and Ideas.* London: Freedom Press, 1965.

ROCKER, Rudolf. *Pioneers of American Freedom.* Los Angeles: Rocker Publications Committee, 1949.

ROSEMONT, Henry P. *Chicago Typographical Union No. 16, 1852-1952.* Chicago: Chicago Typographical Union No. 16, 1952.

SEEGER, Pete and Bob Reiser. *Carry It On! A History in Song and Picture of the Working Men and Women of America.* New York: Simon and Schuster, 1986.

SPIES, August. *August Spies' Autobiography; His Speech in Court and General Notes.* Chicago: Nina van Zandt, 1887.

SCHAACK, Capt. Michael J. *Anarchy and Anarchists.* Chicago: F. J. Schulte, 1889.

SCHMIDT, Frederick R. *He Chose: The Other Was a Treadmill Thing.* Santa Fe: Schmidt, 1968.

TAFT, Philip. *The AFL in the Time of Gompers.* New York: Harper & Row, 1957.

TAX, Meredith. *The Rising of the Women: Feminist Solidarity and Class Conflict, 1880-1917.* New York: Monthly Review, 1980.

THOMPSON, E. P. *William Morris: Romantic to Revolutionary.* London: Merlin Press, 1977.

WALTER, Nicholas. *About Anarchism.* London: Freedom Press, 1971.

WEINBERG, Arthur. *Attorney for the Damned: A Biography of Clarence Darrow.* New York: Simon & Schuster, 1957.

WOODCOCK, George. *Anarchism: A History of Libertarian Ideas and Movements.* Cleveland: World, 1962.

WOODWORTH, Fred. *Anarchism: What Is It? Is it Practical or Utopian? Is Government Necessary?* Tucson: The Match!, 1974.

YELLEN, Samuel. *American Labor Struggles, 1877-1934.* New York: Monad Press, 1974.

YOUNG, Art. *On My Way.* New York: Liveright, 1928.

ZEISLER, Sigmund. *Reminiscences of the Anarchist Case.* Chicago, 1927.

ARTICLES

ABRAMS, Irving S. "The Haymarket Tragedy: Part I—Pioneer Aid," "Part II—Who Threw the Bomb?," *Freedom* (London), November 11 & 18, 1972.

ADELMAN, William J. "Illinois' Forgotten Labor History," *Illinois Issues*, May 1984.

BUHLE, Paul. "The Poet-Prophets: Revolutionary Artists in the U.S., from 1870 to 1930," *Free Spirits: Annals of the Insurgent Imagination*, San Francisco, City Lights Books, 1982.

CARTER, Everett. "The Haymarket Affair in Literature," *American Quarterly* 2, Fall 1950.

DESTLER, Chester M. "Shall Red and Black Unite? An American Revolutionary Document of 1883," *Pacific Historical Review* 14, December 1945.

"*Freedom*: Our First Centenary," *Freedom: Anarchist Monthly* (London), January-February 1986.

GARY, Joseph E. "The Chicago Anarchists of 1886: The Crime, and the Trial, and the Punishment," *The Century Magazine*, April 1893.

HICKS, Clark B. "The Chicago Anarchists of 1886," *Typographical Journal*, November 1947.

JAMES, C. L. "Judge Gary on the Anarchists," *Twentieth Century*, April 30, 1893.

KOGAN, Herman. "William Perkins Black: Haymarket Lawyer," *Chicago History* 5, Summer 1976.

MAROHN, Richard C. "The Haymarket Lightning," *The Gun Report*, April 1977.

McCONNELL, Samuel P. "The Chicago Bomb Case. Personal Recollections of an American Tragedy," *Harper's*, May 1934.

ROSEMONT, Franklin. "Free Play and No Limit: An Introduction to Edward Bellamy's Utopia," *Cultural Correspondence* 10-11, Fall 1979.

RUSSELL, Charles Edward. "The Haymarket and Afterward. Some Personal Recollections," *Appleton's*, October 1907.

SALTER, William M. "What Shall Be Done With the Anarchists?" *Open Court*, October 27, 1887.

SCHNEIROV, Richard. "Chicago's Great Upheaval of 1877," *Chicago History*, Spring 1980.

AFTERWORD

By Ron Sakolsky

Haymarket 1986

one hundred years

of the

eight hour day

is enough!

When this seminal volume was first published for the Haymarket Centennial in 1986, anarchy was at a low ebb in the U.S.A. The Battle of Seattle, which was a defining moment in the global justice movement, was thirteen years away. The subsequent criminalization of anarchists in the throes of the "war on terror" and the "Green Scare" was still to come. Stateside anarchists had heard of the black bloc tactic of the European autonomists in relation to May Day mayhem, but it had not yet been imagined in an American context.

May Day, though originating in Chicago in 1886, was barely remembered in the U.S. as an international day of resistance to the capitalist state in 1986. Instead, it had been usurped in the United States by Labor Day, or even worse by the official Nixonian holiday of Law Day. Instead of depicting its American roots, May Day was represented on television by military parades in the Soviet Union as part of a cold war milieu in which authoritarian state socialism was equated with communism and libertarian socialism was relegated to the dust heap of history. Anarchy was only mentioned as something a country *descended into* when fear reigned and all hope was lost. Given such historical amnesia, it is precisely the power of re-membering that was at the heart of the *Haymarket Scrapbook* project.

The book was intended to vividly recall both the militant refusal of wage slavery in Chicago and the ensuing police state repression that such bold action engendered. In a strange way, the current wave of repression being directed against non-violent direct actionists, insurrectionary anarchists and forest defenders alike is proof positive that anarchy is once again alive and well. Today, anarchism, in all its diversity, is seen as threatening to the powers that be

in some of the same ways that the Haymarket anarchists spooked the established order back in their day, as well as in other ways not yet envisioned in 1886. In retrospect, it might seem somewhat absurd, but in 1986, anarchists often lamented the fact that they were a dying breed. They gloomily asked themselves whether the younger generation that had grown up in Reagan's America would ever pick up the torch of anarchy and carry it into the next century. In truth, back then many of the oldtimers who lamented the death of anarchy were often out of touch with the anarchist cultures of resistance then in formation. Together the later resisters inhabited the cracks in the New World Order, and once they had gathered enough steam, they defiantly made their public debut at the WTO protests just as the century was about to turn.

Compared to 1986, anarchy today seems like a youth movement, but this generational shift has a legacy that goes back to the Haymarket centennial which took place in Chicago in that same year. In spite of the doom and gloom predictions concerning anarchy's demise, even in 1986 Chicago was not completely forgotten as a nexus of anarchist history. Not only was the *Haymarket Scrapbook* published in honor of the 100 year anniversary of the Chicago uprising, but that city was the site of the first of several continental anarchist gatherings in the Eighties. Being a participant in the Haymarket International Anarchist Gathering of 1986 in Chicago, I distinctly remember feeling an excitement and sense of inspiration that I had not felt in many years. This was not the usual stale anarchist gathering bathed in nostalgia for a golden age of anarchy that was now dead. Instead I was surrounded by anarchists of all ages and persuasions who questioned and/or rejected all of the shibboleths of the authoritarian left. Something marvelous was in the air, and the rebellious spirit of Haymarket was invoked at every turn since the 1986 event itself was rooted in the courageous actions of those in the century before whose struggles and words are chronicled in the *Scrapbook*. No doubt some of the seeds that sprouted into the Chicago convergence called Active Resistance a decade later were first planted in this 1986 gathering.

In 1996, Active Resistance would attract 600 anarchists and direct actionists to the Autonomous Zone in Chicago to share the comraderie, ideas, and skills that would prove invaluable three years later on the streets of Seattle. And in the time-honored Chicago tradition that began with Haymarket and had the whole world watching in 1968, the A-Zone was raided during the Democratic National Convention in 1996 by the Chicago police just as Bill Clinton was about to ascend the stage to accept the nomination of his party. And so it was as president that Clinton attended the WTO in 1999, as the blood still caked on his hands from Chicago in 1996 mixed with the tear gas that was being unleashed in Seattle in 1999 to quell a disruption of business as usual fomented by active resisters from across the country, some of whom were the very ones that his party had previously tried to silence in the Windy City. Active Resistance, as well as the seminal anarchist gatherings of the Eighties—the Build the Movement Gathering in Minneapolis (1986), the Anarchist Survival Gathering in Toronto (1988), and San Francisco's Without Borders Gathering in 1989—fanned the flames of anarchy that eventually spread like a wildfire so hot that it could not be extinguished even on that rainy November morning in Seattle. And the convulsive beauty of the collective roar unleashed by the Seattle anarchists, and more recently by the Oakland General Strike of 2011 in the context of the Occupy Movement, had not been heard since 1886.

Just as the Haymarket anarchists in the nineteenth century had not simply called for the eight hour day, but for the abolition of wage slavery itself, contemporary anarchists are often abolitionists when it comes to work. In league with that anti-work emphasis, which is certainly in keeping with surrealism's ongoing war against miserabilism, the *Scrapbook* had, amidst its cornucopia of writers and artists, quite a number of Chicago Surrealist Group members. After all, its editors, Franklin Rosemont and David Roediger had been known for their association with both radical labor history and surrealism. And analagously,

it should come as no surprise that the Chicago Surrealist Group, in the anthology of their 1966–1976 writings, *The Forecast is Hot!*, should entitle the book's introduction, "Surrealism: The Chicago Idea," consciously tracing their lineage back to Haymarket. Among the Chicago Surrealist Group contributors to the *Scrapbook* were Franklin and Penelope Rosemont, Robert Green, Paul and Beth Garon, and Joseph Jablonski. In this sense, the book can be seen as having a surrealist subtext which uniquely illuminates one of the watershed events in the international history of working class radicalism and anarchist resistance.

As I remember it, around the time of the 1986 centennial, hostilities arose between certain Chicago anarchists and left liberals about the commemoration of the Haymarket martyrs to be held at Waldheim Cemetery. A graveyard melee even ensued over which group had the most legitimate claim to the Haymarket legacy. As if in anticipatory response to that question, anarchists were well-represented in the *Scrapbook*. That volume included not only the words of the Haymarket anarchists themselves, but the appearance of pieces by or about Johann Most, Emma Goldman, Voltairine de Cleyre, Peter Kropotkin, Joseph Labadie, Ba Jin, Sam and Esther Dolgoff, Jay Fox, Thomas J. Haggarty, Harry Kelly, Ammon Henacy, Joffre Stewart, Frederico Arcos, and featured artwork by Flavio Costantini and the young Man Ray, who was once a contributor to Emma Goldman's publication, *Mother Earth*. Represented too were such respected historians of anarchism as Paul Avrich, Carolyn Ashbaugh, Sal Salerno, Robert D'Attilio, and Richard Drinnan.

Yet, while anarchism was certainly given its due, the *Scrapbook* was remarkable for its breadth. The expansive universe of the book was not populated by anarchists alone. Its pages bristled with the thoughts of socialists, communists, progressive reformers, soapboxers, hobos, Wobblies, poets, spirit mediums, atheists, free love advocates, race traitors, indigenous rebels, free thought adherents, artists, cranks, dissident historians, and surrealists. This roster was not merely a catalogue of politically-correct inclusivity, but a many-headed hydra of subversive texts and incendiary salvos aimed at the heart of the dominant order. Perhaps this multi-faceted approach to radical history was best exemplified by Franklin Rosemont, among whose last major works in the twenty-first century were biographical studies of the Wobbly bard, Joe Hill, and the French proto-surrealist provocateur, Jacque Vaché.

In a sense, Rosemont's lifetime of creative work as a writer was reflected by the wide variety of his own articles in the *Scrapbook*. Within its pages, we are treated to his sur-realist-tinged homage to Louis Lingg, the militant young anarchist who cheated the hangman's noose with explosives, and an article linking the Chicago novelist Nelson Algren to Lingg, which reveals that, in his later years, the writer even described himself as an anarchist. In fact, as Rosemont pointed out, Algren went so far as to grant Lingg the con-cluding words in his only non-fiction book, *Chicago: City on the Make*: "I despise your order, your laws, your force-propped authority. Hang me for it!" In another article, he focused upon the often unheralded socialist scholar, Joseph Dietzgen, who upon moving to Chicago in 1886 became the editor-in-chief of the anarchist-run *Arbeiter-Zeitung* at the encouragement of the imprisoned Haymarket an-archist, August Spies. Rosemont's final article in the book is a *tour de force* of radical cultural history entitled, "The Image of the Anarchist in Popular Culture," depicting its subject as a bomb-toting, long-haired, wild-eyed fiend (ie. terrorist). It is a rollicking survey of anarchist caricatures that leaves no stone unturned from Thomas Nast to Buster Keaton and from the Marx Brothers to *Mad Magazine*.

And to bring us full circle, it is worth noting that I first met Franklin Rosemont as we proudly marched together with the Wobbly contingent at the annual May Day parade in Chicago many years ago. Upon his death in 2009, he was buried at the Waldheim Cemetery, just a poetic stone's throw from the Haymarket anarchists. In his living mem-ory, I salute the 125th anniversary of both Haymarket and the Charles H. Kerr Publishers.

A BRIEF HISTORY OF THE CHARLES H. KERR COMPANY

John Duda & Kate Khatib

It's a challenge to offer a "brief" history of Charles H. Kerr, because this Chicago radical institution has been in continuous operation since 1886, making it the oldest left publisher in the U.S., and arguably in the world.[1] The project initially emerged from the dissident religious circles that had proliferated as the Unitarian church confronted the issue of slavery. The abolitionist camp, influenced by Transcendentalists like Ralph Waldo Emerson, would drift farther away from any sort of emphasis on supernatural theology and towards a vision of a humanist ethics, becoming excited about the possibility of reconciling the emerging science of Darwinian evolution with a nonsectarian spirituality, and closely connected to the Free Religious Association, started in 1867, which sought to unite freethinking dissidents of all stripes and creeds (or lack thereof). It was in these circles, and specifically working on the tendency's Chicago-based magazine, *Unity*, that a young Charles Hope Kerr, fresh from the study of romance languages at the University of Wisconsin, would get his first taste of the publishing world.

In 1886, Kerr would use the connections with *Unity* to found Charles H. Kerr & Company, an independent publishing house that would take over the business of printing and distributing the magazine. (The "& Company" would remain a convenient fiction for a decade or so. Kerr was largely a one-man operation in its earliest days.) 1886, of course, was also the year that the state of Illinois sentenced seven prominent Chicago anarchists to die on the gallows for their supposed involvement with the bomb that exploded in Haymarket Square. The reactions in the pages of *Unity* were generally timid, afraid of being tarred with the brush of radicalism, the official editorial statements failed to take a stand on behalf of the innocent defendants in the case (although the magazine would also run an article or two with a much more pro-anarchist position).

It wasn't until a few years later, in 1891, that Charles Kerr began to move leftward, taking the publishing house with him. Populism—that late 19th century wave of grassroots agitation sweeping the Midwest—had seized Kerr's imagination, as had Edward Bellamy's utopian socialist novel *Looking Backward*. That very same year, he took it upon himself to publish American anarchist William Henry Van Ornum's *Why Government At All?*, which did little to endear him to the Unitarians behind *Unity*. Kerr would become further radicalized with his

marriage in 1892 to May Walden, a feminist and temperance advocate. In 1893, Kerr made a definitive break with *Unity*, which at this point had become not only increasingly incompatible with his politics, but also a financial drain on the publishing house. He replaced it with the more explicitly political periodical *New Occasions*, firmly tied to the current of populist reform, describing itself as "a magazine of social and industrial progress." The Kerr Company would also get its first taste of conservative reaction that year, with the publication of Matilda Gage's *Woman, Church, and State* drawing the ire of Anthony Comstock and his infamous New York Society for the Suppression of Vice. (Kerr responded by running ads for the book emblazoned with "Condemned by Comstock!")

Kerr's faith in peaceful progress toward socialism was shattered during the 1894 Pullman strike, when federal troops were used to break the Chicago railway strike that had paralyzed the nation's transportation infrastructure. Kerr turned the resources of the publishing company towards the struggle, publishing William H. Carwardine's first-hand account in August of 1894, with all proceeds going towards the families of those workers still out. By 1899, Kerr had left behind populism and resigned from *New Occasions*, becoming aligned with the new Socialist Labor Party under the influence of Algie Simons, who became vice-president of the Kerr Company in 1900. It was really in the context of the Pullman strike and Kerr's growing socialist convictions that the Kerr Company began to take off as a publishing project committed to providing resources to a growing anti-capitalist social movement. Part of this was figuring out ways to keep the project afloat financially if the publishing strategies were going to sacrifice profit for politics. Always an innovator, Kerr hit on the idea of "cooperative publishing bonds"—supporters were able to buy a ten dollar bond (eventually through monthly installments), and for the duration of the time the share in the company was held, supporters received a wholesale discount on the materials they ordered from the press. Not only did this likely encourage small alternative channels of radical book distribution and disperse financial control over the company through a broad base of supporters, it's a strategy that's still integral to movement presses today—just think of South End Press's Community Supported Publishing initiative or the Friends of AK Press program.

With the support of the company's cooperative "investors," the Kerr company would embark on projects like the Pocket Library of Socialism, the so called "little red books" which sought to popularize both American and European socialist theory. In 1899, Kerr would publish "Socialist Songs," which included the first English translation of the working-class anthem, "The Internationale" (translated by Charles H. Kerr himself). In 1900, Kerr began publishing "The Library of Science for Workers," and in 1901 the company released May Walden's socialist-feminist book, *Socialism and the Home*. As Charles Kerr, himself, put it, the aim of the press had become to publish "clear socialism in clear English," making the new radical class politics as widely accessible as possible.

Meanwhile, Algie and May Simons would help the company develop substantial connections with the flourishing European socialist movement, resulting in the first American translation of Engels' *Socialism: Utopian and Scientific* (which was a best-seller for the company). Kerr also distributed the first American edition of Volume 1 of Marx's *Capital*, but it was ultimately the support of autodidact Joseph Dietzgen, whom the Simons brought together with the Kerr company's publishing resources, that allowed Kerr to fund the first complete English translation of all three volumes of *Capital*, a project completed in 1909 by Ernest Untermann, who worked his way through the tomes while living on a chicken farm in Orlando, Florida.

Kerr also began publishing a new magazine in 1900—the *International Socialist Review*,[2] which would quickly become one of the most important nonsectarian journals of radical left thought in the U.S. As Algie Simons eventually distanced himself from the project, becoming more involved with the reformist faction of the Socialist Party that sought to collaborate with the American Federation of Labor, Charles Kerr continued to become even more radical in his outlook, gravitating towards the rank and file militant industrial unionism of the Industrial Workers of the World. The *Review* would correspondingly transition from a theoretical journal for a presumed socialist intellectual elite to a theoretical journal for the revolutionary masses, increasingly providing essential nationwide coverage of working-class insurgency, like the IWW's Free Speech Fights, which erupted in 1909. In 1910, Wobbly poet Ralph Chaplin joined the Company, becoming its chief graphic artist, as did firebrand and muckraker Mary Marcy. With this infusion of new radicals into the Company, Kerr would go on to publish Big Bill Haywood's 1911 anticapitalist manifesto *Industrial Socialism*, and agitate against U.S. intervention in the Mexican Revolution.

Ultimately, as WWI began, the Kerr company proved to be too great a threat for the American government to ignore. Taking a militant anticapitalist and antiwar stance on the conflict and the draft (with, for instance, Marcy's 1915 exhortation for workers to "paralyze the industrial machinery that makes war possible"), the *ISR* became a prime target for the 1917 Espionage Act, which forbade the use of the post to distribute "seditious" material. The 1917 raids targeting the IWW also took a heavy toll on the company (press employee Ralph Chaplin was among those rounded up). The Kerr company threw its support behind Big Bill Haywood in his federal trial, posting $2,000 of company funds and Mary Marcy's house for his bail—all of which was forfeited when Haywood escaped the U.S. for Soviet Russia rather than stand trial. This repression took its heaviest toll on Marcy, who was driven to suicide in 1922.

Kerr, however, persevered until 1928, and continued publishing important left-wing books like the *Autobiography of Mother Jones* and *The Deportations Delirium of 1920*, chronicling the Red Scare and the mass deportation of radicals. Ultimately, after 42 years, Charles Kerr decided to retire, turning over the press to the Proletarian Party, a small Communist organization headed by Scottish immigrant John Keracher, who taught classes on *Capital* in the back of his Detroit shoe store before moving to Chicago. The Proletarian Party was the very first group purged from the newly formed CPU.S.A. in 1919 and played an important role in the sit down strikes of the 1930s that would lead to the emergence of the CIO. Ultimately, it continued, if with lesser intensity, Kerr's legacy in publishing popular, nonsectarian, mass oriented Marxist literature, including in 1935, the first English edition of Engel's *Anti-Dühring*.

Kerr Company continued to survive as the publishing wing of the (dwindling) Proletarian Party throughout the middle decades of the 20th century, until the mid-70s, when the board was repopulated by a new collection of socialist agitators, including the Wobbly historian Fred Thompson. Under the influence of Thompson and other labor activists and historians, the Kerr Company began to delve back into the treasure trove of American labor stories, reissuing some of the company's greatest hits, including the *Autobiography of Mother Jones* and Paul Lafargue's *The Right to Be Lazy*.

It wasn't until the early 80s, though, that the Kerr Company would really come into its own once more as a new incarnation of Charles Hope Kerr's fiery radical spirit. In 1983, control of the company was turned over to Penelope and Franklin Rosemont, artists and labor agitators who had joined the board in the late 1970s. Under the influence of the Rosemonts, the Kerr Company would continue to preserve the history of America's radical agitators and labor activists, with collections like Ben Fletcher's *The Life and Times of a Black Wobbly*, and the collected speeches of Lucy Parsons, widow of the Haymarket martyr Albert Parsons. But like every one of the Kerr Company's many turns, the company's list changed to reflect the concerns and the excitement of the radicals of the era. Under Penelope and Franklin's care, the Kerr Company was responsible for reprinting some of the most important documents to come out of post WWII labor radicalism and the New Left, including CLR James's *Facing Reality*, Marty Glaberman's *Punching Out*, and student-activist manifestos "The New Radicals in the Multiversity" and "The Port Huron Statement." By virtue of the Rosemonts' involvement with the burgeoning young radical movement in Chicago, the Kerr Company became one of the central publishing outlets for the new synthesis of radical political agitation and counter-cultural revolt that emerged in the 1960s and which permanently reshaped the face of American politics.

Not content to simply republish the work of others, the Rosemonts set to work writing their own histories of America's most important radical figures and movements, and encouraging others in their circles to do the same. Driven by a desire to capture history from below, to cast off the "official" record of how things were that seemed to always focus on the viewpoint of the victors, Franklin, Penelope, and others who had come together in Chicago under the mantle of Surrealism,

like the Blues historian and musician Paul Garon, would spend the next thirty years writing a new radical history of America, treating figures like Slim Brundage, Claude McKay, Memphis Minnie, and T-Bone Slim alongside Big Bill Haywood, Lucy Parsons, Mother Jones, and the great Wobbly bard Joe Hill. Hill is, in many ways, the key to this unlikely alliance between these great figures of American counterculture, and these great figures of labor activism—after all, Joe Hill is one of the great songwriters, poets, artists, and cartoonists of American labor. Hill's story, especially in the hands of Franklin Rosemont, in his *Joe Hill*, is the story of a truly cultural union, of the IWW as the singing, dancing, and laughing union. And in its devotion to this kind of vision of revolution—one that's open-minded, experimental, focused on direct action and self-organization rather than orthodoxy and obedience—the Kerr company of today is continuing on the path blazed by Charles Hope Kerr over a century ago.

This article originally appeared in AREA Chicago 10.

Notes:

1) We're fortunate to have a not brief at all history of the Kerr Company's first half-century in Allen Ruff's *We Called Each Other Comrade: Charles H. Kerr & Company, Radical Publisher*, recently reissued by PM Press.

2) No relation to the International Socialist Organization's current magazine of the same name.

INDEX

SUPPORT AK PRESS!

AK Press is one of the world's largest and most productive anarchist publishing houses. We're entirely worker-run and democratically managed. We operate without a corporate structure—no boss, no managers, no bullshit. We publish close to twenty books every year, and distribute thousands of other titles published by other like-minded independent presses from around the globe.

The Friends of AK program is a way that you can directly contribute to the continued existence of AK Press, and ensure that we're able to keep publishing great books just like this one! Friends pay a minimum of $25 per month, for a minimum three month period, into our publishing account. In return, Friends automatically receive (for the duration of their membership), as they appear, one free copy of every new AK Press title. They're also entitled to a 20% discount on everything featured in the AK Press Distribution catalog and on the website, on any and every order. You or your organization can even sponsor an entire book if you should so choose!

There's great stuff in the works—so sign up now to become a Friend of AK Press, and let the presses roll!

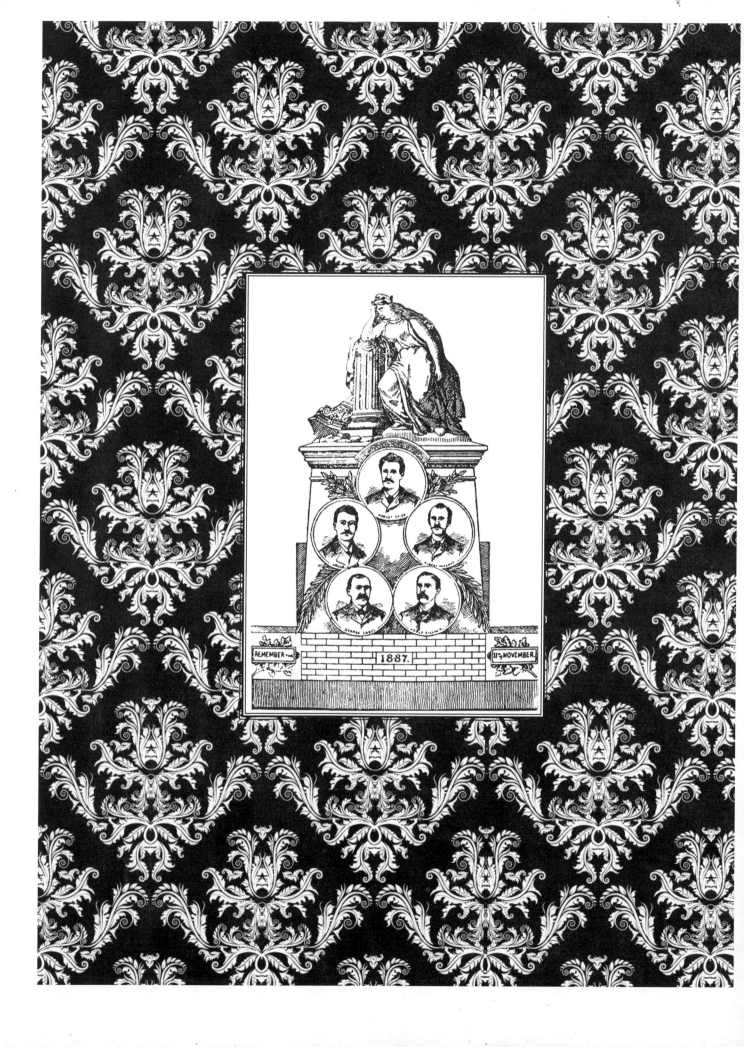